L Michael

Perl Cookbook

Perl Cookbook

Tom Christiansen and
Nathan Torkington

O'REILLY®

Beijing · Cambridge · Farnham · Köln · Paris · Sebastopol · Taipei · Tokyo

Perl Cookbook

by Tom Christiansen and Nathan Torkington

Published by O'Reilly & Associates, Inc., 101 Morris Street, Sebastopol, CA 95472.

Editor: Linda Mui

Production Editor: Clairemarie Fisher O'Leary

Printing History:

August 1998:	First Edition.
September 1998:	Minor corrections.
May 1999:	Minor corrections.

ISBN: 1-56592-243-3 [12/00]

[I]

Table of Contents

List of Examples

Foreword

They say that it's easy to get trapped by a metaphor. But some metaphors are so magnificent that you don't mind getting trapped in them. Perhaps the cooking metaphor is one such, at least in this case. The only problem I have with it is a personal one—I feel a bit like Betty Crocker's mother. The work in question is so monumental that anything I could say here would be either redundant or irrelevant.

However, that never stopped me before.

Cooking is perhaps the humblest of the arts; but to me humility is a strength, not a weakness. Great artists have always had to serve their artistic medium—great cooks just do so literally. And the more humble the medium, the more humble the artist must be in order to lift the medium beyond the mundane. Food and language are both humble media, consisting as they do of an overwhelming profusion of seemingly unrelated and unruly ingredients. And yet, in the hands of someone with a bit of creativity and discipline, things like potatoes, pasta, and Perl are the basis of works of art that "hit the spot" in a most satisfying way, not merely getting the job done, but doing so in a way that makes your journey through life a little more pleasant.

Cooking is also one of the oldest of the arts. Some modern artists would have you believe that so-called ephemeral art is a recent invention, but cooking has always been an ephemeral art. We can try to preserve our art, make it last a little longer, but even the food we bury with our pharoahs gets dug up eventually. So too, much of our Perl programming is ephemeral. This aspect of Perl cuisine has been much maligned. You can call it quick-and-dirty if you like, but there are billions of dollars out there riding on the supposition that fast food is not necessarily dirty food. (We hope.)

Easy things should be easy, and hard things should be possible. For every fast-food recipe, there are countless slow-food recipes. One of the advantages of living in California is that I have ready access to almost every national cuisine ever invented. But even within a given culture, There's More Than One Way To Do It. It's said in Russia that there are more recipes for borscht than there are cooks, and I believe it. My mom's recipe doesn't even have any beets in it! But that's okay, and it's more than okay. Borscht is a cultural differentiator, and different cultures are interesting, and educational, and useful, and exciting.

So you won't always find Tom and Nat doing things in this book the way I would do them. Sometimes they don't even do things the same way as each other. That's okay—again, this is a strength, not a weakness. I have to confess that I learned quite a few things I didn't know before I read this book. What's more, I'm quite confident that I still don't know it all. And I hope I don't any time soon. I often talk about Perl culture as if it were a single, static entity, but there are in fact many healthy Perl subcultures, not to mention sub-subcultures and supercultures and circumcultures in every conceivable combination, all inheriting attributes and methods from each other. It can get confusing. Hey, I'm confused most of the time.

So the essence of a cookbook like this is not to cook for you (it can't), or even to teach you how to cook (though it helps), but rather to pass on various bits of culture that have been found useful, and perhaps to filter out other bits of "culture" that grew in the refrigerator when no one was looking. You in turn will pass on some of these ideas to other people, filtering them through your own experiences and tastes, your creativity and discipline. You'll come up with your own recipes to pass to your children. Just don't be surprised when they in turn cook up some recipes of their own, and ask you what you think. Try not to make a face.

I commend to you these recipes, over which I've made very few faces.

—Larry Wall
June, 1998

Preface

The investment group eyed the entrepreneur with caution, their expressions flickering from scepticism to intrigue and back again.

"Your bold plan holds promise," their spokesman conceded. "But it is very costly and entirely speculative. Our mathematicians mistrust your figures. Why should we entrust our money into your hands? What do you know that we do not?"

"For one thing," he replied, "I know how to balance an egg on its point without outside support. Do you?" And with that, the entrepreneur reached into his satchel and delicately withdrew a fresh hen's egg. He handed over the egg to the financial tycoons, who passed it amongst themselves trying to carry out the simple task. At last they gave up. In exasperation they declared, "What you ask is impossible! No man can balance an egg on its point."

So the entrepreneur took back the egg from the annoyed businessmen and placed it upon the fine oak table, holding it so that its point faced down. Lightly but firmly, he pushed down on the egg with just enough force to crush in its bottom about half an inch. When he took his hand away, the egg stood there on its own, somewhat messy, but definitely balanced. "Was that impossible?" he asked.

"It's just a trick," cried the businessmen. "Once you know how, anyone can do it."

"True enough," came the retort. "But the same can be said for anything. Before you know how, it seems an impossibility. Once the way is revealed, it's so simple that you wonder why you never thought of it that way before. Let me show you that easy way, so others may easily follow. Will you trust me?"

Eventually convinced that this entrepreneur might possibly have something to show them, the skeptical venture capitalists funded his project. From the tiny Andalusian port of Palos de Moguer set forth the *Niña*, the *Pinta*, and the *Santa María*, led by an entrepreneur with a slightly broken egg and his own ideas: Christopher Columbus.

Many have since followed.

Approaching a programming problem can be like balancing Columbus's egg. If no one shows you how, you may sit forever perplexed, watching the egg—and your program—fall over again and again, no closer to the Indies than when you began. This is especially true in a language as idiomatic as Perl.

This book had its genesis in two chapters of the first edition of *Programming Perl*. Chapters 5 and 6 covered "Common Tasks in Perl" and "Real Perl Programs." Those chapters were highly valued by readers because they showed real applications of the language—how to solve day-to-day tasks using Perl. While revising the Camel, we realized that there was no way to do proper justice to those chapters without publishing the new edition on onionskin paper or in multiple volumes. The book you hold in your hands, published two years after the revised Camel, tries to do proper justice to those chapters. We trust it has been worth the wait.

This book isn't meant to be a complete reference book for Perl, although we do describe some parts of Perl previously undocumented. Having a copy of *Programming Perl* handy will allow you to look up the exact definition of an operator, keyword, or function. Alternatively, every Perl installation comes with over 1,000 pages of searchable, online reference materials. If those aren't where you can get at them, see your system administrator.

Neither is this book meant to be a bare-bones introduction for programmers who've never seen Perl before. That's what *Learning Perl*, a kinder and gentler introduction to Perl, is designed for. (If you're on a Microsoft system, you'll probably prefer the *Learning Perl for Win32 Systems* version.)

Instead, this is a book for learning *more* Perl. Neither a reference book nor a tutorial book, the *Perl Cookbook* serves as a companion book to both. It's for people who already know the basics but are wondering how to mix all those ingredients together into a complete program. Spread across 20 chapters and more than 300 focused topic areas affectionately called recipes, this book contains thousands of solutions to everyday challenges encountered by novice and journeyman alike.

We tried hard to make this book useful for both random and sequential access. Each recipe is self-contained, but has a list of references at the end should you need further information on the topic. We've tried to put the simpler, more common recipes toward the front of each chapter and the simpler chapters toward the front of the book. Perl novices should find that these recipes about Perl's basic data types and operators are just what they're looking for. We gradually work our way through topic areas and solutions more geared toward the journeyman Perl programmer. Every now and then we include material that should inspire even the master Perl programmer.

Each chapter begins with an overview of that chapter's topic. This introduction is followed by the main body of each chapter, its recipes. In the spirit of the Perl slogan of TMTOWTDI, "There's more than one way to do it," most recipes show several different techniques for solving the same or closely related problems. These recipes range from short-but-sweet solutions to in-depth mini-tutorials. Where more than one technique is given, we often show costs and benefits of each approach.

As with a traditional cookbook, we expect you to access this book more or less at random. When you want to learn how to do something, you'll look up its recipe. Even if the exact solutions presented don't fit your problem exactly, they'll give you ideas about possible approaches.

Each chapter concludes with one or more complete programs. Although some recipes already include small programs, these longer applications highlight the chapter's principal focus and combine techniques from other chapters, just as any real-world program would. All are useful, and many are used on a daily basis. Some even helped us put this book together.

What's in This Book

The first quarter of the book addresses Perl's basic data types, spread over five chapters. Chapter 1, *Strings*, covers matters like accessing substrings, expanding function calls in strings, and parsing comma-separated data. Chapter 2, *Numbers*, tackles oddities of floating point representation, placing commas in numbers, and pseudo-random numbers. Chapter 3, *Dates and Times*, demonstrates conversions between numeric and string date formats and using timers. Chapter 4, *Arrays*, covers everything relating to list and array manipulation, including finding unique elements in a list, efficiently sorting lists, and randomizing them. Chapter 5, *Hashes*, concludes the basics with a demonstration of the most useful data type, the associative array. The chapter shows how to access a hash in insertion order, how to sort a hash by value, and how to have multiple values per key.

Chapter 6, *Pattern Matching*, is by far the largest chapter. Recipes include converting a shell wildcard into a pattern, matching letters or words, matching multiple lines, avoiding greediness, and matching strings that are close to but not exactly what you're looking for. Although this chapter is the longest in the book, it could easily have been longer still—every chapter contains uses of regular expressions. It's part of what makes Perl Perl.

The next three chapters cover the filesystem. Chapter 7, *File Access*, shows opening files, locking them for concurrent access, modifying them in place, and storing filehandles in variables. Chapter 8, *File Contents*, discusses watching the end of a growing file, reading a particular line from a file, and random access binary I/O. Finally, in Chapter 9, *Directories*, we show techniques to copy, move, or delete a file, manipulate a file's timestamps, and recursively process all files in a directory.

Chapters 10 through 13 focus on making your program flexible and powerful. Chapter 10, *Subroutines*, includes recipes on creating persistent local variables, passing parameters by reference, calling functions indirectly, and handling exceptions. Chapter 11, *References and Records*, is about data structures; basic manipulation of references to data and functions are demonstrated. Later recipes show how to create record-like data structures and how to save and restore these structures from permanent storage. Chapter 12, *Packages, Libraries, and Modules*, concerns breaking up your program into separate files; we discuss how to make variables and functions private to a module, replace built-ins, trap calls to missing modules, and use the *h2ph* and *h2xs* tools to interact with C and C++ code. Lastly, Chapter 13, *Classes, Objects, and Ties*, covers the fundamentals of building your own object-based module to create user-defined types, complete with constructors, destructors, and inheritance. Other recipes show examples of circular data structures, operator overloading, and tied data types.

The next two chapters are about interfaces: one to databases, the other to display devices. Chapter 14, *Database Access*, includes techniques for manipulating indexed text files, locking DBM files and storing data in them, and a demonstration of Perl's SQL interface. Chapter 15, *User Interfaces*, covers topics such as clearing the screen, processing command-line switches, single-character input, moving the cursor using *termcap* and *curses*, and platform independent graphical programming using Tk.

The last quarter of the book is devoted to interacting with other programs and services. Chapter 16, *Process Management and Communication*, is about running other programs and collecting their output, handling zombie processes, named pipes, signal management, and sharing variables between running programs. Chapter 17, *Sockets*, shows how to establish stream connections or use datagrams to create low-level networking applications for client-server programming. Chapter 18, *Internet Services*, is about higher-level protocols such as mail, FTP, Usenet news, and Telnet. Chapter 19, *CGI Programming*, contains recipes for processing web forms, trapping their errors, avoiding shell escapes for security, managing cookies, shopping cart techniques, and saving forms to files or pipes. The final chapter of the book, Chapter 20, *Web Automation*, covers non-interactive uses of the Web. Recipes include fetching a URL, automating form submissions in a script, extracting URLs from a web page, removing HTML tags, finding fresh or stale links, and processing server log files.

Platform Notes

This book was developed using Perl release 5.004_04. That means major release 5, minor release 4, and patch level 4. We tested most programs and examples under BSD, Linux, and SunOS, but that doesn't mean they'll only work on those systems. Perl was *designed* for platform independence. When you use Perl as a general-purpose programming language, employing basic operations like variables, patterns, subroutines, and high-level I/O, your program should work the same everywhere that Perl runs—which is just about everywhere. The first two thirds of this book uses Perl for general-purpose programming.

Perl was originally conceived as a high-level, cross-platform language for systems programming. Although it has long since expanded beyond its original domain, Perl continues to be heavily used for systems programming, both on its native Unix systems and elsewhere. Most recipes in Chapters 14 through 18 deal with classic systems programming. For maximum portability in this area, we've mainly focused on open systems as defined by POSIX, the Portable Operating System Interface, which includes nearly every form of Unix and numerous other systems as well. Most recipes should run with little or no modification on any POSIX system.

You can still use Perl for systems programming work even on non-POSIX systems by using vendor-specific modules, but these are not covered in this book. That's because they're not portable—and to be perfectly honest, because the authors have no such systems at their disposal. Consult the documentation that came with your port of Perl for any proprietary modules that may have been included.

But don't worry. Many recipes for systems programming should work on non-POSIX systems as well, especially those dealing with databases, networking, and web interaction. That's because the modules used for those areas hide platform dependencies. The principal exception is those few recipes and programs that rely upon multitasking constructs, notably the powerful `fork` function, standard on POSIX systems, but few others.

When we needed structured files, we picked the convenient Unix */etc/passwd* database; when we needed a text file to read, we picked */etc/motd*; and when we needed a program to produce output, we picked *who*(1). These were merely chosen to illustrate the principles—the principles work whether or not your system has these files and programs.

Other Books

If you'd like to learn more about Perl, here are some related publications that we (somewhat sheepishly) recommend:

Learning Perl, by Randal Schwartz and Tom Christiansen; O'Reilly & Associates (2nd Edition, 1997).
  A tutorial introduction to Perl for programmers interested in learning Perl from scratch. It's a good starting point if this book is over your head. Erik Olson

refurbished this book for Windows systems, called *Learning Perl for Win32 Systems.*

Programming Perl, by Larry Wall, Tom Christiansen, and Randal Schwartz; O'Reilly & Associates (2nd Edition, 1996).

This book is indispensable for every Perl programmer. Coauthored by Perl's creator, this classic reference is the authoritative guide to Perl's syntax, functions, modules, references, invocation options, and much more.

Advanced Perl Programming, by Sriram Srinivasan; O'Reilly & Associates (1997).

A tutorial for advanced regular expressions, network programming, GUI programming with Tk, and Perl internals. If the *Cookbook* isn't challenging you, buy a copy of the Panther.

Mastering Regular Expressions, by Jeffrey Friedl; O'Reilly & Associates (1997).

This book is dedicated to explaining regular expressions from a practical perspective. It not only covers general regular expressions and Perl patterns very well, it also compares and contrasts these with those used in other popular languages.

How to Set Up and Maintain a Web Site, by Lincoln Stein; Addison-Wesley (2nd Edition, 1997).

If you're trying to manage a web site, configure servers, and write CGI scripts, this is the book for you. Written by the author of Perl's *CGI.pm* module, this book really does cover everything.

Perl: The Programmer's Companion, by Nigel Chapman; John Wiley & Sons (1998).

This small, delightful book is just the book for the experienced programmer wanting to learn Perl. It is not only free of technical errors, it is truly a pleasure to read. It is about Perl as a serious programming language.

Effective Perl Programming, by Joseph N. Hall with Randal Schwartz; Addison-Wesley (1998).

This book includes thorough coverage of Perl's object model, and how to develop modules and contribute them to CPAN. It covers the debugger particularly well.

In addition to the Perl-related publications listed here, the following books came in handy when writing this book. They were used for reference, consultation, and inspiration.

The Art of Computer Programming, by Donald Knuth, Volumes I-III: "Fundamental Algorithms," "Seminumerical Algorithms," and "Sorting and Searching"; Addison-Wesley (3rd Edition, 1998).

Introduction to Algorithms, by Thomas H. Cormen, Charles E. Leiserson, and Ronald L. Rivest; MIT Press and McGraw-Hill (1990).

Algorithms in C, by Robert Sedgewick; Addison-Wesley (1992).

The Art of Mathematics, by Jerry P. King; Plenum (1992).

The Elements of Programming Style, by Brian W. Kernighan and P.J. Plauger; McGraw-Hill (1988).

The UNIX Programming Environment, by Brian W. Kernighan and Rob Pike; Prentice-Hall (1984).

POSIX Programmer's Guide, by Donald Lewine; O'Reilly & Associates (1991).

Advanced Programming in the UNIX Environment, by W. Richard Stevens; Addison-Wesley (1992).

TCP/IP Illustrated, by W. Richard Stevens, et al., Volumes I-III; Addison-Wesley (1992–1996).

Web Client Programming with Perl, by Clinton Wong; O'Reilly & Associates (1997).

HTML: The Definitive Guide, by Chuck Musciano and Bill Kennedy; O'Reilly & Associates (3rd Edition, 1998).

The New Fowler's Modern English Usage, edited by R.W. Burchfield; Oxford (3rd Edition, 1996).

Official Guide to Programming with CGI.pm, by Lincoln Stein; John Wiley & Sons (1997).

Conventions Used in This Book

Programming Conventions

We are firm believers in using Perl's **-w** command-line option and its use strict pragma in every non-trivial program. We start nearly all our longer programs with:

```
#!/usr/bin/perl -w
use strict;
```

We give lots of examples, most of which are pieces of code that should go into a larger program. Some examples are complete programs, which you can recognize because they begin with a #! line.

Still other examples are things to be typed on a command line. We've used % to indicate the shell prompt:

```
% perl -e 'print "Hello, world.\n"'
Hello, world.
```

This style is representative of a standard Unix command line. Quoting and wild-card conventions on other systems vary. For example, most standard command-line interpreters under DOS and VMS require double quotes instead of single ones to group arguments with spaces or wildcards in them. Adjust accordingly.

Typesetting Conventions

The following typographic conventions are used in this book:

Italic

> is used for filenames, command names, and URLs. It is also used to define new terms when they first appear in the text.

Bold

> is used for command-line options.

`Constant Width`

> is used for function and method names and their arguments; in examples to show the text that you enter literally; and in regular text to show any literal code.

`Constant Bold Italic`

> is used in examples to show output produced.

Documentation Conventions

The most up-to-date and complete documentation about Perl is included with Perl itself. If typeset and printed, this massive anthology would use more than a thousand pages of printer pager, greatly contributing to global deforestation. Fortunately, you don't have to print it out because it's available in a convenient and searchable electronic form.

When we refer to a "manpage" in this book, we're talking about this set of online manuals. The name is purely a convention; you don't need a Unix-style **man** program to read them. The *perldoc* command distributed with Perl also works, and you may even have the manpages installed as HTML pages, especially on non-Unix systems. Plus, once you know where they're installed, you can **grep** them directly.* The HTML version of the manpages is available on the Web at *http://www.perl.com/CPAN/doc/manual/html/*.

When we refer to non-Perl documentation, as in "See *kill*(2) in your system manual," this refers to the *kill* manpage from section 2 of the *Unix Programmer's Manual* (system calls). These won't be available on non-Unix systems, but that's probably okay, because you couldn't use them there anyway. If you really do need the

---

* If your system doesn't have *grep*, use the *tcgrep* program supplied at the end of Chapter 6.

documentation for a system call or library function, many organizations have put their manpages on the Web; a quick search of AltaVista for `+crypt(3)` `+man-ual` will find many copies.

We'd Like to Hear from You

We have tested and verified the information in this book to the best of our ability, but you may find that features have changed (which may in fact resemble bugs). Please let us know about any errors you find, as well as your suggestions for future editions, by writing to:

O'Reilly & Associates, Inc.
101 Morris Street
Sebastopol, CA 95472
1-800-998-9938 (in U.S. or Canada)
1-707-829-0515 (international/local)
1-707-829-0104 (fax)

You can also send us messages electronically. To be put on the mailing list or request a catalog, send email to:

info@oreilly.com

To ask technical questions or comment on the book, send email to:

bookquestions@oreilly.com

We have a web site for the book, where we'll list errata and plans for future editions. Here you'll also find all the source code from the book available for download so you don't have to type it all in.

http://www.oreilly.com/catalog/cookbook/

For more information about this book and others, see the O'Reilly web site:

http://www.oreilly.com/

Acknowledgments

This book wouldn't exist but for a legion of people standing, knowing and unknowing, behind the authors. At the head of this legion would have to be our editor, Linda Mui, carrot on a stick in one hand and a hot poker in the other. She was great.

As the author of Perl, Larry Wall was our ultimate reality check. He made sure we weren't documenting things he was planning to change and helped out on wording and style.* If now and then you think you're hearing Larry's voice in this book, you probably are.

Larry's wife, Gloria, a literary critic by trade, shocked us by reading through every single word—and actually liking most of them. Together with Sharon Hopkins, resident Perl Poetess, she helped us rein in our admittedly nearly insatiable tendency to produce pretty prose sentences that could only be charitably described as lying somewhere between the inscrutably complex and the hopelessly arcane, eventually rendering the meandering muddle into something legible even to those whose native tongues were neither PDP-11 assembler nor Mediæval Spanish.

Our three most assiduous reviewers, Mark-Jason Dominus, Jon Orwant, and Abigail, have worked with us on this book nearly as long as we've been writing it. Their rigorous standards, fearsome intellects, and practical experience in Perl applications have been of invaluable assistance. Doug Edwards methodically stress-tested every piece of code from the first seven chapters of the book, finding subtle border cases no one else ever thought about. Other major reviewers include Andy Dougherty, Andy Oram, Brent Halsey, Bryan Buus, Gisle Aas, Graham Barr, Jeff Haemer, Jeffrey Friedl, Lincoln Stein, Mark Mielke, Martin Brech, Matthias Neeracher, Mike Stok, Nate Patwardhan, Paul Grassie, Peter Prymmer, Raphaël Manfredi, and Rod Whitby.

And this is just the beginning. Part of what makes Perl fun is the sense of community and sharing it seems to engender. Many selfless individuals lent us their technical expertise. Some read through complete chapters in formal review. Others provided insightful answers to brief technical questions when we were stuck on something outside our own domain. A few even sent us code. Here's a partial list of these helpful people: Aaron Harsh, Ali Rayl, Alligator Descartes, Andrew Hume, Andrew Strebkov, Andy Wardley, Ashton MacAndrews, Ben Gertzfield, Benjamin Holzman, Brad Hughes, Chaim Frenkel, Charles Bailey, Chris Nandor, Clinton Wong, Dan Klein, Dan Sugalski, Daniel Grisinger, Dennis Taylor, Doug MacEachern, Douglas Davenport, Drew Eckhardt, Dylan Northrup, Eric Eisenhart, Eric Watt Forste, Greg Bacon, Gurusamy Sarathy, Henry Spencer, Jason Ornstein, Jason Stewart, Joel Noble, Jonathan Cohen, Jonathan Scott Duff, Josh Purinton, Julian Anderson, Keith Winstein, Ken Lunde, Kirby Hughes, Larry Rosler, Les Peters, Mark Hess, Mark James, Martin Brech, Mary Koutsky, Michael Parker, Nick Ing-Simmons, Paul Marquess, Peter Collinson, Peter Osel, Phil Beauchamp, Piers Cawley, Randal Schwartz, Rich Rauenzahn, Richard Allan, Rocco Caputo, Roderick Schertler, Roland Walker, Ronan Waide, Stephen Lidie, Steven Owens, Sullivan Beck, Tim Bunce, Todd Miller, Troy Denkinger, and Willy Grimm.

---

* And footnotes.

And let's not forget Perl itself, without which this book could never have been written. Appropriately enough, we used Perl to build endless small tools to aid in the production of this book. Perl tools converted our text in pod format into *troff* for displaying and review and into FrameMaker for production. Another Perl program ran syntax checks on every piece of code in the book. The Tk extension to Perl was used to build a graphical tool to shuffle around recipes using drag-and-drop. Beyond these, we also built innumerable smaller tools for tasks like checking RCS locks, finding duplicate words, detecting certain kinds of grammatical errors, managing mail folders with feedback from reviewers, creating program indices and tables of contents, and running text searches that crossed line boundaries or were restricted to certain sections—just to name a few. Some of these tools found their way into the same book they were used on.

Tom

Thanks first of all to Larry and Gloria for sacrificing some of their European vacation to groom the many nits out of this manuscript, and to my other friends and family—Bryan, Sharon, Brent, Todd, and Drew—for putting up with me over the last couple of years and being subjected to incessant proofreadings.

I'd like to thank Nathan for holding up despite the stress of his weekly drives, my piquant vegetarian cooking and wit, and his getting stuck researching the topics I so diligently avoided.

I'd like to thank those largely unsung titans in our field—Dennis, Linus, Kirk, Eric, and Rich—who were all willing to take the time to answer my niggling operating system and *troff* questions. Their wonderful advice and anecdotes aside, without their tremendous work in the field, this book could never have been written.

Thanks also to my instructors who sacrificed themselves to travel to perilous places like New Jersey to teach Perl in my stead. I'd like to thank Tim O'Reilly and Frank Willison first for being talked into publishing this book, and second for letting time-to-market take a back seat to time-to-quality. Thanks also to Linda, our shamelessly honest editor, for shepherding dangerously rabid sheep through the eye of a release needle.

Most of all, I want to thank my mother, Mary, for tearing herself away from her work in prairie restoration and teaching high school computer and biological sciences to keep both my business and domestic life in smooth working order long enough for me to research and write this book.

Finally, I'd like to thank Johann Sebastian Bach, who was for me a boundless font of perspective, poise, and inspiration—a therapy both mental and physical. I am certain that forevermore the Cookbook will evoke for me the sounds of BWV 849, now indelibly etched into the wetware of head and hand.

Nat

Without my family's love and patience, I'd be baiting hooks in a 10-foot swell instead of mowing my lawn in suburban America. Thank you! My friends have taught me much: Jules, Amy, Raj, Mike, Kef, Sai, Robert, Ewan, Pondy, Mark, and Andy. I owe a debt of gratitude to the denizens of Nerdsholm, who gave sound technical advice and introduced me to my wife (they didn't give me sound technical advice on her, though). Thanks also to my employer, Front Range Internet, for a day job I don't want to quit.

Tom was a great co-author. Without him, this book would be nasty, brutish, and short. Finally, I have to thank Jenine. We'd been married a year when I accepted the offer to write, and we've barely seen each other since then. Nobody will savour the final full-stop in this sentence more than she.

1

Strings

He multiplieth words without knowledge.
—Job 35:16

1.0. Introduction

Many programming languages force you to work at an uncomfortably low level. You think in lines, but your language wants you to deal with pointers. You think in strings, but it wants you to deal with bytes. Such a language can drive you to distraction. Don't despair, though—Perl isn't a low-level language; lines and strings are easy to handle.

Perl was *designed* for text manipulation. In fact, Perl can manipulate text in so many ways that they can't all be described in one chapter. Check out other chapters for recipes on text processing. In particular, see Chapter 6, *Pattern Matching*, and Chapter 8, *File Contents*, which discuss interesting techniques not covered here.

Perl's fundamental unit for working with data is the scalar, that is, single values stored in single (scalar) variables. Scalar variables hold strings, numbers, and references. Array and hash variables hold lists or associations of scalars, respectively. References are used for referring to other values indirectly, not unlike pointers in low-level languages. Numbers are usually stored in your machine's double-precision floating-point notation. Strings in Perl may be of any length (within the limits of your machine's virtual memory) and contain any data you care to put there—even binary data containing null bytes.

A string is not an array of bytes: You cannot use array subscripting on a string to address one of its characters; use `substr` for that. Like all data types in Perl, strings grow and shrink on demand. They get reclaimed by Perl's garbage collection system when they're no longer used, typically when the variables holding them go out of scope or when the expression they were used in has been evaluated. In other words, memory management is already taken care of for you, so you don't have to worry about it.

A scalar value is either defined or undefined. If defined, it may hold a string, number, or reference. The only undefined value is **undef**. All other values are defined, even 0 and the empty string. Definedness is not the same as Boolean truth, though; to check whether a value is defined, use the **defined** function. Boolean truth has a specialized meaning, tested with operators like && and || or in an **if** or **while** block's test condition.

Two defined strings are false: the empty string (`""`) and a string of length one containing the digit zero (`"0"`). This second one may surprise you, but Perl does this because of its on-demand conversion between strings and numbers. The numbers `0.`, `0.00`, and `0.0000000` are all false when unquoted but are not false in strings (the string `"0.00"` is true, not false). All other defined values (e.g., `"false"`, 15, and `\$x`) are true.

The **undef** value behaves like the empty string (`""`) when used as a string, 0 when used as a number, and the null reference when used as a reference. But in all these cases, it's false. Using an undefined value where Perl expects a defined value will trigger a run-time warning message on STDERR if you've used the **-w** flag. Merely asking whether something is true or false does not demand a particular value, so this is exempt from a warning. Some operations do not trigger warnings when used on variables holding undefined values. These include the autoincrement and autodecrement operators, ++ and --, and the addition and catenation assignment operators, += and .=.

Specify strings in your program either with single quotes, double quotes, the quote-like operators q// and qq//, or "here documents." Single quotes are the simplest form of quoting—the only special characters are ' to terminate the string, \' to quote a single quote in the string, and \\ to quote a backslash in the string:

```
$string = '\n';                        # two characters, \ and an n
$string = 'Jon \'Maddog\' Orwant';     # literal single quotes
```

Double quotes interpolate variables (but not function calls—see Recipe 1.10 to find how to do this) and expand a lot of backslashed shortcuts: `"\n"` becomes a newline, `"\033"` becomes the character with octal value 33, `"\cJ"` becomes a Ctrl-J, and so on. The full list of these is given in the *perlop*(1) manpage.

```
$string = "\n";                        # a "newline" character
$string = "Jon \"Maddog\" Orwant";     # literal double quotes
```

The q// and qq// regexp-like quoting operators let you use alternate delimiters for single- and double-quoted strings. For instance, if you want a literal string that

contains single quotes, it's easier to write this than to escape the single quotes
with backslashes:

```
$string = q/Jon 'Maddog' Orwant/;    # literal single quotes
```

You can use the same character as delimiter, as we do with / here, or you can
balance the delimiters if you use parentheses or paren-like characters:

```
$string = q[Jon 'Maddog' Orwant];    # literal single quotes
$string = q{Jon 'Maddog' Orwant};    # literal single quotes
$string = q(Jon 'Maddog' Orwant);    # literal single quotes
$string = q<Jon 'Maddog' Orwant>;    # literal single quotes
```

"Here documents" are borrowed from the shell. They are a way to quote a large
chunk of text. The text can be interpreted as single-quoted, double-quoted, or
even as commands to be executed, depending on how you quote the terminating
identifier. Here we double-quote two lines with a here document:

```
$a = <<"EOF";
This is a multiline here document
terminated by EOF on a line by itself
EOF
```

Note there's no semicolon after the terminating EOF. Here documents are covered
in more detail in Recipe 1.11.

A warning for non-Western programmers: Perl doesn't currently directly support
multibyte characters (expect Unicode support in 5.006), so we'll be using the terms
byte and *character* interchangeably.

1.1. Accessing Substrings

Problem

You want to access or modify just a portion of a string, not the whole thing. For
instance, you've read a fixed-width record and want to extract the individual fields.

Solution

The substr function lets you read from and write to bits of the string.

```
$value = substr($string, $offset, $count);
$value = substr($string, $offset);

substr($string, $offset, $count) = $newstring;
substr($string, $offset)         = $newtail;
```

The unpack function gives only read access, but is faster when you have many
substrings to extract.

```
# get a 5-byte string, skip 3, then grab 2 8-byte strings, then the rest
($leading, $s1, $s2, $trailing) =
    unpack("A5 x3 A8 A8 A*", $data);

# split at five byte boundaries
@fivers = unpack("A5" x (length($string)/5), $string);

# chop string into individual characters
@chars  = unpack("A1" x length($string), $string);
```

Discussion

Unlike many other languages that represent strings as arrays of bytes (or characters), in Perl, strings are a basic data type. This means that you must use functions like unpack or substr to access individual characters or a portion of the string.

The offset argument to substr indicates the start of the substring you're interested in, counting from the front if positive and from the end if negative. If offset is 0, the substring starts at the beginning. The count argument is the length of the substring.

```
$string = "This is what you have";
#            +012345678901234567890  Indexing forwards  (left to right)
#             10987654321098764321-  Indexing backwards (right to left)
#             note that 0 means 10 or 20, etc. above

$first  = substr($string, 0, 1);   # "T"
$start  = substr($string, 5, 2);   # "is"
$rest   = substr($string, 13);     # "you have"
$last   = substr($string, -1);     # "e"
$end    = substr($string, -4);     # "have"
$piece  = substr($string, -8, 3);  # "you"
```

You can do more than just look at parts of the string with substr; you can actually change them. That's because substr is a particularly odd kind of function—an *lvaluable* one, that is, a function that may itself be assigned a value. (For the record, the others are vec, pos, and as of the 5.004 release, keys. If you squint, local and my can also be viewed as lvaluable functions.)

```
$string = "This is what you have";
print $string;
This is what you have
substr($string, 5, 2) = "wasn't"; # change "is" to "wasn't"
This wasn't what you have
substr($string, -12)  = "ondrous";# "This wasn't wondrous"
This wasn't wondrous
substr($string, 0, 1) = "";        # delete first character
his wasn't wondrous
substr($string, -10)  = "";        # delete last 10 characters
his wasn'
```

You can use the =~ operator and the s///, m//, or tr/// operators in conjunction with substr to make them affect only that portion of the string.

```
# you can test substrings with =~
if (substr($string, -10) =~ /pattern/) {
    print "Pattern matches in last 10 characters\n";
}


# substitute "at" for "is", restricted to first five characters
substr($string, 0, 5) =~ s/is/at/g;
```

You can even swap values by using several substrs on each side of an assignment:

```
# exchange the first and last letters in a string
$a = "make a hat";
(substr($a,0,1), substr($a,-1)) = (substr($a,-1), substr($a,0,1));
print $a;
take a ham
```

Although unpack is not lvaluable, it is considerably faster than substr when you extract numerous values at once. It doesn't directly support offsets as substr does. Instead, it uses lowercase "x" with a count to skip forward some number of bytes and an uppercase "X" with a count to skip backward some number of bytes.

```
# extract column with unpack
$a = "To be or not to be";
$b = unpack("x6 A6", $a);   # skip 6, grab 6
print $b;
or not


($b, $c) = unpack("x6 A2 X5 A2", $a); # forward 6, grab 2; backward 5, grab 2
print "$b\n$c\n";
or
be
```

Sometimes you prefer to think of your data as being cut up at specific columns. For example, you might want to place cuts right before positions 8, 14, 20, 26, and 30. Those are the column numbers where each field begins. Although you could calculate that the proper unpack format is "A7 A6 A6 A6 A4 A*", this is too much mental strain for the virtuously lazy Perl programmer. Let Perl figure it out for you. Use the cut2fmt function below:

```
sub cut2fmt {
    my(@positions) = @_;
    my $template   = '';
    my $lastpos    = 1;
    foreach $place (@positions) {
        $template .= "A" . ($place - $lastpos) . " ";
        $lastpos   = $place;
    }
    $template .= "A*";
    return $template;
}
```

```
$fmt = cut2fmt(8, 14, 20, 26, 30);
print "$fmt\n";
A7 A6 A6 A6 A4 A*
```

The powerful **unpack** function goes far beyond mere text processing. It's the gateway between text and binary data.

See Also

The **unpack** and **substr** functions in *perlfunc*(1) and Chapter 3 of *Programming Perl*; the *cut2fmt* subroutine of Recipe 1.18; the binary use of **unpack** in Recipe 8.18

1.2. Establishing a Default Value

Problem

You would like to give a default value to a scalar variable, but only if it doesn't already have one. It often happens that you want a hard-coded default value for a variable that can be overridden from the command-line or through an environment variable.

Solution

Use the || or ||= operator, which work on both strings and numbers:

```
# use $b if $b is true, else $c
$a = $b || $c;

# set $x to $y unless $x is already true
$x ||= $y
```

If 0 or "0" are valid values for your variables, use **defined** instead:

```
# use $b if $b is defined, else $c
$a = defined($b) ? $b : $c;
```

Discussion

The big difference between the two techniques (**defined** and ||) is what they test: definedness versus truth. Three defined values are still false in the world of Perl: 0, "0", and "". If your variable already held one of those, and you wanted to keep that value, a || wouldn't work. You'd have to use the clumsier tests with **defined** instead. It's often convenient to arrange for your program to care only about true or false values, not defined or undefined ones.

Rather than being restricted in its return values to a mere 1 or 0 as in most other languages, Perl's || operator has a much more interesting property: It returns its first operand (the left-hand side) if that operand is true; otherwise it returns its second operand. The && operator also returns the last evaluated expression, but is less often used for this property. These operators don't care whether their operands are strings, numbers, or references—any scalar will do. They just return the first one that makes the whole expression true or false. This doesn't affect the Boolean sense of the return value, but it does make the operators more convenient to use.

This property lets you provide a default value to a variable, function, or longer expression in case the first part doesn't pan out. Here's an example of ||, which would set $foo to be the contents of either $bar or, if $bar is false, "DEFAULT VALUE":

```
$foo = $bar || "DEFAULT VALUE";
```

Here's another example, which sets $dir to be either the first argument to the program or "/tmp" if no argument was given.

```
$dir = shift(@ARGV) || "/tmp";
```

We can do this without altering @ARGV:

```
$dir = $ARGV[0] || "/tmp";
```

If 0 is a valid value for $ARGV[0], we can't use || because it evaluates as false even though it's a value we want to accept. We must resort to the ternary ("hook") operator:

```
$dir = defined($ARGV[0]) ? shift(@ARGV) : "/tmp";
```

We can also write this as follows, although with slightly different semantics:

```
$dir = @ARGV ? $ARGV[0] : "/tmp";
```

This checks the number of elements in @ARGV. Using the hook operator as a condition in a ?: statement evaluates @ARGV in scalar context. It's only false when there are 0 elements, in which case we use "/tmp". In all other cases (when the user gives an argument), we use the first argument.

The following line increments a value in %count, using as the key either $shell or, if $shell is false, "/bin/sh".

```
$count{ $shell || "/bin/sh" }++;
```

You may chain several alternatives together as we have in the following example. The first expression that returns a true value will be used.

```
# find the user name on Unix systems
$user = $ENV{USER}
    || $ENV{LOGNAME}
```

```
|| getlogin()
|| (getpwuid($<))[0]
|| "Unknown uid number $<";
```

The && operator works analogously: It returns its first operand if that operand is false; otherwise, it returns the second one. Because there aren't as many interesting false values as there are true ones, this property isn't used much. One use is demonstrated in Recipe 13.11 or 14.11.

The ||= assignment operator looks odd, but it works exactly like the other binary assignment operators. For nearly all Perl's binary operators, $VAR OP= VALUE means $VAR = $VAR OP VALUE; for example, $a += $b is the same as $a = $a + $b. So ||= is used to set a variable when that variable is itself still false. Since the || check is a simple Boolean one—testing for truth—it doesn't care about undefined values even under -w.

Here's an example of ||= that sets $starting_point to "Greenwich" unless it is already set. Again, we assume $starting_point won't have the value 0 or "0", or that if it does, it's okay to change it.

```
$starting_point ||= "Greenwich";
```

You can't use or in place of || in assignments because or's precedence is too low. $a = $b or $c is equivalent to ($a = $b) or $c. This will always assign $b to $a, which is not the behavior you want.

Don't extend this curious use of || and ||= from scalars to arrays and hashes. It doesn't work because the operators put their left operand into scalar context. Instead, you must do something like this:

```
@a = @b unless @a;          # copy only if empty
@a = @b ? @b : @c;          # assign @b if nonempty, else @c
```

See Also

The || operator in *perlop*(1) or Chapter 2 of *Programming Perl*; the defined and exists functions in *perlfunc*(1) and Chapter 3 of *Programming Perl*

1.3. Exchanging Values Without Using Temporary Variables

Problem

You want to exchange the values of two scalar variables, but don't want to use a temporary variable.

Solution

Use list assignment to reorder the variables.

```
($VAR1, $VAR2) = ($VAR2, $VAR1);
```

Discussion

Most programming languages force you to use an intermediate step when swapping two variables' values:

```
$temp     = $a;
$a        = $b;
$b        = $temp;
```

Not so in Perl. It tracks both sides of the assignment, guaranteeing that you don't accidentally clobber any of your values. This lets you eliminate the temporary variable:

```
$a        = "alpha";
$b        = "omega";
($a, $b) = ($b, $a);          # the first shall be last -- and versa vice
```

You can even exchange more than two variables at once:

```
($alpha, $beta, $production) = qw(January March August);
# move beta        to alpha,
# move production to beta,
# move alpha        to production
($alpha, $beta, $production) = ($beta, $production, $alpha);
```

When this code finishes, `$alpha`, `$beta`, and `$production` have the values `"March"`, `"August"`, and `"January"`.

See Also

The section on "List value constructors" in *perldata*(1) and Chapter 2 of *Programming Perl*

1.4. Converting Between ASCII Characters and Values

Problem

You want to print out the number represented by a given ASCII character, or you want to print out an ASCII character given a number.

Solution

Use `ord` to convert a character to a number, or use `chr` to convert a number to a character:

```
$num  = ord($char);
$char = chr($num);
```

The `%c` format used in `printf` and `sprintf` also converts a number to a character:

```
$char = sprintf("%c", $num);                    # slower than chr($num)
printf("Number %d is character %c\n", $num, $num);
Number 101 is character e
```

A C* template used with `pack` and `unpack` can quickly convert many characters.

```
@ASCII = unpack("C*", $string);
$STRING = pack("C*", @ascii);
```

Discussion

Unlike low-level, typeless languages like assembler, Perl doesn't treat characters and numbers interchangeably; it treats *strings* and numbers interchangeably. That means you can't just assign characters and numbers back and forth. Perl provides Pascal's `chr` and `ord` to convert between a character and its corresponding ordinal value:

```
$ascii_value = ord("e");    # now 101
$character   = chr(101);    # now "e"
```

If you already have a character, it's really represented as a string of length one, so just print it out directly using `print` or the `%s` format in `printf` and `sprintf`. The `%c` format forces `printf` or `sprintf` to convert a number into a character; it's not used for printing a character that's already in character format (that is, a string).

```
printf("Number %d is character %c\n", 101, 101);
```

The `pack`, `unpack`, `chr`, and `ord` functions are all faster than `sprintf`. Here are `pack` and `unpack` in action:

```
@ascii_character_numbers = unpack("C*", "sample");
print "@ascii_character_numbers\n";
115 97 109 112 108 101

$word = pack("C*", @ascii_character_numbers);
$word = pack("C*", 115, 97, 109, 112, 108, 101);   # same
print "$word\n";
sample
```

Here's how to convert from HAL to IBM:

```
$hal = "HAL";
@ascii = unpack("C*", $hal);
foreach $val (@ascii) {
    $val++;                     # add one to each ASCII value
}
$ibm = pack("C*", @ascii);
print "$ibm\n";                 # prints "IBM"
```

The `ord` function can return numbers from 0 to 255. These correspond to C's `unsigned char` data type.

See Also

The `chr`, `ord`, `printf`, `sprintf`, `pack`, and `unpack` functions in *perlfunc*(1) and Chapter 3 of *Programming Perl*

1.5. Processing a String One Character at a Time

Problem

You want to process a string one character at a time.

Solution

Use `split` with a null pattern to break up the string into individual characters, or use `unpack` if you just want their ASCII values:

```
@array = split(//, $string);
```

```
@array = unpack("C*", $string);
```

Or extract each character in turn with a loop:

```
while (/(.)/g) { # . is never a newline here
    # do something with $1
}
```

Discussion

As we said before, Perl's fundamental unit is the string, not the character. Needing to process anything a character at a time is rare. Usually some kind of higher-level Perl operation, like pattern matching, solves the problem more easily. See, for example, Recipe 7.7, where a set of substitutions is used to find command-line arguments.

Splitting on a pattern that matches the empty string returns a list of the individual characters in the string. This is a convenient feature when done intentionally, but it's easy to do unintentionally. For instance, /X*/ matches the empty string. Odds are you will find others when you don't mean to.

Here's an example that prints the characters used in the string "an apple a day", sorted in ascending ASCII order:

```
%seen = ();
$string = "an apple a day";
foreach $byte (split //, $string) {
    $seen{$byte}++;
}
print "unique chars are: ", sort(keys %seen), "\n";
unique chars are:  adelnpy
```

These split and unpack solutions give you an array of characters to work with. If you don't want an array, you can use a pattern match with the /g flag in a while loop, extracting one character at a time:

```
%seen = ();
$string = "an apple a day";
while ($string =~ /(.)/g) {
    $seen{$1}++;
}
print "unique chars are: ", sort(keys %seen), "\n";
unique chars are:  adelnpy
```

In general, if you find yourself doing character-by-character processing, there's probably a better way to go about it. Instead of using index and substr or split and unpack, it might be easier to use a pattern. Instead of computing a 32-bit checksum by hand, as in the next example, the unpack function can compute it far more efficiently.

The following example calculates the checksum of $string with a foreach loop. There are better checksums; this just happens to be the basis of a traditional and computationally easy checksum. See the MD5 module from CPAN if you want a more sound checksum.

```
$sum = 0;
foreach $ascval (unpack("C*", $string)) {
    $sum += $ascval;
}
print "sum is $sum\n";
# prints "1248" if $string was "an apple a day"
```

This does the same thing, but much faster:

```
$sum = unpack("%32C*", $string);
```

This lets us emulate the SysV checksum program:

```
#!/usr/bin/perl
# sum - compute 16-bit checksum of all input files
$checksum = 0;
while (<>) { $checksum += unpack("%16C*", $_) }
$checksum %= (2 ** 16) - 1;
print "$checksum\n";
```

Here's an example of its use:

```
% perl sum /etc/termcap
1510
```

If you have the GNU version of *sum*, you'll need to call it with the **--sysv** option to get the same answer on the same file.

```
% sum --sysv /etc/termcap
1510 851 /etc/termcap
```

Another tiny program that processes its input one character at a time is *slowcat*, shown in Example 1-1. The idea here is to pause after each character is printed so you can scroll text before an audience slowly enough that they can read it.

Example 1-1. slowcat

```
#!/usr/bin/perl
# slowcat - emulate a   s l o w   line printer
# usage: slowcat [-DELAY] [files ...]
$DELAY = ($ARGV[0] =~ /^-([.\d]+)/) ? (shift, $1) : 1;
$| = 1;
while (<>) {
    for (split(//)) {
        print;
        select(undef,undef,undef, 0.005 * $DELAY);
    }
}
```

See Also

The `split` and `unpack` functions in *perlfunc*(1) and Chapter 3 of *Programming Perl;* the use of `select` for timing is explained in Recipe 3.10

1.6. *Reversing a String by Word or Character*

Problem

You want to reverse the characters or words of a string.

Solution

Use the **reverse** function in scalar context for flipping bytes.

```
$revbytes = reverse($string);
```

To flip words, use **reverse** in list context with `split` and `join`:

```
$revwords = join(" ", reverse split(" ", $string));
```

Discussion

The **reverse** function is two different functions in one. When called in scalar context, it joins together its arguments and returns that string in reverse order. When called in list context, it returns its arguments in the opposite order. When using **reverse** for its byte-flipping behavior, use **scalar** to force scalar context unless it's entirely obvious.

```
$gnirts    = reverse($string);      # reverse letters in $string

@sdrow     = reverse(@words);       # reverse elements in @words

$confused = reverse(@words);        # reverse letters in join("", @words)
```

Here's an example of reversing words in a string. Using a single space, " ", as the pattern to `split` is a special case. It causes `split` to use contiguous whitespace as the separator and also discard any leading null fields, just like *awk*. Normally, `split` discards only trailing null fields.

```
# reverse word order
$string = 'Yoda said, "can you see this?"';
@allwords    = split(" ", $string);
$revwords    = join(" ", reverse @allwords);
print $revwords, "\n";
this?" see you "can said, Yoda
```

We could remove the temporary array **@allwords** and do it on one line:

```
$revwords = join(" ", reverse split(" ", $string));
```

Multiple whitespace in **$string** becomes a single space in **$revwords**. If you want to preserve whitespace, use this:

```
$revwords = join("", reverse split(/(\s+)/, $string));
```

One use of **reverse** is to test whether a word is a palindrome (a word that reads the same backward or forward):

```
$word = "reviver";
$is_palindrome = ($word eq reverse($word));
```

We can turn this into a one-liner that finds big palindromes in */usr/dict/words*.

```
% perl -nle 'print if $_ eq reverse && length > 5' /usr/dict/words
deedeed
degged
deified
denned
hallah
kakkak
```

```
murdrum
redder
repaper
retter
reviver
rotator
sooloos
tebbet
terret
tut-tut
```

See Also

The split, reverse, and scalar functions in *perlfunc*(1) and Chapter 3 of *Programming Perl*; the "Switches" section of *perlrun*(1) and Chapter 6 of *Programming Perl*

1.7. *Expanding and Compressing Tabs*

Problem

You want to convert tabs in a string to the appropriate number of spaces, or vice versa. Converting spaces into tabs can be used to reduce file size when the file has many consecutive spaces. Converting tabs into spaces may be required when producing output for devices that don't understand tabs or think they're at different positions than you do.

Solution

Either use a rather funny looking substitution:

```
while ($string =~ s/\t+/' ' x (length($&) * 8 - length($`) % 8)/e) {
    # spin in empty loop until substitution finally fails
}
```

Or the standard Text::Tabs module:

```
use Text::Tabs;
@expanded_lines  = expand(@lines_with_tabs);
@tabulated_lines = unexpand(@lines_without_tabs);
```

Discussion

Assuming that tab stops are set every N positions (where N is customarily eight), it's easy to convert them into spaces. The standard, textbook method does not use the Text::Tabs module but suffers from being difficult to understand. Also, it uses the $` variable, whose very mention currently slows down every pattern match in the program. The reason for this is given in the "Special Variables" section of the Introduction to Chapter 6.

```
while (<>) {
    1 while s/\t+/' ' x (length($&) * 8 - length($`) % 8)/e;
    print;
}
```

If you're looking at the second `while` loop and wondering why it couldn't have been written as part of a simple `s///g` instead, it's because you need to recalculate the length from the start of the line again each time (stored in `$``) rather than merely from where the last match occurred.

The obscure convention `1 while CONDITION` is the same as `while (CONDITION) { }`, but shorter. Its origins date to when Perl ran the first incredibly faster than the second. While the second is now almost as fast, it remains convenient, and the habit has stuck.

The standard Text::Tabs module provides conversion functions to convert both directions, exports a `$tabstop` variable to control the number of spaces per tab, and does not incur the performance hit because it uses $1 and $2 rather than $& and $`.

```
use Text::Tabs;
$tabstop = 4;
while (<>) { print expand($_) }
```

We can also use Text::Tabs to "unexpand" the tabs. This example uses the default `$tabstop` value of 8:

```
use Text::Tabs;
while (<>) { print unexpand($_) }
```

See Also

The manpage for the Text::Tabs module (also in Chapter 7 of *Programming Perl*); the `s///` operator in *perlre*(1) and *perlop*(1) and the "Pattern Matching" and "Regular Expressions" sections of Chapter 2 of *Programming Perl*

1.8. Expanding Variables in User Input

Problem

You've read in a string with an embedded variable reference, such as:

```
You owe $debt to me.
```

Now you want to replace `$debt` in the string with its value.

Solution

Use a substitution with symbolic references if the variables are all globals:

```
$text =~ s/\$(\w+)/${$1}/g;
```

But use a double /ee if they might be lexical (my) variables:

```
$text =~ s/(\$\w+)/$1/gee;
```

Discussion

The first technique is basically "find what looks like a variable name, and then use symbolic dereferencing to interpolate its contents." If $1 contains the string somevar, then ${$1} will be whatever $somevar contains. This won't work if the use strict 'refs' pragma is in effect because that bans symbolic dereferencing.

Here's an example:

```
use vars qw($rows $cols);
no strict 'refs';                    # for ${$1}/g below
my $text;

($rows, $cols) = (24, 80);
$text = q(I am $rows high and $cols long);   # like single quotes!
$text =~ s/\$(\w+)/${$1}/g;
print $text;
I am 24 high and 80 long
```

You may have seen the /e substitution modifier used to evaluate the replacement as code rather than as a string. It's designed for situations such as doubling every whole number in a string:

```
$text = "I am 17 years old";
$text =~ s/(\d+)/2 * $1/eg;
```

When Perl is compiling your program and sees a /e on a substitute, it compiles the code in the replacement block along with the rest of your program, long before the substitution actually happens. When a substitution is made, $1 is replaced with the string that matched. The code to evaluate would then be something like:

```
2 * 17
```

If we tried saying:

```
$text = 'I am $AGE years old';     # note single quotes
$text =~ s/(\$\w+)/$1/eg;          # WRONG
```

assuming $text held a mention of the variable $AGE, Perl would dutifully replace $1 with $AGE and then evaluate code that looked like:

```
'$AGE'
```

which just yields us our original string back again. We need to evaluate the result *again* to get the value of the variable. To do that, just add another /e:

```
$text =~ s/(\$\w+)/$1/eeg;              # finds my() variables
```

Yes, you can have as many /e modifiers as you'd like. Only the first one is compiled and syntax-checked with the rest of your program. This makes it work like the eval {BLOCK} construct, except that it doesn't trap exceptions. Think of it more as a do {BLOCK} instead.

Subsequent /e modifiers are quite different. They're more like the eval "STRING" construct. They don't get compiled until run-time. A small advantage of this scheme is that it doesn't make you put a no strict 'refs' pragma in the block. A tremendous advantage is that unlike the symbolic dereferencing, this mechanism can actually find lexical variables created with my, something symbolic references can never do.

The following example uses the /x modifier to enable whitespace and comments in the pattern part of the substitute and /e to evaluate the right-hand side as code. The /e modifier gives you more control over what happens in case of error or other extenuating circumstances, as we have here:

```
# expand variables in $text, but put an error message in
# if the variable isn't defined
$text =~ s{
    \$                          # find a literal dollar sign
    (\w+)                       # find a "word" and store it in $1
}{
    no strict 'refs';           # for $$1 below
    if (defined $$1) {
        $$1;                    # expand global variables only
    } else {
        "[NO VARIABLE: \$$1]";  # error msg
    }
}egx;
```

Note that the syntax of $$1 has changed for Perl 5.004: it used to mean ${$}1 but now means ${$1}. For backwards compatibility, in strings it still takes the old meaning (but generates a warning with -w). People will write ${$1} within a string to keep from dereferencing the PID variable. If $$ were 23448, then $$1 in a string would turn into 234481, not the contents of the variable whose name was stored in $1.

See Also

The s/// operator in *perlre*(1) and *perlop*(1) and the "Pattern Matching" and "Regular Expressions" sections of Chapter 2 of *Programming Perl*; the eval function in *perlfunc*(1) and Chapter 3 of *Programming Perl*; the similar use of substitutions in Recipe 20.9.

1.9. Controlling Case

Problem

A string in uppercase needs converting to lowercase, or vice versa.

Solution

Use the lc and uc functions or the \L and \U string escapes.

```
use locale;                    # needed in 5.004 or above

$big = uc($little);            # "bo peep" -> "BO PEEP"
$little = lc($big);            # "JOHN"    -> "john"
$big = "\U$little";            # "bo peep" -> "BO PEEP"
$little = "\L$big";            # "JOHN"    -> "john"
```

To alter just one character, use the lcfirst and ucfirst functions or the \l and \u string escapes.

```
$big = "\u$little";            # "bo"      -> "Bo"
$little = "\l$big";            # "BoPeep"    -> "boPeep"
```

Discussion

The functions and string escapes look different, but both do the same thing. You can set the case of either the first character or the whole string. You can even do both at once to force uppercase on initial characters and lowercase on the rest.

The use locale directive tells Perl's case-conversion functions and pattern matching engine to respect your language environment, allowing for characters with diacritical marks, and so on. A common mistake is to use tr/// to convert case. (We're aware that the old Camel book recommended tr/A-Z/a-z/. In our defense, that was the only way to do it back then.) This won't work in all situations because when you say tr/A-Z/a-z/ you have omitted all characters with umlauts, accent marks, cedillas, and other diacritics used in dozens of languages, including English. The uc and \U case-changing commands understand these characters and convert them properly, at least when you've said use locale. (An exception is that in German, the uppercase form of ß is SS, but it's not in Perl.)

```
use locale;                    # needed in 5.004 or above

$beast   = "dromedary";
# capitalize various parts of $beast
$capit   = ucfirst($beast);            # Dromedary
```

```
$capit   = "\u\L$beast";              # (same)
$capall  = uc($beast);                # DROMEDARY
$capall  = "\U$beast";                # (same)
$caprest = lcfirst(uc($beast));       # dROMEDARY
$caprest = "\l\U$beast";              # (same)
```

These capitalization changing escapes are commonly used to make the case in a string consistent:

```
# capitalize each word's first character, downcase the rest
$text = "thIS is a loNG liNE";
$text =~ s/(\w+)/\u\L$1/g;
print $text;
This Is A Long Line
```

You can also use their functional forms to do case-insensitive comparison:

```
if (uc($a) eq uc($b)) {
    print "a and b are the same\n";
}
```

The *randcap* program, shown in Example 1-2, randomly capitalizes 20 percent of the letters of its input. This lets you converse with 14-year-old WaREz d00Dz.

Example 1-2. randcap

```
#!/usr/bin/perl -p
# randcap: filter to randomly capitalize 20% of the letters
# call to srand() is unnecessary in 5.004
BEGIN { srand(time() ^ ($$ + ($$ << 15))) }
sub randcase { rand(100) < 20 ? "\u$_[0]" : "\l$_[0]" }
s/(\w)/randcase($1)/ge;

% randcap < genesis | head -9
boOk 01 genesis

001:001 in the BEginning goD created the heaven and tHe earTh.

001:002 and the earth wAS without ForM, aND void; AnD darkneSS was
        upon The Face of the dEEp. and the spIrit of GOd movEd upOn
        tHe face of the Waters.

001:003 and god Said, let there be ligHt: and therE wAs LigHt.
```

A more interesting approach would have been to take advantage of Perl's ability to use bitwise operators on strings:

```
sub randcase {
    rand(100) < 20 ? ("\040" ^ $1) : $1
}
```

That would, in 20 percent of the cases, switch the case of the letter. However, this misbehaves on 8-bit characters. The original *randcase* program had the same problem, but appying use locale would have easily fixed it.

This example of bitwise string operations quickly strips off all the high bits on a string:

```
$string &= "\177" x length($string);
```

Again, they'll be talking about you all over Europe, and not in the most glowing of terms, if you force all strings to seven bits.

See Also

The uc, lc, ucfirst, and lcfirst functions in *perlfunc*(1) and Chapter 3 of *Programming Perl*; the \L, \U, \l, and \u string escapes in the "Quote and Quote-like Operators" section of *perlop*(1) and Chapter 2 of *Programming Perl*

1.10. Interpolating Functions and Expressions Within Strings

Problem

You want a function call or expression to expand within a string. This lets you construct more complex templates than with simple scalar variable interpolation.

Solution

You can break up your expression into distinct concatenated pieces:

```
$answer = $var1 . func() . $var2;   # scalar only
```

Or you can use the slightly sneaky @{[LIST EXPR]} or ${ \(SCALAR EXPR) } expansions:

```
$answer = "STRING @{[ LIST EXPR ]} MORE STRING";
$answer = "STRING ${\( SCALAR EXPR )} MORE STRING";
```

Discussion

This code shows both techniques. The first line shows concatenation; the second shows the expansion trick:

```
$phrase = "I have " . ($n + 1) . " guanacos.";
$phrase = "I have ${\($n + 1)} guanacos.";
```

The first technique builds the final string by concatenating smaller strings, avoiding interpolation but achieving the same end. Because print effectively concatenates its entire argument list, if we were going to print $phrase, we could have just said:

```
print "I have ",  $n + 1, " guanacos.\n";
```

When you absolutely must have interpolation, you need the punctuation-riddled interpolation from the Solution. Only @, $, and \ are special within double quotes and most backquotes. (As with `m//` and `s///`, the `qx()` synonym is not subject to double-quote expansion if its delimiter is single quotes! `$home = qx'echo home is $HOME';` would get the shell `$HOME` variable, not one in Perl.) So, the only way to force arbitrary expressions to expand is by expanding a `${}` or `@{}` whose block contains a reference.

You can do more than simply assign to a variable after interpolation. It's a general mechanism that can be used in any double-quoted string. For instance, this example will build a string with an interpolated expression and pass the result to a function:

```
some_func("What you want is @{[ split /:/, $rec ]} items");
```

You can interpolate into a here document, as by:

```
die "Couldn't send mail" unless send_mail(<<"EOTEXT", $target);
To: $naughty
From: Your Bank
Cc: @{ get_manager_list($naughty) }
Date: @{[ do { my $now = `date`; chomp $now; $now } ]} (today)

Dear $naughty,

Today, you bounced check number @{[ 500 + int rand(100) ]} to us.
Your account is now closed.

Sincerely,
the management
EOTEXT
```

Expanding backquotes (` `` `) is particularly challenging because you would normally end up with spurious newlines. By creating a braced block following the @ within the `@{[]}` anonymous array dereference, as we did in the last example, you can create private variables.

Although these techniques work, simply breaking your work up into several steps or storing everything in temporary variables is almost always clearer to the reader.

In version 5.004 of Perl, `${\ EXPR }` wrongly evaluates EXPR in list instead of scalar context. This bug is fixed in version 5.005.

See Also

perlref(1) and the "Other Tricks You Can Do with Hard References" section of Chapter 4 of *Programming Perl*

1.11. Indenting Here Documents

Problem

When using the multiline quoting mechanism called a *here document*, the text must be flush against the margin, which looks out of place in the code. You would like to indent the here document text in the code, but not have the indentation appear in the final string value.

Solution

Use a `s///` operator to strip out leading whitespace.

```
# all in one
($var = <<HERE_TARGET) =~ s/^\s+//gm;
    your text
    goes here
HERE_TARGET

# or with two steps
$var = <<HERE_TARGET;
    your text
    goes here
HERE_TARGET
$var =~ s/^\s+//gm;
```

Discussion

The substitution is straightforward. It removes leading whitespace from the text of the here document. The `/m` modifier lets the `^` character match at the start of each line in the string, and the `/g` modifier makes the pattern matching engine repeat the substitution as often as it can (i.e., for every line in the here document).

```
($definition = <<'FINIS') =~ s/^\s+//gm;
    The five varieties of camelids
    are the familiar camel, his friends
    the llama and the alpaca, and the
    rather less well-known guanaco
    and vicuña.
FINIS
```

Be warned: all the patterns in this recipe use `\s`, which will also match newlines. This means they will remove any blank lines in your here document. If you don't want this, replace `\s` with `[^\S\n]` in the patterns.

The substitution makes use of the property that the result of an assignment can be used as the left-hand side of `=~`. This lets us do it all in one line, but it only works when you're assigning to a variable. When you're using the here document directly, it would be considered a constant value and you wouldn't be able to modify it. In fact, you can't change a here document's value *unless* you first put it into a variable.

Not to worry, though, because there's an easy way around this, particularly if you're going to do this a lot in the program. Just write a subroutine to do it:

```
sub fix {
    my $string = shift;
    $string =~ s/^\s+//gm;
    return $string;
}


print fix(<<"END");
    My stuff goes here
END


# With function predeclaration, you can omit the parens:
print fix <<"END";
    My stuff goes here
END
```

As with all here documents, you have to place this here document's target (the token that marks its end, END in this case) flush against the left-hand margin. If you want to have the target indented also, you'll have to put the same amount of whitespace in the quoted string as you use to indent the token.

```
($quote = <<'    FINIS') =~ s/^\s+//gm;
        ...we will have peace, when you and all your works have
        perished--and the works of your dark master to whom you would
        deliver us. You are a liar, Saruman, and a corrupter of men's
        hearts.   --Theoden in /usr/src/perl/taint.c
    FINIS
$quote =~ s/\s+--/\n--/;        #move attribution to line of its own
```

If you're doing this to strings that contain code you're building up for an **eval**, or just text to print out, you might not want to blindly strip off all leading whitespace because that would destroy your indentation. Although **eval** wouldn't care, your reader might.

Another embellishment is to use a special leading string for code that stands out. For example, here we'll prepend each line with @@@, properly indented:

```
if ($REMEMBER_THE_MAIN) {
    $perl_main_C = dequote<<'    MAIN_INTERPRETER_LOOP';
        @@@ int
        @@@ runops() {
        @@@     SAVEI32(runlevel);
        @@@     runlevel++;
        @@@     while ( op = (*op->op_ppaddr)() ) ;
        @@@     TAINT_NOT;
        @@@     return 0;
        @@@ }
    MAIN_INTERPRETER_LOOP
    # add more code here if you want
}
```

Destroying indentation also gets you in trouble with poets.

```
sub dequote;
$poem = dequote<<EVER_ON_AND_ON;
        Now far ahead the Road has gone,
            And I must follow, if I can,
        Pursuing it with eager feet,
            Until it joins some larger way
        Where many paths and errands meet.
            And whither then? I cannot say.
                --Bilbo in /usr/src/perl/pp_ctl.c
EVER_ON_AND_ON
print "Here's your poem:\n\n$poem\n";
```

Here is its sample output:

```
Here's your poem:
Now far ahead the Road has gone,
    And I must follow, if I can,
Pursuing it with eager feet,
    Until it joins some larger way
Where many paths and errands meet.
    And whither then? I cannot say.
        --Bilbo in /usr/src/perl/pp_ctl.c
```

The following **dequote** function handles all these cases. It expects to be called with a here document as its argument. It checks whether each line begins with a common substring, and if so, strips that off. Otherwise, it takes the amount of leading whitespace found on the first line and removes that much off each subsequent line.

```
sub dequote {
    local $_ = shift;
    my ($white, $leader);  # common whitespace and common leading string
    if (/^\s*(?:([^\w\s]+)(\s*).*\n)(?:\s*\1\2?.*\n)+$/) {
        ($white, $leader) = ($2, quotemeta($1));
    } else {
        ($white, $leader) = (/^(\s+)/, '');
    }
    s/^\s*?$leader(?:$white)?//gm;
    return $_;
}
```

If that pattern makes your eyes glaze over, you could always break it up and add comments by adding /x:

```
if (m{
            ^                       # start of line
            \s *                    # 0 or more whitespace chars
            (?:                     # begin first non-remembered grouping
                (                   #   begin save buffer $1
                    [^\w\s]         #     one byte neither space nor word
                    +               #     1 or more of such
                )                   #   end save buffer $1
```

```
            ( \s* )                      #   put 0 or more white in buffer $2
              .* \n                      #   match through the end of first line
          )                              # end of first grouping
          (?:                            # begin second non-remembered grouping
              \s *                       #    0 or more whitespace chars
              \1                         #    whatever string is destined for $1
              \2 ?                       #    what'll be in $2, but optionally
              .* \n                      #    match through the end of the line
          ) +                            # now repeat that group idea 1 or more
          $                              # until the end of the line
        }x
    )
    {
      ($white, $leader) = ($2, quotemeta($1));
    } else {
      ($white, $leader) = (/^(\s+)/, '');
    }
    s{
        ^                                # start of each line (due to /m)
        \s *                             # any amount of leading whitespace
          ?                              #    but minimally matched
        $leader                          # our quoted, saved per-line leader
        (?:                              # begin unremembered grouping
            $white                       #    the same amount
        ) ?                              # optionalize in case EOL after leader
    }{}xgm;
```

There, isn't that much easier to read? Well, maybe not; sometimes it doesn't help to pepper your code with insipid comments that mirror the code. This may be one of those cases.

See Also

The "Scalar Value Constructors" section of *perldata*(1) and the "Here Documents" section of Chapter 2 of *Programming Perl*; the s/// operator in *perlre*(1) and *perlop*(1), and the "Pattern Matching" section of Chapter 2 of *Programming Perl*

1.12. Reformatting Paragraphs

Problem

Your string is too big to fit the screen, and you want to break it up into lines of words, without splitting a word between lines. For instance, a style correction script might read a text file a paragraph at a time, replacing bad phrases with good ones. Replacing a phrase like *utilizes the inherent functionality of* with *uses* will change the length of lines, so it must somehow reformat the paragraphs when they're output.

Solution

Use the standard Text::Wrap module to put line breaks at the right place.

```
use Text::Wrap;
@OUTPUT = wrap($LEADTAB, $NEXTTAB, @PARA);
```

Discussion

The Text::Wrap module provides the **wrap** function, shown in Example 1-3, which takes a list of lines and reformats them into a paragraph having no line more than `$Text::Wrap::columns` characters long. We set `$columns` to 20, ensuring that no line will be longer than 20 characters. We pass **wrap** two arguments before the list of lines: the first is the indent for the first line of output, the second the indent for every subsequent line.

Example 1-3. wrapdemo

```
#!/usr/bin/perl -w
# wrapdemo - show how Text::Wrap works

@input = ("Folding and splicing is the work of an editor,",
          "not a mere collection of silicon",
          "and",
          "mobile electrons!");

use Text::Wrap qw($columns &wrap);

$columns = 20;
print "0123456789" x 2, "\n";
print wrap("    ", "  ", @input), "\n";
```

The result of this program is:

```
01234567890123456789
    Folding and
  splicing is the
  work of an
  editor, not a
  mere collection
  of silicon and
  mobile electrons!
```

We get back a single string, with newlines ending each line but the last:

```
# merge multiple lines into one, then wrap one long line
use Text::Wrap;
undef $/;
print wrap('', '', split(/\s*\n\s*/, <>));
```

If you have the Term::ReadKey module (available from CPAN) on your system, you can use it to determine your window size so you can wrap lines to fit the current screen size. If you don't have the module, sometimes the screen size can be found in $ENV{COLUMNS} or by parsing the output of the *stty* command.

The following program tries to reformat both short and long lines within a paragraph, similar to the *fmt* program, by setting the input record separator $/ to the empty string (causing <> to read paragraphs) and the output record separator $\ to two newlines. Then the paragraph is converted into one long line by changing all newlines (and any surrounding whitespace) to single spaces. Finally, we call the **wrap** function with both leading and subsequent tab strings set to the empty string so we can have block paragraphs.

```
use Text::Wrap        qw(&wrap $columns);
use Term::ReadKey     qw(GetTerminalSize);
($columns) = GetTerminalSize();
($/, $\)  = ('', "\n\n");    # read by paragraph, output 2 newlines
while (<>) {                  # grab a full paragraph
    s/\s*\n\s*/ /g;          # convert intervening newlines to spaces
    print wrap('', '', $_);  # and format
}
```

See Also

The **split** and **join** functions in *perlfunc*(1) and Chapter 3 of *Programming Perl*; the manpage for the standard Text::Wrap module, also in Chapter 7 of *Programming Perl*; the CPAN module Term::ReadKey, and its use in Recipe 15.6

1.13. Escaping Characters

Problem

You need to output a string with certain characters (quotes, commas, etc.) escaped. For instance, you're producing a format string for **sprintf** and want to convert literal % signs into %%.

Solution

Use a substitution to backslash or double each character to be escaped.

```
# backslash
$var =~ s/([CHARLIST])/\\$1/g;

# double
$var =~ s/([CHARLIST])/$1$1/g;
```

Discussion

`$var` is the variable to be altered. The `CHARLIST` is a list of characters to escape and can contain backslash escapes like \t and \n. If you just have one character to escape, omit the brackets:

```
$string =~ s/%/%%/g;
```

The following lets you do escaping when preparing strings to submit to the shell. (In practice, you would need to escape more than just ' and " to make any arbitrary string safe for the shell. Getting the list of characters right is so hard, and the risks if you get it wrong are so great, that you're better off using the list form of `system` and `exec` to run programs, shown in Recipe 16.11. They avoid the shell altogether.)

```
$string = q(Mom said, "Don't do that.");
$string =~ s/(['"])/\\$1/g;
```

We had to use two backslashes in the replacement because the replacement section of a substitution is read as a double-quoted string, and to get one backslash, you need to write two. Here's a similar example for VMS DCL, where you need to double every quote characters to get one through:

```
$string = q(Mom said, "Don't do that.");
$string =~ s/(['"])/$1$1/g;
```

Microsoft command interpreters are harder to work with. In DOS and Windows *COMMAND.COM* recognizes double quotes but not single ones, has no clue what to do with backquotes, and requires a backslash to make a double quote a literal. Almost any of the free or commercial Unix-like shell environments for Windows will improve this depressing situation.

Because we're using character classes in the regular expressions, we can use – to define a range, and ^ at the start to negate. This escapes all characters that aren't in the range A through Z.

```
$string =~ s/([^A-Z])/\\$1/g;
```

If you want to escape all non-word characters, use the \Q and \E string metacharacters or the `quotemeta` function. For example, these are equivalent:

```
$string = "this \Qis a test!\E";
$string = "this is\\ a\\ test\\!";
$string = "this " . quotemeta("is a test!");
```

See Also

The `s///` operator in *perlre*(1) and *perlop*(1) and the "Pattern Matching" section of Chapter 2 of *Programming Perl*; the `quotemeta` function in *perlfunc*(1) and Chap-

ter 3 of *Programming Perl*; the discussion of HTML escaping in Recipe 19.1;
Recipe 19.6 for how to avoid having to escape strings to give the shell

1.14. *Trimming Blanks from the Ends of a String*

Problem

You have read a string that may have leading or trailing whitespace, and you want
to remove it.

Solution

Use a pair of pattern substitutions to get rid of them:

```
$string =~ s/^\s+//;
$string =~ s/\s+$//;
```

You can also write a function that returns the new value:

```
$string = trim($string);
@many   = trim(@many);

sub trim {
    my @out = @_;
    for (@out) {
        s/^\s+//;
        s/\s+$//;
    }
    return wantarray ? @out : $out[0];
}
```

Discussion

This problem has various solutions, but this is the most efficient for the common
case.

If you want to remove the last character from the string, use the chop function.
Version 5 added chomp, which removes the last character if and only if it is contained in the $/ variable, "\n" by default. These are often used to remove the
trailing newline from input:

```
# print what's typed, but surrounded by >< symbols
while (<STDIN>) {
    chomp;
    print ">$_<\n";
}
```

See Also

The s/// operator in *perlre*(1) and *perlop*(1) and the "Pattern Matching" section of Chapter 2 of *Programming Perl*; the chomp and chop functions in *perlfunc*(1) and Chapter 3 of *Programming Perl*; we trim leading and trailing whitespace in the getnum function in Recipe 2.1.

1.15. Parsing Comma-Separated Data

Problem

You have a data file containing comma-separated values that you need to read in, but these data fields may have quoted commas or escaped quotes in them. Most spreadsheets and database programs use comma-separated values as a common interchange format.

Solution

Use the procedure in *Mastering Regular Expressions*.

```
sub parse_csv {
    my $text = shift;       # record containing comma-separated values
    my @new  = ();
    push(@new, $+) while $text =~ m{
        # the first part groups the phrase inside the quotes.
        # see explanation of this pattern in MRE
        "([^\"\\]*(?:\\.[^\"\\]*)*)",?
        |  ([^,]+),?
        |  ,
    }gx;
    push(@new, undef) if substr($text, -1,1) eq ',';
    return @new;          # list of values that were comma-separated
}
```

Or use the standard Text::ParseWords module.

```
use Text::ParseWords;

sub parse_csv {
    return quotewords(",",0, $_[0]);
}
```

Discussion

Comma-separated input is a deceptive and complex format. It sounds simple, but involves a fairly complex escaping system because the fields themselves can contain commas. This makes the pattern matching solution complex and rules out a simple split /,/.

Fortunately, Text::ParseWords hides the complexity from you. Pass its quote-words function two arguments and the CSV string. The first argument is the separator (a comma, in this case) and the second is a true or false value controlling whether the strings are returned with quotes around them.

If you want to represent quotation marks inside a field delimited by quotation marks, escape them with backslashes `"like \"this\""`. Quotation marks and backslashes are the only characters that have meaning backslashed. Any other use of a backslash will be left in the output string.

Here's how you'd use the **parse_csv** subroutines. The q<> is just a fancy quote so we didn't have to backslash everything.

```
$line = q<XYZZY,"","O'Reilly, Inc","Wall, Larry","a \"glug\" bit, ",5,
    "Error, Core Dumped">;
@fields = parse_csv($line);
for ($i = 0; $i < @fields; $i++) {
    print "$i : $fields[$i]\n";
}
0 : XYZZY
1 :
2 : O'Reilly, Inc
3 : Wall, Larry
4 : a \"glug\" bit,
5 : 5
6 : Error, Core Dumped
```

See Also

The explanation of regular expression syntax in *perlre*(1) and Chapter 2 of *Programming Perl*; the documentation for the standard Text::ParseWords module (also in Chapter 7 of *Programming Perl*); the section "An Introductory Example: Parsing CSV Text" in Chapter 7 of *Mastering Regular Expressions*

1.16. Soundex Matching

Problem

You have two English surnames and want to know whether they sound somewhat similar, regardless of spelling. This would let you offer users a "fuzzy search" of names in a telephone book to catch "Smith" and "Smythe" and others within the set, such as "Smite" and "Smote."

Solution

Use the standard Text::Soundex module:

```
use Text::Soundex;

$CODE  = soundex($STRING);
@CODES = soundex(@LIST);
```

Discussion

The soundex algorithm hashes words (particularly English surnames) into a small space using a simple model that approximates an English speaker's pronunciation of the words. Roughly speaking, each word is reduced to a four character string. The first character is an uppercase letter; the remaining three are digits. By comparing the soundex values of two strings, we can guess whether they sound similar.

The following program prompts for a name and looks for similarly sounding names from the password file. This same approach works on any database with names, so you could key the database on the soundex values if you wanted to. Such a key wouldn't be unique, of course.

```
use Text::Soundex;
use User::pwent;

print "Lookup user: ";
chomp($user = <STDIN>);
exit unless defined $user;
$name_code = soundex($user);

while ($uent = getpwent()) {
    ($firstname, $lastname) = $uent->gecos =~ /(\w+)[^,]*\b(\w+)/;

    if ($name_code eq soundex($uent->name) ||
        $name_code eq soundex($lastname)   ||
        $name_code eq soundex($firstname)  )
    {
        printf "%s: %s %s\n", $uent->name, $firstname, $lastname;
    }
}
```

See Also

The documentation for the standard Text::Soundex and User::pwent modules (also in Chapter 7 of *Programming Perl*); your system's *passwd*(5) manpage; Volume 3, Chapter 6 of *The Art of Computer Programming*

1.17. Program: fixstyle

Imagine you have a table with both old and new strings, such as the following.

Old Words	New Words
bonnet	hood
rubber	eraser
lorry	truck
trousers	pants

The program in Example 1-4 is a filter that changes all occurrences of each element in the first set to the corresponding element in the second set.

When called without filename arguments, the program is a simple filter. If filenames are supplied on the command line, an in-place edit writes the changes to
the files, with the original versions safely saved in a file with a ".orig" extension. See Recipe 7.9 for a description. A -v command-line option writes notification of each change to standard error.

The table of original strings and their replacements is stored below __END__ in
the main program as described in Recipe 7.6. Each pair of strings is converted into
carefully escaped substitutions and accumulated into the $code variable like the
popgrep2 program in Recipe 6.10.

A -t check to test for an interactive run check tells whether we're expecting to
read from the keyboard if no arguments are supplied. That way if the user forgets
to give an argument, they aren't wondering why the program appears to be hung.

Example 1-4. fixstyle

```
#!/usr/bin/perl -w
# fixstyle - switch first set of <DATA> strings to second set
#    usage: $0 [-v] [files ...]
use strict;
my $verbose = (@ARGV && $ARGV[0] eq '-v' && shift);

if (@ARGV) {
    $^I = ".orig";              # preserve old files
} else {
    warn "$0: Reading from stdin\n" if -t STDIN;
}

my $code = "while (<>) {\n";
# read in config, build up code to eval
while (<DATA>) {
    chomp;
    my ($in, $out) = split /\s*=>\s*/;
    next unless $in && $out;
```

Example 1-4. fixstyle (continued)

```
        $code .= "s{\\Q$in\\E}{$out}g";
        $code .= "&& printf STDERR qq($in => $out at \$ARGV line \$.\\n)"
                                                    if $verbose;

        $code .= ";\n";
    }
    $code .= "print;\n}\n";

    eval "{ $code } 1" || die;


    __END__
    analysed          => analyzed
    built-in          => builtin
    chastized         => chastised
    commandline       => command-line
    de-allocate       => deallocate
    dropin            => drop-in
    hardcode          => hard-code
    meta-data         => metadata
    multicharacter    => multi-character
    multiway          => multi-way
    non-empty         => nonempty
    non-profit        => nonprofit
    non-trappable     => nontrappable
    pre-define        => predefine
    preextend         => pre-extend
    re-compiling      => recompiling
    reenter           => re-enter
    turnkey           => turn-key
```

One caution: This program is fast, but it doesn't scale if you need to make hundreds of changes. The larger the DATA section, the longer it takes. A few dozen changes won't slow it down, and in fact, the version given in the solution above is faster for that case. But if you run the program on hundreds of changes, it will bog down.

Example 1-5 is a version that's slower for few changes but faster when there are many changes.

Example 1-5. fixstyle2

```
#!/usr/bin/perl -w
# fixstyle2 - like fixstyle but faster for many many matches
use strict;
my $verbose = (@ARGV && $ARGV[0] eq '-v' && shift);
my %change = ();
while (<DATA>) {
    chomp;
    my ($in, $out) = split /\s*=>\s*/;
    next unless $in && $out;
    $change{$in} = $out;
}
```

Example 1-5. fixstyle2 (continued)

```
if (@ARGV) {
    $^I = ".orig";
} else {
    warn "$0: Reading from stdin\n" if -t STDIN;
}

while (<>) {
    my $i = 0;
    s/^(\s+)// && print $1;              # emit leading whitespace
    for (split /(\s+)/, $_, -1) {    # preserve trailing whitespace
        print( ($i++ & 1) ? $_ : ($change{$_} || $_));
    }
}


__END__
analysed            => analyzed
built-in            => builtin
chastized           => chastised
commandline         => command-line
de-allocate         => deallocate
dropin              => drop-in
hardcode            => hard-code
meta-data           => metadata
multicharacter      => multi-character
multiway            => multi-way
non-empty           => nonempty
non-profit          => nonprofit
non-trappable       => nontrappable
pre-define          => predefine
preextend           => pre-extend
re-compiling        => recompiling
reenter             => re-enter
turnkey             => turn-key
```

This version breaks each line into chunks of whitespace and words, which isn't a fast operation. It then uses those words to look up their replacements in a hash, which is much faster than a substitution. So the first part is slower, the second faster. The difference in speed depends on the number of matches.

If we didn't care about keeping the amount of whitespace separating each word constant, the second version can run as fast as the first even for a few changes. If you know a lot about your input, you can collapse whitespace into single blanks by plugging in this loop:

```
# very fast, but whitespace collapse
while (<>) {
    for (split) {
        print $change{$_} || $_, " ";
    }
    print "\n";
}
```

That leaves an extra blank at the end of each line. If that's a problem, you could use the technique from Recipe 16.5 to install an output filter. Place the following code in front of the `while` loop that's collapsing whitespace:

```
my $pid = open(STDOUT, "|-");
die "cannot fork: $!" unless defined $pid;
unless ($pid) {                    # child
        while (<STDIN>) {
        s/ $//;
        print;
    }
    exit;
}
```

1.18. Program: psgrep

Many programs, including *ps*, *netstat*, *lsof*, *ls -l*, *find -ls*, and *tcpdump*, can produce more output than can be conveniently summarized. Logfiles also often grow too long to be easily viewed. You could send these through a filter like *grep* to pick out only certain lines, but regular expressions and complex logic don't mix well; just look at the hoops we jump through in Recipe 6.17.

What we'd really like is to make full queries on the program output or logfile. For example, to ask *ps* something like, "Show me all the processes that exceed 10K in size but which aren't running as the superuser." Or, "Which commands are running on pseudo-ttys?"

The *psgrep* program does this—and infinitely more—because the specified selection criteria are not mere regular expressions; they're full Perl code. Each criterion is applied in turn to every line of output. Only lines matching all arguments are output. The following is a list of things to find and how to find them.

Lines containing "sh" at the end of a word:

```
% psgrep '/sh\b/'
```

Processes whose command names end in "sh":

```
% psgrep 'command =~ /sh$/'
```

Processes running with a user ID below 10:

```
% psgrep 'uid < 10'
```

Login shells with active ttys:

```
% psgrep 'command =~ /^-/' 'tty ne "?"'
```

Processes running on pseudo-ttys:

```
% psgrep 'tty =~ /^[p-t]/'
```

Non-superuser processes running detached:

```
% psgrep 'uid && tty eq "?"'
```

Huge processes that aren't owned by the superuser:

```
% psgrep 'size > 10 * 2**10' 'uid != 0'
```

The last call to *psgrep* produced the following output when run on our system. As one might expect, only *netscape* and its spawn qualified.

FLAGS	UID	PID	PPID	PRI	NI	SIZE	RSS	WCHAN	STA	TTY	TIME	COMMAND
0	101	9751	1	0	0	14932	9652	do_select	S	p1	0:25	netscape
100000	101	9752	9751	0	0	10636	812	do_select	S	p1	0:00	(dns helper)

Example 1-6 shows the *psgrep* program.

Example 1-6. psgrep

```perl
#!/usr/bin/perl -w
# psgrep - print selected lines of ps output by
#          compiling user queries into code

use strict;

# each field from the PS header
my @fieldnames = qw(FLAGS UID PID PPID PRI NICE SIZE
                    RSS WCHAN STAT TTY TIME COMMAND);

# determine the unpack format needed (hard-coded for Linux ps)
my $fmt = cut2fmt(8, 14, 20, 26, 30, 34, 41, 47, 59, 63, 67, 72);

my %fields;                         # where the data will store

die <<Thanatos unless @ARGV;
usage: $0 criterion ...
    Each criterion is a Perl expression involving:
      @fieldnames
    All criteria must be met for a line to be printed.
Thanatos

# Create function aliases for uid, size, UID, SIZE, etc.
# Empty parens on closure args needed for void prototyping.
for my $name (@fieldnames) {
    no strict 'refs';
    *$name = *{lc $name} = sub () { $fields{$name} };
}

my $code = "sub is_desirable { " . join(" and ", @ARGV) . " } ";
unless (eval $code.1) {
    die "Error in code: $@\n\t$code\n";
}

open(PS, "ps wwaxl |")              || die "cannot fork: $!";
print scalar <PS>;                  # emit header line
```

Example 1-6. psgrep (continued)

```
while (<PS>) {
    @fields{@fieldnames} = trim(unpack($fmt, $_));
    print if is_desirable();          # line matches their criteria
}
close(PS)                             || die "ps failed!";

# convert cut positions to unpack format
sub cut2fmt {
    my (@positions) = @_;
    my $template  = '';
    my $lastpos   = 1;
    for my $place (@positions) {
        $template .= "A" . ($place - $lastpos) . " ";
        $lastpos  = $place;
    }
    $template .= "A*";
    return $template;
}

sub trim {
    my @strings = @_;
    for (@strings) {
        s/^\s+//;
        s/\s+$//;
    }
    return wantarray ? @strings : $strings[0];
}

# the following was used to determine column cut points.
# sample input data follows
#123456789012345678901234567890123456789012345678901234567890123456789012345
#         1         2         3         4         5         6         7
# Positioning:
#         8    14    20    26 30 34      41      47        59 63 67   72
#         |     |     |     |  |  |       |       |         |  |  |    |
__END__
```

FLAGS	UID	PID	PPID	PRI	NI	SIZE	RSS	WCHAN	STA	TTY	TIME	COMMAND
100	0	1	0	0	0	760	432	do_select	S	?	0:02	init
140	0	187	1	0	0	784	452	do_select	S	?	0:02	syslogd
100100	101	428	1	0	0	1436	944	do_exit	S	1	0:00	/bin/login
100140	99	30217	402	0	0	1552	1008	posix_lock_	S	?	0:00	httpd
0	101	593	428	0	0	1780	1260	copy_thread	S	1	0:00	-tcsh
100000	101	30639	9562	17	0	924	496		R	p1	0:00	ps axl
0	101	25145	9563	0	0	2964	2360	idetape_rea	S	p2	0:06	trn
100100	0	10116	9564	0	0	1412	928	setup_frame	T	p3	0:00	ssh -C www
100100	0	26560	26554	0	0	1076	572	setup_frame	T	p2	0:00	less
100000	101	19058	9562	0	0	1396	900	setup_frame	T	p1	0:02	nvi /tmp/a

The *psgrep* program integrates many techniques presented throughout this book. Stripping strings of leading and trailing whitespace is found in Recipe 1.14. Converting cut marks into an **unpack** format to extract fixed fields is in Recipe 1.1. Matching strings with regular expressions is the entire topic of Chapter 6.

The multiline string in the here document passed to `die` is discussed in Recipes 1.10 and 1.11. The assignment to `@fields{@fieldnames}` sets many values at once in the hash named `%fields`. Hash slices are discussed in Recipes 4.7 and 5.10.

The sample program input contained beneath `__END__` is described in Recipe 7.6. During development, we used canned input from the `DATA` filehandle for testing purposes. Once the program worked properly, we changed it to read from a piped-in *ps* command but left a remnant of the original filter input to aid in future porting and maintenance. Launching other programs over a pipe is covered in Chapter 16, *Process Management and Communication,* including Recipes 16.10 and 16.13.

The real power and expressiveness in *psgrep* derive from Perl's use of string arguments not as mere strings but directly as Perl code. This is similar to the technique in Recipe 9.9, except that in *psgrep*, the user's arguments are wrapped with a routine called `is_desirable`. That way, the cost of compiling strings into Perl code happens only once, before the program whose output we'll process is even begun. For example, asking for UIDs under 10 creates this string to `eval`:

```
eval "sub is_desirable { uid < 10 } " . 1;
```

The mysterious `".1"` at the end is so that if the user code compiles, the whole `eval` returns true. That way we don't even have to check `$@` for compilation errors as we do in Recipe 10.12.

Specifying arbitrary Perl code in a filter to select records is a breathtakingly powerful approach, but it's not entirely original. Perl owes much to the *awk* programming language, which is often used for such filtering. One problem with *awk* is that it can't easily treat input as fixed-size fields instead of fields separated by something. Another is that the fields are not mnemonically named: *awk* uses $1, $2, etc. Plus Perl can do much that *awk* cannot.

The user criteria don't even have to be simple expressions. For example, this call initializes a variable `$id` to user *nobody*'s number to use later in its expression:

```
% psgrep 'no strict "vars";
          BEGIN { $id = getpwnam("nobody") }
          uid == $id '
```

How can we use unquoted words without even a dollar sign, like `uid`, `command`, and `size`, to represent those respective fields in each input record? We directly manipulate the symbol table by assigning closures to indirect typeglobs, which creates functions with those names. The function names are created using both uppercase and lowercase names, allowing both `"UID < 10"` and `"uid < 10"`. Closures are described in Recipe 11.4, and assigning them to typeglobs to create function aliases is shown in Recipe 10.14.

One twist here not seen in those recipes is empty parentheses on the closure. These allowed us to use the function in an expression anywhere we'd use a single term, like a string or a numeric constant. It creates a void prototype so the field-accessing function named `uid` accepts no arguments, just like the built-in function `time`. If these functions weren't prototyped void, expressions like `"uid < 10"` or `"size / 2 > rss"` would confuse the parser because it would see the unterminated start of a wildcard glob and of a pattern match, respectively. Prototypes are discussed in Recipe 10.11.

The version of *psgrep* demonstrated here expects the output from Red Hat Linux's *ps*. To port to other systems, look at which columns the headers begin at. This approach isn't relevant only to *ps* or only to Unix systems. It's a generic technique for filtering input records using Perl expressions, easily adapted to other record layouts. The input format could be in columns, space separated, comma separated, or the result of a pattern match with capturing parentheses.

The program could even be modified to handle a user-defined database with a small change to the selection functions. If you had an array of records as described in Recipe 11.9, you could let users specify arbitrary selection criteria, such as:

```
sub id()        { $_->{ID}    }
sub title()     { $_->{TITLE} }
sub executive() { title =~ /(?:vice-)?president/i }

# user search criteria go in the grep clause
@slowburners = grep { id < 10 && !executive } @employees;
```

For reasons of security and performance, this kind of power is seldom found in database engines like those described in Chapter 14, *Database Access*. SQL doesn't support this, but given Perl and small bit of ingenuity, it's easy to roll it up on your own. The search engine at *http://mox.perl.com/cgi-bin/MxScreen* uses such a technique, but instead of output from *ps*, its records are Perl hashes loaded from a database.

2

Numbers

*Anyone who considers arithmetical methods
of producing random digits is, of course,
in a state of sin.*

—John von Neumann (1951)

2.0. Introduction

Numbers, the most basic data type of almost any programming language, can be surprisingly tricky. Random numbers, numbers with decimal points, series of numbers, and the conversion of strings to numbers all pose trouble.

Perl works hard to make life easy for you, and the facilities it provides for manipulating numbers are no exception to that rule. If you treat a scalar value as a number, Perl converts it to one. This means that when you read ages from a file, extract digits from a string, or acquire numbers from any of the other myriad textual sources that Real Life pushes your way, you don't need to jump through the hoops created by other languages' cumbersome requirements to turn an ASCII string into a number.

Perl tries its best to interpret a string as a number when you use it as one (such as in a mathematical expression), but it has no direct way of reporting that a string doesn't represent a valid number. Perl quietly converts non-numeric strings to zero, and it will stop converting the string once it reaches a non-numeric character—so "A7" is still 0, and "7A" is just 7. (Note, however, that the -w flag will warn of such improper conversions.) Sometimes (such as when validating input) you need to know if a string represents a valid number. We show you how in Recipe 2.1.

Recipe 2.16 shows how to get a number from strings containing hexadecimal or octal representations of numbers like "0xff". Perl automatically converts literals in your program code (so $a = 3 + 0xff will set $a to 258) but not data read by that program (you can't read "0xff" into $b and then say $a = 3 + $b to make $a become 258).

As if integers weren't giving us enough grief, floating-point numbers can cause even more headaches. Internally, a computer represents numbers with decimal points as floating-point numbers in binary format. Floating-point numbers are not the same as real numbers; they are an approximation of real numbers, with limited precision. Although infinitely many real numbers exist, you only have finite space to represent them, usually about 64 bits or so. You have to cut corners to fit them all in.

When numbers are read from a file or appear as literals in your program, they are converted from decimal representation (e.g., 0.1) to internal representation. 0.1 can't be precisely represented as a binary floating-point number, just as 1/3 can't be exactly represented as a non-repeating decimal number. The computer's binary representation of 0.1, therefore, isn't exactly 0.1. To 20 decimal places, it is 0.10000000000000000555.

Performing arithmetic on binary representations of floating-point numbers can accumulate errors in the representations. In the preceding example, 3 * 0.1 is not stored with the same bit pattern as 0.3. This means you can't blindly test equality with == when you use Perl's floating-point numbers. Working with floating-point numbers is the subject of Recipes 2.2 and 2.3.

Recipe 2.4 shows how to convert an ASCII string representing a binary number (e.g., "1001") into an integer (e.g., 9) and back again. Recipe 2.5 gives three ways to perform one operation on each element of a set of consecutive integers. We show how to convert to and from Roman numerals in Recipe 2.6.

Random numbers are the topic of several recipes. Perl's **rand** function returns a floating-point value between 0 and 1 or between 0 and its argument. We show how to get random numbers in a given range, how to make random numbers more randomly, and how to make **rand** give a different set of random numbers each time you run your program.

We round out the chapter with recipes on trigonometry, logarithms, matrix multiplication, complex numbers, and the often-asked question: "How do you put commas in numbers?"

2.1. Checking Whether a String Is a Valid Number

Problem

You want to check whether a string represents a valid number. This is a common problem when validating input, as in a CGI script.

Solution

Compare it against a regular expression that matches the kinds of numbers you're interested in.

```
if ($string =~ /PATTERN/) {
    # is a number
} else {
    # is not
}
```

Discussion

This problem gets to the heart of what we mean by a number. Even things that sound simple, like *integer*, make you think hard about what you will accept ("Is a leading + for positive numbers optional, mandatory, or forbidden?"). The many ways that floating-point numbers can be represented could overheat your brain.

You must decide what you will and will not accept. Then, construct a regular expression to match those things alone. Here are some precooked solutions (the cookbook's equivalent of just-add-water meals) for most common cases.

```
warn "has nondigits"        if    /\D/;
warn "not a natural number" unless /^\d+$/;               # rejects -3
warn "not an integer"       unless /^-?\d+$/;             # rejects +3
warn "not an integer"       unless /^[+-]?\d+$/;
warn "not a decimal number" unless /^-?\d+\.?\d*$/;       # rejects .2
warn "not a decimal number" unless /^-?(?:\d+(?:\.\d*)?|\.\d+)$/;
warn "not a C float"
      unless /^([+-]?)(?=\d|\.\d)\d*(\.\d*)?([Ee]([+-]?\d+))?$/;
```

These lines do not catch the IEEE notations of "Infinity" and "NaN", but unless you're worried that IEEE committee members will stop by your workplace and beat you over the head with copies of the relevant standards documents, you can probably forget about these strange numbers.

If your number has leading or trailing whitespace, those patterns won't work. Either add the appropriate logic directly, or call the `trim` function from Recipe 1.14.

If you're on a POSIX system, Perl supports the `POSIX::strtod` function. Its semantics are cumbersome, so here's a `getnum` wrapper function for more convenient access. This function takes a string and returns the number it found or `undef` for input that isn't a C float. The `is_numeric` function is a front end to `getnum` for when you just want to say "Is this a float?"

```
sub getnum {
    use POSIX qw(strtod);
    my $str = shift;
    $str =~ s/^\s+//;
    $str =~ s/\s+$//;
    $! = 0;
    my($num, $unparsed) = strtod($str);
    if (($str eq '') || ($unparsed != 0) || $!) {
        return;
    } else {
        return $num;
    }
}

sub is_numeric { defined scalar &getnum }
```

See Also

The regular expression syntax in *perlre*(1) and Chapter 2 of *Programming Perl*; your system's *strtod*(3) manpage; the documentation for the standard POSIX module (also in Chapter 7 of *Programming Perl*)

2.2. Comparing Floating-Point Numbers

Problem

Floating-point arithmetic isn't precise. You want to compare two floating-point numbers and know if they're equal when carried out to a certain number of decimal places. Most of the time, this is the way you *should* compare floating-point numbers for equality.

Solution

Use `sprintf` to format the numbers to a certain number of decimal places, then compare the resulting strings:

```
# equal(NUM1, NUM2, ACCURACY) : returns true if NUM1 and NUM2 are
# equal to ACCURACY number of decimal places

sub equal {
    my ($A, $B, $dp) = @_;
```

```
        return sprintf("%.${dp}g", $A) eq sprintf("%.${dp}g", $B);
    }
```

Alternatively, store the numbers as integers by assuming the decimal place.

Discussion

You need the `equal` routine because most computers' floating-point representations aren't accurate. See the Introduction for a discussion of this issue.

If you have a fixed number of decimal places, as with currency, you can sidestep the problem by storing your values as integers. Storing $3.50 as 350 instead of 3.5 removes the need for floating-point values. Reintroduce the decimal point on output:

```
    $wage = 536;                # $5.36/hour
    $week = 40 * $wage;         # $214.40
    printf("One week's wage is: \$%.2f\n", $week/100);
```

One week's wage is: $214.40

It rarely makes sense to compare to more than 15 decimal places.

See Also

The `sprintf` function in *perlfunc*(1) and Chapter 3 of *Programming Perl*; the entry on $# in the *perlvar*(1) manpage and Chapter 2 of *Programming Perl*; the documentation for the standard Math::BigFloat module (also in Chapter 7 of *Programming Perl*); we use `sprintf` in Recipe 2.3; Volume 2, Section 4.2.2 of *The Art of Computer Programming*

2.3. *Rounding Floating-Point Numbers*

Problem

You want to round a floating-point value to a certain number of decimal places. This problem arises as a result of the same inaccuracies in representation that make testing for equality difficult (see Recipe 2.2), as well as in situations where you must reduce the precision of your answers for readability.

Solution

Use the Perl function `sprintf`, or `printf` if you're just trying to produce output:

```
    $rounded = sprintf("%FORMATf", $unrounded);
```

Discussion

Rounding can seriously affect some algorithms, so the rounding method used should be specified precisely. In sensitive applications like financial computations and thermonuclear missiles, prudent programmers will implement their own rounding function instead of relying on the programming language's built-in logic, or lack thereof.

Usually, though, we can just use `sprintf`. The f format lets you specify a particular number of decimal places to round its argument to. Perl looks at the following digit, rounds up if it is 5 or greater, and rounds down otherwise.

```
$a = 0.255;
$b = sprintf("%.2f", $a);
print "Unrounded: $a\nRounded: $b\n";

printf "Unrounded: $a\nRounded: %.2f\n", $a;

Unrounded: 0.255
Rounded: 0.26
Unrounded: 0.255
Rounded: 0.26
```

Three functions that may be useful if you want to round a floating-point value to an integral value are `int`, `ceil`, and `floor`. `int`, built into Perl, returns the integral portion of the floating-point number passed to it (int will use `$_` if it was called without an argument). The POSIX module's `floor` and `ceil` functions round their argument down and up to the next integer, respectively.

```
use POSIX;

print "number\tint\tfloor\tceil\n";

@a = ( 3.3 , 3.5 , 3.7, -3.3 );
foreach (@a) {
    printf( "%.1f\t%.1f\t%.1f\t%.1f\n",
        $_, int($_), floor($_), ceil($_) );
}
```

number	int	floor	ceil
3.3	3.0	3.0	4.0
3.5	3.0	3.0	4.0
3.7	3.0	3.0	4.0
-3.3	-3.0	-4.0	-3.0

See Also

The `sprintf` and `int` functions in *perlfunc*(1) and Chapter 3 of *Programming Perl*; the `floor` and `ceil` entries in the documentation for the standard POSIX module (also in Chapter 7 of *Programming Perl*); we introduced the `sprintf` technique in Recipe 2.2

2.4. *Converting Between Binary and Decimal*

Problem

You have an integer whose binary representation you'd like to print out, or a binary representation that you'd like to convert into an integer. You might want to do this if you were displaying non-textual data, such as what you get from interacting with certain system programs and functions.

Solution

To convert a Perl integer to a text string of ones and zeros, first pack the integer into a number in network byte order* (the `"N"` format), then unpack it again bit by bit (the `"B32"` format).

```
sub dec2bin {
    my $str = unpack("B32", pack("N", shift));
    $str =~ s/^0+(?=\d)//;    # otherwise you'll get leading zeros
    return $str;
}
```

To convert a text string of ones and zeros to a Perl integer, first massage the string by padding it with the right number of zeros, then just reverse the previous procedure.

```
sub bin2dec {
    return unpack("N", pack("B32", substr("0" x 32 . shift, -32)));
}
```

Discussion

We're talking about converting between strings like `"00100011"` and numbers like 35. The string is the binary representation of the number. We can't solve either problem with `sprintf` (which doesn't have a "print this in binary" format), so we have to resort to Perl's `pack` and `unpack` functions for manipulating strings of data.

The `pack` and `unpack` functions act on strings. You can treat the string as a series of bits, bytes, integers, long integers, floating-point numbers in IEEE representation, checksums—among other strange things. The `pack` and `unpack` functions both take formats, like `sprintf`, specifying what they should do with their arguments.

---

* Also known as *big-endian*, or *MSB* (Most-Significant Bit first) order.

We use `pack` and `unpack` in two ways: "treat this string as a series of bits" and "treat this string as containing a binary representation of an integer." When we treat the string as a series of bits, we have to understand how `pack` will behave. Such a string is treated as a series of bytes, a byte being eight bits. The bytes are always counted from left to right (the first eight bits are the first byte, the next eight bits are the second, and so on), but the bits within each byte can be counted left-to-right as well as right-to-left.

We use `pack` with a template of `"B"` to work with bits within each byte from left to right. This is the order that the `"N"` format expects them in, which we use to treat the series of bits as representing a 32-bit integer.

```
$num = bin2dec('0110110');  # $num is 54
$binstr = dec2bin(54);      # $binstr is 110110
```

See Also

The `pack` and `unpack` functions in *perlfunc*(1) and Chapter 3 of *Programming Perl*; we also use `pack` and `unpack` in Recipe 1.4; to convert between decimal, hexadecimal, and octal, see Recipe 2.16

2.5. Operating on a Series of Integers

Problem

You want to perform an operation on all integers between X and Y, such as when you're working on a contiguous section of an array or in any situations where you want to process all numbers[*] within a range.

Solution

Use a `for` loop, or `..` in conjunction with a `foreach` loop:

```
foreach ($X .. $Y) {
    # $_ is set to every integer from X to Y, inclusive
}

foreach $i ($X .. $Y) {
    # $i is set to every integer from X to Y, inclusive
    }

for ($i = $X; $i <= $Y; $i++) {
    # $i is set to every integer from X to Y, inclusive
}
```

---

[*] Okay, integers. It's hard to find all the reals. Just ask Cantor.

```
for ($i = $X; $i <= $Y; $i += 7) {
    # $i is set to every integer from X to Y, stepsize = 7
}
```

Discussion

The first two methods use the $X .. $Y construct, which creates a list of integers between $X and $Y. This uses a lot of memory when $X and $Y are far apart. (This is fixed in the 5.005 release.) When iterating over consecutive integers, the explicit for loop in the third method is more memory efficient.

The following code shows each technique. Here we only print the numbers we generate:

```
print "Infancy is: ";
foreach (0 .. 2) {
    print "$_ ";
}
print "\n";

print "Toddling is: ";
foreach $i (3 .. 4) {
    print "$i ";
}
print "\n";

print "Childhood is: ";
for ($i = 5; $i <= 12; $i++) {
    print "$i ";
}
print "\n";

Infancy is: 0 1 2
Toddling is: 3 4
Childhood is: 5 6 7 8 9 10 11 12
```

See Also

The for and foreach operators in *perlsyn*(1) and the "For Loops" and "Foreach Loops" sections of Chapter 2 of *Programming Perl*

2.6. Working with Roman Numerals

Problem

You want to convert between regular numbers and Roman numerals. You need to do this with items in outlines, page numbers on a preface, and copyrights for movie credits.

Solution

Use the Roman module from CPAN:

```
use Roman;
$roman = roman($arabic);                        # convert to roman numerals
$arabic = arabic($roman) if isroman($roman);    # convert from roman numerals
```

Discussion

The Roman module provides both **Roman** and **roman** for converting Arabic ("normal") numbers to their Roman equivalents. **Roman** produces uppercase letters, whereas **roman** gives lowercase ones.

The module only deals with Roman numbers from 1 to 3999, inclusive. The Romans didn't represent negative numbers or zero, and 5000 (which 4000 is represented in terms of) uses a symbol outside the ASCII character set.

```
use Roman;
$roman_fifteen = roman(15);                     # "xv"
print "Roman for fifteen is $roman_fifteen\n";
$arabic_fifteen = arabic($roman_fifteen);
print "Converted back, $roman_fifteen is $arabic_fifteen\n";

Roman for fifteen is xv
Converted back, xv is 15
```

See Also

The Encyclopaedia Brittanica article on "Mathematics, History Of"; the documentation with the Roman module; Recipe 6.23

2.7. Generating Random Numbers

Problem

You want to make random numbers in a given range, inclusive, such as when you randomly pick an array index, simulate rolling a die in a game of chance, or generate a random password.

Solution

Use Perl's **rand** function.

```
$random = int( rand( $Y-$X+1 ) ) + $X;
```

Discussion

This code generates and prints a random integer between 25 and 75, inclusive:

```
$random = int( rand(51)) + 25;
print "$random\n";
```

The rand function returns a fractional number, from (and including) 0 up to (but not including) its argument. We give it an argument of 51 to get a number that can be 0 or more, but never 51 or more. We take the integer portion of this to get a number from 0 to 50, inclusive (50.99999.... will be turned to 50 by int). We then add 25 to it, to get a number from 25 to 75, inclusive.

A common application of this is the random selection of an element from an array:

```
$elt = $array[ rand @array ];
```

And generating a random password from a sequence of characters:

```
@chars = ( "A" .. "Z", "a" .. "z", 0 .. 9, qw(! @ $ % ^ & *) );
$password = join("", @chars[ map { rand @chars } ( 1 .. 8 ) ]);
```

We use map to generate eight random indices into @chars, extract the corresponding characters with a slice, and join them together to form the random password. This isn't a *good* random number, though, as its security relies on the choice of seed, which is based on the time the program started. See Recipe 2.8 for a way to better seed your random number generator.

See Also

The int, rand, map, and join functions in *perlfunc*(1) and Chapter 3 of *Programming Perl*; we explore random numbers further in Recipes 2.8, 2.9, and 2.10; we use random numbers in Recipe 1.9

2.8. Generating Different Random Numbers

Problem

Every time you run your program you get the same set of "random" numbers. You want Perl to produce different random numbers each time. This is important in nearly every application of random numbers, especially games.

Solution

Use Perl's srand function:

```
srand EXPR;
```

Discussion

Making random numbers is hard. The best that computers can do, without special hardware, is generate "pseudo-random" numbers, which are evenly distributed in their range of values. These are generated using a mathematical formula, which means that given the same *seed* (starting point), two programs will produce identical pseudo-random numbers.

The `srand` function creates a new seed for the pseudo-random number generator. If given an argument, it uses that number as the seed. If no argument is given, `srand` uses a value that's reasonably difficult to guess as the seed (as of Perl 5.004 or later; before that it just used `time`, which isn't random at all). Don't call `srand` more than once in a program.

If you haven't called `srand` yourself, Perl version 5.004 and later calls `srand` with a "good" seed the first time you call `rand`. Earlier versions did not, so the same program always produced the same sequence. If you prefer that behavior, call `srand` yourself with a particular seed:

```
srand( <STDIN> );
```

Just because Perl tries to use a good default seed does not necessarily guarantee that the numbers generated are cryptographically secure against the most intrepid crackers. Textbooks on cryptography are usually good sources of cryptographically secure random number generators.

See Also

The `srand` function in *perlfunc*(1); Chapter 3 of *Programming Perl*; Recipes 2.7 and 2.9; Bruce Schneier's excellent *Applied Cryptography*; John Wiley & Sons (1995)

2.9. Making Numbers Even More Random

Problem

You want to generate numbers that are more random than Perl's random numbers. Limitations of your C library's random number generator seeds will sometimes cause problems. The sequence of pseudo-random numbers may repeat too soon for some applications.

Solution

Use a different random number generator, such as those provided by the Math::Random and Math::TrulyRandom modules from CPAN:

```
use Math::TrulyRandom;
$random = truly_random_value();

use Math::Random;
$random = random_uniform();
```

Discussion

Perl uses the standard C library routine *rand*(3) to generate pseudo-random numbers. (This can be changed at build time, however.) Some implementations of the rand function return only 16-bit random numbers or have algorithmic weaknesses and may not be sufficiently random.

The Math::TrulyRandom module uses the inadequacies of your system's timers to generate the random numbers. This takes a while, so it isn't useful for generating a lot of random numbers.

The Math::Random module uses the randlib library to generate random numbers. It also includes a wide range of related functions.

See Also

The srand and rand functions in *perlfunc*(1) and Chapter 3 of *Programming Perl*; Recipe 2.7; Recipe 2.8; the documentation for the CPAN modules Math::Random and Math::TrulyRandom

2.10. Generating Biased Random Numbers

Problem

You want to pick a random value where the probabilities of the values are not equal (the distribution is not even). You might be trying to randomly select a banner to display on a web page, given a set of relative weights saying how often each banner is to be displayed. Alternatively, you might want to simulate behavior according to a normal distribution (the bell curve).

Solution

If you want a random value distributed according to a specific function—e.g., the Gaussian (Normal) distribution—consult a statistics textbook to find the appropriate function or algorithm. This subroutine generates random numbers that are normally distributed, with a standard deviation of 1 and a mean of 0.

```
sub gaussian_rand {
    my ($u1, $u2);   # uniformly distributed random numbers
    my $w;           # variance, then a weight
    my ($g1, $g2);   # gaussian-distributed numbers

    do {
        $u1 = 2 * rand() - 1;
        $u2 = 2 * rand() - 1;
        $w = $u1*$u1 + $u2*$u2;
    } while ($w >= 1 || $w == 0)

    $w = sqrt( (-2 * log($w))  / $w );
    $g2 = $u1 * $w;
    $g1 = $u2 * $w;
    # return both if wanted, else just one
    return wantarray ? ($g1, $g2) : $g1;
}
```

If you have a list of weights and values you want to randomly pick from, follow this two-step process: First, turn the weights into a probability distribution with `weight_to_dist` below, and then use the distribution to randomly pick a value with `weighted_rand`:

```
# weight_to_dist: takes a hash mapping key to weight and returns
# a hash mapping key to probability
sub weight_to_dist {
    my %weights = @_;
    my %dist    = ();
    my $total   = 0;
    my ($key, $weight);
    local $_;

    foreach (values %weights) {
        $total += $_;
    }

    while ( ($key, $weight) = each %weights ) {
        $dist{$key} = $weight/$total;
    }

    return %dist;
}

# weighted_rand: takes a hash mapping key to probability, and
# returns the corresponding element
sub weighted_rand {
    my %dist = @_;
    my ($key, $weight);

    while (1) {                        # to avoid floating point inaccuracies
        my $rand = rand;
```

```
            while ( ($key, $weight) = each %dist ) {
                return $key if ($rand -= $weight) < 0;
            }
        }
    }
```

Discussion

The `gaussian_rand` function implements the *polar Box Muller* method for turn-ing two independent uniformly distributed random numbers between 0 and 1 (such as `rand` returns) into two numbers with a mean of 0 and a standard devia-tion of 1 (i.e., a Gaussian distribution). To generate numbers with a different mean and standard deviation, multiply the output of `gaussian_rand` by the new stan-dard deviation, and then add the new mean:

```
# gaussian_rand as above
$mean = 25;
$sdev = 2;
$salary = gaussian_rand() * $sdev + $mean;
printf("You have been hired at \$%.2f\n", $salary);
```

The `weighted_rand` function picks a random number between 0 and 1. It then uses the probabilities generated by `weight_to_dist` to see which element the random number corresponds to. Because of the vagaries of floating-point repre-sentation, the accumulated errors of representation might mean we don't find an element to return. This is why we wrap the code in a `while` to pick a new ran-dom number and try again.

In addition, the CPAN module Math::Random has functions to return random num-bers from a variety of distributions.

See Also

The `rand` function in *perlfunc*(1) and Chapter 3 of *Programming Perl*; Recipe 2.7; the documentation for the CPAN module Math::Random

2.11. Doing Trigonometry in Degrees, not Radians

Problem

You want your trigonometry routines to operate in degrees instead of Perl's native radians.

Solution

Convert between radians and degrees (2π radians equals 360 degrees).

```
BEGIN {
    use constant PI => 3.14159265358979;

    sub deg2rad {
        my $degrees = shift;
        return ($degrees / 180) * PI;
    }

    sub rad2deg {
        my $radians = shift;
        return ($radians / PI) * 180;
    }
}
```

Alternatively, use the Math::Trig module.

```
use Math::Trig;

$radians = deg2rad($degrees);
$degrees = rad2deg($radians);
```

Discussion

If you're doing a lot of trigonometry, look into using either the standard Math::Trig or POSIX modules. They provide many more trigonometric functions than are defined in the Perl core. Otherwise, the first solution above will define the rad2deg and deg2rad functions. The value of π isn't built directly into Perl, but you can calculate it to as much precision as your floating-point hardware provides. If you put it in a BEGIN block, this is done at compile time. In the solution above, the PI function is a constant created with use constant.

If you're looking for the sine in degrees, use this:

```
# deg2rad and rad2deg defined either as above or from Math::Trig
sub degree_sine {
    my $degrees = shift;
    my $radians = deg2rad($degrees);
    my $result = sin($radians);

    return $result;
}
```

See Also

The sin, cos, and atan2 functions in *perlfunc*(1) and Chapter 3 of *Programming Perl*; the documentation for the standard POSIX and Math::Trig modules (also in Chapter 7 of *Programming Perl*)

2.12. Calculating More Trigonometric Functions

Problem

You want to calculate values for trigonometric functions like sine, tangent, or arc-cosine.

Solution

Perl provides only `sin`, `cos`, and `atan2` as standard functions. From these, you can derive `tan` and the other trig functions:

```
sub tan {
    my $theta = shift;

    return sin($theta)/cos($theta);
}
```

The POSIX module provides a wider range of trig functions:

```
use POSIX;

$y = acos(3.7);
```

The Math::Trig module provides a complete set of functions and supports operations on or resulting in complex numbers:

```
use Math::Trig;

$y = acos(3.7);
```

Discussion

The `tan` function will cause a division-by-zero exception when $theta is $\frac{\pi}{2}$, $\frac{3\pi}{2}$, and so on, because the cosine is 0 for these values. Similarly, `tan` and many other functions from Math::Trig may generate the same error. To trap these, use `eval`:

```
eval {
    $y = tan($pi/2);
} or return undef;
```

See Also

The `sin`, `cos`, and `atan2` functions in *perlfunc*(1) and Chapter 3 of *Programming Perl*; we talk about trigonometry in the context of imaginary numbers in Recipe 2.15; we talk about the use of `eval` to catch exceptions in Recipe 10.12

2.13. Taking Logarithms

Problem

You want to take a logarithm in various bases.

Solution

For logarithms to base *e*, use the built-in `log`:

```
$log_e = log(VALUE);
```

For logarithms to base 10, use the POSIX module's `log10` function:

```
use POSIX qw(log10);
$log_10 = log10(VALUE);
```

For other bases, use the mathematical identity:

$$\log_n(x) = \frac{\log_e(x)}{\log_e(n)}$$

where *x* is the number whose logarithm you want, *n* is the desired base, and *e* is the natural logarithm base.

```
sub log_base {
    my ($base, $value) = @_;
    return log($value)/log($base);
}
```

Discussion

The `log_base` function lets you take logarithms to any base. If you know the base you'll want in advance, it's more efficient to cache the log of the base instead of recalculating it every time.

```
# log_base defined as above
$answer = log_base(10, 10_000);
print "log10(10,000) = $answer\n";
log10(10,000) = 4
```

The Math::Complex module does the caching for you via its `logn()` routine, so you can write:

```
use Math::Complex;
printf "log2(1024) = %lf\n", logn(1024, 2); # watch out for argument order!
log2(1024) = 10.000000
```

even though no complex number is involved here. This is not very efficient, but there are plans to rewrite `Math::Complex` in C for speed.

See Also

The `log` function in *perlfunc*(1) and Chapter 3 of *Programming Perl*; the documentation for the standard POSIX module (also in Chapter 7 of *Programming Perl*)

2.14. Multiplying Matrices

Problem

You want to multiply a pair of two-dimensional arrays. Mathematicians and engineers often need this.

Solution

Use the PDL modules, available from CPAN. PDL is the *Perl Data Language*— modules that give fast access to compact matrix and mathematical functions:

```
use PDL;
# $a and $b are both pdl objects
$c = $a * $b;
```

Alternatively, apply the matrix multiplication algorithm to your two-dimensional array:

```
sub mmult {
    my ($m1,$m2) = @_;
    my ($m1rows,$m1cols) = matdim($m1);
    my ($m2rows,$m2cols) = matdim($m2);

    unless ($m1cols == $m2rows) {  # raise exception
        die "IndexError: matrices don't match: $m1cols != $m2rows";
    }

    my $result = [];
    my ($i, $j, $k);

    for $i (range($m1rows)) {
        for $j (range($m2cols)) {
            for $k (range($m1cols)) {
                $result->[$i][$j] += $m1->[$i][$k] * $m2->[$k][$j];
            }
        }
    }
    return $result;
}

sub range { 0 .. ($_[0] - 1) }

sub veclen {
    my $ary_ref = $_[0];
```

```
        my $type = ref $ary_ref;
        if ($type ne "ARRAY") { die "$type is bad array ref for $ary_ref" }
        return scalar(@$ary_ref);
    }

    sub matdim {
        my $matrix = $_[0];
        my $rows = veclen($matrix);
        my $cols = veclen($matrix->[0]);
        return ($rows, $cols);
    }
```

Discussion

If you have the PDL library installed, you can make use of its lightning-fast manipulation of numbers. This requires far less memory and CPU than Perl's array manipulation. When using PDL objects, many numeric operators (such as + and *) are overloaded and work on an element-by-element basis (e.g., * is the so-called *scalar multiplication* operator). To get true matrix multiplication, use the overloaded x operator.

```
use PDL;

$a = pdl [
    [ 3, 2, 3 ],
    [ 5, 9, 8 ],
];

$b = pdl [
    [ 4, 7 ],
    [ 9, 3 ],
    [ 8, 1 ],
];

$c = $a x $b;   # x overload
```

If you don't have the PDL library, or don't feel like pulling it in for a small problem, you can always do the work yourself the good old-fashioned way.

```
# mmult() and other subroutines as above

$x = [
        [ 3, 2, 3 ],
        [ 5, 9, 8 ],
];

$y = [
        [ 4, 7 ],
        [ 9, 3 ],
        [ 8, 1 ],
];

$z = mmult($x, $y);
```

See Also

The documentation with the CPAN module PDL

2.15. Using Complex Numbers

Problem

Your application must manipulate complex numbers, as are often needed in engineering, science, and mathematics.

Solution

Either keep track of the real and imaginary components yourself, or use the Math::Complex class (part of the standard Perl distribution).

Manually

```
# $c = $a * $b manually
$c_real = ( $a_real * $b_real ) - ( $a_imaginary * $b_imaginary );
$c_imaginary = ( $a_real * $b_imaginary ) + ( $b_real * $a_imaginary );
```

Math::Complex

```
# $c = $a * $b using Math::Complex
use Math::Complex;
$c = $a * $b;
```

Discussion

Here's how you'd manually multiply 3+5i and 2-2i:

```
$a_real = 3; $a_imaginary = 5;              # 3 + 5i;
$b_real = 2; $b_imaginary = -2;             # 2 - 2i;
$c_real = ( $a_real * $b_real ) - ( $a_imaginary * $b_imaginary );
$c_imaginary = ( $a_real * $b_imaginary ) + ( $b_real * $a_imaginary );
print "c = ${c_real}+${c_imaginary}i\n";
```

```
c = 16+4i
```

and with Math::Complex:

```
use Math::Complex;
$a = Math::Complex->new(3,5);              # or Math::Complex->new(3,5);
$b = Math::Complex->new(2,-2);
$c = $a * $b;
print "c = $c\n";
```

```
c = 16+4i
```

With the 5.004 version, you may create complex numbers via the `cplx` constructor or via the exported constant *i*:

```
use Math::Complex;
$c = cplx(3,5) * cplx(2,-2);        # easier on the eye
$d = 3 + 4*i;                       # 3 + 4i
printf "sqrt($d) = %s\n", sqrt($d);
```

> **sqrt(3+4i) = 2+i**

The original Math::Complex module distributed with 5.003 did not overload as many functions and operators as the 5.004 version does. Also, the Math::Trig module (new as of 5.004) uses the Math::Complex module internally because some functions can break out from the real axis into the complex plane—for example, the inverse sine of 2.

See Also

The documentation for the standard Math::Complex module (also in Chapter 7 of *Programming Perl*)

2.16. *Converting Between Octal and Hexadecimal*

Problem

You want to convert a string (e.g., `"0x55"` or `"0755"`) containing an octal or hexadecimal number to the correct number.

Perl only understands octal and hexadecimal numbers when they occur as literals in your programs. If they are obtained by reading from files or supplied as command-line arguments, no automatic conversion takes place.

Solution

Use Perl's **oct** and **hex** functions:

```
$number = hex($hexadecimal);        # hexadecimal
$number = oct($octal);              # octal
```

Discussion

The **oct** function converts octal numbers with or without the leading `"0"`: `"0350"` or `"350"`. In fact, it even converts hexadecimal (`"0x350"`) numbers if they have a leading `"0x"`. The **hex** function only converts hexadecimal numbers, with or without a leading "0x": "0x255", "3A", "ff", or "deadbeef". (Letters may be in upper- or lowercase.)

Here's an example that accepts a number in either decimal, octal, or hex, and prints that number in all three bases. It uses the oct function to convert from octal and hexadecimal if the input began with a 0. It then uses printf to convert back into hex, octal, and decimal as needed.

```
print "Gimme a number in decimal, octal, or hex: ";
$num = <STDIN>;
chomp $num;
exit unless defined $num;
$num = oct($num) if $num =~ /^0/; # does both oct and hex
printf "%d %x %o\n", $num, $num, $num;
```

The following code converts Unix file permissions. They're always given in octal, so we use oct instead of hex.

```
print "Enter file permission in octal: ";
$permissions = <STDIN>;
die "Exiting ...\n" unless defined $permissions;
chomp $permissions;
$permissions = oct($permissions);   # permissions always octal
print "The decimal value is $permissions\n";
```

See Also

The "Scalar Value Constructors" section in *perldata*(1) and the "Numeric Literals" section of Chapter 2 of *Programming Perl*; the oct and hex functions in *perlfunc*(1) and Chapter 3 of *Programming Perl*.

2.17. *Putting Commas in Numbers*

Problem

You want to output a number with commas in the right place. People like to see long numbers broken up in this way, especially in reports.

Solution

Reverse the string so you can use backtracking to avoid substitution in the fractional part of the number. Then use a regular expression to find where you need commas, and substitute them in. Finally, reverse the string back.

```
sub commify {
    my $text = reverse $_[0];
    $text =~ s/(\d\d\d)(?=\d)(?!\d*\.)/$1,/g;
    return scalar reverse $text;
}
```

Discussion

It's a lot easier in regular expressions to work from the front than from the back. With this in mind, we reverse the string and make a minor change to the algorithm that repeatedly inserts commas three digits from the end. When all insertions are done, we reverse the final string and return it. Because **reverse** is sensitive to its implicit return context, we force it to scalar context.

This function can be easily adjusted to accommodate the use of periods instead of commas, as are used in some countries.

Here's an example of **commify** in action:

```
# more reasonable web counter :-)
use Math::TrulyRandom;
$hits = truly_random_value();         # negative hits!
$output = "Your web page received $hits accesses last month.\n";
print commify($output);
Your web page received -1,740,525,205 accesses last month.
```

See Also

perllocale(1); the **reverse** function in *perlfunc*(1) and Chapter 3 of *Programming Perl*; the section "Adding Commas to a Number" in Chapter 7 of *Mastering Regular Expressions*

2.18. Printing Correct Plurals

Problem

You're printing something like **"It took $time hours"**, but **"It took 1 hours"** is ungrammatical. You would like to get it right.

Solution

Use **printf** and a ternary conditional (X ? Y : Z) to alter the noun or verb:

```
printf "It took %d hour%s\n", $time, $time == 1 ? "" : "s";

printf "%d hour%s %s enough.\n", $time,
        $time == 1 ? ""   : "s",
        $time == 1 ? "is" : "are";
```

Or, use the Lingua::EN::Inflect module from CPAN as described in the Discussion.

Discussion

The only reason inane messages like "1 file(s) updated" appear is because their authors are too lazy to bother checking whether the count is 1 or not.

If your noun changes by more than an "-s", you'll need to change the printf accordingly:

```
printf "It took %d centur%s", $time, $time == 1 ? "y" : "ies";
```

This is good for simple cases, but you'll get tired of writing it. This leads you to write funny functions like this:

```
sub noun_plural {
    local $_ = shift;
    # order really matters here!
    s/ss$/sses/                                 ||
    s/([psc]h)$/${1}es/                         ||
    s/z$/zes/                                    ||
    s/ff$/ffs/                                   ||
    s/f$/ves/                                    ||
    s/ey$/eys/                                   ||
    s/y$/ies/                                    ||
    s/ix$/ices/                                  ||
    s/([sx])$/$1es/                             ||
    s/$/s/                                       ||
                    die "can't get here";
    return $_;
}
*verb_singular = \&noun_plural;     # make function alias
```

As you find more exceptions, your function will become increasingly convoluted. When you need to handle such morphological changes, turn to the flexible solution provided by the Lingua::EN::Inflect module from CPAN.

```
use Lingua::EN::Inflect qw(PL classical);
classical(1);                       # why isn't this the default?
while (<DATA>) {                    # each line in the data
    for (split) {                  # each word on the line
        print "One $_, two ", PL($_), ".\n";
    }
}
# plus one more
$_ = 'secretary general';
print "One $_, two ", PL($_), ".\n";

__END__
fish fly ox
species genus phylum
cherub radius jockey
index matrix mythos
phenomenon formula
```

That produces the following:

```
One fish, two fish.
One fly, two flies.
One ox, two oxen.
One species, two species.
One genus, two genera.
One phylum, two phyla.
One cherub, two cherubim.
One radius, two radii.
One jockey, two jockeys.
One index, two indices.
One matrix, two matrices.
One mythos, two mythoi.
One phenomenon, two phenomena.
One formula, two formulae.
One secretary general, two secretaries general.
```

This is one of the many things the module can do. It also handles inflections or conjugations for other parts of speech, provides number-insensitive comparison functions, figures out whether to use *a* or *an*, and plenty more.

See Also

The ternary ("hook-colon") operator discussed in *perlop*(1) and in the "Conditional Operator" section of Chapter 2 of *Programming Perl*; the documentation with the CPAN module Lingua::EN::Inflect

2.19. Program: Calculating Prime Factors

The following program takes one or more integer arguments and determines the prime factors. It uses Perl's native numeric representation unless those numbers use floating-point representation and thus lose accuracy. Otherwise (or if the program's -b switch is used), it uses the standard Math::BigInt library, thus allowing for huge numbers. However, it only loads this library if necessary. That's why we use `require` and `import` instead of `use`, which would unconditionally load the library at compile time instead of conditionally at run time.

This is not an efficient way to crack the huge integers used for cryptographic purposes.

Call the program with a list of numbers, and it will show you the prime factors of those numbers:

```
% bigfact 8 9 96 2178
8           2**3
9           3**2
96          2**5 3
2178        2 3**2 11**2
```

You can give it very large numbers:

```
% bigfact 239322000000000000000000
+239322000000000000000000 2**19 3 5**18 +39887

% bigfact 2500000000000000000000000000
+2500000000000000000000000000 2**24 5**26
```

The program is shown in Example 2-1.

Example 2-1. bigfact

```
#!/usr/bin/perl
# bigfact - calculate prime factors
use strict;
use integer;

use vars qw{ $opt_b $opt_d };
use Getopt::Std;

@ARGV && getopts('bd')              or die "usage: $0 [-b] number ...";

load_biglib() if $opt_b;

ARG: foreach my $orig ( @ARGV ) {
    my ($n, %factors, $factor);
    $n = $opt_b ? Math::BigInt->new($orig) : $orig;
    if ($n + 0 ne $n) { # don't use -w for this
        printf STDERR "bigfact: %s would become %s\n", $n, $n+0 if $opt_d;
        load_biglib();
        $n = Math::BigInt->new($orig);
    }
    printf "%-10s ", $n;

    # Here $sqi will be the square of $i. We will take advantage
    # of the fact that ($i + 1) ** 2 == $i ** 2 + 2 * $i + 1.
    for (my ($i, $sqi) = (2, 4); $sqi <= $n; $sqi += 2 * $i ++ + 1) {
        while ($n % $i == 0) {
            $n /= $i;
            print STDERR "<$i>" if $opt_d;
            $factors {$i} ++;
        }
    }

    if ($n != 1 && $n != $orig) { $factors{$n}++ }
    if (! %factors) {
        print "PRIME\n";
        next ARG;
    }
    for $factor ( sort { $a <=> $b } keys %factors ) {
        print "$factor";
        if ($factors{$factor} > 1) {
            print "**$factors{$factor}";
        }
        print " ";
```

Example 2-1. bigfact (continued)

```
    }
    print "\n";
}

# this simulates a use, but at run time
sub load_biglib {
    require Math::BigInt;
    Math::BigInt->import();          #immaterial?
}
```

3

Dates and Times

It is inappropriate to require that a time
represented as seconds since the Epoch precisely
represent the number of seconds between the
referenced time and the Epoch.
—IEEE Std 1003.1b-1993 (POSIX) Section B.2.2.2

3.0. Introduction

Times and dates are important things to be able to manipulate. "How many users logged in last month?", "How many seconds should I sleep, if I want to wake up at midday?", and "Has this user's password expired yet?" are all common questions whose answers involve surprisingly non-obvious manipulations.

Perl represents points in time as intervals, measuring seconds past a point in time called *the Epoch*. On Unix and many other systems, the Epoch was 00:00 Jan 1, 1970, Greenwich Mean Time (GMT).* On a Mac, all dates and times are expressed in the local time zone. The `gmtime` function returns the correct GMT time, based on your Mac's time zone offset. Bear this in mind when considering the recipes in this chapter. The Macintosh's Epoch seconds value ranges from 00:00 Jan 1, 1904 to 06:28:15 Feb 6, 2040.

When we talk about dates and times, we often interchange two different concepts: points in time (dates and times) and intervals between points in time (weeks, months, days, etc.). Epoch seconds represent intervals and points in the same units, so you can do basic arithmetic on them.

---

* These days GMT is increasingly referred to as UTC (Universal Coordinated Time).

However, people are not used to working with Epoch seconds. We are more used to dealing with individual year, month, day, hour, minute, and second values. Furthermore, the month can be represented by its full name or its abbreviation. The day can precede or follow the month. Because of the difficulty of performing calculations with a variety of formats, we typically convert human-supplied strings or lists to Epoch seconds, calculate, and then convert back to strings or lists for output.

For convenience in calculation, Epoch seconds are always calculated in GMT. When converting to or from distinct values, we must always consider whether the time represented is GMT or local. Use different conversion functions depending on whether you need to convert from GMT to local time or vice versa.

Perl's `time` function returns the number of seconds that have passed since the Epoch—more or less.[*] To convert Epoch seconds into distinct values for days, months, years, hours, minutes, and seconds, use the `localtime` and `gmtime` functions. In list context, these functions return a nine-element list with the following elements:

Variable	Values	Range
`$sec`	seconds	0–60
`$min`	minutes	0–59
`$hours`	hours	0–23
`$mday`	day of month	1–31
`$month`	month of year	0–11, 0 == January
`$year`	years since 1900	1-138 (or more)
`$wday`	day of week	0–6, 0 == Sunday
`$yday`	day of year	0–365
`$isdst`	0 or 1	true if daylight savings is in effect

The values for second range from 0–60 to account for leap seconds; you never know when a spare second will leap into existence at the urging of various standards bodies.

From now on, we'll refer to a list of day, month, year, hour, minute, and seconds as DMYHMS, for no better reason than that writing and reading "distinct day, month, year, hour, minute, and seconds values" is wearisome. The abbreviation is not meant to suggest an order of return values.

---

[*] Well, less actually. To be precise, 21 seconds less as of this writing. POSIX requires that `time` not include leap seconds, a peculiar practice of adjusting the world's clock by a second here and there to account for the slowing down of the Earth's rotation due to tidal angular-momentum dissipation. See the *sci.astro* FAQ, section 3, in *http://sciastro.astronomy.net/sci.astro.3.FAQ.*

Perl does *not* return a two-digit year value. It returns the year minus 1900, which just happens to be a two-digit number through 1999. Perl doesn't intrinsically have a Year 2000 problem, unless you make one yourself. (Your computer, and Perl, may have a 2038 problem, though, if we're still using 32 bits by that time.) Add 1900 to get the full year value instead of using the construct `"19$year"`, or soon your programs will refer to the year `"19102"`. We can't pin down the year value's range because it depends on how big an integer your operating system uses for Epoch seconds. Small integers mean a small range; big (64-bit) integers mean a very big range.

In scalar context, `localtime` and `gmtime` return the date and time formatted as an ASCII string:

```
Fri Apr 11 09:27:08 1997
```

The standard Time::tm module provides objects that give you a named interface to these values. The standard Time::localtime and Time::gmtime modules override the list-returning `localtime` and `gmtime` functions, replacing them with versions that return Time::tm objects. Compare these two pieces of code:

```
# using arrays
print "Today is day ", (localtime)[7], " of the current year.\n";
Today is day 117 of the current year.

# using Time::tm objects
use Time::localtime;
$tm = localtime;
print "Today is day ", $tm->yday, " of the current year.\n";
Today is day 117 of the current year.
```

To go *from* a list *to* Epoch seconds, use the standard Time::Local module. It provides the functions `timelocal` and `timegm`, both of which take a nine-element list and return an integer. The list's values have the same meaning and ranges as those returned by `localtime` and `gmtime`.

Epoch seconds values are limited by the size of an integer. If you have a 32-bit signed integer holding your Epoch seconds, you can only represent dates (in GMT) from `Fri Dec 13 20:45:52 1901` to `Tue Jan 19 03:14:07 2038` (inclusive). By 2038, it is assumed, computers will change to use larger integers for Epoch seconds. We hope. For operations on dates outside this range, you must use another representation or work from distinct year, month, and day values.

The Date::Calc and Date::Manip modules on CPAN both work from these distinct values, but be warned: years don't necessarily have 1900 subtracted from them the way the year value returned by `localtime` does, nor do months and weeks always start at 0. As always, consult the manpage of the appropriate module to make sure you're giving it what it expects and getting back from it what you expect. There's little more embarrassing than realizing you've calculated your company payroll based on a calendar that's 1,900 years in the past.

3.1. Finding Today's Date

Problem

You need to find the year, month, and day values for today's date.

Solution

Use `localtime`, which returns values for the current date and time if given no arguments. You can either use `localtime` and extract the information you want from the list it returns:

```
($DAY, $MONTH, $YEAR) = (localtime)[3,4,5];
```

Or, use Time::localtime, which overrides `localtime` to return a Time::tm object:

```
use Time::localtime;
$tm = localtime;
($DAY, $MONTH, $YEAR) = ($tm->mday, $tm->mon, $tm->year);
```

Discussion

Here's how you'd print the current date as "YYYY MM DD", using the non-overridden `localtime`:

```
($day, $month, $year) = (localtime)[3,4,5];
printf("The current date is %04d %02d %02d\n", $year+1900, $month+1, $day);
The current date is 1998 04 28
```

To extract the fields we want from the list returned by `localtime`, we take a list slice. We could also have written it as:

```
($day, $month, $year) = (localtime)[3..5];
```

This is how we'd print the current date as "YYYY-MM-DD" (in approved ISO 8601 fashion), using Time::localtime:

```
use Time::localtime;
$tm = localtime;
printf("The current date is %04d-%02d-%02d\n", $tm->year+1900,
    ($tm->mon)+1, $tm->mday);
The current date is 1998-04-28
```

The object interface might look out of place in a short program. However, when you do a lot of work with the distinct values, accessing them by name makes code much easier to understand.

A more obfuscated way that does not involve introducing temporary variables is:

```
printf("The current date is %04d-%02d-%02d\n",
       sub {($_[5]+1900, $_[4]+1, $_[3])}->(localtime));
```

There is also `strftime` from the POSIX module discussed in Recipe 3.8:

```
use POSIX qw(strftime);
print strftime "%Y-%m-%d\n", localtime;
```

The `gmtime` function works just as `localtime` does, but gives the answer in GMT instead of your local time zone.

See Also

The `localtime` and `gmtime` functions in *perlfunc*(1) and Chapter 3 of *Programming Perl*; the documentation for the standard Time::localtime module

3.2. Converting DMYHMS to Epoch Seconds

Problem

You want to convert a date, a time, or both with distinct values for day, month, year, etc. to Epoch seconds.

Solution

Use the `timelocal` or `timegm` functions in the standard Time::Local module, depending on whether the date and time is in the current time zone or in UTC.

```
use Time::Local;
$TIME = timelocal($sec, $min, $hours, $mday, $mon, $year);
$TIME = timegm($sec, $min, $hours, $mday, $mon, $year);
```

Discussion

The built-in function `localtime` converts an Epoch seconds value to distinct DMYHMS values; the `timelocal` subroutine from the standard Time::Local module converts distinct DMYHMS values to an Epoch seconds value. Here's an example that shows how to find Epoch seconds for a time in the current day. It gets the day, month, and year values from `localtime`:

```
# $hours, $minutes, and $seconds represent a time today,
# in the current time zone
use Time::Local;
$time = timelocal($seconds, $minutes, $hours, (localtime)[3,4,5]);
```

If you're passing month and year values to `timelocal`, it expects values with the same range as those which `localtime` returns. Namely, months start at 0, and years have 1900 subtracted from them.

The `timelocal` function assumes the DMYHMS values represent a time in the current time zone. Time::Local also exports a `timegm` subroutine that assumes the DMYHMS values represent a time in the GMT time zone. Unfortunately, there is no convenient way to convert from a time zone other than the current local time zone or GMT. The best you can do is convert to GMT and add or subtract the time zone offset in seconds.

This code illustrates both the use of `timegm` and how to adjust the ranges of months and years:

```
# $day is day in month (1-31)
# $month is month in year (1-12)
# $year is four-digit year e.g., 1967
# $hours, $minutes and $seconds represent UTC time
use Time::Local;
$time = timegm($seconds, $minutes, $hours, $day, $month-1, $year-1900);
```

As explained in the introduction, Epoch seconds cannot hold values before `Fri Dec 13 20:45:52 1901` or after `Tue Jan 19 03:14:07 2038`. Don't convert such dates to Epoch seconds—use a Date:: module from CPAN, and do your calculations with that instead.

See Also

The documentation for the standard Time::Local module (also in Chapter 7 of *Programming Perl*); convert in the other direction using Recipe 3.3

3.3. Converting Epoch Seconds to DMYHMS

Problem

You have a date and time in Epoch seconds, and you want to calculate individual DMYHMS values from it.

Solution

Use the `localtime` or `gmtime` functions, depending on whether you want the date and time in GMT or your local time zone.

```
($seconds, $minutes, $hours, $day_of_month, $month, $year,
    $wday, $yday, $isdst) = localtime($time);
```

The standard Time::timelocal and Time::gmtime modules override the `localtime` and `gmtime` functions to provide named access to the individual values.

```
use Time::localtime;              # or Time::gmtime
$tm = localtime($TIME);          # or gmtime($TIME)
$seconds = $tm->sec;
# ...
```

Discussion

The `localtime` and `gmtime` functions return strange year and month values; the year has 1900 subtracted from it, and 0 is the month value for January. Be sure to correct the base values for year and month, as this example does:

```
($seconds, $minutes, $hours, $day_of_month, $month, $year,
    $wday, $yday, $isdst) = localtime($time);
printf("Dateline: %02d:%02d:%02d-%04d/%02d/%02d\n",
    $hours, $minutes, $seconds, $year+1900, $month+1,
    $day_of_month);
```

We could have used the Time::localtime module to avoid the temporary variables:

```
use Time::localtime;
$tm = localtime($time);
printf("Dateline: %02d:%02d:%02d-%04d/%02d/%02d\n",
    $tm->hour, $tm->min, $tm->sec, $tm->year+1900,
    $tm->mon+1, $tm->mday);
```

See Also

The `localtime` function in *perlfunc*(1) and Chapter 3 of *Programming Perl*; the documentation for the standard Time::localtime and Time::gmtime modules; convert in the other direction using Recipe 3.2

3.4. Adding to or Subtracting from a Date

Problem

You have a date and time and want to find the date and time of some period in the future or past.

Solution

Simply add or subtract Epoch seconds:

```
$when = $now + $difference;
$then = $now - $difference;
```

If you have distinct DMYHMS values, use the CPAN Date::Calc module. If you're doing arithmetic with days only, use `Add_Delta_Days` (`$offset` is a positive or negative integral number of days):

```
use Date::Calc qw(Add_Delta_Days);
($y2, $m2, $d2) = Add_Delta_Days($y, $m, $d, $offset);
```

If you are concerned with hours, minutes, and seconds (in other words, times as well as dates), use `Add_Delta_DHMS`:

```
use Date::Calc qw(Add_Delta_DHMS);
($year2, $month2, $day2, $h2, $m2, $s2) =
    Add_Delta_DHMS( $year, $month, $day, $hour, $minute, $second,
                    $days_offset, $hour_offset, $minute_offset, $second_offset );
```

Discussion

Calculating with Epoch seconds is easiest, disregarding the effort to get dates and times into and out of Epoch seconds. This code shows how to calculate an offset (55 days, 2 hours, 17 minutes, and 5 seconds, in this case) from a given base date and time:

```
$birthtime = 96176750;                  # 18/Jan/1973, 3:45:50 am
$interval = 5 +                         # 5 seconds
              17 * 60 +                 # 17 minutes
              2  * 60 * 60 +            # 2 hours
              55 * 60 * 60 * 24;        # and 55 days
$then = $birthtime + $interval;
print "Then is ", scalar(localtime($then)), "\n";
Then is Wed Mar 14 06:02:55 1973
```

We could have used Date::Calc's `Add_Delta_DHMS` function and avoided the conversion to and from Epoch seconds:

```
use Date::Calc qw(Add_Delta_DHMS);
($year, $month, $day, $hh, $mm, $ss) = Add_Delta_DHMS(
     1973, 1, 18, 3, 45, 50, # 18/Jan/1973, 3:45:50 am
                   55, 2, 17, 5); # 55 days, 2 hrs, 17 min, 5 sec
print "To be precise: $hh:$mm:$ss, $month/$day/$year\n";
To be precise: 6:2:55, 3/14/1973
```

As usual, we need to know the range of values the function expects. `Add_Delta_DHMS` takes a full year value—that is, one that hasn't had 1900 subtracted from it. The month value for January is 1, not 0. Date::Calc's `Add_Delta_Days` function expects the same kind of values:

```
use Date::Calc qw(Add_Delta_Days);
($year, $month, $day) = Add_Delta_Days(1973, 1, 18, 55);
print "Nat was 55 days old on: $month/$day/$year\n";
Nat was 55 days old on: 3/14/1973
```

See Also

The documentation for the CPAN module Date::Calc

3.5. Difference of Two Dates

Problem

You need to find the number of days between two dates or times.

Solution

If your dates are in Epoch seconds, and fall in the range `Fri Dec 13 20:45:52 1901` to `Tue Jan 19 03:14:07 2038` (inclusive), simply subtract one from the other and convert the seconds to days.

```
$seconds = $recent - $earlier;
```

If you have distinct DMYMHS values, or are worried about the range limitations of Epoch seconds, use the Date::Calc module from CPAN. It can calculate the difference between dates:

```
use Date::Calc qw(Delta_Days);
$days = Delta_Days( $year1, $month1, $day1, $year2, $month2, $day2);
```

It also calculates the difference between dates and times:

```
use Date::Calc qw(Delta_DHMS);
($days, $hours, $minutes, $seconds) =
    Delta_DHMS( $year1, $month1, $day1, $hour1, $minute1, $seconds1,  # earlier
                $year2, $month2, $day2, $hour2, $minute2, $seconds2); # later
```

Discussion

One problem with Epoch seconds is how to convert the large integers back to forms that people can read. The following example shows one way of converting an Epoch seconds value back to its component numbers of weeks, days, hours, minutes, and seconds:

```
$bree = 361535725;          # 16 Jun 1981, 4:35:25
$nat  =  96201950;          # 18 Jan 1973, 3:45:50

$difference = $bree - $nat;
print "There were $difference seconds between Nat and Bree\n";
There were 265333775 seconds between Nat and Bree

$seconds    =  $difference % 60;
$difference = ($difference - $seconds) / 60;
$minutes    =  $difference % 60;
$difference = ($difference - $minutes) / 60;
```

```
$hours      = $difference % 24;
$difference = ($difference - $hours)   / 24;
$days       = $difference % 7;
$weeks      = ($difference - $days)    /  7;
```

```
print "($weeks weeks, $days days, $hours:$minutes:$seconds)\n";
(438 weeks, 4 days, 23:49:35)
```

Date::Calc's functions can ease these calculations. The `Delta_Days` function returns the number of days between two dates. It takes the two dates as a list: year, month, day. The dates are given chronologically—earliest first.

```
use Date::Calc qw(Delta_Days);
@bree = (1981, 6, 16);      # 16 Jun 1981
@nat  = (1973, 1, 18);      # 18 Jan 1973
$difference = Delta_Days(@nat, @bree);
print "There were $difference days between Nat and Bree\n";
There were 3071 days between Nat and Bree
```

The `Delta_DHMS` function returns a four-element list corresponding to the number of days, hours, minutes, and seconds between the two dates you give it.

```
use Date::Calc qw(Delta_DHMS);
@bree = (1981, 6, 16, 4, 35, 25);  # 16 Jun 1981, 4:35:25
@nat  = (1973, 1, 18, 3, 45, 50);  # 18 Jan 1973, 3:45:50
@diff = Delta_DHMS(@nat, @bree);
print "Bree came $diff[0] days, $diff[1]:$diff[2]:$diff[3] after Nat\n";
Bree came 3071 days, 0:49:35 after Nat
```

See Also

The documentation for the CPAN module Date::Calc

3.6. Day in a Week/Month/Year or Week Number

Problem

You have a date, either in Epoch seconds or as distinct year, month, etc. values. You want to find out what week of the year, day of the week, day of the month, or day of the year that the date falls on.

Solution

If you have Epoch seconds, the day of the year, day of the month, and day of the week are returned by `localtime`. The week of the year is easily calculated from the day of the year (but see discussion below, as standards differ).

```
($MONTHDAY, $WEEKDAY, $YEARDAY) = (localtime $DATE)[3,6,7];
$WEEKNUM = int($YEARDAY / 7) + 1;
```

If you have distinct DMYHMS values, you can either convert them to Epoch seconds values as in Recipe 3.3 and then use the solution above, or else use the Day_of_Week, Week_Number, and Day_of_Year functions from the CPAN module Date::Calc:

```
use Date::Calc qw(Day_of_Week Week_Number Day_of_Year);
# you have $year, $month, and $day
# $day is day of month, by definition.
$wday = Day_of_Week($year, $month, $day);
$wnum = Week_Number($year, $month, $day);
$dnum = Day_of_Year($year, $month, $day);
```

Discussion

The Day_of_Week, Week_Number, and Day_of_Year functions all expect years that haven't had 1900 subtracted from them and months where January is 1, not 0. The return value from Day_of_Week can be 1 through 7 (corresponding to Monday through Sunday) or 0 in case of an error (an invalid date, for example).

```
use Date::Calc qw(Day_of_Week Week_Number Day_of_Week_to_Text);

$year  = 1981;
$month = 6;          # (June)
$day   = 16;

$wday = Day_of_Week($year, $month, $day);
print "$month/$day/$year was a ", Day_of_Week_to_Text($wday), "\n";
## see comment above

$wnum = Week_Number($year, $month, $day);
print "in the $wnum week.\n";
6/16/1981 was a Tuesday
in week number 25.
```

The governing standards body of particular countries may have rules about when the first week of the year starts. For example, in Norway the first week must have at least 4 days in it (and weeks start on Mondays). If January 1 falls on a week with 3 or fewer days, it is counted as week 52 (or 53) of the previous year. In America, the first Monday of the year is usually the start of the first work-week. Given such rules, you may have to write your own algorithm, or at least look at the %G, %L, %W, and %U formats to the UnixDate function in Date::Manip.

See Also

The localtime function in *perlfunc*(1) and Chapter 3 of *Programming Perl*; the documentation for the CPAN module Date::Calc

3.7. *Parsing Dates and Times from Strings*

Problem

You read in a date or time specification in an arbitrary format but need to convert that string into distinct year, month, etc. values.

Solution

If your date is already numeric, or in a rigid and easily parsed format, use a regular expression (and possibly a hash mapping month names to numbers) to extract individual day, month, and year values, and then use the standard Time::Local module's `timelocal` and `timegm` functions to turn that into an Epoch seconds value.

```
use Time::Local;
# $date is "1998-06-03" (YYYY-MM-DD form).
($yyyy, $mm, $dd) = ($date =~ /(\d+)-(\d+)-(\d+)/);
# calculate epoch seconds at midnight on that day in this timezone
$epoch_seconds = timelocal(0, 0, 0, $dd, $mm-1, $yyyy-1900);
```

For a more flexible solution, use the `ParseDate` function provided by the CPAN module Date::Manip, and then use `UnixDate` to extract the individual values.

```
use Date::Manip qw(ParseDate UnixDate);
$date = ParseDate($STRING);
if (!$date) {
    # bad date
} else {
    @VALUES = UnixDate($date, @FORMATS);
}
```

Discussion

The flexible `ParseDate` function accepts many formats. It even converts strings like "today", "2 weeks ago Friday", and "2nd Sunday in 1996", and understands the date and time format used in mail and news headers. It returns the decoded date in its own format: a string of the form "YYYYMMDDHH:MM:SS". You can compare two such strings to compare the dates they represent, but arithmetic is difficult. For this reason, we use the `UnixDate` function to extract the year, month, and day values in a preferred format.

`UnixDate` takes a date in the string form returned by `ParseDate` and a list of formats. It applies each format to the string and returns the result. A format is a string describing one or more elements of the date and time and the way that the elements are to be formatted. For example, %Y is the format for the year in four-digit form. Here's an example:

```
use Date::Manip qw(ParseDate UnixDate);

while (<>) {
    $date = ParseDate($_);
    if (!$date) {
        warn "Bad date string: $_\n";
        next;
    } else {
        ($year, $month, $day) = UnixDate($date, "%Y", "%m", "%d");
        print "Date was $month/$day/$year\n";
    }
}
```

See Also

The documentation for the CPAN module Date::Manip; we use this in Recipe 3.11

3.8. Printing a Date

Problem

You need to print a date and time shown in Epoch seconds format in human-readable form.

Solution

Simply call `localtime` or `gmtime` in scalar context, which takes an Epoch second value and returns a string of the form **Tue May 26 05:15:20 1998**:

```
$STRING = localtime($EPOCH_SECONDS);
```

Alternatively, the `strftime` function in the standard POSIX module supports a more customizable output format, and takes individual DMYHMS values:

```
use POSIX qw(strftime);
$STRING = strftime($FORMAT, $SECONDS, $MINUTES, $HOUR,
                   $DAY_OF_MONTH, $MONTH, $YEAR, $WEEKDAY,
                   $YEARDAY, $DST);
```

The CPAN module Date::Manip has a `UnixDate` routine that works like a specialized form `sprintf` designed to handle dates. Pass it a Date::Manip date value. Using Date::Manip in lieu of POSIX::strftime has the advantage of not requiring a POSIX-compliant system.

```
use Date::Manip qw(UnixDate);
$STRING = UnixDate($DATE, $FORMAT);
```

Discussion

The simplest solution is built into Perl already: the localtime function. In scalar context, it returns the string formatted in a particular way:

Sun Sep 21 15:33:36 1997

This makes for simple code, although it restricts the format of the string:

```
use Time::Local;
$time = timelocal(50, 45, 3, 18, 0, 73);
print "Scalar localtime gives: ", scalar(localtime($time)), "\n";
Scalar localtime gives: Thu Jan 18 03:45:50 1973
```

Of course, localtime requires the date and time in Epoch seconds. The POSIX::strftime function takes a set of individual DMYMHS values and a format and returns a string. The format is similar to a printf format; % directives specify fields in the output string. A full list of these directives is available in your system's documentation for strftime. strftime expects the individual values representing the date and time to be the same range as the values returned by localtime:

```
use POSIX qw(strftime);
use Time::Local;
$time = timelocal(50, 45, 3, 18, 0, 73);
print "strftime gives: ", strftime("%A %D", localtime($time)), "\n";
strftime gives: Thursday 01/18/73
```

All values are shown in their national representation when using POSIX::strftime. So, if you run it in France, your program would print "Sunday" as "Dimanche". Be warned: Perl's interface to the POSIX function strftime always converts the date, assuming that it falls in the current time zone.

If you don't have access to POSIX's strftime function, there's always the trusty Date::Manip CPAN module, described in Recipe 3.6.

```
use Date::Manip qw(ParseDate UnixDate);
$date = ParseDate("18 Jan 1973, 3:45:50");
$datestr = UnixDate($date, "%a %b %e %H:%M:%S %z %Y");    # as scalar
print "Date::Manip gives: $datestr\n";
Date::Manip gives: Thu Jan 18 03:45:50 GMT 1973
```

See Also

The gmtime and localtime functions in *perlfunc*(1) and Chapter 3 of *Programming Perl*; *perllocale*(1); your system's *strftime*(3) manpage; the documentation for the POSIX module (also in Chapter 7 of *Programming Perl*); the documentation for the CPAN module Date::Manip

3.9. High-Resolution Timers

Problem

You need to measure time with a finer granularity than the full seconds that `time` returns.

Solution

This might not be possible. If your system supports both the `syscall` function in Perl as well as a system call like *gettimeofday*(2), then you could possibly use them to measure the time. The procedure for using `syscall` varies from system to system. The Discussion has sample code using it, but this is not necessarily portable.

The Time::HiRes module (available from CPAN) encapsulates this functionality for some systems:

```
use Time::HiRes;
$t0 = Time::HiRes::time;
## do your operation here
$t1 = gettimeofday Time::HiRes::time;
$elapsed = $t1-$t0;
# $elapsed is a floating point value, representing number
# of seconds between $t1 and $t2
```

Discussion

Here's some code that uses Time::HiRes to time how long the user takes to press RETURN:

```
use Time::HiRes ;
print "Press return when ready: ";
$before = Time::HiRes::time();
$line = <>;
$elapsed = Time::HiRes::time()-$before;
print "You took $elapsed seconds.\n";
Press return when ready:
You took 0.228149 seconds.
```

Compare this to the equivalent `syscall` code:

```
require 'sys/syscall.ph';

# initialize the structures returned by gettimeofday
$TIMEVAL_T = "LL";
$done = $start = pack($TIMEVAL_T, ());

# prompt
print "Press return when ready: ";
```

```
# read the time into $start
syscall(&SYS_gettimeofday, $start, 0) != -1
            || die "gettimeofday: $!";

# read a line
$line = <>;

# read the time into $done
syscall(&SYS_gettimeofday, $done, 0) != -1
            || die "gettimeofday: $!";

# expand the structure
@start = unpack($TIMEVAL_T, $start);
@done  = unpack($TIMEVAL_T, $done);

# fix microseconds
for ($done[1], $start[1]) { $_ /= 1_000_000 }

# calculate time difference
$delta_time = sprintf "%.4f", ($done[0]  + $done[1]  )
                                         -
                              ($start[0] + $start[1] );

print "That took $delta_time seconds\n";
Press return when ready:
That took 0.3037 seconds
```

It's longer because it's doing system calls in Perl, while Time::HiRes does them in C providing a single function. It's complex because directly accessing system calls peculiar to your operating system requires you to know details about the underlying C structures that the system call takes and returns. Some programs that come with the Perl distribution try to automatically calculate the formats to pack and unpack for you, if fed the appropriate C header file. In the example, *sys/syscall.ph* is a Perl library file generated with *h2ph*, which converts the *sys/syscall.h* header file into *sys/syscall.ph* that defines (among other things) &SYS_gettimeofday as a subroutine that returns the system call number of gettimeofday.

Here's another example of Time::HiRes, showing how you could use it to benchmark a sort:

```
use Time::HiRes qw(gettimeofday);
# take mean sorting time
$size = 500;
$number_of_times = 100;
$total_time = 0;

for ($i = 0; $i < $number_of_times; $i++) {
    my (@array, $j, $begin, $time);
    # populate array
    @array = ();
    for ($j=0; $j<$size; $j++) { push(@array, rand) }

    # sort it
```

```
    $begin = gettimeofday;
    @array = sort { $a <=> $b } @array;
    $time = gettimeofday-$begin;
    $total_time += $time;
}

printf "On average, sorting %d random numbers takes %.5f seconds\n",
    $size, ($total_time/$number_of_times);
On average, sorting 500 random numbers takes 0.02821 seconds
```

See Also

The documentation for the CPAN modules Time::HiRes and Benchmark; the
syscall function in *perlfunc*(1) and Chapter 3 of *Programming Perl*; your system's *syscall*(2) manpage

3.10. Short Sleeps

Problem

You need to sleep for less than a second.

Solution

Use the select() function, if your system supports it:

```
    select(undef, undef, undef, $time_to_sleep);
```

Some systems don't support a four-argument select. The Time::HiRes module
provides a sleep function that takes a floating point number of seconds:

```
    use Time::HiRes qw(sleep);
    sleep($time_to_sleep);
```

Discussion

Here's an example of select. It's a simpler version of the program in Recipe 1.5.
Think of it as your very own 300-baud terminal.

```
    while (<>) {
        select(undef, undef, undef, 0.25);
        print;
    }
```

Using Time::HiRes, we'd write it as:

```
    use Time::HiRes qw(sleep);
    while (<>) {
        sleep(0.25);
        print;
    }
```

See Also

The documentation for the CPAN modules Time::HiRes and BenchMark; the `sleep` and `select` functions in *perlfunc*(1) and Chapter 3 of *Programming Perl*; we use the `select` function for short sleeps in the `slowcat` program in Recipe 1.5

3.11. Program: hopdelta

Have you ever wondered why it took so long for someone's mail to get to you? With postal mail, you can't trace how long each intervening post office let your letter gather dust in their back office. But with electronic mail, you can. The message carries in its header `Received:` lines showing when each intervening mail transport agent along the way got the message.

The dates in the headers are hard to read. You have to read them backwards, bottom to top. They are written in many varied formats, depending on the whim of each transport agent. Worst of all, each date is written in its own local time zone. It's hard to eyeball `"Tue, 26 May 1998 23:57:38 -0400"` and `"Wed, 27 May 1998 05:04:03 +0100"` and realize these two dates are only 6 minutes and 25 seconds apart.

The `ParseDate` and `DateCalc` functions in the Date::Manip module from CPAN can help this:

```
use Date::Manip qw(ParseDate DateCalc);
$d1 = ParseDate("Tue, 26 May 1998 23:57:38 -0400");
$d2 = ParseDate("Wed, 27 May 1998 05:04:03 +0100");
print DateCalc($d1, $d2);
+0:0:0:0:0:6:25
```

That's a nice format for a program to read, but it's still not what the casual reader wants to see. The *hopdelta* program, shown in Example 3-1, takes a mailer header and tries to analyze the deltas (difference) between each hop (mail stop). Its output is shown in the local time zone.

Example 3-1. hopdelta

```
#!/usr/bin/perl
# hopdelta - feed mail header, produce lines
#            showing delay at each hop.
use strict;
use Date::Manip qw (ParseDate UnixDate);

# print header; this should really use format/write due to
# printf complexities
printf "%-20.20s %-20.20s %-20.20s   %s\n",
        "Sender", "Recipient", "Time", "Delta";
```

Example 3-1. hopdelta (continued)

```perl
$/ = '';                    # paragraph mode
$_ = <>;                    # read header
s/\n\s+/ /g;                # join continuation lines

# calculate when and where this started
my($start_from) = /^From.*\@([^\s>]*)/m;
my($start_date) = /^Date:\s+(.*)/m;
my $then = getdate($start_date);
printf "%-20.20s %-20.20s %s\n", 'Start', $start_from, fmtdate($then);

my $prevfrom = $start_from;

# now process the headers lines from the bottom up
for (reverse split(/\n/)) {
    my ($delta, $now, $from, $by, $when);
    next unless /^Received:/;
    s/\bon (.*?) (id.*)/; $1/s;         # qmail header, I think
    unless (($when) = /;\s+(.*)$/) {    # where the date falls
        warn "bad received line: $_";
        next;
    }
    ($from) = /from\s+(\S+)/;
    ($from) = /\((.*?)\)/ unless $from; # some put it here
    $from =~ s/\)$//;                   # someone was too greedy
    ($by)   = /by\s+(\S+\.\S+)/;        # who sent it on this hop

    # now random mungings to get their string parsable
    for ($when) {
        s/ (for|via) .*$//;
        s/([+-]\d\d\d\d) \(\S+\)/$1/;
        s/id \S+;\s*//;
    }
    next unless $now = getdate($when);          # convert to Epoch
    $delta = $now - $then;

    printf "%-20.20s %-20.20s %s  ", $from, $by, fmtdate($now);
    $prevfrom = $by;
    puttime($delta);
    $then = $now;
}

exit;

# convert random date strings into Epoch seconds
sub getdate {
    my $string      = shift;
    $string         =~ s/\s+\(.*\)\s*$//;       # remove nonstd tz
    my $date        = ParseDate($string);
    my $epoch_secs  = UnixDate($date,"%s");
    return $epoch_secs;
}
```

Example 3-1. hopdelta (continued)

```
# convert Epoch seconds into a particular date string
sub fmtdate {
    my $epoch = shift;
    my($sec,$min,$hour,$mday,$mon,$year) = localtime($epoch);
    return sprintf "%02d:%02d:%02d %04d/%02d/%02d",
        $hour, $min, $sec,
        $year + 1900, $mon + 1, $mday,
}


# take seconds and print in pleasant-to-read format
sub puttime {
    my($seconds) = shift;
    my($days, $hours, $minutes);

    $days    = pull_count($seconds, 24 * 60 * 60);
    $hours   = pull_count($seconds, 60 * 60);
    $minutes = pull_count($seconds, 60);

    put_field('s', $seconds);
    put_field('m', $minutes);
    put_field('h', $hours);
    put_field('d', $days);

    print "\n";
}


# usage: $count = pull_count(seconds, amount)
# remove from seconds the amount quantity, altering caller's version.
# return the integral number of those amounts so removed.
sub pull_count {
    my($answer) = int($_[0] / $_[1]);
    $_[0] -= $answer * $_[1];
    return $answer;
}


# usage: put_field(char, number)
# output number field in 3-place decimal format, with trailing char
# suppress output unless char is 's' for seconds
sub put_field {
    my ($char, $number) = @_;
    printf " %3d%s", $number, $char if $number || $char eq 's';
}
```

Sender	Recipient	Time	Delta	
Start	wall.org	09:17:12 1998/05/23		
wall.org	mail.brainstorm.net	09:20:56 1998/05/23	44s	3m
mail.brainstorm.net	jhereg.perl.com	09:20:58 1998/05/23	2s	

4

Arrays

> *Works of art, in my opinion, are the only objects in*
> *the material universe to possess internal order, and*
> *that is why, though I don't believe that only art*
> *matters, I do believe in Art for Art's sake.*
>
> —E.M. Forster

4.0. Introduction

If you are asked about the contents of your pockets, or the names of the last three presidents, or how to get to the highway, you recite a list: you name one thing after another in a particular order. Lists are part of your conception of the world. With Perl's powerful list- and array-handling primitives, you can translate this world view directly into code.

In this chapter, we'll use the terms *list* and *array* as the Perl language thinks of them. Take ("Reagan", "Bush", "Clinton"); that's a *list* of the last three American presidents, in order. To store that list into a variable, use an *array*, as in @presidents = ("Reagan", "Bush", "Clinton"). Both are ordered groups of scalar values; the difference is that an array is a named variable, one whose array length can be directly changed, whereas a list is a more ephemeral notion. You might think of an array as a variable and a list as the values it contains.

This distinction may seem arbitrary, but operations that modify the length of these groupings (like push and pop) require a proper array and not merely a list. Think of the difference between $a and 4. You can say $a++ but not 4++. Likewise, you can say pop(@a) but not pop (1,2,3).

The most important thing to glean from this is that Perl's lists and arrays are both ordered groupings of scalars. Operators and functions that work on lists or arrays are designed to provide faster or more convenient access to the elements than manual access would provide. Since few actually deal with modifying the array's length, you can usually use arrays and lists interchangeably.

You can't use nested parentheses to create a list of lists. If you try that in Perl, your lists get *flattened*, meaning that both these lines are equivalent:

```
@nested = ("this", "that", "the", "other");
@nested = ("this", "that", ("the", "other"));
```

Why doesn't Perl (usefully) just support nested lists directly? Although partially for historical reasons, this easily allows for operations (like `print` or `sort`) that work on arbitrarily long lists of arbitrary contents.

What happens if you want a more complex data structure, such as an array of arrays or an array of hashes? Remember that scalars aren't restricted to containing just numbers or strings; they can also hold references. Complex (multilevel) data structures in Perl are always put together using references. Therefore, what appear to be "two-dimensional arrays" or "arrays of arrays" are always implemented as arrays of array *references*, in the same way that two-dimensional arrays in C can be arrays of pointers to arrays.

Most recipes in this chapter don't care what you keep in your arrays; for example, the problem of merging two arrays is the same whether the arrays contains strings, numbers, or references. Some problems are intrinsically tied to the contents of your arrays; recipes for those are in Chapter 11, *References and Records*. This chapter's recipes deal with generic arrays.

Let's have some more terminology. The scalar items in an array or list are called *elements*, which you access by specifying their position, or *index*. Indices in Perl start at 0. So, given this list:

```
@tune = ( "The", "Star-Spangled", "Banner" );
```

`"The"` is in the first position, but you'd access it as `$tune[0]`. `"Star-Spangled"` is in the second position, but you'd access it as `$tune[1]`. This structure is doubly justified: the contrariness of computers, whose first representable number is 0, and the contrariness of language designers, who chose 0 because it is an *offset* into the array, not the *ordinal* number of the element.

4.1. *Specifying a List In Your Program*

Problem

You want to include a list in your program. This is how you initialize arrays.

Solution

You can write out a comma-separated list of elements:

```
@a = ("quick", "brown", "fox");
```

If you have a lot of single-word elements, use the qw() operator:

```
@a = qw(Why are you teasing me?);
```

If you have a lot of multi-word elements, use a here document and extract lines:

```
@lines = (<<"END_OF_HERE_DOC" =~ m/^\s*(.+)/gm);
    The boy stood on the burning deck,
    It was as hot as glass.
END_OF_HERE_DOC
```

Discussion

The first technique is the most commonly used, often because only small arrays are normally initialized as program literals. Initializing a large array would fill your program with values and make it hard to read, so such arrays are either initialized in a separate library file (see Chapter 12, *Packages, Libraries, and Modules*), or the values are simply read from a file:

```
@bigarray = ();
open(DATA, "< mydatafile")         or die "Couldn't read from datafile: $!\n";
while (<DATA>) {
    chomp;
    push(@bigarray, $_);
}
```

The second technique uses the qw() operator, one of the quoting operators. Along with q(), qq(), and qx(), qw() provides another way to quote values for your program. q() behaves like single quotes, so these two lines are equivalent:

```
$banner = 'The Mines of Moria';
$banner = q(The Mines of Moria);
```

Similarly, qq() behaves like double quotes:

```
$name   =  "Gandalf";
$banner = "Speak, $name, and enter!";
$banner = qq(Speak, $name, and welcome!);
```

And qx() is almost exactly like backticks; that is, it runs a command through the shell complete with variable interpolation and backslash escapes. You can't stop interpolation with backticks, but you can with qx. If you don't want Perl variables to be expanded, you can use a single-quote delimiter on qx to suppress this:

```
$his_host   = 'www.perl.com';
$host_info  = `nslookup $his_host`; # expand Perl variable
```

```
$perl_info  = qx(ps $$);            # that's Perl's $$
$shell_info = qx'ps $$';            # that's the new shell's $$
```

Whereas q(), qq(), and qx() quote single strings, qw() quotes a list of single-word strings by splitting its argument on whitespace, without variable interpolation. These are all the same:

```
@banner = ('Costs', 'only', '$4.95');
@banner = qw(Costs only $4.95);
@banner = split(' ', 'Costs only $4.95');
```

All quoting operators behave like regular expression matches, in that you can select your quote delimiters, including paired brackets. All four kinds of brackets (angle, square, curly, and round ones) nest properly. That means you can easily use parentheses or braces (or the other two) without fear, provided that they match up:

```
@brax   = qw! ( ) < > { } [ ] !;
@rings  = qw(Nenya Narya Vilya);
@tags   = qw<LI TABLE TR TD A IMG H1 P>;
@sample = qw(The vertical bar (|) looks and behaves like a pipe.);
```

If you don't want to change the quoting character, use a backslash to escape the delimiter in the string:

```
@banner = qw|The vertical bar (\|) looks and behaves like a pipe.|;
```

You may only use qw() when each separate, space-separated component is an element in the return list. Be careful not to give Columbus four ships instead of three:

```
@ships  = qw(Niña Pinta Santa María);           # WRONG
@ships  = ('Niña', 'Pinta', 'Santa María');     # right
```

See Also

The "List Value Constructors" section of *perldata*(1); the "List Values and Arrays" section of Chapter 2 of *Programming Perl*; the "Quote and Quote-Like Operators" section of *perlop*(1); the s/// operator in *perlop*(1) and Chapter 2 of *Programming Perl*

4.2. Printing a List with Commas

Problem

You'd like to print out a list with an unknown number of elements with an "and" before the last element, and with commas between each element if there are more than two.

Solution

Use this function, which returns the formatted string:

```
sub commify_series {
    (@_ == 0) ? ''                                                   :
    (@_ == 1) ? $_[0]                                                :
    (@_ == 2) ? join(" and ", @_)                                    :
                join(", ", @_[0 .. ($#_-1)], "and $_[-1]");
}
```

Discussion

It often looks odd to print out arrays:

```
@array = ("red", "yellow", "green");
print "I have ", @array, " marbles.\n";
print "I have @array marbles.\n";
```
I have redyellowgreen marbles.
I have red yellow green marbles.

What you really want it to say is, `"I have red, yellow, and green marbles"`. The function given in the solution generates strings in that format. The word `"and"` is placed between the last two list elements. If there are more than two elements in the list, a comma is placed between every element.

Example 4-1 gives a complete demonstration of the function, with one addition: If any element in the list already contains a comma, a semi-colon is used for the separator character instead.

Example 4-1. commify_series

```
#!/usr/bin/perl -w
# commify_series - show proper comma insertion in list output

@lists = (
    [ 'just one thing' ],
    [ qw(Mutt Jeff) ],
    [ qw(Peter Paul Mary) ],
    [ 'To our parents', 'Mother Theresa', 'God' ],
    [ 'pastrami', 'ham and cheese', 'peanut butter and jelly', 'tuna' ],
    [ 'recycle tired, old phrases', 'ponder big, happy thoughts' ],
    [ 'recycle tired, old phrases',
      'ponder big, happy thoughts',
      'sleep and dream peacefully' ],
);

foreach $aref (@lists) {
    print "The list is: " . commify_series(@$aref) . ".\n";
}

sub commify_series {
    my $sepchar = grep(/,/ => @_) ? ";" : ",";
```

Example 4-1. commify_series (continued)

```
(@_ == 0) ? ''                                       :
(@_ == 1) ? $_[0]                                    :
(@_ == 2) ? join(" and ", @_)                        :
            join("$sepchar ", @_[0 .. ($#_-1)], "and $_[-1]");
}
```

Here's the output from the program:

```
The list is: just one thing.
The list is: Mutt and Jeff.
The list is: Peter, Paul, and Mary.
The list is: To our parents, Mother Theresa, and God.
The list is: pastrami, ham and cheese, peanut butter and jelly, and tuna.
The list is: recycle tired, old phrases and ponder big, happy thoughts.
The list is: recycle tired, old phrases; ponder
    big, happy thoughts; and sleep and dream peacefully.
```

As you see, we don't follow the ill-advised practice of omitting the final comma from a series under any circumstances. To do so introduces unfortunate ambiguities and unjustifiable exceptions. The examples above would have claimed that we were the offspring of Mother Theresa and God, and would have had us eating sandwiches made of jelly and tuna fish fixed together atop the peanut butter.

See Also

Fowler's *Modern English Usage*; we explain the nested list syntax in Recipe 11.1; the grep function in *perlfunc*(1) and Chapter 3 of *Programming Perl*; the conditional operator ("?:") is discussed in *perlop*(1) and in the "Conditional Operator" section of Chapter 2 of *Programming Perl*

4.3. *Changing Array Size*

Problem

You want to enlarge or truncate an array. For example, you might truncate an array of employees that's already sorted by salary to list the five highest-paid employees. Or, if you know how big your array will get and that it will grow piecemeal, it's more efficient to get memory for it in one step by enlarging it just once than it is to keep pushing values onto the end.

Solution

Assign to $#ARRAY:

```
# grow or shrink @ARRAY
$#ARRAY = $NEW_LAST_ELEMENT_INDEX_NUMBER;
```

Assigning to an element past the end automatically extends the array:

```
$ARRAY[$NEW_LAST_ELEMENT_INDEX_NUMBER] = $VALUE;
```

Discussion

`$#ARRAY` is the number of the last valid index in `@ARRAY`. If we assign it a number smaller than its current value, we truncate the array. Truncated elements are lost forever. If we assign `$#ARRAY` a number larger than its current value, the array grows. New elements have the undefined value.

`$#ARRAY` is not `@ARRAY`, though. Although `$#ARRAY` is the last valid index in the array, `@ARRAY` (in scalar context, as when treated as a number) is the *number* of elements. `$#ARRAY` is one less than `@ARRAY` because array indices start at 0.

Here's some code that uses both:

```
sub what_about_that_array {
    print "The array now has ", scalar(@people), " elements.\n";
    print "The index of the last element is $#people.\n";
    print "Element #3 is '$people[3]'.\n";
}

@people = qw(Crosby Stills Nash Young);
what_about_that_array();
```

prints:

```
The array now has 4 elements.
The index of the last element is 3.
Element #3 is 'Young'.
```

whereas:

```
$#people--;
what_about_that_array();
```

prints:

```
The array now has 3 elements.
The index of the last element is 2.
Element #3 is ''.
```

Element #3 disappeared when we shortened the array. If we'd used the **-w** flag on this program, Perl would also have warned "use of uninitialized value" because `$people[3]` is undefined.

```
$#people = 10_000;
what_about_that_array();
```

prints:

```
The array now has 10001 elements.
The index of the last element is 10000.
Element #3 is ''.
```

The "Young" element is now gone forever. Instead of assigning to $#people, we could have said:

```
$people[10_000] = undef;
```

Perl arrays are not sparse. In other words, if you have a 10,000th element, you must have the 9,999 other elements, too. They may be undefined, but they still take up memory. For this reason, $array[time], or any other construct that uses a very large integer as an array index, is a bad idea. Use a hash instead.

We have to say scalar @array in the print because Perl gives list context to (most) functions' arguments, but we want @array in scalar context.

See Also

The discussion of the $#ARRAY notation in *perldata*(1), also explained in the "List Values and Arrays" section of Chapter 2 of *Programming Perl*

4.4. Doing Something with Every Element in a List

Problem

You want to repeat a procedure for every element in a list.

Often you use an array to collect information you're interested in; for instance, login names of users who have exceeded their disk quota. When you finish collecting the information, you want to process it by doing something with every element in the array. In the disk quota example, you might send each user a stern mail message.

Solution

Use a foreach loop:

```
foreach $item (LIST) {
    # do something with $item
}
```

Discussion

Let's say we've used @bad_users to compile a list of users over their allotted disk quota. To call some complain() subroutine for each one we'd use:

```
foreach $user (@bad_users) {
    complain($user);
}
```

Rarely is this recipe so simply applied. Instead, we often use functions to generate
the list:

```
foreach $var (sort keys %ENV) {
    print "$var=$ENV{$var}\n";
}
```

Here we're using `sort` and `keys` to build a sorted list of environment variable
names. In situations where the list will be used more than once, you'll obviously
keep it around by saving in an array. But for one-shot processing, it's often tidier
to process the list directly.

Not only can we add complexity to this formula by building up the list in the
`foreach`, we can also add complexity by doing more work inside the code block.
A common application of `foreach` is to gather information on every element of a
list, and then decide (based on that information) whether to do something. For
instance, returning to the disk quota example:

```
foreach $user (@all_users) {
    $disk_space = get_usage($user);      # find out how much disk space in use
    if ($disk_space > $MAX_QUQTA) {      # if it's more than we want ...
        complain($user);                 # ... then object vociferously
    }
}
```

More complicated program flow is possible. The code can call `last` to jump out
of the loop, `next` to move on to the next element, or `redo` to jump back to the
first statement inside the block. Use these to say "no point continuing with this
one, I know it's not what I'm looking for" (`next`), "I've found what I'm looking
for, there's no point in my checking the rest" (`last`), or "I've changed some
things, I'd better do my tests and calculations again" (`redo`).

The variable set to each value in the list is called a *loop variable* or *iterator variable*. If no iterator variable is supplied, the global variable $_ is used. $_ is the
default variable for many of Perl's string, list, and file functions. In brief code
blocks, omitting $_ improves readability. (In long ones, though, too much implicit
use hampers readability.) For example:

```
foreach ('who') {
    if (/tchrist/) {
        print;
    }
}
```

or combining with a `while` loop:

```
while (<FH>) {                   # $_ is set to the line just read
    chomp;                       # $_ has a trailing \n removed, if it had one
    foreach (split) {            # $_ is split on whitespace, into @_
                                 # then $_ is set to each chunk in turn
        $_ = reverse;            # the characters in $_ are reversed
```

```
        print;              # $_ is printed
    }
}
```

Perhaps all these uses of $_ are starting to make you nervous. In particular, the foreach and the while both give values to $_. You might fear that at the end of the foreach, the full line as read into $_ with <FH> would be forever gone.

Fortunately, your fears would be unfounded, at least in this case. Perl won't permanently clobber $_'s old value, because the foreach's iterator variable ($_ in this case) is automatically preserved during the loop. It saves away any old value on entry and restores it upon exit.

There is cause for some concern though. If the while had been the inner loop and the foreach the outer one, then your fears would have been realized. Unlike a foreach loop, the while <FH> construct clobbers the value of the global $_ without first localizing it! So any routine—or block for that matter—that uses such a construct with $_ should always declare local $_ at its front.

If a lexical variable (one declared with my) is in scope, the temporary variable will be lexically scoped, private to that loop. Otherwise, it will be a dynamically scoped global variable. To avoid strange magic at a distance, as of release 5.004 you can write this more obviously and more clearly as:

```
foreach my $item (@array) {
    print "i = $item\n";
}
```

The foreach looping construct has another feature: each time through the loop, the iterator variable becomes not a copy of but rather an *alias* for the current element. This means that when you change that iterator variable, you really change each element in the list:

```
@array = (1,2,3);
foreach $item (@array) {
    $item--;
}
print "@array\n";
0 1 2

# multiply everything in @a and @b by seven
@a = ( .5, 3 ); @b =( 0, 1 );
foreach $item (@a, @b) {
    $item *= 7;
}
print "@a @b\n";
3.5 21 0 7
```

This aliasing means that using a foreach loop to modify list values is both more readable and faster than the equivalent code using a three-part for loop and explicit indexing would be. This behavior is a feature, not a bug, that was introduced by design. If you didn't know about it, you might accidentally change something. Now you know about it.

For example, if we used `s///` on elements of the list returned by the `values` function, we would only be changing copies, not the real hash itself. The hash slice (`@hash{keys %hash}` is a hash slice, explained in Chapter 5, *Hashes*), however, gives us something we *can* usefully change:

```
# trim whitespace in the scalar, the array, and all the values
# in the hash
foreach ($scalar, @array, @hash{keys %hash}) {
    s/^\s+//;
    s/\s+$//;
}
```

For reasons hearkening back to the equivalent construct in the Unix Bourne shell, the `for` and `foreach` keywords are interchangeable:

```
for $item (@array) {  # same as foreach $item (@array)
    # do something
}

for (@array)       {  # same as foreach $_ (@array)
    # do something
}
```

This style often indicates that its author writes or maintains shell scripts, perhaps for Unix systems administration. As such, their life is probably hard enough, so don't speak too harshly of them. Remember, TMTOWTDI. This is just one of those ways.

If you aren't fluent in Bourne shell, you might find it clearer to express "for each `$thing` in this `@list`," by saying `foreach` to make your code less like the shell and more like English. (But don't try to make your English look like your code!)

See Also

The "For Loops," "Foreach Loops," and "Loop Control" sections of *perlsyn*(1) and Chapter 2 of *Programming Perl*; the "Temporary Values via local()" section of *perlsub*(1); the "Scoped Declarations" section of Chapter 2 of *Programming Perl*; we talk about `local()` in Recipe 10.13; we talk about `my()` in Recipe 10.2

4.5. Iterating Over an Array by Reference

Problem

You have a reference to an array, and you want to use `foreach` to work with the array's elements.

Solution

Use `foreach` or `for` to loop over the dereferenced array:

```
# iterate over elements of array in $ARRAYREF
foreach $item (@$ARRAYREF) {
    # do something with $item
}

for ($i = 0; $i <= $#$ARRAYREF; $i++) {
    # do something with $ARRAYREF->[$i]
}
```

Discussion

The solutions assume you have a scalar variable containing the array reference. This lets you do things like this:

```
@fruits = ( "Apple", "Blackberry" );
$fruit_ref = \@fruits;
foreach $fruit (@$fruit_ref) {
    print "$fruit tastes good in a pie.\n";
}
```
Apple tastes good in a pie.
Blackberry tastes good in a pie.

We could have rewritten the `foreach` loop as a `for` loop like this:

```
for ($i=0; $i <= $#$fruit_ref; $i++) {
    print "$fruit_ref->[$i] tastes good in a pie.\n";
}
```

Frequently, though, the array reference is the result of a more complex expression. You need to use the `@{ EXPR }` notation to turn the result of the expression back into an array:

```
$namelist{felines} = \@rogue_cats;
foreach $cat ( @{ $namelist{felines} } ) {
    print "$cat purrs hypnotically..\n";
}
print "--More--\nYou are controlled.\n";
```

Again, we can replace the `foreach` with a `for` loop:

```
for ($i=0; $i <= $#{ $namelist{felines} }; $i++) {
    print "$namelist{felines}[$i] purrs hypnotically.\n";
}
```

See Also

perlref(1) and *perllol*(1); Chapter 4 of *Programming Perl*; Recipe 11.1; Recipe 4.4

4.6. *Extracting Unique Elements from a List*

Problem

You want to eliminate duplicate values from a list, such as when you build the list
from a file or from the output of another command. This recipe is equally applicable to removing duplicates as they occur in input and to removing duplicates from
an array you've already populated.

Solution

Use a hash to record which items have been seen, then **keys** to extract them. You
can use Perl's idea of truth to shorten and speed up your code.

Straightforward

```
%seen = ();
@uniq = ();
foreach $item (@list) {
    unless ($seen{$item}) {
        # if we get here, we have not seen it before
        $seen{$item} = 1;
        push(@uniq, $item);
    }
}
```

Faster

```
%seen = ();
foreach $item (@list) {
    push(@uniq, $item) unless $seen{$item}++;
}
```

Similar but with user function

```
%seen = ();
foreach $item (@list) {
    some_func($item) unless $seen{$item}++;
}
```

Faster but different

```
%seen = ();
foreach $item (@list) {
    $seen{$item}++;
}
@uniq = keys %seen;
```

Faster and even more different

```
%seen = ();
@uniqu = grep { ! $seen{$_} ++ } @list;
```

Discussion

The question at the heart of the matter is "Have I seen this element before?" Hashes are ideally suited to such lookups. The first technique ("Straightforward") builds up the array of unique values as we go along, using a hash to record whether something is already in the array.

The second technique ("Faster") is the most natural way to write this sort of thing in Perl. It creates a new entry in the hash every time it sees an element that hasn't been seen before, using the ++ operator. This has the side effect of making the hash record the number of times the element was seen. This time we only use the hash for its property of working like a set.

The third example ("Similar but with user function") is similar to the second but rather than storing the item away, we call some user-defined function with that item as its argument. If that's all we're doing, keeping a spare array of those unique values is unnecessary.

The next mechanism ("Faster but different") waits until it's done processing the list to extract the unique keys from the %seen hash. This may be convenient, but the original order has been lost.

The final approach, ("Faster and even more different") merges the construction of the %seen hash with the extraction of unique elements. This preserves the original order of elements.

Using a hash to record the values has two side effects: processing long lists can take a lot of memory and the list returned by **keys** is not in alphabetical, numeric, or insertion order.

Here's an example of processing input as it is read. We use `who` to gather information on the current user list, and then we extract the username from each line before updating the hash:

```
# generate a list of users logged in, removing duplicates
%ucnt = ();
for (`who`) {
    s/\s.*\n//;   # kill from first space till end-of-line, yielding username
    $ucnt{$_}++;  # record the presence of this user
}
# extract and print unique keys
@users = sort keys %ucnt;
print "users logged in: @users\n";
```

See Also

The "Foreach Loops" section of *perlsyn*(1) and Chapter 2 of *Programming Perl*; the **keys** function in *perlfunc*(1) and Chapter 3 of *Programming Perl*; the "Hashes

(Associative Arrays)" section of Chapter 2 of *Programming Perl*; Chapter 5, *Hashes*; we use hashes in a similar fashion in Recipe 4.7 and Recipe 4.8

4.7. *Finding Elements in One Array but Not Another*

Problem

You want to find elements that are in one array but not another.

Solution

You want to find elements in @A that aren't in @B. Build a hash of the keys of @B to use as a lookup table. Then check each element in @A to see if it is in @B.

Straightforward implementation

```
# assume @A and @B are already loaded
%seen = ();                     # lookup table to test membership of B
@aonly = ();                    # answer

# build lookup table
foreach $item (@B) { $seen{$item} = 1 }

# find only elements in @A and not in @B
foreach $item (@A) {
    unless ($seen{$item}) {
        # it's not in %seen, so add to @aonly
        push(@aonly, $item);
    }
}
```

More idiomatic version

```
my %seen; # lookup table
my @aonly;# answer

# build lookup table
@seen{@B} = ();

foreach $item (@A) {
    push(@aonly, $item) unless exists $seen{$item};
}
```

Discussion

As with nearly any problem in Perl that asks whether a scalar is in one list or another, this one uses a hash. First, process @B so that the %seen hash records each element from @B by setting its value to 1. Then process @A one element at a time, checking whether that particular element had been in @B by consulting the %seen hash.

The given code retains duplicate elements in @A. This can be easily fixed by adding the elements of @A to %seen as they are processed:

```
foreach $item (@A) {
    push(@aonly, $item) unless $seen{$item};
    $seen{$item} = 1;                    # mark as seen
}
```

The two solutions differ mainly in how they build the hash. The first iterates through @B. The second uses a *hash slice* to initialize the hash. A hash slice is easiest illustrated by example:

```
$hash{"key1"} = 1;
$hash{"key2"} = 2;
```

is equivalent to:

```
@hash{"key1", "key2"} = (1,2);
```

The list in the curly braces holds the keys; the list on the right holds the values. We initialize %seen in the first solution by looping over each element in @B and setting the appropriate value of %seen to 1. In the second, we simply say:

```
@seen{@B} = ();
```

This uses items in @B as keys for %seen, setting each corresponding value to undef, because there are fewer values on the right than places to put them. This works out here because we check for existence of the key, not logical truth or definedness of the value. If we needed true values, a slice could still shorten our code:

```
@seen{@B} = (1) x @B;
```

See Also

Hash slices are explained in *perldata*(1) and the "Variables" section of Chapter 2 of *Programming Perl*; Chapter 5; we use hashes in a similar fashion in Recipe 4.6 and Recipe 4.8

4.8. Computing Union, Intersection, or Difference of Unique Lists

Problem

You have a pair of lists, each having unduplicated items. You'd like to find out which items are in both lists (*intersection*), one but not the other (*difference*), or either (*union*).

Solution

The following solutions need the listed initializations:

```
@a = (1, 3, 5, 6, 7, 8);
@b = (2, 3, 5, 7, 9);

@union = @isect = @diff = ();
%union = %isect = ();
%count = ();
```

Simple solution for union and intersection

```
foreach $e (@a) { $union{$e} = 1 }

foreach $e (@b) {
    if ( $union{$e} ) { $isect{$e} = 1 }
    $union{$e} = 1;
}
@union = keys %union;
@isect = keys %isect;
```

More idiomatic version

```
foreach $e (@a, @b) { $union{$e}++ && $isect{$e}++ }

@union = keys %union;
@isect = keys %isect;
```

Union, intersection, and symmetric difference

```
foreach $e (@a, @b) { $count{$e}++ }

foreach $e (keys %count) {
    push(@union, $e);
    if ($count{$e} == 2) {
        push @isect, $e;
    } else {
        push @diff, $e;
    }
}
```

Indirect solution

```
@isect = @diff = @union = ();

foreach $e (@a, @b) { $count{$e}++ }

foreach $e (keys %count) {
    push(@union, $e);
    push @{ $count{$e} == 2 ? \@isect : \@diff }, $e;
}
```

Discussion

The first solution most directly computes the union and intersection of two lists, neither containing duplicates. Two different hashes are used to record whether a particular item goes in the union or the intersection. We first put every element of the first array in the union hash, giving it a true value. Then processing each element of the second array, we check whether that element is already present in the union. If it is, then we put it in the intersection as well. In any event, it is put into the union. When we're done, we extract the keys of both the union and intersection hashes. The values aren't needed.

The second solution ("More idiomatic version") is essentially the same but relies on familiarity with the Perl (and *awk*, C, C++, and Java) ++ and && operators. By placing the ++ after the variable, we first look at its old value before incrementing it. The first time through it won't be in the union, which makes the first part of the && false, and the second part is consequently ignored. The second time that we encounter the same element, it's already present in the union, so we put it in the intersection as well.

The third solution uses just one hash to track how many times each element has been seen. Once both arrays have their elements recorded in the hash, we process those hash keys one at a time. If it's there, it goes in the union array. Keys whose values are 2 were in both arrays, so they are put in the intersection array. Keys whose values are 1 were in just one of the two arrays, so they are put in the difference array. The elements of the output arrays are not in the same order as the elements in the input arrays.

The last solution, like the previous one, uses just one hash to count how many times each element has been encountered. However, this time we choose the array within the @{ .... } block.

We compute the symmetric difference here, not the simple difference. These are set theoretic terms. A *symmetric* difference is the set of all the elements that are members of either @A or @B, but not of both. A *simple difference* is the set of members of @A but not of @B, which we calculated in Recipe 4.7.

See Also

The "Hashes (Associative Arrays)" section of Chapter 2 of *Programming Perl*; Chapter 5; we use hashes in a similar fashion in Recipe 4.6 and Recipe 4.7

4.9. Appending One Array to Another

Problem

You want to join two arrays by appending all the elements of one to the end of the other.

Solution

Use push:

```
# push
push(@ARRAY1, @ARRAY2);
```

Discussion

The push function is optimized for appending a list to the end of an array. You can take advantage of Perl's list flattening to join two arrays, but it results in significantly more copying than push:

```
@ARRAY1 = (@ARRAY1, @ARRAY2);
```

Here's an example of push in action:

```
@members = ("Time", "Flies");
@initiates = ("An", "Arrow");
push(@members, @initiates);
# @members is now ("Time", "Flies", "An", "Arrow")
```

If you want to insert the elements of one array into the middle of another, use the splice function:

```
splice(@members, 2, 0, "Like", @initiates);
print "@members\n";
splice(@members, 0, 1, "Fruit");
splice(@members, -2, 2, "A", "Banana");
print "@members\n";
```

This is output:

```
Time Flies Like An Arrow
Fruit Flies Like A Banana
```

See Also

The splice and push functions in *perlfunc*(1) and Chapter 3 of *Programming Perl*; the "List Values and Arrays" section of Chapter 2 of *Programming Perl*; the "List Value Constructors" section of *perldata*(1)

4.10. Reversing an Array

Problem

You want to reverse an array.

Solution

Use the **reverse** function:

```
# reverse @ARRAY into @REVERSED
@REVERSED = reverse @ARRAY;
```

Or use a **for** loop:

```
for ($i = $#ARRAY; $i >= 0; $i--) {
    # do something with $ARRAY[$i]
}
```

Discussion

The **reverse** function actually reverses a list; the **for** loop simply processes the list in reverse order. If you don't need a reversed copy of the list, **for** saves memory and time.

If you're using **reverse** to reverse a list that you just sorted, you should have sorted it in the correct order to begin with. For example:

```
# two-step: sort then reverse
@ascending = sort { $a cmp $b } @users;
@descending = reverse @ascending;

# one-step: sort with reverse comparison
@descending = sort { $b cmp $a } @users;
```

See Also

The **reverse** function in *perlfunc*(1) and Chapter 3 of *Programming Perl*; we use reverse in Recipe 1.6

4.11. *Processing Multiple Elements of an Array*

Problem

You want to pop or shift multiple elements at a time.

Solution

Use splice:

```
# remove $N elements from front of @ARRAY (shift $N)
@FRONT = splice(@ARRAY, 0, $N);

# remove $N elements from the end of the array (pop $N)
@END = splice(@ARRAY, -$N);
```

Discussion

It's often convenient to wrap these as functions:

```
sub shift2 (\@) {
    return splice(@{$_[0]}, 0, 2);
}

sub pop2 (\@) {
    return splice(@{$_[0]}, -2);
}
```

This makes their behavior more apparent when you use them:

```
@friends = qw(Peter Paul Mary Jim Tim);
($this, $that) = shift2(@friends);
# $this contains Peter, $that has Paul, and
# @friends has Mary, Jim, and Tim

@beverages = qw(Dew Jolt Cola Sprite Fresca);
@pair = pop2(@beverages);
# $pair[0] contains Sprite, $pair[1] has Fresca,
# and @beverages has (Dew, Jolt, Cola)
```

splice returns the elements removed from the array, so shift2 replaces the first two elements in @ARRAY with nothing (i.e., deletes them) and returns the two elements it deleted. In pop2, the last two elements at end of the array are removed and returned.

These two functions are prototyped to take an array reference as their argument to better mimic the built-in shift and pop functions. The caller doesn't pass in an explicit reference using a backslash. Instead, the compiler, having seen the array reference prototype, arranges to pass the array by reference anyway. Advantages to this approach include efficiency, transparency, and compile-time parameter checking. One disadvantage is that the thing passed in must look like a real array with a leading @ sign, not just a scalar containing an array reference. If it did, you'd have to prepend an @, making it less transparent:

```
$line[5] = \@list;
@got = pop2( @{ $line[5] } );
```

This is another example of where a proper array and not a mere list is called for. The `\@` prototype requires that whatever goes in that argument slot be an array. `$line[5]` isn't an array, but an array reference. That's why we need the "extra" @ sign.

See Also

The `splice` function in *perlfunc*(1) and Chapter 3 of *Programming Perl*; the "Prototypes" sections of *perlsub*(1) and Chapter 2 of *Programming Perl*; we use `splice` in Recipe 4.9

4.12. Finding the First List Element That Passes a Test

Problem

You want the first element in the list (or its index) that passes a test. Alternatively, you want to know whether any element passes the test. The test can be simple identity ("Is this element in the list?")* or more complex ("I have a list of Employee objects, sorted from highest salary to lowest. Which manager has the highest salary?"). Simple cases normally only require the value of the element, but when the array itself will be altered, you probably need to know the index number of the first matching element.

Solution

To find a matching value, use `foreach` to loop over every element, and call `last` as soon as you find a match:

```
my($match, $found, $item);
foreach $item (@array) {
    if ($criterion) {
        $match = $item;  # must save
        $found = 1;
```

---

* But why didn't you use a hash then?

```
        last;
    }
}
if ($found) {
    ## do something with $match
} else {
    ## unfound
}
```

To find a matching index, use for to loop a variable over every array index, and call last as soon as you find a match:

```
my($i, $match_idx);
for ($i = 0; $i < @array; $i++) {
    if ($criterion) {
        $match_idx = $i;     # save the index
        last;
    }
}

if (defined $match_idx) {
    ## found in $array[$match_idx]
} else {
    ## unfound
}
```

Discussion

Not having a built-in mechanism to do this, we must write our own code to go through the list and test each element. We use foreach and for and call last to ensure that we stop as soon as we find a match. Before we use last to stop looking, though, we save the value or index.

A common mistake is to try to use grep here. The problem is that grep always tests all elements and finds all matches, so it's inefficient if you only want the first match.

We have to set $match when we want the value of the first matching element. We can't just test $item at the end of the loop, because foreach automatically localizes the iterator variable and this prevents us from getting to its last loop value after the loop ends. See Recipe 4.4.

Here's an example. Assume that @employees has a list of Employee objects, sorted in descending order by salary. We wish to find out the highest paid engineer, who will be the first engineer in the array. We only want to print the engineer's name, so we want the value, not the index.

```
foreach $employee (@employees) {
    if ( $employee->category() eq 'engineer' ) {
        $highest_engineer = $employee;
        last;
```

```
        }
    }
    print "Highest paid engineer is: ", $highest_engineer->name(), "\n";
```

When we're searching and only want the index, we can save some code by remembering that $i will not be an acceptable array index if we don't find a match. This mainly saves us code space, as not doing an assignment doesn't really win us much compared to the time we'll have spent testing the list elements. It's more obscure, because it tests if ($i < @ARRAY) to check whether we found a match, instead of the more obvious defined test as in the previous Solution.

```
for ($i = 0; $i < @ARRAY; $i++) {
    last if $criterion;
}
if ($i < @ARRAY) {
    ## found and $i is the index
} else {
    ## not found
}
```

See Also

The "For Loops," "Foreach Loops," and "Loop Control" sections of *perlsyn*(1) and Chapter 2 of *Programming Perl*; the grep function in *perlfunc*(1) and Chapter 3 of *Programming Perl*

4.13. Finding All Elements in an Array Matching Certain Criteria

Problem

From a list, you want only the elements that match certain criteria.

This notion of extracting a subset of a larger list is common. It's how you find all engineers in a list of employees, all users in the "staff" group, and all the filenames you're interested in.

Solution

Use grep to apply a condition to all elements in the list and return only those for which the condition was true:

```
@MATCHING = grep { TEST ($_) } @LIST;
```

Discussion

This could also be accomplished with a `foreach` loop:

```
@matching = ();
foreach (@list) {
    push(@matching, $_) if TEST ($_);
}
```

The Perl `grep` function is shorthand for all that looping and mucking about. It's not really like the Unix `grep` command; it doesn't have options to return line numbers or to negate the test, and it isn't limited to regular-expression tests. For example, to filter out just the large numbers from an array or to find out which keys in a hash have very large values:

```
@bigs = grep { $_ > 1_000_000 } @nums;
@pigs = grep { $users{$_} > 1e7 } keys %users;
```

Here's something that sets `@matching` to lines from the *who* command that start with "gnat ":

```
@matching = grep { /^gnat / } `who`;
```

Here's another example:

```
@engineers = grep { $_->position() eq 'Engineer' } @employees;
```

It extracts only those objects from the array `@employees` whose `position()` method returns the string `Engineer`.

You could have even more complex tests in a `grep`:

```
@secondary_assistance = grep { $_->income >= 26_000 &&
                               $_->income <  30_000 }
                        @applicants;
```

But at that point you may decide it would be more legible to write a proper loop instead.

See Also

The "For Loops," "Foreach Loops," and "Loop Control" sections of *perlsyn*(1) and Chapter 2 of *Programming Perl*; the `grep` function in *perlfunc*(1) and Chapter 3 of *Programming Perl*; your system's *who*(1) manpage, if it exists; Recipe 4.12

4.14. Sorting an Array Numerically

Problem

You want to sort a list of numbers, but Perl's sort (by default) sorts alphabetically in ASCII order.

Solution

Use Perl's sort function and the <=> numerical comparison operator:

```
@sorted = sort { $a <=> $b } @unsorted;
```

Discussion

The sort function takes an optional code block, which lets you replace the default alphabetic comparison subroutine with your own. This comparison function is called each time sort has to compare two values. The values to compare are loaded into the special package variables $a and $b, which are automatically localized.

The comparison function should return a negative number if $a ought to appear before $b in the output list, 0 if they're the same and their order doesn't matter, or a positive number if $a ought to appear after $b. Perl has two operators that behave this way: <=> for sorting numbers in ascending numeric order, and cmp for sorting strings in ascending alphabetic order. By default, sort uses cmp-style comparisons.

Here's code that sorts the list of PIDs in @pids, lets the user select one, then sends it a TERM signal followed by a KILL signal. We use a code block that compares $a to $b with <=> to sort numerically:

```
# @pids is an unsorted array of process IDs
foreach my $pid (sort { $a <=> $b } @pids) {
    print "$pid\n";
}
print "Select a process ID to kill:\n";
chomp ($pid = <>);
die "Exiting ... \n" unless $pid && $pid =~ /^\d+$/;
kill('TERM',$pid);
sleep 2;
kill('KILL',$pid);
```

If you use $a <=> $b or $a cmp $b, the list will be sorted in ascending order. For a descending sort, all we have to do is swap $a and $b in the sort subroutine:

```
@descending = sort { $b <=> $a } @unsorted;
```

Comparison routines must be consistent; that is, they should always return the same answer when called with the same values. Inconsistent comparison routines lead to infinite loops or core dumps, especially in older releases of Perl.

You can also say sort SUBNAME LIST where SUBNAME is the name of a comparison subroutine returning -1, 0, or +1. In the interests of speed, the normal calling conventions are bypassed, and the values to be compared magically appear for the duration of the subroutine in the global package variables $a and $b. Because of the odd way Perl calls this subroutine, it may not be recursive.

A word of warning: $a and $b are set in the package active in the call to sort, which may not be the same as the one that the SUBNAME function passed to sort was compiled in! For example:

```
package Sort_Subs;
sub revnum { $b <=> $a }

package Other_Pack;
@all = sort Sort_Subs::revnum 4, 19, 8, 3;
```

This will silently fail (unless you have -w in effect, in which case it will vocally fail), because the sort call sets the package variables $a and $b in its own package, Other_Pack, but the revnum function uses its own package's versions. This is another reason why in-lining sort functions is easier, as in:

```
@all = sort { $b <=> $a } 4, 19, 8, 3;
```

For more on packages, see Chapter 10, *Subroutines*.

See Also

The cmp and <=> operators in *perlop*(1) and Chapter 2 of *Programming Perl*; the kill, sort, and sleep functions in *perlfunc*(1) and Chapter 3 of *Programming Perl*; Recipe 4.15

4.15. Sorting a List by Computable Field

Problem

You want to sort a list by something more complex than a simple string or numeric comparison.

This is common when working with objects ("sort by the employee's salary") or complex data structures ("sort by the third element in the array that this is a reference to"). It's also applicable when you want to sort by more than one key, for instance, sorting by birthday and then by name when multiple people have the same birthday.

Solution

Use the customizable comparison routine in `sort`:

```
@ordered = sort { compare() } @unordered;
```

You can speed this up by precomputing the field.

```
@precomputed = map { [compute(),$_] } @unordered;
@ordered_precomputed = sort { $a->[0] <=> $b->[0] } @precomputed;
@ordered = map { $_->[1] } @ordered_precomputed;
```

And, finally, you can combine the three steps:

```
@ordered = map { $_->[1] }
           sort { $a->[0] <=> $b->[0] }
           map { [compute(), $_] }
           @unordered;
```

Discussion

The use of a comparison routine was explained in Recipe 4.14. As well as using built-in operators like `<=>`, you can construct more complex tests:

```
@ordered = sort { $a->name cmp $b->name } @employees;
```

You often see `sort` used like this in part of a `foreach` loop:

```
foreach $employee (sort { $a->name cmp $b->name } @employees) {
    print $employee->name, " earns \$", $employee->salary, "\n";
}
```

If you're going to do a lot of work with elements in a particular order, it's more efficient to sort it once and work from that:

```
@sorted_employees = sort { $a->name cmp $b->name } @employees;
foreach $employee (@sorted_employees) {
    print $employee->name, " earns \$", $employee->salary, "\n";
}
# load %bonus
foreach $employee (@sorted_employees) {
    if ( $bonus{ $employee->ssn } ) {
        print $employee->name, " got a bonus!\n";
    }
}
```

We can put multiple comparisons in the routine and separate them with `||`. `||` is a short-circuit operator: it returns the first true (non-zero) value it finds. This means we can sort by one kind of comparison, but if the elements are equal (the comparison returns 0) we can sort by another. This has the effect of a sort within a sort:

```
@sorted = sort { $a->name cmp $b->name
                         ||
                 $b->age <=> $a->age } @employees;
```

This first considers the names of the two employees to be compared. If they're not equal, || stops and returns the result of the cmp (effectively sorting them in ascending order by name). If the names are equal, though, || keeps testing and returns the result of the <=> (sorting them in descending order by age). The result is a list that is sorted by name and by age within groups of the same name.

Let's look at a real-life example of sorting. Here we fetch all users, as User::pwent objects. Then we sort them by name and print the sorted list:

```
use User::pwent qw(getpwent);
@users = ();
# fetch all users
while (defined($user = getpwent)) {
    push(@users, $user);
}
    @users = sort { $a->name cmp $b->name } @users;
foreach $user (@users) {
    print $user->name, "\n";
}
```

We can have more than simple comparisons, or combinations of simple comparisons. This code sorts a list of names by comparing the *second* letters of the names. It gets the second letters by using substr:

```
@sorted = sort { substr($a,1,1) cmp substr($b,1,1) } @names;
```

and here we sort by length of the strings:

```
@sorted = sort { length $a <=> length $b } @strings;
```

The sort function calls the code block each time it needs to compare two elements, and the number of comparisons grows dramatically with the number of elements we're sorting. Sorting 10 elements requires (on average) 46 comparisons, but sorting 1,000 elements requires 14,000 comparisons. A time-consuming operation like a split or a subroutine call for each comparison can easily make your program crawl.

Fortunately, we can remove this bottleneck by running the operation once per element prior to the sort. Use map to store the results of the operation in an array whose elements are anonymous arrays containing both the computed field and the original field. Then we sort this array of arrays on the precomputed field, and use map to get the sorted original data. This map-sort-map concept is useful and common, so let's look at it in more depth.

Let's apply map-sort-map to the sorting by string length example:

```
@temp = map { [ length $_, $_ ] } @strings;
@temp = sort { $a->[0] <=> $b->[0] } @temp;
@sorted = map { $_->[1] } @temp;
```

The first line creates a temporary array of strings and their lengths, using map. The second line sorts the temporary array by comparing the precomputed lengths. The third line turns the sorted temporary array of strings and lengths back into a sorted array of strings. This way we calculated the length of each string only once.

Because the input to each line is the output of the previous line (the @temp array we make in line 1 is fed to sort in line 2, and that output is fed to map in line 3), we can combine it into one statement and eliminate the temporary array:

```
@sorted = map   { $_->[1] }
          sort { $a->[0] <=> $b->[0] }
          map   { [ length $_, $_ ] }
          @strings;
```

The operations now appear in reverse order. When you meet a map-sort-map, you should read it from the bottom up to determine the function:

@strings

> The last part is the data to be sorted. Here it's just an array, but later we'll see that this can be a subroutine or even backticks. Anything that returns a list to be sorted is fair game.

map

> The map closest to the bottom builds the temporary list of anonymous arrays. This list contains the precomputed fields (length $_) and also records the original element ($_) by storing them both in an anonymous array. Look at this map line to find out how the fields are computed.

sort

> The sort line sorts the list of anonymous arrays by comparing the precomputed fields. It won't tell you much, other than whether the list is sorted in ascending or descending order.

map

> The map at the top of the statement turns the sorted list of anonymous arrays back into a list of the sorted original elements. It will generally be the same for every map-sort-map.

Here's a more complicated example, which sorts by the first number that appears on each line in @fields:

```
@temp = map { [ /(\d+)/, $_ ] } @fields;
@sorted_temp = sort { $a->[0] <=> $b->[0] } @temp;
@sorted_fields = map { $_->[1] } @sorted_temp;
```

The regular expression mumbo-jumbo in the first line extracts the first number from the line being processed by map. We use the regular expression /(\d+)/ in a list context to extract the number.

We can remove the temporary arrays in that code, giving us:

```
@sorted_fields = map  { $_->[1] }
                sort { $a->[0] <=> $b->[0] }
                map  { [ /(\d+)/, $_ ] }
                @fields;
```

This final example compactly sorts colon-separated data, as from Unix's *passwd* file. It sorts the file numerically by fourth field (group id), then numerically by the third field (user id), and then alphabetically by the first field (user name).

```
print map  { $_->[0] }              # whole line
     sort {
                $a->[1] <=> $b->[1]  # gid
                ||
                $a->[2] <=> $b->[2]  # uid
                ||
                $a->[3] cmp $b->[3]  # login
         }
     map  { [ $_, (split /:/)[3,2,0] ] }
     `cat /etc/passwd';
```

This compact, map-sort-map technique is more reminiscent of the functional world of Lisp and Scheme programming than Perl's normal C and *awk* heritage. Because it was first pointed out by Randal Schwartz, this black art is often referred to as the *Schwartzian Transform*.

See Also

The sort function in *perlfunc*(1) and Chapter 3 of *Programming Perl*; the cmp and <=> operators in *perlop*(1) and Chapter 2 of *Programming Perl*; Recipe 4.14

4.16. Implementing a Circular List

Problem

You want to create and manipulate a circular list.

Solution

Use unshift and pop (or push and shift) on a normal array.

Procedure

```
unshift(@circular, pop(@circular));  # the last shall be first
push(@circular, shift(@circular));   # and vice versa
```

Discussion

Circular lists are commonly used to repeatedly process things in order; for example, connections to a server. The code shown above isn't a true computer science circular list, with pointers and true circularity. Instead, the operations provide for moving the last element to the first position, and vice versa.

```
sub grab_and_rotate ( \@ ) {
    my $listref = shift;
    my $element = $listref->[0];
    push(@$listref, shift @$listref);
    return $element;
}

@processes = ( 1, 2, 3, 4, 5 );
while (1) {
    $process = grab_and_rotate(@processes);
    print "Handling process $process\n";
    sleep 1;
}
```

See Also

The unshift and push functions in *perlfunc*(1) and Chapter 3 of *Programming Perl*; Recipe 13.13

4.17. Randomizing an Array

Problem

You want to shuffle the elements of an array randomly. The obvious application is writing a card game, where you must shuffle a deck of cards, but it is equally applicable to any situation where you want to deal with elements of an array in a random order.

Solution

Swap each element in the array with another randomly selected, element:

```
# fisher_yates_shuffle( \@array ) : generate a random permutation
# of @array in place
sub fisher_yates_shuffle {
    my $array = shift;
    my $i;
    for ($i = @$array; --$i; ) {
        my $j = int rand ($i+1);
        next if $i == $j;
        @$array[$i,$j] = @$array[$j,$i];
    }
```

```
    }

    fisher_yates_shuffle( \@array );     # permutes @array in place
```

Or, pick a random permutation using the code in Example 4-4:

```
    $permutations = factorial( scalar @array );
    @shuffle = @array [ n2perm( 1+int(rand $permutations), $#array ) ];
```

Discussion

Shuffling is a surprisingly tricky process. It's easy to write a bad shuffle:

```
    sub naive_shuffle {                              # don't do this
        for (my $i = 0; $i < @_; $i++) {
            my $j = int rand @_;                     # pick random element
            ($_[$i], $_[$j]) = ($_[$j], $_[$i]);     # swap 'em
        }
    }
```

This algorithm is biased; the list's possible permutations don't all have the same probability of being generated. The proof of this is simple: take the case where we're passed a 3-element list. We generate three random numbers, each of which can have three possible values, yielding 27 possible outcomes here. There are only 6 permutations of the 3-element list, though. Because 27 isn't evenly divisible by 6, some outcomes are more likely than others.

The Fisher-Yates shuffle avoids this bias by changing the range of the random numbers it selects.

See Also

The rand function, in *perlfunc*(1) and Chapter 3 of *Programming Perl*; for more on random numbers, see Recipes 2.7, 2.8, and 2.9; Recipe 4.19 provides another way to select a random permutation

4.18. Program: words

Description

Have you ever wondered how programs like *ls* generate columns of sorted output that you read down the columns instead of across the rows? For example:

awk	cp	ed	login	mount	rmdir	sum
basename	csh	egrep	ls	mt	sed	sync
cat	date	fgrep	mail	mv	sh	tar
chgrp	dd	grep	mkdir	ps	sort	touch
chmod	df	kill	mknod	pwd	stty	vi
chown	echo	ln	more	rm	su	

Example 4-2 does this.

Example 4-2. words

```perl
#!/usr/bin/perl -w
# words - gather lines, present in columns

use strict;

my ($item, $cols, $rows, $maxlen);
my ($xpixel, $ypixel, $mask, @data);

getwinsize();

# first gather up every line of input,
# remembering the longest line length seen
$maxlen = 1;
while (<>) {
    my $mylen;
    s/\s+$//;
    $maxlen = $mylen if (($mylen = length) > $maxlen);
    push(@data, $_);
}

$maxlen += 1;                    # to make extra space

# determine boundaries of screen
$cols = int($cols / $maxlen) || 1;
$rows = int(($#data+$cols) / $cols);

# pre-create mask for faster computation
$mask = sprintf("%%-%ds ", $maxlen-1);

# subroutine to check whether at last item on line
sub EOL { ($item+1) % $cols == 0 }

# now process each item, picking out proper piece for this position
for ($item = 0; $item < $rows * $cols; $item++) {
    my $target =  ($item % $cols) * $rows + int($item/$cols);
    my $piece = sprintf($mask, $target < @data ? $data[$target] : "");
    $piece =~ s/\s+$// if EOL();  # don't blank-pad to EOL
    print $piece;
    print "\n" if EOL();
}

# finish up if needed
print "\n" if EOL();

# not portable -- linux only
sub getwinsize {
    my $winsize = "\0" x 8;
    my $TIOCGWINSZ = 0x40087468;
    if (ioctl(STDOUT, $TIOCGWINSZ, $winsize)) {
        ($rows, $cols, $xpixel, $ypixel) = unpack('S4', $winsize);
```

Example 4-2. words (continued)

```
    } else {
        $cols = 80;
    }
}
```

The most obvious way to print out a sorted list in columns is to print each element of the list, one at a time, padded out to a particular width. When you're about to hit the end of the line, generate a newline. But that only works if you're planning on reading each row left to right. If you instead expect to read it down each column, this approach won't do.

The *words* program is a filter that generates output going down the columns. It reads all input, keeping track of the length of the longest line seen. Once everything has been read in, it divides the screen width by the length of the longest input record seen, yielding the expected number of columns.

Then the program goes into a loop that executes once per input record, but the output order isn't in the obvious order. Imagine you had a list of nine items:

```
    Wrong        Right
    -----        -----
    1 2 3        1 4 7
    4 5 6        2 5 8
    7 8 9        3 6 9
```

The *words* program does the necessary calculations to print out elements (1,4,7) on one line, (2,5,8) on the next, and (3,6,9) on the last.

To figure out the current window size, this program does an `ioctl` call. This works fine—on the system it was written for. On any other system, it won't work. If that's good enough for you, then good for you. Recipe 12.14 shows how to find this on your system using the *ioctl.ph* file, or with a C program. Recipe 15.4 shows a more portable solution, but that requires installing a CPAN module.

See Also

Recipe 15.4

4.19. Program: permute

Problem

Have you ever wanted to generate all possible permutations of an array or to execute some code for every possible permutation? For example:

```
% echo man bites dog | permute
```

dog bites man
bites dog man
dog man bites
man dog bites
bites man dog
man bites dog

The number of permutations of a set is the factorial of the size of the set. This grows big extremely fast, so you don't want to run it on many permutations:

```
Set Size            Permutations
1                   1
2                   2
3                   6
4                   24
5                   120
6                   720
7                   5040
8                   40320
9                   362880
10                  3628800
11                  39916800
12                  479001600
13                  6227020800
14                  87178291200
15                  1307674368000
```

Doing something for each alternative takes a correspondingly large amount of time. In fact, factorial algorithms exceed the number of particles in the universe with very small inputs. The factorial of 500 is greater than ten raised to the *thousandth* power!

```
use Math::BigInt;
sub factorial {
    my $n = shift;
    my $s = 1;
    $s *= $n-- while $n > 0;
    return $s;
}
print factorial(Math::BigInt->new("500"));
+1220136... (1035 digits total)
```

The two solutions that follow differ in the order of the permutations they return.

The solution in Example 4-3 uses a classic list permutation algorithm used by Lisp hackers. It's relatively straightforward but makes unnecessary copies. It's also hard-wired to do nothing but print out its permutations.

Example 4-3. tsc-permute

```
#!/usr/bin/perl -n
# tsc_permute: permute each word of input
permute([split], []);
sub permute {
```

Example 4-3. tsc-permute (continued)

```
my @items = @{ $_[0] };
my @perms = @{ $_[1] };
unless (@items) {
    print "@perms\n";
} else {
    my(@newitems,@newperms,$i);
    foreach $i (0 .. $#items) {
        @newitems = @items;
        @newperms = @perms;
        unshift(@newperms, splice(@newitems, $i, 1));
        permute([@newitems], [@newperms]);
    }
}
}
```

The solution in Example 4-4, provided by Mark-Jason Dominus, is faster (by around 25%) and more elegant. Rather than precalculate all permutations, his code generates the nth particular permutation. It is elegant in two ways. First, it avoids recursion except to calculate the factorial, which the permutation algorithm proper does not use. Second, it generates a permutation of integers rather than permute the actual data set.

He also uses a time-saving technique called *memoizing*. The idea is that a function that always returns a particular answer when called with a particular argument memorizes that answer. That way, the next time it's called with the same argument, no further calculations are required. The `factorial` function uses a private array `@fact` to remember previously calculated factorial values as described in Recipe 10.3.

You call n2perm with two arguments: the permutation number to generate (from 0 through `factorial(N)-1`, where N is the size of your array) and the subscript of the array's last element. The n2perm function calculates directions for the permutation in the n2pat subroutine. Then it converts those directions into a permutation of integers in the pat2perm subroutine. The directions are a list like (0 2 0 1 0), which means: "Splice out the 0th element, then the second element from the remaining list, then the 0th element, then the first, then the 0th."

Example 4-4. mjd-permute

```
#!/usr/bin/perl -w
# mjd_permute: permute each word of input
use strict;

while (<>) {
    my @data = split;
    my $num_permutations = factorial(scalar @data);
    for (my $i=0; $i < $num_permutations; $i++) {
        my @permutation = @data[n2perm($i, $#data)];
```

Example 4-4. mjd-permute (continued)

```
        print "@permutation\n";
    }
}

# Utility function: factorial with memoizing
BEGIN {
  my @fact = (1);
  sub factorial($) {
      my $n = shift;
      return $fact[$n] if defined $fact[$n];
      $fact[$n] = $n * factorial($n - 1);
  }
}

# n2pat($N, $len) : produce the $N-th pattern of length $len
sub n2pat {
    my $i   = 1;
    my $N   = shift;
    my $len = shift;
    my @pat;
    while ($i <= $len + 1) {    # Should really be just while ($N) { ...
        push @pat, $N % $i;
        $N = int($N/$i);
        $i++;
    }
    return @pat;
}

# pat2perm(@pat) : turn pattern returned by n2pat() into
# permutation of integers.   XXX: splice is already O(N)
sub pat2perm {
    my @pat    = @_;
    my @source = (0 .. $#pat);
    my @perm;
    push @perm, splice(@source, (pop @pat), 1) while @pat;
    return @perm;
}

# n2perm($N, $len) : generate the Nth permutation of $len objects
sub n2perm {
    pat2perm(n2pat(@_));
}
```

See Also

unshift and splice in *perlfunc*(1) or Chapter 3 of *Programming Perl*; the sections discussing closures in *perlsub*(1) and *perlref*(1) and Chapter 2 of *Programming Perl*; Recipe 2.7; Recipe 10.3

5

Hashes

*Doing linear scans over an associative array is like
trying to club someone to death with a loaded Uzi.*

—Larry Wall

5.0. Introduction

People and parts of computer programs interact in all sorts of ways. Single scalar variables are like hermits, living a solitary existence whose only meaning comes from within the individual. Arrays are like cults, where multitudes marshal themselves under the name of a charismatic leader. In the middle lies the comfortable, intimate ground of the one-to-one relationship that is the hash. (Older documentation for Perl often called hashes *associative arrays*, but that's a mouthful. Other languages that support similar constructs sometimes use different terms for them; you may hear about *hash tables*, *tables*, *dictionaries*, *mappings*, or even *alists*, depending on the language.)

Unfortunately, this isn't a relationship of equals. Hashes are an *of* relationship, like saying "Andy is the boss of Nat," "The blood pressure of our patient is 112/62," and "The name of journal ISSN 1087-903X is *The Perl Journal*." Hashes only give convenient ways to access values for "Nat's boss" and "1087-903X's name"; you can't ask "Whose boss is Andy?" Finding the answer to that question is a recipe in this chapter.

Fortunately, hashes have their benefits, just like relationships. Hashes are a built-in data type in Perl. Their use reduces many complex algorithms to simple variable accesses. They are also fast and convenient ways to build indices and quick lookup tables.

It's time to put a name to these notions. The relationship embodied in a hash is a good thing to use for its name. For instance, the relationships in the examples above are *boss of, blood pressure of,* and *name of.* We'd give them Perl names `%boss`, `%blood_pressure`, and `%name`. Where a lone scalar has `$` as its type identifier and an entire array has `@`, a hash has `%`.

Only use the `%` when referring to the hash as a whole, such as `%boss`. When referring to the value for a key, it's a single scalar value and so a `$` is called for, just as when referring to one element of an array you also use a `$`. This means that "the boss of Nat" would be written as `$boss{"Nat"}`.

A regular array uses whole numbers for indices, but the indices of a hash are always strings. Its values may be any arbitrary scalar values, including references. Using references as values, you can create hashes that hold not merely strings or numbers, but also arrays, other hashes, or objects. (Or rather, references to arrays, hashes, or objects.)

A hash can be initialized with a list, where elements of the list are key and value pairs:

```
%age = ( "Nat",   24,
         "Jules", 25,
         "Josh",  17  );
```

This is equivalent to:

```
$age{"Nat"}   = 24;
$age{"Jules"} = 25;
$age{"Josh"}  = 17;
```

To make it easier to read and write hash initializations, the `=>` operator, sometimes known as a *comma arrow*, was created. Mostly it behaves as a better-looking comma. For example, you can write a hash initialization this way:

```
%food_color = (
              "Apple"  => "red",
              "Banana" => "yellow",
              "Lemon"  => "yellow",
              "Carrot" => "orange"
              );
```

(This particular hash is used in many examples in this chapter.) This initialization is also an example of *hash-list equivalence*—hashes behave in some ways as though they were lists of key-value pairs. We'll use this in a number of recipes, including the merging and inverting recipes.

Unlike a regular comma, the comma arrow has a special property: It quotes any word preceding it, which means you can safely omit the quotes and improve legibility. Single-word hash keys are also automatically quoted, which means you can write $hash{somekey} instead of $hash{"somekey"}. You could rewrite the preceding initialization of %food_color as:

```
%food_color = (
                Apple   => "red",
                Banana  => "yellow",
                Lemon   => "yellow",
                Carrot  => "orange"
              );
```

One important issue to be aware of regarding hashes is that their elements are stored in an internal order convenient for efficient retrieval. This means that no matter what order you insert your data, it will come out in an unpredictable disorder.

See Also

The unshift and splice functions in *perlfunc*(1) and Chapter 3 of *Programming Perl*; the discussions of closures in *perlsub*(1) and *perlref*(1); and Chapter 4 of *Programming Perl*

5.1. Adding an Element to a Hash

Problem

You need to add an entry to a hash.

Solution

Simply assign to the hash key:

```
$HASH{$KEY} = $VALUE;
```

Discussion

Putting something into a hash is straightforward. In languages that don't provide the hash as an intrinsic data type, you have to worry about overflows, resizing, and collisions in your hash table. In Perl, all that is taken care of for you with a simple assignment. If that entry was already occupied (had a previous value), memory for that value is automatically freed, just as when assigning to a simple scalar.

```
# %food_color defined per the introduction
$food_color{Raspberry} = "pink";
print "Known foods:\n";
foreach $food (keys %food_color) {
    print "$food\n";
}
```

```
Known foods:
Banana
Apple
Raspberry
Carrot
Lemon
```

If you store undef as a hash key, it gets stringified to "" (and generates a warning if your program is running under -w). Using undef as a key is probably not
what you want. On the other hand, undef is a valid *value* in a hash. But if you
fetch the value for a key that isn't in the hash, you'll also get undef. This means
you can't use the simple Boolean test if ($hash{$key}) to see whether there is
an entry in %hash for $key. Use exists($hash{$key}) to test whether a key is
in the hash, defined($hash{$key}) to test if the corresponding value is not
undef, and if ($hash{$key}) to test if the corresponding value is a true value.

In Perl's hashing algorithm, permutations of a string hash to the same spot internally. If your hash contains as keys many permutations of the same string, like
"sparc" and "craps", hash performance can degrade noticeably. In practice, this
seldom occurs.

See Also

The "List Value Constructors" section of *perldata*(1); the "List Values and Arrays"
section of Chapter 2 of *Programming Perl*; Recipe 5.2

5.2. Testing for the Presence of a Key in a Hash

Problem

You need to know whether a hash has a particular key, regardless of any possible
associated value.

Solution

Use the exists function.

```
# does %HASH have a value for $KEY ?
if (exists($HASH{$KEY})) {
    # it exists
} else {
    # it doesn't
}
```

Discussion

This code uses `exists` to check whether a key is in the `%food_color` hash:

```
# %food_color per the introduction
foreach $name ("Banana", "Martini") {
    if (exists $food_color{$name}) {
        print "$name is a food.\n";
    } else {
        print "$name is a drink.\n";
    }
}
```

Banana is a food.
Martini is a drink.

The `exists` function tests whether a key is in the hash. It doesn't test whether the value corresponding to that key is defined, nor whether the value is true or false. We may be splitting hairs, but problems caused by confusing existence, defined-ness, and truth can multiply like rabbits. Take this code:

```
%age = ();
$age{"Toddler"} = 3;
$age{"Unborn"} = 0;
$age{"Phantasm"} = undef;

foreach $thing ("Toddler", "Unborn", "Phantasm", "Relic") {
    print "$thing: ";
    print "Exists " if exists $age{$thing};
    print "Defined " if defined $age{$thing};
    print "True " if $age{$thing};
    print "\n";
}
```

Toddler: Exists Defined True
Unborn: Exists Defined
Phantasm: Exists
Relic:

`$age{"Toddler"}` passes the existence, definedness, and truth tests. It exists because we gave `"Toddler"` a value in the hash, it's defined because that value isn't `undef`, and it's true because the value isn't one of Perl's false values.

`$age{"Unborn"}` passes only the existence and definedness tests. It exists because we gave `"Unborn"` a value in the hash, and it's defined because that value isn't `undef`. It isn't *true*, however, because 0 is one of Perl's false values.

`$age{"Phantasm"}` passes only the existence test. It exists because we gave `"Phantasm"` a value in the hash. Because that value was `undef`, it doesn't pass the definedness test. Because `undef` is also one of Perl's false values, it doesn't pass the truth test either.

$age{"Relic"} passes none of the tests. We didn't put a value for "Relic" into the hash, so the existence test fails. Because we didn't put a value in, $age{"Relic"} is undef whenever we try to access it. We know from "Phantasm" that undef fails the definedness and truth tests.

Sometimes it's useful to store undef in a hash. This indicates "I've seen this key, but it didn't have a meaningful value associated with it." Take, for instance, a program to look up file sizes given a list of files as input. This version tries to skip files we've seen before, but it doesn't skip zero-length files, and it doesn't skip files that we've seen before but don't exist.

```
%size = ();
while (<>) {
    chomp;
    next if $size{$_};              # WRONG attempt to skip
    $size{$_} = -s $_;
}
```

If we change the incorrect line to call exists, we also skip files that couldn't be statted, instead of repeatedly trying (and failing) to look them up:

```
    next if exists $size{$_};
```

The food and drink code above assumes that which is not food must be a drink. This is a dangerous assumption to make in the real world.

See Also

The exists and defined functions in *perlfunc*(1) and Chapter 3 of *Programming Perl*; the discussion of truth in the "Scalar Values" section of *perldata*(1), and the "Boolean Context" section of Chapter 2 of *Programming Perl*.

5.3. Deleting from a Hash

Problem

You want to remove an entry from a hash so that it doesn't show up with keys, values, or each. If you were using a hash to associate salaries with employees, and an employee resigned, you'd want to remove their entry from the hash.

Solution

Use the delete function:

```
# remove $KEY and its value from %HASH
delete($HASH{$KEY});
```

Discussion

Sometimes people mistakenly try to use undef to remove an entry from a hash.
undef $hash{$key} and $hash{$key} = undef both make %hash have an entry
with key $key and value undef.

The delete function is the only way to remove a specific entry from a hash. Once
you've deleted a key, it no longer shows up in a keys list or an each iteration,
and exists will return false for that key.

This demonstrates the difference between undef and delete:

```
# %food_color as per Introduction
sub print_foods {
    my @foods = keys %food_color;
    my $food;

    print "Keys: @foods\n";
    print "Values: ";

    foreach $food (@foods) {
        my $color = $food_color{$food};

        if (defined $color) {
            print "$color ";
        } else {
            print "(undef) ";
        }
    }
    print "\n";
}

print "Initially:\n";
print_foods();

print "\nWith Banana undef\n";
undef $food_color{"Banana"};
print_foods();

print "\nWith Banana deleted\n";
delete $food_color{"Banana"};
print_foods();

Initially:
Keys: Banana Apple Carrot Lemon
Values: yellow red orange yellow

With Banana undef
Keys: Banana Apple Carrot Lemon
Values: (undef) red orange yellow

With Banana deleted
Keys: Apple Carrot Lemon
Values: red orange yellow
```

As you see, if we set `$food_color{"Banana"}` to `undef`, `"Banana"` still shows up as a key in the hash. The entry is still there; we only succeeded in making the value `undef`. On the other hand, `delete` actually removed it from the hash—`"Banana"` is no longer in the list returned by `keys`.

`delete` can also take a hash slice, deleting all listed keys at once:

```
delete @food_color{"Banana", "Apple", "Cabbage"};
```

See Also

The `delete` and `keys` functions in *perlfunc*(1) and in Chapter 3 of *Programming Perl*; we use keys in Recipe 5.4

5.4. Traversing a Hash

Problem

You want to perform an action on each entry (i.e., each key-value pair) in a hash.

Solution

Use `each` with a `while` loop:

```
while(($key, $value) = each(%HASH)) {
    # do something with $key and $value
}
```

Or use `keys` with a `foreach` loop, unless the hash is potentially very large:

```
foreach $key (keys %HASH) {
    $value = $HASH{$key};
    # do something with $key and $value
}
```

Discussion

Here's a simple example, iterating through the `%food_color` hash from the introduction.

```
# %food_color per the introduction
while(($food, $color) = each(%food_color)) {
    print "$food is $color.\n";
}
Banana is yellow.
Apple is red.
Carrot is orange.
Lemon is yellow.
```

```
foreach $food (keys %food_color) {
    my $color = $food_color{$food};
    print "$food is $color.\n";
}
```
Banana is yellow.
Apple is red.
Carrot is orange.
Lemon is yellow.

We didn't really need the $color variable in the foreach example because we only use it once. Instead, we could have just written:

```
print "$food is $food_color{$food}.\n"
```

Every time each is called on the same hash, it returns the "next" key-value pair. We say "next" because the pairs are returned in the order the underlying lookup structure imposes on them, and this order is almost never alphabetic or numeric. When each runs out of hash elements, it returns the empty list (), which tests false and terminates the while loop.

The foreach example uses keys, which constructs an entire list containing every key from hash, before the loop even begins executing. The advantage to using each is that it gets the keys and values one pair at a time. If the hash contains many keys, not having to pre-construct a complete list of them can save substantial memory. The each function, however, doesn't let you control the order in which pairs are processed.

Using foreach and keys to loop over the list lets you impose an order. For instance, if we wanted to print the food names in alphabetical order:

```
foreach $food (sort keys %food_color) {
    print "$food is $food_color{$food}.\n";
}
```
Apple is red.
Banana is yellow.
Carrot is orange.
Lemon is yellow.

This is a common use of foreach. We use keys to obtain a list of keys in the hash, and then we use foreach to iterate over them. The danger is that if the hash contains a large number of elements, the list returned by keys will use a lot of memory. The trade-off lies between memory use and the ability to process the entries in a particular order. We cover sorting in more detail in Recipe 5.9.

Because keys, values, and each all use the same internal data structures, be careful about mixing calls to these functions or prematurely exiting an each loop. Each time you call keys or values, the current location for each is reset. This code loops forever, printing the first key returned by each:

```
while ( ($k,$v) = each %food_color ) {
    print "Processing $k\n";
    keys %food_color;                # goes back to the start of %food_color
}
```

Modifying a hash while looping over it with **each** or **foreach** is, in general, fraught with danger. The **each** function can behave differently with **tied** and untied hashes when you add or delete keys from a hash. A **foreach** loops over a pre-generated list of keys, so once the loop starts, **foreach** can't know whether you've added or deleted keys. Keys added in the body of the loop aren't automatically appended to the list of keys to loop over, nor are keys deleted by the body of the loop deleted from this list.

Example 5-1 reads a mailbox file and reports on the number of messages from each person. It uses the **From:** line to determine the sender. (It isn't smart in this respect, but we're showing hash manipulation, not mail-file processing.) Supply the mailbox filename as a command-line argument, or use "**-**" to indicate you're piping the mailbox to the program.

Example 5-1. countfrom

```
#!/usr/bin/perl
# countfrom - count number of messages from each sender

$filename = $ARGV[0] || "-";

open(FILE, "<$filename")            or die "Can't open $filename : $!";

while(<FILE>) {
    if (/^From: (.*)/) { $from{$1}++ }
}

foreach $person (sort keys %from) {
    print "$person: $from{$person}\n";
}
```

See Also

The **each** and **keys** functions in *perlfunc*(1) and in Chapter 3 of *Programming Perl*; we talk about for and foreach in Recipe 4.5

5.5. *Printing a Hash*

Problem

You want to print a hash, but neither print "**%hash**" nor print **%hash** works.

Solution

One of several approaches is to iterate over every key-value pair in the hash using Recipe 5.4, and print them:

```
while ( ($k,$v) = each %hash ) {
    print "$k => $v\n";
}
```

Or use **map** to generate a list of strings:

```
print map { "$_ => $hash{$_}\n" } keys %hash;
```

Or use the interpolation trick from Recipe 1.10 to interpolate the hash as a list:

```
print "@{[ %hash ]}\n";
```

Or use a temporary array variable to hold the hash, and print that:

```
{
    my @temp = %hash;
    print "@temp";
}
```

Discussion

The methods differ in the degree that their output is customizable in order and formatting and in their efficiency.

The first method, iterating over the hash, is very flexible and space-efficient. You can format the output as you like it, and it only requires two scalar variables: the current key and value. You can print the hash in key order (at the cost of building a list of sorted keys) if you use a **foreach** loop.

```
foreach $k (sort keys %hash) {
    print "$k => $hash{$k}\n";
}
```

The **map** function is just as flexible. You can still process the list in any order by sorting the keys. You can customize the output to your heart's content. But it builds up a list of strings like "KEY =>VALUE\n" to pass to **print**.

The last two methods are interpolation tricks. By treating the hash as an list, you can't predict or control the output order of the key-value pairs. Furthermore, the output will consist of a list of keys and values, each separated by whatever $" happens to hold. You can't put newlines between pairs or "=>" within them, as we could with the other methods.

See Also

The `$"` variable in *perlvar*(1) and in the "Global Special Variables" section of Chapter 2 of *Programming Perl*; the `foreach`, `map`, `keys`, `sort`, and `each` functions in *perlfunc*(1) and Chapter 3 of *Programming Perl*; we give a technique for interpolating into strings in Recipe 1.10; we discuss the techniques for hash traversal in Recipe 5.4

5.6. Retrieving from a Hash in Insertion Order

Problem

The `keys` and `each` functions give you the hash elements in a strange order, and you want them in the order in which you inserted them.

Solution

Use the Tie::IxHash module.

```
use Tie::IxHash;
tie %HASH, "Tie::IxHash";
# manipulate %HASH
@keys = keys %HASH;          # @keys is in insertion order
```

Discussion

Tie::IxHash makes `keys`, `each`, and `values` return the hash elements in the order they were added. This often removes the need to preprocess the hash keys with a complex `sort` comparison or maintain a distinct array containing the keys in the order they were inserted into the hash.

Tie::IxHash also provides an object-oriented interface to `splice`, `push`, `pop`, `shift`, `unshift`, `keys`, `values`, and `delete`, among others.

Here's an example, showing both `keys` and `each`:

```
# initialize
use Tie::IxHash;

tie %food_color, "Tie::IxHash";
$food_color{Banana} = "Yellow";
$food_color{Apple}  = "Green";
$food_color{Lemon}  = "Yellow";

print "In insertion order, the foods are:\n";
foreach $food (keys %food_color) {
```

```
        print "  $food\n";
    }

    print "Still in insertion order, the foods' colors are:\n";
    while (( $food, $color ) = each %food_color ) {
        print "$food is colored $color.\n";
    }
```

In insertion order, the foods are:
  Banana
  Apple
  Lemon
Still in insertion order, the foods' colors are:
Banana is colored Yellow.
Apple is colored Green.
Lemon is colored Yellow.

See Also

The documentation for the CPAN module Tie::IxHash; Recipe 13.15

5.7. Hashes with Multiple Values Per Key

Problem

You want to store more than one value for each key.

Solution

Store an array reference in $hash{$key}, and put the values into that array.

Discussion

You can only store scalar values in a hash. References, however, are scalars. This solves the problem of storing multiple values for one key by making $hash{$key} a reference to an array containing values for $key. The normal hash operations—insertion, deletion, iteration, and testing for existence—can now be written in terms of array operations like push, splice, and foreach.

This code shows simple insertion into the hash. It processes the output of *who*(1) on Unix machines and outputs a terse listing of users and the ttys they're logged in on:

```
%ttys = ();

open(WHO, "who|")                      or die "can't open who: $!";
while (<WHO>) {
    ($user, $tty) = split;
```

```
        push( @{$ttys{$user}}, $tty );
    }

    foreach $user (sort keys %ttys) {
        print "$user: @{$ttys{$user}}\n";
    }
```

The heart of the code is the push line, the multihash version of $ttys{$user} =
$tty. We interpolate all the tty names in the print line with @{$ttys{$user}}.
We'd loop over the anonymous array if, for instance, we wanted to print the
owner of each tty:

```
    foreach $user (sort keys %ttys) {
        print "$user: ", scalar( @{$ttys{$user}} ), " ttys.\n";
        foreach $tty (sort @{$ttys{$user}}) {
            @stat = stat("/dev/$tty");
            $user = @stat ? ( getpwuid($stat[4]) )[0] : "(not available)";
            print "\t$tty (owned by $user)\n";
        }
    }
```

The exists function can have two meanings: "Is there at least one value for this
key?" and "Does this value exist for this key?" Implementing the second approach
requires searching the array for the value. The delete function and the first sense
of exists are interrelated: If we can guarantee that no anonymous array is ever
empty, we can use the built-in exists. We ensure that no anonymous array is
ever empty by checking for such a situation after deleting an element:

```
    sub multihash_delete {
        my ($hash, $key, $value) = @_;
        my $i;

        return unless ref( $hash->{$key} );
        for ($i = 0; $i < @{ $hash->{$key} }; $i++) {
            if ($hash->{$key}->[$i] eq $value) {
                splice( @{$hash->{$key}}, $i, 1);
                last;
            }
        }

        delete $hash->{$key} unless @{$hash->{$key}};
    }
```

The alternative approach to multivalued hashes is given in Chapter 13, *Classes,
Objects, and Ties*, implemented as tied normal hashes.

See Also

The splice, delete, push, foreach, and exists functions in *perlfunc*(1) and
Chapter 3 of *Programming Perl*; Recipe 11.1; we cover ties in Recipe 13.15

5.8. *Inverting a Hash*

Problem

Hashes map keys to values. You have a hash and a value for which you want to find the corresponding key.

Solution

Use **reverse** to create an inverted hash whose values are the original hash's keys and vice versa.

```
# %LOOKUP maps keys to values
%REVERSE = reverse %LOOKUP;
```

Discussion

This technique uses the list equivalence of hashes mentioned in the introduction. In list context, **reverse** treats %LOOKUP as a list and reverses the order of its elements. The significant property of a hash treated as a list is that the list elements come in pairs: the first element is the key; the second, the value. When you **reverse** such a list, the first element is the value, and the second is a key. Treating *this* list as a hash results in a hash whose values are the keys of the original hash and vice versa.

Here's an example:

```
%surname = ( "Mickey" => "Mantle", "Babe" => "Ruth" );
%first_name = reverse %surname;
print $first_name{"Mantle"}, "\n";
Mickey
```

When we treat %surname as a list, it becomes:

```
("Mickey", "Mantle", "Babe", "Ruth")
```

(or maybe (`"Babe"`, `"Ruth"`, `"Mickey"`, `"Mantle"`) because we can't predict the order). Reversing this list gives us:

```
("Ruth", "Babe", "Mantle", "Mickey")
```

When we treat this list as a hash, it becomes:

```
("Ruth" => "Babe", "Mantle" => "Mickey")
```

Now instead of turning first names into surnames, it turns surnames into first names.

Example 5-2 is a program called `foodfind`. If you give it a food name, it'll tell you the color of that food. If you give it a color, it'll tell you a food of that color.

Example 5-2. foodfind

```
#!/usr/bin/perl -w
# foodfind - find match for food or color

$given = shift @ARGV or die "usage: foodfind food_or_color\n";

%color = (
            "Apple"  => "red",
            "Banana" => "yellow",
            "Lemon"  => "yellow",
            "Carrot" => "orange"
        );

%food = reverse %color;

if (exists $color{$given}) {
print "$given is a food with color $color{$given}.\n";
}
if (exists $food{$given}) {
print "$food{$given} is a food with color $given.\n";
}
```

If two keys in the original hash have the same value (as `"Lemon"` and `"Banana"` do in the color example), then the inverted hash will only have one (which is dependent on the hashing order, and you shouldn't try to predict it). This is because hashes have, by Perl definition, unique keys.

If you want to invert a hash with non-unique values, you must use the techniques shown in Recipe 5.7. That is, build up a hash whose values are a list of keys in the original hash:

```
# %food_color as per the introduction
while (($food,$color) = each(%food_color)) {
    push(@{$foods_with_color{$color}}, $food);
}

print "@{$foods_with_color{yellow}} were yellow foods.\n";
Banana Lemon were yellow foods.
```

This also lets us change the `foodfind` program to handle colors represented by more than one food. For instance, `foodfind yellow` reports bananas and lemons.

If any values in the original hash were references instead of just strings and numbers, the inverted hash poses a problem because references don't work well as hash keys unless you use the Tie::RefHash module described in Recipe 5.12.

See Also

The **reverse** function in *perlfunc*(1) and in Chapter 3 of *Programming Perl*;
Recipe 13.15

5.9. Sorting a Hash

Problem

You need to work with the elements of a hash in a particular order.

Solution

Use **keys** to get a list of the keys, then **sort** them based on the ordering you
want:

```
# %HASH is the hash to sort
@keys = sort { criterion() } (keys %hash);
foreach $key (@keys) {
    $value = $hash{$key};
    # do something with $key, $value
}
```

Discussion

Even though you can't directly maintain a hash in a specific order (unless you use
the Tie::IxHash module mentioned in Recipe 5.6), you can access its entries in any
order.

This technique offers many variations on the same basic mechanism: You extract
the keys, reorder them using the **sort** function, and then process the entries in
the new order. All the sorting tricks shown in Chapter 4, *Arrays*, can be used here.
Let's look at some applications.

The following code simply uses **sort** to order the keys alphabetically:

```
foreach $food (sort keys %food_color) {
    print "$food is $food_color{$food}.\n";
}
```

This sorts the keys by their associated values:

```
foreach $food (sort { $food_color{$a} cmp $food_color{$b} }
                keys %food_color)
{
    print "$food is $food_color{$food}.\n";
}
```

This sorts by length of the values:

```
@foods = sort { length($food_color{$a}) <=> length($food_color{$b}) }
    keys %food_color;
foreach $food (@foods) {
    print "$food is $food_color{$food}.\n";
}
```

See Also

The sort and keys functions in *perlfunc*(1) and in Chapter 3 of *Programming Perl*; Recipe 5.6; we discuss sorting lists in Recipe 4.15

5.10. Merging Hashes

Problem

You need to make a new hash with the entries of two existing hashes.

Solution

Treat them as lists, and join them as you would lists.

```
%merged = (%A, %B);
```

To save memory, loop over the hashes' elements and build a new hash that way:

```
%merged = ();
while ( ($k,$v) = each(%A) ) {
    $merged{$k} = $v;
}
while ( ($k,$v) = each(%B) ) {
    $merged{$k} = $v;
}
```

Discussion

The first method, like the earlier recipe on inverting a hash, uses the hash-list equivalence explained in the introduction. (%A, %B) evaluates to a list of paired keys and values. When we assign it to %merged, Perl turns that list of pairs back into a hash.

Here's an example of that technique:

```
# %food_color as per the introduction
%drink_color = ( Galliano  => "yellow",
                 "Mai Tai" => "blue" );

%ingested_color = (%drink_color, %food_color);
```

Keys in both input hashes appear only once in the output hash. If a food and a drink shared the same name, for instance, then the last one seen by the first merging technique would be the one that showed up in the resultant hash.

This style of direct assignment, as in the first example, is easier to read and write, but requires a lot of memory if the hashes are large. That's because Perl has to unroll both hashes into a temporary list before the assignment to the merged hash is done. Step-by-step merging using each, as in the second technique, spares you that cost and lets you decide what to do with duplicate keys.

The first example could be rewritten to use the each technique:

```
# %food_color per the introduction, then
%drink_color = ( Galliano  => "yellow",
                 "Mai Tai" => "blue" );

%substance_color = ();
while (($k, $v) = each %food_color) {
    $substance_color{$k} = $v;
}
while (($k, $v) = each %drink_color) {
    $substance_color{$k} = $v;
}
```

That technique duplicated the while and assignment code. Here's a sneaky way to get around that:

```
foreach $substanceref ( \%food_color, \%drink_color ) {
    while (($k, $v) = each %$substanceref) {
        $substance_color{$k} = $v;
    }
}
```

If we were merging hashes with duplicates, we can insert our own code to decide what to do with those duplicates:

```
foreach $substanceref ( \%food_color, \%drink_color ) {
    while (($k, $v) = each %$substanceref) {
        if (exists $substance_color{$k}) {
            print "Warning: $k seen twice.  Using the first definition.\n";
            next;
        }
        $substance_color{$k} = $v;
    }
}
```

In the special case of appending one hash to another, we can use the hash slice notation to give an elegant shorthand:

```
@all_colors{keys %new_colors} = values %new_colors;
```

This requires enough memory for lists of the keys and values of `%new_colors`. As with the first technique, the memory requirement might make this technique infeasible when such lists would be large.

See Also

This is a variation on Recipe 4.9; the each function in *perlfunc*(1) and in Chapter 3 of *Programming Perl*

5.11. *Finding Common or Different Keys in Two Hashes*

Problem

You need to find keys in one hash that are present in another hash or keys in one hash that are not present in another.

Solution

Use keys to loop through the keys of one hash, checking whether each key is also in the other hash.

Find common keys

```
my @common = ();
foreach (keys %hash1) {
    push(@common, $_) if exists $hash2{$_};
}
# @common now contains common keys
```

Find keys from one hash that aren't in both

```
my @this_not_that = ();
foreach (keys %hash1) {
    push(@this_not_that, $_) unless exists $hash2{$_};
}
```

Discussion

Because we're finding common or different keys of the hashes, we can apply our earlier array recipes for finding common or different elements to arrays of the hashes' keys. For an explanation, see Recipe 4.8.

This code uses the difference technique to find non-citrus foods:

```
# %food_color per the introduction
```

```
# %citrus_color is a hash mapping citrus food name to its color.
%citrus_color = ( Lemon  => "yellow",
                  Orange => "orange",
                  Lime   => "green" );

# build up a list of non-citrus foods
@non_citrus = ();

foreach (keys %food_color) {
    push (@non_citrus, $_) unless exists $citrus_color{$_};
}
```

See Also

The "Variables" section of Chapter 2 of *Programming Perl*; the **each** function in *perlfunc*(1) and in Chapter 3 of *Programming Perl*

5.12. Hashing References

Problem

When you use **keys** on a hash whose keys are references, the references that **keys** returns no longer work. This situation often arises when you want to cross-reference two different hashes.

Solution

Use Tie::RefHash:

```
use Tie::RefHash;
tie %hash, "Tie::RefHash";
# you may now use references as the keys to %hash
```

Discussion

Hash keys are automatically "stringified," that is, treated as though they appeared between double quotes. In the case of numbers or strings, nothing is lost. This isn't the case with references, though.

Stringified references look like these:

```
Class::Somewhere=HASH(0x72048)
ARRAY(0x72048)
```

A stringified reference can't be dereferenced, because it is just a string and no longer a reference. This means you can't use references as the keys to a hash without losing their "magic."

Hand-rolled solutions to this problem involve maintaining a distinct hash whose keys are stringified references and whose values are the actual references. This is what Tie::RefHash does. We'll use IO objects for filehandles here to show you that even such strange references can be used to index a hash tied with Tie::RefHash.

Here's an example:

```
use Tie::RefHash;
use IO::File;

tie %name, "Tie::RefHash";
foreach $filename ("/etc/termcap", "/vmunix", "/bin/cat") {
    $fh = IO::File->new("< $filename") or next;
    $name{$fh} = $filename;
}
print "open files: ", join(", ", values %name), "\n";
foreach $file (keys %name) {
    seek($file, 0, 2);          # seek to the end
    printf("%s is %d bytes long.\n", $name{$file}, tell($file));
}
```

If you're storing objects as the keys to a hash, though, you almost always should be storing a unique attribute of the object (e.g., name or ID number) instead.

See Also

The documentation for the standard Tie::RefHash module; the "Hard References Don't Work as Hash Keys" section of Chapter 4 of *Programming Perl*, and the "Warning" section of *perlref*(1)

5.13. Presizing a Hash

Problem

You want to preallocate memory for a hash to speed up your program so Perl won't have to incrementally allocate memory each time a new entry is added to the hash. Often you know the final size of a hash before you start building it up, and it's possible to use this information to speed up your program.

Solution

Assign the number of key-value pairs your hash will have to keys %HASH.

```
# presize %hash to $num
keys(%hash) = $num;
```

Discussion

This new feature, first introduced in release 5.004 of Perl, may or may not improve your performance. Perl already shares keys between hashes, so if you already have a hash with "Apple" as a key, Perl won't need to allocate memory for another copy of "Apple" when you add an entry whose key is "Apple" to another hash.

```
# will have 512 users in %users
keys(%users) = 512;
```

Perl's internal data structures require the number of keys to be a power of 2. If we had said:

```
keys(%users) = 1000;
```

Perl would have internally allocated 1024 "buckets" for the hash. Keys and buckets aren't always one to one. You get the best performance when they are, but the distribution of keys to buckets is dependent on your keys and Perl's (immutable) hash algorithm.

See Also

The keys function in *perlfunc*(1) and Chapter 3 of *Programming Perl*; Recipe 4.3

5.14. Finding the Most Common Anything

Problem

You have an aggregate data structure, such as an array or a hash. You want to know how often each element in the array (or key or value in the hash) occurs. For instance, if your array contains web server transactions, you might want to find the most commonly requested file. If your hash maps usernames to number of logins, you want to find the most common number of logins.

Solution

Use a hash to count how many times each element, key, or value appears:

```
%count = ();
foreach $element (@ARRAY) {
    $count{$element}++;
}
```

Discussion

Any time you want to count how often different things appear, you should probably be using a hash. The `foreach` adds one to `$count{$element}` for every occurrence of `$element`.

See Also

Recipe 4.6; Recipe 4.7

5.15. Representing Relationships Between Data

Problem

You want to represent relationships between elements of data—for instance, the *mother of* relationship in a family tree or *parent process* for a process table. This is closely related to representing tables in relational databases (tables represent relationships between information) and to representing computer science graph structures (edges represent relationships between nodes).

Solution

Use a hash to represent the relationship.

Discussion

Here's part of the family tree from the Bible:

```
%father = ( 'Cain'       => 'Adam',
            'Abel'       => 'Adam',
            'Seth'       => 'Adam',
            'Enoch'      => 'Cain',
            'Irad'       => 'Enoch',
            'Mehujael'   => 'Irad',
            'Methusael'  => 'Mehujael',
            'Lamech'     => 'Methusael',
            'Jabal'      => 'Lamech',
            'Jubal'      => 'Lamech',
            'Tubalcain'  => 'Lamech',
            'Enos'       => 'Seth' );
```

This lets us, for instance, easily trace a person's lineage:

```
while (<>) {
    chomp;
    do {
```

```
            print "$_ ";              # print the current name
            $_ = $father{$_};         # set $_ to $_'s father
      } while defined;                # until we run out of fathers
      print "\n";
}
```

We can already ask questions like "Who begat Seth?" by checking the %father
hash. By inverting this hash, we invert the relationship. This lets us use Recipe 5.8
to answer questions like "Whom did Lamech beget?"

```
while ( ($k,$v) = each %father ) {
    push( @{ $children{$v} }, $k );
}


$" = ', ';                          # separate output with commas
while (<>) {
    chomp;
    if ($children{$_}) {
        @children = @{$children{$_}};
    } else {
        @children = "nobody";
    }
    print "$_ begat @children.\n";
}
```

Hashes can also represent relationships such as the C language #includes. A
includes B if A contains #include B. This code builds the hash (it doesn't look for
files in /usr/include as it should, but that is a minor change):

```
foreach $file (@files) {
    local *F;                        # just in case we want a local FH
    unless (open (F, "<$file")) {
        warn "Couldn't read $file: $!; skipping.\n";
        next;
    }

    while (<F>) {
        next unless /^\s*#\s*include\s*<([^>]+)>/;
        push(@{$includes{$1}}, $file);
    }
    close F;
}
```

This shows which files with include statements are not included in other files.

```
@include_free = ();                       # list of files that don't include others
@uniq{map { @$_ } values %includes} = undef;
foreach $file (sort keys %uniq) {
        push( @include_free , $file ) unless $includes{$file};
}
```

The values of %includes are anonymous arrays because a single file can (and
often does) include more than one other file. We use map to build up a big list of
all the included files and remove duplicates by using a hash.

See Also

Recipe 4.6; the more complex data structures in Recipe 11.9 through Recipe 11.14

5.16. Program: dutree

The *dutree* program, shown in Example 5-3, turns the output of *du*.

```
% du pcb
19        pcb/fix
20        pcb/rev/maybe/yes
10        pcb/rev/maybe/not
705       pcb/rev/maybe
54        pcb/rev/web
1371      pcb/rev
3         pcb/pending/mine
1016      pcb/pending
2412      pcb
```

into sorted, indented output:

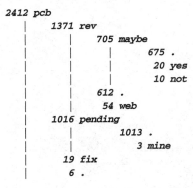

```
2412 pcb
  |      1371 rev
  |       |       705 maybe
  |       |        |        675 .
  |       |        |         20 yes
  |       |        |         10 not
  |       |       612 .
  |       |        54 web
  |      1016 pending
  |       |        1013 .
  |       |           3 mine
  |        19 fix
  |         6 .
```

The arguments you give *dutree* are passed through to *du*. That way you could call *dutree* in any of these ways, or maybe more if your *du* supports other options.

```
% dutree
% dutree /usr
% dutree -a
% dutree -a /bin
```

The %Dirsize hash maintains the mapping of names to sizes. For example, $Dirsize{"pcb"} contains 2412 in this sample run. We'll use that hash both for output and for sorting each directory's subdirectories by size.

%Kids is more interesting. For any given path $path, $Kids{$path} contains a (reference to an) array of names of subdirectories of this one. The "pcb" entry contains a reference to an anonymous array containing "fix", "rev", and "pending". The "rev" entry contains "maybe" and "web". The "maybe" entry contains **"yes"** and **"not"**, which do not have their own entries because they are end nodes in the tree.

The output function is passed the start of the tree—the last line read in from the output of *du*. First it prints that directory and its size. Then the function sorts the directory's children (if any) so that those with the most disk usage float to the top. Finally, output calls itself, recursing on each child in order. The extra arguments are used in formatting.

This program is inherently recursive because the filesystem is recursive. However, its data structure is not recursive; at least, not the way a circular linked list is. Each value is an array of further keys to process. The recursion resides in the processing, not in the storage.

Example 5-3. dutree

```perl
#!/usr/bin/perl -w
# dutree - print sorted indented rendition of du output
use strict;

my %Dirsize;
my %Kids;

getdots(my $topdir = input());
output($topdir);

# run du, read in input, save sizes and kids
# return last directory (file?) read
sub input {
    my($size, $name, $parent);
    @ARGV = ("du @ARGV |");          # prep the arguments
    while (<>) {                     # magic open is our friend
        ($size, $name) = split;
        $Dirsize{$name} = $size;
        ($parent = $name) =~ s#/[^/]+$##;    # dirname
        push @{ $Kids{$parent} }, $name unless eof;
    }
    return $name;
}


# figure out how much is taken up in each directory
# that isn't stored in subdirectories.  add a new
# fake kid called "." containing that much.
sub getdots {
    my $root = $_[0];
    my($size, $cursize);
    $size = $cursize = $Dirsize{$root};
    if ($Kids{$root}) {
        for my $kid (@{ $Kids{$root} }) {
            $cursize -= $Dirsize{$kid};
            getdots($kid);
        }
    }
```

Example 5-3. dutree (continued)

```
    }
    if ($size != $cursize) {
        my $dot = "$root/.";
        $Dirsize{$dot} = $cursize;
        push @{ $Kids{$root} }, $dot;
    }
}

# recursively output everything,
# passing padding and number width in as well
# on recursive calls
sub output {
    my($root, $prefix, $width) = (shift, shift || '', shift || 0);
    my $path;
    ($path = $root) =~ s#.*/##;       # basename
    my $size = $Dirsize{$root};
    my $line = sprintf("%${width}d %s", $size, $path);
    print $prefix, $line, "\n";
    for ($prefix .= $line) {          # build up more output
        s/\d /| /;
        s/[^|]/ /g;
    }
    if ($Kids{$root}) {               # not a bachelor node
        my @Kids = @{ $Kids{$root} };
        @Kids = sort { $Dirsize{$b} <=> $Dirsize{$a} } @Kids;
        $Dirsize{$Kids[0]} =~ /(\d+)/;
        my $width = length $1;
        for my $kid (@Kids) { output($kid, $prefix, $width) }
    }
}
```

Before Perl supported hashes of arrays directly, Herculean efforts were required to emulate these higher order constructs. Some folks used repeated calls to split and join, but these were exceedingly slow.

Example 5-4 is a version of *dutree* from those days of Perl arcana. Because we didn't have proper array references, we had to usurp the Perl symbol table itself. This program created variables on the fly with bizarre names. Can you find which hash this program is using?

The @{"pcb"} array contains "pcb/fix", "pcb/rev", and "pcb/pending". The @{"pcb/rev"} array contains "pcb/rev/maybe" and "pcb/rev/web". The @{"pcb/rev/maybe"} array contains "pcb/rev/yes" and "pcb/rev/not".

When you assign something like "pcb/fix" to *kid, it promotes the string on the right-hand side to a typeglob. This makes @kid an alias for @{"pcb/fix"}— among other things. It would also alias &kid to &{"pcb/fix"}, and so on.

If that isn't interesting enough, consider how the local is using dynamic scoping of global variables to avoid passing in extra arguments. Check out what's happening with the $width variable in the output routine.

Example 5-4. dutree-orig

```perl
#!/usr/bin/perl
# dutree_orig: the old version pre-perl5 (early 90s)

@lines = `du @ARGV`;
chop(@lines);
&input($top = pop @lines);
&output($top);
exit;

sub input {
    local($root, *kid, $him) = @_[0,0];
    while (@lines && &childof($root, $lines[$#lines])) {
        &input($him = pop(@lines));
        push(@kid, $him);
    }
    if (@kid) {
        local($mysize) = ($root =~ /^(\d+)/);
        for (@kid) { $mysize -= (/^(\d+)/)[0]; }
        push(@kid, "$mysize .") if $size != $mysize;
    }
    @kid = &sizesort(*kid);
}

sub output {
    local($root, *kid, $prefix) = @_[0,0,1];
    local($size, $path) = split(' ', $root);
    $path =~ s!.*/!!;
    $line = sprintf("%${width}d %s", $size, $path);
    print $prefix, $line, "\n";
    $prefix .= $line;
    $prefix =~ s/\d /| /;
    $prefix =~ s/[^|]/ /g;
    local($width) = $kid[0] =~ /(\d+)/ && length("$1");
    for (@kid) { &output($_, $prefix); };
}

sub sizesort {
    local(*list, @index) = shift;
    sub bynum { $index[$b] <=> $index[$a]; }
    for (@list) { push(@index, /(\d+)/); }
    @list[sort bynum 0..$#list];
}

sub childof {
    local(@pair) = @_;
    for (@pair) { s/^\d+\s+//g; s/$/\//; }
    index($pair[1], $pair[0]) >= 0;
}
```

The answer to the question posed above, "Which hash is the old *dutree* using?" is %main::, that is, the Perl symbol table itself. Needless to say, this program will never run under use strict. We're happy to report that the updated version runs three times as fast as the old one. That's because the old one keeps looking up variables in the symbol table, and the new one doesn't have to. It's also because we avoid all that slow splitting of the space used and the directory name. But we thought we'd show you the old version because it is instructive too.

6

Pattern Matching

[Art is] pattern informed by sensibility.
—Sir Herbert Read
The Meaning of Art

6.0. Introduction

Although most modern programming languages offer primitive pattern matching tools, usually through an extra library, Perl's patterns are integrated directly into the language core. Perl's patterns boast features not found in pattern matching in other languages, features that encourage a whole different way of looking at data. Just as chess players see patterns in the board positions that their pieces control, Perl adepts look at data in terms of patterns. These patterns, expressed in the punctuation-intensive language of regular expressions,* provide access to powerful algorithms normally available only to computer science scholars.

"If this pattern matching thing is so powerful and so fantastic," you may be saying, "why don't you have a hundred different recipes on regular expressions in this chapter?" Regular expressions are the natural solution to many problems involving numbers, strings, dates, web documents, mail addresses, and almost everything else in this book; we used pattern matching over 100 times in other chapters. This chapter mostly presents recipes in which pattern matching forms part of the questions, not just part of the answers.

Perl's extensive and ingrained support for regular expressions means that you not only have features available that you won't find in any other language, but you

---

* To be honest, *regular expressions* in the classic sense of the word do not by definition contain backreferences, the way Perl's patterns do.

have new ways of using them, too. Programmers new to Perl often look for functions like these:

```
match( $string, $pattern );
subst( $string, $pattern, $replacement );
```

But matching and substituting are such common tasks that they merit their own syntax:

```
$meadow =~ m/sheep/;    # True if $meadow contains "sheep"
$meadow !~ m/sheep/;    # True if $meadow doesn't contain "sheep"
$meadow =~ s/old/new/;  # Replace "old" with "new" in $meadow
```

Pattern matching isn't like direct string comparison, even at its simplest. It's more like string searching with mutant wildcards on steroids. Without anchors, the position where the match occurs can float freely throughout the string. Any of the following lines would also be matched by the expression $meadow =~ /ovine/, giving false positives when looking for lost sheep:

```
Fine bovines demand fine toreadors.
Muskoxen are a polar ovibovine species.
Grooviness went out of fashion decades ago.
```

Sometimes they're right in front of you but they still don't match:

```
Ovines are found typically in oviaries.
```

The problem is that while you are probably thinking in some human language, the pattern matching engine most assuredly is not. When the engine is presented with the pattern /ovine/ and a string to match this against, it searches the string for an "o" that is immediately followed by a "v", then by an "i", then by an "n", and then finally by an "e". What comes before or after that sequence doesn't matter.

As you find your patterns matching some strings you don't want them to match and not matching other strings that you do want them to match, you start embellishing. If you're really looking for nothing but sheep, you probably want to match more like this:

```
if ($meadow =~ /\bovines?\b/i) { print "Here be sheep!" }
```

Don't be tricked by the phantom cow lurking in that string. That's not a bovine. It's an ovine with a \b in front, which matches at a word boundary only. The s? indicates an optional "s" so we can find one or more ovines. The trailing /i makes whole pattern match case insensitive.

As you see, some characters or sequences of characters have special meaning to the pattern-matching engine. These metacharacters let you *anchor* the pattern to the start or end of the string, give alternatives for parts of a pattern, allow repetition and wildcarding, and remember part of the matching substring for use later in the pattern or in subsequent code.

Learning the syntax of pattern matching isn't as daunting as it might appear. Sure, there are a lot of symbols, but each has a reason for existing. Regular expressions aren't random jumbles of punctuation—they're carefully thought out jumbles of punctuation! If you forget one, you can always look it up. Summary tables are included in *Programming Perl, Learning Perl, Mastering Regular Expressions*, and the *perlre*(1) and *perlop*(1) manpages included with every Perl installation.

The Tricky Bits

Much trickier than the syntax of regular expressions is their sneaky semantics. The three aspects of pattern-matching behavior that seem to cause folks the most trouble are greed, eagerness, and backtracking (and also how these three interact with each other).

Greed is the principle that if a quantifier (like `*`) can match a varying number of times, it will prefer to match as long a substring as it can. This is explained in Recipe 6.15.

Eagerness is the notion that the leftmost match wins. The engine is very eager to return you a match as quickly as possible, sometimes even before you are expecting it. Consider the match `"Fred" =~ /x*/`. If asked to explain this in plain language, you might say "Does the string `"Fred"` contain any x's?" If so, you might be surprised to learn that it seems to. That's because `/x*/` doesn't truly mean "any x's", unless your idea of "any" includes nothing at all. Formally, it means *zero or more* of them, and in this case, zero sufficed for the eager matcher.

A more illustrative example of eagerness would be the following:

```
$string = "good food";
$string =~ s/o*/e/;
```

Can you guess which of the following is in `$string` after that substitution?

```
good food
geod food
geed food
geed feed
ged food
ged fed
egood food
```

The answer is the last one because the earliest point at which zero or more occurrences of `"o"` could be found was right at the beginning of the string. Surprised? Regular expressions can do that to you.

Can you guess what adding /g modifier to make the substitution global will do? Think of it this way: that string has many places where zero or more instances of `"o"` occur—eight, to be precise. The answer is `"egeede efeede"`.

Here's another example of where greed takes a back seat to eagerness:

```
$ echo longest | perl -ne 'print "$&\n" if /(long|longer|longest)+/'
long
```

That's because Perl uses what's called a traditional NFA,[*] a non-deterministic finite automaton. This kind of matching engine is not guaranteed to return the longest *overall* match, just the longest, leftmost match. You might think of Perl's greed as being left-to-right directed, not globally greedy.

But it doesn't have to be that way. Here's an example using *awk*, a language that Perl borrows a lot from:

```
$ echo longest |
    awk 'match($0, /(long|longer|longest)+/) \
        { print substr($0, RSTART, RLENGTH) }'
longest
```

Choosing how to implement pattern matching depends mainly on two factors: are the expressions nonregular (do they use backreferences), and what needs to be returned (yes/no, range of whole match, ranges of subexpressions). Tools like *awk*, *egrep*, and *lex* use regular expressions and only need a yes/no answer or the range of the whole match. This is exactly what DFAs can support, and because DFAs are faster and simpler, these tools have traditionally used DFA implementations. Pattern matching within programs and libraries, such as *ed*, *regex*, and *perl*, is another kettle of fish; typically, we need to support nonregular expressions and we need to know what parts of the string were matched by various parts of the pattern. This is a much harder problem with potentially exponential run times. The natural algorithm for this problem is an NFA, and therein lies both a problem and an opportunity. The problem is that NFAs are slow. The opportunity is that significant performance gains can be made by rewriting the patterns to exploit how the particular NFA implementation runs. This is a major part of Jeffrey Friedl's book, *Mastering Regular Expressions*.

The last and most powerful of the three tricky bits in pattern matching is backtracking. For a pattern to match, the entire regular expression must match, not just part of it. So if the beginning of a pattern containing a quantifier succeeds in a way that causes later parts in the pattern to fail, the matching engine backs up and tries to find another match for the beginning part—that's why it's called backtracking. Essentially, it means that the engine is going to try different possibilities, systematically investigating alternate matches until it finds one that works. In some pattern matching implementations, you keep backtracking in case other submatches make the overall match longer. Perl's matcher doesn't do that; as soon as one possibility works, it uses that—until and unless something later on in the pattern

---

[*] As opposed to a POSIX-style NFA. See *Mastering Regular Expressions* for the differences.

fails, forcing a backtrack to retry another possible way of matching. This is discussed in Recipe 6.16.

Pattern-Matching Modifiers

Pattern-matching modifiers are a lot easier to list and learn than the different metacharacters. Here's a brief summary of them:

/i	Ignore alphabetic case (locale-aware)
/x	Ignore most whitespace in pattern and permit comments
/g	Global—match/substitute as often as possible
/gc	Don't reset search position on failed match
/s	Let . match newline; also, ignore deprecated $*
/m	Let ^ and $ match next to embedded \n
/o	Compile pattern once only
/e	Righthand side of a s/// is code to eval
/ee	Righthand side of a s/// is a string to eval, then run as code, and its return value eval'led again.

/i and /g are the most commonly used modifiers. The pattern /ram/i matches "ram", "RAM", "Ram", and so forth. Backreferences will be checked case-insensitively if this modifier is on; see Recipe 6.16 for an example. This comparison can be made aware of the user's current locale settings if the use locale pragma has been invoked. As currently implemented, /i slows down a pattern match because it disables several performance optimizations.

The /g modifier is used with s/// to replace every match, not just the first one. /g is also used with m// in loops to find (but not replace) every matching occurrence:

```
while (m/(\d+)/g) {
    print "Found number $1\n";
}
```

Used in list context, /g pulls out all matches:

```
@numbers = m/(\d+)/g;
```

That finds only non-overlapping matches. You have to be much sneakier to get overlapping ones by making a zero-width look-ahead with the (?=...) construct. Because it's zero-width, the match engine hasn't advanced at all. Within the look-ahead, capturing parentheses are used to grab the thing anyway. Although we've saved something, Perl notices we haven't made any forward progress on the /g so bumps us forward one character position.

This shows the difference:

```
$digits = "123456789";
@nonlap = $digits =~ /(\d\d\d)/g;
@yeslap = $digits =~ /(?=(\d\d\d))/g;
print "Non-overlapping:  @nonlap\n";
```

```
print "Overlapping:        @yeslap\n";
Non-overlapping:  123 456 789
Overlapping:      123 234 345 456 567 678 789
```

The /s and /m modifiers are used when matching strings with embedded new-lines. /s makes dot match "\n", something it doesn't normally do; it also makes the match ignore the value of the old, deprecated $* variable. /m makes ^ and $ match after and before "\n" respectively. They are useful with paragraph slurping mode as explained in the introduction to Chapter 8, *File Contents*, and in Recipe 6.6.

The /e switch is used so that the right-hand part is run as code and its return value is used as the replacement string. s/(\d+)/sprintf("%#x", $1)/ge would convert all numbers into hex, changing, for example, 2581 into 0xb23.

Because different countries have different ideas of what constitutes an alphabet, the POSIX standard provides systems (and thus programs) with a standard way of representing alphabets, character set ordering, and so on. Perl gives you access to some of these through the use locale pragma; see the perllocale manpage for more information. When use locale is in effect, the \w character class includes accented and other exotic characters. The case-changing \u, \U, \l, and \L (and the corresponding uc, ucfirst, etc. functions) escapes also respect use locale, so σ will be turned into Σ with \u if the locale says it should.

Special Variables

Perl sets special variables as the result of certain kinds of matches: $1, $2, $3, and so on *ad infinitum* (Perl doesn't stop at $9) are set when a pattern contains back-references (parentheses around part of the pattern). Each left parenthesis as you read left to right in the pattern begins filling a new, numbered variable. The variable $+ contains the contents of the last backreference of the last successful match. This helps you tell which of several alternate matches was found (for example, if / (x.*y) | (y.*z) / matches, $+ contains whichever of $1 or $2 got filled). $& contains the complete text matched in the last successful pattern match. $' and $` are the strings before and after the successful match, respectively:

```
$string = "And little lambs eat ivy";
$string =~ /l[^s]*s/;
print "($`) ($&) ($')\n";
(And ) (little lambs) ( eat ivy)
```

$`, $&, and $' are tempting, but dangerous. Their very presence anywhere in a program slows down every pattern match because the engine must populate these variables for every match. This is true even if you use one of these variables only once, or, for that matter, if you never actually use them at all but merely mention them. As of release 5.005, $& is no longer as expensive.

All this power may make patterns seem omnipotent. Surprisingly enough, this is not (quite) the case. Regular expressions are fundamentally incapable of doing some things. For some of those, special modules lend a hand. Regular expressions are unable to deal with balanced input, that is, anything that's arbitrarily nested, like matching parentheses, matching HTML tags, etc. For that, you have to build up a real parser, like the HTML::Parser recipes in Chapter 20, *Web Automation*. Another thing Perl patterns can't do yet is fuzzy matches; Recipe 6.13 shows how to use a module to work around that.

To learn far more about regular expressions than you ever thought existed, check out *Mastering Regular Expressions*, written by Jeffrey Friedl and published by O'Reilly & Associates. This book is dedicated to explaining regular expressions from a practical perspective. It not only covers general regular expressions and Perl patterns well, it also compares and contrasts these with those used in other popular languages.

6.1. Copying and Substituting Simultaneously

Problem

You're tired of constantly using two separate statements with redundant information, one to copy and another to substitute.

Solution

Instead of:

```
$dst = $src;
$dst =~ s/this/that/;
```

use:

```
($dst = $src) =~ s/this/that/;
```

Discussion

Sometimes what you wish you could have is the new string, but you don't care to write it in two steps.

For example:

```
# strip to basename
($progname = $0)        =~ s!^.*/!!;

# Make All Words Title-Cased
```

```
($capword   = $word)       =~ s/(\w+)/\u\L$1/g;

# /usr/man/man3/foo.1 changes to /usr/man/cat3/foo.1
($catpage   = $manpage)   =~ s/man(?=\d)/cat/;
```

You can even use this technique on an entire array:

```
@bindirs = qw( /usr/bin /bin /usr/local/bin );
for (@libdirs = @bindirs) { s/bin/lib/ }
print "@libdirs\n";
/usr/lib /lib /usr/local/lib
```

The parentheses are required when combining an assignment if you wish to
change the result in the leftmost variable. Normally, the result of a substitution is
its success: either " " for failure, or the number of times the substitution was done.
Contrast this with the preceding examples where the parentheses surround the
assignment itself. For example:

```
($a =   $b) =~ s/x/y/g;     # copy $b to $a, then change $b
$a = ($b  =~ s/x/y/g);      # change $b, count goes in $a
```

See Also

The "Variables" section of Chapter 2 of *Programming Perl*, and the "Assignment
Operators" section of *perlop*(1)

6.2. *Matching Letters*

Problem

You want to see whether a value only consists of alphabetic characters.

Solution

The obvious character class for matching regular letters isn't good enough in the
general case:

```
if ($var =~ /^[A-Za-z]+$/) {
    # it is purely alphabetic
}
```

That's because it doesn't respect the user's locale settings. If you need to match
letters with diacritics as well, use `locale` and match against a negated character
class:

```
use locale;
if ($var =~ /^[^\W\d_]+$/) {
    print "var is purely alphabetic\n";
}
```

Discussion

Perl can't directly express "something alphabetic" independent of locale, so we have to be more clever. The \w regular expression notation matches one alphabetic, numeric, or underscore character. Therefore, \W is not one of those. The negated character class [^\W\d_] specifies a byte that must not be an alphanumunder, a digit, or an underscore. That leaves us with nothing but alphabetics, which is what we were looking for.

Here's how you'd use this in a program:

```
use locale;
use POSIX 'locale_h';

# the following locale string might be different on your system
unless (setlocale(LC_ALL, "fr_CA.ISO8859-1")) {
    die "couldn't set locale to French Canadian\n";
}

while (<DATA>) {
    chomp;
    if (/^[^\W\d_]+$/) {
        print "$_: alphabetic\n";
    } else {
        print "$_: line noise\n";
    }
}

__END__
silly
façade
coöperate
niño
Renée
Molière
hæmoglobin
naïve
tschüß
random!stuff#here
```

See Also

The treatment of locales in Perl in *perllocale*(1); your system's *locale*(3) manpage; we discuss locales in greater depth in Recipe 6.12; the "Perl and the POSIX Locale" section of Chapter 7 of *Mastering Regular Expressions*

6.3. Matching Words

Problem

You want to pick out words from a string.

Solution

Think long and hard about what you want a word to be and what separates one word from the next, then write a regular expression that embodies your decisions. For example:

```
/\S+/                 # as many non-whitespace bytes as possible
/[A-Za-z'-]+/         # as many letters, apostrophes, and hyphens
```

Discussion

Because words vary between applications, languages, and input streams, Perl does not have built-in definitions of words. You must make them from character classes and quantifiers yourself, as we did previously. The second pattern is an attempt to recognize `"shepherd's"` and `"sheep-shearing"` each as single words.

Most approaches will have limitations because of the vagaries of written human languages. For instance, although the second pattern successfully identifies `"spank'd"` and `"counter-clockwise"` as words, it will also pull the `"rd"` out of `"23rd Psalm"`. If you want to be more precise when you pull words out from a string, you can specify the stuff surrounding the word. Normally, this should be a word-boundary, not whitespace:

```
/\b([A-Za-z]+)\b/        # usually best
/\s([A-Za-z]+)\s/        # fails at ends or w/ punctuation
```

Although Perl provides \w, which matches a character that is part of a valid Perl identifier, Perl identifiers are rarely what you think of as words, since we really mean a string of alphanumerics and underscores, but not colons or quotes. Because it's defined in terms of \w, \b may surprise you if you expect to match an English word boundary (or, even worse, a Swahili word boundary).

\b and \B can still be useful. For example, /\Bis\B/ matches the string `"is"` only within a word, not at the edges. And while `"thistle"` would be found, `"vis-à-vis"` wouldn't.

See Also

The treatment of \b, \w, and \s in *perlre*(1) and in the "Regular Expression Bestiary" section of Chapter 2 of *Programming Perl*; the words-related patterns in Recipe 6.23

6.4. Commenting Regular Expressions

Problem

You want to make your complex regular expressions understandable and maintainable.

Solution

You have four techniques at your disposal: comments outside the pattern, comments inside the pattern with the /x modifier, comments inside the replacement part of s///, and alternate delimiters.

Discussion

The piece of sample code in Example 6-1 uses all four techniques. The initial comment describes the overall intent of the regular expression. For relatively simple patterns, this may be all that is needed. More complex patterns, as in the example, will require more documentation.

Example 6-1. resname

```
#!/usr/bin/perl -p
# resname - change all "foo.bar.com" style names in the input stream
# into "foo.bar.com [204.148.40.9]" (or whatever) instead

use Socket;                 # load inet_addr
s{                          #  .
    (                       # capture the hostname in $1
        (?:                 # these parens for grouping only
            (?! [-_] )      # lookahead for neither underscore nor dash
            [\w-] +         # hostname component
            \.              # and the domain dot
        ) +                 # now repeat that whole thing a bunch of times
        [A-Za-z]            # next must be a letter
        [\w-] +             # now trailing domain part
    )                       # end of $1 capture
}{                          # replace with this:
    "$1 " .                 # the original bit, plus a space
    ( ($addr = gethostbyname($1))    # if we get an addr
      ? "[" . inet_ntoa($addr) . "]" #      format it
      : "[???]"                       # else mark dubious
```

Example 6-1. resname (continued)

```
        )
}gex;                       # /g for global
                            # /e for execute
                            # /x for nice formatting
```

For aesthetics, the example uses alternate delimiters. When you split your match or substitution over multiple lines, it helps readability to have matching braces. Another common reason to use alternate delimiters is when your pattern or replacement contains slashes, as in s/\/\//\/..\//g, alternate delimiters makes such patterns easier to read, as in s!//!/..!g or s{//}{/../}g.

The /x modifier makes Perl ignore most whitespace in the pattern (it still counts in a bracketed character class) and treat # characters and their following text as comments. Although useful, this can prove troublesome if you want literal whitespace or # characters in your pattern. If you do want these characters, you'll have to quote them with a backslash, as in the escaped pound signs here:

```
s/                      # replace
  \#                    #    a pound sign
  (\w+)                 #    the variable name
  \#                    #    another pound sign
/${$1}/xg;              # with the value of the global variable
```

Remember that comments should explain the text, not just restate the code. Using "$i++ # add one to i" is apt to lose marks in your programming course or get you talked about by your coworkers.

The final technique is /e, which evaluates the replacement portion as a full Perl expression, not just as a (double-quote interpolated) string. The result of running this code is used as the replacement string. Because it is evaluated as code, you can put comments in it. This slows your code down somewhat, but not as much as you'd think (until you write a benchmark on your own, a good idea that will allow you to develop a feel for the efficiency of different constructs). That's because the right-hand side of the substitute is syntax-checked and compiled at compile-time along with the rest of your program. This may be overkill in the case of a simple string replacement, but it is marvelous for more complex cases.

Doubling up the /e to make /ee (or even more, like /eee!) is like the eval "STRING" construct. This allows you to use lexical variables instead of globals in the previous replacement example.

```
s/                      # replace
  \#                    #    a pound sign
  (\w+)                 #    the variable name
  \#                    #    another pound sign
/'$' . $1/xeeg;         # with the value of *any* variable
```

After a /ee substitution, you can test the $@ variable. It contains any error messages resulting from running your code, because this is real run-time code generation—unlike /e.

See Also

The /x modifier in *perlre*(1) and the "Pattern Matching" section of Chapter 2 of *Programming Perl*; the "Comments Within a Regular Expression" section of Chapter 7 of *Mastering Regular Expressions*

6.5. Finding the Nth Occurrence of a Match

Problem

You want to find the Nth match in a string, not just the first one. For example, you'd like to find the word preceding the third occurrence of "fish":

```
One fish two fish red fish blue fish
```

Solution

Use the /g modifier in a while loop, keeping count of matches:

```
$WANT = 3;
$count = 0;
while (/(\w+)\s+fish\b/gi) {
    if (++$count == $WANT) {
        print "The third fish is a $1 one.\n";
        # Warning: don't 'last' out of this loop
    }
}
The third fish is a red one.
```

Or use a repetition count and repeated pattern like this:

```
/(?:\w+\s+fish\s+){2}(\w+)\s+fish/i;
```

Discussion

As explained in the chapter introduction, using the /g modifier in scalar context creates something of a *progressive match*, useful in while loops. This is commonly used to count the number of times a pattern matches in a string:

```
# simple way with while loop
$count = 0;
while ($string =~ /PAT/g) {
    $count++;                    # or whatever you'd like to do here
}
```

```
# same thing with trailing while
$count = 0;
$count++ while $string =~ /PAT/g;

# or with for loop
for ($count = 0; $string =~ /PAT/g; $count++) { }

# Similar, but this time count overlapping matches
$count++ while $string =~ /(?=PAT)/g;
```

To find the Nth match, it's easiest to keep your own counter. When you reach the appropriate N, do whatever you care to. A similar technique could be used to find every N^{th} match by checking for multiples of N using the modulus operator. For example, (++$count % 3) == 0 would be every third match.

If this is too much bother, you can always extract all matches and then hunt for the ones you'd like.

```
$pond  = 'One fish two fish red fish blue fish';

# using a temporary
@colors = ($pond =~ /(\w+)\s+fish\b/gi);     # get all matches
$color  = $colors[2];                        # then the one we want

# or without a temporary array
$color = ( $pond =~ /(\w+)\s+fish\b/gi )[2]; # just grab element 3

print "The third fish in the pond is $color.\n";
The third fish in the pond is red.
```

Or finding all even-numbered fish:

```
$count = 0;
$_ = 'One fish two fish red fish blue fish';
@evens = grep { $count++ % 2 == 1 } /(\w+)\s+fish\b/gi;
print "Even numbered fish are @evens.\n";
Even numbered fish are two blue.
```

For substitution, the replacement value should be a code expression that returns the proper string. Make sure to return the original as a replacement string for the cases you aren't interested in changing. Here we fish out the fourth specimen and turn it into a snack:

```
$count = 0;
s{
    \b                  # makes next \w more efficient
    ( \w+ )             # this is what we'll be changing
    (
      \s+ fish \b
    )
}{
    if (++$count == 4) {
        "sushi" . $2;
    } else {
```

```
            $1   . $2;
        }
}gex;
One fish two fish red fish sushi fish
```

Picking out the last match instead of the first one is a fairly common task. The easiest way is to skip the beginning part greedily. After `/.*\b(\w+)\s+fish\b/`, for example, the $1 variable would have the last fish.

Another way to get arbitrary counts is to make a global match in list context to produce all hits, then extract the desired element of that list:

```
$pond = 'One fish two fish red fish blue fish swim here.';
$color = ( $pond =~ /\b(\w+)\s+fish\b/gi )[-1];
print "Last fish is $color.\n";
Last fish is blue.
```

If you need to express this same notion of finding the last match in a single pattern without /g, you can do so with the negative lookahead assertion `(?!THING)`. When you want the last match of arbitrary pattern A, you find A followed by any number of characters not followed by A. The general construct is `A(?!.*A)`, which can be broken up for legibility:

```
m{
    A               # find some pattern A
    (?!             # mustn't be able to find
        .*          # something
        A           # and A
    )
}x
```

That leaves us with this approach for selecting the last fish:

```
$pond = 'One fish two fish red fish blue fish swim here.';
if ($pond =~ m{
                    \b  (  \w+) \s+ fish \b
                (?! .* \b fish \b )
            }six )
{
    print "Last fish is $1.\n";
} else {
    print "Failed!\n";
}
Last fish is blue.
```

This approach has the advantage that it can fit in just one pattern, which makes it suitable for similar situations as shown in Recipe 6.17. It has its disadvantages, though. It's obviously much harder to read and understand, although once you learn the formula, it's not too bad. But it also runs more slowly though—around twice as slowly on the data set tested above.

See Also

The behavior of m//g in scalar context is given in the "Regexp Quote-like Operators" section of *perlop*(1), and in the "Pattern Matching Operators" section of Chapter 2 of *Programming Perl*; zero-width positive lookahead assertions are shown in the "Regular Expressions" section of *perlre*(1), and in the "Rules of Regular Expression Matching" section of Chapter 2 of *Programming Perl*

6.6. Matching Multiple Lines

Problem

You want to use regular expressions on a string containing more than one line, but the special characters . (any character but newline), ^ (start of string), and $ (end of string) don't seem to work for you. This might happen if you're reading in multiline records or the whole file at once.

Solution

Use /m, /s, or both as pattern modifiers. /s lets . match newline (normally it doesn't). If the string had more than one line in it, then /foo.*bar/s could match a "foo" on one line and a "bar" on a following line. This doesn't affect dots in character classes like [#%.], since they are regular periods anyway.

The /m modifier lets ^ and $ match next to a newline. /^=head[1-7]$/m would match that pattern not just at the beginning of the record, but anywhere right after a newline as well.

Discussion

A common, brute-force approach to parsing documents where newlines are not significant is to read the file one paragraph at a time (or sometimes even the entire file as one string) and then extract tokens one by one. To match across newlines, you need to make . match a newline; it ordinarily does not. In cases where newlines are important and you've read more than one line into a string, you'll probably prefer to have ^ and $ match beginning- and end-of-line, not just beginning- and end-of-string.

The difference between /m and /s is important: /m makes ^ and $ match next to a newline, while /s makes . match newlines. You can even use them together— they're not mutually exclusive options.

Example 6-2 creates a filter to strip HTML tags out of each file in @ARGV and send the results to STDOUT. First we undefine the record separator so each read operation fetches one entire file. (There could be more than one file, because @ARGV has several arguments in it. In this case, each read would get a whole file.) Then we strip out instances of beginning and ending angle brackets, plus anything in between them. We can't use just `.*` for two reasons: first, it would match closing angle brackets, and second, the dot wouldn't cross newline boundaries. Using `.*?` in conjunction with `/s` solves these problems—at least in this case.

Example 6-2. killtags

```perl
#!/usr/bin/perl
# killtags - very bad html tag killer
undef $/;               # each read is whole file
while (<>) {            # get one whole file at a time
    s/<.*?>//gs;        # strip tags (terribly)
    print;             # print file to STDOUT
}
```

Because this is just a single character, it would be much faster to use `s/<[^>]*>//gs`, but that's still a naïve approach: It doesn't correctly handle tags inside HTML comments or angle brackets in quotes (`<IMG SRC="here.gif" ALT="<<Ooh la la!>>">`). Recipe 20.6 explains how to avoid these problems.

Example 6-3 takes a plain text document and looks for lines at the start of paragraphs that look like `"Chapter 20: Better Living Through Chemisery"`. It wraps these with an appropriate HTML level one header. Because the pattern is relatively complex, we use the `/x` modifier so we can embed whitespace and comments.

Example 6-3. headerfy

```perl
#!/usr/bin/perl
# headerfy: change certain chapter headers to html
$/ = '';
while ( <> ) {                  # fetch a paragraph
    s{
            \A                  # start of record
            (                   # capture in $1
                Chapter         # text string
                \s+             # mandatory whitespace
                \d+             # decimal number
                \s*             # optional whitespace
                :               # a real colon
                . *             # anything not a newline till end of line
            )
    }{<H1>$1</H1>}gx;
    print;
}
```

Here it is as a one-liner from the command line if those extended comments just get in the way of understanding:

```
% perl -00pe 's{\A(Chapter\s+\d+\s*:.*)}{<H1>$1</H1>}gx' datafile
```

This problem is interesting because we need to be able to specify both start-of-record and end-of-line in the same pattern. We could normally use ^ for start-of-record, but we need $ to indicate not only end-of-record, but also end-of-line as well. We add the /m modifier, which changes both ^ and $. So instead of using ^ to match beginning-of-record, we use \A instead. (We're not using it here, but in case you're interested, the version of $ that always matches end-of-record even in the presence of /m is \Z.)

The following example demonstrates using both /s and /m together. That's because we want ^ to match the beginning of any line in the paragraph and also want dot to be able to match a newline. (Because they are unrelated, using them together is simply the sum of the parts. If you have the questionable habit of using "single line" as a mnemonic for /s and "multiple line" for /m, then you may think you can't use them together.) The predefined variable $. represents the record number of the last read file. The predefined variable $ARGV is the file automatically opened by implicit <ARGV> processing.

```
$/ = '';              # paragraph read mode for readline access
while (<ARGV>) {
    while (m#^START(.*?)^END#sm) {  # /s makes . span line boundaries
                                    # /m makes ^ match near newlines
        print "chunk $. in $ARGV has <<$1>>\n";
    }
}
```

If you've already committed to using the /m modifier, you can use \A and \Z to get the old meanings of ^ and $ respectively. But what if you've used the /s modifier and want to get the original meaning of .? You can use [^\n]. If you don't care to use /s but want the notion of matching any character, you could construct a character class that matches any one byte, such as [\000-\377] or even [\d\D]. You can't use [.\n] because . is not special in a character class.

See Also

The $/ variable in *perlvar*(1) and in the "Special Variables" section of Chapter 2 of *Programming Perl*; the /s and /m modifiers in *perlre*(1) and "The Fine Print" section of Chapter 2 of *Programming Perl*; the "String Anchors" section of *Mastering Regular Expressions*; we talk more about the special variable $/ in Chapter 8

6.7. *Reading Records with a Pattern Separator*

Problem

You want to read in records separated by a pattern, but Perl doesn't allow its input record separator variable to be a regular expression.

Many problems, most obviously those involving the parsing of complex file formats, become a lot simpler when you are easily able to extract records that might be separated by a number of different strings.

Solution

Read the whole file and use `split`:

```
undef $/;
@chunks = split(/pattern/, <FILEHANDLE>);
```

Discussion

Perl's record separator must be a fixed string, not a pattern. (After all, *awk* has to be better at *something*.) To sidestep this limitation, undefine the input record separator entirely so that the next line-read operation gets the rest of the file. This is sometimes called *slurp* mode, because it slurps in the whole file as one big string. Then `split` that huge string using the record separating pattern as the first argument.

Here's an example, where the input stream is a text file that includes lines consisting of ".Se", ".Ch", and ".Ss", which are special codes in the *troff* macro set that this book was developed under. These lines are the separators, and we want to find text that falls between them.

```
# .Ch, .Se and .Ss divide chunks of STDIN
{
    local $/ = undef;
    @chunks = split(/^\.(Ch|Se|Ss)$/m, <>);
}
print "I read ", scalar(@chunks), " chunks.\n";
```

We create a localized version of $/ so its previous value gets restored after the block finishes. By using `split` with parentheses in the pattern, captured separators are also returned. This way the data elements in the return list alternate with elements containing "Se", "Ch", or "Ss".

If you didn't want delimiters returned but still needed parentheses, you could use non-capturing parentheses in the pattern: `/^\.(?:Ch|Se|Ss)$/m`.

If you just want to split *before* a pattern but include the pattern in the return, use a look-ahead assertion: /^(?=\.(?:Ch|Se|Ss))/m. That way each chunk starts with the pattern.

Be aware that this uses a lot of memory if the file is large. However, with today's machines and your typical text files, this is less often an issue now than it once was. Just don't try it on a 200-MB logfile unless you have plenty of virtual memory to use to swap out to disk with! Even if you do have enough swap space, you'll likely end up thrashing.

See Also

The $/ variable in *perlvar*(1) and in the "Special Variables" section of Chapter 2 of *Programming Perl*; the split function in *perlfunc*(1) and Chapter 3 of *Programming Perl*; we talk more about the special variable $/ in Chapter 8

6.8. Extracting a Range of Lines

Problem

You want to extract all lines from one starting pattern through an ending pattern or from a starting line number up to an ending line number.

A common example of this is extracting the first 10 lines of a file (line numbers 1 to 10) or just the body of a mail message (everything past the blank line).

Solution

Use the operators .. or ... with patterns or line numbers. The operator ... doesn't return true if both its tests are true on the same line, but .. does.

```
while (<>) {
    if (/BEGIN PATTERN/ .. /END PATTERN/) {
        # line falls between BEGIN and END in the
        # text, inclusive.
    }
}

while (<>) {
    if ($FIRST_LINE_NUM .. $LAST_LINE_NUM) {
        # operate only between first and last line, inclusive.
    }
}
```

The ... operator doesn't test both conditions at once if the first one is true.

```
while (<>) {
    if (/BEGIN PATTERN/ ... /END PATTERN/) {
        # line is between BEGIN and END on different lines
    }
}

while (<>) {
    if ($FIRST_LINE_NUM ... $LAST_LINE_NUM) {
        # operate only between first and last line, but not same
    }
}
```

Discussion

The range operators, .. and ..., are probably the least understood of Perl's myriad operators. They were designed to allow easy extraction of ranges of lines without forcing the programmer to retain explicit state information. When used in a scalar sense, such as in the test of if and while statements, these operators return a true or false value that's partially dependent on what they last returned. The expression left_operand .. right_operand returns false until left_operand is true, but once that test has been met, it stops evaluating left_operand and keeps returning true until right_operand becomes true, after which it restarts the cycle. To put it another way, the first operand turns on the construct as soon as it returns a true value, whereas the second one turns it off as soon as *it* returns true.

These conditions are absolutely arbitrary. In fact, you could write mytestfunc1() .. mytestfunc2(), although in practice this is seldom done. Instead, the range operators are usually used either with line numbers as operands (the first example), patterns as operands (the second example), or both.

```
# command-line to print lines 15 through 17 inclusive (see below)
perl -ne 'print if 15 .. 17' datafile

# print out all <XMP> .. </XMP> displays from HTML doc
while (<>) {
    print if m#<XMP>#i .. m#</XMP>#i;
}

# same, but as shell command
% perl -ne 'print if m#<XMP>#i .. m#</XMP>#i' document.html
```

If either operand is a numeric literal, the range operators implicitly compare against the $. variable ($NR or $INPUT_LINE_NUMBER if you use English). Be careful with implicit line number comparisons here. You must specify literal numbers in your code, not variables containing line numbers. That means you can simply say 3 .. 5 in a conditional, but not $n .. $m where $n and $m are 3 and 5 respectively. You have to be more explicit and test the $. variable directly.

```
perl -ne 'BEGIN { $top=3; $bottom=5 }  print if $top .. $bottom' /etc/passwd
          # previous command FAILS
perl -ne 'BEGIN { $top=3; $bottom=5 } \
    print if $. == $top .. $. ==     $bottom' /etc/passwd     # works
perl -ne 'print if 3 .. 5' /etc/passwd   # also works
```

The difference between .. and ... is their behavior when both operands can be true on the same line. Consider these two cases:

```
print if /begin/ .. /end/;
print if /begin/ ... /end/;
```

Given the line "You may not end ere you begin", both the double- and triple-dot versions of the range operator above return true. But the code using .. will not print any further lines. That's because .. tests both conditions on the same line once the first test matches, and the second test tells it that it's reached the end of its region. On the other hand, ... will continue until the *next* line that matches /end/ because it never tries to test both operands on the same time.

You may mix and match conditions of different sorts, as in:

```
while (<>) {
    $in_header =   1  .. /^$/;
    $in_body   = /^$/ .. eof();
}
```

The first assignment sets $in_header to be true from the first input line until after the blank line separating the header, such as from a mail message, a news posting, or even an HTTP header. (Technically speaking, an HTTP header should have both linefeeds and carriage returns as network line terminators, but in practice, servers are liberal in what they accept.) The second assignment sets $in_body to be true starting as soon as the first blank line is encountered, up through end of file. Because range operators do not retest their initial condition, any further blank lines (such as those between paragraphs) won't be noticed.

Here's an example. It reads files containing mail messages and prints addresses it finds in headers. Each address is printed only once. The extent of the header is from a line beginning with a "From:" up through the first blank line. If we're not within that range, go on to the next line. This isn't an RFC-822 notion of an address, but it's easy to write.

```
%seen = ();
while (<>) {
    next unless /^From:?\s/i .. /^$/;
    while (/([^<>(),;\s]+\@[^<>(),;\s]+)/g) {
        print "$1\n" unless $seen{$1}++;
    }
}
```

If this all range business seems mighty strange, chalk it up to trying to support the *s2p* and *a2p* translators for converting *sed* and *awk* code into Perl. Both those tools have range operators that must work in Perl.

See Also

The `..` and `...` operators in the "Range Operator" sections of *perlop*(1) and Chapter 2 of *Programming Perl*; the entry for `$NR` in *perlvar*(1) and the "Special Variables" section of Chapter 2 of *Programming Perl*

6.9. Matching Shell Globs as Regular Expressions

Problem

You want to allow users to specify matches using traditional shell wildcards, not full Perl regular expressions. Wildcards are easier to type than full regular expressions for simple cases.

Solution

Use the following subroutine to convert four shell wildcard characters into their equivalent regular expression; all other characters will be quoted to render them literals.

```
sub glob2pat {
    my $globstr = shift;
    my %patmap = (
        '*' => '.*',
        '?' => '.',
        '[' => '[',
        ']' => ']',
    );
    $globstr =~ s{(.)} { $patmap{$1} || "\Q$1" }ge;
    return '^' . $globstr . '$';
}
```

Discussion

A Perl pattern is not the same as a shell wildcard pattern. The shell's `*.*` is not a valid regular expression. Its meaning as a pattern would be `/^.*\..*$/`, which is admittedly much less fun to type.

The function given in the Solution makes these conversions for you, following the standard wildcard rules used by the `glob` built-in.

Shell	Perl
`list.?`	`^list\..$`
`project.*`	`^project\..*$`
`*old`	`^.*old$`
`type*.[ch]`	`^type.*\.[ch]$`
`*.*`	`^.*\..*$`
`*`	`^.*$`

In the shell, the rules are different. The entire pattern is implicitly anchored at the ends. A question mark maps into any character, an asterisk is any amount of anything, and brackets are character ranges. Everything else is normal.

Most shells do more than simple one-directory globbing. For instance, you can say `*/*` to mean "all the files in all the subdirectories of the current directory." Furthermore, most shells don't list files whose names begin with a period, unless you explicitly put that leading period into your glob pattern. Our `glob2pat` function doesn't do these things—if you need them, use the File::KGlob module from CPAN.

See Also

Your system's *csh*(1) and *ksh*(1) manpages; the `glob` function in *perlfunc*(1) and Chapter 3 of *Programming Perl*; the documentation for the CPAN module Glob::DosGlob; the "I/O Operators" section of *perlop*(1) and the "Filename Globbing Operator" section of Chapter 2 of *Programming Perl*; we talk more about globbing in Recipe 9.6

6.10. Speeding Up Interpolated Matches

Problem

You want your function or program to take one or more regular expressions as arguments, but doing so seems to run slower than using literals.

Solution

To overcome this bottleneck, if you have only one pattern whose value won't change during the entire run of a program, store it in a string and use `/$pattern/o`.

```
while ($line = <>) {
    if ($line =~ /$pattern/o) {
        # do something
    }
}
```

If you have more than one pattern, however, that won't work. Use one of the three techniques outlined in the Discussion for a speed-up of an order of magnitude or so.

Discussion

When Perl compiles a program, it converts patterns into an internal form. This conversion occurs at compile time for patterns without variables in them, but at run time for those that do contain variables. That means that interpolating variables into patterns, as in /$pattern/, can slow your program down. This is particularly noticeable when $pattern changes often.

The /o modifier is a promise from the script's author that the values of any variables interpolated into that pattern will not change—or that if they do, Perl should disregard any such changes. Given such a promise, Perl need only interpolate the variable and compile the pattern the first time it encounters the match. But if the interpolated variable were to change, Perl wouldn't notice. Make sure to use it only on unchanging variables, or else wrong answers will result.

Using /o on patterns without interpolated variables does not speed anything up. The /o modifier is also of no help when you have an unknown number of regular expressions and need to check one or more strings against all of these patterns. Nor is it of any use when the interpolated variable is a function argument, since each call of the function gives the variable a new value.

Example 6-4 is an example of the slow but straightforward technique for matching many patterns against many lines. The array @popstates contains the standard two-letter abbreviations for some of the places in the heartland of North America where we normally refer to soft drinks as *pop* (*soda* to us means either plain soda water or else handmade delicacies from the soda fountain at the corner drugstore, preferably with ice cream). The goal is to print out any line of input that contains any of those places, matching them at word boundaries only. It doesn't use /o because the variable that holds the pattern keeps changing.

Example 6-4. popgrep1

```
#!/usr/bin/perl
# popgrep1 - grep for abbreviations of places that say "pop"
# version 1: slow but obvious way
@popstates = qw(CO ON MI WI MN);
LINE: while (defined($line = <>)) {
    for $state (@popstates) {
        if ($line =~ /\b$state\b/) {
            print; next LINE;
        }
    }
}
```

Such a direct, obvious, brute-force approach is also horribly slow because it has to recompile all patterns with each line of input. Three different ways of addressing this are described in this section. One builds a string of Perl code and `eval`s it; one caches the internal representations of regular expressions in closures; and one uses the Regexp module from CPAN to hold compiled regular expressions.

The traditional way to get Perl to speed up a multiple match is to build up a string containing the code and `eval "$code"` it. Example 6-5 contains a version that uses this technique.

Example 6-5. popgrep2

```perl
#!/usr/bin/perl
# popgrep2 - grep for abbreviations of places that say "pop"
# version 2: eval strings; fast but hard to quote
@popstates = qw(CO ON MI WI MN);
$code = 'while (defined($line = <>)) {';
for $state (@popstates) {
    $code .= "\tif (\$line =~ /\\b$state\\b/) { print \$line; next; }\n";
}
$code .= '}';
print "CODE IS\n----\n$code\n----\n" if 0;   # turn on to debug
eval $code;
die if $@;
```

The `popgrep2` program builds strings like this:

```perl
    while (defined($line = <>)) {
        if ($line =~ /\bCO\b/) { print $line; next; }
        if ($line =~ /\bON\b/) { print $line; next; }
        if ($line =~ /\bMI\b/) { print $line; next; }
        if ($line =~ /\bWI\b/) { print $line; next; }
        if ($line =~ /\bMN\b/) { print $line; next; }
    }
```

As you see, those end up looking like constant strings to `eval`. We put the entire loop and pattern match in the `eval` text, too, which makes it run faster.

The worst thing about this `eval "STRING"` approach is that it's difficult to get the quoting and escaping right. The `dequote` function from Recipe 1.11 can make it easier to read, but escaping variables whose use is delayed will still be an issue. Also, none of the strings can contain a slash, since that's what we're using as a delimiter for the `m//` operator.

A solution to these problems is a subtle technique first developed by Jeffrey Friedl. The key here is building an anonymous subroutine that caches the compiled patterns in the closure it creates. To do this, we `eval` a string containing the definition of an anonymous subroutine to match any of the supplied patterns. Perl compiles the pattern once, when the subroutine is defined. The string is evaluated to give you comparatively quick matching ability. An explanation of the algorithm

can be found at the end of the section "Regex Compilation, the /o Modifier, and
Efficiency" in Chapter 7 of *Mastering Regular Expressions*.

Example 6-6 is a version of our pop grepper that uses that technique.

Example 6-6. popgrep3

```perl
#!/usr/bin/perl
# popgrep3 - grep for abbreviations of places that say "pop"
# version 3: use build_match_func algorithm
@popstates = qw(CO ON MI WI MN);
    $expr = join('||', map { "m/\\b\$popstates[$_]\\b/o" } 0..$#popstates);
$match_any = eval "sub { $expr }";
die if $@;
while (<>) {
    print if &$match_any;
}
```

The string that gets evaluated ends up looking like this, modulo formatting:

```perl
sub {
        m/\b$popstates[0]\b/o || m/\b$popstates[1]\b/o ||
        m/\b$popstates[2]\b/o || m/\b$popstates[3]\b/o ||
        m/\b$popstates[4]\b/o
    }
```

The reference to the @popstates array is locked up inside the closure. Each one
is different, so the /o is safe here.

Example 6-7 is a generalized form of this technique showing how to create functions that return true if any of the patterns match or if all match.

Example 6-7. grepauth

```perl
#!/usr/bin/perl
# grepauth - print lines that mention both Tom and Nat

$multimatch = build_match_all(q/Tom/, q/Nat/);
while (<>) {
    print if &$multimatch;
}
exit;

sub build_match_any { build_match_func('||', @_) }
sub build_match_all { build_match_func('&&', @_) }
sub build_match_func {
    my $condition = shift;
    my @pattern = @_;   # must be lexical variable, not dynamic one
    my $expr = join $condition => map { "m/\$pattern[$_]/o" } (0..$#pattern);
    my $match_func = eval "sub { local \$_ = shift if \@_; $expr }";
    die if $@;   # propagate $@; this shouldn't happen!
    return $match_func;
}
```

Using eval "STRING" on interpolated strings as we did in *popgrep2* is a hack that happens to work. Using lexical variables that get bound up in a closure as in *popgrep3* and the build_match_* functions is deep enough magic that even Perl wizards stare at it a while before they believe in it. Of course, it still works whether they believe in it or not.

What you really need is some way to get Perl to compile each pattern once and let you directly refer to the compiled form later on. Such functionality is directly supported in the 5.005 release in the form of a qr// regular-expression quoting operator. For prior releases, that's exactly what the experimental Regexp module from CPAN was designed for. Objects created by this module represent compiled regular expression patterns. Using the match method on these objects matches the pattern against the string argument. Methods in the class exist for extracting backreferences, determining where pattern matched, and passing flags corresponding to modifiers like /i.

Example 6-8 is a version of our program that demonstrates a simple use of this module.

Example 6-8. popgrep4

```
#!/usr/bin/perl
# popgrep4 - grep for abbreviations of places that say "pop"
# version 4: use Regexp module
use Regexp;
@popstates = qw(CO ON MI WI MN);
@poppats   = map { Regexp->new( '\b' . $_ . '\b') } @popstates;
while (defined($line = <>)) {
    for $patobj (@poppats) {
        print $line if $patobj->match($line);
    }
}
```

You might wonder about the comparative speeds of these approaches. When run against the 22,000 line text file (the Jargon File, to be exact), version 1 ran in 7.92 seconds, version 2 in merely 0.53 seconds, version 3 in 0.79 seconds, and version 4 in 1.74 seconds. The last technique is a lot easier to understand than the others, although it does run slightly slower than they do. It's also more flexible.

See Also

Interpolation is explained in the "Scalar Value Constructors" section of *perldata*(1), and in the "String Literals" section of Chapter 2 of *Programming Perl*; the /o modifier in *perlre*(1) and the "Pattern Matching" section of Chapter 2 of *Programming Perl*; the "Regex Compilation, the /o Modifier, and Efficiency" section of Chapter 7 of *Mastering Regular Expressions*; the documentation with the CPAN module Regexp

6.11. *Testing for a Valid Pattern*

Problem

You want to let users enter their own patterns, but an invalid one would abort your program the first time you tried to use it.

Solution

Test the pattern in an `eval {}` construct first, matching against some dummy string. If `$@` is not set, no exception occurred, so you know the pattern successfully compiled as a valid regular expression. Here is a loop that continues prompting until the user supplies a valid pattern:

```
do {
    print "Pattern? ";
    chomp($pat = <>);
    eval { "" =~ /$pat/ };
    warn "INVALID PATTERN $@" if $@;
} while $@;
```

Here's a standalone subroutine that verifies whether a pattern is valid.

```
sub is_valid_pattern {
    my $pat = shift;
    return eval { "" =~ /$pat/; 1 } || 0;
}
```

That one relies upon the block returning 1 if it completes, which in the case of an exception, never happens.

Discussion

There's no end to patterns that won't compile. The user could mistakenly enter `"<I\s*[^>"`, `"*** GET RICH ***"`, or `"+5-i"`. If you blindly use the proffered pattern in your program, it will cause an exception, normally a fatal event.

The tiny program in Example 6-9 demonstrates this.

Example 6-9. paragrep

```
#!/usr/bin/perl
# paragrep - trivial paragraph grepper
die "usage: $0 pat [files]\n" unless @ARGV;
$/ = '';
$pat = shift;
eval { "" =~ /$pat/; 1 }      or die "$0: Bad pattern $pat: $@\n";
while (<>) {
    print "$ARGV $.: $_" if /$pat/o;
}
```

That /o is a promise to Perl that the interpolated variable's contents are constant over the program's entire run. It's an efficiency hack. Even if $pat changes, Perl won't notice.

You could encapsulate this in a function call that returns 1 if the block completes and 0 if not as shown in the Solution section. Although eval "/$pat/" would also work to trap the exception, it has two other problems. First of all, there couldn't be any slashes (or whatever your chosen pattern delimiter is) in the string the user entered. More importantly, it would open a drastic security hole that you almost certainly want to avoid. Strings like this could really ruin your day:

```
$pat = "You lose @{[ system('rm -rf *')]} big here";
```

If you don't wish to provide the user with a real pattern, you can always meta-quote the string first:

```
$safe_pat = quotemeta($pat);
something() if /$safe_pat/;
```

Or, even easier, use:

```
something() if /\Q$pat/;
```

But if you're going to do that, why are you using pattern matching at all? In that case, a simple use of **index** would be enough.

By letting the user supply a real pattern, you give them the power into do interesting and useful things. This is a good thing. You just have to be slightly careful, that's all. Suppose they wanted to enter a case-insensitive pattern, but you didn't provide the program with an option like *grep*'s -i option. By permitting full patterns, the user can enter an embedded /i modifier as (?i), as in /(?i)stuff/.

What happens if the interpolated pattern expands to nothing? If $pat is the empty string, what does /$pat/ match—that is, what does a blank // match? It doesn't match the start of all possible strings. Surprisingly enough, matching the null pattern exhibits the dubiously useful semantics of reusing the previous successfully matched pattern. In practice, this is hard to make good use of in Perl.

Even if you use **eval** to check the pattern for validity, beware: matching certain patterns takes time that is exponentially proportional to the length of the string being matched. There is no good way to detect one of these, and if the user sticks you with one, your program will appear to hang as it and the entropic heat death of the universe have a long race to see who finishes first. Setting a timer to jump out of a long-running command offers some hope for a way out of this but (as of the 5.004 release) still carries with it the possibility of a core dump if you interrupt Perl at an inopportune moment.

See Also

The `eval` function in *perlfunc*(1) and in Chapter 2 of *Programming Perl*;
Recipe 10.12

6.12. Honoring Locale Settings in Regular Expressions

Problem

You want to translate case when in a different locale, or you want to make \w
match letters with diacritics, such as *José* or *déjà vu.*

For example, let's say you're given half a gigabyte of text written in German and
told to index it. You want to extract words (with \w+) and convert them to lowercase (with `lc` or \L), but the normal versions of \w and `lc` neither match the German words nor change the case of accented letters.

Solution

Perl's regular-expression and text-manipulation routines have hooks to POSIX
locale setting. If you use the `use locale` pragma, accented characters are taken
care of—assuming a reasonable `LC_CTYPE` specification and system support for
the same.

```
use locale;
```

Discussion

By default, \w+ and case-mapping functions operate on upper- and lowercase letters, digits, and underscores. This works only for the simplest of English words,
failing even on many common imports. The `use locale` directive lets you redefine what a "word character" means.

In Example 6-10 you can see the difference in output between having selected the
English ("en") locale and the German ("de") one.

Example 6-10. localeg

```
#!/usr/bin/perl -w
# localeg - demonstrate locale effects

use locale;
use POSIX 'locale_h';

$name = "andreas k\xF6nig";
@locale{qw(German English)} = qw(de_DE.ISO_8859-1 us-ascii);
```

Example 6-10. localeg

```
setlocale(LC_CTYPE, $locale{English})
  or die "Invalid locale $locale{English}";
@english_names = ();
while ($name =~ /\b(\w+)\b/g) {
        push(@english_names, ucfirst($1));
}
setlocale(LC_CTYPE, $locale{German})
  or die "Invalid locale $locale{German}";
@german_names = ();
while ($name =~ /\b(\w+)\b/g) {
        push(@german_names, ucfirst($1));
}

print "English names: @english_names\n";
print "German names:  @german_names\n";
```
English names: Andreas K Nig
German names: Andreas König

This approach relies on POSIX locale support, which your system may or may not
provide. Even if your system does claim to provide POSIX locale support, the standard does not specify the locale names. As you can tell, portability of this
approach is not assured.

See Also

The treatment of \b, \w, and \s in *perlre*(1) and in the "Regular Expression Bestiary" section of Chapter 2 of *Programming Perl*; the treatment of locales in Perl in
perllocale(1); your system's *locale*(3) manpage; we discuss locales in greater depth
in Recipe 6.2; the "Perl and the POSIX locale" section of Chapter 7 of *Mastering
Regular Expressions*

6.13. Approximate Matching

Problem

You want to match something fuzzily.

Any time you want to be forgiving of misspellings in user input, you want to do
fuzzy matching.

Solution

Use the String::Approx module, available from CPAN:

```
use String::Approx qw(amatch);

if (amatch("PATTERN", @list)) {
```

```
        # matched
    }

@matches = amatch("PATTERN", @list);
```

Discussion

String::Approx calculates the difference between the pattern and each string in the list. If less than a certain number (by default, 10 percent of the length of the pattern) one-character insertions, deletions, or substitutions are required to make the string from the pattern, the string "matches" the pattern. In scalar context, `amatch` returns the number of successful matches. In list context, it returns those strings that matched.

```
use String::Approx qw(amatch);
open(DICT, "/usr/dict/words")                    or die "Can't open dict: $!";
while(<DICT>) {
    print if amatch("balast");
}

ballast
balustrade
blast
blastula
sandblast
```

You can also pass options to `amatch` to control case-insensitivity and the number of insertions, deletions, or substitutions to have. These options are passed in as a list reference; they're fully described in the String::Approx documentation.

It must be noted that using the module's matching function seems to run between 10 and 40 times slower than Perl's built-in matching function. Only use String::Approx if you're after fuzziness in your matching that Perl's regular expressions can't provide.

See Also

The documentation for the CPAN module String::Approx; Recipe 1.16

6.14. Matching from Where the Last Pattern Left Off

Problem

You want to match again from where the last pattern left off.

This is a useful approach to take when repeatedly extracting data in chunks from a string.

Solution

Use a combination of the /g match modifier, the \G pattern anchor, and the pos function.

Discussion

If you use the /g modifier on a match, the regular expression engine keeps track of its position in the string when it finished matching. The next time you match with /g, the engine starts looking for a match from this remembered position. This lets you use a while loop to extract the information you want from the string.

```
while (/(\d+)/g) {
    print "Found $1\n";
}
```

You can also use \G in your pattern to anchor it to the end of the previous match. For example, if you had a number stored in a string with leading blanks, you could change each leading blank into the digit zero this way:

```
$n = "   49 here";
$n =~ s/\G /0/g;
print $n;
00049 here
```

You can also make good use of \G in a while loop. Here we use \G to parse a comma-separated list of numbers (e.g., "3,4,5,9,120"):

```
while (/\G,?(\d+)/g) {
    print "Found number $1\n";
}
```

By default, when your match fails (when we run out of numbers in the examples, for instance) the remembered position is reset to the start. If you don't want this to happen, perhaps because you want to continue matching from that position but with a different pattern, use the modifier /c with /g:

```
$_ = "The year 1752 lost 10 days on the 3rd of September";

while (/(\d+)/gc) {
    print "Found number $1\n";
}

if (/\G(\S+)/g) {
    print "Found $1 after the last number.\n";
}

Found number 1752
Found number 10
Found number 3
Found rd after the last number.
```

As you can see, successive patterns can use /g on a string and in doing so change the location of the last successful match. The position of the last successful match is associated with the scalar being matched against, not with the pattern. Further, the position is not copied when you copy the string, nor saved if you use the ill-named `local` operator.

The location of the last successful match can be read and set with the `pos` function, which takes as its argument the string whose position you want to get or set. If no argument is given, `pos` operates on `$_`:

```
print "The position in \$a is ", pos($a);
pos($a) = 30;
print "The position in \$_ is ", pos;
pos = 30;
```

See Also

The /g modifier is discussed in *perlre*(1) and the "The Rules of Regular Expression Matching" section of Chapter 2 of *Programming Perl*

6.15. *Greedy and Non-Greedy Matches*

Problem

You have a pattern with a greedy quantifier like *, +, ?, or {}, and you want to stop it from being greedy.

A classic case of this is the naïve substitution to remove tags from HTML. Although it looks appealing, `s#<TT>.*</TT>##gsi`, actually deletes everything from the first open TT tag through the last closing one. This would turn `"Even <TT>vi</TT> can edit <TT>troff</TT> effectively."` into `"Even  effectively"`, completely changing the meaning of the sentence!

Solution

Replace the offending greedy quantifier with the corresponding non-greedy version. That is, change *, +, ?, and {} into *?, +?, ??, and {}?, respectively.

Discussion

Perl has two sets of quantifiers: the *maximal* ones *, +, ?, and {} (sometimes called *greedy*) and the *minimal* ones *?, +?, ??, and {}? (sometimes called *stingy*). For instance, given the string `"Perl is a Swiss Army Chainsaw!"`, the pattern `/(r.*s)/` matches `"rl is a Swiss Army Chains"` whereas `/(r.*?s)/` matches `"rl is"`.

With maximal quantifiers, when you ask to match a variable number of times, such as zero or more times for * or one or more times for +, the matching engine prefers the "or more" portion of that description. Thus `/foo.*bar/` matches from the first `"foo"` up to the last `"bar"` in the string, rather than merely the next `"bar"`, as some might expect. To make any of the regular expression repetition operators prefer stingy matching over greedy matching, add an extra ?. So *? matches zero or more times, but rather than match as much as it possibly can the way * would, it matches as little as possible.

```
# greedy pattern
s/<.*>//gs;                    # try to remove tags, very badly

# non-greedy pattern
s/<.*?>//gs;                   # try to remove tags, still rather badly
```

This approach doesn't remove tags from all possible HTML correctly, because a single regular expression is not an acceptable replacement for a real parser. See Recipe 20.6 for the right way to do this.

Minimal matching isn't all it's cracked up to be. Don't fall into the trap of thinking that including the partial pattern `BEGIN.*?END` in a pattern amidst other elements will always match the shortest amount of text between occurrences of `BEGIN` and `END`. Imagine the pattern `/BEGIN(.*?)END/`. If matched against the string `"BEGIN and BEGIN and END"`, $1 would contain `"and BEGIN and"`. This is probably not what you want.

Imagine if we were trying to pull out everything between bold-italic pairs:

```
<b><i>this</i> and <i>that</i> are important</b> Oh, <b><i>me too!</i></b>
```

A pattern to find only text *between* bold-italic HTML pairs, that is, text that doesn't include them, might appear to be this one:

```
m{ <b><i>(.*?)</i></b> }sx
```

You might be surprised to learn that the pattern doesn't do that. Many people incorrectly understand this as matching a `"<b><i>"` sequence, then something that's not `"<b><i>"`, and then `"</i></b>"`, leaving the intervening text in $1. While often it works out that way due to the input data, that's not really what it says. It just matches the shortest leftmost substring that satisfies the *entire pattern*. In this case, that's the entire string. If the intention were to extract only stuff between `"<b><i>"` and its corresponding `"</i></b>"`, with no other bold-italic tags in between, it would be incorrect.

If the string in question is just one character, a negated class is remarkably more efficient than a minimal match, as in `/X([^X]*)X/`. But the general way to say "match BEGIN, then not BEGIN, then END" for any arbitrary values of BEGIN and END is as follows (this also stores the intervening part in $1):

```
/BEGIN((?:(?!BEGIN).)*)END/
```

Applying this to the HTML-matching code, we end up with something like:

```
m{ <b><i>(  (?: (?!</b>|</i>). )*  ) </i></b> }sx
```

or perhaps:

```
m{ <b><i>(  (?: (?!</[ib]>). )*  ) </i></b> }sx
```

Jeffrey Friedl points out that this quick-and-dirty method isn't particularly efficient. He suggests crafting a more elaborate pattern when speed really matters, such as:

```
m{
    <b><i>
    [^<]*  # stuff not possibly bad, and not possibly the end.
    (?:
# at this point, we can have '<' if not part of something bad
      (?!  </?[ib]>  )   # what we can't have
      <                  # okay, so match the '<'
      [^<]*              # and continue with more safe stuff
    ) *
    </i></b>
}sx
```

This is a variation on Jeffrey's unrolling-the-loop technique, described in Chapter 5 of *Mastering Regular Expressions.*

See Also

The non-greedy quantifiers in the "Regular Expressions" section of *perlre*(1), and in the "The Rules of Regular Expression Matching" section of Chapter 2 of *Programming Perl*

6.16. *Detecting Duplicate Words*

Problem

You want to check for doubled words in a document.

Solution

Use backreferences in your regular expression.

Discussion

Parentheses in a pattern make the regular expression engine remember what matched that part of the pattern. Later in your pattern, you can refer to the actual string that matched with \1 (indicating the string matched by the first set of parentheses), \2 (for the second string matched by the second set of parentheses), and so on. Don't use $1; it would be treated as a variable and interpolated before the match began. If you match /([A-Z])\1/, that says to match a capital letter followed not just by any capital letter, but by whichever one was captured by the first set of parentheses in that pattern.

This sample code reads its input files by paragraph, with the definition of *paragraph* following Perl's notion of two or more contiguous newlines. Within each paragraph, it finds all duplicate words. It ignores case and can match across newlines.

Here we use /x to embed whitespace and comments to make the regular expression readable. /i lets us match both instances of "is" in the sentence "Is is this ok?". We use /g in a while loop to keep finding duplicate words until we run out of text. Within the pattern, use \b (word boundary) and \s (whitespace) to help pick out whole words and avoid matching "This".

```
$/ = '';                      # paragrep mode
while (<>) {
    while ( m{
                \b            # start at a word boundary (begin letters)
                (\S+)         # find chunk of non-whitespace
                \b            # until another word boundary (end letters)
                (
                    \s+       # separated by some whitespace
                    \1        # and that very same chunk again
                    \b        # until another word boundary
                ) +           # one or more sets of those
            }xig
        )
    {
        print "dup word '$1' at paragraph $.\n";
    }
}
```

That code finds the duplicated *test* in the following paragraph:

```
This is a test
test of the duplicate word finder.
```

The use of a word boundary anchor surrounding \S+ is usually a bad idea because word boundaries are defined as transitions between alphanumunders (that's a \w) and either the edge of the string or a non-alphanumunder. Surrounding it by \b changes \S+ from its normal meaning of one or more non-whitespace characters to a stretch of non-whitespace whose first and last character must be an alphanumunder.

Here's another interesting demonstration of using backreferences. Imagine you had two words in which the end of the first word was the same as the start of the next one, such as "nobody" and "bodysnatcher". You'd like to find that overlapping part and come up with `"nobodysnatcher"`. This is just a variant on the duplicate word problem.

Conventional byte-by-byte processing the way a C programmer would write it would take a great deal of tricky code to solve this problem. But with a backtracking pattern matcher, it just takes one simple pattern match.

```
$a = 'nobody';
$b = 'bodysnatcher';
if ("$a $b" =~ /^(\w+)(\w+) \2(\w+)$/) {
    print "$2 overlaps in $1-$2-$3\n";
}
```
body overlaps in no-body-snatcher

You might think that $1 would first grab up all of `"nobody"` due to greediness. In fact, it does—for a while. But once it's done so, there aren't any more characters to put in $2. So the engine backs up and $1 begrudgingly gives up one character to $2. The space character matches successfully, but then it sees \2, which currently holds merely `"y"`. The next character in the string is not a `"y"`, but a `"b"`. This makes the engine back up all the way, eventually forcing $1 to surrender enough to $2 that the pattern can match something, a space, then that same thing.

Actually, that won't quite work out if the overlap is itself the product of a doubling, as in `"rococo"` and `"cocoon"`. The preceding algorithm would have decided that the overlapping string, $2, must be just `"co"` rather than `"coco"`. But we don't want a `"rocococoon"`; we want a `"rococoon"`. Adding a minimal matching quantifier to the $1 part gives the much better pattern:

```
/^(\w+?)(\w+) \2(\w+)$/,
```

which solves this problem.

Backtracking is more powerful than you imagine. Example 6-11 offers another take on the prime factorization problem from Chapter 2, *Numbers*.

Example 6-11. prime-pattern
```
#!/usr/bin/perl
# prime_pattern -- find prime factors of argument using pattern matching
for ($N = ('o' x shift); $N =~ /^(oo+?)\1+$/; $N =~ s/$1/o/g) {
    print length($1), " ";
}
print length ($N), "\n";
```

Although not practical, this approach marvelously demonstrates the power of backtracking and is therefore very instructional.

Here's another example. Using a brilliant insight first illustrated by Doug McIlroy (or so says Andrew Hume), you can find solutions to Diophantine equations of order one with regular expressions. Consider the equation 12x + 15y + 16z = 281. Can you think of possible values for *x*, *y*, and *z*? Perl can!

```
# solve for 12x + 15y + 16z = 281, maximizing x
if (($X, $Y, $Z)  =
       (('o' x 281)  =~ /^(o*)\1{11}(o*)\2{14}(o*)\3{15}$/))
{
       ($x, $y, $z) = (length($X), length($Y), length($Z));
       print "One solution is: x=$x; y=$y; z=$z.\n";
} else {
       print "No solution.\n";
}
One solution is: x=17; y=3; z=2.
```

Because the first o* was greedy, *x* was allowed to grow as large as it could. Changing one or more of the * quantifiers to *?, +, or +? can produce different solutions.

```
('o' x 281)  =~ /^(o+)\1{11}(o+)\2{14}(o+)\3{15}$/
One solution is: x=17; y=3; z=2
('o' x 281)  =~ /^(o*?)\1{11}(o*)\2{14}(o*)\3{15}$/
One solution is: x=0; y=7; z=11.
('o' x 281)  =~ /^(o+?)\1{11}(o*)\2{14}(o*)\3{15}$/
One solution is: x=1; y=3; z=14.
```

An important lesson to be learned from these amazing feats of mathematical prowess by a lowly pattern matcher is that a pattern matching engine, particularly a backtracking one, very much wants to give you an answer and will work phenomenally hard to do so. But solving a regular expression with backreferences can take time exponentially proportional to the length of the input to complete. For all but trivial inputs, such algorithms make continental drift seem brisk.

See Also

The explanation of backreferences in the "Regular Expressions" section of *perlre*(1), and in "The Fine Print" section of Chapter 2 of *Programming Perl*; the "The Doubled-Word Thing" section in Chapter 2 of *Mastering Regular Expressions*

6.17. *Expressing AND, OR, and NOT in a Single Pattern*

Problem

You have an existing program that accepts a pattern as an argument or input. It doesn't allow you to add extra logic, like case insensitive options, ANDs, or NOTs. So you need to write a single pattern that matches either of two different patterns (the "or" case), both of two patterns (the "and" case), or that reverses the sense of the match ("not").

This situation arises often in a configuration files, web forms, or command-line arguments. Imagine there's a program that does this:

```
chomp($pattern = <CONFIG_FH>);
if ( $data =~ /$pattern/ ) { ..... }
```

As the one maintaining the contents of CONFIG_FH, you need to convey Booleans through to the matching program through that one, measly pattern without explicit connectives.

Solution

True if either /ALPHA/ or /BETA/ matches, like /ALPHA/ || /BETA/:

```
/ALPHA|BETA/
```

True if both /ALPHA/ and /BETA/ match, but may overlap, meaning "BETALPHA" should be okay, like /ALPHA/ && /BETA/:

```
/^(?=.*ALPHA)(?=.*BETA)/s
```

True if both /ALPHA/ and /BETA/ match, but may not overlap, meaning that "BETALPHA" should fail:

```
/ALPHA.*BETA|BETA.*ALPHA/s
```

True if pattern /PAT/ does not match, like $var !~ /PAT/:

```
/^(?:(?!PAT).)*$/s
```

True if pattern BAD does not match, but pattern GOOD does:

```
/(?=^(?:(?!BAD).)*$)GOOD/s
```

Discussion

When you're writing a regular program and want to know if something doesn't match, say one of:

```
if (!($string =~ /pattern/)) { something() }   # ugly
if (  $string !~ /pattern/)  { something() }   # preferred
```

If you want to see if two patterns both match, use:

```
if ($string =~ /pat1/ && $string =~ /pat2/ ) { something() }
```

If you want to see if either of two patterns matches:

```
if ($string =~ /pat1/ || $string =~ /pat2/ ) { something() }
```

In short, use Perl's normal Boolean connectives to combine regular expressions, rather than doing it all within a single pattern. However, imagine a *minigrep* program, one that reads its single pattern as an argument, as shown in Example 6-12.

Example 6-12. minigrep

```
#!/usr/bin/perl
# minigrep - trivial grep
$pat = shift;
while (<>) {
    print if /$pat/o;
}
```

If you want to tell *minigrep* that some pattern must not match, or that it has to match both of two subpatterns in any order, then you're at an impasse. The program isn't built to accept those constructs. How can you do it using one pattern? That is, you'd like to execute the *minigrep PAT* program where PAT can't match or has more than one connected patterns in it. This need comes up often in program reading patterns from configuration files.

The OR case is pretty easy, since the | symbol provides for alternation. The AND and NOT cases, however, require special encoding.

For AND, you have to distinguish between overlapping and non-overlapping cases. You want to see if a string matches both `"bell"` and `"lab"`. If you allow overlapping, then the word `"labelled"` qualifies. But if you didn't want to count overlaps, then it shouldn't qualify. The overlapping case uses two look-ahead assertions:

```
"labelled" =~ /^(?=.*bell)(?=.*lab)/s
```

Remember: in a normal program, you don't have to go through these contortions. You can simply say:

```
$string =~ /bell/ && $string =~ /lab/
```

To unravel this, we'll spell it out using /x and comments. Here's the long version:

```
if ($murray_hill =~ m{
                ^                   # start of string
                (?=                 # zero-width lookahead
                    .*              # any amount of intervening stuff
                    bell            # the desired bell string
                )                   # rewind, since we were only looking
                (?=                 # and do the same thing
                    .*              # any amount of intervening stuff
                    lab             # and the lab part
                )
            }sx )                   # /s means . can match newline
    {
        print "Looks like Bell Labs might be in Murray Hill!\n";
    }
```

We didn't use .*? to end it early because minimal matching is more expensive than maximal matching. So it's more efficient to use .* over .*?, given random input where the occurrence of matches at the front or the end of the string is completely unpredictable. Of course, sometimes choosing between .* and .*? may depend on correctness rather than efficiency, but not here.

To handle the non-overlapping case, you need two parts separated by an OR. The first branch is THIS followed by THAT; the second is the other way around.

```
"labelled" =~ /(?:^.*bell.*lab)|(?:^.*lab.*bell)/
```

or in long form:

```
$brand = "labelled";
if ($brand =~ m{
        (?:                      # non-capturing grouper
          ^ .*?                  # any amount of stuff at the front
              bell               # look for a bell
              .*?                # followed by any amount of anything
              lab                # look for a lab
          )                      # end grouper
        |                        # otherwise, try the other direction
        (?:                      # non-capturing grouper
          ^ .*?                  # any amount of stuff at the front
              lab                # look for a lab
              .*?                # followed by any amount of anything
              bell               # followed by a bell
          )                      # end grouper
      }sx )                      # /s means . can match newline
    {
        print "Our brand has bell and lab separate.\n";
    }
```

These patterns aren't necessarily faster. $murray_hill =~ /bell/ && $murray_hill =~ /lab/ will scan the string at most twice, but the pattern matching engine's only option is to try to find a "lab" for each occurrence of "bell" in (?=^.*?bell)(?=^.*?lab), leading to quadratic worst case running times.

If you followed those two, then the NOT case should be a breeze. The general form looks like this:

```
$map =~ /^(?:(?!waldo).)*$/s
```

Spelled out in long form, this yields:

```
if ($map =~ m{
        ^                        # start of string
        (?:                      # non-capturing grouper
          (?!                    # look ahead negation
              waldo              # is he ahead of us now?
          )                      # is so, the negation failed
          .                      # any character (cuzza /s)
        ) *                      # repeat that grouping 0 or more
```

```
        $                       # through the end of the string
    }sx )                       # /s means . can match newline
{

    print "There's no waldo here!\n";

}
```

How would you combine AND, OR, and NOT? It's not a pretty picture, and in a regular program, you'd almost never do this, but from a config file or command line where you only get to specify one pattern, you have no choice. You just have to combine what we've learned so far. Carefully.

Let's say you wanted to run the Unix *w* program and find out whether user tchrist were logged on anywhere but a terminal whose name began with ttyp; that is, tchrist must match, but ttyp must not.

Here's sample input from *w* on my Linux system:

```
 7:15am  up 206 days, 13:30,  4 users,   load average: 1.04, 1.07, 1.04
USER      TTY      FROM            LOGIN@  IDLE    JCPU   PCPU  WHAT
tchrist   tty1                     5:16pm 36days 24:43   0.03s  xinit
tchrist   tty2                     5:19pm  6days  0.43s  0.43s  -tcsh
tchrist   ttyp0    chthon          7:58am  3days 23.44s  0.44s  -tcsh
gnat      ttyS4    coprolith       2:01pm 13:36m  0.30s  0.30s  -tcsh
```

Here's how to do that using the *minigrep* program outlined previously or with the *tcgrep* program at the end of this chapter:

```
% w | minigrep '^(?!.*ttyp).*tchrist'
```

Decoding that pattern:

```
m{
        ^                       # anchored to the start
        (?!                     # zero-width look-ahead assertion
          .*                    # any amount of anything (faster than .*?)
          ttyp                  # the string you don't want to find
        )                       # end look-ahead negation; rewind to start
        .*                      # any amount of anything (faster than .*?)
        tchrist                 # now try to find Tom
}x
```

Never mind that any sane person would just call *grep* twice, once with a -v option to select only non-matches.

```
% w | grep tchrist | grep -v ttyp
```

The point is that Boolean conjunctions and negations *can* be coded up in one single pattern. You should comment this kind of thing, though, having pity on those who come after you—before they do.

How would you embed that /s in a pattern passed to a program from the command line? The same way as you would a /i switch: by using (?i) in the pattern. The /s and /m modifiers can be painlessly included in a pattern as well, using /(?s) or /(?m). These can even cluster, as in /(?smi). That would make these two reasonably interchangeable:

```
% grep -i 'pattern' files
% minigrep '(?i)pattern' files
```

See Also

Lookahead assertions are shown in the "Regular Expressions" section of *perlre*(1), and in the "Rules of Regular Expression Matching" section of Chapter 2 of *Programming Perl*; your system's *grep*(1) and *w*(1) manpages; we talk about configuration files in Recipe 8.16

6.18. Matching Multiple-Byte Characters

Problem

You need to perform regular-expression searches against multiple-byte characters.

A *character encoding* is a set mapping from characters and symbols to digital representations. ASCII is an encoding where each character is represented as exactly one byte, but complex writing systems, such as those for Chinese, Japanese, and Korean, have so many characters that their encodings need to use multiple bytes to represent characters.

Perl works on the principle that each byte represents a single character, which works well in ASCII but makes regular expression matches on strings containing multiple-byte characters tricky, to say the least. The regular expression engine does not understand the character boundaries in your string of bytes, and so can return "matches" from the middle of one character to the middle of another.

Solution

Exploit the encoding by tailoring the pattern to the sequences of bytes that constitute characters. The basic approach is to build a pattern that matches a single (multiple byte) character in the encoding, and then use that "any character" pattern in larger patterns.

Discussion

As an example, we'll examine one of the encodings for Japanese, called *EUC-JP*, and then show how we use this in solving a number of multiple-byte encoding issues. EUC-JP can represent thousands of characters, but it's basically a superset of ASCII. Bytes with values ranging from 0 to 127 (0x00 to 0x7F) are almost exactly their ASCII counterparts, so those bytes represent one-byte characters. Some characters are represented by a pair of bytes, the first with value 0x8E and the second with a value in the range 0xA0–0xDF. Some others are represented by three bytes, the first with the value 0x8F and the others in the range 0xA1–0xFE, while others still are represented by two bytes, each in the 0xA1–0xFE range.

We can convey this information—what bytes can make up characters in this encoding—as a regular expression. For ease of use later, here we'll define a string, $eucjp, that holds the regular expression to match a single EUC-JP character:

```
my $eucjp = q{                    # EUC-JP encoding subcomponents:
    [\x00-\x7F]                    # ASCII/JIS-Roman (one-byte/character)
  | \x8E[\xA0-\xDF]                # half-width katakana (two bytes/char)
  | \x8F[\xA1-\xFE][\xA1-\xFE]     # JIS X 0212-1990 (three bytes/char)
  | [\xA1-\xFE][\xA1-\xFE]         # JIS X 0208:1997 (two bytes/char)
};
```

(Because we've inserted comments and whitespace for pretty-printing, we'll have to use the /x modifier when we use this in a match or substitution.)

With this template in hand, the following sections show how to:

- Perform a normal match without any "false" matches

- Count, convert (to another encoding), and/or filter characters

- Verify whether the target text is valid according to an encoding

- Detect which encoding the target text uses

All the examples are shown using EUC-JP as the encoding of interest, but they will work with any of the many multiple-byte encodings commonly used for text processing, such as Unicode, Big-5, etc.

Avoiding false matches

A false match is where the regular expression engine finds a match that begins in the middle of a multiple-byte character sequence. We can get around the problem by carefully controlling the match, ensuring that the pattern matching engine stays synchronized with the character boundaries at all times.

This can be done by anchoring the match to the start of the string, then manually bypassing characters ourselves when the real match can't happen at the current location. With the EUC-JP example, the "bypassing characters" part is /(?: $eucjp)*?/. $eucjp is our template to match any valid character, and because it is applied via the non-greedy *?, it can match a character only when whatever follows (presumably the desired real match) can't match. Here's a real example:

```
/^ (?: $eucjp )*?  \xC5\xEC\xB5\xFE/ox # Trying to find Tokyo
```

In the EUC-JP encoding, the Japanese word for Tokyo is written with two characters, the first encoded by the two bytes \xC5\xEC, the second encoded by the two
bytes \xB5\xFE. As far as Perl is concerned, we're looking merely for the four-
byte sequence \xC5\xEC\xB5\xFE, but because we use (?: $eucjp)*? to move
along the string only by characters of our target encoding, we know we'll stay in
synch.

Don't forget to use the /ox modifiers. The /x modifier is especially crucial due to
the whitespace used in the encoding template $eucjp. The /o modifier is for effi-
ciency, since we know $eucjp won't change from use to use.

Use in a replacement is similar, but since the text leading to the real match is also
part of the overall match, we must capture it with parentheses, being sure to
include it in the replacment text. Assuming that $Tokyo and $Osaka have been set
to the bytes sequences for their respective words in the EUC-JP encoding, we
could use the following to replace Osaka for Tokyo:

```
/^ (  (?:eucjp)*? ) $Tokyo/$1$Osaka/ox
```

If used with /g, we want to anchor the match to the end of the previous match,
rather than to the start of the string. That's as simple as changing ^ to \G:

```
/\G (  (?:eucjp)*? ) $Tokyo/$1$Osaka/gox
```

Splitting multiple-byte strings

Another common task is to split an input string into its individual charcters. With a
one-byte-per-character encoding, you can simply split //, but with a multiple-byte
encoding, we need something like:

```
@chars = /$eucjp/gox; # One character per list element
```

Now, @chars contains one character per element. The following snippet shows
how you might use this to write a filter of some sort:

```
while (<>) {
  my @chars = /$eucjp/gox; # One character per list element
  for my $char (@chars) {
    if (length($char) == 1) {
      # Do something interesting with this one-byte character
    } else {
      # Do something interesting with this multiple-byte character
    }
  }
  my $line = join("",@chars); # Glue list back together
  print $line;
}
```

In the two "do something interesting" parts, any change to $char will be reflected
in the output when @chars is glued back together.

Validating multiple-byte strings

The use of /$eucjp/gox in this kind of technique relies strongly on the input string indeed being properly formatted in our target encoding, EUC-JP. If it's not, the template /$eucjp/ won't be able to match, and bytes will be skipped.

One way to address this is to use /\G$eucjp/gox instead. This prohibits the pattern matching engine from skipping bytes in order to find a match (since the use of \G indicates that any match must immediately follow the previous match). This is still not a perfect approach, since it will simply stop matching on ill-formatted input data.

A better approach to confirm that a string is valid with respect to an encoding is to use something like:

```
$is_eucjp = m/^(?:$eucjp)*$/xo;
```

If a string has only valid characters from start to end, you know the string as a whole is valid.

There is one potential for a problem, and that's due to how the end-of-string meta-character $ works: it can be true at the end of the string (as we want), and also just before a newline at the end of the string. That means you can still match successfully even if the newline is not a valid character in the encoding. To get around this problem, you could use the more-complicated (?!\n)$ instead of $.

You can use the basic validation technique to detect which encoding is being used. For example, Japanese is commonly encoded with either EUC-JP, or another encoding called Shift-JIS. If you've set up the templates, as with $eucjp, you can do something like:

```
$is_eucjp = m/^(?:$eucjp)*$/xo;
$is_sjis  = m/^(?:$sjis)*$/xo;
```

If both are true, the text is likely ASCII (since, essentially, ASCII is a sub-component of both encodings). (It's not quite fool-proof, though, since some strings with multi-byte characters might appear to be valid in both encodings. In such a case, automatic detection becomes impossible, although one might use character-frequency data to make an educated guess.)

Converting between encodings

Converting from one encoding to another can be as simple as an extension of the process-each-character routine above. Conversions for some closely related encodings can be done by a simple mathematical computation on the bytes, while others might require huge mapping tables. In either case, you insert the code at the "do something interesting" points in the routine.

Here's an example to convert from EUC-JP to Unicode, using a `%euc2uni` hash as a mapping table:

```
while (<>) {
    my @chars = /$eucjp/gox; # One character per list element
    for my $euc (@chars) {
        my $uni = $euc2uni{$char};
        if (defined $uni) {
            $euc = $uni;
        } else {
            ## deal with unknown EUC->Unicode mapping here.
        }
    }
    my $line = join("",@chars);
    print $line;
}
```

The topic of multiple-byte matching and processing is of particular importance when dealing with Unicode, which has a variety of possible representations. UCS-2 and UCS-4 are fixed-length encodings. UTF-8 defines a mixed one- through six-byte encoding. UTF-16, which represents the most common instance of Unicode encoding, is a variable-length 16-bit encoding.

See Also

Jeffrey Friedl's article in Issue 5 of *The Perl Journal*; *CJKV Information Processing* by Ken Lunde; O'Reilly & Associates, (due 1999)

6.19. Matching a Valid Mail Address

Problem

You want to find a pattern that will verify the validity of a supplied mail address.

Solution

There isn't one. You cannot do real-time validation of mail addresses. You must pick from a number of compromises.

Discussion

The common patterns that people try to use for this are all quite incorrect. As an example, the address fred&barney@stonehenge.com is valid and deliverable (as of this writing), but most patterns that allegedly match valid mail addresses fail miserably.

RFC-822 documents have a formal specification for what constitutes a syntactically valid mail address. However, complete processing requires recursive parsing of nested comments, something that one single regular expression cannot do. If you first strip off legal comments:

```
1 while $addr =~ s/\(([^()]*\)//g;
```

You could then in theory use the 6598-byte pattern given on the last page of *Mastering Regular Expressions* to test for RFC-conformance, but that's still not good enough, for three reasons.

First, not all RFC-valid address are deliverable. For example, `foo@foo.foo.foo.foo` is valid in form, but in practice is not deliverable. Some people try to do DNS lookups for MX records, even trying to connect to the host handling that address's mail to check if it's valid at that site. This is a poor approach because most sites can't do a direct connect to any other site, and even if they could, mail receiving sites increasingly either ignore the SMTP VRFY command or fib about its answer.

Second, some RFC-invalid addresses, in practice, are perfectly deliverable. For example, a lone `postmaster` is almost certainly deliverable but doesn't pass RFC-822 muster. It doesn't have an `@` in it.

Thirdly and most important, just because the address happens to be both valid and deliverable doesn't mean that it's the right one. `president@whitehouse.gov`, for example, is valid by the RFC and deliverable. But it's very unlikely that would really be the mail address of the person submitting information to your CGI script.

The script at *http://www.perl.com/CPAN/authors/Tom_Christiansen/scripts/ckaddr.gz* makes a valiant (albeit provably imperfect) attempt at doing this incorrectly. It jumps through many hoops, including the RFC-822 regular expression from *Mastering Regular Expressions*, DNS MX record look-up, and stop lists for naughty words and famous people. But this is still a very weak approach.

Our best advice for verifying a person's mail address is to have them enter their address twice, just as you would when changing a password. This usually weeds out typos. If both versions match, send mail to that address with a personal message such as:

```
Dear someuser@host.com,

Please confirm the mail address you gave us Wed May  6 09:38:41
MDT 1998 by replying to this message.  Include the string
"Rumpelstiltskin" in that reply, but spelled in reverse; that is,
start with "Nik...".  Once this is done, your confirmed address will
be entered into our records.
```

If you get the message back and they've followed your directions, you can be reasonably assured that it's real.

A related strategy that's less open to forgery is to give them a PIN (personal identification number). Record the address and PIN (preferably a random one) for later processing. In the mail you send, ask them to include the PIN in their reply. If it bounces, or the message is included via a vacation script, it'll be there anyway. So ask them to mail back the PIN slightly altered, such as with the characters reversed, one added or subtracted to each digit, etc.

See Also

The "Matching an Email Address" section of Chapter 7 of *Mastering Regular Expressions*; Recipe 18.9

6.20. *Matching Abbreviations*

Problem

Suppose you had a list of commands, such as `"send"`, `"abort"`, `"list"`, and `"edit"`. The user types one in, but you don't want to make them type out the whole thing.

Solution

You can use the following technique if the strings all start with different characters or if you want to arrange the matches so one takes precedence over another, as `"SEND"` has precedence over `"STOP"` here:

```
chomp($answer = <>);
if    ("SEND"  =~ /^\Q$answer/i) { print "Action is send\n"  }
elsif ("STOP"  =~ /^\Q$answer/i) { print "Action is stop\n"  }
elsif ("ABORT" =~ /^\Q$answer/i) { print "Action is abort\n" }
elsif ("LIST"  =~ /^\Q$answer/i) { print "Action is list\n"  }
elsif ("EDIT"  =~ /^\Q$answer/i) { print "Action is edit\n"  }
```

Or you can use the Text::Abbrev module:

```
use Text::Abbrev;
$href = abbrev qw(send abort list edit);
for (print "Action: "; <>; print "Action: ") {
    chomp;
    my $action = $href->{ lc($_) };
    print "Action is $action\n";
}
```

Discussion

The first technique switches the typical order of a match. Normally you have a variable on the left side of the match and a known pattern on the right side. We might try to decide which action the user wanted us to take by saying $answer =~ /^ABORT/i, which is true if $answer begins with the string "ABORT". It matches whether $answer has anything after "ABORT", so "ABORT LATER" would still match. Handling abbreviations generally requires quite a bit of ugliness: $answer =~ /^A(B(O(R(T)?)?)?)?$/i.

Compare the classic "variable =~ pattern" with "ABORT" =~ /^\Q$answer/i. The \Q escapes any characters that would otherwise be treated as regular expression, so your program won't blow up if the user enters an invalid pattern. When the user enters something like "ab", the expanded match becomes "ABORT" =~ /^ab/i after variable substitution and metaquoting. This matches.

The standard Text::Abbrev module takes a different approach. You give it a list of words, and it returns a reference to a hash whose keys are all unambiguous abbreviations and whose values are the fully expanded strings. So if $href were created as in the Solution example, $href->{"a"} would return the string "abort".

This technique is commonly used to call a function based on the name of the string the user types in. Do this by using a symbolic reference, like:

```
$name = 'send';
&$name();
```

But that's scary, because it allows the user to run any function in our program, assuming they know its name. It also runs afoul of that pesky use strict 'refs' pragma.

Here's a partial program that creates a hash in which the key is the command name and the value is a reference to the function to call for that command:

```
# assumes that &invoke_editor, &deliver_message,
# $file and $PAGER are defined somewhere else.
use Text::Abbrev;
my($href, %actions, $errors);
%actions = (
    "edit"  => \&invoke_editor,
    "send"  => \&deliver_message,
    "list"  => sub { system($PAGER, $file) },
    "abort" => sub {
                    print "See ya!\n";
                    exit;
                },
    ""      => sub {
                    print "Unknown command: $cmd\n";
                    $errors++;
                },
);

$href = abbrev(keys %actions);
```

```
    local $_;
    for (print "Action: "; <>; print "Action: ") {
        s/^\s+//;          # trim leading  white space
        s/\s+$//;          # trim trailing white space
        next unless $_;
        $actions->{ $href->{ lc($_) } }->();
    }
```

The last statement could have been written like this if you're not into tight expressions or need practice typing:

```
    $abbreviation = lc($_);
    $expansion    = $href->{$abbreviation};
    $coderef      = $actions->{$expansion};
    &$coderef();
```

See Also

The documentation for the standard Text::Abbrev module (also in Chapter 7 of *Programming Perl*); interpolation is explained in the "Scalar Value Constructors" section of *perldata*(1), and in the "String Literals" section of Chapter 2 of *Programming Perl*

6.21. Program: urlify

This program puts HTML links around URLs in files. It doesn't work on all possible URLs, but does hit the most common ones. It tries hard to avoid including end-of-sentence punctuation in the marked-up URL.

It is a typical Perl filter, so it can be used by feeding it input:

```
    % gunzip -c ~/mail/archive.gz | urlify > archive.urlified
```

or by supplying files on the command line:

```
    % urlify ~/mail/*.inbox > ~/allmail.urlified
```

The program is shown in Example 6-13.

Example 6-13. urlify

```
#!/usr/bin/perl
# urlify - wrap HTML links around URL-like constructs

$urls = '(http|telnet|gopher|file|wais|ftp)';
$ltrs = '\w';
$gunk = '/#~:.?+=&%@!\-';
$punc = '.:?\-';
$any  = "${ltrs}${gunk}${punc}";

while (<>) {
    s{
```

Example 6-13. urlify (continued)

```
        \b                          # start at word boundary
        (                           # begin $1  {
          $urls      :              # need resource and a colon
          [$any] +?                 # followed by on or more
                                    #  of any valid character, but
                                    #  be conservative and take only
                                    #  what you need to....
        )                           # end     $1  }
        (?=                         # look-ahead non-consumptive assertion
          [$punc]*                  # either 0 or more punctuation
          [^$any]                   #    followed by a non-url char
          |                         # or else
          $                         #    then end of the string
        )
      }{<A HREF="$1">$1</A>}igox;
    print;
}
```

6.22. Program: tcgrep

This program is a Perl rewrite of the Unix *grep* program. Although it runs slower than C versions (especially the GNU *grep*s), it offers many more features.

The first, and perhaps most important, feature is that it runs anywhere Perl does. Other enhancements are that it can ignore anything that's not a plain text file, automatically expand compressed or *gzip*ped files, recurse down directories, search complete paragraphs or user-defined records, look in younger files before older ones, and add underlining or highlighting of matches. It also supports both the -c option to indicate a count of matching records as well as -C for a count of matching patterns when there could be more than one per record.

This program uses *gzcat* or *zcat* to decompress compressed files, so this feature is unavailable on systems without these programs and systems without the ability to run external programs (such as the Macintosh).

Run the program with no arguments for a usage message (see the usage subroutine in the following code). This command line recursively and case-insensitively greps every file in *~/mail* for mail messages from someone called "kate", reporting the filenames that contained matches.

```
    % tcgrep -ril '^From: .*kate' ~/mail
```

The program is shown in Example 6-14.

Example 6-14. tcgrep

```
#!/usr/bin/perl -w
# tcgrep: tom christiansen's rewrite of grep
# v1.0: Thu Sep 30 16:24:43 MDT 1993
```

Example 6-14. tcgrep (continued)

```
# v1.1: Fri Oct  1 08:33:43 MDT 1993
# v1.2: Fri Jul 26 13:37:02 CDT 1996
# v1.3: Sat Aug 30 14:21:47 CDT 1997
# v1.4: Mon May 18 16:17:48 EDT 1998

use strict;
                                    # globals
use vars qw($Me $Errors $Grand_Total $Mult %Compress $Matches);

my ($matcher, $opt);                # matcher - anon. sub to check for matches
                                    # opt - ref to hash w/ command line options

init();                             # initialize globals

($opt, $matcher) = parse_args();  # get command line options and patterns

matchfile($opt, $matcher, @ARGV); # process files

exit(2) if $Errors;
exit(0) if $Grand_Total;
exit(1);

###################################

sub init {
    ($Me = $0) =~ s!.*/!!;          # get basename of program, "tcgrep"
    $Errors = $Grand_Total = 0;     # initialize global counters
    $Mult = "";                     # flag for multiple files in @ARGV
    $| = 1;                         # autoflush output

    %Compress = (                   # file extensions and program names
        z  => 'gzcat',              # for uncompressing
        gz => 'gzcat',
        Z  => 'zcat',
    );
}

###################################

sub usage {
        die <<EOF
usage: $Me [flags] [files]

Standard grep options:
        i    case insensitive
        n    number lines
        c    give count of lines matching
        C    ditto, but >1 match per line possible
        w    word boundaries only
        s    silent mode
        x    exact matches only
        v    invert search sense (lines that DON'T match)
```

Example 6-14. tcgrep (continued)

```
        h   hide filenames
        e   expression (for exprs beginning with -)
        f   file with expressions
        l   list filenames matching

Specials:
        1   1 match per file
        H   highlight matches
        u   underline matches
        r   recursive on directories or dot if none
        t   process directories in 'ls -t' order
        p   paragraph mode (default: line mode)
        P   ditto, but specify separator, e.g. -P '%%\\n'
        a   all files, not just plain text files
        q   quiet about failed file and dir opens
        T   trace files as opened

May use a TCGREP environment variable to set default options.
EOF
}

#####################################

sub parse_args {
    use Getopt::Std;

    my ($optstring, $zeros, $nulls, %opt, $pattern, @patterns, $match_code);
    my ($SO, $SE);

    if ($_ = $ENV{TCGREP}) {            # get envariable TCGREP
        s/^([^\-])/-$1/;                # add leading - if missing
        unshift(@ARGV, $_);             # add TCGREP opt string to @ARGV
    }

    $optstring = "incCwsxvhe:f:l1HurtpP:aqT";

    $zeros = 'inCwxvhelut';             # options to init to 0 (prevent warnings)
    $nulls = 'pP';                      # options to init to "" (prevent warnings)

    @opt{ split //, $zeros } = ( 0 )  x length($zeros);
    @opt{ split //, $nulls } = ( '' ) x length($nulls);

    getopts($optstring, \%opt)                  or usage();

    if ($opt{f}) {                      # -f patfile
        open(PATFILE, $opt{f})                  or die qq($Me: Can't open '$opt{f}': $!);

                                        # make sure each pattern in file is valid
        while ( defined($pattern = <PATFILE>) ) {
            chomp $pattern;
            eval { 'foo' =~ /$pattern/, 1 } or
                die "$Me: $opt{f}:$.: bad pattern: $@";
```

Example 6-14. tcgrep (continued)

```
            push @patterns, $pattern;
        }
        close PATFILE;
    }
    else {                          # make sure pattern is valid
        $pattern = $opt{e} || shift(@ARGV) || usage();
        eval { 'foo' =~ /$pattern/, 1 } or
            die "$Me: bad pattern: $@";
        @patterns = ($pattern);
    }

    if ($opt{H} || $opt{u}) {       # highlight or underline
        my $term = $ENV{TERM} || 'vt100';
        my $terminal;

        eval {                      # try to look up escapes for stand-out
            require POSIX;          # or underline via Term::Cap
            use Term::Cap;

            my $termios = POSIX::Termios->new();
            $termios->getattr;
            my $ospeed = $termios->getospeed;

            $terminal = Tgetent Term::Cap { TERM=>undef, OSPEED=>$ospeed }
        };

        unless ($@) {               # if successful, get escapes for either
            local $^W = 0;          # stand-out (-H) or underlined (-u)
            ($SO, $SE) = $opt{H}
                ? ($terminal->Tputs('so'), $terminal->Tputs('se'))
                : ($terminal->Tputs('us'), $terminal->Tputs('ue'));
        }
        else {                      # if use of Term::Cap fails,
            ($SO, $SE) = $opt{H}    # use tput command to get escapes
                ? (`tput -T $term smso`, `tput -T $term rmso`)
                : (`tput -T $term smul`, `tput -T $term rmul`)
        }
    }

    if ($opt{i}) {
        @patterns = map {"(?i)$_"} @patterns;
    }

    if ($opt{p} || $opt{P}) {
        @patterns = map {"(?m)$_"} @patterns;
    }

    $opt{p}   && ($/ = '');
    $opt{P}   && ($/ = eval(qq("$opt{P}")));      # for -P '%%\n'
    $opt{w}   && (@patterns = map {'\b' . $_ . '\b'} @patterns);
    $opt{'x'} && (@patterns = map {"^$_\$"} @patterns);
    if (@ARGV) {
```

Example 6-14. tcgrep (continued)

```perl
        $Mult = 1 if ($opt{r} || (@ARGV > 1) || -d $ARGV[0]) && !$opt{h};
    }
    $opt{1}   += $opt{l};                    # that's a one and an ell
    $opt{H}   += $opt{u};
    $opt{c}   += $opt{C};
    $opt{'s'} += $opt{c};
    $opt{1}   += $opt{'s'} && !$opt{c};      # that's a one

    @ARGV = ($opt{r} ? '.' : '-') unless @ARGV;
    $opt{r} = 1 if !$opt{r} && grep(-d, @ARGV) == @ARGV;

    $match_code = '';
    $match_code .= 'study;' if @patterns > 5; # might speed things up a bit

    foreach (@patterns) { s(/)(\\/)g }

    if ($opt{H}) {
        foreach $pattern (@patterns) {
            $match_code .= "\$Matches += s/($pattern)/${SO}\$1${SE}/g;";
        }
    }
    elsif ($opt{v}) {
        foreach $pattern (@patterns) {
            $match_code .= "\$Matches += !/$pattern/;";
        }
    }
    elsif ($opt{C}) {
        foreach $pattern (@patterns) {
            $match_code .= "\$Matches++ while /$pattern/g;";
        }
    }
    else {
        foreach $pattern (@patterns) {
            $match_code .= "\$Matches++ if /$pattern/;";
        }
    }

    $matcher = eval "sub { $match_code }";
    die if $@;

    return (\%opt, $matcher);
}

###################################

sub matchfile {
    $opt = shift;                # reference to option hash
    $matcher = shift;            # reference to matching sub

    my ($file, @list, $total, $name);
    local($_);
    $total = 0;
```

Example 6-14. tcgrep (continued)

```
FILE: while (defined ($file = shift(@_))) {

        if (-d $file) {
            if (-l $file && @ARGV != 1) {
                warn "$Me: \"$file\" is a symlink to a directory\n"
                    if $opt->{T};
                next FILE;

            }
            if (!$opt->{r}) {
                warn "$Me: \"$file\" is a directory, but no -r given\n"
                    if $opt->{T};
                next FILE;
            }
            unless (opendir(DIR, $file)) {
                unless ($opt->{'q'}) {
                    warn "$Me: can't opendir $file: $!\n";
                    $Errors++;
                }
                next FILE;
            }
            @list = ();
            for (readdir(DIR)) {
                push(@list, "$file/$_") unless /^\.{1,2}$/;
            }
            closedir(DIR);
            if ($opt->{t}) {
                my (@dates);
                for (@list) { push(@dates, -M) }
                @list = @list[sort { $dates[$a] <=> $dates[$b] } 0..$#dates];
            }
            else {
                @list = sort @list;
            }
            matchfile($opt, $matcher, @list);    # process files
            next FILE;
        }


        if ($file eq '-') {
            warn "$Me: reading from stdin\n" if -t STDIN && !$opt->{'q'};
            $name = '<STDIN>';
        }
        else {
            $name = $file;
            unless (-e $file) {
                warn qq($Me: file "$file" does not exist\n) unless $opt->{'q'};
                $Errors++;
                next FILE;
            }
            unless (-f $file || $opt->{a}) {
                warn qq($Me: skipping non-plain file "$file"\n) if $opt->{T};
                next FILE;
            }
```

Example 6-14. tcgrep (continued)

```
            }

        my ($ext) = $file =~ /\.([^.]+)$/;
        if (defined $ext && exists $Compress{$ext}) {
            $file = "$Compress{$ext} <$file |";
        }
        elsif (! (-T $file  || $opt->{a})) {
            warn qq($Me: skipping binary file "$file"\n) if $opt->{T};
            next FILE;
        }
    }

    warn "$Me: checking $file\n" if $opt->{T};

    unless (open(FILE, $file)) {
        unless ($opt->{'q'}) {
            warn "$Me: $file: $!\n";
            $Errors++;
        }
        next FILE;
    }

    $total = 0;

    $Matches = 0;

LINE:   while (<FILE>) {
        $Matches = 0;

        #############
        &{$matcher}();          # do it! (check for matches)
        #############

        next LINE unless $Matches;

        $total += $Matches;

        if ($opt->{p} || $opt->{P}) {
            s/\n{2,}$/\n/ if $opt->{p};
            chomp          if $opt->{P};
        }

        print("$name\n"), next FILE if $opt->{l};

        $opt->{'s'} || print $Mult && "$name:",
            $opt->{n} ? "$.:" : "",
            $_,
            ($opt->{p} || $opt->{P}) && ('-' x 20) . "\n";

        next FILE if $opt->{1};                     # that's a one
    }
}
```

Example 6-14. tcgrep (continued)

```
continue {
    print $Mult && "$name:", $total, "\n" if $opt->{c};
}
$Grand_Total += $total;
}
```

6.23. Regular Expression Grabbag

We have found these regular expressions useful or interesting.

Roman numbers

```
m/^m*(d?c{0,3}|c[dm])(l?x{0,3}|x[lc])(v?i{0,3}|i[vx])$/i
```

Swap first two words

```
s/(\S+)(\s+)(\S+)/$3$2$1/
```

Keyword = Value

```
m/(\w+)\s*=\s*(.*?)\s*$/          # keyword is $1, value is $2
```

Line of at least 80 characters

```
m/.{80,}/
```

MM/DD/YY HH:MM:SS

```
m|(\d+)/(\d+)/(\d+) (\d+):(\d+):(\d+)|
```

Changing directories

```
s(/usr/bin)(/usr/local/bin)g
```

Expanding %7E (hex) escapes

```
s/%([0-9A-Fa-f][0-9A-Fa-f])/chr hex $1/ge
```

Deleting C comments (imperfectly)

```
s{
    /\*                     # Match the opening delimiter
    .*?                     # Match a minimal number of characters
    \*/                     # Match the closing delimiter
} []gsx;
```

Removing leading and trailing whitespace

```
s/^\s+//;
s/\s+$//;
```

Turning \ followed by n into a real newline

```
s/\\n/\n/g;
```

Removing package portion of fully qualified symbols

```
s/^.*:://
```

Dotted quads (most IP addresses)

```
# XXX: fails on legal IPs 127.1 and 2130706433.
```

```
    m{
        ^   ( \d | [01]?\d\d | 2[0-4]\d | 25[0-5] )
        \.  ( \d | [01]?\d\d | 2[0-4]\d | 25[0-5] )
        \.  ( \d | [01]?\d\d | 2[0-4]\d | 25[0-5] )
        \.  ( \d | [01]?\d\d | 2[0-4]\d | 25[0-5] )
        $
    }x
```

Removing leading path from filename

```
    s(^.*/)()
```

Extracting columns setting from TERMCAP

```
    $cols = ( ($ENV{TERMCAP} || " ") =~ m/:co#(\d+):/ ) ? $1 : 80;
```

Removing directory components from program name and arguments

```
    ($name = " $0 @ARGV") =~ s, /\S+/,  ,g;
```

Checking your operating system

```
    die "This isn't Linux" unless $^O =~ m/linux/i;
```

Joining continuation lines in multiline string

```
    s/\n\s+/ /g
```

Extracting all numbers from a string

```
    @nums = m/(\d+\.?\d*|\.\d+)/g;
```

Finding all-caps words

```
    @capwords = m/(\b[^\Wa-z0-9_]+\b)/g;
```

Finding all-lowercase words

```
    @lowords = m/(\b[^\WA-Z0-9_]+\b)/g;
```

Finding initial-caps word

```
    @icwords = m/(\b[^\Wa-z0-9_][^\WA-Z0-9_]*\b)/;
```

Finding links in simple HTML

```
    @links = m/<A[^>]+?HREF\s*=\s*["']?([^'" >]+?)[ '"]?>/sig;
```

Finding middle initial in $_

```
    ($initial) = m/^\S+\s+(\S)\S*\s+\S/ ? $1 : "";
```

Changing inch marks to quotes

```
    s/"([^"]*)"/``$1''/g
```

Extracting sentences (two spaces required)

```
    { local $/ = "";
      while (<>) {
        s/\n/ /g;
        s/ {3,}/ /g;
        push @sentences, m/(\S.*?[!?.])(?=  |\Z)/g;
      }
    }
```

YYYY-MM-DD

```
    m/(\d{4})-(\d\d)-(\d\d)/              # YYYY in $1, MM in $2, DD in $3
```

North American telephone numbers

```
    m/ ^
        (?:
          1 \s (?: \d\d\d \s)?            # 1, or 1 and area code
          |                              # ... or ...
          \(\d\d\d\) \s                  # area code with parens
          |                              # ... or ...
          (?: \+\d\d?\d? \s)?            # optional +country code
          \d\d\d ([\s\-])                # and area code
        )
        \d\d\d (\s|\1)                    # prefix (and area code separator)
        \d\d\d\d                          # exchange
          $
    /x
```

Exclamations

```
    m/\boh\s+my\s+gh?o(d(dess(es)?|s?)|odness|sh)\b/i
```

Extracting lines regardless of line terminator

```
    push(@lines, $1)
        while ($input =~ s/^([^\012\015]*)(\012\015?|\015\012?)//);
```

7

File Access

> *I the heir of all the ages, in the*
> *foremost files of time.*
> —Alfred, Lord Tennyson
> *Locksley Hall*

7.0. Introduction

Nothing is more central to data processing than the file. As with everything else in Perl, easy things are easy and hard things are possible. Common tasks (opening, reading data, writing data) use simple I/O functions and operators, whereas fancier functions do hard things like non-blocking I/O and file locking.

This chapter deals with the mechanics of file *access*: opening a file, telling subroutines which files to work with, locking files, and so on. Chapter 8, *File Contents*, deals with techniques for working with the *contents* of a file: reading, writing, shuffling lines, and other operations you can do once you have access to the file.

Here's Perl code for printing all lines in the file */usr/local/widgets/data* that contain the word `"blue"`:

```
open(INPUT, "< /usr/local/widgets/data")
    or die "Couldn't open /usr/local/widgets/data for reading: $!\n";

while (<INPUT>) {
    print if /blue/;
}
close(INPUT);
```

Getting a Handle on the File

Central to Perl's file access is the *filehandle*, like INPUT in the preceding program. This is a symbol you use to represent the file when you read and write. Because filehandles aren't variables (they don't have a $, @, or % type marker on their names—but they are part of Perl's symbol table just as subroutines and variables are), storing filehandles in variables and passing them to subroutines won't always work. You should use the odd-looking *FH notation, indicating a typeglob, the basic unit of Perl's symbol table:

```
$var = *STDIN;
mysub($var, *LOGFILE);
```

When you store filehandles in variables like this, you don't use them directly. They're called *indirect filehandles* because they indirectly refer to the real filehandle. Two modules, IO::File (standard since 5.004) and FileHandle (standard since 5.000), can create anonymous filehandles.

When we use IO::File or IO::Handle in our examples, you could obtain identical results by using FileHandle instead, since it's now just a wrapper module.

Here's how we'd write the "blue"-finding program with the IO::File module using purely object-oriented notation:

```
use IO::File;

$input = IO::File->new("< /usr/local/widgets/data")
    or die "Couldn't open /usr/local/widgets/data for reading: $!\n";

while (defined($line = $input->getline())) {
    chomp($line);
    STDOUT->print($line) if $line =~ /blue/;
}
$input->close();
```

As you see, it's much more readable to use filehandles directly. It's also a lot faster.

But here's a little secret for you: you can skip all that arrow and method-call business altogether. Unlike most objects, you don't actually *have* to use IO::File objects in an object-oriented way. They're essentially just anonymous filehandles, so you can use them anywhere you'd use a regular indirect filehandle. Recipe 7.16 covers these modules and the *FH notation. We use both IO::File and symbolic filehandles in this chapter.

Standard FileHandles

Every program starts out with three global filehandles already opened: STDIN, STDOUT, and STDERR. STDIN (*standard input*) is the default source of input, STDOUT (*standard output*) is the default destination for output, and STDERR (*standard error*) is the default place to send warnings and errors. For interactive programs, STDIN is the keyboard, STDOUT and STDERR are the screen:

```
while (<STDIN>) {                       # reads from STDIN
    unless (/\d/) {
        warn "No digit found.\n";       # writes to STDERR
    }
    print "Read: ", $_;                  # writes to STDOUT
}
END { close(STDOUT)                      or die "couldn't close STDOUT: $!" }
```

Filehandles live in packages. That way, two packages can have filehandles with the same name and be separate, just as they can with subroutines and variables. The **open** function associates a filehandle with a file or program, after which you use that filehandle for I/O. When done, **close** the filehandle to break the association.

Files are accessed at the operating system through numeric file descriptors. You can learn a filehandle's descriptor number using the **fileno** function. Perl's filehandles are sufficient for most file operations, but Recipe 7.19 tells you how to deal with the situation where you're given an file descriptor and want to turn it into a filehandle you can use.

I/O Operations

Perl's most common operations for file interaction are **open**, **print**, <FH> to read a record, and **close**. These are wrappers around routines from the C buffered input/output library called *stdio*. Perl's I/O functions are documented in Chapter 3 of *Programming Perl*, *perlfunc*(1), and your system's *stdio*(3S) manpages. The next chapter details I/O operations like <>, **print**, **seek**, and **tell**.

The most important I/O function is **open**. It takes two arguments, the filehandle and a string containing the filename and access mode. To open */tmp/log* for writing and to associate it with the filehandle LOGFILE, say:

```
open(LOGFILE, "> /tmp/log")     or die "Can't write /tmp/log: $!";
```

The three most common access modes are < for reading, > for overwriting, and >> for appending. The **open** function is discussed in more detail in Recipe 7.1.

When opening a file or making virtually any other system call,* checking the return value is indispensable. Not every **open** succeeds; not every file is readable; not every piece of data you **print** can reach its destination. Most programmers check **open**, **seek**, **tell**, and **close** in robust programs. You might also want to check other functions. The Perl documentation lists return values from all functions

---

* The term *system call* denotes a call into your operating system. It is unrelated to the C and Perl function that's actually named **system**.

and operators. If a system call fails, it returns `undef`, except for `wait`, `waitpid`, and `syscall`, which return –1 on failure. The system error message or number is available in the `$!` variable. This is often used in `die` or `warn` messages.

To read a record in Perl, use the circumfix operator `<FILEHANDLE>`, whose behavior is also available through the `readline` function. A record is normally a line, but you can change the record terminator, as detailed in Chapter 8. If `FILEHANDLE` is omitted, Perl opens and reads from the filenames in `@ARGV` or from STDIN if there aren't any. Customary and curious uses of this are described in Recipe 7.7.

Abstractly, files are simply streams of bytes. Each filehandle has associated with it a number representing the current byte position in the file, returned by the `tell` function and set by the `seek` function. In Recipe 7.10, we rewrite a file without closing and reopening by using `seek` to move back to the start, rewinding it.

When you no longer have use for a filehandle, `close` it. The `close` function takes a single filehandle and returns true if the filehandle could be successfully flushed and closed, false otherwise. You don't need to explicitly close every filehandle. When you open a filehandle that's already open, Perl implicitly closes it first. When your program exits, any open filehandles also get closed.

These implicit closes are for convenience, not stability, because they don't tell you whether the system call succeeded or failed. Not all closes succeed. Even a `close` on a read-only file can fail. For instance, you could lose access to the device because of a network outage. It's even more important to check the `close` if the file was opened for writing. Otherwise you wouldn't notice if the disk filled up.

```
close(FH)            or die "FH didn't close: $!";
```

The prudent programmer even checks the `close` on standard output stream at the program's end, in case STDOUT was redirected from the command line the output filesystem filled up. Admittedly, your run-time system should take care of this for you, but it doesn't.

Checking standard error, though, is probably of dubious value. After all, if STDERR fails to close, what are you planning to do about it?

STDOUT is the default destination for output from the `print`, `printf`, and `write` functions. Change this with `select`, which takes the new default output filehandle and returns the previous one. The new output filehandle should have been opened before calling `select`:

```
$old_fh = select(LOGFILE);                    # switch to LOGFILE for output
print "Countdown initiated ...\n";
select($old_fh);                              # return to original output
print "You have 30 seconds to reach minimum safety distance.\n";
```

Some of Perl's special variables change the behavior of the currently selected output filehandle. Most important is $|, which controls output buffering for each filehandle. Buffering is explained in Recipe 7.12.

Perl provides functions for buffered and unbuffered input and output. Although there are some exceptions, you shouldn't mix calls to buffered and unbuffered I/O functions. The following table shows the two sets of functions you should not mix. Functions on a particular row are only loosely associated; for instance, `sysread` doesn't have the same semantics as `<>`, but they are on the same row because they both read input from a filehandle.

Action	Buffered	Unbuffered
opening	`open`, `sysopen`	`sysopen`
closing	`close`	`close`
input	`<FILE>`, `readline`	`sysread`
output	`print`	`syswrite`
repositioning	`seek`, `tell`	`sysseek`

Repositioning is addressed in Chapter 8, but we also use it in Recipe 7.10.

7.1. Opening a File

Problem

You want to read or write to a filename from Perl.

Solution

Use **open** for convenience, **sysopen** for precision, or the IO::File module to get an anonymous filehandle.

The **open** function takes two arguments: the filehandle to open and one string containing the filename and special characters indicating how to open it (the mode):

```
open(SOURCE, "< $path")
    or die "Couldn't open $path for reading: $!\n";

open(SINK, "> $path")
    or die "Couldn't open $path for writing: $!\n";
```

The **sysopen** function takes three or four arguments: filehandle, filename, mode, and an optional permissions value. The mode is a number constructed from constants provided by the Fcntl module:

```
use Fcntl;

sysopen(SOURCE, $path, O_RDONLY)
    or die "Couldn't open $path for reading: $!\n";

sysopen(SINK, $path, O_WRONLY)
    or die "Couldn't open $path for writing: $!\n";
```

The IO::File module's **new** method accepts both **open** and **sysopen** style arguments and returns an anonymous filehandle. The **new** method also accepts a mode in the style of *fopen(3)*:

```
use IO::File;

# like Perl's open
$fh = IO::File->new("> $filename")
    or die "Couldn't open $filename for writing: $!\n";

# like Perl's sysopen
$fh = IO::File->new($filename, O_WRONLY|O_CREAT)
    or die "Couldn't open $filename for writing: $!\n";

# like stdio's fopen(3)
$fh = IO::File->new($filename, "r+")
    or die "Couldn't open $filename for read and write: $!\n";
```

Discussion

All input and output goes through filehandles, whether filehandles are mentioned or not. Filehandles aren't exclusively connected to files—they're also used to communicate with other programs (see Chapter 16, *Process Management and Communication*) and for network communication (see Chapter 17, *Sockets*). The **open** function can also be used to manipulate file descriptors, discussed in Recipe 7.19.

The **open** function quickly and conveniently solves the problem of associating a filehandle with a file. It permits a shorthand for common modes (reading, writing, reading and writing, appending) passed in with the filename. It doesn't let you control the permission that files are created with or even whether files are created. For this level of control, you need **sysopen**, which uses constants provided by the Fcntl module to control individual settings like read, write, create, and truncate.

Most programmers meet **open** long before they meet **sysopen**. The following table shows how **open** modes (the *Filename* column) correspond to **sysopen** constants (*O_flags*) and to the *fopen(3)* strings that IO::File->new can take (*Char*).

Read and *Write* indicate that the filehandle may be read from or written to. *Append* means no matter where you are in the file, output goes to the end of the file (on most systems). *Create* indicates whether the open statement creates a file if one having the given name doesn't already exist. *Trunc* indicates open will clobber any existing data if the file already exists.

Filename	Read	Write	Append	Create	Trunc	O_flags	Char
< *file*	yes	no	no	no	no	RDONLY	"r"
> *file*	no	yes	no	yes	yes	WRONLY TRUNC CREAT	"w"
>> *file*	no	yes	yes	yes	no	WRONLY APPEND CREAT	"a"
+< *file*	yes	yes	no	no	no	RDWR	"r+"
+> *file*	yes	yes	no	yes	yes	RDWR TRUNC CREAT	"w+"
+>> *file*	yes	yes	yes	yes	no	RDWR APPEND CREAT	"a+"

Here's a tip: you almost never want to use +> or +>>. The first clobbers your file before you can read it, and the second one is confusing because your read pointer can be anywhere, but on many systems, the writer always jumps to the end of the file.

The `sysopen` function takes three or four arguments:

```
sysopen(FILEHANDLE, $name, $flags)          or die "Can't open $name : $!";
sysopen(FILEHANDLE, $name, $flags, $perms) or die "Can't open $name : $!";
```

`$name` is the name of the file, without any < or + funny business. `$flags` is a number, formed by ORing together separate mode values for O_CREAT, O_WRONLY, O_TRUNC, etc. The exact availability of O_* constants depends on your operating system, so consult the online documentation for this (usually *open*(2), but not always), or look in */usr/include/fcntl.h*. Common ones are:

O_RDONLY	Read only
O_WRONLY	Write only
O_RDWR	Read and write
O_CREAT	Create the file if it doesn't exist
O_EXCL	Fail if the file already exists
O_APPEND	Append to the file
O_TRUNC	Truncate the file
O_NONBLOCK	Non-blocking access

Less common O_* flags sometimes available include O_SHLOCK, O_EXLOCK, O_BINARY, O_NOCTTY, and O_SYNC. Consult your *open*(2) manpage or its local equivalent for details.

If you omit the $perms argument to sysopen, Perl uses the octal value 0666. These permissions values need to be in octal and are modified by your process's current umask. A umask value is a number representing disabled permissions bits—if your umask were 027 (group can't write; others can't read, write, or execute), then passing sysopen 0666 would create a file with mode 0640 (mathematically: 0666 &~ 027 is 0640).

If umask seems confusing, here's some advice: supply a creation mode of 0666 for regular files and one of 0777 for directories and executable files. This gives users a choice: if they want protected files, they can choose process umasks of 022, 027, or even the particularly antisocial mask of 077. Programs should rarely if ever make policy decisions better left to the user. One exception is when writing files that should be kept private: mail files, web browser cookies, *.rhosts* files, and so on. In short, seldom if ever use 0644 as argument to sysopen because that takes away the user's option to have a more permissive umask.

Here are examples of open and sysopen in action.

To open file for reading:

```
open(FH, "< $path")                                        or die $!;
sysopen(FH, $path, O_RDONLY)                               or die $!;
```

To open file for writing, create new file if needed, or else truncate old file:

```
open(FH, "> $path")                                        or die $!;
sysopen(FH, $path, O_WRONLY|O_TRUNC|O_CREAT)               or die $!;
sysopen(FH, $path, O_WRONLY|O_TRUNC|O_CREAT, 0600)         or die $!;
```

To open file for writing, create new file, file must not exist:

```
sysopen(FH, $path, O_WRONLY|O_EXCL|O_CREAT)                or die $!;
sysopen(FH, $path, O_WRONLY|O_EXCL|O_CREAT, 0600)          or die $!;
```

To open file for appending, create if necessary:

```
open(FH, ">> $path")                                       or die $!;
sysopen(FH, $path, O_WRONLY|O_APPEND|O_CREAT)              or die $!;
sysopen(FH, $path, O_WRONLY|O_APPEND|O_CREAT, 0600)        or die $!;
```

To open file for appending, file must exist:

```
sysopen(FH, $path, O_WRONLY|O_APPEND)                      or die $!;
```

To open file for update, file must exist:

```
open(FH, "+< $path")                                       or die $!;
sysopen(FH, $path, O_RDWR)                                 or die $!;
```

To open file for update, create file if necessary:

```
sysopen(FH, $path, O_RDWR|O_CREAT)                         or die $!;
sysopen(FH, $path, O_RDWR|O_CREAT, 0600)                   or die $!;
```

To open file for update, file must not exist:

```
sysopen(FH, $path, O_RDWR|O_EXCL|O_CREAT)         or die $!;
sysopen(FH, $path, O_RDWR|O_EXCL|O_CREAT, 0600)   or die $!;
```

We demonstrate using a creation mask of 0600 here only to show how to create a private file. The argument is normally omitted.

See Also

The open, sysopen, and umask functions in *perlfunc*(1) and Chapter 3 of *Programming Perl*; the documentation for the standard IO::File and Fcntl modules (also in Chapter 7 of *Programming Perl*); your system's *open*(2), *fopen*(3), and *umask*(2) manpages; Recipe 7.2

7.2. Opening Files with Unusual Filenames

Problem

You want to open a file with a funny filename, like "-" or one that starts with <, >, or |, has leading or trailing whitespace; or ends with |. You don't want these to trigger open's do-what-I-mean behavior, since in this case, that's *not* what you mean.

Solution

Use open like this:

```
$filename =~ s#^(\s)#./$1#;
open(HANDLE, "< $filename\0")         or die "cannot open $filename : $!\n";
```

Or simply use sysopen:

```
sysopen(HANDLE, $filename, O_RDONLY)   or die "cannot open $filename: $!\n";
```

Discussion

The open function uses a single string to determine both the filename and the mode—the way the file is to be opened. If your filename begins with the characters used to indicate the mode, open can easily do something unexpected. Imagine the following code:

```
$filename = shift @ARGV;
open(INPUT, $filename)               or die "Couldn't open $filename : $!\n";
```

If the user gave `">/etc/passwd"` as the filename on the command line, this code would attempt to open */etc/passwd* for writing—definitely unsafe! We can try to give an explicit mode, say for writing:

```
open(OUTPUT, ">$filename")
    or die "Couldn't open $filename for writing: $!\n";
```

but even this would let the user give a filename of `">data"` and the code would append to the file **data** instead of erasing the old contents.

The easiest solution is **sysopen**, which takes the mode and filename as separate arguments:

```
use Fcntl;                              # for file constants

sysopen(OUTPUT, $filename, O_WRONLY|O_TRUNC)
    or die "Can't open $filename for writing: $!\n";
```

To get the same effect with **open** requires chicanery if the filename has leading or trailing whitespace:

```
$file =~ s#^(\s)#./$1#;
open(OUTPUT, "> $file\0")
        or die "Couldn't open $file for OUTPUT : $!\n";
```

The substitution protects initial whitespace (this cannot occur in fully specified filenames like `"/etc/passwd"`, but only in relative filenames like `" passwd"`). The NULL byte (`"\0"`) isn't considered part of the filename by **open**, but it does prevent any trailing whitespace from being ignored.

The magic way **open** interprets filenames is nearly always a good thing. You never have to use the special case of `"-"` to mean standard input or output. If you write a filter and use a simple **open**, users can pass `"gzip -dc bible.gz|"` as a filename, and your filter will automatically run the decoding program.

It's only those programs that run under special privilege that should worry about security with **open**. When designing programs that will be run on someone else's behalf, like setuid programs or CGI scripts, the prudent programmer always considers whether the user can supply their own filename and thereby cajole what would otherwise appear to be a normal **open** used for simple reading into overwriting a file or even running another program. Perl's -T command-line flag to enable taint-checking would take care of this.

See Also

The **open** and **sysopen** functions in *perlfunc*(1) and Chapter 3 of *Programming Perl*; Recipe 7.1; Recipe 7.7; Recipe 16.2; Recipe 19.4; Recipe 19.6

7.3. *Expanding Tildes in Filenames*

Problem

You want to open filenames like *~username/blah*, but **open** doesn't interpret the tilde to mean a home directory.

Solution

Expand the filename manually with a substitution:

```
$filename =~ s{ ^ ~ ( [^/]* ) }
             { $1
                  ? (getpwnam($1))[7]
                  : ( $ENV{HOME} || $ENV{LOGDIR}
                      || (getpwuid($>))[7]
                    )
}ex;
```

Discussion

The uses of tilde that we want to catch are:

```
~user
~user/blah
~
~/blah
```

If no name follows the ~, the current user's home directory is used.

This substitution uses /e to evaluate the replacement as Perl code. If a username follows the tilde, it's stored in $1, which **getpwnam** uses to extract the user's home directory out of the return list. This directory becomes the replacement string. If the tilde was not followed by a username, substitute in either the current HOME environment variable or the LOGDIR one. If neither of those environment variables is valid, look up the effective user ID's home directory.

See Also

Your system's *getpwnam*(2) manpage; the **getpwnam** function in *perlfunc*(1) and Chapter 3 of *Programming Perl*; Recipe 9.6

7.4. Making Perl Report Filenames in Errors

Problem

Your program works with files, but Perl's errors and warnings only report the last used filehandle, not the name of the file.

Solution

Use the filename as the filehandle:

```
open($path, "< $path")
    or die "Couldn't open $path for reading : $!\n";
```

Discussion

Ordinarily, error messages say:

```
Argument "3\n" isn't numeric in multiply at tallyweb line 16, <LOG> chunk 17.
```

The filehandle LOG doesn't help much because you don't know which file the handle was connected to. By using the filename itself as indirect filehandle, Perl produces more informative errors and warnings:

```
Argument "3\n" isn't numeric in multiply at tallyweb
   line 16, </usr/local/data/mylog3.dat> chunk 17.
```

Unfortunately, this doesn't work with `strict refs` turned on because the variable $path doesn't really have a filehandle in it, but just a string that sometimes behaves as one. The chunk mentioned in warnings and error messages is the current value of the `$.` variable.

See Also

Recipe 7.1; the open function in *perlfunc*(1) and Chapter 3 of *Programming Perl*

7.5. Creating Temporary Files

Problem

You need to create a temporary file and have it automatically deleted when your program exits. For instance, you want to write a temporary configuration file to feed a program you launch. In this case, you want to know the temporary file's name to tell the utility program. In other cases, you may just want a temporary file to write to and read from, and don't need to know its filename.

Solution

If you don't need to know the file's name, use the **new_tmpfile** class method
from the IO::File module to get a filehandle opened for reading and writing:

```
use IO::File;

$fh = IO::File->new_tmpfile
          or die "Unable to make new temporary file: $!";
```

If you need to know the file's name, use the **tmpnam** function from the POSIX
module to get a filename that you then open yourself:

```
use IO::File;
use POSIX qw(tmpnam);

# try new temporary filenames until we get one that didn't already exist
do { $name = tmpnam() }
    until $fh = IO::File->new($name, O_RDWR|O_CREAT|O_EXCL);

# install atexit-style handler so that when we exit or die,
# we automatically delete this temporary file
END { unlink($name) or die "Couldn't unlink $name : $!" }

# now go on to use the file ...
```

Discussion

If you only need scratch space, the IO::File module's **new_tmpfile** class method
returns a filehandle connected to a temporary file that's been opened read-write
by using the following code:

```
for (;;) {
    $name = tmpnam();
    sysopen(TMP, $tmpnam, O_RDWR | O_CREAT | O_EXCL) && last;
}
unlink $tmpnam;
```

This file will be automatically deleted when your program finally exits or the file is
closed. You cannot find its name to tell another process, because it doesn't have a
name. In fact, on systems that support such semantics, the filename was already
deleted before the method returned. A child process could inherit the open file
descriptor, however.[*]

This shows **new_tmpfile** in action. We create a temporary file, write to it, rewind,
and print what we wrote:

```
use IO::File;

$fh = IO::File->new_tmpfile            or die "IO::File->new_tmpfile: $!";
```

---

[*] But you'd better set $^F to at least `fileno($fh)` before you **exec** anything.

```
$fh->autoflush(1);
print $fh "$i\n" while $i++ < 10;
seek($fh, 0, 0)                          or die "seek: $!";
print "Tmp file has: ", <$fh>;
```

The second solution gets a temporary file whose name you can give to another process. We use the POSIX::tmpnam function, open the file ourselves, and delete it when we're done. We don't test whether a file of that name exists before opening it because that would introduce a race condition—someone might create the file between our checking whether it exists and our creating the file.* Instead, we wrap tmpnam in a loop to make sure we get a new file and don't accidentally clobber someone else's. Two processes shouldn't get the same filename from new_tmpfile, in theory.

See Also

The documentation for the standard IO::File and POSIX modules (also in Chapter 7 of *Programming Perl*); Recipe 7.19; your system's *tmpnam*(3) manpage

7.6. *Storing Files Inside Your Program Text*

Problem

You have data that you want to bundle with your program and treat as though it were in a file, but you don't want it to be in a different file.

Solution

Use the __DATA__ or __END__ tokens after your program code to mark the start of a data block, which can be read inside your program or module from the DATA filehandle.

Use __DATA__ within a module:

```
while (<DATA>) {
    # process the line
}
__DATA__
# your data goes here
```

Similarly, use __END__ within the main program file:

```
while (<main::DATA>) {
    # process the line
}
```

---

* Race conditions are explained in Recipe 19.4.

```
__END__
# your data goes here
```

Discussion

__DATA__ and __END__ indicate the logical end of a module or script before the physical end of file is reached. Text after __DATA__ or __END__ can be read through the per-package DATA filehandle. For example, take the hypothetical module Primes. Text after __DATA__ in *Primes.pm* can be read from the Primes::DATA filehandle.

__END__ behaves as a synonym for __DATA__ in the main package. Text after __END__ tokens in modules is inaccessible.

This lets you write self-contained programs that would ordinarily keep data kept in separate files. Often this is used for documentation. Sometimes it's configuration data or old test data that the program was originally developed with, left lying about in case it ever needs to be recreated.

Another trick is to use DATA to find out the current program's or module's size or last modification date. On most systems, the $0 variable will contain the full pathname to your running script. On systems where $0 is not correct, you could try the DATA filehandle instead. This can be used to pull in the size, modification date, etc. Put a special token __DATA__ at the end of the file (and maybe a warning not to delete it), and the DATA filehandle will be to the script itself.

```
use POSIX qw(strftime);

$raw_time = (stat(DATA))[9];
$size     = -s DATA;
$kilosize = int($size / 1024) . 'k';

print "<P>Script size is $kilosize\n";
print strftime("<P>Last script update: %c (%Z)\n", localtime($raw_time));

__DATA__
DO NOT REMOVE THE PRECEDING LINE.
Everything else in this file will be ignored.
```

See Also

The "Scalar Value Constructors" section of *perldata*(1), and the "Other Literal Tokens" section of Chapter 2 of *Programming Perl*

7.7. *Writing a Filter*

Problem

You want to write a program that takes a list of filenames on the command line and reads from STDIN if no filenames were given. You'd like the user to be able to give the file "-" to indicate STDIN or "someprogram |" to indicate the output of another program. You might want your program to modify the files in place or to produce output based on its input.

Solution

Read lines with <>:

```
while (<>) {
    # do something with the line
}
```

Discussion

When you say:

```
while (<>) {
    # ...
}
```

Perl translates this into:*

```
unshift(@ARGV, '-') unless @ARGV;
while ($ARGV = shift @ARGV) {
    unless (open(ARGV, $ARGV)) {
        warn "Can't open $ARGV: $!\n";
        next;
    }
    while (defined($_ = <ARGV>)) {
        # ...
    }
}
```

You can access ARGV and $ARGV inside the loop to read more from the filehandle or to find the filename currently being processed. Let's look at how this works.

Behavior

If the user supplies no arguments, Perl sets @ARGV to a single string, "-". This is shorthand for STDIN when opened for reading and STDOUT when opened for writing. It's also what lets the user of your program specify "-" as a filename on the command line to read from STDIN.

---

* Except that the code written here won't work because ARGV has internal magic.

Next, the file processing loop removes one argument at a time from @ARGV and copies the filename into the global variable $ARGV. If the file cannot be opened, Perl goes on to the next one. Otherwise, it processes a line at a time. When the file runs out, the loop goes back and opens the next one, repeating the process until @ARGV is exhausted.

The open statement didn't say open(ARGV, "< $ARGV"). There's no extra greater-than symbol supplied. This allows for interesting effects, like passing the string "gzip -dc file.gz |" as an argument, to make your program read the output of the command "gzip -dc file.gz". See Recipe 16.6 for more about this use of magic open.

You can change @ARGV before or inside the loop. Let's say you don't want the default behavior of reading from STDIN if there aren't any arguments—you want it to default to all the C or C++ source and header files. Insert this line before you start processing <ARGV>:

```
@ARGV = glob("*.[Cch]") unless @ARGV;
```

Process options before the loop, either with one of the Getopt libraries described in Chapter 15, *User Interfaces*, or manually:

```
# arg demo 1: Process optional -c flag
if (@ARGV && $ARGV[0] eq '-c') {
    $chop_first++;
    shift;
}

# arg demo 2: Process optional -NUMBER flag
if (@ARGV && $ARGV[0] =~ /^-(\d+)$/) {
    $columns = $1;
    shift;
}

# arg demo 3: Process clustering -a, -i, -n, or -u flags
while (@ARGV && $ARGV[0] =~ /^-(.+)/ && (shift, ($_ = $1), 1)) {
    next if /^$/;
    s/a// && (++$append,      redo);
    s/i// && (++$ignore_ints, redo);
    s/n// && (++$nostdout,    redo);
    s/u// && (++$unbuffer,    redo);
    die "usage: $0 [-ainu] [filenames] ...\n";
}
```

Other than its implicit looping over command-line arguments, <> is not special. The special variables controlling I/O still apply; see Chapter 8 for more on them. You can set $/ to set the line terminator, and $. contains the current line (record) number. If you undefine $/, you don't get the concatenated contents of all files at once; you get one complete file each time:

```
undef $/;
while (<>) {
```

```
        # $_ now has the complete contents of
        # the file whose name is in $ARGV
    }
```

If you localize $/, the old value is automatically restored when the enclosing block exits:

```
    {                       # create block for local
        local $/;   # record separator now undef
        while (<>) {
            # do something; called functions still have
            # undeffed version of $/
        }
    }                       # $/ restored here
```

Because processing <ARGV> never explicitly closes filehandles, the record number in $. is not reset. If you don't like that, you can explicitly close the file yourself to reset $.:

```
    while (<>) {
        print "$ARGV:$.:$_";
        close ARGV if eof;
    }
```

The eof function defaults to checking the end of file status of the last file read. Since the last handle read was ARGV, eof reports whether we're at the end of the current file. If so, we close it and reset the $. variable. On the other hand, the special notation eof() with parentheses but no argument checks if we've reached the end of all files in the <ARGV> processing.

Command-line options

Perl has command-line options, -n, -p, and -i, to make writing filters and one-liners easier.

The -n option adds the while (<>) loop around your program text. It's normally used for filters like *grep* or programs that summarize the data they read. The program is shown in Example 7-1.

Example 7-1. findlogin1

```
#!/usr/bin/perl
# findlogin1 - print all lines containing the string "login"
while (<>) {# loop over files on command line
    print if /login/;
}
```

The program in Example 7-1 could be written as shown in Example 7-2.

Example 7-2. findlogin2

```
#!/usr/bin/perl -n
# findlogin2 - print all lines containing the string "login"
print if /login/;
```

You can combine the **-n** and **-e** options to run Perl code from the command line:

```
% perl -ne 'print if /login/'
```

The **-p** option is like **-n** but it adds a **print** at the end of the loop. It's normally used for programs that translate their input. This program is shown in Example 7-3.

Example 7-3. lowercase1

```
#!/usr/bin/perl
# lowercase - turn all lines into lowercase

use locale;
while (<>) {                # loop over lines on command line
    s/([^\WO-9_])/\l$1/g;   # change all letters to lowercase
    print;
}
```

The program in Example 7-3 could be written as shown in Example 7-4.

Example 7-4. lowercase2

```
#!/usr/bin/perl -p
# lowercase - turn all lines into lowercase
use locale;
s/([^\WO-9_])/\l$1/g;# change all letters to lowercase
```

Or written from the command line as:

```
% perl -Mlocale -pe 's/([^\WO-9_])/\l$1/g'
```

While using **-n** or **-p** for implicit input looping, the special label **LINE:** is silently created for the whole input loop. That means that from an inner loop, you can go on the following input record by using **next LINE** (this is like *awk*'s **next**). Go on to the file by closing ARGV (this is like *awk*'s **nextfile**). This is shown in Example 7-5.

Example 7-5. countchunks

```
#!/usr/bin/perl -n
# countchunks - count how many words are used.
# skip comments, and bail on file if __END__
# or __DATA__ seen.
for (split /\W+/) {
    next LINE if /^#/;
    close ARGV if /__(DATA|END)__/;
    $chunks++;
}
END { print "Found $chunks chunks\n" }
```

The *tcsh* keeps a *.history* file in a format such that every other line contains a commented out timestamp in Epoch seconds:

```
#+0894382237
less /etc/motd
#+0894382239
vi ~/.exrc
#+0894382242
date
#+0894382242
who
#+0894382288
telnet home
```

A simple one-liner can render that legible:

```
% perl -pe 's/^#\+(\d+)\n/localtime($1) . " "/e'
Tue May  5 09:30:37 1998    less /etc/motd
Tue May  5 09:30:39 1998    vi ~/.exrc
Tue May  5 09:30:42 1998    date
Tue May  5 09:30:42 1998    who
Tue May  5 09:31:28 1998    telnet home
```

The -i option changes each file on the command line. It is described in Recipe 7.9, and is normally used in conjunction with -p.

You have to say use locale to handle current character set.

See Also

perlrun(1), and the "Switches" section of Chapter 6 of *Programming Perl*; Recipe 7.9; Recipe 16.6

7.8. Modifying a File in Place with Temporary File

Problem

You need to update a file in place, and you can use a temporary file.

Solution

Read from the original file, write changes to a temporary file, and then rename the temporary back to the original:

```
open(OLD, "< $old")          or die "can't open $old: $!";
open(NEW, "> $new")          or die "can't open $new: $!";
select(NEW);                 # new default filehandle for print
while (<OLD>) {
    # change $_, then...
```

```
        print NEW $_            or die "can't write $new: $!";
    }
    close(OLD)                  or die "can't close $old: $!";
    close(NEW)                  or die "can't close $new: $!";
    rename($old, "$old.orig")   or die "can't rename $old to $old.orig: $!";
    rename($new, $old)          or die "can't rename $new to $old: $!";
```

This is the best way to update a file "in place."

Discussion

This technique uses little memory compared to the approach that doesn't use a temporary file. It has the added advantages of giving you a backup file and being easier and safer to program.

You can make the same changes to the file using this technique that you can with the version that uses no temporary file. For instance, to insert lines at line 20:

```
while (<OLD>) {
    if ($. == 20) {
        print NEW "Extra line 1\n";
        print NEW "Extra line 2\n";
    }
    print NEW $_;
}
```

Or delete lines 20 through 30:

```
while (<OLD>) {
    next if 20 .. 30;
    print NEW $_;
}
```

Note that **rename** won't work across filesystems, so you should create your temporary file in the same directory as the file being modified.

The truly paranoid programmer would lock the file during the update.

See Also

Recipe 7.1; Recipe 7.9; Recipe 7.10

7.9. Modifying a File in Place with -i Switch

Problem

You need to modify a file in place from the command line, and you're too lazy[*] for the file manipulation of Recipe 7.8.

---

[*] Lazy-as-virtue, not lazy-as-sin.

Solution

Use the -i and -p switches to Perl. Write your program on the command line:

```
% perl -i.orig -p -e 'FILTER COMMAND' file1 file2 file3 ...
```

Or use the switches in programs:

```
#!/usr/bin/perl -i.orig -p
# filter commands go here
```

Discussion

The -i command-line switch modifies each file in place. It creates a temporary file as in the previous recipe, but Perl takes care of the tedious file manipulation for you. Use it with -p (explained in Recipe 7.7) to turn:

```
while (<>) {
    if ($ARGV ne $oldargv) {                 # are we at the next file?
        rename($ARGV, $ARGV . '.orig');
        open(ARGVOUT, ">$ARGV");             # plus error check
        select(ARGVOUT);
        $oldargv = $ARGV;
    }
    s/DATE/localtime/e;
}
continue{
    print;
}
select (STDOUT);                             # restore default output
```

into:

```
% perl -pi.orig -e 's/DATE/localtime/e'
```

The -i switch takes care of making a backup (say −i instead of −i.orig to discard the original file contents instead of backing them up), and -p makes Perl loop over filenames given on the command line (or STDIN if no files were given).

The preceding one-liner would turn a file containing the following:

```
Dear Sir/Madam/Ravenous Beast,
     As of DATE, our records show your account
is overdue.  Please settle by the end of the month.
Yours in cheerful usury,
     --A. Moneylender
```

into:

```
Dear Sir/Madam/Ravenous Beast,
     As of Sat Apr 25 12:28:33 1998, our records show your account
is overdue.  Please settle by the end of the month.
Yours in cheerful usury,
     --A. Moneylender
```

This switch makes in-place translators a lot easier to write and to read. For instance, this changes isolated instances of **"hisvar"** to **"hervar"** in all C, C++, and *yacc* files:

```
% perl -i.old -pe 's{\bhisvar\b}{hervar}g' *.[Cchy]
```

Turn on and off the -i behavior with the special variable $^I. Set @ARGV, and then use <> as you would with -i on the command line:

```
# set up to iterate over the *.c files in the current directory,
# editing in place and saving the old file with a .orig extension
local $^I   = '.orig';            # emulate -i.orig
local @ARGV = glob("*.c");        # initialize list of files
while (<>) {
    if ($. == 1) {
        print "This line should appear at the top of each file\n";
    }
    s/\b(p)earl\b/${1}erl/ig;     # Correct typos, preserving case
    print;
} continue {close ARGV if eof}
```

Beware that creating a backup file under a particular name when that name already exists clobbers the previously backed up version.

See Also

perlrun(1), and the "Switches" section of Chapter 6 of *Programming Perl*; the $^I and $. variables in *perlvar*(1), and in the "Special Variables" section of Chapter 2 of *Programming Perl*; the .. operator in the "Range Operator" sections of *perlop*(1) and Chapter 2 of *Programming Perl*

7.10. Modifying a File in Place Without a Temporary File

Problem

You need to insert, delete, or change one or more lines in a file, and you don't want to (or can't) use a temporary file.

Solution

Open the file in update mode ("+<"), read the whole file into an array of lines, change the array, then rewrite the file and truncate it to its current seek pointer.

```
open(FH, "+< FILE")                  or die "Opening: $!";
@ARRAY = <FH>;
```

```
# change ARRAY here
seek(FH,0,0)                    or die "Seeking: $!";
print FH @ARRAY                 or die "Printing: $!";
truncate(FH,tell(FH))           or die "Truncating: $!";
close(FH)                       or die "Closing: $!";
```

Discussion

As explained in the Introduction, the operating system treats files as unstructured streams of bytes. This makes it impossible to insert, modify, or change bits of the file in place. (Except for the special case of fixed-record-length files, discussed in Recipe 8.13.) You can use a temporary file to hold the changed output, or you can read the entire file into memory, change it, and write it back out again.

Reading everything into memory works for small files, but it doesn't scale well. Trying it on your 800 MB web server log files will either deplete your virtual memory or thrash your machine's VM system. For small files, though, this works:

```
open(F, "+< $infile")       or die "can't read $infile: $!";
$out = '';
while (<F>) {
    s/DATE/localtime/eg;
    $out .= $_;
}
seek(F, 0, 0)               or die "can't seek to start of $infile: $!";
print F $out                or die "can't print to $infile: $!";
truncate(F, tell(F))        or die "can't truncate $infile: $!";
close(F)                    or die "can't close $infile: $!";
```

For other examples of the things you can do in-place, look at the recipes in Chapter 8.

This approach is for the truly determined. It's harder to write, takes more memory (potentially a *lot* more), doesn't keep a backup file, and may confuse other processes trying to read from the file you're updating. For most purposes, therefore, we suggest it's probably not worth it.

Remember to lock if you're paranoid.

See Also

The seek, truncate, open, sysopen functions in *perlfunc*(1) and in Chapter 3 of *Programming Perl*; Recipe 7.8; Recipe 7.9

7.11. Locking a File

Problem

Many processes need to update the same file simultaneously.

Solution

Have all processes honor advisory locking by using flock:

```
open(FH, "+< $path")          or die "can't open $path: $!";
flock(FH, 2)                  or die "can't flock $path: $!";
# update file, then...
close(FH)                     or die "can't close $path: $!";
```

Discussion

Operating systems vary greatly in the type and reliability of locking techniques available. Perl tries hard to give you something that works, even if your operating system uses its own underlying technique. The flock function takes two arguments: a filehandle and a number representing what to do with the lock on that filehandle. The numbers are normally represented by names like LOCK_EX, which you can get from the Fcntl or IO::File modules.

The LOCK_SH, LOCK_EX, LOCK_UN, and LOCK_NB symbolic values were not available in the Fcntl module before the 5.004 release, and even now they are available only if you ask for them specifically using the :flock tag. Their values are 1, 2, 4, and 8 respectively, which you may supply yourself instead of using the symbolic constants. You'll therefore often see people write:

```
sub LOCK_SH()  { 1 }     #  Shared lock (for reading)
sub LOCK_EX()  { 2 }     #  Exclusive lock (for writing)
sub LOCK_NB()  { 4 }     #  Non-blocking request (don't stall)
sub LOCK_UN()  { 8 }     #  Free the lock (careful!)
```

Locks come in two varieties: shared and exclusive. Despite what you might infer by "exclusive," processes aren't required to obey locks on files. Another way of saying this is that flock implements *advisory locking*. It allows processes to let the operating system suspend would-be writers of a file until any readers are finished with it.

Flocking files is like putting up a stoplight at an intersection. It works only if people pay attention to whether the light is red or green—or yellow in the case of a shared lock. The red light doesn't stop traffic; it merely signals that traffic should stop. A desperate, ignorant, or rude person will still go flying through the intersection no matter what the light says. Likewise, flock only blocks out other flockers—not processes trying to do I/O. Unless everyone is polite, accidents can (and will) happen.

The polite process customarily indicates its intent to read from the file by requesting a LOCK_SH. Many processes can have simultaneous shared locks on the file because they (presumably) won't be changing the data. If a process intends to write to the file, it should request an exclusive lock via LOCK_EX. The operating system then suspends the requesting process until all other processes have released their locks, at which point it grants the lock to the suspended process and unblocks it. You are guaranteed that no other process will be able to run flock(FH, LOCK_EX) on the same file while you hold the lock. This is almost but not quite like saying that there can be only one exclusive lock on the file. Forked children inherit not only their parents' open files, but, on some systems, also any locks held. That means if you hold an exclusive lock and fork without execing, your child may also have that same exclusive lock on the file.

The flock function is therefore by default a blocking operation. You can also acquire a lock without wedging your process by using the LOCK_NB flag when you request a lock. This lets you warn the user that there may be a wait until other processes with locks are done:

```
unless (flock(FH, LOCK_EX|LOCK_NB)) {
    warn "can't immediately write-lock the file ($!), blocking ...";
    unless (flock(FH, LOCK_EX)) {
        die "can't get write-lock on numfile: $!";
    }
}
```

If you use LOCK_NB and are refused a LOCK_SH, then you know that someone else has a LOCK_EX and is updating the file. If you are refused a LOCK_EX, then someone holds either a LOCK_SH or a LOCK_EX, so you shouldn't try to update the file.

Locks dissolve when the file is closed, which may not be until your process exits. Manually unlocking the file without closing can be perilous due to buffering. The buffer might not have been flushed, leading to a time between unlocking and closing when another process could read data that the contents of your buffer were supposed to replace. A safer way to deal with this is:

```
if ($] < 5.004) {                    # test Perl version number
    my $old_fh = select(FH);
    local $| = 1;                     # enable command buffering
    local $\ = '';                    # clear output record separator
    print "";                         # trigger output flush
    select($old_fh);                  # restore previous filehandle
}
flock(FH, LOCK_UN);
```

Before version 5.004 of Perl, you had to force a flush. Because folks would often forget to do that, 5.004 changed LOCK_UN so that any pending unwritten buffers are automatically flushed right before the lock is released.

Here's how you increment a number in a file, using `flock`:

```perl
use Fcntl qw(:DEFAULT :flock);

sysopen(FH, "numfile", O_RDWR|O_CREAT)
                                or die "can't open numfile: $!";
flock(FH, LOCK_EX)              or die "can't write-lock numfile: $!";
# Now we have acquired the lock, it's safe for I/O
$num = <FH> || 0;              # DO NOT USE "or" THERE!!
seek(FH, 0, 0)                  or die "can't rewind numfile : $!";
truncate(FH, 0)                 or die "can't truncate numfile: $!";
print FH $num+1, "\n"           or die "can't write numfile: $!";
close(FH)                       or die "can't close numfile: $!";
```

Closing the filehandle flushes the buffers and unlocks the file. The `truncate` function is discussed in Chapter 8.

File locking is not as easy as you might think—or wish. Because locks are advisory, if one process uses locking and another doesn't, all bets are off. Never use the existence of a file as a locking indication because there exists a race condition between the test for the existence of the file and its creation. Furthermore, because file locking is an intrinsically stateful concept, it doesn't get along well with the stateless model embraced by network filesystems such as NFS. Although some vendors claim that `fcntl` addresses such matters, practical experience suggests otherwise.

NFS locking intimately involves both server and client. Consequently, we know of no general mechanism for guaranteed reliable locking over NFS. You can do it if you know certain operations are atomic in the server or client implementation. You can do it if you know that both server and client support `flock` or `fcntl`; most don't. But in general you can't hope to write code that works everywhere.

Don't confuse Perl's `flock` with the SysV function `lockf`. Unlike `lockf`, `flock` locks entire files at once. Perl doesn't support `lockf` directly. The only way to lock a portion of a file is to use the `fnctl` function, as demonstrated in the *lock-area* program at the end of this chapter.

See Also

The `flock` and `fcntl` functions in *perlfunc*(1) and in Chapter 3 of *Programming Perl*; the documentation for the standard Fcntl and DB_File modules (also in Chapter 7 of *Programming Perl*); Recipe 7.21; Recipe 7.22

7.12. Flushing Output

Problem

When printing to a filehandle, output doesn't appear immediately. This is a problem in CGI scripts running on some programmer-hostile web servers where, if the web server sees warnings from Perl before it sees the (buffered) output of your script, it sends the browser an uninformative 500 **Server Error**. These buffering problems arise with concurrent access to files by multiple programs and when talking with devices or sockets.

Solution

Disable buffering by setting the per-filehandle variable $| to a true value, customarily 1:

```
$old_fh = select(OUTPUT_HANDLE);
$| = 1;
select($old_fh);
```

Or, if you don't mind the expense, disable it by calling the `autoflush` method from the IO modules:

```
use IO::Handle;
OUTPUT_HANDLE->autoflush(1);
```

Discussion

In most stdio implementations, buffering varies with the type of output device. Disk files are block buffered, often with a buffer size of more than 2K. Pipes and sockets are often buffered with a buffer size between ½ and 2K. Serial devices, including terminals, modems, mice, and joysticks, are normally line-buffered; stdio sends the entire line out only when it gets the newline.

Perl's `print` function does not support truly unbuffered output—a physical write for each individual character. Instead, it supports *command buffering*, in which one physical write is made after every separate output command. This isn't as hard on your system as no buffering at all, and it still gets the output where you want it, when you want it.

Control output buffering through the $| special variable. Enable command buffering by setting it to a true value. It has no effect upon input; see Recipes 15.6 and

15.8 for unbuffered input. Set this variable to a false value to use default stdio buffering. Example 7-6 illustrates the difference.

Example 7-6. seeme

```
#!/usr/bin/perl -w
# seeme - demo stdio output buffering
$| = (@ARGV > 0);        # command buffered if arguments given
print "Now you don't see it...";
sleep 2;
print "now you do\n";
```

If you call this program with no arguments, STDOUT is not command buffered. Your terminal (console, window, telnet session, whatever) doesn't receive output until the entire line is completed, so you see nothing for two seconds and then get the full line "Now you don't see it ... now you do". If you call the program with at least one argument, STDOUT is command buffered. That means you first see "Now you don't see it...", and then after two seconds you finally see "now you do".

The dubious quest for increasingly compact code has led programmers to use the return value of select, the filehandle that *was* currently selected, as part of the second select:

```
select((select(OUTPUT_HANDLE), $| = 1)[0]);
```

There's another way. The FileHandle and IO modules provide a class method called autoflush. Call it with true or false values (the default value is true) to control autoflushing on a particular output handle:

```
use FileHandle;

STDERR->autoflush;          # already unbuffered in stdio
$filehandle->autoflush(0);
```

If you're willing to accept the oddities of indirect object notation covered in Chapter 13, *Classes, Objects, and Ties*, you can even write something reasonably close to English:

```
use IO::Handle;
# assume REMOTE_CONN is an interactive socket handle,
# but DISK_FILE is a handle to a regular file.
autoflush REMOTE_CONN  1;          # unbuffer for clarity
autoflush DISK_FILE    0;          # buffer this for speed
```

This avoids the bizarre select business, and makes your code much more readable. Unfortunately, your program takes longer to compile because you're now including the IO::Handle module, so thousands and thousands of lines must first be read and compiled. Learn to manipulate $| directly, and you'll be happy.

To ensure that your output gets where you want it, when you want it, buffer flushing is important. It's particularly important with sockets, pipes, and devices, because you may be trying to do interactive I/O with these—more so, in fact, because you can't assume line-buffering. Consider the program in Example 7-7.

Example 7-7. getpcomidx

```perl
#!/usr/bin/perl
# getpcomidx - fetch www.perl.com's index.html document
use IO::Socket;
$sock = new IO::Socket::INET (PeerAddr => 'www.perl.com',
                              PeerPort => 'http(80)');
die "Couldn't create socket: $@" unless $sock;
# the library doesn't support $! setting; it uses $@

$sock->autoflush(1);

# Mac *must* have \015\012\015\012 instead of \n\n here.
# It's a good idea for others, too, as that's the spec,
# but implementations are encouraged to accept "\cJ\cJ" too,
# and as far as we've seen, they do.
$sock->print("GET /index.html http/1.1\n\n");
$document = join('', $sock->getlines());
print "DOC IS: $document\n";
```

There's no way to control input buffering using any kind of flushing discussed so far. For that, you need to see Recipes 15.6 and 15.8.

See Also

The $| entry in *perlvar*(1), and in the "Special Variables" section of Chapter 2 of *Programming Perl*; the documentation for the standard FileHandle and IO::Handle modules (also in Chapter 7 of *Programming Perl*); the `select` function in *perlfunc*(1) and in Chapter 3 of *Programming Perl*

7.13. Reading from Many Filehandles Without Blocking

Problem

You want to learn whether input is available to be read, rather than blocking for input as <> does. This is useful when reading from pipes, sockets, devices, and other programs.

Solution

Use **select** with a timeout value of 0 seconds, if you're comfortable with manipulating bit-vectors representing file descriptor sets:

```
$rin = '';
# repeat next line for all filehandles to poll
vec($rin, fileno(FH1), 1) = 1;
vec($rin, fileno(FH2), 1) = 1;
vec($rin, fileno(FH3), 1) = 1;

$nfound = select($rout=$rin, undef, undef, 0);
if ($nfound) {
   # input waiting on one or more of those 3 filehandles
   if (vec($rout,fileno(FH1),1)) {
       # do something with FH1
   }
   if (vec($rout,fileno(FH2),1)) {
       # do something with FH2
   }
   if (vec($rout,fileno(FH3),1)) {
       # do something with FH3
   }
}
```

The IO::Select module provides an abstraction to hide the bit-vector operations:

```
use IO::Select;

$select = IO::Select->new();
# repeat next line for all filehandles to poll
$select->add(*FILEHANDLE);
if (@ready = $select->can_read(0)) {
    # input waiting on the filehandles in @ready
}
```

Discussion

The **select** function is really two functions in one. If you call it with one argument, you change the current default output filehandle (see Recipe 7.12). If you call it with four arguments, it tells you which filehandles have input waiting or are ready to receive output. This recipe only deals with four-argument **select**.

The first three arguments to **select** are strings containing bit-vectors. Each bit-vector represents a set of file descriptors to inspect for pending input, pending output, and pending expedited data (like out-of-band or urgent data on a socket), respectively. The final argument is the timeout—how long **select** should spend waiting for status to change. A timeout value of 0 indicates a poll. Timeout can also be a floating-point number of seconds, or **undef** to wait (block) until status changes:

```
$rin = '';
vec($rin, fileno(FILEHANDLE), 1) = 1;
$nfound = select($rin, undef, undef, 0);    # just check
if ($nfound) {
    $line = <FILEHANDLE>;
    print "I read $line";
}
```

This code isn't perfect, though. If someone connects and sends a character but never sends a newline, your program will block in the <FILE>. We get around this by reading characters one at a time and processing completed lines when we read a "\n". This removes the need for the blocking <FILE> call. Another solution (if you're not testing files) is detailed in Recipe 7.15.

The IO::Select module hides the bit-vectors from you. IO::Select->new() returns a new object on which you call the **add** method to add one or more filehandles to the set. When you've added all the filehandles you are interested in, call **can_read**, **can_write**, or **has_exception**. These functions return a list of filehandles you can safely read from, write to, or that have unread exceptional data (TCP out-of-band data, for example).

Don't mix calls to four-argument **select** with calls to any of the buffered I/O functions listed in this chapter's Introduction (**read**, <>, **seek**, **tell**, etc.). Instead, you must use **sysread**—and **sysseek** if you want to reposition the filehandle within the file.

If you want to read whatever is available on a socket or pipe and return immediately, see Recipe 7.14. If you're trying to do non-blocking reads on a terminal, see Recipes 15.6 and 15.8.

See Also

The **select** function in *perlfunc*(1) and in Chapter 3 of *Programming Perl*; the documentation for the standard module IO::Select; Recipe 7.14

7.14. Doing Non-Blocking I/O

Problem

You want to read from or write to a filehandle without the system blocking your process until the program, file, socket, or device at the other end is ready. This is desired less often of regular files than of special files.

Solution

Open the file with **sysopen**, and specify the O_NONBLOCK option:

```
use Fcntl;

sysopen(MODEM, "/dev/cua0", O_NONBLOCK|O_RDWR)
    or die "Can't open modem: $!\n";
```

If you already have a filehandle, use **fcntl** to change the flags:

```
use Fcntl;

$flags = '';
fcntl(HANDLE, F_GETFL, $flags)
    or die "Couldn't get flags for HANDLE : $!\n";
$flags |= O_NONBLOCK;
fcntl(HANDLE, F_SETFL, $flags)
    or die "Couldn't set flags for HANDLE: $!\n";
```

Once a filehandle is set for non-blocking I/O, the **sysread** or **syswrite** calls that would block will instead return **undef** and set $! to EAGAIN:

```
use POSIX qw(:errno_h);

$rv = syswrite(HANDLE, $buffer, length $buffer);
if (!defined($rv) && $! == EAGAIN) {
    # would block
} elsif ($rv != length $buffer) {
    # incomplete write
} else {
    # successfully wrote
}

$rv = sysread(HANDLE, $buffer, $BUFSIZ);
if (!defined($rv) && $! == EAGAIN) {
    # would block
} else {
    # successfully read $rv bytes from HANDLE
}
```

Discussion

The O_NONBLOCK constant is part of the POSIX standard, so most machines should support it. We use the POSIX module to get the numeric value for the error EAGAIN.

See Also

The sysopen and fcntl functions in *perlfunc*(1) and in Chapter 3 of *Program-ming Perl*; the documentation for the standard POSIX module; your system's *open*(2) and *fcntl*(2) manpages; Recipe 7.13; Recipe 7.15

7.15. Determining the Number of Bytes to Read

Problem

You want to know how many bytes to read from a filehandle with read or sys-read.

Solution

Use the FIONREAD ioctl call:

```
$size = pack("L", 0);
ioctl(FH, $FIONREAD, $size)        or die "Couldn't call ioctl: $!\n";
$size = unpack("L", $size);

# $size bytes can be read
```

Discussion

The Perl ioctl function is a direct interface to the operating system's *ioctl(2)* sys-tem call. If your system doesn't have the FIONREAD request or the *ioctl(2)* call, you can't use this recipe. FIONREAD and the other *ioctl*(2) requests are numeric values normally found lurking in C include files.

Perl's *h2ph* tool tries to convert C include files to Perl code, which can be required. FIONREAD ends up defined as a function in the *sys/ioctl.ph* file:

```
require 'sys/ioctl.ph';

$size = pack("L", 0);
ioctl(FH, FIONREAD(), $size)       or die "Couldn't call ioctl: $!\n";
$size = unpack("L", $size);
```

If *h2ph* wasn't installed or doesn't work for you, you can manually *grep* the include files:

```
% grep FIONREAD /usr/include/*/*
/usr/include/asm/ioctls.h:#define FIONREAD        0x541B
```

Or write a small C program using the editor of champions:

```
% cat > fionread.c
#include <sys/ioctl.h>
main() {
    printf("%#08x\n", FIONREAD);
}
^D
% cc -o fionread fionread.c
% ./fionread
0x4004667f
```

Then hard-code it, leaving porting as an exercise to your successor.

```
$FIONREAD = 0x4004667f;          # XXX: opsys dependent

$size = pack("L", 0);
ioctl(FH, $FIONREAD, $size)      or die "Couldn't call ioctl: $!\n";
$size = unpack("L", $size);
```

FIONREAD requires a filehandle connected to a stream, which means sockets, pipes, and tty devices work, but files don't.

If this is too much system programming for you, try to think outside the problem. Read from the filehandle in non-blocking mode (see Recipe 7.14). If you manage to read something, then that's how much was waiting to be read. If you couldn't read anything, there was nothing to be read.

See Also

Recipe 7.14; your system's *ioctl*(2) manpage; the `ioctl` function in *perlfunc*(1) and in Chapter 3 of *Programming Perl*

7.16. Storing Filehandles in Variables

Problem

You want to use a filehandle like a normal variable so you can pass it to or return it from a function, store it in a data structure, and so on.

Solution

If you already have a regular symbolic filehandle like STDIN or LOGFILE, use the typeglob notation, *FH. This is the most efficient approach.

```
$variable = *FILEHANDLE;         # save in variable
subroutine(*FILEHANDLE);         # or pass directly

sub subroutine {
    my $fh = shift;
    print $fh "Hello, filehandle!\n";
}
```

If you want anonymous filehandles, see the *return_fh* function below, or use the
new method from the IO::File or IO::Handle module, store that in a scalar variable, and use it as though it were a normal filehandle:

```
use FileHandle;                        # make anon filehandle
$fh = FileHandle->new();

use IO::File;                          # 5.004 or higher
$fh = IO::File->new();
```

Discussion

You have many choices for passing filehandles into a subroutine or storing them
in a data structure. The simplest and fastest way is through the typeglob notation,
*FH. It may help you to conceptualize the asterisk as the type symbol for a file-
handle. Like the little colored balls from high school chemistry that stood for
atomic particles, it's not really true, but it is a convenient mental shorthand. By the
time you understand where this model breaks down, you won't need it anymore.

That works cleanly for simple things, but what if you wanted to make an array of
filehandles whose names you didn't know? As shown in Chapter 11, *References
and Records*, generating anonymous arrays, hashes, and even functions on the fly
can prove extremely convenient. It would be nice to be able to do the same with
filehandles. That's where the IO modules come in.

You can generate an anonymous handle with the IO::Handle or IO::File module's
new method. This returns a filehandle you can pass to subroutines, store in arrays,
and use however you would use a named filehandle's typeglob—plus more. You
can also use those modules as object classes for inheritance purposes because the
return values from the new constructor are fully fledged objects, complete with
available method calls.

You can use these as indirect filehandles, which saves you the trouble of thinking
up filehandle names. Instead, you think up names to store the anonymous filehandles in.

To capture the typeglob from a named filehandle, prefix it with *:

```
$fh_a = IO::File->new("< /etc/motd")     or die "open /etc/motd: $!";
$fh_b = *STDIN;
some_sub($fh_a, $fh_b);
```

This isn't the only way, but it is the simplest and most convenient. Its only limitation is that you can't bless it to turn it into an object. To do this, you must bless
a *reference* to a typeglob—that's what IO::Handle does. Like typeglobs, references to typeglobs can be safely used as indirect filehandles, whether blessed or
not.

To create and return a new filehandle from a function, do this:

```
sub return_fh {             # make anon filehandle
    local *FH;              # must be local, not my
    # now open it if you want to, then...
    return *FH;
}

$handle = return_fh();
```

A subroutine accepting a filehandle argument can either store the argument into a (preferably lexical) variable and use that as an indirect filehandle:

```
sub accept_fh {
    my $fh = shift;
    print $fh "Sending to indirect filehandle\n";
}
```

or it can localize a typeglob and use the filehandle directly:

```
sub accept_fh {
    local *FH = shift;
    print  FH "Sending to localized filehandle\n";
}
```

Both styles work with either IO::Handle objects or typeglobs of real filehandles:

```
accept_fh(*STDOUT);
accept_fh($handle);
```

Perl accepts many things as indirect filehandles (strings, typeglobs, and references to typeglobs), but unless you pass typeglobs or IO::Handle objects you may run into trouble. Strings ("LOGFILE" instead of *LOGFILE) require special finessing to work between packages, and references to typeglobs can't be usefully returned from functions.

In the preceding examples, we assigned the filehandle to a scalar variable before using it. That is because only simple scalar variables, not expressions or subscripts into hashes or arrays, can be used with built-ins like print, printf, or the diamond operator. These are illegal and won't even compile:

```
@fd = (*STDIN, *STDOUT, *STDERR);
print $fd[1] "Type it: ";                    # WRONG
$got = <$fd[0]>                              # WRONG
print $fd[2] "What was that: $got";          # WRONG
```

With print and printf, you get around this by using a block and an expression where you would place the filehandle:

```
print  { $fd[1] } "funny stuff\n";
printf { $fd[1] } "Pity the poor %x.\n", 3_735_928_559;
Pity the poor deadbeef.
```

That block is a proper block, so you can put more complicated code there. This sends the message out to one of two places:

```
$ok = -x "/bin/cat";
print { $ok ? $fd[1] : $fd[2] } "cat stat $ok\n";
print { $fd[ 1 + ($ok || 0) ]  } "cat stat $ok\n";
```

This approach of treating `print` and `printf` like object methods calls doesn't work for the diamond operator, because it's a real operator, not just a function with a comma-less argument. Assuming you've been storing typeglobs in your structure as we did above, you can use the built-in function named `readline` to read a record just as `<FH>` does. Given the preceding initialization of `@fd`, this would work:

```
$got = readline($fd[0]);
```

See Also

The `open` function in *perlfunc*(1) and in Chapter 3 of *Programming Perl*; Recipe 7.1; the documentation with the standard FileHandle module (also in Chapter 7 of *Programming Perl*); the "Typeglobs and Filehandles" sections of Chapter 2 of *Programming Perl* and Chapter 2 of *Programming Perl*

7.17. *Caching Open Output Filehandles*

Problem

You need more output files open simultaneously than your system allows.

Solution

Use the standard FileCache module:

```
use FileCache;
cacheout ($path);          # each time you use a filehandle
print $path "output";
```

Discussion

FileCache's `cacheout` function lets you work with more output files than your operating system lets you have open at any one time. If you use it to open an existing file that FileCache is seeing for the first time, the file is truncated to length zero, no questions asked. However, in its opening and closing of files in the background, `cacheout` tracks the files it has opened before and does not overwrite them, but appends to them instead. This does not create directories for you, so if you give it */usr/local/dates/merino.ewe* to open but the directory */usr/local/dates* doesn't exist, `cacheout` will `die`.

The `cacheout()` function checks the value of the C-level constant NOFILE from the standard system include file `sys/param.h` to determine how many concurrently open files are allowed on your system. This value can be incorrect on some systems and even missing on a few (for instance, on those where the maximum number of open file descriptors is a process resource limit that can be set with the *limit* or *ulimit* commands). If `cacheout()` can't get a value for NOFILE, just set `$FileCache::maxopen` to be four less than the correct value, or choose a reasonable number by trial and error.

Example 7-8 splits an *xferlog* file created by the popular *wuftpd* FTP server into files named after the authenticated user. The fields in `xferlog` files are space-separated, and the fourth from last field is the authenticated username.

Example 7-8. splitwulog

```
#!/usr/bin/perl
# splitwulog - split wuftpd log by authenticated user
use FileCache;
$outdir = '/var/log/ftp/by-user';
while (<>) {
    unless (defined ($user = (split)[-4])) {
        warn "Invalid line: $.\n";
        next;
    }
    $path = "$outdir/$user";
    cacheout $path;
    print $path $_;
}
```

See Also

Documentation for the standard FileCache module (also in Chapter 7 of *Programming Perl*); the `open` function in *perlfunc*(1) and in Chapter 3 of *Programming Perl*

7.18. Printing to Many Filehandles Simultaneously

Problem

You need to output the same data to several different filehandles.

Solution

If you want to do it without forking, write a `foreach` loop that iterates across the
filehandles:

```
foreach $filehandle (@FILEHANDLES) {
    print $filehandle $stuff_to_print;
}
```

If you don't mind forking, open a filehandle that's a pipe to a *tee* program:

```
open(MANY, "| tee file1 file2 file3 > /dev/null")    or die $!;
print MANY "data\n"                                   or die $!;
close(MANY)                                           or die $!;
```

Discussion

A filehandle sends output to one file or program only. To duplicate output to several places, you must call `print` multiple times or make a filehandle connected to
a program like `tee`, which distributes its input elsewhere. If you use the first
option, it's probably easiest to put the filehandles in a list or array and loop
through them:

```
# 'use strict' complains about this one:
for $fh ('FH1', 'FH2', 'FH3')    { print $fh "whatever\n" }
# but not this one:
for $fh (*FH1, *FH2, *FH3)       { print $fh "whatever\n" }
```

However, if your system supports the *tee* program, or if you've installed the Perl
version from Recipe 8.19, you may open a pipe to *tee* and let it do the work of
copying the file to several places. Remember that *tee* normally also copies its output to STDOUT, so you must redirect *tee*'s standard output to */dev/null* if you
don't want an extra copy:

```
open (FH, "| tee file1 file2 file3 >/dev/null");
print FH "whatever\n";
```

You could even redirect your own STDOUT to the *tee* process, and then you're
able to use a regular `print` directly:

```
# make STDOUT go to three files, plus original STDOUT
open (STDOUT, "| tee file1 file2 file3") or die "Teeing off: $!\n";
print "whatever\n"                        or die "Writing: $!\n";
close(STDOUT)                             or die "Closing: $!\n";
```

See Also

The `print` function in *perlfunc*(1) and in Chapter 3 of *Programming Perl*; the
"Typeglobs and Filehandles" sections of Chapter 2 of *Programming Perl* and Chapter 2 of *Programming Perl*; we use this technique in Recipe 8.19 and Recipe 13.15

7.19. Opening and Closing File Descriptors by Number

Problem

You know which file descriptors you'd like to do I/O on, but Perl requires filehandles, not descriptor numbers.

Solution

To open the file descriptor, use the `"<&="` or `"<&"` open modes or the IO::Handle module's `fdopen` class method:

```
open(FH, "<&=$FDNUM");      # open FH to the descriptor itself
open(FH, "<&$FDNUM");       # open FH to a copy of the descriptor

use IO::Handle;

$fh->fdopen($FDNUM, "r");   # open file descriptor 3 for reading
```

To close one by number, either use the `POSIX::close` function or else first open it as we did previously.

Discussion

Occasionally you have a file descriptor but no filehandle. Perl's I/O system uses filehandles instead of file descriptors, so you have to make a new filehandle for an already open file descriptor. The `"<&"`, `">&"`, and `"+<&"` modes to `open` will do this for reading, writing, and updating respectively. Adding an equal sign to these to make `"<&="`, `">&="`, and `"+<&="` is more parsimonious of file descriptors and nearly always what you want to do. That's because it used only a C-level `fdopen` function, not a `dup2` system call.

If you have version 5.004 or better installed, you can use the IO::Handle object method. This is the same as:

```
use IO::Handle;
$fh = IO::Handle->new();

$fh->fdopen(3, "r");          # open fd 3 for reading
```

Closing a file descriptor by number is even rarer. The `POSIX::close` function does so directly. If your system doesn't have a working POSIX library but does have a working `syscall` (and your sysadmin has installed the *sys/syscall.ph* file created with the *h2ph* translator), you can call the not very portable `syscall` function. It has peculiar parameters and return values: You have to add 0 to numbers and append the empty string (`""`) to strings to coerce them to the right types for C, and the error return value is -1 rather than false as in other Perl calls. Needless to say, use `syscall` only as a last resort.

Here's how you'd open the file descriptors that the MH mail system feeds its child processes. It identifies them in the environment variable MHCONTEXTFD:

```
$fd = $ENV{MHCONTEXTFD};
open(MHCONTEXT, "<&=$fd")     or die "couldn't fdopen $fd: $!";
# after processing
close(MHCONTEXT)              or die "couldn't close context file: $!";
```

If you want to close a descriptor by number, just `open` it first.

See Also

The `open` function in *perlfunc*(1) and in Chapter 3 of *Programming Perl*; the documentation for the standard POSIX and IO::Handle modules (also in Chapter 7 of *Programming Perl*); your system's *fdopen*(3) manpages

7.20. Copying Filehandles

Problem

You want to make a copy of a filehandle.

Solution

To create an alias for a filehandle, say:

```
*ALIAS = *ORIGINAL;
```

Use `open` with the & mode to create an independent copy of the file descriptor for the filehandle:

```
open(OUTCOPY, ">&STDOUT")     or die "Couldn't dup STDOUT: $!";
open(INCOPY,  "<&STDIN" )     or die "Couldn't dup STDIN : $!";
```

Use `open` with the &= mode to create an alias for that filehandle's file descriptor:

```
open(OUTALIAS, ">&=STDOUT")  or die "Couldn't alias STDOUT: $!";
open(INALIAS,  "<&=STDIN")   or die "Couldn't alias STDIN : $!";
open(BYNUMBER, ">&=5")        or die "Couldn't alias file descriptor 5: $!";
```

Discussion

If you create an alias for a filehandle with typeglobs, only one Perl I/O object is still being accessed. If you close one of these aliased filehandles, the I/O object is closed. Any subsequent attempt to use a copy of that filehandle will give you an error like `"print on closed filehandle"`. When alternating access through the aliased filehandles, writes work as you'd expect because there's no duplicated stdio data structure to get out of sync.

If you create a copy of a file descriptor with open(COPY, ">&HANDLE"), you're really calling the *dup*(2) system call. You get two independent file descriptors whose file position, locks, and flags are shared, but which have independent stdio buffers. Closing one filehandle doesn't affect its copy. Simultaneously accessing the file through both filehandles is a recipe for disaster. Instead, this technique is normally used to save and restore STDOUT and STDERR:

```
# take copies of the file descriptors
open(OLDOUT, ">&STDOUT");
open(OLDERR, ">&STDERR");

# redirect stdout and stderr
open(STDOUT, "> /tmp/program.out")   or die "Can't redirect stdout: $!";
open(STDERR, ">&STDOUT")             or die "Can't dup stdout: $!";

# run the program
system($joe_random_program);

# close the redirected filehandles
close(STDOUT)                        or die "Can't close STDOUT: $!";
close(STDERR)                        or die "Can't close STDERR: $!";

# restore stdout and stderr
open(STDERR, ">&OLDERR")             or die "Can't restore stderr: $!";
open(STDOUT, ">&OLDOUT")             or die "Can't restore stdout: $!";

# avoid leaks by closing the independent copies
close(OLDOUT)                        or die "Can't close OLDOUT: $!";
close(OLDERR)                        or die "Can't close OLDERR: $!";
```

If you create an alias of a file descriptor using open(ALIAS, ">&=HANDLE"), you're really calling the *fdopen*(3) stdio function. You get a single file descriptor with two stdio buffers accessed through two filehandles. Closing one filehandle closes the file descriptor of any aliases, but not their filehandles—if you tried to print to a filehandle whose alias had been closed, Perl wouldn't give a "print on closed filehandle warning" even though the print didn't succeed. In short, accessing the file through both filehandles is also a recipe for disaster. This is really used only to open a file descriptor by number. See Recipe 7.19 for more information on this.

See Also

The open function in *perlfunc*(1) and in Chapter 3 of *Programming Perl*; your system's *dup*(2) manpage

7.21. *Program: netlock*

When locking files, we recommend that you use `flock` when possible. However, on some systems, `flock`'s locking strategy is not reliable. For example, the person who built Perl on your system configured `flock` to use a version of file locking that didn't even try to work over the Net, or you're on the increasingly rare system where no `flock` emulation exists at all.

The following program and module provide a basic implementation of a file locking mechanism. Unlike a normal `flock`, with this module you lock file *names*, not file descriptors.

Thus, you can use it to lock directories, domain sockets, and other non-regular files. You can even lock files that don't exist yet. It uses a directory created at the same level in the directory structure as the locked file, so you must be able to write to the enclosing directory of the file you wish to lock. A sentinel file within the lock directory contains the owner of the lock. This is also useful with Recipe 7.8, because you can lock the filename even though the file that has that name changes.

The `nflock` function takes one or two arguments. The first is the pathname to lock; the second is the optional amount of time to wait for the lock. The function returns true if the lock is granted, false if the timeout expired, and raises an exception should various improbable events occur, like being unable to write the directory.

Set the `$File::LockDir::Debug` variable to true to make the module emit messages if it stalls waiting for a lock. If you forget to free a lock and try to exit the program, the module will remove them for you. This won't happen if your program is sent a signal it doesn't trap.

Example 7-9 shows a driver program to demonstrate the File::LockDir module.

Example 7-9. drivelock

```perl
#!/usr/bin/perl -w
# drivelock - demo File::LockDir module
use strict;
use File::LockDir;
$SIG{INT} = sub { die "outta here\n" };
$File::LockDir::Debug = 1;
my $path = shift                          or die "usage: $0 <path>\n";
unless (nflock($path, 2)) {
    die "couldn't lock $path in 2 seconds\n";
}
sleep 100;
nunflock($path);
```

The module itself is shown in Example 7-10. For more on building your own modules, see Chapter 12, *Packages, Libraries, and Modules.*

Example 7-10. File::LockDir

```
package File::LockDir;
# module to provide very basic filename-level
# locks.  No fancy systems calls.  In theory,
# directory info is sync'd over NFS.  Not
# stress tested.

use strict;

use Exporter;
use vars qw(@ISA @EXPORT);
@ISA       = qw(Exporter);
@EXPORT    = qw(nflock nunflock);

use vars qw($Debug $Check);
$Debug  ||= 0;   # may be predefined
$Check  ||= 5;   # may be predefined

use Cwd;
```

```
                                              return



                                       pathname";



                               ...: $!" if $missed++ > 10
              && !-d $lockname;
```

Example 7-10. File::LockDir (continued)

```
        if ($Debug) {{
            open(OWNER, "< $whosegot") || last; # exit "if"!
            my $lockee = <OWNER>;
            chomp($lockee);
            printf STDERR "%s $0\[$$]: lock on %s held by %s\n",
                scalar(localtime), $pathname, $lockee;
            close OWNER;
        }}
        sleep $Check;
        return if $naptime && time > $start+$naptime;
    }
    sysopen(OWNER, $whosegot, O_WRONLY|O_CREAT|O_EXCL)
                            or croak "can't create $whosegot: $!";
    printf OWNER "$0\[$$] on %s since %s\n",
            hostname(), scalar(localtime);
    close(OWNER)
        or croak "close $whosegot: $!";
    $Locked_Files{$pathname}++;
    return 1;
}


# free the locked file
sub nunflock($) {
    my $pathname = shift;
    my $lockname = name2lock($pathname);
    my $whosegot = "$lockname/owner";
    unlink($whosegot);
    carp "releasing lock on $lockname" if $Debug;
    delete $Locked_Files{$pathname};
    return rmdir($lockname);
}


# helper function
sub name2lock($) {
    my $pathname = shift;
    my $dir  = dirname($pathname);
    my $file = basename($pathname);
    $dir = getcwd() if $dir eq '.';
    my $lockname = "$dir/$file.LOCKDIR";
    return $lockname;
}


# anything forgotten?
END {
    for my $pathname (keys %Locked_Files) {
        my $lockname = name2lock($pathname);
        my $whosegot = "$lockname/owner";
        carp "releasing forgotten $lockname";
        unlink($whosegot);
        return rmdir($lockname);
    }
}


1;
```

7.22. *Program: lockarea*

Perl's `flock` function only locks complete files, not regions of the file. Although `fcntl` supports locking of a file's regions, this is difficult to access from Perl, largely because no one has written an XS module that portably packs up the necessary structure.

The program in Example 7-11 implements *fcntl*, but only for the three architectures it already knows about: SunOS, BSD, and Linux. If you're running something else, you'll have to figure out the layout of the `flock` structure. We did this by eyeballing the C-language *sys/fcntl.h* #include file—and running the *c2ph* program to figure out alignment and typing. This program, while included with Perl, only works on systems with a strong Berkeley heritage, like those listed above. As with Unix—or Perl itself—you don't *have* to use *c2ph*, but it sure makes life easier if you can.

The `struct_flock` function in the *lockarea* program packs and unpacks in the proper format for the current architectures by consulting the `$^O` variable, which contains your current operating system name. There is no `struct_flock` function declaration. It's just aliased to the architecture-specific version. Function aliasing is discussed in Recipe 10.14.

The *lockarea* program opens a temporary file, clobbering any existing contents and writing a screenful (80 by 23) of blanks. Each line is the same length.

The program then forks one or more times and lets all the child processes try to update the file at the same time. The first argument, *N*, is the number of times to fork to produce 2 ** N processes. So *lockarea 1* makes two children, *lockarea 2* makes four, *lockarea 3* makes eight, *lockarea 4* makes sixteen, etc. The more kids, the more contention for the locks.

Each process picks a random line in the file, locks just that line, and updates it. It writes its process ID into the line, prepended with a count of how many times the line has been updated:

```
4: 18584 was just here
```

If the line was already locked, when the lock is finally granted, the line is updated with a message indicating the process that was in the way of this process:

```
29: 24652 ZAPPED 24656
```

A fun demo is to run the *lockarea* program in the background and the *rep* program from Chapter 15 watching the file change. Think of it as a video game for systems programmers.

```
% lockarea 5 &
% rep -1 'cat /tmp/lkscreen'
```

When you interrupt the original parent, usually with Ctrl-C or by sending it a SIG-
INT from the command line, it kills all its children by sending its entire process
group a signal.

Example 7-11. lockarea

```perl
#!/usr/bin/perl -w
# lockarea - demo record locking with fcntl

use strict;

my $FORKS = shift || 1;
my $SLEEP = shift || 1;

use Fcntl;
use POSIX qw(:unistd_h :errno_h);

my $COLS = 80;
my $ROWS = 23;

# when's the last time you saw *this* mode used correctly?
open(FH, "+> /tmp/lkscreen")                      or  die $!;

select(FH);
$| = 1;
select STDOUT;

# clear screen
for (1 .. $ROWS) {
        print FH " " x $COLS, "\n";
}

my $progenitor = $$;
fork while $FORKS-- > 0;

print "hello from $$\n";

if ($progenitor == $$) {
        $SIG{INT} = \&genocide;
} else {
        $SIG{INT} = sub { die "goodbye from $$" };
}

while (1) {
        my $line_num = int rand($ROWS);
        my $line;
        my $n;

        # move to line
        seek(FH, $n = $line_num * ($COLS+1), SEEK_SET)             or next;

        # get lock
        my $place = tell(FH);
        my $him;
```

Example 7-11. lockarea (continued)

```
        next unless defined($him = lock(*FH, $place, $COLS));

        # read line
        read(FH, $line, $COLS) == $COLS                        or next;
        my $count = ($line =~ /(\d+)/) ? $1 : 0;
        $count++;

        # update line
        seek(FH, $place, 0)                                    or die $!;
        my $update = sprintf($him
                        ? "%6d: %d ZAPPED %d"
                        : "%6d: %d was just here",
                      $count, $$, $him);
        my $start = int(rand($COLS - length($update)));
        die "XXX" if $start + length($update) > $COLS;
        printf FH "%*.*s\n", -$COLS, $COLS, " " x $start . $update;

        # release lock and go to sleep
        unlock(*FH, $place, $COLS);
        sleep $SLEEP if $SLEEP;
}
die "NOT REACHED";                          # just in case

# lock($handle, $offset, $timeout) - get an fcntl lock
sub lock {
        my ($fh, $start, $till) = @_;
        ##print "$$: Locking $start, $till\n";
        my $lock = struct_flock(F_WRLCK, SEEK_SET, $start, $till, 0);
        my $blocker = 0;
        unless (fcntl($fh, F_SETLK, $lock)) {
            die "F_SETLK $$ @_: $!" unless $! == EAGAIN || $! == EDEADLK;
            fcntl($fh, F_GETLK, $lock)          or die "F_GETLK $$ @_: $!";
            $blocker = (struct_flock($lock))[-1];
            ##print "lock $$ @_: waiting for $blocker\n";
            $lock = struct_flock(F_WRLCK, SEEK_SET, $start, $till, 0);
            unless (fcntl($fh, F_SETLKW, $lock)) {
                warn "F_SETLKW $$ @_: $!\n";
                return;  # undef
            }
        }
        return $blocker;
}

# unlock($handle, $offset, $timeout) - release an fcntl lock
sub unlock {
        my ($fh, $start, $till) = @_;
        ##print "$$: Unlocking $start, $till\n";
        my $lock = struct_flock(F_UNLCK, SEEK_SET, $start, $till, 0);
        fcntl($fh, F_SETLK, $lock) or die "F_UNLCK $$ @_: $!";
}

# OS-dependent flock structures
```

Example 7-11. lockarea (continued)

```
# Linux struct flock
#    short l_type;
#    short l_whence;
#    off_t l_start;
#    off_t l_len;
#    pid_t l_pid;
BEGIN {
        # c2ph says: typedef='s2 12 i', sizeof=16
        my $FLOCK_STRUCT = 's s l l i';

        sub linux_flock {
            if (wantarray) {
                my ($type, $whence, $start, $len, $pid) =
                    unpack($FLOCK_STRUCT, $_[0]);
                return ($type, $whence, $start, $len, $pid);
            } else {
                my ($type, $whence, $start, $len, $pid) = @_;
                return pack($FLOCK_STRUCT,
                        $type, $whence, $start, $len, $pid);
            }
        }

}


# SunOS struct flock:
#    short   l_type;         /* F_RDLCK, F_WRLCK, or F_UNLCK */
#    short   l_whence;       /* flag to choose starting offset */
#    long    l_start;        /* relative offset, in bytes */
#    long    l_len;          /* length, in bytes; 0 means lock to EOF */
#    short   l_pid;          /* returned with F_GETLK */
#    short   l_xxx;          /* reserved for future use */
BEGIN {
        # c2ph says: typedef='s2 12 s2', sizeof=16
        my $FLOCK_STRUCT = 's s l l s s';

        sub sunos_flock {
            if (wantarray) {
                my ($type, $whence, $start, $len, $pid, $xxx) =
                    unpack($FLOCK_STRUCT, $_[0]);
                return ($type, $whence, $start, $len, $pid);
            } else {
                my ($type, $whence, $start, $len, $pid) = @_;
                return pack($FLOCK_STRUCT,
                        $type, $whence, $start, $len, $pid, 0);
            }
        }

}


# (Free)BSD struct flock:
#    off_t   l_start;        /* starting offset */
#    off_t   l_len;          /* len = 0 means until end of file */
```

Example 7-11. lockarea (continued)

```
#    pid_t   l_pid;          /* lock owner */
#    short   l_type;         /* lock type: read/write, etc. */
#    short   l_whence;       /* type of l_start */
BEGIN {
        # c2ph says: typedef="q2 i s2", size=24
        my $FLOCK_STRUCT = 'll ll i s s';    # XXX: q is ll


        sub bsd_flock {
            if (wantarray) {
                my ($xxstart, $start, $xxlen, $len, $pid, $type, $whence) =
                    unpack($FLOCK_STRUCT, $_[0]);
                return ($type, $whence, $start, $len, $pid);
            } else {
                my ($type, $whence, $start, $len, $pid) = @_;
                my ($xxstart, $xxlen) = (0,0);
                return pack($FLOCK_STRUCT,
                        $xxstart, $start, $xxlen, $len, $pid, $type, $whence);
            }
        }
}


# alias the fcntl structure at compile time
BEGIN {
        for ($^O) {
            *struct_flock =                    do                                  {

                                /bsd/   &&   \&bsd_flock
                                         ||
                                    /linux/   &&      \&linux_flock
                                         ||
                                  /sunos/   &&       \&sunos_flock
                                         ||
                        die "unknown operating system $^O, bailing out";
            };
        }
}


# install signal handler for children
BEGIN {
        my $called = 0;

        sub genocide {
            exit if $called++;
            print "$$: Time to die, kiddies.\n" if $$ == $progenitor;
            my $job = getpgrp();
            $SIG{INT} = 'IGNORE';
            kill -2, $job if $job;    # killpg(SIGINT, job)
            1 while wait > 0;
            print "$$: My turn\n" if $$ == $progenitor;
            exit;
        }
```

Example 7-11. lockarea (continued)

```
}

END { &genocide }
```

8

File Contents

*The most brilliant decision in all of Unix
was the choice of a single character
for the newline sequence.*

—Mike O'Dell, only half jokingly

8.0. Introduction

Before the Unix Revolution, every kind of data source and destination was inherently different. Getting two programs merely to understand each other required heavy wizardry and the occasional sacrifice of a virgin stack of punch cards to an itinerant mainframe repairman. This computational Tower of Babel made programmers dream of quitting the field to take up a less painful hobby, like autoflagellation.

These days, such cruel and unusual programming is largely behind us. Modern operating systems work hard to provide the illusion that I/O devices, network connections, process control information, other programs, the system console, and even users' terminals are all abstract streams of bytes called *files*. This lets you easily write programs that don't care where their input came from or where their output goes.

Because programs read and write via byte streams of simple text, every program can communicate with every other program. It is difficult to overstate the power and elegance of this approach. No longer dependent upon troglodyte gnomes with secret tomes of JCL (or COM) incantations, users can now create custom tools from smaller ones by using simple command-line I/O redirection, pipelines, and backticks.

Treating files as unstructured byte streams necessarily governs what you can do with them. You can read and write sequential, fixed-size blocks of data at any location in the file, increasing its size if you write past the current end. Perl uses the standard C I/O library to implement reading and writing of variable-length records like lines, paragraphs, and words.

What can't you do to an unstructured file? Because you can't insert or delete bytes anywhere but at end of file, you can't change the length of, insert, or delete records. An exception is the last record, which you can delete by truncating the file to the end of the previous record. For other modifications, you need to use a temporary file or work with a copy of the file in memory. If you need to do this a lot, a database system may be a better solution than a raw file (see Chapter 14, *Database Access*).

The most common files are text files, and the most common operations on text files are reading and writing lines. Use <FH> (or the internal function implementing it, `readline`) to read lines, and use **print** to write them. These functions can also be used to read or write any record that has a specific record separator. Lines are simply records that end in "\n".

The <FH> operator returns **undef** on error or when end of the file is reached, so use it in loops like this:

```
while (defined ($line = <DATAFILE>)) {
    chomp $line;
    $size = length $line;
    print "$size\n";                    # output size of line
}
```

Because this is a common operation and that's a lot to type, Perl gives it a shorthand notation. This shorthand reads lines into $_ instead of $line. Many other string operations use $_ as a default value to operate on, so this is more useful than it may appear at first:

```
while (<DATAFILE>) {
    chomp;
    print length, "\n";                 # output size of line
}
```

Call <FH> in scalar context to read the next line. Call it in list context to read all remaining lines:

```
@lines = <DATAFILE>;
```

Each time <FH> reads a record from a filehandle, it increments the special variable $. (the "current input record number"). This variable is only reset when **close** is called explicitly, which means that it's not reset when you reopen an already opened filehandle.

Another special variable is $/, the input record separator. It is set to "\n", the default end-of-line marker. You can set it to any string you like, for instance "\0" to read null-terminated records. Read paragraphs by setting $/ to the empty string,

"". This is almost like setting $/ to "\n\n", in that blank lines function as record separators, but "" treats two or more consecutive empty lines as a single record separator, whereas "\n\n" returns empty records when more than two consecutive empty lines are read. Undefine $/ to read the rest of the file as one scalar:

```
undef $/;
$whole_file = <FILE>;                # 'slurp' mode
```

The -0 option to Perl lets you set $/ from the command line:

```
% perl -040 -e '$word = <>; print "First word is $word\n";'
```

The digits after -0 are the octal value of the single character that $/ is to be set to. If you specify an illegal value (e.g., with -0777) Perl will set $/ to undef. If you specify -00, Perl will set $/ to "". The limit of a single octal value means you can't set $/ to a multibyte string, for instance, "%%\n" to read *fortune* files. Instead, you must use a BEGIN block:

```
% perl -ne 'BEGIN { $/="%%\n" } chomp; print if /Unix/i' fortune.dat
```

Use print to write a line or any other data. The print function writes its arguments one after another and doesn't automatically add a line or record terminator by default.

```
print HANDLE "One", "two", "three"; # "Onetwothree"
print "Baa baa black sheep.\n";      # Sent to default output handle
```

There is no comma between the filehandle and the data to print. If you put a comma in there, Perl gives the error message "No comma allowed after file-handle". The default output handle is STDOUT. Change it with the select function. (See the introduction to Chapter 7, *File Access*.)

All systems use the virtual "\n" to represent a line terminator, called a *newline*. There is no such thing as a newline character. It is an illusion that the operating system, device drivers, C libraries, and Perl all conspire to preserve. Sometimes, this changes the number of characters in the strings you read and write. The conspiracy is revealed in Recipe 8.11.

Use the read function to read a fixed-length record. It takes three arguments: a filehandle, a scalar variable, and the number of bytes to read. It returns undef if an error occurred or else the number of bytes read. To write a fixed-length record, just use print.

```
$rv = read(HANDLE, $buffer, 4096)
          or die "Couldn't read from HANDLE : $!\n";
# $rv is the number of bytes read,
# $buffer holds the data read
```

The truncate function changes the length of a file, which can be specified as a filehandle or as a filename. It returns true if the file was successfully truncated, false otherwise:

```
truncate(HANDLE, $length)
    or die "Couldn't truncate: $!\n";
truncate("/tmp/$$.pid", $length)
    or die "Couldn't truncate: $!\n";
```

Each filehandle keeps track of where it is in the file. Reads and writes occur from this point, unless you've specified the O_APPEND flag (see Recipe 7.1). Fetch the file position for a filehandle with tell, and set it with seek. Because the stdio library rewrites data to preserve the illusion that "\n" is the line terminator, you cannot portably seek to offsets calculated by counting characters. Instead, only seek to offsets returned by tell.

```
$pos = tell(DATAFILE);
print "I'm $pos bytes from the start of DATAFILE.\n";
```

The seek function takes three arguments: the filehandle, the offset (in bytes) to go to, and a numeric argument indicating how to interpret the offset. 0 indicates an offset from the start of the file (the kind of value returned by tell); 1, an offset from the current location (a negative number means move backwards in the file, a positive number means move forward); and 2, an offset from end of file.

```
seek(LOGFILE, 0, 2)       or die "Couldn't seek to the end: $!\n";
seek(DATAFILE, $pos, 0)   or die "Couldn't seek to $pos: $!\n";
seek(OUT, -20, 1)         or die "Couldn't seek back 20 bytes: $!\n";
```

So far we've been describing buffered I/O. That is, <FH>, print, read, seek, and tell are all operations that use buffers for speed. Perl also provides unbuffered I/O operations: sysread, syswrite, and sysseek, all discussed in Chapter 7.

The sysread and syswrite functions are different from their <FH> and print counterparts. They both take a filehandle to act on, a scalar variable to either read into or write out from, and the number of bytes to read or write. They can also take an optional fourth argument, the offset in the scalar variable to start reading or writing at:

```
$written = syswrite(DATAFILE, $mystring, length($mystring));
die "syswrite failed: $!\n" unless $written == length($mystring);
$read = sysread(INFILE, $block, 256, 5);
warn "only read $read bytes, not 256" if 256 != $read;
```

The syswrite call sends the contents of $mystring to DATAFILE. The sysread call reads 256 bytes from INFILE and stores them 5 characters into $block, leaving its first 5 characters intact. Both sysread and syswrite return the number of bytes transferred, which could be different than the amount of data you were attempting to transfer. Maybe the file didn't have all the data you thought it did, so you got a short read. Maybe the filesystem that the file lives on filled up. Maybe your process was interrupted part of the way through the write. Stdio takes care of finishing the transfer in cases of interruption, but if you use the `sysread` and `syswrite` calls, you must do it yourself. See Recipe 9.3 for an example of this.

The `sysseek` function doubles as an unbuffered replacement for both `seek` and `tell`. It takes the same arguments as `seek`, but it returns either the new position if successful or `undef` on error. To find the current position within the file:

```
$pos = sysseek(HANDLE, 0, 1);        # don't change position
die "Couldn't sysseek: $!\n" unless defined $pos;
```

These are the basic operations available to you. The art and craft of programming lies in using these basic operations to solve complex problems like finding the number of lines in a file, reversing the order of lines in a file, randomly selecting a line from a file, building an index for a file, and so on.

8.1. Reading Lines with Continuation Characters

Problem

You have a file with long lines split over two or more lines, with backslashes to indicate that a continuation line follows. You want to rejoin those split lines. Makefiles, shell scripts, and many other scripting or configuration languages let you break a long line into several shorter ones in this fashion.

Solution

Build up the complete lines one at a time until reaching one without a backslash:

```
while (defined($line = <FH>) ) {
    chomp $line;
    if ($line =~ s/\\$//) {
        $line .= <FH>;
        redo unless eof(FH);
    }
    # process full record in $line here
}
```

Discussion

Here's an example input file:

```
DISTFILES = $(DIST_COMMON) $(SOURCES) $(HEADERS) \
            $(TEXINFOS) $(INFOS) $(MANS) $(DATA)
```

```
DEP_DISTFILES = $(DIST_COMMON) $(SOURCES) $(HEADERS) \
        $(TEXINFOS) $(INFO_DEPS) $(MANS) $(DATA) \
        $(EXTRA_DIST)
```

You'd like to process that file with the escaped newlines ignored. That way the first record would in this case be the first two lines, the second record the next three lines, etc.

Here's how the algorithm works. The `while` loop reads lines, which may or may not be complete records—they might end in backslash (and a newline). The substitution operator `s///` tries to remove a trailing backslash. If the substitution fails, we've found a line without a backslash at the end. Otherwise, read another record, concatenate it onto the accumulating `$line` variable, and use `redo` to jump back to just inside the opening brace of the `while` loop. This lands us back on the `chomp`.

A common problem with files in this format is invisible blanks between the backslash and end of line. It would be more forgiving if the substitute were like this:

```
if ($line =~ s/\\\s*$//) {
    # as before
}
```

Unfortunately, even if your program is forgiving, others doubtlessly aren't. Just remember to be liberal in what you accept and conservative in what you produce.

See Also

The `chomp` function in *perlfunc*(1) and in Chapter 3 of *Programming Perl*; the `redo` keyword in the "Loop Control" sections of *perlsyn*(1) and Chapter 2 of *Programming Perl*

8.2. Counting Lines (or Paragraphs or Records) in a File

Problem

You need to compute the number of lines in a file.

Solution

Many systems have a *wc* program to count lines in a file:

```
$count = `wc -l < $file`;
die "wc failed: $?" if $?;
chomp($count);
```

You could also open the file and read line-by-line until the end, counting lines as
you go:

```
open(FILE, "< $file") or die "can't open $file: $!";
$count++ while <FILE>;
# $count now holds the number of lines read
```

Here's the fastest solution, assuming your line terminator really *is* "\n":

```
$count += tr/\n/\n/ while sysread(FILE, $_, 2 ** 16);
```

Discussion

Although you can use -s $file to determine the file size in bytes, you generally
cannot use it to derive a line count. See the Introduction to Chapter 9, *Directories*,
for more on -s.

If you can't or don't want to call another program to do your dirty work, you can
emulate *wc* by opening up and reading the file yourself:

```
open(FILE, "< $file") or die "can't open $file: $!";
$count++ while <FILE>;
# $count now holds the number of lines read
```

Another way of writing this is:

```
open(FILE, "< $file") or die "can't open $file: $!";
for ($count=0; <FILE>; $count++) { }
```

If you're not reading from any other files, you don't need the $count variable in
this case. The special variable $. holds the number of lines read since a filehan-
dle was last explicitly closed:

```
1 while <FILE>;
$count = $.;
```

This reads all the records in the file and discards them.

To count paragraphs, set the global input record separator variable $/ to the
empty string ("") before reading to make <> read a paragraph at a time.

```
$/ = '';                    # enable paragraph mode for all reads
open(FILE, $file) or die "can't open $file: $!";
1 while <FILE>;
$para_count = $.;
```

See Also

Your system's *wc*(1) manpage; the $/ entry in *perlvar*(1), and in the "Special Vari-
ables" section of Chapter 2 of *Programming Perl*; the Introduction to Chapter 9

8.3. *Processing Every Word in a File*

Problem

You need to do something to every word in a file, similar to the `foreach` function of *csh*.

Solution

Either `split` each line on whitespace:

```
while (<>) {
    for $chunk (split) {
        # do something with $chunk
    }
}
```

Or use the m//g operator to pull out one chunk at a time:

```
while (<>) {
    while ( /(\w[\w'-]*)/g ) {
        # do something with $1
    }
}
```

Discussion

Decide what you mean by "word." Sometimes you want anything but whitespace, sometimes you only want program identifiers, and sometimes you want English words. Your definition governs which regular expression to use.

The preceding two approaches work differently. Patterns are used in the first approach to decide what is *not* a word. In the second, they're used to decide what *is* a word.

With these techniques, it's easy to make a word frequency counter. Use a hash to store how many times each word has been seen:

```
# Make a word frequency count
%seen = ();
while (<>) {
    while ( /(\w['\w-]*)/g ) {
        $seen{lc $1}++;
    }
}

# output hash in a descending numeric sort of its values
foreach $word ( sort { $seen{$b} <=> $seen{$a} } keys %seen) {
    printf "%5d %s\n", $seen{$word}, $word;
}
```

To make the example program count line frequency instead of word frequency, omit the second `while` loop and do `$seen{lc $_}++` instead:

```
# Line frequency count
%seen = ();
while (<>) {
    $seen{lc $_}++;
}
foreach $line ( sort { $seen{$b} <=> $seen{$a} } keys %seen ) {
    printf "%5d %s", $seen{$line}, $line;
}
```

Odd things that may need to be considered as words include "M.I.T.", "Micro$oft", "o'clock", "49ers", "street-wise", "and/or", "&", "c/o", "St.", "Tschüß", and "Niño". Bear this in mind when you choose a pattern to match. The last two require you to place a use locale in your program and then employ \w for a word character in the current locale.

See Also

The `split` function in *perlfunc*(1) and in Chapter 3 of *Programming Perl*; Recipe 6.3; Recipe 6.23

8.4. Reading a File Backwards by Line or Paragraph

Problem

You want to process each line or paragraph of a text file in reverse.

Solution

Read all lines into an array, then process that array from the end to the start:

```
@lines = <FILE>;
while ($line = pop @lines) {
    # do something with $line
}
```

Or store an array of lines in reverse order:

```
@lines = reverse <FILE>;
foreach $line (@lines) {
    # do something with $line
}
```

Discussion

The limitations of file access mentioned in this chapter's Introduction prevent you from reading a line at a time starting from the end. You must read the lines into memory, then process them in reverse order. Needless to say, this requires at least as much available memory as the size of the file.

The first technique moves through the array of lines, in reverse order. This *destructively* processes the array, popping an element off the end of the array each time through the loop. We could do it non-destructively with:

```
for ($i = $#lines; $i != -1; $i--) {
    $line = $lines[$i];
}
```

The second approach generates an array of lines that is already in reverse order. This array can then be processed non-destructively. We get the reversed lines because the assignment to @lines forces list context on **reverse**, which in turn forces it on <FILE>. <> in a list context returns a list of all lines in the file.

These approaches are easily extended to paragraphs just by changing $/:

```
# this enclosing block keeps local $/ temporary
{
    local $/ = '';
    @paragraphs = reverse <FILE>;
}

foreach $paragraph (@paragraphs) {
    # do something
}
```

See Also

The **reverse** function in *perlfunc*(1) and in Chapter 3 of *Programming Perl*; the $/ entry in *perlvar*(1), and in the "Special Variables" section of Chapter 2 of *Programming Perl*; Recipe 4.10; Recipe 1.6

8.5. Trailing a Growing File

Problem

You want to read from a continually growing file, but the read fails when you reach the (current) end of file.

Solution

Read until the end of file. Sleep, clear the EOF flag, and read some more. Repeat until interrupted. To clear the EOF flag, either use **seek**:

```
for (;;) {
    while (<FH>) { .... }
    sleep $SOMETIME;
    seek(FH, 0, 1);
}
```

or the IO::Handle module's **clearerr** method:

```
use IO::Seekable;

for (;;) {
    while (<FH>) { .... }
    sleep $SOMETIME;
    FH->clearerr();
}
```

Discussion

When you read to the end of a file, an internal flag is set that prevents further reading. The most direct way to clear this flag is the **clearerr** method, if supported: it's in the IO::Handle and FileHandle modules.

```
$naptime = 1;

use IO::Handle;
open (LOGFILE, "/tmp/logfile") or die "can't open /tmp/logfile: $!";
for (;;) {
    while (<LOGFILE>) { print }      # or appropriate processing
    sleep $naptime;
    LOGFILE->clearerr();             # clear stdio error flag
}
```

If that simple approach doesn't work on your system, you may need to use **seek**. The **seek** code given above tries to move zero bytes from the current position, which nearly always works. It doesn't change the current position, but it should clear the end-of-file condition on the handle so that the next <LOGFILE> picks up new data.

If that still doesn't work (e.g., it relies on features of your C library's (so-called) standard I/O implementation), then you may need to use the following **seek** code, which remembers the old file position explicitly and returns there directly.

```
for (;;) {
    for ($curpos = tell(LOGFILE); <LOGFILE>; $curpos = tell(LOGFILE)) {
        # process $_ here
    }
```

```
        sleep $naptime;
        seek(LOGFILE, $curpos, 0);   # seek to where we had been
    }
```

On some kinds of filesystems, the file could be removed while you are reading it. If so, there's probably little reason to continue checking whether it grows. To make the program exit in that case, stat the handle and make sure its link count (the third field in the return list) hasn't gone to 0:

```
    exit if (stat(LOGFILE))[3] == 0
```

If you're using the File::stat module, you could write that more readably as:

```
    use File::stat;
    exit if stat(*LOGFILE)->nlink == 0;
```

See Also

The seek function in *perlfunc*(1) and in Chapter 3 of *Programming Perl*; your system's *tail*(1) and *stdio*(3) manpages

8.6. *Picking a Random Line from a File*

Problem

You want to return a random line from a file.

Solution

Use rand and $. (the current line number) to decide which line to print:

```
    srand;
    rand($.) < 1 && ($line = $_) while <>;
    # $line is the random line
```

Discussion

This is a beautiful example of a solution that may not be obvious. We read every line in the file but don't have to store them all in memory. This is great for large files. Each line has a 1 in N (where N is the number of lines read so far) chance of being selected.

Here's a replacement for *fortune* using this algorithm:

```
    $/ = "%%\n";
    @ARGV = qw( /usr/share/games/fortunes );
    srand;
    rand($.) < 1 && ($adage = $_) while <>;
    print $adage;
```

If you know line offsets (for instance, you've created an index) and the number of lines, you can randomly select a line and jump to its offset in the file, but you usually don't have such an index.

Here's a more rigorous explanation of how the algorithm works. The function call `rand ($.)` picks a random number between 0 and the current line number. Therefore, you have a one in N chance, that is, $1/N$, of keeping the Nth line. Therefore you've a 100% chance of keeping the first line, a 50% chance of keeping the second, a 33% chance of keeping the third, and so on. The question is whether this is fair for all N, where N is any positive integer.

First, some concrete examples, then abstract ones.

Obviously, a file with one line (N=1) is fair: you always keep the first line because $1/1 = 100\%$, making it fair for files of 1 line. For a file with two lines, N=2. You always keep the first line; then when reaching the second line, you have a 50% chance of keeping it. Thus, both lines have an equal chance of being selected, which shows that N=2 is fair. For a file with three lines, N=3. You have a one-third chance, 33%, of keeping that third line. That leaves a two-thirds chance of retaining one of the first two out of the three lines. But we've already shown that for those first two lines there's a 50-50 chance of selecting either one. 50 percent of two-thirds is one-third. Thus, you have a one-third chance of selecting each of the three lines of the file.

In the general case, a file of N+1 lines will choose the last line $\frac{1}{N+1}$ times and one of the previous N lines $\frac{N}{N+1}$ times. Dividing $\frac{N}{N+1}$ by N leaves us with $\frac{1}{N+1}$ for each the first N lines in our N+1 line file, and also $\frac{1}{N+1}$ for line number N+1. The algorithm is therefore fair for all N, where N is a positive integer.

We've managed to choose fairly a random line from a file with speed directly proportional to the size of the file, but using no more memory than it takes to hold the longest line, even in the worst case.

See Also

The `$.` entry in *perlvar*(1) and in the "Special Variables" section of Chapter 2 of *Programming Perl*; Recipe 2.7; Recipe 2.8

8.7. Randomizing All Lines

Problem

You want to copy a file and randomly reorder its lines.

Solution

Read all lines into an array, shuffle the array using the algorithm from Recipe 4.17, and write the shuffled lines back out:

```
# assumes the &shuffle sub from Chapter 4
while (<INPUT>) {
    push(@lines, $_);
}
fisher_yates_shuffle(\@lines);
foreach (@reordered) {
    print OUTPUT $_;
}
```

Discussion

The easiest approach is to read all lines into memory and shuffle them there. Because you don't know where lines start in the file, you can't just shuffle a list of line numbers and then extract the lines in the order they'll appear in the shuffled file. Even if you *did* know their starts, it would probably still be slower because you'd be **seeking** around in the file instead of simply reading it from start to finish.

See Also

Recipe 2.7; Recipe 2.8; Recipe 4.17

8.8. *Reading a Particular Line in a File*

Problem

You want to extract a single line from a file.

Solution

The simplest solution is to read the lines until you get to the one you want:

```
# looking for line number $DESIRED_LINE_NUMBER
$. = 0;
do { $LINE = <HANDLE> } until $. == $DESIRED_LINE_NUMBER || eof;
```

If you are going to be doing this a lot and the file fits into memory, read the file into an array:

```
@lines = <HANDLE>;
$LINE = $lines[$DESIRED_LINE_NUMBER];
```

If you will be retrieving lines by number often and the file doesn't fit into memory, build a byte-address index to let you **seek** directly to the start of the line:

```perl
# usage: build_index(*DATA_HANDLE, *INDEX_HANDLE)
sub build_index {
    my $data_file  = shift;
    my $index_file = shift;
    my $offset     = 0;

    while (<$data_file>) {
        print $index_file pack("N", $offset);
        $offset = tell($data_file);
    }
}

# usage: line_with_index(*DATA_HANDLE, *INDEX_HANDLE, $LINE_NUMBER)
# returns line or undef if LINE_NUMBER was out of range
sub line_with_index {
    my $data_file    = shift;
    my $index_file   = shift;
    my $line_number  = shift;

    my $size;               # size of an index entry
    my $i_offset;           # offset into the index of the entry
    my $entry;              # index entry
    my $d_offset;           # offset into the data file

    $size = length(pack("N", 0));
    $i_offset = $size * ($line_number-1);
    seek($index_file, $i_offset, 0) or return;
    read($index_file, $entry, $size);
    $d_offset = unpack("N", $entry);
    seek($data_file, $d_offset, 0);
    return scalar(<$data_file>);
}

# usage:
open(FILE, "< $file")           or die "Can't open $file for reading: $!\n";
open(INDEX, "+>$file.idx")
        or die "Can't open $file.idx for read/write: $!\n";
build_index(*FILE, *INDEX);
$line = line_with_index(*FILE, *INDEX, $seeking);
```

If you have the DB_File module, its DB_RECNO access method ties an array to a file, one line per array element:

```perl
use DB_File;
use Fcntl;

$tie = tie(@lines, $FILE, "DB_File", O_RDWR, 0666, $DB_RECNO) or die
    "Cannot open file $FILE: $!\n";
# extract it
$line = $lines[$sought-1];
```

Discussion

Each strategy has different features, useful in different circumstances. The linear access approach is easy to write and best for short files. The index method gives quick two-step lookup, but requires that the index be pre-built, so it is best when the file being indexed doesn't change often compared to the number of lookups. The DB_File mechanism has some initial overhead, but subsequent accesses are much faster than with linear access, so use it for long files that are accessed more than once and are accessed out of order.

It is important to know whether you're counting lines from 0 or 1. The `$.` variable is 1 after the first line is read, so count from 1 when using linear access. The index mechanism uses lots of offsets, so count from 0. DB_File treats the file's records as an array indexed from 0, so count lines from 0.

Here are three different implementations of the same program, *print_line*. The program takes two arguments, a filename, and a line number to extract.

The version in Example 8-1 simply reads lines until it finds the one it's looking for.

Example 8-1. print_line-v1

```perl
#!/usr/bin/perl -w
# print_line-v1 - linear style

@ARGV == 2 or die "usage: print_line FILENAME LINE_NUMBER\n";

($filename, $line_number) = @ARGV;
open(INFILE, "< $filename") or die "Can't open $filename for reading: $!\n";
while (<INFILE>) {
    $line = $_;
    last if $. == $line_number;
}
if ($. != $line_number) {
    die "Didn't find line $line_number in $filename\n";
}
print;
```

The index version in Example 8-2 must build an index. For many lookups, you could build the index once and then use it for all subsequent lookups:

Example 8-2. print_line-v2

```perl
#!/usr/bin/perl -w
# print_line-v2 - index style
# build_index and line_with_index from above
@ARGV == 2 or
    die "usage: print_line FILENAME LINE_NUMBER";

($filename, $line_number) = @ARGV;
open(ORIG, "< $filename")
```

Example 8-2. print_line-v2 (continued)

```
        or die "Can't open $filename for reading: $!";

# open the index and build it if necessary
# there's a race condition here: two copies of this
# program can notice there's no index for the file and
# try to build one.  This would be easily solved with
# locking
$indexname = "$filename.index";
sysopen(IDX, $indexname, O_CREAT|O_RDWR)
        or die "Can't open $indexname for read/write: $!";
build_index(*ORIG, *IDX) if -z $indexname;   # XXX: race unless lock

$line = line_with_index(*ORIG, *IDX, $line_number);
die "Didn't find line $line_number in $filename" unless defined $line;
print $line;
```

The DB_File version in Example 8-3 is indistinguishable from magic.

Example 8-3. print_line-v3

```
#!/usr/bin/perl -w
# print_line-v3 - DB_File style
use DB_File;
use Fcntl;

@ARGV == 2 or
    die "usage: print_line FILENAME LINE_NUMBER\n";

($filename, $line_number) = @ARGV;
$tie = tie(@lines, "DB_File", $filename, O_RDWR, 0666, $DB_RECNO)
        or die "Cannot open file $filename: $!\n";

unless ($line_number < $tie->length) {
    die "Didn't find line $line_number in $filename\n"
}

print $lines[$line_number-1];                        # easy, eh?
```

See Also

The documentation for the standard DB_File module (also in Chapter 7 of *Programming Perl*); the `tie` function in *perlfunc*(1) and in Chapter 3 of *Programming Perl*; the entry on `$.` in *perlvar*(1) and in the "Special Variables" section of Chatper 2 of *Programming Perl*

8.9. *Processing Variable-Length Text Fields*

Problem

You want to extract variable length fields from your input.

Solution

Use `split` with a pattern matching the field separators.

```
# given $RECORD with field separated by PATTERN,
# extract @FIELDS.
@FIELDS = split(/PATTERN/, $RECORD);
```

Discussion

The `split` function takes up to three arguments: PATTERN, EXPRESSION, and LIMIT. The LIMIT parameter is the maximum number of fields to split into. (If the input contains more fields, they are returned unsplit in the final list element.) If LIMIT is omitted, all fields (except any final empty ones) are returned. EXPRESSION gives the string value to split. If EXPRESSION is omitted, `$_` is split. PATTERN is a pattern matching the field separator. If PATTERN is omitted, contiguous stretches of whitespace are used as the field separator and leading empty fields are silently discarded.

If your input field separator isn't a fixed string, you might want `split` to return the field separators as well as the data by using parentheses in PATTERN to save the field separators. For instance:

```
split(/([+-])/, "3+5-2");
```

returns the values:

```
(3, '+', 5, '-', 2)
```

To split colon-separated records in the style of the */etc/passwd* file, use:

```
@fields = split(/:/, $RECORD);
```

The classic application of `split` is whitespace-separated records:

```
@fields = split(/\s+/, $RECORD);
```

If `$RECORD` started with whitespace, this last use of `split` would have put an empty string into the first element of `@fields` because `split` would consider the record to have an initial empty field. If you didn't want this, you could use this special form of `split`:

```
@fields = split(" ", $RECORD);
```

This behaves like `split` with a pattern of `/\s+/`, but ignores leading whitespace.

When the record separator can appear in the record, you have a problem. The usual solution is to escape occurrences of the record separator in records by prefixing them with a backslash. See Recipe 1.13.

See Also

The split function in *perlfunc*(1) and in Chapter 3 of *Programming Perl*

8.10. Removing the Last Line of a File

Problem

You'd like to remove the last line from a file.

Solution

Read the file a line at a time and keep track of the byte address of the last line you've seen. When you've exhausted the file, truncate to the last address you saved:

```
open (FH, "+< $file")                    or die "can't update $file: $!";
while ( <FH> ) {
    $addr = tell(FH) unless eof(FH);
}
truncate(FH, $addr)                      or die "can't truncate $file: $!";
```

Discussion

This is much more efficient than reading the file into memory all at once, since it only holds one line at a time. Although you still have to grope your way through the whole file, you can use this program on files larger than available memory.

See Also

The open and binmode functions in *perlfunc*(1) and in Chapter 3 of *Programming Perl*; your system's *open*(2) and *fopen*(3) manpages

8.11. Processing Binary Files

Problem

Your system distinguishes between text and binary files. How do you?

Solution

Use the `binmode` function on the filehandle:

```
binmode(HANDLE);
```

Discussion

Not everyone agrees what constitutes a line in a text file, because one person's textual character set is another's binary gibberish. Even when everyone is using ASCII instead of EBCDIC, Rad50, or Unicode, discrepancies arise.

As mentioned in the Introduction, there is no such thing as a newline character. It is purely virtual, a figment of the operating system, standard libraries, device drivers, and Perl.

Under Unix or Plan9, a `"\n"` represents the physical sequence `"\cJ"` (the Perl double-quote escape for Ctrl-J), a linefeed. However, on a terminal that's not in raw mode, an Enter key generates an incoming `"\cM"` (a carriage return) which turns into `"\cJ"`, whereas an outgoing `"\cJ"` turns into `"\cM\cJ"`. This strangeness doesn't happen with normal files, just terminal devices, and it is handled strictly by the device driver.

On a Mac, a `"\n"` is usually represented by `"\cM"`; just to make life interesting (and because the standard requires that `"\n"` and `"\r"` be different), a `"\r"` represents a `"\cJ"`. This is exactly the opposite of the way that Unix, Plan9, VMS, CP/M, or nearly anyone else does it. So, Mac programmers writing files for other systems or talking over a network have to be careful. If you send out `"\n"`, you'll deliver a `"\cM"`, and no `"\cJ"` will be seen. Most network services prefer to receive and send `"\cM\cJ"` as a line terminator, but most accept merely a `"\cJ"`.

Under VMS, DOS, or their derivatives, a `"\n"` represents `"\cJ"`, similar to Unix and Plan9. From the perspective of a tty, Unix and DOS behave identically: a user who hits Enter generates a `"\cM"`, but this arrives at the program as a `"\n"`, which is `"\cJ"`. A `"\n"` (that's a `"\cJ"`, remember) sent to a terminal shows up as a `"\cM\cJ"`.

These strange conversions happen to Windows files as well. A DOS text file actually physically contains two characters at the end of every line, `"\cM\cJ"`. The last block in the file has a `"\cZ"` to indicate where the text stops. When you write a line like `"bad news\n"` on those systems, the file contains `"bad news\cM\cJ"`, just as if it were a terminal.

When you read a line on such systems, it's even stranger. The file itself contains `"bad news\cM\cJ"`, a 10-byte string. When you read it in, your program gets nothing but `"bad news\n"`, where that `"\n"` is the virtual newline character, that is, a linefeed (`"\cJ"`). That means to get rid of it, a single chop or chomp will do.

But your poor program has been tricked into thinking it's only read nine bytes from the file. If you were to read 10 such lines, you would appear to have read just 90 bytes into the file, but in fact would be at position 100. That's why the `tell` function must always be used to determine your location. You can't infer your position just by counting what you've read.

This legacy of the old CP/M filesystem, whose equivalent of a Unix inode stored only block counts and not file sizes, has frustrated programmers for decades, and no end is in sight. Because DOS is compatible with CP/M file formats, Windows with DOS, and NT with Windows, the sins of the fathers have truly been visited unto the children of the fourth generation.

You can circumvent the single `"\n"` terminator by telling Perl (and the operating system) that you're working with binary data. The `binmode` function indicates that data read or written through the given filehandle should not be mangled the way a text file would likely be on those systems.

```
$gifname = "picture.gif";
open(GIF, $gifname)              or die "can't open $gifname: $!";

binmode(GIF);                   # now DOS won't mangle binary input from GIF
binmode(STDOUT);                # now DOS won't mangle binary output to STDOUT

while (read(GIF, $buff, 8 * 2**10)) {
    print STDOUT $buff;
}
```

Calling `binmode` on systems that don't make this distinction (including Unix, the Mac, and Plan 9) is harmless. Inappropriately doing so (such as on a text file) on systems that do (including MVS, VMS, and DOS, regardless of its GUI) can mangle your files.

If you're *not* using `binmode`, the data you read using stdio (`<>`) will automatically have the native system's line terminator changed to `"\n"`, even if you change $/. Similarly, any `"\n"` you `print` to the filehandle will be turned into the native line terminator. See this chapter's Introduction for more details.

If you want to get what was on the disk, byte for byte, you should set `binmode` if you're on one of the odd systems listed above. Then, of course, you also have to set $/ to the real record separator if you want to use `<>` on it.

See Also

The `open` and `binmode` functions in *perlfunc*(1) and in Chapter 3 of *Programming Perl*; your system's *open*(2) and *fopen*(3) manpages

8.12. *Using Random-Access I/O*

Problem

You have to read a binary record from the middle of a large file but don't want to read a record at a time to get there.

Solution

Once you know the record's size, multiply it by the record number to get the byte address, and then seek to that byte address and read the record:

```
$ADDRESS = $RECSIZE * $RECNO;
seek(FH, $ADDRESS, 0) or die "seek:$!";
read(FH, $BUFFER, $RECSIZE);
```

Discussion

The Solution assumes the first record has a RECNO of 0. If you're counting from one, use:

```
$ADDRESS = $RECSIZE * ($RECNO-1);
```

This won't work on a text file unless all lines are the same length. This is rarely the case.

See Also

The **seek** function in *perlfunc*(1) and in Chapter 3 of *Programming Perl*; Recipe 8.13

8.13. *Updating a Random-Access File*

Problem

You want to read in an old record from a binary file, change its values, and write back the record.

Solution

After **reading** the old record, **pack** up the updated values, **seek** to the previous address, and write it back.

```
use Fcntl;                          # for SEEK_SET and SEEK_CUR

$ADDRESS = $RECSIZE * $RECNO;
```

```
seek(FH, $ADDRESS, SEEK_SET)          or die "Seeking: $!";
read(FH, $BUFFER, $RECSIZE) == $RECSIZE
                                      or die "Reading: $!";
@FIELDS = unpack($FORMAT, $BUFFER);
# update fields, then
$BUFFER = pack($FORMAT, @FIELDS);
seek(FH, -$RECSIZE, SEEK_CUR)         or die "Seeking: $!";
print FH $BUFFER;
close FH                              or die "Closing: $!";
```

Discussion

You don't have to use anything fancier than `print` in Perl to output a record. Remember that the opposite of `read` is not `write` but `print`, although oddly enough, the opposite of `sysread` actually is `syswrite`. (`split` and `join` are opposites, but there's no `speak` to match `listen`, no `resurrect` for `kill`, and no `curse` for `bless`.)

The example program shown in Example 8-4, *weekearly*, takes one argument: the user whose record you want to backdate by a week. (Of course, in practice, you wouldn't really want to (nor be able to!) mess with the system accounting files.) This program requires write access to the file to be updated, since it opens the file in update mode. After fetching and altering the record, it packs it up again, skips backwards in the file one record, and writes it out.

Example 8-4. weekearly

```
#!/usr/bin/perl
# weekearly -- set someone's login date back a week
use User::pwent;
use IO::Seekable;

$typedef = 'L A12 A16';          # linux fmt; sunos is "L A8 A16"
$sizeof  = length(pack($typedef, ()));
$user    = shift(@ARGV) || $ENV{USER} || $ENV{LOGNAME};

$address = getpwnam($user)->uid * $sizeof;

open (LASTLOG, "+</var/log/lastlog")
    or die "can't update /var/log/lastlog: $!";
seek(LASTLOG, $address, SEEK_SET)
    or die "seek failed: $!";
read(LASTLOG, $buffer, $sizeof) == $sizeof
    or die "read failed: $!";

($time, $line, $host) = unpack($typedef, $buffer);
$time  -= 24 * 7 * 60 * 60;        # back-date a week
$buffer = pack($typedef, $time, $line, $host);

seek(LASTLOG, -$sizeof, SEEK_CUR)    # backup one record
    or die "seek failed: $!";
print LASTLOG $record;
```

Example 8-4. weekearly (continued)

```
close(LASTLOG)
    or die "close failed: $!";
```

See Also

The open, seek, read, pack, and unpack functions in the *perlfunc*(1) and in Chapter 3 of *Programming Perl*; Recipe 8.12; Recipe 8.14

8.14. Reading a String from a Binary File

Problem

You want to read a NUL-terminated string from a file, starting at a particular address.

Solution

Set $/ to an ASCII NUL, and read the string with <>:

```
$old_rs = $/;                          # save old $/
$/ = "\0";                             # NULL
seek(FH, $addr, SEEK_SET)              or die "Seek error: $!\n";
$string = <FH>;                        # read string
chomp $string;                         # remove NULL
$/ = $old_rs;                          # restore old $/
```

You can use local to save and restore $/ if you want:

```
{
    local $/ = "\0";
    # ...
}                                      # $/ is automatically restored
```

Discussion

The example program shown in Example 8-5, *bgets*, accepts a filename and one or more byte addresses as arguments. Decimal, octal, or hexadecimal addresses may be specified. For each address, the program reads and prints the NULL- or EOF-terminated string at that position:

Example 8-5. bgets

```
#!/usr/bin/perl
# bgets - get a string from an address in a binary file
use IO::Seekable;
($file, @addrs) = @ARGV              or die "usage: $0 file addr ...";
open(FH, $file)                      or die "cannot open $file: $!";
$/ = "\000";
```

Example 8-5. bgets (continued)

```
foreach $addr (@addrs) {
    $addr = oct $addr if $addr =~ /^0/;
    seek(FH, $addr, SEEK_SET)
        or die "can't seek to $addr in $file: $!";
    printf qq{%#x %#o %d "%s"\n}, $addr, $addr, $addr, scalar <>;
}
```

Here's a simple implementation of the Unix *strings* program:

Example 8-6. strings

```
#!/usr/bin/perl
# strings - pull strings out of a binary file
$/ = "\0";
while (<>) {
    while (/([\040-\176\s]{4,})/g) {
        print $1, "\n";
    }
}
```

See Also

The seek, getc, and ord functions in *perlfunc*(1) and in Chapter 3 of *Programming Perl*; the discussion of qq// in the "Quote and Quote-Like Operators" section of the *perlop*(1) manpage, and in the "Pick Your Own Quotes" section of Chapter 2 of *Programming Perl*

8.15. *Reading Fixed-Length Records*

Problem

You want to read a file whose records have a fixed length.

Solution

Use read and unpack:

```
    # $RECORDSIZE is the length of a record, in bytes.
    # $TEMPLATE is the unpack template for the record
    # FILE is the file to read from
    # @FIELDS is an array, one element per field

    until ( eof(FILE) ) {
        read(FILE, $record, $RECORDSIZE) == $RECORDSIZE
            or die "short read\n";
        @FIELDS = unpack($TEMPLATE, $record);
    }
```

Discussion

Because the file in question is not a text file, you can't use <FH> or IO:: modules' getline method to read in records. Instead, you must simply read a particular number of bytes into a buffer. This buffer then contains one record's data, which you decode using unpack with the right format.

For binary data, the catch is often determining the right format. If you're reading data written by a C program, this can mean peeking at C include files or manpages describing the structure layout, and this requires knowledge of C. It also requires that you become unnaturally chummy with your C compiler, because otherwise it's hard to predict field padding and alignment (such as the x2 in the format used in Recipe 8.18). If you're lucky enough to be on a Berkeley Unix system or a system supporting *gcc*, then you may be able to use the *c2ph* tool distributed with Perl to cajole your C compiler into helping you with this.

The *tailwtmp* program at the end of this chapter uses the format described in *utmp*(5) under Linux and works on its */var/log/wtmp* and */var/run/utmp* files. Once you commit to working in a binary format, machine dependencies creep in fast. It probably won't work unaltered on your system, but the procedure is still illustrative. Here is the relevant layout from the C include file on Linux:

```
#define UT_LINESIZE        12
#define UT_NAMESIZE        8
#define UT_HOSTSIZE        16

struct utmp {                       /* here are the pack template codes */
    short ut_type;                  /* s for short, must be padded      */
    pid_t ut_pid;                   /* i for integer                    */
    char ut_line[UT_LINESIZE];      /* A12 for 12-char string           */
    char ut_id[2];                  /* A2, but need x2 for alignment     */
    time_t ut_time;                 /* l for long                       */
    char ut_user[UT_NAMESIZE];      /* A8 for 8-char string             */
    char ut_host[UT_HOSTSIZE];      /* A16 for 16-char string           */
    long ut_addr;                   /* l for long                       */
};
```

Once you figure out the binary layout, feed that (in this case, "s x2 i A12 A2 x2 l A8 A16 l") to pack with an empty field list to determine the record's size. Remember to check the return value of read when you read in your record to make sure you got back the number of bytes you asked for.

If your records are text strings, use the "a" or "A" unpack templates.

Fixed-length records are useful in that the *n*th record begins at byte offset SIZE * (*n*-1) in the file, where SIZE is the size of a single record. See the indexing code in Recipe 8.8 for an example of this.

See Also

The unpack, pack, and read functions in *perlfunc*(1) and in Chapter 3 of *Programming Perl*; Recipe 1.1

8.16. Reading Configuration Files

Problem

You want to allow the users of your program to change its behavior through configuration files.

Solution

Either process a file in trivial VAR=VALUE format, setting a hash key-value pair for each setting:

```
while (<CONFIG>) {
    chomp;                    # no newline
    s/#.*//;                  # no comments
    s/^\s+//;                 # no leading white
    s/\s+$//;                 # no trailing white
    next unless length;       # anything left?
    my ($var, $value) = split(/\s*=\s*/, $_, 2);
    $User_Preferences{$var} = $value;
}
```

Or better yet, treat the config file as full Perl code:

```
do "$ENV{HOME}/.progrc";
```

Discussion

The first solution lets you read in config files in a trivial format like this (comments and blank lines are allowed):

```
# set class C net
NETMASK = 255.255.255.0
MTU     = 296

DEVICE  = cua1
RATE    = 115200
MODE    = adaptive
```

After you're done, you can pull in a setting by something like $User_Preferences{"RATE"} to find the value 115200. If you wanted the config file to directly set a variable in your program using that name, instead of assigning to the hash, do this:

```
no strict 'refs';
$$var = $value;
```

and the $RATE variable would contain 115200.

The second solution uses do to pull in raw Perl code directly. When used with an expression instead of a block, do interprets the expression as a filename. This is nearly identical to using **require**, but without risk of taking a fatal exception. In the second format, the config file would look like:

```
# set class C net
$NETMASK = '255.255.255.0';
$MTU     = 0x128;
# Brent, please turn on the modem
$DEVICE  = 'cua1';
$RATE    = 115_200;
$MODE    = 'adaptive';
```

If you don't see the point of having extra punctuation and live code, consider this: you can have all of Perl at your disposal. You can now add arbitrary logic and tests to your simple assignments:

```
if ($DEVICE =~ /1$/) {
    $RATE = 28_800;
} else {
    $RATE = 115_200;
}
```

Many programs support system and personal configuration files. If you want the user's choices to override the system ones, load the user file second:

```
$APPDFLT = "/usr/local/share/myprog";

do "$APPDFLT/sysconfig.pl";
do "$ENV{HOME}/.myprogrc";
```

If you want to ignore the system config file when the user has their own, test the return value of the do.

```
do "$ENV{HOME}/.myprogrc";
    or
do "$APPDFLT/sysconfig.pl"
```

You might wonder what context those files will be executed under. They will be in the same package that do itself was compiled into. Typically you'll direct users to set particular variables, which, being unqualified globals, will end up in the current package. If you'd prefer unqualified variables go into a particular package, do this:

```
{ package Settings; do "$ENV{HOME}/.myprogrc" }
```

As with a file read in using `require` or `use`, those read in using `do` count as a separate and unrelated lexical scope. That means the configuration file can't access its caller's lexical (`my`) variables, nor can the caller find any such variables that might have been set in the file. It also means that the user's code isn't held accountable to a pragma like *use strict* or *use integer* that may be in effect in the caller.

If you don't want clean partitioning of variable visibility, you can get the config file's code executed in your own lexical scope. If you have a `cat` program or its technical equivalent handy, you could write yourself a hand-rolled `do`:

```
eval `cat $ENV{HOME}/.myprogrc`;
```

We've never actually seen anyone (except Larry) use that approach in production code.

For one thing, `do` is a lot easier to type. Also, it respects the `@INC` path, which is normally searched if a full path is not specified, but, unlike using a `require`, no implicit error checking happens under `do`. This means you don't have to wrap it in an `eval` to catch exceptions that would otherwise cause your program to die, because `do` already functions as an `eval`.

You can still check for errors on your own if you'd like:

```
$file = "someprog.pl";
unless ($return = do $file) {
    warn "couldn't parse $file: $@"      if $@;
    warn "couldn't do $file: $!"         unless defined $return;
    warn "couldn't run $file"            unless $return;
}
```

This is much simpler for the programmer to source in code than it would be to invent and then parse a complicated, new syntax. It's also much easier on the user than forcing them to learn the syntax rules of yet another configuration file. Even better, you give the user access to a powerful algorithmic programming language.

One reasonable concern is security. How do you know that the file hasn't been tampered with by someone other than the user? The traditional approach here is to do nothing, trusting the directory and file permissions. Nine times out of ten, this is also the right approach. Most projects just aren't worth being that paranoid over. For those that are, see the next recipe.

See Also

The `eval` and `require` functions in *perlfunc*(1) and in Chapter 3 of *Programming Perl*; Recipe 8.17; Recipe 10.12

8.17. *Testing a File for Trustworthiness*

Problem

You want to read from a file, perhaps because it has configuration information. You only want to use the file if it can't be written to (or perhaps not even be read from) by anyone else than its owner.

Solution

Use the `stat` call to retrieve ownership and file permissions information. You can use the built-in version, which returns a list:

```
( $dev, $ino, $mode, $nlink,
  $uid, $gid, $rdev, $size,
  $atime, $mtime, $ctime,
  $blksize, $blocks )        = stat($filename)
        or die "no $filename: $!";

$mode &= 07777;               # discard file type info
```

Or you can use the by-name interface in:

```
$info = stat($filename)      or die "no $filename: $!";
if ($info->uid == 0) {
    print "Superuser owns $filename\n";
}
if ($info->atime > $info->mtime) {
    print "$filename has been read since it was written.\n";
}
```

Discussion

Usually you trust users to set file permissions as they wish. If they want others to read their files, or even to write to them, that's their business. Applications like editors, mailers, and shells are often more discerning, though, refusing to evaluate code in configuration files if anyone but the owner can write to them. This helps avoid Trojan horses attacks. Security-minded programs like *ftp* and *rlogin* may even reject config files that can be read by anyone but their owner.

If the file is writable by someone other than the owner or is owned by someone other than the current user or the superuser, it shouldn't be trusted. To figure out file ownership and permissions, the `stat` function is used. The following function returns true if the file is deemed safe and false otherwise. If the `stat` fails, `undef` is returned.

```
use File::stat;

sub is_safe {
```

```
    my $path = shift;
    my $info = stat($path);
    return unless $info;

    # owner neither superuser nor me
    # the real uid is in stored in the $< variable
    if (($info->uid != 0) && ($info->uid != $<)) {
        return 0;
    }

    # check whether group or other can write file.
    # use 066 to detect either reading or writing
    if ($info->mode & 022) {    # someone else can write this
        return 0 unless -d _;   # non-directories aren't safe
            # but directories with the sticky bit (01000) are
        return 0 unless $info->mode & 01000;
    }
    return 1;
}
```

A directory is considered safe even if others can write to it, provided that its mode 01000 (owner delete only) bit is set.

Careful programmers also ensure that no enclosing directory is writable. This is due to systems with the "chown giveaway" problem in which any user can give away a file they own and make it owned by someone else. The following function handles that by using the is_safe function to check every enclosing directory up to the root if it detects that you have the chown problem, for which it queries the POSIX::sysconf. If you don't have an unrestricted version of chown, the is_verysafe subroutine just calls is_safe. If you do have the problem, it walks up the filesystem tree until it reaches the root.

```
    use Cwd;
    use POSIX qw(sysconf _PC_CHOWN_RESTRICTED);
    sub is_verysafe {
        my $path = shift;
        return is_safe($path) if sysconf(_PC_CHOWN_RESTRICTED);
        $path = getcwd() . '/' . $path if $path !~ m{^/};
        do {
            return unless is_safe($path);
            $path =~ s#([^/]+|/)$##;                  # dirname
            $path =~ s#/$## if length($path) > 1;  # last slash
        } while length $path;

        return 1;
    }
```

To use this in a program, try something like this:

```
    $file = "$ENV{HOME}/.myprogrc";
    readconfig($file) if is_safe($file);
```

This has potential for a race condition, because it's presumed that the hypothetical `readconfig` function will open the file. Between the time when `is_safe` checks the file's stats and when `readconfig` opens it, something wicked could theoretically occur. To avoid this, pass `is_safe` the already open filehandle, which is set up to handle this:

```
$file = "$ENV{HOME}/.myprogrc";
if (open(FILE, "< $file")) {
    readconfig(*FILE) if is_safe(*FILE);
}
```

You would still have to arrange for `readconfig` to accept a filehandle instead of a filename, though.

8.18. Program: tailwtmp

Every time a user logs into or out of a Unix system, a record is added to the *wtmp* file. You can't use the normal *tail* program on it because it's in binary format. The *tailwtmp* program in Example 8-7 knows the format of the binary file and shows every new record as it appears. You'll have to adjust the **pack** format for your own system.

Example 8-7. tailwtmp

```
#!/usr/bin/perl
# tailwtmp - watch for logins and logouts;
# uses linux utmp structure, from utmp(5)
$typedef = 's x2 i A12 A4 l A8 A16 l';
$sizeof = length pack($typedef, () );
use IO::File;
open(WTMP, '/var/log/wtmp') or die "can't open /var/log/wtmp: $!";
seek(WTMP, 0, SEEK_END);
for (;;) {
while (read(WTMP, $buffer, $sizeof) == $sizeof) {
        ($type, $pid,  $line, $id, $time, $user, $host, $addr)
            = unpack($typedef, $buffer);
        next unless $user && ord($user) && $time;
        printf "%1d %-8s %-12s %2s %-24s %-16s %5d %08x\n",
            $type,$user,$line,$id,scalar(localtime($time)),
            $host,$pid,$addr;
    }
    for ($size = -s WTMP; $size == -s WTMP; sleep 1) {}
    WTMP->clearerr();
}
```

8.19. Program: tctee

Not all systems support the classic *tee* program for splitting output pipes to multiple destinations. This command sends the output from *someprog* to */tmp/output* and to the mail pipe beyond.

```
% someprog | tee /tmp/output | Mail -s 'check this' user@host.org
```

This program helps not only users who aren't on Unix systems and don't have a regular *tee*. It also helps those who are, because it offers features not found on other version of *tee*.

The four flag arguments are -i to ignore interrupts, -a to append to output files, -u for unbuffered output, and -n to omit copying the output on to standard out.

Because this program uses Perl's magic open, you can specify pipes as well as files.

```
% someprog | tctee f1 "|cat -n" f2 ">>f3"
```

That sends the output from *someprog* to the files *f1* and *f2*, appends it to *f3*, sends a copy to the program *cat -n*, and also produces the stream on standard output.

The program in Example 8-8 is one of many venerable Perl programs written nearly a decade ago that still runs perfectly well. If written from scratch now, we'd probably use strict, warnings, and ten to thirty thousand lines of modules. But if it ain't broke . . .

Example 8-8. tctee

```perl
#!/usr/bin/perl
# tctee - clone that groks process tees
# perl3 compatible, or better.

while ($ARGV[0] =~ /^-(.+)/ && (shift, ($_ = $1), 1)) {
    next if /^$/;
    s/i// && (++$ignore_ints, redo);
    s/a// && (++$append,      redo);
    s/u// && (++$unbuffer,    redo);
    s/n// && (++$nostdout,    redo);
    die "usage $0 [-aiun] [filenames] ...\n";
}

if ($ignore_ints) {
    for $sig ('INT', 'TERM', 'HUP', 'QUIT') { $SIG{$sig} = 'IGNORE'; }
}

$SIG{'PIPE'} = 'PLUMBER';
$mode = $append ? '>>' : '>';
$fh = 'FH000';

unless ($nostdout) {
    %fh = ('STDOUT', 'standard output'); # always go to stdout
}

$| = 1 if $unbuffer;

for (@ARGV) {
    if (!open($fh, (/^[^>|]/ && $mode) . $_)) {
```

Example 8-8. tctee (continued)

```
        warn "$0: cannot open $_: $!\n"; # like sun's; i prefer die
        $status++;
        next;
    }
    select((select($fh), $| = 1)[0]) if $unbuffer;
    $fh{$fh++} = $_;
}

while (<STDIN>) {
    for $fh (keys %fh) {
        print $fh $_;
    }
}

for $fh (keys %fh) {
    next if close($fh) || !defined $fh{$fh};
    warn "$0: couldnt close $fh{$fh}: $!\n";
    $status++;
}

exit $status;

sub PLUMBER {
    warn "$0: pipe to \"$fh{$fh}\" broke!\n";
    $status++;
    delete $fh{$fh};
}
```

8.20. Program: laston

When you log in to a Unix system, it tells you when you last logged in. That information is stored in a binary file called *lastlog*. Each user has their own record; UID 8 is at record 8, UID 239 at record 239, and so on. To find out when a given user last logged in, convert their login name to a number, seek to their record in that file, read, and unpack. Doing so with shell tools is very hard, but it's very easy with the *laston* program. Here's an example:

```
% laston gnat
gnat    UID 314 at Mon May 25 08:32:52 1998 on ttyp0 from below.perl.com
```

The program in Example 8-9 is much newer than the `tctee` program in Example 8-8, but it's less portable. It uses the Linux binary layout of the *lastlog* file. You'll have to change this for other systems.

Example 8-9. laston

```
#!/usr/bin/perl
# laston - find out when given user last logged on
use User::pwent;
use IO::Seekable qw(SEEK_SET);
```

Example 8-9. laston (continued)

```perl
open (LASTLOG, "/var/log/lastlog") or die "can't open /var/log/lastlog: $!".

$typedef = 'L A12 A16';   # linux fmt; sunos is "L A8 A16"
$sizeof  = length(pack($typedef, ()));

for $user (@ARGV) {
    $U = ($user =~ /^\d+$/) ? getpwuid($user) : getpwnam($user);
    unless ($U) { warn "no such uid $user\n"; next; }
    seek(LASTLOG, $U->uid * $sizeof, SEEK_SET) or warn "seek failed: $!";
    read(LASTLOG, $buffer, $sizeof) == $sizeof or next;
    ($time, $line, $host) = unpack($typedef, $buffer);
    printf "%-8s UID %5d %s%s%s\n", $U->name, $U->uid,
            $time ? ("at " . localtime($time)) : "never logged in",
            $line && " on $line",
            $host && " from $host";
}
```

9

Directories

*Unix has its weak points
but its file system is not one of them.*
—Chris Torek

9.0. Introduction

To fully understand directories, you need to be acquainted with the underlying mechanics. The following explanation is slanted towards the Unix filesystem, for whose system calls and behavior Perl's directory access routines were designed, but it is applicable to some degree to most other platforms.

A filesystem consists of two parts: a set of data blocks where the contents of files and directories are kept, and an index to those blocks. Each entity in the filesystem has an entry in the index, be it a plain file, a directory, a link, or a special file like those in /dev. Each entry in the index is called an *inode* (short for *index node*). Since the index is a flat index, inodes are addressed by number.

A directory is a specially formatted file, whose inode entry marks it as a directory. A directory's data blocks contain a set of pairs. Each pair consists of the name of something in that directory and the inode number of that thing. The data blocks for */usr/bin* might contain:

Name	Inode
bc	17
du	29
nvi	8
pine	55
vi	8

Every directory is like this, even the root directory (/). To read the file */usr/bin/vi*, the operating system reads the inode for /, reads its data blocks to find the entry for */usr*, reads */usr*'s inode, reads its data block to find */usr/bin*, reads */usr/bin*'s inode, reads its data block to find */usr/bin/vi*, reads */usr/bin/vi*'s inode, and then reads the data from its data block.

The name in a directory entry isn't fully qualified. The file */usr/bin/vi* has an entry with the name *vi* in the */usr/bin* directory. If you open the directory */usr/bin* and read entries one by one, you get filenames like *patch*, *rlogin*, and *vi* instead of fully qualified names like */usr/bin/patch*, */usr/bin/rlogin*, and */usr/bin/vi*.

The inode has more than a pointer to the data blocks. Each inode also contains the type of thing it represents (directory, plain file, etc.), the size of the thing, a set of permissions bits, owner and group information, the time the thing was last modified, the number of directory entries that point to this inode, and so on.

Some operations on files change the contents of the file's data blocks; some change just the inode. For instance, appending to or truncating a file updates its inode by changing the size field. Other operations change the directory entry that points to the file's inode. Changing a file's name changes only the directory entry; it updates neither the file's data nor its inode.

Three fields in the inode structure contain the last access, change, and modification times: `atime`, `ctime`, and `mtime`. The `atime` field is updated each time the pointer to the file's data blocks is followed and the file's data is read. The `mtime` field is updated each time the file's data changes. The `ctime` field is updated each time the file's inode changes. The `ctime` is *not* creation time; there is no way under standard Unix to find a file's creation time.

Reading a file changes its `atime` only. Changing a file's name doesn't change `atime`, `ctime`, or `mtime` because it was only the directory entry that changed (it does change the `atime` and `mtime` of the directory the file is in, though). Truncating a file doesn't change its `atime` (because we haven't read, we've just changed the size field in its directory entry), but it does change its `ctime` because we changed its size field and its `mtime` because we changed its contents (even though we didn't follow the pointer to do so).

We can access a file or directory's inode by calling the built-in function `stat` on its name. For instance, to get the inode for */usr/bin/vi*, say:

```
@entry = stat("/usr/bin/vi") or die "Couldn't stat /usr/bin/vi : $!";
```

To get the inode for the directory */usr/bin*, say:

```
@entry = stat("/usr/bin")    or die "Couldn't stat /usr/bin : $!";
```

You can stat filehandles, too:

```
@entry = stat(INFILE)          or die "Couldn't stat INFILE : $!";
```

The **stat** function returns a list of the values of the fields in the directory entry. If it couldn't get this information (for instance, if the file doesn't exist), it returns an empty list. It's this empty list we test for with the **or die** construct. Be careful of using || **die** because that throws the expression into scalar context, in which case **stat** only reports whether it worked. It doesn't return the list of values. The _ cache referred to below will still be updated, though.

The values returned by **stat** are listed in the following table.

Element	Abbreviation	Description
0	dev	Device number of filesystem
1	ino	Inode number (the "pointer" field)
2	mode	File mode (type and permissions)
3	nlink	Number of (hard) links to the file
4	uid	Numeric user ID of file's owner
5	gid	Numeric group ID of file's owner
6	rdev	The device identifier (special files only)
7	size	Total size of file, in bytes
8	atime	Last access time, in seconds, since the Epoch
9	mtime	Last modify time, in seconds, since the Epoch
10	ctime	Inode change time, in seconds, since the Epoch
11	blksize	Preferred block size for filesystem I/O
12	blocks	Actual number of blocks allocated

The standard File::stat module provides a named interface to these values. It overrides the **stat** function, so instead of returning the preceding array, it returns an object with a method for each attribute:

```
use File::stat;

$inode = stat("/usr/bin/vi");
$ctime = $inode->ctime;
$size  = $inode->size;
```

In addition, Perl provides a set of operators that call **stat** and return one value only. These are collectively referred to as the -X operators because they all take

the form of a dash followed by a single character. They're modelled on the shell's
test operators:

-X	Stat field	Meaning
-r	mode	File is readable by effective UID/GID
-w	mode	File is writable by effective UID/GID
-x	mode	File is executable by effective UID/GID
-o	mode	File is owned by effective UID
-R	mode	File is readable by real UID/GID
-W	mode	File is writable by real UID/GID
-X	mode	File is executable by real UID/GID
-O	mode	File is owned by real UID
-e		File exists
-z	size	File has zero size
-s	size	File has nonzero size (returns size)
-f	mode,rdev	File is a plain file
-d	mode,rdev	File is a directory
-l	mode	File is a symbolic link
-p	mode	File is a named pipe (FIFO)
-S	mode	File is a socket
-b	rdev	File is a block special file
-c	rdev	File is a character special file
-t	rdev	Filehandle is opened to a tty
-u	mode	File has setuid bit set
-g	mode	File has setgid bit set
-k	mode	File has sticky bit set
-T	N/A	File is a text file
-B	N/A	File is a binary file (opposite of -T)
-M	mtime	Age of file in days when script started
-A	atime	Same for access time
-C	ctime	Same for inode change time (not creation)

The `stat` and the -X operators cache the values that the *stat*(2) system call
returned. If you then call `stat` or a -X operator with the special filehandle _ (a

single underscore), it won't call `stat` again but will instead return information from its cache. This lets you test many properties of a single file without calling *stat*(2) many times or introducing a race condition:

```
open( F, "< $filename" )
    or die "Opening $filename: $!\n";
unless (-s F && -T _) {
    die "$filename doesn't have text in it.\n";
}
```

The `stat` call just returns the information in one inode, though. How do we get a list of the contents of a directory? For that, Perl provides `opendir`, `readdir`, and `closedir`:

```
opendir(DIRHANDLE, "/usr/bin") or die "couldn't open /usr/bin : $!";
while ( defined ($filename = readdir(DIRHANDLE)) ) {
    print "Inside /usr/bin is something called $filename\n";
}
closedir(DIRHANDLE);
```

These directory reading functions are designed to look like the file open and close functions. Where `open` takes a filehandle, though, `opendir` takes a directory handle. They look the same (a bare word) but they are different: you can `open(BIN, "/a/file")` and `opendir(BIN, "/a/dir")` and Perl won't get confused. You might, but Perl won't. Because filehandles and directory handles are different, you can't use the `<>` operator to read from a directory handle.

The filenames in a directory aren't necessarily stored alphabetically. If you want to get an alphabetical list of files, you'll have to read all the entries and sort them yourself.

The separation of directory information from inode information can create some odd situations. Operations that change the directory only require write permission on the directory, not on the file. Most operations that change information in the file's data require write permission to the file. Operations that alter the permissions of the file require that the caller be the file's owner or the superuser. This can lead to the interesting situation of being able to delete a file you can't read, or write to a file you can't remove.

Although these situations make the filesystem structure seem odd at first, they're actually the source of much of Unix's power. Links, two filenames that refer to the same file, are now extremely simple. The two directory entries just list the same inode number. The inode structure includes a count of the number of directory entries referring to the file (`nlink` in the values returned by `stat`), but it lets the operating system store and maintain only one copy of the modification times, size, and other file attributes. When one directory entry is `unlinked`, data blocks are only deleted if the directory entry was the last one that referred to the file's inode—and no processes still have the file open. You can unlink an open file, but its disk space won't be released until the last close.

Links come in two forms. The kind described above, where two directory entries list the same inode number (like *vi* and *nvi* in the earlier table), are called *hard links*. The operating system cannot tell the first directory entry of a file (the one created when the file was created) from any subsequent hard links to it. The other kind, *soft* or *symbolic links*, are very different. A soft link is a special type of file whose data block stores the filename the file is linked to. Soft links have a different mode value, indicating they're not regular files. The operating system, when asked to open a soft link, instead opens the filename contained in the data block.

Executive Summary

Filenames are kept in a directory, separate from the size, protections, and other metadata kept in an inode.

The stat function returns the inode information (metadata).

opendir, readdir, and friends provide access to filenames in a directory through a *directory handle*.

Directory handles look like filehandles, but they are not the same. In particular, you can't use <> on directory handles.

The permissions on a directory determine whether you can read and write the list of filenames. The permissions on a file determine whether you can change the file's metadata or contents.

Three different times are stored in an inode. None of them is the file's creation time.

9.1. Getting and Setting Timestamps

Problem

You need to retrieve or alter when a file was last modified (written or changed) or accessed (read).

Solution

Use stat to get those times and utime to set them. Both functions are built into Perl:

```
($READTIME, $WRITETIME) = (stat($filename))[8,9];

utime($NEWREADTIME, $NEWWRITETIME, $filename);
```

Discussion

As explained in the Introduction, three different times are associated with an inode in the traditional Unix filesystem. Of these, any user can set the `atime` and `mtime` with `utime`, assuming the user has write access to the parent directory of the file. There is effectively no way to change the `ctime`. This example shows how to call `utime`:

```
$SECONDS_PER_DAY = 60 * 60 * 24;
($atime, $mtime) = (stat($file))[8,9];
$atime -= 7 * $SECONDS_PER_DAY;
$mtime -= 7 * $SECONDS_PER_DAY;

utime($atime, $mtime, $file)
    or die "couldn't backdate $file by a week w/ utime: $!";
```

You must call `utime` with both `atime` and `mtime` values. If you only want to change one, you must call `stat` first to get the other:

```
$mtime = (stat $file)[9];
utime(time, $mtime, $file);
```

This is easier to understand if you use File::stat:

```
use File::stat;
utime(time, stat($file)->mtime, $file);
```

Use `utime` to make it appear as though you never touched a file at all (beyond its `ctime` being updated). For example, to edit a file, use the program in Example 9-1.

Example 9-1. uvi

```
#!/usr/bin/perl -w
# uvi - vi a file without changing its access times

$file = shift or die "usage: uvi filename\n";
($atime, $mtime) = (stat($file))[8,9];
system($ENV{EDITOR} || "vi", $file);
utime($atime, $mtime, $file)
    or die "couldn't restore $file to orig times: $!";
```

See Also

The `stat` and `utime` functions in *perlfunc*(1) and in Chapter 3 of *Programming Perl*; the standard File::stat module (also in Chapter 7 of *Programming Perl*); your system's *utime*(3) manpage

9.2. Deleting a File

Problem

You want to delete a file. Perl's `delete` function isn't what you want.

Solution

Use Perl's standard `unlink` function:

```
unlink($FILENAME)                      or die "Can't delete $FILENAME: $!\n";
unlink(@FILENAMES) == @FILENAMES  or die "Couldn't unlink all of
@FILENAMES: $!\n";
```

Discussion

The `unlink` function takes its name from the Unix system call. Perl's `unlink` takes a list of filenames and returns the number of filenames successfully deleted. This return value can then be tested with `||` or `or`:

```
unlink($file) or die "Can't unlink $file: $!";
```

`unlink` doesn't report which filenames it couldn't delete, only how many it did delete. Here's one way to test for successful deletion of many files and to report the number deleted:

```
unless (($count = unlink(@filelist)) == @filelist) {
    warn "could only delete $count of "
            . (@filelist) . " files";
}
```

A `foreach` over `@filelist` would permit individual error messages.

Under Unix, deleting a file from a directory requires write access to the directory,[*] not to the file, because it's the directory you're changing. Under some circumstances, you could remove a file you couldn't write to or write to a file you couldn't remove.

If you delete a file that some process still has open, the operating system removes the directory entry but doesn't free up data blocks until all processes have closed the file. This is how the `new_tmpfile` function in IO::File (see Recipe 7.5) works.

---

[*] Unless the sticky bit, mode 01000, is turned on for the directory, which further restricts deletions to be by the file's owner only. Shared directories like */tmp* are usually mode 01777 for security reasons.

See Also

The unlink function in *perlfunc*(1) and in Chapter 3 of *Programming Perl*; your system's *unlink*(2) manpage; we use the idea of a file that has been deleted but is still accessible in Recipe 7.5

9.3. Copying or Moving a File

Problem

You need to copy a file, but Perl has no built-in copy command.

Solution

Use the copy function from the standard File::Copy module:

```
use File::Copy;
copy($oldfile, $newfile);
```

You can do it by hand:

```
open(IN,  "< $oldfile")                     or die "can't open $oldfile: $!";
open(OUT, "> $newfile")                     or die "can't open $newfile: $!";

$blksize = (stat IN)[11] || 16384;          # preferred block size?
while ($len = sysread IN, $buf, $blksize) {
    if (!defined $len) {
        next if $! =~ /^Interrupted/;       # ^Z and fg
        die "System read error: $!\n";
    }
    $offset = 0;
    while ($len) {                # Handle partial writes.
        defined($written = syswrite OUT, $buf, $len, $offset)
            or die "System write error: $!\n";
        $len     -= $written;
        $offset += $written;
    };
}

close(IN);
close(OUT);
```

Or you can call your system's copy program:

```
system("cp $oldfile $newfile");        # unix
system("copy $oldfile $newfile");      # dos, vms
```

Discussion

The File::Copy module provides copy and move functions. These are more convenient than resorting to low-level I/O calls and more portable than calling system. move works across file-system boundaries; the standard Perl built-in rename (usually) does not.

```
use File::Copy;

copy("datafile.dat", "datafile.bak")
    or die "copy failed: $!";

move("datafile.dat", "datafile.new")
    or die "move failed: $!";
```

Because these functions return only a simple success status, you can't easily tell which file prevented the copy or move from being done. Copying the files manually lets you pinpoint which files didn't copy, but it fills your program with complex sysreads and syswrites.

See Also

Documentation for the standard File::Copy module (also in Chapter 7 of *Programming Perl*); the rename, read, and syswrite functions in *perlfunc*(1) and in Chapter 3 of *Programming Perl*

9.4. Recognizing Two Names for the Same File

Problem

You want to identify if two filenames in a list correspond to the same file on disk (because of hard and soft links, two filenames can refer to a single file). You might do this to make sure that you don't change a file you've already worked with.

Solution

Maintain a hash, keyed by the device and inode number of the files you've seen. The values are the names of the files:

```
%seen = ();

sub do_my_thing {
    my $filename = shift;
    my ($dev, $ino) = stat $filename;

    unless ($seen{$dev, $ino}++) {
```

```
        # do something with $filename because we haven't
        # seen it before
    }
}
```

Discussion

A key in %seen is made by combining the device number ($dev) and inode number ($ino) of each file. Files that are the same will have the same device and inode numbers, so they will have the same key.

If you want to maintain a list of all files of the same name, instead of counting the number of times seen, save the name of the file in an anonymous array.

```
foreach $filename (@files) {
    ($dev, $ino) = stat $filename;
    push( @{ $seen{$dev,$ino} }, $filename);
}

foreach $devino (sort keys %seen) {
    ($dev, $ino) = split(/$;/o, $devino);
    if (@{$seen{$devino}} > 1) {
        # @{$seen{$devino}} is a list of filenames for the same file
    }
}
```

The $; variable contains the separator string using the old multidimensional associative array emulation syntax, $hash{$x,$y,$z}. It's still a one-dimensional hash, but it has composite keys. The key is really join($; => $x, $y, $z). The split separates them again. Although you'd normally just use a real multilevel hash directly, here there's no need, and it's cheaper not to.

See Also

The $; variable in *perlvar*(1), and in the "Special Variables" section of Chapter 2 of *Programming Perl*; the stat function in *perlfunc*(1) and in Chapter 3 of *Programming Perl*; Chapter 5, *Hashes*

9.5. Processing All Files in a Directory

Problem

You want to do something to each file in a particular directory.

Solution

Use `opendir` to open the directory and then `readdir` to retrieve every filename:

```
opendir(DIR, $dirname) or die "can't opendir $dirname: $!";
while (defined($file = readdir(DIR))) {
    # do something with "$dirname/$file"
}
closedir(DIR);
```

Discussion

The `opendir`, `readdir`, and `closedir` functions operate on directories as `open`, `<>`, and `close` operate on files. Both use handles, but the directory handles used by `opendir` and friends are different from the file handles used by `open` and friends. In particular, you can't use `<>` on a directory handle.

In scalar context, `readdir` returns the next filename in the directory until it reaches the end of the directory when it returns `undef`. In list context it returns the rest of the filenames in the directory or an empty list if there were no files left. As explained in the Introduction, the filenames returned by `readdir` do not include the directory name. When you work with the filenames returned by `readdir`, you must either move to the right directory first or prepend the directory to the filename.

This shows one way of prepending:

```
$dir = "/usr/local/bin";
print "Text files in $dir are:\n";
opendir(BIN, $dir) or die "Can't open $dir: $!";
while( defined ($file = readdir BIN) ) {
    print "$file\n" if -T "$dir/$file";
}
closedir(BIN);
```

We test `$file` with `defined` because simply saying `while ($file = readdir BIN)` would only be testing truth and not definedness. Although the loop would end when `readdir` ran out of files to return, it would also end prematurely if a file had the name "0".

The `readdir` function will return the special directories "." (the directory itself) and ".." (the parent of the directory). Most people skip the files with code like:

```
while ( defined ($file = readdir BIN) ) {
    next if $file =~ /^\.\.?$/;    # skip . and ..
    # ...
}
```

Like filehandles, directory handles are per-package constructs. Further, you have two ways of getting a local directory handle: use `local *DIRHANDLE` or use an

object module (see Recipe 7.16). The appropriate module in this case is `DirHan-`
`dle`. The following code uses DirHandle and produces a sorted list of plain files
that aren't dotfiles (that is, whose names don't begin with a "`.`"):

```
use DirHandle;

sub plainfiles {
    my $dir = shift;
    my $dh = DirHandle->new($dir)    or die "can't opendir $dir: $!";
    return sort                      # sort pathnames
        grep {    -f    }            # choose only "plain" files
        map   { "$dir/$_" }          # create full paths
        grep {  !/^\./  }            # filter out dot files
        $dh->read();                 # read all entries
}
```

DirHandle's `read` method behaves just like `readdir`, returning the rest of the filenames. The bottom `grep` only returns those that don't begin with a period. The
`map` turns the filenames returned by `read` into fully qualified filenames, and the
top `grep` filters out directories, links, etc. The resulting list is then `sorted` and
returned.

In addition to `readdir`, there's also `rewinddir` (to move the directory handle
back to the start of the filename list), `seekdir` (to move to a specific offset in the
list), and `telldir` (to find out how far from the start of the list you are).

See Also

The `closedir`, `opendir`, `readdir`, `rewinddir`, `seekdir`, and `telldir` functions in *perlfunc*(1) and in Chapter 3 of *Programming Perl*; documentation for the
standard DirHandle module (also in Chapter 7 of *Programming Perl*)

9.6. Globbing, or Getting a List of Filenames Matching a Pattern

Problem

You want to get a list of filenames similar to MS-DOS's `*.*` and Unix's `*.h` (this is
called *globbing*).

Solution

Perl provides globbing with the semantics of the Unix C shell through the `glob`
keyword and `<>`:

```
@list = <*.c>;
@list = glob("*.c");
```

You can also use `readdir` to extract the filenames manually:

```
opendir(DIR, $path);
@files = grep { /\.c$/ } readdir(DIR);
closedir(DIR);
```

The CPAN module File::KGlob does globbing without length limits:

```
use File::KGlob;

@files = glob("*.c");
```

Discussion

Perl's built-in `glob` and <WILDCARD> notation (not to be confused with <FILE-HANDLE>) currently use an external program to get the list of filenames on most platforms. This program is *csh* on Unix,* and a program called *dosglob.exe* on Windows. On VMS and the Macintosh, file globs are done internally without an external program. Globs are supposed to give C shell semantics on non-Unix systems to encourage portability. The use of the shell on Unix also makes this inappropriate for setuid scripts.

To get around this, you can either roll your own selection mechanism using the built-in `opendir` or CPAN's File::KGlob, neither of which uses external programs. File::KGlob provides Unix shell-like globbing semantics, whereas `opendir` lets you select files with Perl's regular expressions.

At its simplest, an `opendir` solution uses `grep` to filter the list returned by `readdir`:

```
@files = grep { /\.[ch]$/i } readdir(DH);
```

You could also do this with the DirHandle module:

```
use DirHandle;

$dh = DirHandle->new($path)    or die "Can't open $path : $!\n";
@files = grep { /\.[ch]$/i } $dh->read();
```

As always, the filenames returned don't include the directory. When you use the filename, you'll need to prepend the directory name:

```
opendir(DH, $dir)        or die "Couldn't open $dir for reading: $!";

@files = ();
while( defined ($file = readdir(DH)) ) {
    next unless /\.[ch]$/i;

    my $filename = "$dir/$file";
```

---

* Usually. If *tcsh* is installed, Perl uses that because it's safer. If neither is installed, */bin/sh* is used.

```
    push(@files, $filename) if -T $filename;
}
```

The following example combines directory reading and filtering with the Schwartzian Transform from Chapter 4, *Arrays*, for efficiency. It sets @dirs to a sorted list
of the subdirectories in a directory whose names are all numeric:

```
@dirs = map  { $_->[1] }                  # extract pathnames
        sort { $a->[0] <=> $b->[0] }      # sort names numeric
        grep { -d $_->[1] }               # path is a dir
        map  { [ $_, "$path/$_" ] }       # form (name, path)
        grep { /^\d+$/ }                  # just numerics
        readdir(DIR);                     # all files
```

Recipe 4.15 explains how to read these strange-looking constructs. As always, formatting and documenting your code can make it much easier to read and understand.

See Also

The opendir, readdir, closedir, grep, map, and sort functions in *perlfunc*(1)
and in Chapter 3 of *Programming Perl*; documentation for the standard DirHandle module (also in Chapter 7 of *Programming Perl*); the "I/O Operators" section
of *perlop*(1), and the "Filename Globbing Operator" section of Chapter 2 of *Programming Perl*; we talk more about globbing in Recipe 6.9; Recipe 9.7

9.7. Processing All Files in a Directory Recursively

Problem

You want to do something to each file and subdirectory in a particular directory.

Solution

Use the standard File::Find module.

```
use File::Find;
sub process_file {
    # do whatever;
}
find(\&process_file, @DIRLIST);
```

Discussion

File::Find provides a convenient way to process a directory recursively. It does the
directory scans and recursion for you. All you do is pass find a code reference

and a list of directories. For each file in those directories, recursively, find calls
your function.

Before calling your function, find changes to the directory being visited, whose
path relative to the starting directory is stored in the $File::Find::dir variable.
$_ is set to the basename of the file being visited, and the full path of that file can
be found in $File::Find::name. Your code can set $File::Find::prune to
true to tell find not to descend into the directory just seen.

This simple example demonstrates File::Find. We give find an anonymous subroutine that prints the name of each file visited and adds a / to the names of
directories:

```
@ARGV = qw(.) unless @ARGV;
use File::Find;
find sub { print $File::Find::name, -d && '/', "\n" }, @ARGV;
```

This prints a / after directory names using the -d file test operator, which returns
the empty string ' ' if it fails.

The following program prints the sum of everything in a directory. It gives find
an anonymous subroutine to keep a running sum of the sizes of each file it visits.
That includes all inode types, including the sizes of directories and symbolic links,
not just regular files. Once the find function returns, the accumulated sum is displayed.

```
use File::Find;
@ARGV = ('.') unless @ARGV;
my $sum = 0;
find sub { $sum += -s }, @ARGV;
print "@ARGV contains $sum bytes\n";
```

This code finds the largest single file within a set of directories:

```
use File::Find;
@ARGV = ('.') unless @ARGV;
my ($saved_size, $saved_name) = (-1, '');
sub biggest {
    return unless -f && -s _ > $saved_size;
    $saved_size = -s _;
    $saved_name = $File::Find::name;
}
find(\&biggest, @ARGV);
print "Biggest file $saved_name in @ARGV is $saved_size bytes long.\n";
```

We use $saved_size and $saved_name to keep track of the name and the size
of the largest file visited. If we find a file bigger than the largest seen so far, we
replace the saved name and size with the current ones. When the find is done
running, the largest file and its size are printed out, rather verbosely. A more general tool would probably just print the filename, its size, or both. This time we

used a named function rather than an anonymous one because the function was getting big.

It's simple to change this to find the most recently changed file:

```
use File::Find;
@ARGV = ('.') unless @ARGV;
my ($age, $name);
sub youngest {
    return if defined $age && $age > (stat($_))[9];
    $age = (stat(_))[9];
    $name = $File::Find::name;
}
find(\&youngest, @ARGV);
print "$name " . scalar(localtime($age)) . "\n";
```

The File::Find module doesn't export its $name variable, so always refer to it by its fully qualified name. The example in Example 9-2 is more a demonstration of namespace munging than of recursive directory traversal, although it does find all the directories. It makes $name in our current package an alias for the one in File::Find, which is essentially how Exporter works. Then it declares its own version of **find** with a prototype that lets it be called like **grep** or **map**.

Example 9-2. fdirs

```
#!/usr/bin/perl -lw
# fdirs - find all directories
@ARGV = qw(.) unless @ARGV;
use File::Find ();
sub find(&@) { &File::Find::find }
*name = *File::Find::name;
find { print $name if -d } @ARGV;
```

Our **find** only calls the **find** in File::Find, which we were careful not to import by specifying an () empty list in the **use** statement. Rather than write this:

```
find sub { print $File::Find::name if -d }, @ARGV;
```

we can write the more pleasant:

```
find { print $name if -d } @ARGV;
```

See Also

The documentation for the standard File::Find and Exporter modules (also in Chapter 7 of *Programming Perl*); your system's *find*(1) manpage; Recipe 9.6

9.8. Removing a Directory and Its Contents

Problem

You want to remove a directory tree recursively without using rm -r.

Solution

Use the finddepth function from File::Find, shown in Example 9-3.

Example 9-3. rmtree1

```perl
#!/usr/bin/perl
# rmtree1 - remove whole directory trees like rm -r
use File::Find qw(finddepth);
die "usage: $0 dir ..\n" unless @ARGV;
*name = *File::Find::name;
finddepth \&zap, @ARGV;
sub zap {
    if (!-l && -d _) {
        print "rmdir $name\n";
        rmdir($name)  or warn "couldn't rmdir $name: $!";
    } else {
        print "unlink $name";
        unlink($name) or warn "couldn't unlink $name: $!";
    }
}
```

Or use rmtree from File::Path, as shown in Example 9-4.

Example 9-4. rmtree2

```perl
#!/usr/bin/perl
# rmtree2 - remove whole directory trees like rm -r
use File::Path;
die "usage: $0 dir ..\n" unless @ARGV;
foreach $dir (@ARGV) {
    rmtree($dir);
}
```

WARNING   These programs remove an entire directory tree. Use with extreme
           caution!

Discussion

The File::Find module exports both a find function, which traverses a tree in the (essentially random) order the files occur in the directory, as well as a finddepth function, which is guaranteed to visit all the files underneath a directory before visiting the directory itself. This is exactly what we need to remove a directory and its contents.

We have to use two different functions, rmdir and unlink. The unlink function deletes only files, and rmdir only deletes empty directories. We need to use finddepth to make sure that we've first removed the directory's contents before we rmdir the directory itself.

Check first that the file isn't a symbolic link before determining if it's a directory. −d returns true for both a directory and a symbol link to a directory. stat, lstat, and the file test operators like −d all use the operating system call *stat*(2), which returns all the information kept about a file in an inode. These functions and operators retain that information and let you do more tests on the same file with the special underscore (_) filehandle. This avoids redundant system calls that would return the same information, slowly.

See Also

The unlink, rmdir, lstat, and stat functions in *perlfunc*(1) and in Chapter 3 of *Programming Perl*; the documentation for the standard File::Find module; your system's *rm*(1) and *stat*(2) manpages; the −X section of *perlfunc*(1), and the "Named Unary and File Test Operators" section of Chapter 2 of *Programming Perl*

9.9. Renaming Files

Problem

You have a lot of files whose names you want to change.

Solution

Use a foreach loop and the rename function:

```
foreach $file (@NAMES) {
    my $newname = $file;
    # change $newname
    rename($file, $newname) or
        warn "Couldn't rename $file to $newname: $!\n";
}
```

Discussion

This is straightforward. rename takes two arguments. The first is the filename to change, and the second is its new name. Perl's rename is a front end to the operating system's rename system call, which typically won't let you rename files across filesystem boundaries.

A small change turns this into a generic **rename** script, such as the one by Larry Wall shown in Example 9-5.

Example 9-5. rename

```perl
#!/usr/bin/perl -w
# rename - Larry's filename fixer
$op = shift or die "Usage: rename expr [files]\n";
chomp(@ARGV = <STDIN>) unless @ARGV;
for (@ARGV) {
    $was = $_;
    eval $op;
    die $@ if $@;
    rename($was,$_) unless $was eq $_;
}
```

This script's first argument is Perl code that alters the filename (stored in $_) to reflect how you want the file renamed. It can do this because it uses an **eval** to do the hard work. It also skips **rename** calls when the filename is untouched. This lets you simply use wildcards like **rename EXPR *** instead of making long lists of filenames.

Here are five examples of calling the *rename* program from your shell:

```
% rename 's/\.orig$//'  *.orig
% rename 'tr/A-Z/a-z/ unless /^Make/'  *
% rename '$_ .= ".bad"'  *.f
% rename 'print "$_: "; s/foo/bar/ if <STDIN> =~ /^y/i'  *
% find /tmp -name '*~' -print | rename 's/^(.+)~$/.#$1/'
```

The first shell command removes a trailing "`.orig`" from each filename.

The second converts uppercase to lowercase. Because a translation is used rather than the **lc** function, this conversion won't be locale-aware. To fix that, you'd have to write:

```
% rename 'use locale; $_ = lc($_) unless /^Make/'  *
```

The third appends "`.bad`" to each Fortran file ending in "`.f`", something a lot of us have wanted to do for a long time.

The fourth prompts the user for the change. Each file's name is printed to standard output and a response is read from standard input. If the user types something starting with a "`y`" or "`Y`", any "`foo`" in the filename is changed to "`bar`".

The fifth uses *find* to locate files in `/tmp` that end with a tilde. It renames these so that instead of ending with a tilde, they start with a dot and a pound sign. In effect, this switches between two common conventions for backup files.

The *rename* script exemplifies the powerful Unix tool-and-filter philosophy. Even though we could have created a dedicated command to do the lowercase conversion, it's nearly as easy to write a flexible, reusable tool by embedding an `eval`. By allowing the filenames to be read from standard input, we don't have to build in the recursive directory walk. Instead, we just use *find*, which performs this function well. There's no reason to recreate the wheel, although using File::Find we could have.

See Also

The `rename` function in *perlfunc*(1) and in Chapter 3 of *Programming Perl*; your system's *mv*(1) and *rename*(2) manpages; the documentation for the standard File::Find module (also in Chapter 7 of *Programming Perl*)

9.10. *Splitting a Filename into Its Component Parts*

Problem

You want to extract a filename, its enclosing directory, or the extension(s) from a string that contains a full pathname.

Solution

Use routines from the standard File::Basename module.

```
use File::Basename;

$base = basename($path);
$dir  = dirname($path);
($base, $dir, $ext) = fileparse($path);
```

Discussion

The standard File::Basename module contains routines to split up a filename. `dirname` and `basename` supply the directory and filename portions respectively:

```
$path = '/usr/lib/libc.a';
$file = basename($path);
$dir  = dirname($path);

print "dir is $dir, file is $file\n";
# dir is /usr/lib, file is libc.a
```

The `fileparse` function can be used to extract the extension. To do so, pass `fileparse` the path to decipher and a regular expression that matches the extension. You must give `fileparse` this pattern because an extension isn't necessarily dot-separated. Consider ".tar.gz"—is the extension ".tar", ".gz", or ".tar.gz"? By specifying the pattern, you control which of these you get.

```
$path = '/usr/lib/libc.a';
($name,$dir,$ext) = fileparse($path,'\..*');

print "dir is $dir, name is $name, extension is $ext\n";
# dir is /usr/lib/, name is libc, extension is .a
```

By default, these routines parse pathnames using your operating system's normal conventions for directory separators by looking at the $^O variable, which holds a string identifying the system you're running on. That value was determined when Perl was built and installed. You can change the default by calling the `fileparse_set_fstype` routine. This alters the behavior of subsequent calls to the File::Basename functions:

```
fileparse_set_fstype("MacOS");
$path = "Hard%20Drive:System%20Folder:README.txt";
($name,$dir,$ext) = fileparse($path,'\..*');

print "dir is $dir, name is $name, extension is $ext\n";
# dir is Hard%20Drive:System%20Folder, name is README, extension is .txt
```

To pull out just the extension, you might use this:

```
sub extension {
    my $path = shift;
    my $ext = (fileparse($path,'\..*'))[2];
    $ext =~ s/^\.//;
    return $ext;
}
```

When called on a file like *source.c.bak*, this returns an extension of "c.bak", not just "bak". If you wanted just ".bak" returned, use '\..*?' as the second argument to `fileparse`.

When passed a pathname with a trailing directory separator, such as `lib/`, `fileparse` considers the directory name to be "lib/", whereas `dirname` considers it to be ".".

See Also

The documentation for the standard File::Basename module (also in Chapter 7 of *Programming Perl*); the entry for $^O in *perlvar*(1), and in the "Special Variables" section of Chapter 2 of *Programming Perl*

9.11. Program: symirror

The program in Example 9-6 recursively duplicates a directory tree, making a shadow forest full of symlinks pointing back at the real files.

Example 9-6. symirror

```perl
#!/usr/bin/perl -w
# symirror - build spectral forest of symlinks
use strict;
use File::Find;
use Cwd;

my ($srcdir, $dstdir);
my $cwd = getcwd();
die "usage: $0 realdir mirrordir" unless @ARGV == 2;

for (($srcdir, $dstdir) = @ARGV) {
    my $is_dir = -d;
    next if $is_dir;                         # cool
    if (defined ($is_dir)) {
        die "$0: $_ is not a directory\n";
    } else {                                 # be forgiving
        mkdir($dstdir, 0777) or die "can't mkdir $dstdir: $!";
    }
} continue {
    s#^(?!/)#$cwd/#;                         # fix relative paths
}

chdir $srcdir or die "Can't chdir to $srchdir: $!";
find(\&wanted, '.');

sub wanted {
    my($dev, $ino, $mode) = lstat($_);
    my $name = $File::Find::name;
    $mode &= 07777;                     # preserve directory permissions
    $name =~ s!^\./!!;                  # correct name
    if (-d _) {                         # then make a real directory
        mkdir("$dstdir/$name", $mode)
            or die "can't mkdir $dstdir/$name: $!";
    } else {                            # shadow everything else
        symlink("$srcdir/$name", "$dstdir/$name")
            or die "can't symlink $srcdir/$name to $dstdir/$name: $!";
    }
}
```

9.12. Program: lst

Have you ever wondered what the newest or biggest files within a directory are? The standard *ls* program has options for listing out directories sorted in time order (the -t flag) and for recursing into subdirectories (the -R flag). However, it pauses at each directory to display the sorted contents of just that directory. It doesn't descend through all the subdirectories first and then sort everything it finds.

The following *lst* program does that. Here's an example using its -l flag to get a long listing:

```
% lst -l /etc
12695 0600      1      root    wheel       512 Fri May 29 10:42:41 1998
    /etc/ssh_random_seed
12640 0644      1      root    wheel     10104 Mon May 25  7:39:19 1998
    /etc/ld.so.cache
12626 0664      1      root    wheel     12288 Sun May 24 19:23:08 1998
    /etc/psdevtab
12304 0644      1      root    root        237 Sun May 24 13:59:33 1998
    /etc/exports
12309 0644      1      root    root       3386 Sun May 24 13:24:33 1998
    /etc/inetd.conf
12399 0644      1      root    root      30205 Sun May 24 10:08:37 1998
    /etc/sendmail.cf
18774 0644      1      gnat    perldoc    2199 Sun May 24  9:35:57 1998
    /etc/X11/XMetroconfig
12636 0644      1      root    wheel       290 Sun May 24  9:05:40 1998
    /etc/mtab
12627 0640      1      root    root          0 Sun May 24  8:24:31 1998
    /etc/wtmplock
12310 0644      1      root    tchrist      65 Sun May 24  8:23:04 1998
    /etc/issue
....
```

/etc/X11/XMetroconfig showed up in the middle of the listing for */etc* because it wasn't just for */etc*, but for everything within that directory, recursively.

Other supported options include sorting on read time instead of write time using -u and sorting on size rather than time with -s. The -i flag takes the list of filenames from standard input instead of recursing with find. That way, if you already had a list of filenames, you could feed them to *lst* for sorting.

The program is shown in Example 9-7.

Example 9-7. lst

```
#!/usr/bin/perl
# lst - list sorted directory contents (depth first)

use Getopt::Std;
use File::Find;
use File::stat;
use User::pwent;
use User::grent;

getopts('lusrcmi')      or die <<DEATH;
Usage: $0 [-mucsril] [dirs ...]
  or    $0 -i [-mucsrl] < filelist

Input format:
    -i   read pathnames from stdin
Output format:
    -l   long listing
Sort on:
    -m  use mtime (modify time) [DEFAULT]
```

Example 9-7. lst (continued)

```
    -u  use atime (access time)
    -c  use ctime (inode change time)
    -s  use size for sorting
Ordering:
    -r  reverse sort
NB: You may only use select one sorting option at a time.
DEATH

unless ($opt_i || @ARGV) { @ARGV = ('.') }

if ($opt_c + $opt_u + $opt_s + $opt_m > 1) {
    die "can only sort on one time or size";
}

$IDX = 'mtime';
$IDX = 'atime' if $opt_u;
$IDX = 'ctime' if $opt_c;
$IDX = 'size'  if $opt_s;

$TIME_IDX = $opt_s ? 'mtime' : $IDX;

*name = *File::Find::name;  # forcibly import that variable

# the $opt_i flag tricks wanted into taking
# its filenames from ARGV instead of being
# called from find.

if ($opt_i) {
    *name = *_;  # $name now alias for $_
    while (<>) { chomp; &wanted; }    # ok, not stdin really
} else {
    find(\&wanted, @ARGV);
}

# sort the files by their cached times, youngest first
@skeys = sort { $time{$b} <=> $time{$a} } keys %time;

# but flip the order if -r was supplied on command line
@skeys = reverse @skeys if $opt_r;

for (@skeys) {
    unless ($opt_l) {  # emulate ls -l, except for permissions
        print "$_\n";
        next;
    }
    $now = localtime $stat{$_}->$TIME_IDX();
    printf "%6d %04o %6d %8s %8s %8d %s %s\n",
    $stat{$_}->ino(),
    $stat{$_}->mode() & 07777,
    $stat{$_}->nlink(),
    user($stat{$_}->uid()),
    group($stat{$_}->gid()),
```

Example 9-7. lst (continued)

```
        $stat{$_}->size(),
        $now, $_;
}


# get stat info on the file, saving the desired
# sort criterion (mtime, atime, ctime, or size)
# in the %time hash indexed by filename.
# if they want a long list, we have to save the
# entire stat object in %stat.  yes, this is a
# hash of objects
sub wanted {
    my $sb = stat($_);   # XXX: should be stat or lstat?
    return unless $sb;
    $time{$name} = $sb->$IDX();   # indirect method call
    $stat{$name} = $sb if $opt_l;
}


# cache user number to name conversions
sub user {
    my $uid = shift;
    $user{$uid} = getpwuid($uid) ? getpwuid($uid)->name : "#$uid"
        unless defined $user{$uid};
    return $user{$uid};
}


# cache group number to name conversions
sub group {
    my $gid = shift;
    $group{$gid} = getgrgid($gid) ? getpwuid($gid)->name : "#$gid"
        unless defined $group{$gid};
    return $group{$gid};
}
```

10

Subroutines

Composing mortals with immortal fire.

—W. H. Auden
"Three Songs for St Cecilia's Day"

10.0. Introduction

To avoid the dangerous practice of copying and pasting code throughout a program, your larger programs will probably reuse chunks of code with subroutines. We'll use the terms *subroutine* and *function* interchangeably, because Perl doesn't distinguish between the two any more than C does. Even object-oriented methods are just subroutines that are called using a special syntax, described in Chapter 13, *Classes, Objects, and Ties.*

A subroutine is declared with the sub keyword. Here's a simple subroutine definition:

```
sub hello {
    $greeted++;          # global variable
    print "hi there!\n";
}
```

The typical way of calling that subroutine is:

```
hello();                 # call subroutine hello with no arguments/parameters
```

Because Perl compiles your program before executing it, it doesn't matter where your subroutines are declared. These definitions don't have to be in the same file as your main program. They can be pulled in from other files using the do, require, or use operators, as described in Chapter 12, *Packages, Libraries, and Modules.* They can even be created on the fly using eval or the AUTOLOAD mechanism, or generated using closures, which can be used as function templates.

If you are familiar with other programming languages, several characteristics of Perl's functions may surprise you if you're not prepared. Most of the recipes in this chapter illustrate how to take advantage of—and be aware of—these properties.

- Perl functions have no formal, named parameters, but this is not necessarily a bad thing. See Recipes 10.1 and 10.7.

- All variables are global unless declared otherwise. See Recipes 10.2, 10.3, and 10.13 for details.

- Passing or returning more than one array or hash normally causes them to lose their separate identities. See Recipes 10.5, 10.8, 10.9, and 10.11 to avoid this.

- A function can know whether it was called in list or scalar context, how many arguments it was called with, and even the name of the function that called it. See Recipes 10.4 and 10.6 to find out how.

- Perl's undef value can be used to indicate an error condition since no valid string or number ever has that value. Recipe 10.10 covers subtle pitfalls with undef you should avoid, and Recipe 10.12 shows how to deal with other catastrophic conditions.

- Perl supports interesting operations on functions you might not see in other languages, like anonymous functions, creating functions on the fly, and calling them indirectly using function pointers. See Recipes 10.14 and 10.16 for these esoteric topics.

Calling a function as $x = &func; does not supply any arguments, but rather provides direct access to its caller's @_ array! If you omit the ampersand and use either func() or func, then a new and empty @_ is provided instead.

10.1. Accessing Subroutine Arguments

Problem

You have written a function and want to use the arguments supplied by its caller.

Solution

All values passed as arguments to a function are in the special array @_. Thus, the first argument to the function is in $_[0], the second is in $_[1], and so on. The number of arguments is therefore scalar(@_).

For example:

```
sub hypotenuse {
    return sqrt( ($_[0] ** 2) + ($_[1] ** 2) );
```

```
    }

    $diag = hypotenuse(3,4);   # $diag is 5
```

Your subroutines will almost always start by copying arguments into named private variables for safer and more convenient access:

```
    sub hypotenuse {
        my ($side1, $side2) = @_;
        return sqrt( ($side1 ** 2) + ($side2 ** 2) );
    }
```

Discussion

It's been said that programming has only three nice numbers: zero, one, and however many you please. Perl's subroutine mechanism was designed to facilitate writing functions with as many—or as few—elements in the parameter and return lists as you wish. All incoming parameters appear as separate scalar values in the special array @_, which is automatically local to each function (see Recipe 10.13). To return a value from a subroutine, use the **return** statement with an argument. If there is no **return** statement, the return value is the result of the last evaluated expression.

Here are some sample calls to the **hypotenuse** function defined in the Solution:

```
    print hypotenuse(3, 4), "\n";                    # prints 5

    @a = (3, 4);
    print hypotenuse(@a), "\n";                       # prints 5
```

If you look at the arguments used in the second call to **hypotenuse**, it might appear that only one argument was passed: the array @a. This isn't what happens—the elements of @a are copied into the @_ array separately. Similarly, if we called a function with (@a, @b), we'd be giving it all the arguments in both arrays. This is the same principle of flattened lists at work as when we say:

```
    @both = (@men, @women);
```

The scalars in @_ are implicit aliases for the ones passed in, not copies. That means changing the elements of @_ in a subroutine changes the values in the subroutine's caller. This is a holdover from before Perl had proper references.

So, we can write functions that leave their arguments intact, by copying the arguments to private variables like this:

```
    @nums = (1.4, 3.5, 6.7);
    @ints = int_all(@nums);          # @nums unchanged
    sub int_all {
        my @retlist = @_;                    # make safe copy for return
        for my $n (@retlist) { $n = int($n) }
        return @retlist;
    }
```

We can also write functions that change their caller's variables:

```
@nums = (1.4, 3.5, 6.7);
trunc_em(@nums);                    # @nums now (1,3,6)
sub trunc_em {
    for (@_) { $_ = int($_) }   # truncate each argument
}
```

Don't pass constants to this kind of function, as in `trunc_em(1.4, 3.5, 6.7)`. If you try, you'll get a run-time exception saying `Modification of a read-only value attempted at ....`

The built-in functions `chop` and `chomp` work like this, modifying their caller's variables and returning the character(s) removed. People are used to such functions returning the changed values, so they often write things like:

```
$line = chomp(<>);                     # WRONG
```

until they get the hang of how it works. Given this vast potential for confusion, you might want to think twice before modifying `@_` in your subroutines.

See Also

The section on "Subroutines" in Chapter 2 of *Programming Perl* and *perlsub*(1)

10.2. *Making Variables Private to a Function*

Problem

Your subroutine needs temporary variables. You shouldn't use global variables, because another subroutine might also use the same variables.

Solution

Use `my` to declare a variable private to a region of your program:

```
sub somefunc {
    my $variable;                      # $variable is invisible outside somefunc()
    my ($another, @an_array, %a_hash);    # declaring many variables at once

    # ...
}
```

Discussion

The my operator confines a variable to a particular region of code in which it can be used and accessed. Outside that region, it can't be accessed. This region is called its *scope*.

Variables declared with my have *lexical scope*, which means that they exist only within a particular textual area of code. For instance, the scope of $variable in the Solution is the function it was defined in, somefunc. When a call to some-func is made, the variable is created. The variable is destroyed when the function call ends. The variable can be accessed within the function, but not outside of it.

A lexical scope is usually a block of code with a set of braces around it, such as those defining the body of the somefunc subroutine or those marking the code blocks of if, while, for, foreach, and eval statements. Lexical scopes may also be an entire file or strings given to eval. Since a lexical scope is usually a block, we'll sometimes talk about lexical variables (variables with lexical scope) being only visible in their block when we mean that they're only visible in their scope. Forgive us. Otherwise, we'll be using the words "scope" and "sub" more than a WWII Navy movie.

Because the parts of code that can see a my variable are determined at compile time and don't change after that, lexical scoping is sometimes misleadingly referred to as static scoping. Lexical scoping is in contrast to *dynamic* scoping, which we'll cover in Recipe 10.13.

You can combine a my declaration with an assignment. Use parentheses when defining more than one variable:

```
my ($name, $age) = @ARGV;
my $start        = fetch_time();
```

These lexical variables behave as you would expect a local variable to. Nested blocks can see lexicals declared in outer blocks, but not in unrelated blocks:

```
my ($a, $b) = @pair;
my $c = fetch_time();

sub check_x {
    my $x = $_[0];
    my $y = "whatever";
    run_check();
    if ($condition) {
        print "got $x\n";
    }
}
```

In the preceding code, the if block inside the function can access the private $x variable. However, the run_check function called from within that scope cannot access $x or $y because run_check was presumably defined in another scope. However, check_x could access $a, $b, or $c from the outer scope because the function was defined in the same scope as those three variables.

Don't nest the declaration of named subroutines within the declarations of other named subroutines. Such subroutines, unlike proper closures, will not get the right bindings of the lexical variables. Recipe 10.16 shows how to cope with this restriction.

When a lexical goes out of scope, its storage is freed unless a reference to its value's storage space still exists, as with @arguments in the following code:

```
sub save_array {
    my @arguments = @_;
    push(@Global_Array, \@arguments);
}
```

Perl's garbage collection system knows not to deallocate things until they're no longer used. This is why we can return a reference to a private variable without leaking memory.

See Also

The section on "Scoped Declarations" in Chapter 2 of *Programming Perl* and the section on "Private Variables via my()" in *perlsub*(1)

10.3. *Creating Persistent Private Variables*

Problem

You want a variable to retain its value between calls to a subroutine but not be visible outside that routine. For instance, you'd like your function to keep track of how many times it was called.

Solution

Wrap the function in another block, and declare my variables in that block's scope rather than the function's:

```
{
    my $variable;
    sub mysub {
        # ... accessing $variable
    }
}
```

If the variables require initialization, make that block a BEGIN so the variable is guaranteed to be set before the main program starts running:

```
BEGIN {
    my $variable = 1;              # initial value
    sub othersub {                 # ... accessing $variable
    }
}
```

Discussion

Unlike local variables in C or C++, Perl's lexical variables don't necessarily get recycled just because their scope has exited. If something more permanent is still aware of the lexical, it will stick around. In this case, mysub uses $variable, so Perl doesn't reclaim the variable when the block around the definition of mysub ends.

Here's how to write a counter:

```
{
    my $counter;
    sub next_counter { return ++$counter }
}
```

Each time next_counter is called, it increments and returns the $counter variable. The first time next_counter is called, $counter is undefined, so it behaves as though it were 0 for the ++. The variable is not part of next_counter's scope, but rather part of the block surrounding it. No code from outside can change $counter except by calling next_counter.

Generally, you should use a BEGIN for the extra scope. Otherwise, you could call the function before its variable were initialized.

```
BEGIN {
    my $counter = 42;
    sub next_counter { return ++$counter }
    sub prev_counter { return --$counter }
}
```

This technique creates the Perl equivalent of C's static variables. Actually, it's a little better. Rather than being limited to just one function, both functions share their private variable.

See Also

The sections on "Closures" and on "Package Constructors and Destructors: BEGIN and END" in Chapters 4 and 5 of *Programming Perl*, respectively; the section on "Private Variables via my()" in *perlsub*(1); the section on "Package Constructors and Destructors" in *perlmod*(1); Recipe 11.4

10.4. *Determining Current Function Name*

Problem

You want to determine the name of the currently running function. This is useful for creating error messages that don't need to be changed if you copy and paste the subroutine code.

Solution

Use the `caller` function:

```
$this_function = (caller(0))[3];
```

Discussion

Code can always find the current line number in the special symbol __LINE__, the current file in __FILE__, and the current package in __PACKAGE__. But there's no such symbol for the current subroutine name, let alone the name of the one that called this subroutine.

The built-in function `caller` handles all of these. In scalar context it returns the calling function's package name. But in list context, it returns a wealth of information. You can also pass it a number indicating how many frames (nested subroutine calls) back you'd like information about: 0 is your own function, 1 is your caller, and so on.

Here's the full syntax, where $i is how far back you're interested in:

```
($package, $filename, $line, $subr, $has_args, $wantarray )= caller($i);
#    0         1         2       3        4           5
```

Here's what each of those return values means:

$package
:   The package that the code was compiled in.

$filename
:   The name of the file the code was compiled in, reporting -e if launched from the command-line switch of the same name, or - if the script was read from STDIN.

$line
:   The line number that frame was called from.

$subr

> The name of that frame's function, including its package. Closures return names like `main::__ANON__`, which are not callable. In `eval` it returns `"(eval)"`.

$has_args

> Whether the function was called with arguments.

$wantarray

> The value the `wantarray` function would return for that stack frame; either true, false but defined, or else undefined (respectively). This tells you whether the function was called in list, scalar, or void context.

Rather than using `caller` directly as in the solution, you might want to write functions instead:

```
$me  = whoami();
$him = whowasi();

sub whoami  { (caller(1))[3] }
sub whowasi { (caller(2))[3] }
```

These use arguments 1 and 2 for parent and grandparent functions because the call to `whoami` or `whowasi` would be number 0.

See Also

The `wantarray` and `caller` functions in Chapter 3 of *Programming Perl* and in *perlfunc*(1); Recipe 10.6

10.5. Passing Arrays and Hashes by Reference

Problem

You want to pass a function more than one array or hash and have each remain distinct. For example, you want to put the "Find elements in one array but not in another" algorithm from Recipe 4.7 in a subroutine. This subroutine must then be called with two arrays that remain distinct.

Solution

Pass arrays and hashes by reference, using the backslash operator:

```
array_diff( \@array1, \@array2 );
```

Discussion

See Chapter 11, *References and Records*, for more about manipulation of references. Here's a subroutine that takes array references and a subroutine call that generates them:

```
@a = (1, 2);
@b = (5, 8);
@c = add_vecpair( \@a, \@b );
print "@c\n";
6 10

sub add_vecpair {        # assumes both vectors the same length
    my ($x, $y) = @_;    # copy in the array references
    my @result;

    for (my $i=0; $i < @$x; $i++) {
        $result[$i] = $x->[$i] + $y->[$i];
    }

    return @result;
}
```

A potential difficulty with this function is that it doesn't check to make sure it got exactly two arguments that were both array references. You could check explicitly this way:

```
unless (@_ == 2 && ref($x) eq 'ARRAY' && ref($y) eq 'ARRAY') {
    die "usage: add_vecpair ARRAYREF1 ARRAYREF2";
}
```

If all you plan to do is die on error (see Recipe 10.12), you can usually omit this check, since dereferencing the wrong kind of reference triggers an exception anyway.

See Also

The section on "Passing References" in Chapter 2 of *Programming Perl* and on "Pass by Reference" in *perlsub*(1); the section on "Prototypes" in Chapter 2 of *Programming Perl* or in *perlsub*(1); Recipe 10.11; Chapter 11; Chapter 4 of *Programming Perl*.

10.6. Detecting Return Context

Problem

You want to know whether your function was called in scalar context or list context. This lets you have one function that does different things, like most of Perl's built-in functions.

Solution

Use the `wantarray()` function, which has three possible return values depending on how the current function was called:

```
if (wantarray()) {
    # list context
}
elsif (defined wantarray()) {
    # scalar context
}
else {
    # void context
}
```

Discussion

Many built-in functions act differently when called in scalar context than in list context. A user-defined function can learn the context it was called in by examining the return value from the `wantarray` built-in. List context is indicated by a true return value. If it returns a value that is false but defined, then the function's return value will be used in scalar context. If it returns `undef`, it isn't being asked to provide a value at all.

```
if (wantarray()) {
    print "In list context\n";
    return @many_things;
} elsif (defined wantarray()) {
    print "In scalar context\n";
    return $one_thing;
} else {
    print "In void context\n";
    return;   # nothing
}

mysub();                    # void context

$a = mysub();              # scalar context
if (mysub()) {   }         # scalar context

@a = mysub();              # list context
print mysub();             # list context
```

See Also

The `return` and `wantarray` functions in Chapter 3 of *Programming Perl* and *perlfunc*(1)

10.7. Passing by Named Parameter

Problem

You want to make a function with many parameters easy to invoke so that programmers remember what the arguments do, rather than having to memorize their order.

Solution

Name each parameter in the call:

```
thefunc(INCREMENT => "20s", START => "+5m", FINISH => "+30m");
thefunc(START => "+5m", FINISH => "+30m");
thefunc(FINISH => "+30m");
thefunc(START => "+5m", INCREMENT => "15s");
```

Then in the subroutine, create a hash loaded up with default values plus the array of named pairs.

```
sub thefunc {
    my %args = (
        INCREMENT   => '10s',
        FINISH      => 0,
        START       => 0,
        @_,                # argument pair list goes here
    );
    if ($args{INCREMENT}  =~ /m$/ ) { ..... }
}
```

Discussion

Functions whose arguments require a particular order work well for short argument lists, but as the number of parameters increases, it's awkward to make some of them optional or have default values. You can only leave out trailing arguments, never initial ones.

Having the caller supply value pairs is a more flexible approach. The first element of the pair is the argument name, and the second is its value. This makes for self-documenting code, because you can see the parameters' intended meanings without having to read the full function definition. Even better, programmers using your function no longer have to remember the order of the arguments and can omit any arguments.

This works by having the function declare a private hash variable to hold the default parameter values. Put the current arguments, @_, after the default values, so the actual arguments will override the defaults because of the order of the values in the assignment.

See Also

Chapter 4, *Arrays*

10.8. *Skipping Selected Return Values*

Problem

You have a function that returns many values, but you only care about some of them. The stat function is a classic example: often you only want one value from its long return list (mode, for instance).

Solution

Either assign to a list with undef in some of the slots:

```
($a, undef, $c) = func();
```

or else take a slice of the return list, selecting only what you want:

```
($a, $c) = (func())[0,2];
```

Discussion

Using dummy temporary variables is wasteful:

```
($dev,$ino,$DUMMY,$DUMMY,$uid) = stat($filename);
```

Use undef instead of dummy variables to discard a value:

```
($dev,$ino,undef,undef,$uid)   = stat($filename);
```

Or take a slice, selecting just the values you care about:

```
($dev,$ino,$uid,$gid)   = (stat($filename))[0,1,4,5];
```

If you want to put an expression into list context and discard all its return values (calling it simply for side effects), as of version 5.004 you can assign to the empty list:

```
() = some_function();
```

See Also

The discussion on `slices` in Chapter 2 of *Programming Perl* and *perlsub*(1); Recipe 3.1

10.9. Returning More Than One Array or Hash

Problem

You want a function to return more than one array or hash, but the return list flattens into just one long list of scalars.

Solution

Return references to the hashes or arrays:

```
($array_ref, $hash_ref) = somefunc();

sub somefunc {
    my @array;
    my %hash;

    # ...

    return ( \@array, \%hash );
}
```

Discussion

Just as all arguments collapse into one flat list of scalars, return values do, too. Functions that want to return separate arrays of hashes need to return those by reference, and the caller must be prepared to receive references. If a function wants to return three separate hashes, for example, it should use one of the following:

```
sub fn {
    .....
    return (\%a, \%b, \%c); # or
    return \(%a,  %b,  %c); # same thing
}
```

The caller must expect a list of hash references returned out of the function. It cannot just assign to three hashes.

```
(%h0, %h1, %h2)   = fn();     # WRONG!
@array_of_hashes = fn();     # eg: $array_of_hashes[2]->{"keystring"}
($r0, $r1, $r2)   = fn();     # eg: $r2->{"keystring"}
```

See Also

The general discussions on references in Chapter 11, and in Chapter 4 of *Programming Perl*; Recipe 10.5

10.10. Returning Failure

Problem

You want to return a value indicating that your function failed.

Solution

Use a bare **return** statement without any argument, which returns **undef** in scalar context and the empty list **()** in list context.

```
return;
```

Discussion

A **return** without an argument means:

```
sub empty_retval {
    return ( wantarray ? () : undef );
}
```

You can't use just **return undef** because in list context you will get a list of one value: **undef**. If your caller says:

```
if (@a = yourfunc()) { ... }
```

Then the "error" condition will be perceived as true, because **@a** will be assigned (**undef**) and then evaluated in scalar context. This yields 1, the number of elements in **@a**, which is true. You could use the **wantarray** function to see what context you were called in, but a bare **return** is a clear and tidy solution that always works:

```
unless ($a = sfunc()) { die "sfunc failed" }
unless (@a = afunc()) { die "afunc failed" }
unless (%a = hfunc()) { die "hfunc failed" }
```

Some of Perl's built-in functions have a peculiar return value. Both **fcntl** and **ioctl** have the curious habit of returning the string **"0 but true"** in some circumstances. (This magic string is conveniently exempt from the -w flag's incessant numerical conversion warnings.) This has the advantage of letting you write code like this:

```
ioctl(....) or die "can't ioctl: $!";
```

That way, code doesn't have to check for a defined zero as distinct from the undefined value, as it would for the read or glob functions. "0 but true" is zero when used numerically. It's rare that this kind of return value is needed. A more common (and spectacular) way to indicate failure in a function is to raise an exception, as described in Recipe 10.12.

See Also

The undef, wantarray, and return functions in Chapter 3 of *Programming Perl* and *perlfunc*(1); Recipe 10.12

10.11. Prototyping Functions

Problem

You want to use function prototypes so the compiler can check your argument types.

Solution

Perl has something of a prototype facility, but it isn't what you're thinking. Perl's function prototypes are more like a context coercion used to write functions that behave like some of Perl's built-ins, such as push and pop.

Discussion

Manually checking the validity of a function's arguments can't happen until runtime. If you make sure the function is declared before it is used, you can tickle the compiler into using a very limited form of prototype checking to help you here. Don't confuse Perl's function prototypes with those found in any other language. Perl prototypes serve only to emulate the behavior of built-in functions.

A Perl function prototype is zero or more spaces, backslashes, or type characters enclosed in parentheses after the subroutine definition or name. A backslashed type symbol means that the argument is passed by reference, and the argument in that position must start with that type character.

A prototype forces context on the arguments to the prototyped function call. This is done when Perl compiles your program, and in most cases this does not necessarily mean that Perl checks the number or type of the arguments to your function. If Perl sees func(3, 5) for a function prototyped as sub func ($), it will stop with a compile-time error. But if it sees func(@array) with the same prototype, it will merely put **@array** into scalar context instead of saying "you can't pass an array—I'm expecting a scalar."

This is so important that it bears repeating: don't use Perl prototypes expecting the compiler to check type and number of arguments for you.

So what use are they? They have two main uses, although as you experiment with them you may find others. The first use is to tell Perl how many arguments your subroutine has, so you can leave off parentheses when you call the function. The second is to create a subroutine that has the same calling syntax as a built-in.

Omitting parentheses

Ordinarily your subroutines take a list of arguments, and you can omit parentheses on the function call if you like:

```
@results = myfunc 3, 5;
```

Without prototypes, this is the same as:

```
@results = myfunc(3, 5);
```

In the absence of parentheses, Perl will put the right hand side of the subroutine call into list context. You can use prototypes to change this behavior:

```
sub myfunc($);
@results = myfunc 3, 5;
```

Now this is the same as:

```
@results = ( myfunc(3), 5 );
```

You can also provide an empty prototype to indicate the function takes no arguments, like the built-in function **time**. This is how Fcntl provides the LOCK_SH, LOCK_EX, and LOCK_UN constants. They are exported functions defined to have an empty prototype:

```
sub LOCK_SH () { 1 }
sub LOCK_EX () { 2 }
sub LOCK_UN () { 4 }
```

Mimicking built-ins

The other common use of prototypes is to give the convenient pass-without-flattening behavior of built-in functions like **push** and **shift**. When you call **push** as **push(@array, 1, 2, 3)** the function gets a *reference* to **@array** instead of the actual array. This is accomplished by backslashing the @ character in the prototype:

```
sub mypush (\@@) {
  my $array_ref = shift;
  my @remainder = @_;

  # ...
}
```

The \@ in the prototype says "require the first argument to begin with an @ character, and pass it by reference." The second @ says "the rest of the arguments are a (possibly empty) list." A backslash in a prototype requires that the argument actually begin with the literal type character, which can sometimes be annoying. You can't even use the conditional ?: construct to pick which array to pass:

```
    mypush( $x > 10 ? @a : @b , 3, 5 );          # WRONG
```

Instead, you must play games with references:

```
    mypush( @{ $x > 10 ? \@a : \@b }, 3, 5 );     # RIGHT
```

Here's an **hpush** function that works like push, but on hashes. It appends a list of key/value pairs to an existing hash, overwriting previous contents for those keys.

```
sub hpush(\%@) {
    my $href = shift;
    while ( my ($k, $v) = splice(@_, 0, 2) ) {
        $href->{$k} = $v;
    }
}
hpush(%pieces, "queen" => 9, "rook" => 5);
```

See Also

The prototype function in *perlfunc*(1); the section on "Prototypes" in Chapter 2 of *Programming Perl* and in *perlsub*(1); Recipe 10.5

10.12. Handling Exceptions

Problem

How do you safely call a function that might raise an exception? How do you create a function that raises an exception?

Solution

Sometimes you encounter a problem so exceptional that merely returning an error isn't strong enough, because the caller could ignore the error. Use die STRING from your function to trigger an exception:

```
    die "some message";          # raise exception
```

The caller can wrap the function call in an eval to intercept that exception, and then consult the special variable $@ to see what happened:

```
eval { func() };
if ($@) {
    warn "func raised an exception: $@";
}
```

Discussion

Raising exceptions is not a facility to be used lightly. Most functions should return an error using a bare `return` statement. Wrapping every call in a trap is tedious and unsightly, removing the appeal of using exceptions in the first place.

But on rare occasion, failure in a function should cause the entire program to abort. Rather than calling the irrecoverable `exit` function, you should call `die` instead, which at least gives the programmer the chance to cope. If no exception handler has been installed via `eval`, then the program aborts at that point.

To detect such a failure program, wrap the call to the function with a block `eval`. The `$@` variable will be set to the offending exception if one occurred; otherwise, it will be false.

```
eval { $val = func() };
warn "func blew up: $@" if $@;
```

Any `eval` catches all exceptions, not just specific ones. Usually you should propagate unexpected exceptions to an enclosing handler. For example, suppose your function raised an exception containing the string `"Full moon!"`. You could safely trap that exception while letting the others through by inspecting the `$@` variable. Calling `die` without an argument uses the contents of `$@` and the current context to construct a new exception string.

```
eval { $val = func() };
if ($@ && $@ !~ /Full moon!/) {
    die;     # re-raise unknown errors
}
```

If the function is part of a module, consider using the Carp module and call `croak` or `confess` instead of `die`. The only difference between `die` and `croak` is that with `croak`, the error appears to be from the caller's perspective, not the module's. The `confess` function, on the other hand, creates a full stack backtrace of who called whom and with what arguments.

Another intriguing possibility is for the function to detect that its return value is being completely ignored; that is, it is being called in a void context. In that case, returning an error indication would be useless, so raise an exception instead.

Of course, just because it's not voided doesn't mean the return value is being dealt with appropriately. But if it is voided, it's certainly not being checked.

```
if (defined wantarray()) {
        return;
} else {
    die "pay attention to my error!";
}
```

See Also

The $@ variable in Chapter 2 of *Programming Perl* and *perlvar*(1); the `die` and `eval` functions in Chapter 3 of *Programming Perl* and *perlfunc*(1); Recipe 10.15; Recipe 12.2; Recipe 16.21

10.13. Saving Global Values

Problem

You need to temporarily save away the value of a global variable.

Solution

Use the `local` operator to save a previous global value, automatically restoring it when the current block exits:

```
$age = 18;          # global variable
if (CONDITION) {
    local $age = 23;
    func();         # sees temporary value of 23
} # restore old value at block exit
```

Discussion

Unfortunately, Perl's `local` operator does not create a local variable. That's what my does. Instead, `local` merely preserves an existing value for the duration of its enclosing block. Hindsight shows that if `local` had been called *save_value* instead, much confusion could have been avoided.

Still, there are three places where you *must* use `local` instead of my:

1. You need to give a global variable a temporary value, especially $_.

2. You need to create a local file or directory handle or a local function.

3. You want to temporarily change just one element of an array or hash.

Using local() for temporary values for globals

The first situation is more apt to happen with predefined, built-in variables than it is with user variables. These are often variables that Perl will use as hints for its high-level operations. In particular, any function that uses $_, implicitly or explicitly, should certainly have a local $_. This is annoyingly easy to forget to do. See Recipe 13.15 for one solution to this.

Here's an example of using a lot of global variables. The $/ variable is a global
that implicitly affects the behavior of the readline operator used in <FH> operations.

```
$para = get_paragraph(*FH);         # pass filehandle glob
$para = get_paragraph(\*FH);        # pass filehandle by glob reference
$para = get_paragraph(*IO{FH});     # pass filehandle by IO reference
sub get_paragraph {
    my $fh = shift;
    local $/ = '';
    my $paragraph = <$fh>;
    chomp($paragraph);
    return $paragraph;
}
```

Using local() for local handles

The second situation arises when you need a local filehandle or directory handle,
or, rarely, a local function. You can, in post 5.000 Perls, use one of the standard
Symbol, Filehandle, or IO::Handle modules, but this simple typeglob technique
still works. For example:

```
$contents = get_motd();
sub get_motd {
    local *MOTD;
    open(MOTD, "/etc/motd")          or die "can't open motd: $!";
    local $/ = undef;  # slurp full file;
    local $_ = <MOTD>;
    close (MOTD);
    return $_;
}
```

If you wanted to return the open filehandle, you'd use:

```
return *MOTD;
```

Using local() on parts of aggregates

The third situation almost never occurs. Because the local operator is really a "save
value" operator, you can use it to save off just one element of an array or hash,
even if that array or hash is itself a lexical!

```
my @nums = (0 .. 5);
sub first {
    local $nums[3] = 3.14159;
    second();
}
sub second {
    print "@nums\n";
}
second();
0 1 2 3 4 5
first();
0 1 2 3.14159 4 5
```

The only common use for this kind of thing is for temporary signal handlers.

```
sub first {
    local $SIG{INT} = 'IGNORE';
    second();
}
```

Now while `second()` is running, interrupt signals will be ignored. When `first()` returns, the previous value of `$SIG{INT}` will be automatically restored.

Although a lot of old code uses `local`, it's definitely something to steer clear of when it can be avoided. Because `local` still manipulates the values of global variables, not local variables, you'll run afoul of **use strict.**

The `local` operator produces *dynamic scoping* or *run-time scoping*. This is in contrast with the other kind of scoping Perl supports, which is much more intuitive. That's the kind of scoping that **my** provides, known as *lexical scoping*, or sometimes as *static* or *compile-time scoping*.

With dynamic scoping, a variable is accessible if it's in the current scope—or the scope of any frames (blocks) in its subroutine call stack, as determined at run time. Any functions called have full access to dynamic variables, because they're still globals, just ones with temporary values. Only lexical variables are safe from tampering. If that's not enough reason to change, you might be interested to know that lexicals are about 10 percent faster to access than dynamics.

Old code that says:

```
sub func {
    local($x, $y) = @_;
    #....
}
```

can almost always be replaced without ill effect by the following:

```
sub func {
    my($x, $y) = @_;
    #....
}
```

The only case where code can't be so upgraded is when it relies on dynamic scoping. That would happen if one function called another, and the latter relied upon access to the former's temporary versions of the global variables `$x` and `$y`. Code that handles global variables and expects strange action at a distance instead of using proper parameters is fragile at best. Good programmers avoid this kind of thing like the plague.

If you come across old code that uses:

```
&func(*Global_Array);
sub func {
```

```
        local(*aliased_array) = shift;
        for (@aliased_array) { .... }
    }
```

this should probably be changed into something like this:

```
    func(\@Global_Array);
    sub func {
        my $array_ref = shift;
        for (@$array_ref) { .... }
    }
```

They're using the old pass-the-typeglob strategy devised before Perl supported proper references. It's not a pretty thing.

See Also

The `local` and `my` functions in Chapter 3 of *Programming Perl* and *perlfunc*(1); the section on "Subroutines" in Chapter 2 of *Programming Perl*; the sections on "Private Variables via my()" "Temporary Values via local()" in *perlsub*(1); Recipe 10.2; Recipe 10.16

10.14. Redefining a Function

Problem

You want to temporarily or permanently redefine a function, but functions can't be assigned to.

Solution

To redefine a function, assign a new code reference to the typeglob of the name of the function. Use a `local` if you want it to be temporary.

```
    undef &grow;                    # silence -w complaints of redefinition
    *grow = \&expand;
    grow();                         # calls expand()

    {
        local *grow = \&shrink;     # only until this block exists
        grow();                     # calls shrink()
    }
```

Discussion

Unlike a variable but like a handle, a function cannot be directly assigned to. It's just a name. You can manipulate it almost as though it were a variable, because you can directly manipulate the run-time symbol table using typeglobs like `*foo` to produce interesting aliasing effects.

Assigning a reference to a typeglob changes what is accessed the next time a symbol of that type is needed. This is what the Exporter does when you import a function or variable from one package into another. Since this is direct manipulation of the package symbol table, it only works on package variables (globals), not lexicals.

```
*one::var = \%two::Table;    # make %one::var alias for %two::Table
*one::big = \&two::small;    # make &one::big alias for &two::small
```

A typeglob is something you can use `local` on, but not `my`. Because of the `local`, this aliasing effect is then limited to the duration of the current block.

```
local *fred = \&barney;     # temporarily alias &fred to &barney
```

If the value assigned to a typeglob is not a reference but itself another typeglob, then *all* types by that name are aliased. The types aliased in a full typeglob assignment are scalar, array, hash, function, filehandle, directory handle, and format. That means that assigning `*Top = *Bottom` would make the current package variable `$Top` an alias for `$Bottom`, `@Top` for `@Bottom`, `%Top` for `%Bottom`, and `&Top` for `&Bottom`. It would even alias the corresponding file and directory handles and formats! You probably don't want to do this.

Use assignments to typeglobs together with closures to clone a bunch of similar functions cheaply and easily. Imagine you wanted a function for HTML generation to help with colors. For example:

```
$string =  red("careful here");
print $string;
<FONT COLOR='red'>careful here</FONT>
```

You could write the `red` function this way:

```
sub red { "<FONT COLOR='red'>@_</FONT>" }
```

If you need more colors, you could do something like this:

```
sub color_font {
    my $color = shift;
    return "<FONT COLOR='$color'>@_</FONT>";
}
sub red    { color_font("red", @_)    }
sub green  { color_font("green", @_)  }
sub blue   { color_font("blue", @_)   }
sub purple { color_font("purple", @_) }
# etc
```

The similar nature of these functions suggests that there may be a way to factor out the common bit. To do this, use an assignment to an indirect typeglob. If you're running with the highly recommended use strict pragma, you must first disable strict 'refs' for that block.

```
@colors = qw(red blue green yellow orange purple violet);
for my $name (@colors) {
    no strict 'refs';
    *$name = sub { "<FONT COLOR='$name'>@_</FONT>" };
}
```

These functions all seem independent, but the real code was in fact only compiled once. This technique saves on both compile time and memory use. To create a proper closure, any variables in the anonymous subroutine *must* be lexicals. That's the reason for the my on the loop iteration variable.

This is one of the few places where giving a prototype to a closure is sensible. If you wanted to impose scalar context on the arguments of these functions (probably not a wise idea), you could have written it this way instead:

```
*$name = sub ($) { "<FONT COLOR='$name'>$_[0]</FONT>" };
```

However, since prototype checking happens at compile time, the preceding assignment happens too late to be useful. So, put the whole loop of assignments within a BEGIN block, forcing it to occur during compilation.

See Also

The sections on "Symbol Tables" in Chapter 5 of *Programming Perl* and in *perlmod*(1); the section on "Closures" in Chapter 4 of *Programming Perl* and the discussion of closures in *perlref*(1); Recipe 10.11; Recipe 11.4

10.15. Trapping Undefined Function Calls with AUTOLOAD

Problem

You want to intercept calls to undefined functions so you can handle them gracefully.

Solution

Declare a function called AUTOLOAD for the package whose undefined function calls you'd like to trap. While running, that package's $AUTOLOAD variable contains the name of the undefined function being called.

Discussion

Another strategy for creating similar functions is to use a proxy function. If you call an undefined function, instead of automatically raising an exception, you can trap the call. If the function's package has a function named AUTOLOAD, then this function is called in its place, with the special package global $AUTOLOAD set to the fully qualified function name. The AUTOLOAD subroutine can then do whatever that function would do.

```
sub AUTOLOAD {
    use vars qw($AUTOLOAD);
    my $color = $AUTOLOAD;
    $color =~ s/.*:://;
    return "<FONT COLOR='$color'>@_</FONT>";
}
#note: sub chartreuse isn't defined.
print chartreuse("stuff");
```

When the nonexistent `main::chartreuse` function is called, rather than raising an exception, `main::AUTOLOAD` is called with the same arguments as you passed `chartreuse`. The package variable $AUTOLOAD would contain the string `main::chartreuse` because that's the function it's proxying.

The technique using typeglob assignments shown in Recipe 10.14 is faster and more flexible than using AUTOLOAD. It's faster because you don't have to run the copy and substitute. It's more flexible because it lets you do this:

```
{
    local *yellow = \&violet;
    local (*red, *green) = (\&green, \&red);
    print_stuff();
}
```

While `print_stuff()` is running, or while in any functions it calls, anything printed in yellow will come out violet, and the red and green texts will exchange colors.

Aliasing subroutines like this won't handle calls to undefined subroutines. AUTO-LOAD does.

See Also

The section on "Autoloading" in Chapter 5 of *Programming Perl* and in *perlsub*(1); the documentation for the standard modules AutoLoader and AutoSplit, also in Chapter 7 of *Programming Perl*; Recipe 10.12; Recipe 12.10, Recipe 13.11

10.16. Nesting Subroutines

Problem

You want to have nested subroutines, such that one subroutine is only visible and callable from another. When you try the obvious approach of nesting sub FOO { sub BAR { } ... } Perl gives you warnings about variables that will not stay shared.

Solution

Instead of having the inner functions be normal subroutines, make them closures and temporarily assign them to the typeglob of the right name to create a localized function.

Discussion

If you use nested subroutines in other programming languages with their own private variables, you'll have to work at it a bit in Perl. The intuitive coding of this kind of thing gives the warning "will not stay shared". For example, this won't work:

```
sub outer {
    my $x = $_[0] + 35;
    sub inner { return $x * 19 }    # WRONG
    return $x + inner();
}
```

The following is a workaround:

```
sub outer {
    my $x = $_[0] + 35;
    local *inner = sub { return $x * 19 };
    return $x + inner();
}
```

Now inner() can only be called from within outer() because of the temporary assignments of the closure. But when it does, it has normal access to the lexical variable $x from the scope of outer().

This essentially creates a function local to another function, something not directly supported in Perl; however, the programming isn't always clear.

See Also

The sections on "Symbol Tables" in Chapter 5 of *Programming Perl* and in *perlmod*(1); the section on "Closures" in Chapter 4 of *Programming Perl* and the discussion of closures in *perlref*(1); Recipe 10.13; Recipe 11.4

10.17. Program: Sorting Your Mail

The program in Example 10-1 sorts a mailbox by subject by reading input a paragraph at a time, looking for one with a `"From"` at the start of a line. When it finds one, it searches for the subject, strips it of any `"Re: "` marks, and stores its lowercased version in the `@sub` array. Meanwhile, the messages themselves are stored in a corresponding `@msgs` array. The `$msgno` variable keeps track of the message number.

Example 10-1. bysub1

```perl
#!/usr/bin/perl
# bysub1 - simple sort by subject
my(@msgs, @sub);
my $msgno = -1;
$/ = '';                         # paragraph reads
while (<>) {
    if (/^From/m) {
        /^Subject:\s*(?:Re:\s*)*(.*)/mi;
        $sub[++$msgno] = lc($1) || '';
    }
    $msgs[$msgno] .= $_;
}
for my $i (sort { $sub[$a] cmp $sub[$b] || $a <=> $b } (0 .. $#msgs)) {
    print $msgs[$i];
}
```

That `sort` is only sorting array indices. If the subjects are the same, `cmp` returns 0, so the second part of the `||` is taken, which compares the message numbers in the order they originally appeared.

If `sort` were fed a list like `(0,1,2,3)`, that list would get sorted into a different permutation, perhaps `(2,1,3,0)`. We iterate across them with a `for` loop to print out each message.

Example 10-2 shows how an *awk* programmer might code this program, using the -00 switch to read paragraphs instead of lines.

Example 10-2. bysub2

```perl
#!/usr/bin/perl -n00
# bysub2 - awkish sort-by-subject
BEGIN { $msgno = -1 }
$sub[++$msgno] = (/^Subject:\s*(?:Re:\s*)*(.*)/mi)[0] if /^From/m;
```

Example 10-2. bysub2 (continued)

```
$msg[$msgno] .= $_;
END { print @msg[ sort { $sub[$a] cmp $sub[$b] || $a <=> $b } (0 .. $#msg) ] }
```

Perl has kept parallel arrays since its early days. Keeping each message in a hash is a more elegant solution. We'll sort on each field in the hash, by making an anonymous hash as described in Chapter 11.

Example 10-3 is a program similar in spirit to Example 10-1 and Example 10-2.

Example 10-3. bysub3

```
#!/usr/bin/perl -00
# bysub3 - sort by subject using hash records
use strict;
my @msgs = ();
while (<>) {
    push @msgs, {
        SUBJECT => /^Subject:\s*(?:Re:\s*)*(.*)/mi,
        NUMBER  => scalar @msgs,   # which msgno this is
        TEXT    => '',
    } if /^From/m;
    $msgs[-1]{TEXT} .= $_;
}

for my $msg (sort {
                      $a->{SUBJECT} cmp $b->{SUBJECT}
                                    ||
                      $a->{NUMBER}  <=> $b->{NUMBER}
                   } @msgs
            )
{
    print $msg->{TEXT};
}
```

Once we have real hashes, adding further sorting criteria is simple. A common way to sort a folder is subject major, date minor order. The hard part is figuring out how to parse and compare dates. Date::Manip does this, returning a string we can compare; however, the *datesort* program in Example 10-4, which uses Date::Manip, runs more than 10 times slower than the previous one. Parsing dates in unpredictable formats is extremely slow.

Example 10-4. datesort

```
#!/usr/bin/perl -00
# datesort - sort mbox by subject then date
use strict;
use Date::Manip;
my @msgs = ();
while (<>) {
    next unless /^From/m;
    my $date = '';
```

Example 10-4. datesort (continued)

```
    if (/^Date:\s*(.*)/m) {
        ($date = $1) =~ s/\s+\(.*//;   # library hates (MST)
        $date = ParseDate($date);
    }
    push @msgs, {
        SUBJECT => /^Subject:\s*(?:Re:\s*)*(.*)/mi,
        DATE    => $date,
        NUMBER  => scalar @msgs,
        TEXT    => '',
    };
} continue {
    $msgs[-1]{TEXT} .= $_;
}

for my $msg (sort {
                    $a->{SUBJECT} cmp $b->{SUBJECT}
                             ||
                    $a->{DATE}    cmp $b->{DATE}
                             ||
                    $a->{NUMBER}  <=> $b->{NUMBER}


                } @msgs
        )
{
    print $msg->{TEXT};
}
```

Example 10-4 is written to draw attention to the continue block. When a loop's end is reached, either because it fell through to that point or got there from a next, the whole continue block is executed. It corresponds to the third portion of a three-part for loop, except that the continue block isn't restricted to an expression. It's a full block, with separate statements.

See Also

The sort function in Chapter 3 of *Programming Perl* and in *perlfunc*(1); the discussion of the $/ variable in Chapter 2 of *Programming Perl*, *perlvar*(1), and the Introduction to Chapter 8, *File Contents*; Recipe 3.7; Recipe 4.15; Recipe 5.9; Recipe 11.9

11

References and Records

> *With as little a web as this will I*
> *ensnare as great a fly as Cassio.*
>
> —Shakespeare
> *Othello, Act II, scene i*

11.0. Introduction

Perl provides three fundamental data types: scalars, arrays, and hashes. It's certainly possible to write many programs without recourse to complex records, but most programs need something more complex than simple variables and lists.

Perl's three built-in types combine with references to produce arbitrarily complex and powerful data structures, the records that users of ancient versions of Perl desperately yearned for. Selecting the proper data structure and algorithm can make the difference between an elegant program that does its job quickly and an ungainly concoction that's glacially slow to execute and consumes system resources voraciously.

The first part of this chapter shows how to create and use plain references. The second part shows how to use references to create higher order data structures.

References

To grasp the concept of references, you must first understand how Perl stores values in variables. Each defined variable has a name and the address of a chunk of memory associated with it. This idea of storing addresses is fundamental to references because a reference is a value that holds the location of another value. The scalar value that contains the memory address is called a *reference*. Whatever value lives at that memory address is called a *referent.* (You may also call it a "thingie" if you prefer to live a whimsical existence.) See Figure 11-1.

The referent could be any of Perl's built-in types (scalar, array, hash, ref, code, or glob) or a user-defined type based on one of the built-in ones.

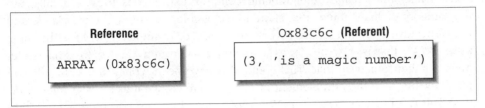

Reference	Ox83c6c **(Referent)**
ARRAY (0x83c6c)	(3, 'is a magic number')

Figure 11-1. Reference and referent

Referents in Perl are *typed.* This means you can't treat a reference to an array as though it were a reference to a hash, for example. Attempting to do so produces a runtime exception. No mechanism for type casting exists in Perl. This is considered a feature.

So far, it may look as though a reference were little more than a raw address with strong typing. But it's far more than that. Perl takes care of automatic memory allocation and deallocation (garbage collection) for references, just as it does for everything else. Every chunk of memory in Perl has a *reference count* associated with it, representing how many places know about that referent. The memory used by a referent is not returned to the process's free pool until its reference count reaches zero. This ensures that you never have a reference that isn't valid— no more core dumps and general protection faults from mismanaged pointers as in C.

Freed memory is returned to Perl for later use, but few operating systems reclaim it and decrease the process's memory footprint. This is because most memory allocators use a stack, and if you free up memory in the middle of the stack, the operating system can't take it back without moving the rest of the allocated memory around. That would destroy the integrity of your pointers and blow XS code out of the water.

To follow a reference to its referent, preface the reference with the appropriate type symbol for the data you're accessing. For instance, if $sref is a reference to a scalar, you can say:

```
print $$sref;     # prints the scalar value that the reference $sref refers to
$$sref = 3;       # assigns to $sref's referent
```

To access one element of an array or hash whose reference you have, use the infix pointer-arrow notation, as in $rv->[37] or $rv->{"wilma"}. Besides dereferencing array references and hash references, the arrow is also used to call an indirect function through its reference, as in `$code_ref->("arg1", "arg2")`; this is discussed Recipe 11.4. If you're using an object, use an arrow to call a method, `$object->methodname("arg1", "arg2")`, as shown in Chapter 13, *Classes, Objects, and Ties.*

Perl's syntax rules make dereferencing complex expressions tricky—it falls into the category of "hard things that should be possible." Mixing right associative and left associative operators doesn't work out well. For example, `$$x[4]` is the same as `$x->[4]`; that is, it treats `$x` as a reference to an array and then extracts element number four from that. This could also have been written `${$x}[4]`. If you really meant "take the fifth element of `@x` and dereference it as a scalar reference," then you need to use `${$x[4]}`. You should avoid putting two type signs (`$@%&`) side-by-side, unless it's simple and unambiguous like `%hash = %$hashref`.

In the simple cases using `$$sref` above, you could have written:

```
    print ${$sref};            # prints the scalar $sref refers to
    ${$sref} = 3;              # assigns to $sref's referent
```

For safety, some programmers use this notation exclusively.

When passed a reference, the **ref** function returns a string describing its referent. (It returns false if passed a non-reference.) This string is usually one of SCALAR, ARRAY, HASH, or CODE, although the other built-in types of GLOB, REF, IO, Regexp, and LVALUE also occasionally appear. If you call **ref** on a non-reference, it returns an empty string. If you call **ref** on an object (a reference whose referent has been blessed), it returns the class the object was blessed into: CGI, IO::Socket, or even ACME::Widget.

You can create references in Perl by taking references to things that are already there or by using the [ ], { }, and **sub** { } composers. The backslash operator is simple to use: put it before the thing you want a reference to. For instance, if you want a reference to the contents of `@array`, just say:

```
    $aref = \@array;
```

You can even create references to constant values; future attempts to change the value of the referent will cause a runtime error:

```
    $pi = \3.14159;
    $$pi = 4;                 # runtime error
```

Anonymous Data

Taking references to existing data is helpful when you're using pass-by-reference in a function call, but for dynamic programming, it becomes cumbersome. You need to be able to grow data structures at will, to allocate new arrays and hashes (or scalars or functions) on demand. You don't want to be bogged down with having to give them names each time.

Perl can explicitly create anonymous arrays and hashes, which allocate a new array or hash and return a reference to that memory:

```
$aref = [ 3, 4, 5 ];                              # new anonymous array
$href = { "How" => "Now", "Brown" => "Cow" };     # new anonymous hash
```

Perl can also create a reference implicitly by *autovivification*. This is what happens when you try to assign through undefined references and Perl automatically creates the reference you're trying to use.

```
undef $aref;
@$aref = (1, 2, 3);
print $aref;
ARRAY(0x80c04f0)
```

Notice how we went from an undefined variable to one with an array reference in it without actually assigning anything? Perl filled in the undefined reference for you. This is the property that permits something like this to work as the first statement in your program:

```
$a[4][23][53][21] = "fred";
print $a[4][23][53][21];
fred
print $a[4][23][53];
ARRAY(0x81e2494)
print $a[4][23];
ARRAY(0x81e0748)
print $a[4];
ARRAY(0x822cd40)
```

The following table shows mechanisms for producing references to both named and anonymous scalars, arrays, hashes, and functions. (Anonymous typeglobs are too scary to show—and virtually never used. It's best to use `Symbol::gensym()` or `IO::Handle->new()` for them.)

Reference to	Named	Anonymous
Scalar	`\$scalar`	`\do{my $anon}`
Array	`\@array`	`[ LIST ]`
Hash	`\%hash`	`{ LIST }`
Code	`\&function`	`sub { CODE }`

These diagrams illustrate the differences between named and anonymous values. Figure 11-2 shows named values.

In other words, saying $a = \$b makes $$a and $b the *same piece of memory*. If you say $$a = 3, then the value of $b is set to 3.

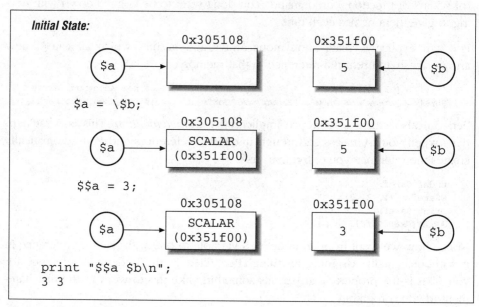

Figure 11-2. Named values

Figure 11-3 shows anonymous values.

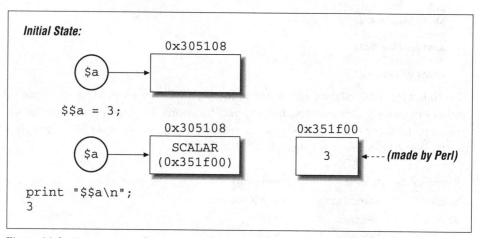

Figure 11-3. Anonymous values

Every reference evaluates as true, by definition, so if you write a subroutine that returns a reference, you can return `undef` on error and check for it with:

```
$op_cit = cite($ibid)          or die "couldn't make a reference";
```

The `undef` operator can be used on any variable or function in Perl to free its memory. This does not necessarily free memory, call object destructors, etc. It just decrements the reference count by one. Without an argument, undef produces an undefined value.

Records

The classic use of references in Perl is to circumvent the restriction that arrays and hashes may hold scalars only. References are scalars, so to make an array of arrays, make an array of array *references*. Similarly, hashes of hashes are implemented as hashes of hash references, arrays of hashes as arrays of hash references, hashes of arrays as hashes of array references, and so on.

Once you have these complex structures, you can use them to implement records. A record is a single logical unit composed of different attributes. For instance, a name, an address, and a birthday might comprise a record representing a person. C calls such things *structs*, and Pascal calls them *RECORDs*. Perl doesn't have a particular name for these because you can implement this notion in different ways.

The most common technique in Perl is to treat a hash as a record, where the keys of the hash are the record's field names and the values of the hash are those fields' values.

For instance, we might create a "person" record like this:

```
$Nat = { "Name"     => "Leonhard Euler",
         "Address"  => "1729 Ramanujan Lane\nMathworld, PI 31416",
         "Birthday" => 0x5bb5580,
       };
```

Because $Nat is a scalar, it can be stored in an array or hash element, thus creating groups of people. Now apply the array and hash techniques from Chapters 4 and 5 to sort the sets, merge hashes, pick a random record, and so on.

The attributes of a record, including the "person" record, are always scalars. You can certainly use numbers as readily as strings there, but that's no great trick. The real power play happens when you use even more references for values in the record. "Birthday", for instance, might be stored as an anonymous array with three elements: day, month, and year. You could then say $person-> {"Birthday"}->[0] to access just the day field. Or a date might be represented as a hash record, which would then lend itself to access such as $person-> {"Birthday"}->{"day"}. Adding references to your collection of skills makes possible many more complex and useful programming strategies.

At this point, we've conceptually moved beyond simple records. We're now creating elaborate data structures that represent complicated relationships between the data they hold. Although we *can* use these to implement traditional data structures like linked lists, the recipes in the second half of this chapter don't deal specifically with any particular structure. Instead, they give generic techniques for loading, printing, copying, and saving generic data structures. The final program example demonstrates how to manipulate binary trees.

See Also

Chapter 4 of *Programming Perl*; *perlref*(1), *perllol*(1), and *perldsc*(1)

11.1. *Taking References to Arrays*

Problem

You need to manipulate an array by reference.

Solution

To get a reference to an array:

```
$aref                = \@array;
$anon_array          = [1, 3, 5, 7, 9];
$anon_copy           = [ @array ];
@$implicit_creation  = (2, 4, 6, 8, 10);
```

To deference an array reference, precede it with an at sign (@):

```
push(@$anon_array, 11);
```

Or use a pointer arrow plus a bracketed subscript for a particular element:

```
$two = $implicit_creation->[0];
```

To get the last index number by reference, or the number of items in that referenced array:

```
$last_idx = $#$aref;
$num_items = @$aref;
```

Or defensively embracing and forcing context:

```
$last_idx = $#{ $aref };
$num_items = scalar @{ $aref };
```

Discussion

Here are array references in action:

```
# check whether $someref contains a simple array reference
if (ref($someref) ne 'ARRAY') {
    die "Expected an array reference, not $someref\n";
}

print "@{$array_ref}\n";              # print original data
```

```
@order = sort @{ $array_ref };   # sort it

push @{ $array_ref }, $item;     # append new element to orig array
```

If you can't decide whether to use a reference to a named array or to create a new one, here's a simplistic guideline that will prove right more often than not. Only take a reference to an existing array either to return the reference out of scope, thereby creating an anonymous array, or to pass the array by reference to a function. For virtually all other cases, use [@array] to create a new array reference with a copy of the old values.

Automatic reference counting and the backslash operator make a powerful combination:

```
sub array_ref {
    my @array;
    return \@array;
}


$aref1 = array_ref();
$aref2 = array_ref();
```

Each time **array_ref** is called, the function allocates a new piece of memory for **@array**. If we hadn't returned a reference to **@array**, its memory would have been freed when its block, the subroutine, ended. However, because a reference to **@array** is still accessible, Perl doesn't free that storage, and we end up with a reference to a piece of memory that can no longer be accessed through the symbol table. Such a piece of memory is called *anonymous* because no name is associated with it.

To access a particular element of the array referenced by $aref, you could write $$aref[4], but writing $aref->[4] is the same thing, and it is clearer.

```
print $array_ref->[$N];     # access item in position N (best)
print $$array_ref[$N];      # same, but confusing
print ${$array_ref}[$N];    # same, but still confusing, and ugly to boot
```

If you have an array reference, you can only access a slice of the referenced array in this way:

```
@$pie[3..5];         # array slice, but a little confusing to read
@{$pie}[3..5];       # array slice, easier (?) to read
```

Array slices, even when accessed through array references, are assignable. In the next line, the array dereference happens first, and then the slice:

```
@{$pie}[3..5] = ("blackberry", "blueberry", "pumpkin");
```

An array slice is exactly the same as a list of individual array elements. Because you can't take a reference to a list, you can't take a reference to an array slice:

```
$sliceref = \@{$pie}[3..5];    # WRONG!
```

To iterate through the entire array, use either a **foreach** loop or a **for** loop:

```
foreach $item ( @{$array_ref} ) {
    # $item has data
}

for ($idx = 0; $idx <= $#{ $array_ref }; $idx++) {
    # $array_ref->[$idx] has data
}
```

See Also

Chapter 4 of *Programming Perl*; *perlref*(1) and *perllol*(1); Recipe 2.14; Recipe 4.5

11.2. Making Hashes of Arrays

Problem

For each key in a hash, only one scalar value is allowed, but you'd like to use one key to store and retrieve multiple values. That is, you'd like the value to be a list.

Solution

Use references to arrays as the hash values. Use **push** to append:

```
push(@{ $hash{"KEYNAME"} }, "new value");
```

Then, dereference the value as an array reference when printing out the hash:

```
foreach $string (keys %hash) {
    print "$string: @{$hash{$string}}\n";
}
```

Discussion

You can only store scalar values in a hash. References, however, are scalars. This solves the problem of storing multiple values for one key by making $hash{$key} a reference to an array containing the values for $key. The normal hash operations (insertion, deletion, iteration, and testing for existence) can now be written in terms of array operations like push, splice, and foreach.

Here's how to give a key many values:

```
$hash{"a key"} = [ 3, 4, 5 ];        # anonymous array
```

Once you have a key with many values, here's how to use them:

```
@values = @{ $hash{"a key"} };
```

To append a new value to the array of values associated with a particular key, use push:

```
push @{ $hash{"a key"} }, $value;
```

The classic application of these data structures is inverting a hash that has many keys with the same associated value. When inverted, you end up with a hash that has many values for the same key. This is addressed in Recipe 5.8.

Be warned that this:

```
@residents = @{ $phone2name{$number} };
```

causes a runtime exception under use strict because you're dereferencing an undefined reference where autovivification won't occur. You must do this instead:

```
@residents = exists( $phone2name{$number} )
                ? @{ $phone2name{$number} }
                : ();
```

See Also

The section on "Hashs of Arrays" in Chapter 4 of *Programming Perl* and in *perldsc*(1); Recipe 5.8; the example "Tie Example: Make a Hash That Always Appends" in Recipe 13.15

11.3. Taking References to Hashes

Problem

You need to manipulate a hash by reference. This might be because it was passed into a function that way or because it's part of a larger data structure.

Solution

To get a hash reference:

```
$href = \%hash;
$anon_hash = { "key1" => "value1", "key2" => "value2", ... };
$anon_hash_copy = { %hash };
```

To dereference a hash reference:

```
%hash  = %$href;
$value = $href->{$key};
@slice = @$href{$key1, $key2, $key3};  # note: no arrow!
@keys  = keys %$href;
```

To check whether something is a hash reference:

```
if (ref($someref) ne 'HASH') {
    die "Expected a hash reference, not $someref\n";
}
```

Discussion

This example prints out all the keys and values in two predefined hashes:

```
foreach $href ( \%ENV, \%INC ) {          # OR: for $href ( \(%ENV,%INC) ) {
    foreach $key ( keys %$href ) {
        print "$key => $href->{$key}\n";
    }
}
```

Accessing slices of hashes by reference works just as it does with slices of arrays by reference. For example:

```
@values = @$hash_ref{"key1", "key2", "key3"};

for $val (@$hash_ref{"key1", "key2", "key3"}) {
    $val += 7;    # add 7 to each value in hash slice
}
```

See Also

Chapter 5, *Hashes*; Chapter 4 of *Programming Perl*; *perlref*(1); Recipe 11.9

11.4. Taking References to Functions

Problem

You need to manipulate a subroutine by reference. This might happen if you need to create a signal handler, a Tk callback, or a hash of function pointers.

Solution

To get a code reference:

```
$cref = \&func;
$cref = sub { ... };
```

To call a code reference:

```
@returned = $cref->(@arguments);
@returned = &$cref(@arguments);
```

Discussion

If the name of a function is `func`, you can produce a reference to this code by preceding that name with `\&`. You can also create anonymous functions using the `sub {}` notation. These code references can be stored just like any other reference.

Perl 5.004 introduced the postfix arrow notation for dereferencing a code reference. Prior to that, to call a subroutine by reference, you had to say `&$func-`

name(@ARGS), where $funcname contained the name of a function. Although it is
still possible to store the name of a function in a variable, such as:

```
$funcname = "thefunc";
&$funcname();
```

that's not a very good solution for several reasons. First, it uses symbolic references, not real (hard) references, so it is forbidden under the use strict 'refs'
pragma. Symbolic references to variables are usually a bad idea, since they can't
access lexical variables, only globals, and aren't reference counted.

Second, it doesn't include package information, so if executed in a different package, it would try to call the wrong function. Finally, in the odd case that the function were redefined at some point, the symbolic reference would get whatever the
current definition for the function was, whereas the hard reference would retain its
old definition.

Instead of placing the name of the function in the variable, use the backslash
operator to create a reference to the function. This is the normal way to store a
function in a variable or pass it to another function. You can mix and match references to named functions with references to unnamed ones:

```
my %commands = (
    "happy" => \&joy,
    "sad"   => \&sullen,
    "done"  => sub { die "See ya!" },
    "mad"   => \&angry,
);

print "How are you? ";
chomp($string = <STDIN>);
if ($commands{$string}) {
    $commands{$string}->();
} else {
    print "No such command: $string\n";
}
```

If you create an anonymous function that refers to a lexical (my) variable from an
enclosing scope, Perl's reference counting ensures that the lexical variable is never
deallocated so long as that function reference exists:

```
sub counter_maker {
    my $start = 0;
    return sub {                    # this is a closure
        return $start++;            # lexical from enclosing scope
    };
}

$counter = counter_maker();

for ($i = 0; $i < 5; $i ++) {
    print &$counter, "\n";
}
```

Even though `counter_maker` has ended and `$start` has gone out of scope, Perl doesn't free it because the anonymous subroutine referenced by `$counter` still has a reference to `$start`. If we call `counter_maker` again, it'll return another anonymous subroutine reference that uses a *different* `$start`:

```
$counter1 = counter_maker();
$counter2 = counter_maker();

for ($i = 0; $i < 5; $i ++) {
    print &$counter1, "\n";
}

print &$counter1, " ", &$counter2, "\n";
0
1
2
3
4
5 0
```

Closures are often used in callback routines. In graphical and other event-based programming, you associate code with a keypress, mouse click, window expose event, etc. The code will be called much later, probably from an entirely different scope. Variables mentioned in the closure must be available when it's finally called. To work properly, such variables must be lexicals, not globals.

Another use for closures is function generators, that is, functions that create and return brand new functions. `counter_maker` is a function generator. Here's another simple one:

```
sub timestamp {
    my $start_time = time();
    return sub { return time() - $start_time };
}
$early = timestamp();
sleep 20;
$later = timestamp();
sleep 10;
printf "It's been %d seconds since early.\n", $early->();
printf "It's been %d seconds since later.\n", $later->();
It's been 30 seconds since early.
It's been 10 seconds since later.
```

Each call to `timestamp` generates and returns a brand new function. The timestamp function creates a lexical called `$start_time` that contains the current clock time (in epoch seconds). Every time that closure is called, it returns how many seconds have passed since it was created by subtracting its starting time from the current time.

See Also

The section on "Closures" in Chapter 4 of *Programming Perl* and the discussion on closures in *perlref*(1); Recipe 10.11; Recipe 11.4

11.5. Taking References to Scalars

Problem

You want to create and manipulate a reference to a scalar value.

Solution

To create a reference to a scalar variable, use the backslash operator:

```
$scalar_ref = \$scalar;       # get reference to named scalar
```

To create a reference to an anonymous scalar value (a value that isn't in a variable), assign through a dereference of an undefined variable:

```
undef $anon_scalar_ref;
$$anon_scalar_ref = 15;
```

This creates a reference to a constant scalar:

```
$anon_scalar_ref = \15;
```

Use `${...}` to dereference:

```
print ${ $scalar_ref };       # dereference it
${ $scalar_ref } .= "string"; # alter referent's value
```

Discussion

If you want to create many new anonymous scalars, use a subroutine that returns a reference to a lexical variable out of scope, as explained in the Introduction:

```
sub new_anon_scalar {
    my $temp;
    return \$temp;
}
```

Perl almost never implicitly dereferences for you. Exceptions include references to filehandles, code references to `sort`, and the reference argument to `bless`. Because of this, you can only dereference a scalar reference by prefacing it with $ to get at its contents:

```
$sref = new_anon_scalar();
$$sref = 3;
print "Three = $$sref\n";
@array_of_srefs = ( new_anon_scalar(), new_anon_scalar() );
```

```
${ $array[0] } = 6.02e23;
${ $array[1] } = "avocado";
print "\@array contains: ", join(", ", map { $$_ } @array ), "\n";
```

Notice we have to put braces around $array[0] and $array[1]. If we tried to say $$array[0], the tight binding of dereferencing would turn it into $array->[0]. It would treat $array as an array reference and return the element at index zero.

Here are other examples where it is safe to omit the braces:

```
$var        = 'uptime';      # $var holds text
$vref       = \$var;         # $vref "points to" $var
if ($$vref =~ /load/) {}     # look at $var, indirectly
chomp $$vref;                # alter $var, indirectly
```

As mentioned in the introduction, you may use the **ref** built-in to inspect a reference for its referent's type. Calling **ref** on a scalar reference returns the string "SCALAR":

```
# check whether $someref contains a simple scalar reference
if (ref($someref) ne 'SCALAR') {
    die "Expected a scalar reference, not $someref\n";
}
```

See Also

Chapter 4 of *Programming Perl* and *perlref*(1)

11.6. Creating Arrays of Scalar References

Problem

You want to create and manipulate an array of references to scalars. This arises when you pass variables by reference to a function to let the function change their values.

Solution

To create an array, either backslash each scalar in the list to store in the array:

```
@array_of_scalar_refs = ( \$a, \$b );
```

or simply backslash the entire list, taking advantage of the backslash operator's distributive property:

```
@array_of_scalar_refs = \( $a, $b );
```

To get or set the value of an element of the list, use ${ ... }:

```
${ $array_of_scalar_refs[1] } = 12;        # $b = 12
```

Discussion

In the following examples, @array is a simple array containing references to sca-lars (an array of references is not a reference to an array). To access the original data indirectly, braces are critical.

```
($a, $b, $c, $d) = (1 .. 4);       # initialize
@array =   (\$a, \$b, \$c, \$d);   # refs to each scalar
@array = \( $a,  $b,  $c,  $d);    # same thing!
@array = map { \my $anon } 0 .. 3; # allocate 4 anon scalarresf

${ $array[2] } += 9;               # $c now 12

${ $array[ $#array ] } *= 5;       # $d now 20
${ $array[-1] }        *= 5;       # same; $d now 100

$tmp   = $array[-1];               # using temporary
$$tmp *= 5;                        # $d now 500
```

The two assignments to @array are equivalent—the backslash operator is distrib-utive across a list. So preceding a list (not an array) with a backslash is the same as applying a backslash to everything in that list. The ensuing code changes the val-ues of the variables whose references were stored in the array.

Here's how to deal with such an array without explicit indexing.

```
use Math::Trig qw(pi);             # load the constant pi
foreach $sref (@array) {           # prepare to change $a,$b,$c,$d
    ($$sref **= 3) *= (4/3 * pi);  # replace with spherical volumes
}
```

This code uses the formula for deriving the volume of a sphere:

$$Volume = \frac{4}{3}\pi r^3$$

The $sref loop index variable is each reference in @array, and $$sref is the number itself, that is, the original variables $a, $b, $c, and $d. Changing $$sref in the loop changes those variables as well. First we replace $$sref with its cube, then multiply the resulting value by ⁴⁄₃ π. This takes advantage of the fact that assignment in Perl returns an lvalue, letting you chain assignment operators together as we've done using the **= and *= assignment operators.

Actually, anonymous scalars are pretty useless, given that a scalar value fits in the same space as a scalar reference. That's why there's no explicit composer. Scalar references exist only to allow aliasing—which can be done in other ways.

See Also

The section on "Assignment Operators" in Chapter 2 of *Programming Perl* and in *perlop*(1)

11.7. Using Closures Instead of Objects

Problem

You want records with private state, behavior, and identity, but you don't want to learn object-oriented programming to accomplish this.

Solution

Write a function that returns (by reference) a hash of code references. These code references are all closures created in the same scope, so when they execute, they'll all share the same set of bindings to private variables.

Discussion

Because a closure is a binding of code and data, it can implement what might be thought of as an object.

Here's an example that creates and returns a hash of anonymous functions. mkcounter takes an argument of a seed counter and returns a hash reference that you can use to manipulate the counter indirectly.

```
$c1 = mkcounter(20);
$c2 = mkcounter(77);

printf "next c1: %d\n", $c1->{NEXT}->();   # 21
printf "next c2: %d\n", $c2->{NEXT}->();   # 78
printf "next c1: %d\n", $c1->{NEXT}->();   # 22
printf "last c1: %d\n", $c1->{PREV}->();   # 21
printf "old  c2: %d\n", $c2->{RESET}->();  # 77
```

The code values in the hash references in $c1 and $c2 maintain their own separate state. Here's how to set that up:

```
sub mkcounter {
    my $count  = shift;
    my $start  = $count;
    my $bundle = {
        "NEXT"   => sub { return ++$count  },
        "PREV"   => sub { return --$count  },
        "GET"    => sub { return $count    },
        "SET"    => sub { $count = shift    },
        "BUMP"   => sub { $count += shift   },
```

```
            "RESET"  => sub { $count = $start  },
        };
        $bundle->{"LAST"} = $bundle->{"PREV"};
        return $bundle;
    }
```

Because the lexical variables used by the closures in the `$bundle` hash reference are returned by the function, they are not deallocated. The next time `mkcounter` is called, the closures get a different set of variable bindings for the same code. Because no one outside of those closures can access these two variables, this assures you of true privacy.

The assignment right before the return makes both the `"PREV"` and `"LAST"` values point to the same closure. Depending on your object-oriented background, you might think of these as being two different messages, both implemented using the same method.

The bundle we return is not an object in that it has no obvious inheritance and polymorphism. (Yet.) But it certainly does have state, behavior, and identity, as well as encapsulation.

See Also

The section on "Closures" in Chapter 4 of *Programming Perl* and the discussion on closures in *perlref*(1); Recipe 11.4; Recipe 11.9; Chapter 13

11.8. Creating References to Methods

Problem

You want to store a reference to a method.

Solution

Create a closure that makes the proper method call on the appropriate object.

Discussion

When you ask for a reference to a method, you're asking for more than just a raw function pointer. You also need to record which object the method needs to be called upon as the object contains the data the method will work with. The best way to do this is using a closure. Assuming `$obj` is lexically scoped, you can say:

```
$mref = sub { $obj->meth(@_) };
# later...
$mref->("args", "go", "here");
```

Even when $obj goes out of scope, the closure stored in $mref has captured it. Later when it's called indirectly, the correct object is used for the method call.

Be aware that the notation:

```
$sref = \$obj->meth;
```

doesn't do what you probably expected. It first calls the method on that object and gives you either a reference to the return value or a reference to the last of the return values if the method returns a list.

The can method from the UNIVERSAL base class, while appealing, is also unlikely to produce what you want.

```
$cref = $obj->can("meth");
```

This produces a code ref to the appropriate method (should one be found), one that carries no object information. Think of it as a raw function pointer. The information about the object is lost. That's why you need a closure to capture both the object state as well as the method to call.

See Also

The discussion on methods in the Introduction to Chapter 13; Recipe 11.7; Recipe 13.7

11.9. Constructing Records

Problem

You want to create a record data type.

Solution

Use a reference to an anonymous hash.

Discussion

Suppose you wanted to create a data type that contained various data fields, akin to a C struct or a Pascal RECORD. The easiest way is to use an anonymous hash. For example, here's how to initialize and use that record:

```
$record = {
    NAME   => "Jason",
    EMPNO  => 132,
    TITLE  => "deputy peon",
    AGE    => 23,
    SALARY => 37_000,
```

```
    PALS   => [ "Norbert", "Rhys", "Phineas"],
};

printf "I am %s, and my pals are %s.\n",
    $record->{NAME},
    join(", ", @{$record->{PALS}});
```

Just having one of these records isn't much fun—you'd like to build larger structures. For example, you might want to create a %ByName hash that you could initialize and use this way:

```
# store record
$byname{ $record->{NAME} } = $record;

# later on, look up by name
if ($rp = $byname{"Aron"}) {          # false if missing
    printf "Aron is employee %d.\n", $rp->{EMPNO};
}

# give jason a new pal
push @{$byname{"Jason"}->{PALS}}, "Theodore";
printf "Jason now has %d pals\n", scalar @{$byname{"Jason"}->{PALS}};
```

That makes %byname a hash of hashes, because its values are hash references. Looking up employees by name would be easy using such a structure. If we find a value in the hash, we store a reference to the record in a temporary variable, $rp, which we then use to get any field we want.

We can use our existing hash tools to manipulate %byname. For instance, we could use the each iterator to loop through it in an arbitrary order:

```
# Go through all records
while (($name, $record) = each %byname) {
    printf "%s is employee number %d\n", $name, $record->{EMPNO};
}
```

What about looking employees up by employee number? Just build and use another data structure, an array of hashes called @employees. If your employee numbers aren't consecutive (for instance, they jump from 1 to 159997) an array would be a bad choice. Instead, you should use a hash mapping employee number to record. For consecutive employee numbers, use an array:

```
# store record
$employees[ $record->{EMPNO} ] = $record;

# lookup by id
if ($rp = $employee[132]) {
    printf "employee number 132 is %s\n", $rp->{NAME};
}
```

With a data structure like this, updating a record in one place effectively updates it everywhere. For example, this gives Jason a 3.5% raise:

```
$byname{"Jason"}->{SALARY} *= 1.035;
```

This change is reflected in all views of these records. Remember that both `$byname{"Jason"}` and `$employees[132]` refer to the same record because the references they contain refer to the same anonymous hash.

How would you select all records matching a particular criterion? This is what `grep` is for. Here's how to get everyone with "peon" in their titles or all the 27-year-olds:

```
@peons   = grep { $_->{TITLE} =~ /peon/i } @employees;
@tsevens = grep { $_->{AGE}   == 27 }      @employees;
```

Each element of `@peons` and `@tsevens` is itself a reference to a record, making them arrays of hashes, like `@employees`.

Here's how to print all records sorted in a particular order, say by age:

```
# Go through all records
foreach $rp (sort { $a->{AGE} <=> $b->{AGE} } values %byname) {
    printf "%s is age %d.\n", $rp->{NAME}, $rp->{AGE};
    # or with a hash slice on the reference
    printf "%s is employee number %d.\n", @$rp{'NAME','EMPNO'};
}
```

Rather than take time to sort them by age, you could just create another view of these records, `@byage`. Each element in this array, `$byage[27]` for instance, would be an array of all the records with that age. In effect, this is an array of arrays of hashes. You would build it this way:

```
# use @byage, an array of arrays of records
push @{ $byage[ $record->{AGE} ] }, $record;
```

Then you could find them all this way:

```
for ($age = 0; $age <= $#byage; $age++) {
    next unless $byage[$age];
    print "Age $age: ";
    foreach $rp (@{$byage[$age]}) {
        print $rp->{NAME}, " ";
    }
    print "\n";
}
```

A similar approach is to use `map` to avoid the `foreach` loop:

```
for ($age = 0; $age <= $#byage; $age++) {
    next unless $byage[$age];
    printf "Age %d: %s\n", $age,
        join(", ", map {$_->{NAME}} @{$byage[$age]});
}
```

See Also

Recipe 4.13; Recipe 11.3

11.10. *Reading and Writing Hash Records to Text Files*

Problem

You want to read or write hash records to text files.

Solution

Use a simple file format with one field per line:

```
FieldName: Value
```

and separate records with blank lines.

Discussion

If you have an array of records that you'd like to store and retrieve from a text file, you can use a simple format based on mail headers. The format's simplicity requires that the keys have neither colons nor newlines, and the values not have newlines.

This code writes them out:

```
foreach $record (@Array_of_Records) {
    for $key (sort keys %$record) {
        print "$key: $record->{$key}\n";
    }
    print "\n";
}
```

Reading them in is easy, too.

```
$/ = "";                    # paragraph read mode
while (<>) {
    my @fields = split /^([^:]+):\s*/m;
    shift @fields;          # for leading null field
    push(@Array_of_Records, { map /(.*)/, @fields });
}
```

The `split` acts upon `$_`, its default second argument, which contains a full paragraph. The pattern looks for start of line (not just start of record, thanks to the `/m`) followed by one or more non-colons, followed by a colon and optional white space. When `split`'s pattern contains parentheses, these are returned along with the values. The return values placed in `@fields` are in key-value order, with a leading null field we shift off. The braces in the call to **push** produces a reference to a new anonymous hash, which we copy `@fields` into. Since that array was stored in order of the needed key-value pairing, this makes for well-ordered hash contents.

All you're doing is reading and writing a plain text file, so you can use related recipes for additional components. You could use Recipe 7.11 to ensure that you have clean, concurrent access; Recipe 1.13 to store colons and newlines in keys and values; and Recipe 11.3 store more complex structures.

If you are willing to sacrifice the elegance of a plain textfile for a quick, random-access database of records, use a DBM file, as described in Recipe 11.14.

See Also

The `split` function in *perlfunc*(1) and Chapter 3 of *Programming Perl*; Recipe 11.9; Recipe 11.13; Recipe 11.14

11.11. Printing Data Structures

Problem

You want to print out a data structure.

Solution

If the output's legibility and layout are important, write your own custom printing routine.

If you are in the Perl debugger, use the **x** command:

```
DB<1> $reference = [ { "foo" => "bar" }, 3, sub { print "hello, world\n" } ];
DB<2> x $reference
  0  ARRAY(0x1d033c)
     0  HASH(0x7b390)
        'foo' = 'bar'>
     1  3
     2  CODE(0x21e3e4)
        - & in ???>
```

From within your own programs, use the **Dumper** function from the CPAN module Data::Dumper:

```
use Data::Dumper;
print Dumper($reference);
```

Discussion

Sometimes you'll want to make a dedicated function for your data structure that delivers a particular output format, but often this is overkill. If you're running under the Perl debugger, the **x** and **X** commands provide nice pretty-printing. The **x** command is more useful because it works on both global and lexical variables, whereas X only works on globals. Pass x a reference to the data structure you want to print.

```
D<1> x \@INC
   0  ARRAY(0x807d0a8)
      0  '/home/tchrist/perllib'
      1  '/usr/lib/perl5/i686-linux/5.00403'
      2  '/usr/lib/perl5'
      3  '/usr/lib/perl5/site_perl/i686-linux'
      4  '/usr/lib/perl5/site_perl'
      5  '.'
```

These commands use the *dumpvar.pl* library. Here's an example:

```
{ package main; require "dumpvar.pl" }
*dumpvar = \&main::dumpvar if __PACKAGE__ ne 'main';
dumpvar("main", "INC");          # show both @INC and %INC
```

The *dumpvar.pl* library isn't a module, but we wish it were—so we cajole it into exporting its dumpvar function anyway. The first two lines forcibly import the main::dumpvar function from package main into the current package, assuming it's different. Here's the output of that call:

```
@INC = (
   0  '/home/tchrist/perllib/i686-linux'
   1  '/home/tchrist/perllib'
   2  '/usr/lib/perl5/i686-linux/5.00404'
   3  '/usr/lib/perl5'
   4  '/usr/lib/perl5/site_perl/i686-linux'
   5  '/usr/lib/perl5/site_perl'
   6  '.'
)
%INC = (
   'dumpvar.pl' = '/usr/lib/perl5/i686-linux/5.00404/dumpvar.pl'
   'strict.pm' = '/usr/lib/perl5/i686-linux/5.00404/strict.pm'
)
```

The Data::Dumper module, located on CPAN, has a more flexible solution. It provides a Dumper function that takes a list of references and returns a string with a printable (and evalable) form of those references.

```
use Data::Dumper;
print Dumper(\@INC);
$VAR1 = [
        '/home/tchrist/perllib',
        '/usr/lib/perl5/i686-linux/5.00403',
        '/usr/lib/perl5',
        '/usr/lib/perl5/site_perl/i686-linux',
        '/usr/lib/perl5/site_perl',
        '.'
     ];
```

Data::Dumper supports a variety of output formats. Check its documentation for details.

See Also

The documentation for the CPAN module Data::Dumper; the section "The Perl Debugger" from Chapter 8 of *Programming Perl* or *perldebug*(1)

11.12. Copying Data Structures

Problem

You need to copy a complex data structure.

Solution

Use the `dclone` function from the Storable module from CPAN:

```
use Storable;

$r2 = dclone($r1);
```

Discussion

Two types of "copy" are sometimes confused. A *surface copy* (also known as *shallow copy*) simply copies references without creating copies of the data behind them:

```
@original = ( \@a, \@b, \@c );
@surface = @original;
```

A *deep copy* creates an entirely new structure with no overlapping references. This copies references to 1 layer deep:

```
@deep = map { [ @$_ ] } @original;
```

If `@a`, `@b`, and `@c` themselves contain references, the preceding `map` is no longer adequate. Writing your own code to deep-copy structures is laborious and rapidly becomes tiresome.

The Storable module, found on CPAN, provides a function called `dclone` that recursively copies its argument:

```
use Storable qw(dclone);
$r2 = dclone($r1);
```

This only works on references or blessed objects of type SCALAR, ARRAY, or HASH; references of type CODE, GLOB, and IO and more esoteric types are not supported. The `safeFreeze` function from the `FreezeThaw` module supports these when used in the same address space by using a reference cache that could interfere with garbage collection and object destructors under some circumstances.

Because `dclone` takes and returns references, you must add extra punctuation if you have a hash of arrays that you want to copy:

```
%newhash = %{ dclone(\%oldhash) };
```

See Also

The documentation for the CPAN modules Storable, Data::Dumper, and Freeze-Thaw

11.13. Storing Data Structures to Disk

Problem

You want to save your large, complex data structure to disk so you don't have to build it up each time your program runs.

Solution

Use the CPAN module Storable's `store` and `retrieve` functions:

```
use Storable;
store(\%hash, "filename");

# later on...
$href = retrieve("filename");           # by ref
%hash = %{ retrieve("filename") };    # direct to hash
```

Discussion

The Storable module uses C functions and a binary format to walk Perl's internal data structures and lay out its data. It's more efficient than a pure Perl and string-based approach, but it's also more fragile.

The `store` and `retrieve` functions expect binary data using the machine's own byte-ordering. This means files created with these functions cannot be shared across different architectures. `nstore` does the same job `store` does, but keeps data in canonical (network) byte order, at a slight speed cost:

```
use Storable qw(nstore);
nstore(\%hash, "filename");
# later ...
$href = retrieve("filename");
```

No matter whether `store` or `nstore` was used, you need to call the same `retrieve` routine to restore the objects in memory. The producer must commit to portability, but the consumer doesn't have to. Code needs only to be changed in one place when the producer changes their mind and the code thus offers a consistent interface on the consumer side, who does not need to know or care.

The `store` and `nstore` functions don't lock any of the files they work on. If you're worried about concurrent access, open the file yourself, lock it using Recipe 7.11, and then use `store_fd` or its slower but machine-independent version `nstore_fd`.

Here's code to save a hash to a file, with locking. We don't open with the O_TRUNC flag because we have to wait to get the lock before we can clobber the file.

```
use Storable qw(nstore_fd);
use Fcntl qw(:DEFAULT :flock);
sysopen(DF, "/tmp/datafile", O_RDWR|O_CREAT, 0666)
    or die "can't open /tmp/datafile: $!";
flock(DF, LOCK_EX)              or die "can't lock /tmp/datafile: $!";
nstore_fd(\%hash, *DF)
    or die "can't store hash\n";
truncate(DF, tell(DF));
close(DF);
```

Here's code to restore that hash from a file, with locking:

```
use Storable;
use Fcntl qw(:DEFAULT :flock);
open(DF, "< /tmp/datafile")     or die "can't open /tmp/datafile: $!";
flock(DF, LOCK_SH)              or die "can't lock /tmp/datafile: $!";
$href = retrieve(*DF);
close(DF);
```

With care, you can pass large data objects efficiently between processes with this strategy, since a filehandle connected to a pipe or socket is still a byte stream, just like a plain file.

Unlike the various DBM bindings, Storable does not restrict you to using only hashes (or arrays, with DB_File). Arbitrary data structures, including objects, can be stored to disk. The whole structure must be read in or written out in its entirety.

See Also

The section on "Remote Procedure Calls (RPC)" in Chapter 13 of *Advanced Perl Programming*; Recipe 11.14

11.14. *Transparently Persistent Data Structures*

Problem

You have a complex data structure that you want to persist outside your program.

Solution

Use MLDBM and either (preferably) DB_File, or else GDBM_File:

```
use MLDBM qw(DB_File);
use Fcntl;

tie(%hash, 'MLDBM', 'testfile.db', O_CREAT|O_RDWR, 0666)
    or die "can't open tie to testfile.db: $!";

# ... act on %hash

untie %hash;
```

Discussion

A hash with 100,000 items in it would undoubtably take considerable time to build. Storing this to disk, either slowly by hand or quickly with Storable, is still an expensive operation in memory and computation.

The DBM modules solve this by tying hashes to disk database files. Rather than reading the whole structure in at once, they only pull in what they need, when they need it. To the user, it looks like a hash that persists across program invocations.

Unfortunately, the values in this persistent hash must be plain strings. You cannot readily use a database file as a backing store for a hash of hashes, a hash of arrays, and so on, just for a hash of strings.

However, the MLDBM module from CPAN allows you to store references in a database. It uses Data::Dumper to stringify these references for external storage:

```
use MLDBM qw(DB_File);
use Fcntl;
tie(%hash, 'MLDBM', 'testfile.db', O_CREAT|O_RDWR, 0666)
    or die "can't open tie to testfile.db: $!";
```

Now you can use %hash to fetch or store complex records from disk. The only drawback is that you can't access the references piecemeal. You have to pull in the reference from the database, work with it, and then store it back.

```
# this doesn't work!
$hash{"some key"}[4] = "fred";

# RIGHT
$aref = $hash{"some key"};
$aref->[4] = "fred";
$hash{"some key"} = $aref;
```

See Also

The documentation for the CPAN module MLDBM; Recipe 14.1; Recipe 14.7; Recipe 14.11

11.15. Program: Binary Trees

Because Perl's built-in data types are already powerful, high-level, dynamic data types in their own right, most code can use what's already provided. If you just want quick lookups, you nearly always want to use a simple hash. As Larry has said, "The trick is to use Perl's strengths rather than its weaknesses."

However, hashes provide no inherent ordering. To traverse the hash in a particular order, you must first extract its keys and then sort them. If you find yourself doing so many times, performance will suffer, but probably not enough to justify the time required to craft a fancy algorithm.

A tree structure provides ordered traversals. How do you write a tree in Perl? First, you grab one of your favorite textbooks on data structures; the authors recommend Cormen et al., as mentioned in the "Other Books" section of the Preface. Using an anonymous hash to represent each node in the tree, translate the algorithms in the book into Perl. This is usually much more straightforward than you would imagine.

The program code in Example 11-1 demonstrates a simple binary tree implementation using anonymous hashes. Each node has three fields: a left child, a right child, and a value. The crucial property of an ordered binary tree is that all its left children have values less than the current node's value, and all right children have values greater than the current node's value.

The main program does three things. First, it creates a tree with 20 random nodes. Then it shows the in-order, pre-order, and post-order traversals of that tree. Finally, it allows the user to enter a key, and it reports whether that key is in the tree.

The **insert** function takes advantage of Perl's implicit pass-by-reference behavior on scalars to initialize an empty tree when asked to insert into an empty node. The assignment of the new node back to $_[0] alters the value in its caller.

Although this data structure takes much more memory than a simple hash and the lookups are slower, the ordered traversals themselves are faster.

If you want to learn more about binary trees, *Introduction to Algorithms* by Cormen, Leiserson, and Rivest and *Algorithms in C* by Robert Sedgewick both cover the material. A B-Tree is not a binary tree; it is a more flexible tree structure normally maintained on disk. DB_File has a BTREE interface (see *DB_File*(3)), and Mark-Jason Dominus has an excellent article on B-Trees in *The Perl Journal*, Volume 2, Issue 4, Winter 1997, pp. 35-42.

The program is shown in Example 11-1.

Example 11-1. bintree

```perl
#!/usr/bin/perl -w
# bintree - binary tree demo program
use strict;
my($root, $n);

# first generate 20 random inserts
while ($n++ < 20) { insert($root, int(rand(1000)))}

# now dump out the tree all three ways
print "Pre order:  ";  pre_order($root);  print "\n";
print "In order:   ";  in_order($root);   print "\n";
print "Post order: ";  post_order($root); print "\n";

# prompt until EOF
for (print "Search? "; <>; print "Search? ") {
    chomp;
    my $found = search($root, $_);
    if ($found) { print "Found $_ at $found, $found->{VALUE}\n" }
    else        { print "No $_ in tree\n" }
}

exit;

########################################

# insert given value into proper point of
# provided tree.  If no tree provided,
# use implicit pass by reference aspect of @_
# to fill one in for our caller.
sub insert {
    my($tree, $value) = @_;
    unless ($tree) {
        $tree = {};                         # allocate new node
        $tree->{VALUE} = $value;
        $tree->{LEFT}  = undef;
        $tree->{RIGHT} = undef;
        $_[0] = $tree;                  # $_[0] is reference param!
        return;
    }
```

Example 11-1. bintree (continued)

```
    if    ($tree->{VALUE} > $value) { insert($tree->{LEFT},  $value) }
    elsif ($tree->{VALUE} < $value) { insert($tree->{RIGHT}, $value) }
    else                            { warn "dup insert of $value\n"  }
                                    # XXX: no dups
}


# recurse on left child,
# then show current value,
# then recurse on right child.
sub in_order {
    my($tree) = @_;
    return unless $tree;
    in_order($tree->{LEFT});
    print $tree->{VALUE}, " ";
    in_order($tree->{RIGHT});
}


# show current value,
# then recurse on left child,
# then recurse on right child.
sub pre_order {
    my($tree) = @_;
    return unless $tree;
    print $tree->{VALUE}, " ";
    pre_order($tree->{LEFT});
    pre_order($tree->{RIGHT});
}


# recurse on left child,
# then recurse on right child,
# then show current value.
sub post_order {
    my($tree) = @_;
    return unless $tree;
    post_order($tree->{LEFT});
    post_order($tree->{RIGHT});
    print $tree->{VALUE}, " ";
}


# find out whether provided value is in the tree.
# if so, return the node at which the value was found.
# cut down search time by only looking in the correct
# branch, based on current value.
sub search {
    my($tree, $value) = @_;
    return unless $tree;
    if ($tree->{VALUE} == $value) {
        return $tree;
    }
    search($tree->{ ($value < $tree->{VALUE}) ? "LEFT" : "RIGHT"}, $value)
}
```

12

Packages, Libraries, and Modules

12.0. Introduction

Imagine that you have two separate programs, both of which work fine by themselves, and you decide to make a third program that combines the best features from the first two. You copy both programs into a new file or cut and paste selected pieces. You find that the two programs had variables and functions with the same names that should remain separate. For example, both might have an init function or a global $count variable. When merged into one program, these separate parts would interfere with each other.

The solution to this problem is *packages*. Perl uses packages to partition the global namespace. The package is the basis for both traditional modules and object-oriented classes. Just as directories contain files, packages contain identifiers. Every global identifier (variables, functions, file and directory handles, and formats) has two parts: its package name and the identifier proper. These two pieces are separated from one another with a double colon. For example, the variable $CGI::needs_binmode is a global variable named $needs_binmode, which resides in package CGI.

Where the filesystem uses slashes to separate the directory from the filename, Perl uses a double colon (prior to release 5.000, you could only use a single quote mark, as in $CGI'needs_bin_mode). $Names::startup is the variable named $startup in the package Names, whereas $Dates::startup is the $startup variable in package Dates. Saying $startup by itself without a package name means the global variable $startup in the current package. (This assumes that no lexical $startup variable is currently visible. Lexical variables are explained in Chapter 10, *Subroutines*.) When looking at an unqualified variable name, a lexical takes precedence over a global. Lexicals live in scopes; globals live in packages. If you really want the global instead, you need to fully qualify it.

package is a compile-time declaration that sets the default package prefix for unqualified global identifiers, just as chdir sets the default directory prefix for relative pathnames. This effect lasts until the end of the current scope (a brace-enclosed block, file, or eval). The effect is also terminated by any subsequent package statement in the same scope. (See the following code.) All programs are in package main until they use a package statement to change this.

```
package Alpha;
$name = "first";

package Omega;
$name = "last";

package main;
print "Alpha is $Alpha::name, Omega is $Omega::name.\n";
Alpha is first, Omega is last.
```

Unlike user-defined identifiers, built-in variables with punctuation names (like $_ and $.) and the identifiers STDIN, STDOUT, STDERR, ARGV, ARGVOUT, ENV, INC, and SIG are all forced to be in package main when unqualified. That way things like STDIN, @ARGV, %ENV, and $_ are always the same no matter what package you're in; for example, @ARGV always means @main::ARGV, even if you've used package to change the default package. A fully qualified @ElseWhere::ARGV would not (and carries no special built-in meaning). Make sure to localize $_ if you use it in your module.

Modules

The unit of software reuse in Perl is the *module*, a file that has a collection of related functions designed to be used by other programs and library modules. Every module has a public interface, a set of variables and functions that outsiders are encouraged to use. From inside the module, the interface is defined by initializing certain package variables that the standard Exporter module looks at. From outside the module, the interface is accessed by importing symbols as a side effect of the use statement. The public interface of a Perl module is whatever is documented to be public. In the case of undocumented interfaces, it's whatever is vaguely intended to be public. When we talk about modules in this chapter, and traditional modules in general, we mean those that use the Exporter.

The **require** or **use** statements both pull a module into your program, although their semantics are slightly different. **require** loads modules at runtime, with a check to avoid the redundant loading of a given module. **use** is like **require**, with two added properties: compile-time loading and automatic importing.

Modules included with **use** are processed at compile time, but **require** processing happens at run time. This is important because if a module that a program needs is missing, the program won't even start because the **use** fails during compilation of your script. Another advantage of compile-time **use** over run-time **require** is that function prototypes in the module's subroutines become visible to the compiler. This matters because only the compiler cares about prototypes, not the interpreter. (Then again, we don't usually recommend prototypes except for replacing built-in commands, which do have them.)

use is suitable for giving hints to the compiler because of its compile-time behavior. A *pragma* is a special module that acts as directive to the compiler to alter how Perl compiles your code. A pragma's name is always all lowercase, so when writing a regular module instead of a pragma, choose a name that starts with a capital letter. Pragmas supported by Perl 5.004 include autouse, constant, diagnostics, integer, lib, locale, overload, sigtrap, strict, subs, and vars. Each has its own manpage.

The other difference between **require** and **use** is that **use** performs an implicit *import* on the included module's package. Importing a function or variable from one package to another is a form of aliasing; that is, it makes two different names for the same underlying thing. It's like linking in files from another directory to your current one by the command *ln /somedir/somefile*. Once it's linked in, you no longer have to use the full pathname to access the file. Likewise, an imported symbol no longer needs to be fully qualified by package name (or predeclared with **use vars** or **use subs**). You can use imported variables as though they were part of your package. If you imported $English::OUTPUT_AUTOFLUSH in the current package, you could refer to it as $OUTPUT_AUTOFLUSH.

The required file extension for a Perl module is ".pm". The module named FileHandle would be stored in the file *FileHandle.pm*. The full path to the file depends on your include path, which is stored in the global @INC variable. Recipe 12.7 shows how to manipulate this array to your own purposes.

If the module name itself contains one or more double colons, these are translated into your system's directory separator. That means that the File::Find module resides in the file *File/Find.pm* under most filesystems. For example:

```
require "FileHandle.pm";        # run-time load
require FileHandle;             # ".pm" assumed; same as previous
use FileHandle;                 # compile-time load
```

```
require "Cards/Poker.pm";        # run-time load
require Cards::Poker;            # ".pm" assumed; same as previous
use Cards::Poker;               # compile-time load
```

Import/Export Regulations

The following is a typical setup for a hypothetical module named Cards::Poker that demonstrates how to manage its exports. The code goes in the file named *Poker.pm* within the directory *Cards*: that is, *Cards/Poker.pm*. (See Recipe 12.7 for where the *Cards* directory should reside.) Here's that file, with line numbers included for reference:

```
1    package Cards::Poker;
2    use Exporter;
3    @ISA = ('Exporter');
4    @EXPORT = qw(&shuffle @card_deck);
5    @card_deck = ();                    # initialize package global
6    sub shuffle { }                     # fill-in definition later
7    1;                                  # don't forget this
```

Line 1 declares the package that the module will put its global variables and functions in. Typically, a module first switches to a particular package so that it has its own place for global variables and functions, one that won't conflict with that of another program. This *must* be written exactly as the corresponding use statement will be written when the module is loaded.

Don't say **package Poker** just because the basename of your file is *Poker.pm*. Rather, say **package Cards::Poker** because your users will say use Cards::Poker. This common problem is hard to debug. If you don't make the package and use statements exactly the same, you won't see a problem until you try to call imported functions or access imported variables, which will be mysteriously missing.

Line 2 loads in the Exporter module, which manages your module's public interface as described below. Line 3 initializes the special, per-package array @ISA to contain the word "Exporter". When a user says use Cards::Poker, Perl implicitly calls a special method, Cards::Poker->import(). You don't have an import method in your package, but that's OK, because the Exporter package does, and you're *inheriting* from it because of the assignment to @ISA (*is a*). Perl looks at the package's @ISA for resolution of undefined methods. Inheritance is a topic of Chapter 13, *Classes, Objects, and Ties*. You may ignore it for now—so long as you put code as shown in lines 2 and 3 into each module you write.

Line 4 assigns the list ('&shuffle', '@card_deck') to the special, per-package array @EXPORT. When someone imports this module, variables and functions listed in that array are aliased into the caller's own package. That way they don't have to call the function Cards::Poke::shuffle(23) after the import. They can just write `shuffle(23)` instead. This won't happen if they load Cards::Poker with `require Cards::Poker`; only a `use` imports.

Lines 5 and 6 set up the package global variables and functions to be exported. (We presume you'll actually flesh out their initializations and definitions more than in these examples.) You're free to add other variables and functions to your module as well, including ones you don't put in the public interface via `@EXPORT`. See Recipe 12.1 for more about using the Exporter.

Finally, line 7 is a simple 1, indicating the overall return value of the module. If the last evaluated expression in the module doesn't produce a true value, an exception will be raised. Trapping this is the topic of Recipe 12.2. Any old true value will do, like 6.02e23 or `"Because tchrist and gnat told us to put this here"`; however, 1 is the canonical true value used by almost every module.

Packages group and organize global identifiers. They have nothing to do with privacy. Code compiled in package `Church` can freely examine and alter variables in package `State`. Package variables are always global and are used for sharing. But that's okay, because a module is more than just a package; it's also a file, and files count as their own scope. So if you want privacy, use lexical variables instead of globals. This is the topic of Recipe 12.4.

Other Kinds of Library Files

A library is a collection of loosely related functions designed to be used by other programs. It lacks the rigorous semantics of a Perl module. The file extension `.pl` indicates that it's a Perl library file. Examples include *syslog.pl* and *chat2.pl*.

Perl libraries—or in fact, any arbitrary file with Perl code in it—can be loaded in using `do 'file.pl'` or with `require 'file.pl'`. The latter is preferred in most situations, because unlike `do`, `require` does implicit error checking. It raises an exception if the file can't be found in your `@INC` path, doesn't compile, or if it doesn't return a true value when any initialization code is run. (The last part is what the `1;` was for earlier.) Another advantage of `require` is that it keeps track of which files have already been loaded in the global hash `%INC`. It doesn't reload the file if `%INC` indicates that the file has already been read in.

Libraries work well when used by a program, but problems can arise when libraries use one another. Consequently, simple Perl libraries have been rendered mostly obsolete, replaced by the more modern modules. But some programs still use libraries, usually loading them in with `require` instead of `do`.

Other file extensions are occasionally seen in Perl. A `".ph"` is used for C header files that have been translated into Perl libraries using the *h2ph* tool, as discussed in Recipe 12.14. A `".xs"` indicates an augmented C source file, possibly created by the *h2xs* tool, which will be compiled by the *xsubpp* tool and your C compiler into native machine code. This process of creating mixed-language modules is discussed in Recipe 12.15.

So far we've only talked about traditional modules, which export their interface by allowing the caller direct access to particular subroutines and variables. Most modules fall into this category. But some problems—and some programmers—lend themselves to more intricately designed modules, those involving objects. An object-oriented module seldom uses the import-export mechanism at all. Instead, it provides an object-oriented interface full of constructors, destructors, methods, inheritance, and operator overloading. This is the subject of Chapter 13.

Not Reinventing the Wheel

CPAN, the Comprehensive Perl Archive Network, is a gigantic repository of nearly everything about Perl you could imagine, including source, documentation, alternate ports, and above all, modules. Before you write a new module, check with CPAN to see whether one already exists that does what you need. Even if one doesn't, something close enough might give you ideas.

You can access CPAN at *http://www.perl.com/CPAN/CPAN.html* (or *ftp://www.perl.com/pub/perl/CPAN/CPAN.html*). This file briefly describes each of CPAN's modules, but because it's manually edited, it may not always have the very latest modules' descriptions. You can find out about those in the *CPAN/RECENT* or *CPAN/RECENT.html* file.

The module directory itself is in *CPAN/modules*. It contains indices of all registered modules plus three convenient subdirectories: *by-module, by-author,* and *by-category*. All modules are available through each of these, but the *by-category* directory is probably the most useful. There you will find directories covering specific applications areas including operating system interfaces; networking, modems, and interprocess communication; database interfaces; user interfaces; interfaces to other programming languages; authentication, security, and encryption; World Wide Web, HTML, HTTP, CGI, and MIME; images, pixmap and bitmap manipulation, drawing, and graphing—just to name a few.

See Also

The sections on "Packages" and on "Modules" in Chapter 5 of *Programming Perl* and in *perlmod*(1)

12.1. Defining a Module's Interface

Problem

You want the standard Exporter module to define the external interface to your module.

Solution

In module file *YourModule.pm*, place the following code. Fill in the ellipses as explained in the Discussion section.

```
package YourModule;
use strict;
use vars qw(@ISA @EXPORT @EXPORT_OK %EXPORT_TAGS $VERSION);

use Exporter;
$VERSION = 1.00;            # Or higher
@ISA = qw(Exporter);

@EXPORT     = qw(...);      # Symbols to autoexport (:DEFAULT tag)
@EXPORT_OK  = qw(...);      # Symbols to export on request
%EXPORT_TAGS = (            # Define names for sets of symbols
    TAG1 => [...],
    TAG2 => [...],
    ...
);

#######################
# your code goes here
#######################

1;                         # this should be your last line
```

In other files where you want to use YourModule, choose one of these lines:

```
use YourModule;            # Import default symbols into my package.
use YourModule qw(...);    # Import listed symbols into my package.
use YourModule ();         # Do not import any symbols
use YourModule qw(:TAG1);  # Import whole tag set
```

Discussion

The standard Exporter module handles the module's external interface. Although you could define your own `import` method for your package, almost no one does this.

When someone says `use YourModule`, this does a `require "YourModule.pm"` statement followed a `YourModule->import()` method call, both during compile time. The `import` method inherited from the Exporter package looks for global variables in your package to govern its behavior. Because they must be package globals, we've declared them with the use vars pragma to satisfy use strict. These variables are:

$VERSION

When a module is loaded, a minimal required version number can be supplied. If the version isn't at least this high, the use will raise an exception.

```
use YourModule 1.86;        # If $VERSION < 1.86, fail
```

@EXPORT

This array contains a list of functions and variables that will be exported into the caller's own namespace so they can be accessed without being fully qualified. Typically, a qw() list is used.

```
@EXPORT = qw(&F1 &F2 @List);
@EXPORT = qw( F1  F2 @List);        # same thing
```

When a simple use YourModule call is made, the function &F1 can be called as F1() rather than YourModule::F1() and the array can be accessed as @List instead of @YourModule::List. The ampersand is optional in front of an exported function specification.

To load the module at compile time but request that no symbols be exported, use the special form use Exporter (), with empty parentheses.

@EXPORT_OK

This array contains symbols that can be imported if they're specifically asked for. If the array were loaded this way:

```
@EXPORT_OK = qw(Op_Func %Table);
```

Then the user could load the module like so:

```
use YourModule qw(Op_Func %Table F1);
```

and import only the Op_Func function, the %Table hash, and the F1 function. The F1 function was listed in the @EXPORT array. Notice that this does not automatically import F2 or @List, even though they're in @EXPORT. To get everything in @EXPORT plus extras from @EXPORT_OK, use the special :DEFAULT tag, such as:

```
use YourModule qw(:DEFAULT %Table);
```

%EXPORT_TAGS

This hash is used by large modules like CGI or POSIX to create higher-level groupings of related import symbols. Its values are references to arrays of symbol names, all of which must be in either @EXPORT or @EXPORT_OK. Here's a sample initialization:

```
%EXPORT_TAGS = (
    Functions => [ qw(F1 F2 Op_Func) ],
    Variables => [ qw(@List %Table)  ],
);
```

An import symbol with a leading colon means to import a whole group of symbols. Here's an example:

```
use YourModule qw(:Functions %Table);
```

That pulls in all the symbols from

```
@{ $YourModule::EXPORT_TAGS{Functions} },
```

that is, it pulls in the F1, F2, and Op_Func functions and then the %Table hash.

Although you don't list it in %EXPORT_TAGS, the implicit tag :DEFAULT automatically means everything in @EXPORT.

You don't have to have all those variables defined in your module. You just need the ones that you expect people to be able to use.

See Also

The documentation for the standard Exporter module, also found in Chapter 7 of *Programming Perl*; Recipe 12.7; Recipe 12.18

12.2. Trapping Errors in require or use

Problem

You need to load in a module that might not be present on your system. This normally results in a fatal exception. You want to detect and trap these failures.

Solution

Wrap the require or use in an eval, and wrap the eval in a BEGIN block:

```
# no import
BEGIN {
    unless (eval "require $mod") {
        warn "couldn't load $mod: $@";
    }
}

# imports into current package
BEGIN {
eval "use $mod;
if ($@) { warn "$@"}
}
```

Discussion

You usually want a program to fail if it tries to load a module that is missing or doesn't compile. Sometimes, though, you'd like to recover from that error, perhaps trying an alternative module instead. As with any other exception, you insulate yourself from compilation errors with an eval.

You don't want to use eval { BLOCK }, because this only traps run-time exceptions and use is a compile-time event. Instead, you must use eval "string", to catch compile-time problems as well. Remember, require on a bareword has a slightly different meaning than require on a variable. It adds a ".pm" and translates double-colons into your operating system's path separators, canonically / (as in URLs), but sometimes \, :, or even . on some systems.

If you need to try several modules in succession, stopping at the first one that works, you could do something like this:

```
BEGIN {
    my($found, @DBs, $mod);
    $found = 0;
    @DBs = qw(Giant::Eenie Giant::Meanie Mouse::Mynie Moe);
    for $mod (@DBs) {
        if (eval "require $mod") {
            $mod->import();              # if needed
            $found = 1;
            last;
        }
    }
    die "None of @DBs loaded" unless $found;
}
```

We wrap the eval in a BEGIN block to ensure the module-loading happens at compile time instead of run time.

See Also

The eval, die, use, and require functions in Chapter 3 of *Programming Perl* and in *perlfunc*(1); Recipe 10.12; Recipe 12.3

12.3. Delaying use Until Run Time

Problem

You have a module that you don't need to load each time the program runs, or whose inclusion you wish to delay until after the program starts up.

Solution

Either break up the use into its separate **require** and **import** components, or else employ the use autouse pragma.

Discussion

Programs that check their arguments and abort with a usage message on error have no reason to load modules they'll never use. This delays the inevitable and annoys users. But those use statements happen during compilation, not execution, as explained in the Introduction.

Here, an effective strategy is to place argument checking in a **BEGIN** block before loading the modules. The following is the start of a program that checks to make sure it was called with exactly two arguments, which must be whole numbers, before going on to load the modules it will need:

```
BEGIN {
    unless (@ARGV == 2 && (2 == grep {/^\d+$/} @ARGV)) {
        die "usage: $0 num1 num2\n";
    }
}
use Some::Module;
use More::Modules;
```

A related situation arises in programs that don't always use the same set of modules every time they're run. For example, the *factors* program from Chapter 2, *Numbers*, needs the infinite precision arithmetic library only when the -b command-line flag is supplied. A use statement would be pointless within a conditional because it's evaluated at compile time, long before the if can be checked. So we'll use a **require** instead:

```
if ($opt_b) {
    require Math::BigInt;
}
```

Because Math::BigInt is an object-oriented module instead of a traditional one, no import was needed. If you have an import list, specify it with a qw() construct as you would with use. For example, rather than this:

```
use Fcntl qw(O_EXCL O_CREAT O_RDWR);
```

you might say this instead:

```
require Fcntl;
Fcntl->import(qw(O_EXCL O_CREAT O_RDWR));
```

Delaying the import until run time means that the rest of your program will not be subject to any imported semantic changes that the compiler would have seen if you'd used a use. In particular, subroutine prototypes and the overriding of built-in functions will not be seen in time.

You might want to encapsulate this delayed loading in a subroutine. The following deceptively simple approach does not work:

```
sub load_module {
    require $_[0];   #WRONG
    import  $_[0];   #WRONG
}
```

It fails for subtle reasons. Imagine calling **require** with an argument of `"Math::BigFloat"`. If that's a bareword, the double colon is converted into your operating system's path separator and a trailing .pm is added. But as a simple variable, it's a literal filename. Worse, Perl doesn't have a built-in **import** function. Instead, there's a class method named **import** that we're using the dubious indirect object syntax on. As with indirect filehandles, you can't use indirect objects on anything but a plain scalar variable, or a bareword or a block returning the object, not an expression or one element from an array or hash.

A better implementation might look more like:

```
load_module('Fcntl', qw(O_EXCL O_CREAT O_RDWR));

sub load_module {
    eval "require $_[0]";
    die if $@;
    $_[0]->import(@_[1 .. $#_]);
}
```

But this still isn't perfectly correct in the general case. It really shouldn't import those symbols into its own package. It should put them into its caller's package. We could account for this, but the whole procedure is getting increasingly messy.

A convenient alternative is the use autouse pragma. New as of Perl 5.004, this directive can save time on infrequently loaded functions by delaying their loading until they're actually used:

```
use autouse Fcntl => qw( O_EXCL() O_CREAT() O_RDWR() );
```

We put parentheses after O_EXCL, O_CREAT, and O_RDWR when we autoused them but not when we used them or imported them. The autouse pragma doesn't just take function names, it can also take a prototype for the function. The Fcntl constants are prototyped to take no arguments, so we can use them as barewords in our program without use strict kvetching.

Remember, too, that use strict's checks take place at compile time. If we use Fcntl, the prototypes in the Fcntl module will be compiled and we can use the constants without parentheses. If we require or wrap the use in an eval, as we did earlier, we prevent the compiler from reading the prototypes, so we can't use the Fcntl constants without parentheses.

Read the `autouse` pragma's online documentation to learn its various caveats and provisos.

See Also

Recipe 12.2; the discussion on the `import` method in the documentation for the standard Exporter module, also found in Chapter 7 of *Programming Perl*; the documentation for the standard `use autouse` pragma

12.4. Making Variables Private to a Module

Problem

You want to make a variable or function private to a package.

Solution

You can't. But you can make them private to the file that the module sits in, which usually suffices.

Discussion

Remember that a package is just a way of grouping variables and functions together, conferring no privacy. Anything in a package is by definition global and accessible from anywhere. Packages only group; they don't hide.

For privacy, only lexical variables will do. A module is implemented in a *Module.pm*, with all its globals in the package named Module. Because that whole file is by definition a scope and lexicals are private to a scope, creating file-scoped lexicals is effectively the same thing as a module-private variable.

If you alternate packages within a scope, though, you may be surprised that the scope's lexicals are visible no matter where you are. That's because a package statement only sets a different prefix for a global identifier.

```
package Alpha;
my $aa = 10;
    $x = "azure";

package Beta;
my $bb = 20;
    $x = "blue";
```

```
package main;
print "$aa, $bb, $x, $Alpha::x, $Beta::x\n";
10, 20, , azure, blue
```

Was that the output you expected? The two lexicals, $aa and $bb, are still in scope because we haven't left the current block, file, or eval. You might think of globals and lexicals as existing in separate dimensions, forever unrelated to each other. Package statements have nothing to do with lexicals. By setting the current prefix, the first global variable $x is really $Alpha::x, whereas the second $x is now $Beta::x because of the intervening package statement changing the default prefix. Package identifiers, if fully qualified, can be accessed from anywhere, as we've done in the print statement.

So, packages can't have privacy—but modules can because they're in a file, which is always its own scope. Here's a simple module, placed in the file *Flipper.pm*, that exports two functions, flip_words and flip_boundary. The module provides code to reverse words in a line, and to change the definition of a word boundary.

```
# Flipper.pm
package Flipper;
use strict;

require Exporter;
use vars qw(@ISA @EXPORT $VERSION);
@ISA     = qw(Exporter);
@EXPORT  = qw(flip_words flip_boundary);
$VERSION = 1.0;

my $Separatrix = ' ';   # default to blank; must precede functions

sub flip_boundary {
    my $prev_sep = $Separatrix;
    if (@_) { $Separatrix = $_[0] }
    return $prev_sep;
}
sub flip_words {
    my $line  = $_[0];
    my @words = split($Separatrix, $line);
    return join($Separatrix, reverse @words);
}
1;
```

This module sets three package variables needed by the Exporter and also initializes a lexical variable at file level called $Separatrix. Again, this variable is private to the file, not to the package. All code beneath its declaration in the same scope (or nested within that scope, as are the functions' blocks) can see $Separatrix perfectly. Even though they aren't exported, global variables could be accessed using the fully qualified name, as in $Flipper::VERSION.

A scope's lexicals cannot be examined or tinkered with from outside that scope, which in this case is the entire file below their point of declaration. You cannot fully qualify lexicals or export them either; only globals can be exported. If someone outside the module needs to look at or change the file's lexicals, they must ask the module itself. That's where the `flip_boundary` function comes into play, allowing indirect access to the module's private parts.

This module would work the same even if its `$Separatrix` variable were a package global rather than a file lexical. Someone from the outside could theoretically play with it without the module realizing this. On the other hand, if they really want to that badly, perhaps you should let them do so. Peppering your module with file-scoped lexicals is not necessary. You already have your own namespace (Flipper, in this case) where you can store all the identifiers you want. That's what it's there for, after all. Good Perl programming style nearly always avoids fully qualified identifiers.

Speaking of style, the case of identifiers used in the Flipper module was not random. Following the Perl style guide, identifiers in all capitals are reserved for those with special meaning to Perl itself. Functions and local variables are all lowercase. The module's persistent variables (either file lexicals or package globals) are capitalized. Identifiers with multiple words have each of these separated by an underscore to make it easier to read. Please don't use mixed capitals without underscores—you wouldn't like reading this book without spaces, either.

See Also

The discussion on file-scoped lexicals in *perlmod*(1); the "Scoped Declarations" section in Chapter 2 of *Programming Perl*; the section on "Programming in Style" in Chapter 8 of *Programming Perl* or *perlstyle*(1); Recipe 10.2; Recipe 10.3

12.5. Determining the Caller's Package

Problem

You need to find out the current or calling package.

Solution

To find the current package:

```
$this_pack = __PACKAGE__;
```

To find the caller's package:

```
$that_pack = caller();
```

Discussion

The `__PACKAGE__` symbol returns the package that the code is currently being compiled into. This doesn't interpolate into double-quoted strings:

```
print "I am in package __PACKAGE__\n";                    # WRONG!
I am in package _ _PACKAGE_ _
```

Needing to figure out the caller's package arose more often in older code that received as input a string of code to be evaluated, or a filehandle, format, or directory handle name. Consider a call to a hypothetical `runit` function:

```
package Alpha;
runit('$line = <TEMP>');

package Beta;
sub runit {
    my $codestr = shift;
    eval $codestr;
    die if $@;
}
```

Because `runit` was compiled in a different package than was currently executing, when the eval runs, it will act as though it were passed $Beta::line and Beta::TEMP. The old workaround was to include your caller's package first:

```
package Beta;
sub runit {
    my $codestr = shift;
    my $hispack = caller;
    eval "package $hispack; $codestr";
    die if $@;
}
```

That approach only works when `$line` is a global variable. If it's lexical, that won't help at all. Instead, arrange for `runit` to accept a reference to a subroutine:

```
package Alpha;
runit( sub { $line = <TEMP> } );

package Beta;
sub runit {
    my $coderef = shift;
    &$coderef();
}
```

This not only works with lexicals, it has the added benefit of checking the code's syntax at compile time, which is a major win.

If all that's being passed in is a filehandle, it's more portable to use the `Symbol::qualify` function. This function takes a name and package to qualify the name into. If the name needs qualification, it fixes it; otherwise, it's left alone. But that's considerably less efficient than a `*` prototype.

Here's an example that reads and returns *n* lines from a filehandle. The function qualifies the handle before working with it.

```
open (FH, "< /etc/termcap")
    or die "can't open /etc/termcap: $!";
($a, $b, $c) = nreadline(3, 'FH');

use Symbol ();
use Carp;
sub nreadline {
    my ($count, $handle) = @_;
    my(@retlist,$line);

    croak "count must be > 0" unless $count > 0;
    $handle = Symbol::qualify($handle, (caller())[0]);
    croak "need open filehandle" unless defined fileno($handle);

    push(@retlist, $line) while defined($line = <$handle>) && $count--;
    return @retlist;
}
```

If everyone who called your `nreadline` function passed in the filehandle as a typeglob *FH, as a glob reference *FH, or using FileHandle or IO::Handle objects, you wouldn't need to do this. It's only the possibility of a bare `"FH"` that requires qualification.

See Also

The documentation for the standard Symbol module, also found in Chapter 7 of *Programming Perl*; the descriptions of the special symbols __FILE__, __LINE__, and __PACKAGE__ in *perldata*(1); Recipe 12.12

12.6. *Automating Module Clean-Up*

Problem

You need to create setup code and clean-up code for a module that gets called automatically, without user intervention.

Solution

For setup code, put executable statements outside subroutine definitions in the module file. For clean-up code, use an END subroutine in that module.

Discussion

In some languages, the programmer must call a module's initialization code before any of that module's regular functions can be safely accessed. Similarly, when the program is done, the programmer may have to call module-specific finalization code.

Not so in Perl. For per-module initialization code, executable statements outside of any subroutines in your module suffice. When the module is loaded in, that code runs right then and there. The user never has to remember to do this, because it's done automatically.

Now, why would you want automatic clean-up code? It depends on the module. You might want to write a shutdown message to a logfile, tell a database server to commit any pending state, refresh a screen, or return the tty to its original state.

Suppose you want a module to log quietly whenever a program using it starts up or finishes. Add code in an END subroutine to run after your program finishes:

```perl
$Logfile = "/tmp/mylog" unless defined $Logfile;
open(LF, ">>$Logfile")
    or die "can't append to $Logfile: $!";
select((((select(LF), $|=1))[0]);   # unbuffer LF
logmsg("startup");

sub logmsg {
    my $now = scalar gmtime;
    print LF "$0 $$ $now: @_\n"
        or die "write to $Logfile failed: $!";
}

END {
    logmsg("shutdown");
    close(LF)
        or die "close $Logfile failed: $!";
}
```

The first part of code, outside any subroutine declaration, is executed at module load time. The module user doesn't have to do anything special to make this happen. Someone might be unpleasantly surprised, however, if the file can't be accessed, since the **die** would make the **use** or **require** fail.

END routines work like exit handlers, such as **trap 0** in the shell, **atexit** in C programming, or global destructors or finalizers in object-oriented languages. All the ENDs in a program are run in the opposite order that they were loaded; that is, last seen, first run. These get called whether the program finishes through normal process termination by implicitly reaching the end of your main program, through an explicit call to the **exit** function, or via an uncaught exception such as **die** or a mistake involving division by zero.

Uncaught signals are a different matter, however. Death by signal does not run your exit handlers. The following pragma takes care of them:

```
use sigtrap qw(die normal-signals error-signals);
```

END also isn't called when a process polymorphs itself via the **exec** function because you are still in the same process, just a different program. All normal process attributes remain, like process ID and parent PID, user and group IDs, umask, current directory, environment variables, resource limits and accumulated statistics, open file descriptors (however, see the $^F variable in *perlvar*(1) or Camel:2). If it didn't work this way, exit handlers would execute redundantly in programs managing **fork** and **exec** manually. This would not be good.

See Also

The standard **use sigtrap** pragma, also in Chapter 7 of *Programming Perl*; the section on "Package Constructors and Destructors" in Chapter 5 of *Programming Perl* and in *perlmod*(1); the $^F variable in the section on "Global Special Variables" in Chapter 2 of *Programming Perl* and in *perldata*(1); the **fork** and **exec** functions in Chapter 3 of *Programming Perl* and in *perlmod*(1)

12.7. Keeping Your Own Module Directory

Problem

You don't want to install your own personal modules in the standard per-system extension library.

Solution

You have several choices: use Perl's -I command line switch; set your PERL5LIB environment variable; or employ the **use lib** pragma, possibly in conjunction with the FindBin module.

Discussion

The @INC array contains a list of directories that are consulted every time a do, require, or use compiles code from another file, library, or module. You can print these out easily from the command line:

```
% perl -e 'for (@INC) { printf "%d %s\n", $i++, $_ }'
0 /usr/local/perl/lib/i686-linux/5.004
1 /usr/local/perl/lib
2 /usr/local/perl/lib/site_perl/i686-linux
3 /usr/local/perl/lib/site_perl
4 .
```

The first two directories, elements 0 and 1 of @INC, are the standard architecture-dependent and architecture-independent directories, which all standard libraries, modules, and pragmas will go into. You have two of them because some modules contain information or formatting that makes sense only on that particular architecture. For example, the Config module contains information that cannot be shared across several architectures, so it goes in the 0th array element. Modules that include compiled C components, such as *Socket.so*, are also placed there. Most modules, however, go in the platform-independent directory in the 1st element.

The next pair, elements 2 and 3 above, fulfills roles analogous to elements 0 and 1, but on a site-specific basis. Suppose you have a module that didn't come with Perl, like a module from CPAN or one you wrote yourself. When you or (more likely) your system administrator installs this module, its components go into one of the site-specific directories. You are encouraged to use these for any modules that your entire site should be able to access conveniently.

The last standard component, "." (your current working directory), is useful only when developing and testing your software, not when deploying it. If your modules are in the same directory that you last chdired to, you're fine. If you're anywhere else, it doesn't work.

So sometimes none of the @INC directories work out. Maybe you have your own personal modules. Perhaps your project group has particular modules that are relevant only to that project. In these cases, you need to augment the standard @INC search.

The first approach involves using a command-line flag, -I*dirlist*. The *dirlist* is a colon-separated[*] list of one or more directories, which will be prepended to the front of the @INC array. This works well for simple command lines, and thus can be used on a per-command basis, such as when you call a quick one-liner from a shell script.

This technique should not be included in the #! (pound-bang) line. First, it's not much fun to modify each program. More importantly, some older operating systems have bugs related to how long that line can be, typically 32 characters, including the #! part. That means if you have a very long path, such as #!/opt/languages/free/extrabits/perl, you may get the mysterious "Command not found" error. Perl does its best to rescan the line manually, but it's still too dicey to rely on.

Often, a better solution is to set the PERL5LIB environment variable. This can be done in your shell start-up file. Or, your system administrator may want to do so in a systemwide start-up file so all users can benefit. For example, suppose you

---

[*] Comma-separated on MacOS.

have all your own modules in a directory called *~/perllib*. You would place one of
the following lines in your shell start-up file, depending on which shell you use:

```
# syntax for sh, bash, ksh, or zsh
$ export PERL5LIB=$HOME/perllib

# syntax for csh or tcsh
% setenv PERL5LIB ~/perllib
```

Probably the most convenient solution from your users' perspective is for you to
add a **use lib** pragma near the top of your script. That way the users of the program don't need to take any special action to run your program. Imagine a hypothetical project called Spectre whose programs rely on its own set of libraries.
Those programs could have a statement like this at their start:

```
use lib "/projects/spectre/lib";
```

What happens when you don't know the exact path to the library? Perhaps you've
allowed the whole project to be installed in an arbitrary path. You could create an
elaborate installation procedure to dynamically update the script, but even if you
did, paths would still be frozen at installation time. If someone moved the files
later, the libraries wouldn't be found.

The FindBin module conveniently solves this problem. This module tries to compute the full path to the executing script's enclosing directory, setting an import-
able package variable called $Bin to that directory. Typical usage is either to look
for modules in the same directory as the program or in a *lib* directory at the same
level.

To demonstrate the first case, suppose you have a program called */wherever/spectre/
myprog* that needs to look in */wherever/spectre* for its modules, but you don't want
to hardcode that path.

```
use FindBin;
use lib $FindBin::Bin;
```

The second case would be used if your program lives in */wherever/spectre/bin/
myprog* but needs to look at */wherever/spectre/lib* for its modules.

```
use FindBin qw($Bin);
use lib "$Bin/../lib";
```

See Also

The documentation for the standard **use lib** pragma and the standard FindBin
module; the discussion of the PERL5LIB environment in *perl*(1); your shell's syntax for setting environment variables

12.8. Preparing a Module for Distribution

Problem

You want to prepare your module in standard distribution format so you can easily send your module to a friend. Better yet, you plan to contribute your module to CPAN so everyone can use it.

Solution

It's best to start with Perl's standard *h2xs* tool. Let's say you want to make a Planets module or an Astronomy::Orbits module. You'd type:

```
% h2xs -XA -n Planets
% h2xs -XA -n Astronomy::Orbits
```

These commands make subdirectories called *./Planets/* and *./Astronomy/Orbits/* respectively, where you will find all the components you need to get you started. The **-n** flag names the module you want to make, **-X** suppresses creation of XS (external subroutine) components, and **-A** means the module won't use the Auto-Loader.

Discussion

Writing modules is easy—once you know how. Writing a proper module is like filling out a legal contract: it's full of places to initial, sign, and date exactly right. If you miss any, it's not valid. Instead of hiring a contract lawyer, you can get a quick start on writing modules using the *h2xs* program. This tool gives you a skeletal module file with all the right parts filled in, and it also gives you the other files needed to correctly install your module and its documentation or to bundle it up for inclusion in CPAN or sending off to a friend.

h2xs is something of a misnomer because XS is Perl's external subroutine interface for linking with C or C++. But the *h2xs* tool is also extremely convenient for preparing a distribution even when you aren't using the XS interface.

Let's look at one of the modules file that *h2xs* has made. Because the module is to be called Astronomy::Orbits, the user will specify not **use Orbits** but rather **use Astronomy::Orbits**. Therefore an extra *Astronomy* subdirectory is made, in which an *Orbits* directory is placed. Here is the first and perhaps most important line of *Orbit.pm*:

```
package Astronomy::Orbits;
```

This sets the package—the default prefix—on all global identifiers (variables, functions, filehandles, etc.) in the file. Therefore a variable like @ISA is really the global variable @Astronomy::Orbits::ISA.

As we said in the Introduction, you must not make the mistake of saying **package Orbits** because it's in the file *Orbits.pm*. The **package** statement in the module must be exactly match the target of the **use** or **require** statement, which means the leading directory portion needs to be there and the characters' case must be the same. Furthermore, it must be installed in an *Astronomy* subdirectory. The *h2xs* command will set this all up properly, including the installation rule in the Makefile. But if you're doing this by hand, you must keep this in mind. See Recipe 12.1 for that.

If you plan to use autoloading, described in Recipe 12.10, omit the -A flag to *h2xs*, which produces lines like this:

```
require Exporter;
require AutoLoader;
@ISA = qw(Exporter AutoLoader);
```

If your module is bilingual in Perl and C as described in Recipe 12.15, omit the -**X** flag to *h2xs* to produce lines like this:

```
require Exporter;
require DynaLoader;
@ISA = qw(Exporter DynaLoader);
```

Following this is the Exporter's variables as explained in Recipe 12.1. If you're writing an object-oriented module as described in Chapter 13, you probably won't use the Exporter at all.

That's all there is for setup. Now, write your module code. When you're ready to ship it off, use the **make dist** directive from your shell to bundle it all up into a tar archive for easy distribution. (The name of the *make* program may vary from system to system.)

```
% make dist
```

This will leave you with a file whose name is something like *Astronomy-Orbits-1.03.tar.Z*.

To register as a CPAN developer, check out *http://www.perl.com/CPAN/modules/04pause.html*.

See Also

http://www.perl.com/CPAN to find a mirror near you and directions for submission; *h2xs*(1); the documentation for the standard Exporter, AutoLoader, AutoSplit, and ExtUtils::MakeMaker modules, also found in Chapter 7 of *Programming Perl*

12.9. Speeding Module Loading with SelfLoader

Problem

You'd like to load a very large module quickly.

Solution

Use the SelfLoader module:

```
require Exporter;
require SelfLoader;
@ISA = qw(Exporter SelfLoader);
#
# other initialization or declarations here
#
__DATA__
sub abc { .... }
sub def { .... }
```

Discussion

When you load a module using `require` or `use`, the entire module file must be read and compiled (into internal parse trees, not into byte code or native machine code) right then. For very large modules, this annoying delay is unnecessary if you need only a few functions from a particular file.

To address this problem, the SelfLoader module delays compilation of each subroutine until it is actually called. SelfLoader is easy to use: just place your module's subroutines underneath the `__DATA__` marker so the compiler will ignore them, use a `require` to pull in the SelfLoader, and include SelfLoader in the module's `@ISA` array. That's all there is to it. When your module is loaded, the SelfLoader creates stub functions for all the routines below `__DATA__`. The first time a function gets called, the stub replaces itself by compiling the real function and then calling it.

There is one significant restriction on modules that employ the SelfLoader (or the AutoLoader for that matter, which is described in Recipe 12.10). SelfLoaded or AutoLoaded subroutines have no access to lexical variables in the file whose `__DATA__` block they are in because they are compiled via `eval` in an imported AUTOLOAD block. Such dynamically generated subroutines are therefore compiled in the scope of SelfLoader's or AutoLoader's AUTOLOAD.

Whether using the SelfLoader helps or hinders performance depends on how many subroutines the module has, how large they are, and whether they'll all end up getting called over the lifetime of the program or not.

You should initially develop and test your module without the SelfLoader. Commenting out the __DATA__ line will take care of that, allowing those functions to be visible at compile time.

See Also

The documentation for the standard module SelfLoader, also in Chapter 7 of *Programming Perl*; Recipe 12.10

12.10. Speeding Up Module Loading with Autoloader

Problem

You want to use the AutoLoader module.

Solution

The easiest solution is to use the *h2xs* facility to create a directory and all the files you'll need. Here we assume you have your own directory, *~/perllib/*, which contains your personal library modules.

```
% h2xs -Xn Sample
% cd Sample
% perl Makefile.PL LIB=~/perllib
% (edit Sample.pm)
% make install
```

Discussion

The AutoLoader addresses the same performance issues as the SelfLoader. It also provides stub functions that get replaced by the real ones the first time they're called. But instead of looking for functions all in the same file, hidden below a __DATA__ marker, the AutoLoader expects to find the real definition for each function in its own file. If your *Sample.pm* module had two functions, foo and bar, then the AutoLoader would expect to find them in *Sample/auto/foo.al* and *Sample/auto/bar.al*, respectively. Modules employing the AutoLoader load faster than those using the SelfLoader, but at the cost of extra files, disk space, and complexity.

This setup sounds complicated. If you were doing it manually, it probably would be. Fortunately, *h2xs* helps out tremendously here. Besides creating a module directory with templates for your *Sample.pm* file and other files you'll need, it also generates a Makefile that uses the AutoSplit module to break your module's functions into little files, one function per file. The `make install` rule installs these so they will be found automatically. All you have to do is put the module functions down below an __END__ line (rather than a __DATA__ line as in SelfLoader) that you'll find has already been created.

As with the SelfLoader, it's easier to develop and test your module without the AutoLoader. Just comment out the __END__ line while developing it.

The same restrictions about the invisibility of file lexicals that apply to modules using the SelfLoader also apply when using the AutoLoader, so using file lexicals to maintain private state doesn't work. If state is becoming that complex and significant issue, consider writing an object module instead of a traditional one.

See Also

The documentation for the standard module AutoLoader, also in Chapter 7 of *Programming Perl*; *h2xs*(1); Recipe 12.9

12.11. Overriding Built-In Functions

Problem

You want to replace a standard, built-in function with your own version.

Solution

Import that function from another module into your own namespace.

Discussion

Many (but not all) of Perl's built-in functions may be overridden. This is not something to be attempted lightly, but it is possible. You might do this, for example, if you are running on a platform that doesn't support the function that you'd like to emulate. Or, you might want to add your own wrapper around the built-in.

Not all reserved words have the same status. Those that return a negative number in the C-language `keyword()` function in the *toke.c* file in your Perl source kit may be overridden. Keywords that cannot be overridden as of 5.004 are `chop`, `defined`, `delete`, `do`, `dump`, `each`, `else`, `elsif`, `eval`, `exists`, `for`, `foreach`, `format`, `glob`, `goto`, `grep`, `if`, `keys`, `last`, `local`, `m`, `map`, `my`, `next`, `no`, `pack-`

age, pop, pos, print, printf, prototype, push, q, qq, qw, qx, redo, return, s, scalar, shift, sort, splice, split, study, sub, tie, tied, tr, undef, unless, unshift, untie, until, use, while, and y. The rest can.

A standard Perl module that does this is Cwd, which can overload chdir. Others are the by-name versions of the functions returning lists: File::stat, Net::hostent, Net::netent, Net::protoent, Net::servent, Time::gmtime, Time::localtime, Time::tm, User::grent, and User::pwent. These modules all override built-in functions like stat or getpwnam to return an object that can be accessed using a name, like getpwnam("daemon")->dir. To do this, they have to override the original, list-returning versions of those functions.

Overriding may be done uniquely by importing the function from another package. This import only takes effect in the importing package, not in all possible packages. It's not enough simply to predeclare the function. You have to import it. This is a guard against accidentally redefining built-ins.

Let's say that you'd like to replace the built-in time function, whose answer is in integer seconds, with one that returns a floating point number instead. You could make a FineTime module with an optionally exported time function as follows:

```
package FineTime;
use strict;
require Exporter;
use vars qw(@ISA @EXPORT_OK);
@ISA = qw(Exporter);
@EXPORT_OK = qw(time);

sub time() { ..... }   # TBA
```

Then the user who wants to use this augmented version of time would say something like:

```
use FineTime qw(time);
$start = time();
1 while print time() - $start, "\n";
```

This code assumes that your system has a function you can stick in the "TBA" definition above. See Recipe 12.14 for strategies that may work on your system.

For overriding of methods and operators, see Chapter 13.

See Also

The section on "Overriding Built-in Functions" in Chapter 5 of *Programming Perl* and in *perlsub*(1)

12.12. Reporting Errors and Warnings Like Built-Ins

Problem

You want to generate errors and warnings in your modules, but when you use warn or die, the user sees your own filename and line number. You'd like your functions to act like built-ins and report messages from the perspective of the user's code not your own.

Solution

The standard Carp module provides functions to do this. Use carp instead of warn. Use croak (for a short message) and confess (for a long message) instead of die.

Discussion

Like built-ins, some of your module's functions generate warnings or errors if all doesn't go well. Think about sqrt: when you pass it a negative number (and you haven't used the Math::Complex module), an exception is raised, producing a message such as "Can't take sqrt of -3 at /tmp/negroot line 17", where */tmp/negroot* is the name of your own program. But if you write your own function that dies, perhaps like this:

```
sub even_only {
    my $n = shift;
    die "$n is not even" if $n & 1;  # one way to test
    #....
}
```

then the message will say it's coming from the file your even_only function was itself compiled in, rather than from the file the user was in when they called your function. That's where the Carp module comes in handy. Instead of using die, use croak instead:

```
use Carp;
sub even_only {
    my $n = shift;
    croak "$n is not even" if $n % 2;  # here's another
    #....
}
```

If you just want to complain about something, but have the message report where in the user's code the problem occurred, call carp instead of warn. (carp and

croak do not share **warn**'s and **die**'s sensitivity to a trailing newline on the message.) For example:

```
use Carp;
sub even_only {
    my $n = shift;
    if ($n & 1) {          # test whether odd number
        carp "$n is not even, continuing";
        ++$n;
    }
    #....
}
```

Many built-ins emit warnings only when the **-w** command-line switch has been used. The $^W variable (which is not meant to be a control character but rather a ^ followed by a W) reflects whether that switch was used. You could choose to grouse only if the user asked for complaints:

```
carp "$n is not even, continuing" if $^W;
```

Finally, the Carp module provides a third function: **confess**. This works just like **croak**, except that it provides a full stack backtrace as it dies, reporting who called whom and with what arguments.

See Also

The **warn** and **die** functions in Chapter 3 of *Programming Perl* and in *perlmod*(1); the documentation for the standard Carp module, also in Chapter 7 of *Programming Perl*; Recipe 19.2; the discussion on __WARN__ and __DIE__ in the section on "Global Special Arrays" in Chapter 2 of *Programming Perl*, in *perlvar*(1), and in Recipe 16.15

12.13. Referring to Packages Indirectly

Problem

You want to refer to a variable or function in a package unknown until runtime, but syntax like $packname::$varname is illegal.

Solution

Use symbolic references:

```
{
    no strict 'refs';
    $val  = ${ $packname . "::" . $varname };
    @vals = @{ $packname . "::" . $aryname };
    &{ $packname . "::" . $funcname }("args");
```

```
        ($packname . "::" . $funcname) -> ("args");
    }
```

Discussion

A package declaration has meaning at compile time. If you don't know the name of the package or variable until run time, you'll have to resort to symbolic references for direct access to the package symbol table. Assuming you normally run with use strict in effect, you must disable part of it to use symbolic references. Once you've used the no strict 'refs' directive in that block, build up a string with the fully qualified name of the variable or function you're interested in. Then dereference this name as though it were a proper Perl reference.

Prior to version 5 of Perl, programmers were forced to use an eval for this kind of thing:

```
    eval "package $packname; \$'$val = \$$varname"; # set $main'val
    die if $@;
```

As you see, this approach makes quoting difficult. It's also comparatively slow. Fortunately, you never need to do this just to access variables indirectly by name. Symbolic references are a necessary compromise.

Similarly, eval could be used to define functions on the fly. Suppose you wanted to be able to get the base 2 or base 10 logs of numbers:

```
    printf "log2  of 100 is %.2f\n", log2(100);
    printf "log10 of 100 is %.2f\n", log10(100);
```

Perl has only the natural log function. Here's how one could use eval to create these functions at run time. Here we'll create functions named log2 up through log999:

```
    $packname = 'main';
    for ($i = 2; $i < 1000; $i++) {
        $logN = log($i);
        eval "sub ${packname}::log$i { log(shift) / $logN }";
        die if $@;
    }
```

Here, at least, you don't need to do that. The following code does the same thing, but instead of compiling a new function 998 times, we compile it only once, as a closure. Then we use symbolic dereferencing of the symbol table to assign the same subroutine reference to many function names:

```
    $packname = 'main';
    for ($i = 2; $i < 1000; $i++) {
        my $logN = log($i);
        no strict 'refs';
        *{"${packname}::log$i"} = sub { log(shift) / $logN };
    }
```

When you assign a reference to a typeglob, you create an alias just for the type of that name. That's how the Exporter does its job. The first line in the next code sample manually imports the function name `Colors::blue` into the current package. The second makes the `main::blue` function an alias for the `Colors::azure` function.

```
*blue       = \&Colors::blue;
*main::blue = \&Colors::azure;
```

Given the flexibility of typeglob assignments and symbolic references, a full-blown `eval "STRING"` is nearly always unnecessary, the last resort of the desperate programmer. The only thing worse would be if it weren't available at all.

See Also

The section on "Symbolic References" in Chapter 4 of *Programming Perl* and in the start of *perlsub*(1); Recipe 11.4

12.14. Using h2ph to Translate C #include Files

Problem

Someone gave you code that generates the bizarre error message:

```
Can't locate sys/syscall.ph in @INC (did you run h2ph?)
(@INC contains: /usr/lib/perl5/i686-linux/5.00404 /usr/lib/perl5
/usr/lib/perl5/site_perl/i686-linux /usr/lib/perl5/site_perl .)
at some_program line 7.
```

You want to know what it means and how to fix it.

Solution

Get your system administrator to do this, running as the superuser:

```
% cd /usr/include; h2ph sys/syscall.h
```

However, most include files require other include files, which means you should probably just translate them all:

```
% cd /usr/include; h2ph *.h */*.h
```

If that reports too many filenames or misses some that are more deeply nested, try this instead:

```
% cd /usr/include; find . -name '*.h' -print | xargs h2ph
```

Discussion

A file whose name ends in " .ph" has been created by the *h2ph* tool, which translates C preprocessor directives from C #include files into Perl. The goal is to allow Perl code to access the same constants as C code. The *h2xs* tool is a better approach in most cases because it provides compiled C code for your modules, not Perl code simulating C code. However, using *h2xs* requires a lot more programming savvy (at least, for accessing C code) than *h2ph* does.

When *h2ph*'s translation process works, it's wonderful. When it doesn't, you're probably out of luck. As system architectures and include files become more complex, *h2ph* fails more frequently. If you're lucky, the constants you need are already in the Fcntl, Socket, or POSIX modules. The POSIX module implements constants from *sys/file.h*, *sys/errno.h*, and *sys/wait.h*, among others. It also allows fancy tty handling, as described in Recipe 15.8.

So what can you do with these *.ph* files? Here are a few examples. The first uses the pessimally non-portable syscall function to access your operating system's gettimeofday system call. This implements the FineTime module described in Recipe 12.11.

```
# file FineTime.pm
package main;
require 'sys/syscall.ph';
die "No SYS_gettimeofday in sys/syscall.ph"
    unless defined &SYS_gettimeofday;

package FineTime;
    use strict;
require Exporter;
use vars qw(@ISA @EXPORT_OK);
@ISA = qw(Exporter);
@EXPORT_OK = qw(time);

sub time() {
    my $tv = pack("LL", ());  # presize buffer to two longs
    syscall(&main::SYS_gettimeofday, $tv, undef) >= 0
        or die "gettimeofday: $!";
    my($seconds, $microseconds) = unpack("LL", $tv);
    return $seconds + ($microseconds / 1_000_000);
}

1;
```

If you are forced to require an old-style *.pl* or *.ph* file, do so from the main package (package main in the preceding code). These old libraries always put their symbols in the current package, and main serves as a reasonable rendezvous point. To use a symbol, use its fully qualified name, as we did with main::SYS_gettimeofday.

The *sys/ioctl.ph* file, if you can get it to build on your system, is the gateway to your system's idiosyncratic I/O functions through the `ioctl` function. One such function is the TIOCSTI ioctl, shown in Example 12-1. That abbreviation stands for "terminal I/O control, simulate terminal input." On systems that implement this function, it will push one character into your device stream so that the next time any process reads from that device, it gets the character you put there.

Example 12-1. jam

```perl
#!/usr/bin/perl -w
# jam - stuff characters down STDIN's throat
require 'sys/ioctl.ph';
die "no TIOCSTI" unless defined &TIOCSTI;
sub jam {
    local $SIG{TTOU} = "IGNORE"; # "Stopped for tty output"
    local *TTY;  # make local filehandle
    open(TTY, "+</dev/tty")                 or die "no tty: $!";
    for (split(//, $_[0])) {
        ioctl(TTY, &TIOCSTI, $_)            or die "bad TIOCSTI: $!";
    }
    close(TTY);
}
jam("@ARGV\n");
```

Since *sys/ioctl.h* translation is so dodgy, you'll probably have to run this C program to get your TIOCSTI value.

```
% cat > tio.c <<EOF && cc tio.c && a.out
#include <sys/ioctl.h>
main() { printf("%#08x\n", TIOCSTI); }
EOF
0x005412
```

Another popular use for `ioctl` is for figuring out your current window size in rows and columns, and maybe even in pixels. This is shown in Example 12-2.

Example 12-2. winsz

```perl
#!/usr/bin/perl
# winsz - find x and y for chars and pixels
require 'sys/ioctl.ph';
die "no TIOCGWINSZ " unless defined &TIOCGWINSZ;
open(TTY, "+</dev/tty")                        or die "No tty: $!";
unless (ioctl(TTY, &TIOCGWINSZ, $winsize='')) {
    die sprintf "$0: ioctl TIOCGWINSZ (%08x: $!)\n", &TIOCGWINSZ;
}
($row, $col, $xpixel, $ypixel) = unpack('S4', $winsize);
print "(row,col) = ($row,$col)";
print "  (xpixel,ypixel) = ($xpixel,$ypixel)" if $xpixel || $ypixel;
print "\n";
```

As you see, as soon as you start playing with *.ph* files, unpacking binary data, and calling `syscall` and `ioctl`, you need to know about the C APIs that Perl normally hides. The only other thing that requires this much C knowledge is using the XS interface. Some suggest you should resist the temptation to descend into such unportable convolutions. Others feel that the demands put upon the trenchworkers are such that they must be forgiven these desperate measures.

Fortunately, less fragile mechanisms are increasingly available. CPAN modules for most of these functions now exist, which should theoretically prove more robust than sourcing *.ph* files.

See Also

h2ph(1); the instructions on running *h2ph* in the *INSTALL* file from the *perl* source distribution; the `syscall` and `ioctl` functions in Chapter 3 of *Programming Perl* and in *perlmod*(1); Recipe 12.15

12.15. *Using h2xs to Make a Module with C Code*

Problem

You'd like to access your system's unique C functions from Perl.

Solution

Use the *h2xs* tool to generate the necessary template files, fill the files in appropriately, and then type:

```
% perl Makefile.PL
% make
```

Discussion

A Perl module need not be written solely in Perl. As with any other module, first pick a module name and use *h2xs* on it. We'll make a `FineTime::time` function with the same semantics as in the previous recipe, but this time around, we'll implement it using real C.

First, we run the following command:

```
% h2xs -cn FineTime
```

If we had a *.h* file with function prototype declarations, we could include that, but because we're writing this one from scratch, we'll use the -c flag to omit building

code to translate any #define symbols. The -n flag says to create a module directory named *FineTime/*, which will have the following files:

Manifest	List of files in the distribution
Changes	change log
Makefile.PL	a meta-makefile
FineTime.pm	the Perl parts
FineTime.xs	the soon-to-be C parts
test.pl	a test driver

Before we can type make, we'll have to generate a Makefile based on our system's configuration using the *Makefile.PL* template. Here's how to do that:

```
% perl Makefile.PL
```

If the XS code calls library code that isn't in the normal set of libraries Perl links
from, add one more line to *Makefile.PL* first. For example, if we wanted to link
against the *librpm.a* library, which lives in the */usr/redhat/lib* directory, we'd
change the line of *Makefile.PL* that reads:

```
'LIBS'      => [''],   # e.g., '-lm'
```

so that it says:

```
'LIBS'      => ['-L/usr/redhat/lib -lrpm'],
```

If the module is to be installed somewhere other than the local *site_lib* directory,
specify that on the command line:

```
% perl Makefile.PL LIB=~/perllib
```

Finally, edit the *FineTime.pm* and *FineTime.xs* files. In the first case, most of the
work has been done for us. We just set up the export list with the function to be
exported. This time we put it in @EXPORT_OK so that if the user wants the function, they must ask for it by name. Here's *FineTime.pm*:

```
package FineTime;
use strict;
use vars qw($VERSION @ISA @EXPORT_OK);
require Exporter;
require DynaLoader;
@ISA = qw(Exporter DynaLoader);
@EXPORT_OK = qw(time);
$VERSION = '0.01';
bootstrap FineTime $VERSION;
1;
```

The *make* process will automatically translate *FineTime.xs* into a *FineTime.c* file
and eventually into a shared library, probably called *FineTime.so* on most platforms.

The utility that does this translation is *xsubpp*, which is described in its own manpage and *perlxstut*(1). The build will call *xsubpp* automatically.

Besides a strong C background, you also need to understand the C-to-Perl interface, called XS (external subroutine). The details and nuances of XS are beyond the scope of this book. The automatically generated *FineTime.xs* had the Perl-specific include files in it, as well as the MODULE declaration. We've added some extra includes and written the code for the new `time` function. Although this doesn't look entirely like C, it will, once *xsubpp* gets done with it.

Here's the *FineTime.xs* we used:

```
#include <unistd.h>
#include <sys/time.h>
#include "EXTERN.h"
#include "perl.h"
#include "XSUB.h"

MODULE = FineTime              PACKAGE = FineTime

double
time()
    CODE:
        struct timeval tv;
        gettimeofday(&tv,0);
        RETVAL = tv.tv_sec + ((double) tv.tv_usec) / 1000000;
    OUTPUT:
        RETVAL
```

Defining a function by the same name as one from the standard C library won't cause a problem when it's compiled because that's not its real name. That's just what Perl calls it. The C linker will see it as `XS_FineTime_time`, so no conflict exists.

Here's what happened with make install (with some edits):

```
% make install
mkdir ./blib/lib/auto/FineTime
cp FineTime.pm ./blib/lib/FineTime.pm
/usr/local/bin/perl -I/usr/lib/perl5/i686-linux/5.00403  -I/usr/lib/perl5
/usr/lib/perl5/ExtUtils/xsubpp -typemap
    /usr/lib/perl5/ExtUtils/typemap FineTime.xs
FineTime.tc && mv FineTime.tc FineTime.c && cc -c -Dbool=char -DHAS_BOOL
    -O2-DVERSION=\"0.01\" -DXS_VERSION=\"0.01\" -fpic
    -I/usr/lib/perl5/i686-linux/5.00403/CORE FineTime.c
Running Mkbootstrap for FineTime ()
chmod 644 FineTime.bs
LD_RUN_PATH="" cc -o blib/arch/auto/FineTime/FineTime.so
    -shared -L/usr/local/lib FineTime.o
chmod 755 blib/arch/auto/FineTime/FineTime.so
cp FineTime.bs ./blib/arch/auto/FineTime/FineTime.bs
chmod 644 blib/arch/auto/FineTime/FineTime.bs
```

```
Installing /home/tchrist/perllib/i686-linux/./auto/FineTime/FineTime.so
Installing /home/tchrist/perllib/i686-linux/./auto/FineTime/FineTime.bs
Installing /home/tchrist/perllib/./FineTime.pm
Writing /home/tchrist/perllib/i686-linux/auto/FineTime/.packlist
Appending installation info to /home/tchrist/perllib/i686-linux/perllocal.pod
```

Once this is all done, we'll be able to type something like this into the shell:

```
% perl -I ~/perllib -MFineTime=time -le '1 while print time()' | head
888177070.090978
888177070.09132
888177070.091389
888177070.091453
888177070.091515
888177070.091577
888177070.091639
888177070.0917
888177070.091763
888177070.091864
```

See Also

Chapters 18 through 20 in *Advanced Perl Programming*; *perlxstut*(1) and *perlxs*(1) to learn how to call C from Perl; *perlcall*(1) and *perlguts*(1) to understand the internal Perl API; *perlembed*(1) to learn how to call Perl from C; the the documentation for the standard ExtUtils::MakeMaker module, *h2ph*(1) and *xsubpp*(1); *http://www.perl.com/CPAN/authors/Dean_Roehrich/*, which contains Dean's comprehensive XS cookbook that includes directions on interface with C++

12.16. Documenting Your Module with Pod

Problem

You need to document your module, but don't know what format to use.

Solution

Embed your documentation in the your module file using pod format.

Discussion

Pod stands for *plain old documentation*. It's documentation embedded in your program using a very simple markup format. Programmers are notorious for writing the code first and the documentation never, so pod was designed to make writing documentation so easy that anyone can and will do so. Sometimes this even works.

When Perl is parsing your source code, a line starting with an equal sign (where a new statement is expected) says to ignore all text until it finds a line beginning with =cut, after which it will start parsing code again. This lets you mix code and documentation throughout your Perl program or module file. Since it's mostly plain text, type in your documentation as literal text, or nearly so. The translators try to be clever and make output-specific decisions so the programmer doesn't have to specifically format variable names, function calls, etc.

Along with Perl are shipped several translators that filter generic pod format into specific output styles. These include *pod2man* to change your pods into *troff* for use with the *man* program or for phototypesetting and printing; *pod2html* for creating web pages (which works even on non-Unix systems); and *pod2text* for plain ASCII. Other translators, like *pod2ipf*, *pod2fm*, *pod2texi*, *pod2latex*, and *pod2ps*, may also be available or can be found on CPAN.

Many books are written using proprietary word processors with limited scripting capabilities. Not this one! It was written in pod format using common text editors (*vi* for Tom, *emacs* for Nat) before being translated into *troff* for printing during technical review using a special translator written by Larry called *pod2ora*. The final book was produced by converting the pod source files to FrameMaker.

Although formally documented in *perlpod*(1), pod is probably easiest to learn by reading existing module files. If you started making your module using *h2xs*, then you already have the sample pods right there. The *Makefile* knows to convert these into *man* format and install those manpages so others can read them. Alternatively, the *perldoc* program can translate pods on the fly using *pod2text*.

Indented paragraphs will be left verbatim. Other paragraphs will be reformatted to fit the page. Only two kinds of markups are used in pod: paragraphs beginning with an equal sign and one or more words, and interior sequences starting with a single letter followed by text enclosed in angle brackets. Paragraph tags are for headers, list enumeration, and per-translator escapes. Angle bracket sequences are mainly used for font changes, such as selecting bold, italic, or constant-width fonts. Here's an example of an =head2 pod directive and various bracket escapes for font changes:

```
=head2 Discussion

    If we had a I<.h> file with function prototype declarations, we
    could include that, but since we're writing this one from scratch,
    we'll use the B<-c> flag to omit building code to translate any
    C<#define> symbols. The B<-n> flag says to create a module directory
    named I<FineTime/>, which will have the following files.
```

The =for escape introduces specific code that is only *for* a particular output filter. This book, for example, written mostly in pod, includes calls to the standard *troff* tools *eqn*, *tbl*, and *pic*. Here's an example of embedded *eqn*. Only translators that produce *troff* will heed this paragraph.

```
=for troff
.EQ
log sub n (x) = { {log sub e (x)} over {log sub e (n)} }
.EN
```

Pod can also create multiline comments. In C, the sequence `/* .... */` can comment out many lines of text all at once—there's no need to put a marker on each line. Since Perl ignores pod directives, use these for block commenting. The trick is to find a directive that the pod filters ignore. You could specify that a block is "for later" or "for nobody":

```
=for later
next if 1 .. ?^$?;
s/^(.)/>$1/;
s/(.{73})........*/$1<SNIP>/;

=cut back to perl
```

or you could use a =begin and =end pair:

```
=begin comment

if (!open(FILE, $file)) {
    unless ($opt_q) {
        warn "$me: $file: $!\n";
        $Errors++;
    }
    next FILE;
}

$total = 0;
$matches = 0;

=end comment
```

See Also

The section on "PODs: Embedded Documentation" in *perlsyn*(1), as well as *perlpod*(1), *pod2man*(1), *pod2html*(1), and *pod2text*(1)

12.17. Building and Installing a CPAN Module

Problem

You want to install a module file that you downloaded from CPAN over the Net or obtained from a CD.

Solution

Type the following commands into your shell. It will build and install version 4.54 of the Some::Module package.

```
% gunzip Some-Module-4.54.tar.gz
% tar xf Some-Module-4.54
% cd Some-Module-4.54
% perl Makefile.PL
% make
% make test
% make install
```

Discussion

Like most programs on the Net, Perl modules are available in source kits stored as *tar* archives in GNU zip format.* If *tar* warns of "Directory checksum errors", then you downloaded the binary file in text format, mutilating it.

You'll probably have to become a privileged user with adequate permissions to install the module in the system directories. Standard modules are installed in a directory like */usr/lib/perl5* while third-party modules are installed in */usr/lib/perl5/ site_perl*.

Here's a sample run, showing the installation of the MD5 module:

```
% gunzip MD5-1.7.tar.gz
% tar xf MD5-1.7.tar
% cd MD5-1.7
% perl Makefile.PL
Checking if your kit is complete...
Looks good
Writing Makefile for MD5
% make
mkdir ./blib
mkdir ./blib/lib
```

---

* This is not the same as the zip format common on Windows machines, but newer version of Windows *winzip* will read it. Prior to Perl 5.005, you'll need the standard port of Perl for Win32, not the ActiveState port, to build CPAN modules. Free versions of *tar* and *gnutar* are also available for Microsoft systems.

```
cp MD5.pm ./blib/lib/MD5.pm
AutoSplitting MD5 (./blib/lib/auto/MD5)
/usr/bin/perl -I/usr/local/lib/perl5/i386 ...
...
cp MD5.bs ./blib/arch/auto/MD5/MD5.bs
chmod 644 ./blib/arch/auto/MD5/MD5.bsmkdir ./blib/man3
Manifying ./blib/man3/MD5.3
% make test
PERL_DL_NONLAZY=1 /usr/bin/perl -I./blib/arch -I./blib/lib
-I/usr/local/lib/perl5/i386-freebsd/5.00404 -I/usr/local/lib/perl5 test.pl
1..14
ok 1
ok 2
...
ok 13
ok 14
% sudo make install
Password:
Installing /usr/local/lib/perl5/site_perl/i386-freebsd/./auto/MD5/
    MD5.so
Installing /usr/local/lib/perl5/site_perl/i386-freebsd/./auto/MD5/
    MD5.bs
Installing /usr/local/lib/perl5/site_perl/./auto/MD5/autosplit.ix
Installing /usr/local/lib/perl5/site_perl/./MD5.pm
Installing /usr/local/lib/perl5/man/man3/./MD5.3
Writing /usr/local/lib/perl5/site_perl/i386-freebsd/auto/MD5/.packlist
Appending installation info to /usr/local/lib/perl5/i386-freebsd/
5.00404/perllocal.pod
```

If your system manager isn't around or can't be prevailed upon to run the installation, don't worry. When you use Perl to generate the Makefile from template *Makefile.PL*, you can specify alternate installation directories.

```
# if you just want the modules installed in your own directory
% perl Makefile.PL LIB=~/lib

# if you have your own complete distribution
% perl Makefile.PL PREFIX=~/perl5-private
```

See Also

The documentation for the standard ExtUtils::MakeMaker module, also in Chapter 7 of *Programming Perl*; the INSTALL file in the Perl source distribution for information on building a staticly linked *perl* binary.

12.18. *Example: Module Template*

Following is the skeleton of a module. If you want to write a module of your own, you can copy this and customize it.

```
package Some::Module;  # must live in Some/Module.pm

use strict;

require Exporter;
use vars        qw($VERSION @ISA @EXPORT @EXPORT_OK %EXPORT_TAGS);

# set the version for version checking
$VERSION        = 0.01;


@ISA          = qw(Exporter);
@EXPORT       = qw(&func1 &func2 &func4);
%EXPORT_TAGS = ( );      # eg: TAG => [ qw!name1 name2! ],

# your exported package globals go here,
# as well as any optionally exported functions
@EXPORT_OK    = qw($Var1 %Hashit &func3);

use vars qw($Var1 %Hashit);
# non-exported package globals go here
use vars        qw(@more $stuff);

# initialize package globals, first exported ones
$Var1   = '';
%Hashit = ();

# then the others (which are still accessible as $Some::Module::stuff)
$stuff  = '';
@more   = ();

# all file-scoped lexicals must be created before
# the functions below that use them.

# file-private lexicals go here
my $priv_var    = '';
my %secret_hash = ();

# here's a file-private function as a closure,
# callable as &$priv_func.
my $priv_func = sub {
    # stuff goes here.
};

# make all your functions, whether exported or not;
# remember to put something interesting in the {} stubs
sub func1       { .... }    # no prototype
sub func2()     { .... }    # proto'd void
sub func3($$)   { .... }    # proto'd to 2 scalars

# this one isn't auto-exported, but could be called!
sub func4(\%)   { .... }    # proto'd to 1 hash ref

END { }         # module clean-up code here (global destructor)

1;
```

12.19. Program: Finding Versions and Descriptions of Installed Modules

Perl is shipped with many modules. Even more can be found on CPAN. The following program prints out the names, versions, and descriptions of all modules installed on your system. It uses standard modules like File::Find and includes several techniques described in this chapter.

To run it, type:

```
% pmdesc
```

It prints a list of modules and their descriptions:

```
FileHandle (2.00) - supply object methods for filehandles
IO::File (1.06021) - supply object methods for filehandles
IO::Select (1.10) - OO interface to the select system call
IO::Socket (1.1603) - Object interface to socket communications
...
```

With the -v flag, *pmdesc* provides the names of the directories the files are in:

```
% pmdesc -v

<<<Modules from /usr/lib/perl5/i686-linux/5.00404>>>

FileHandle (2.00) - supply object methods for filehandles
    ...
```

The **-w** flag warns if a module doesn't come with a pod description, and -s sorts the module list within each directory.

The program is given in Example 12-3.

Example 12-3. pmdesc

```perl
#!/usr/bin/perl -w
# pmdesc - describe pm files
# tchrist@perl.com

use strict;
use File::Find      qw(find);
use Getopt::Std     qw(getopts);
use Carp;

use vars (
    q!$opt_v!,              # give debug info
    q!$opt_w!,              # warn about missing descs on modules
    q!$opt_a!,              # include relative paths
    q!$opt_s!,              # sort output within each directory
);

$| = 1;
```

Example 12-3. pmdesc (continued)

```perl
getopts('wvas')                 or die "bad usage";

@ARGV = @INC unless @ARGV;

# Globals.  wish I didn't really have to do this.
use vars (
    q!$Start_Dir!,              # The top directory find was called with
    q!%Future!,                 # topdirs find will handle later
);

my $Module;

# install an output filter to sort my module list, if wanted.
if ($opt_s) {
    if (open(ME, "-|")) {
        $/ = '';
        while (<ME>) {
            chomp;
            print join("\n", sort split /\n/), "\n";
        }
        exit;
    }
}

MAIN: {
    my %visited;
    my ($dev, $ino);

    @Future{@ARGV} = (1) x @ARGV;

    foreach $Start_Dir (@ARGV) {
        delete $Future{$Start_Dir};

        print "\n<<Modules from $Start_Dir>>\n\n"
            if $opt_v;

        next unless ($dev,$ino) = stat($Start_Dir);
        next if $visited{$dev,$ino}++;
        next unless $opt_a || $Start_Dir =~ m!^/!;

        find(\&wanted, $Start_Dir);
    }
    exit;
}

# calculate module name from file and directory
sub modname {
    local $_ = $File::Find::name;

    if (index($_, $Start_Dir . '/') == 0) {
        substr($_, 0, 1+length($Start_Dir)) = '';
```

Example 12-3. pmdesc (continued)

```
    }

    s { /              }    {::}gx;
    s { \.p(m|od)$     }    {}x;

    return $_;
}


# decide if this is a module we want
sub wanted {
    if ( $Future{$File::Find::name} ) {
        warn "\t(Skipping $File::Find::name, qui venit in futuro.)\n"
            if 0 and $opt_v;
        $File::Find::prune = 1;
        return;
    }
    return unless /\.pm$/ && -f;
    $Module = &modname;
    # skip obnoxious modules
    if ($Module =~ /^CPAN(\Z|::)/) {
        warn("$Module -- skipping because it misbehaves\n");
        return;
    }

    my   $file = $_;

    unless (open(POD, "< $file")) {
        warn "\tcannot open $file: $!";
            # if $opt_w;
        return 0;
    }

    $: = " -:";

    local $/ = '';
    local $_;
    while (<POD>) {
        if (/=head\d\s+NAME/) {
            chomp($_ = <POD>);
            s/^.*?-\s+//s;
            s/\n/ /g;
            #write;
            my $v;
            if (defined ($v = getversion($Module))) {
                print "$Module ($v) ";
            } else {
                print "$Module ";
            }
            print "- $_\n";
            return 1;
        }
    }
}
```

Example 12-3. pmdesc (continued)

```
    warn "\t(MISSING DESC FOR $File::Find::name)\n"
        if $opt_w;

    return 0;
}

# run Perl to load the module and print its verson number, redirecting
# errors to /dev/null
sub getversion {
    my $mod = shift;

    my $vers = `$^X -m$mod -e 'print \$${mod}::VERSION' 2>/dev/null`;
    $vers =~ s/^\s*(.*?)\s*$/$1/; # remove stray whitespace
    return ($vers || undef);
}

format =
^<<<<<<<<<<<<<<<<<~~^<<<<<<<<<<<<<<<<<<<<<<<<<<<<<<<<<<<<<<<<<<<<<<<<<<<<<<<<<<<<<<<
$Module,          $_
.
```

13

Classes, Objects, and Ties

All the world over, I will back the masses
against the classes.

—William E. Gladstone
Speech at Liverpool, 28 June 1886

13.0. Introduction

Along with references and modules, release 5.000 of Perl added objects. As usual, Perl doesn't try to enforce one true style but embraces many. This helps more people do their job the way they want to do it.

You don't have to use objects to write programs, unlike Java, where programs are instances of objects. If you want to, though, you can write Perl programs that use nearly every weapon in the object-oriented arsenal. Perl supports classes and objects, single and multiple inheritance, instance methods and class methods, access to overridden methods, constructors and destructors, operator overloading, proxy methods through autoloading, delegation, a rooted hierarchy for all objects, and two levels of garbage collection.

You can use as many or as few object-oriented techniques as you want and need. Ties are the only parts of Perl where you must use object orientation. And even then, only the module implementor need be aware of this; the casual user gets to remain blissfully unaware of the internal mechanics. Ties, discussed in Recipe 13.15, let you transparently intercept access to a variable. For example, you can use ties to make a hash that allows lookups by key or value.

Under the Hood

If you ask ten people what object orientation is, you'll get ten different answers. People bandy about terms like abstraction and encapsulation, trying to isolate the basic units of object-oriented programming languages and give them big names to write papers and books about. Not all object-oriented languages offer the same features, yet they are still deemed object-oriented. This, of course, produces more papers and books.

We'll follow the nomenclature used in Perl's documentation, the *perlobj*(1) manpage, and Chapter 5 of *Programming Perl*, "Libraries, Modules, and Classes." An *object* is a variable that belongs to a *class*. *Methods* are functions associated with a class or object. In Perl, a class is a package — and usually a module. An object is a reference to something that's been *blessed* into a class. Blessing associates a referent with a class. This is done with the **bless** function, which takes one or two arguments. The first is a reference to the thing to bless, and the optional second argument is the package to bless it into.

```
$object = {};                          # hash reference
bless($object, "Data::Encoder");       # bless $object into Data::Encoder class
bless($object);                        # bless $object into current package
```

The class name is the package name (**Data::Encoder** in the example above). Because classes are modules (usually), the code for the **Data::Encoder** class resides in the file *Data/Encoder.pm*. As with traditional modules, the directory structure is purely for convenience; it implies nothing about inheritance, variable sharing, or anything else. Unlike a traditional module, though, an object module seldom if ever uses the Exporter. Access should be through method calls only, not imported functions or variables.

Once an object has been blessed, calling the **ref** function on its reference returns the name of its class instead of the fundamental type of referent:

```
$obj = [3,5];
print ref($obj), " ", $obj->[1], "\n";
bless($obj, "Human::Cannibal");
print ref($obj), " ", $obj->[1], "\n";

ARRAY 5
Human::Cannibal 5
```

As you can see, you can still dereference a reference once it has been blessed. Most frequently, objects are implemented as blessed hash references. You may use any kind of reference you want, but hash references are the most flexible. They let you have arbitrarily named data fields in an object.

```
$obj->{Stomach} = "Empty";    # directly accessing an object's contents
$obj->{NAME}    = "Thag";
# uppercase field name to make it stand out (optional)
```

Although Perl permits it, it's considered poor form for any code outside the class to directly access the contents of an object. The point of objects, everyone agrees, is to give you a nominally opaque handle to *something* that you access through designated methods only. This lets the maintainer of the class change its implementation without needing to change all application code that uses the class.

Methods

To call a method, use ->. Here, we call the `encode()` method of $object with the argument `"data"` and store the return value in $encoded:

```
$encoded = $object->encode("data");
```

This is an *object method*, because we call the method on an object. We can also have *class methods*, methods called on class names.

```
$encoded = Data::Encoder->encode("data");
```

Invoking a method calls the function in the corresponding class, implicitly passing as the initial argument either a reference for object methods or a string for class methods. Recipe 13.7 shows how to make method calls where the method is determined at runtime.

Most classes provide *constructor* methods, which return new objects. Unlike some object-oriented languages, constructor methods in Perl are not specially named. In fact, you can name them anything you like. C++ programmers have a penchant for calling their constructors in Perl `new`. We recommend that you name your constructors whatever makes sense in the context of the problem you're solving. For example, constructors in the Tk extension to Perl are named after the widgets they create. A less common approach is to export a function with the same name as the class; see "Example: Overloaded StrNum Class" in Recipe 13.14 for an example.

A typical constructor looks like this:

```
sub new {
    my $class = shift;
    my $self  = {};        # allocate new hash for object
    bless($self, $class);
    return $self;
}
```

Call the constructor with:

```
$object = Class->new();
```

If there isn't any inheritance or other monkey business working behind the scenes, this is effectively the same as:

```
$object = Class::new("Class");
```

The new() function's first argument here is the class name to bless the new reference into. A constructor should pass that string as the second argument to bless().

Recipe 13.1 also talks about functions that return blessed references. Constructors don't have to be class methods; it's often useful to have object methods that themselves return new objects, as discussed in Recipe 13.6.

A *destructor* is a subroutine that runs when an object's referent is garbage collected. Unlike constructors, you have no choice in naming it. You must name your destructor method DESTROY. This method, if it exists, will be called for all objects immediately prior to memory deallocation. Destructors, described in Recipe 13.2, are optional.

Some languages syntactically allow the compiler to restrict access to a class's methods. Perl does not—it allows code to call any method of an object. The author of a class should document clearly the *public* methods (those which may be used), and the user of a class should avoid undocumented (implicitly *private*) methods.

Perl doesn't distinguish between methods that can be called on a class (*class methods*) and methods that can be called on an object (*instance methods*). If you want a particular method to be called as a class method only, do something like this:

```
sub class_only_method {
    my $class = shift;
    die "class method called on object" if ref $class;
    # more code here
}
```

If you want to allow a particular method to be called as an instance method only, do something like this:

```
sub instance_only_method {
    my $self = shift;
    die "instance method called on class" unless ref $self;
    # more code here
}
```

If your code calls an undefined method on an object, Perl won't complain at compile time; the program will instead trigger an exception at run time. Likewise, the compiler can't catch situations where you pass a non-prime value to a method expecting a prime number. Methods are just function calls whose package is determined at run time. Like all indirect functions, they have no prototype checking— because that happens at compile time. Even if method calls were aware of prototypes, in Perl the compiler is unable to automatically check the precise types or ranges of arguments to functions. Perl prototypes are used to *coerce* a function argument's context, not to check ranges. Recipe 10.11 details Perl's strange perspective on prototypes.

You can prevent Perl from triggering an exception for undefined methods by using the AUTOLOAD mechanism to catch calls to nonexistent methods. We show an application of this in Recipe 13.11.

Inheritance

Inheritance defines a hierarchy of classes. Calls to methods not defined in a class search this hierarchy for a method of that name. The first method found is used. Inheritance means allowing one class to piggy-back on top of another so you don't have to write the same code again and again. This is a form of software reuse, and therefore related to Laziness, the principal virtue of a programmer.

Some languages provide special syntax for inheritance. In Perl, each class (package) can put its list of *superclasses* (parents in the hierarchy) into the package global (not a my) variable @ISA. This list is searched at runtime when a call is made to a method not defined in the object's class. If the first package listed in @ISA doesn't have the method but that package has its own @ISA, Perl looks first in *that* package's own @ISA, recursively, before going on.

If the inheritance search fails, the same check is run again, this time looking for a method named AUTOLOAD. The lookup sequence for $ob->meth(), where $ob is of class P, is:

- P::meth
- All packages S in @P::ISA, recursively, for any S::meth()
- UNIVERSAL::meth
- The P::AUTOLOAD subroutine
- All packages S in @P::ISA, recursively, for any S::AUTOLOAD()
- The UNIVERSAL::AUTOLOAD subroutine

Most classes have just one item in their @ISA array, a situation called *single inheritance*. Classes with more than one element in @ISA represent *multiple inheritance*. The benefits of multiple inheritance are widely contested, but it is supported by Perl.

Recipe 13.9 talks about the basics of inheritance and designing a class so it can be easily subclassed. In Recipe 13.10 we show how a subclass can call overridden methods in its superclasses.

Perl doesn't support inheritance of data values. A class can, but should not, touch another's data directly. This violates the envelope and ruins the abstraction. If you follow the advice in Recipes 13.10 and 13.12, this won't be much of an issue.

A Warning on Indirect Object Notation

The *indirect* notation for method calls:

```
$lector = new Human::Cannibal;
feed $lector "Zak";
move $lector "New York";
```

is an alternative syntax for:

```
$lector = Human::Cannibal->new();
$lector->feed("Zak");
$lector->move("New York");
```

This indirect object notation is appealing to English speakers and familiar to C++ programmers (who use **new** this way). Do not be seduced. It has two grave problems. One is that it follows the same quirky rules as the filehandle slot in print and printf:

```
printf STDERR "stuff here\n";
```

This slot, if filled, must contain a bare symbol, a block, or a scalar variable name; it can't be any old scalar expression. This can lead to horribly confusing precedence problems, as in these next two lines:

```
move $obj->{FIELD};                   # probably wrong
move $ary[$i];                        # probably wrong
```

Surprisingly, those actually parse as:

```
$obj->move->{FIELD};                  # Surprise!
$ary->move->[$i];                     # Surprise!
```

rather than as you might have expected:

```
$obj->{FIELD}->move();                # Nope, you wish
$ary[$i]->move;                       # Nope, you wish
```

The second problem is that Perl must guess at compile time whether **name** and **move** are functions or methods. Usually Perl gets it right, but when it doesn't, you get a function call compiled as a method, or vice versa. This can introduce incredibly subtle bugs that are hard to unravel. The infix arrow notation using -> doesn't suffer from either of these disturbing ambiguities, so we recommend you use it exclusively.

Some Notes on Object Terminology

In the object-oriented world, many words describe only a few concepts. If you've programmed in another object-oriented language, you might like to know how familiar terms and concepts map onto Perl.

For example, it's common to call objects *instances* of a class and those objects' methods *instance methods*. Data fields peculiar to each object are often called *instance data* or *object attributes*, and data fields common to all members of that class are *class data*, *class attributes*, or *static data members*.

Also, *base class*, *generic class*, and *superclass* all describe the same notion (a parent or similar ancestor in the inheritance hierarchy), whereas *derived class*, *specific class*, and *subclass* describe the opposite relationship (a child or descendent in the inheritance hierarchy).

C++ programmers have *static methods*, *virtual methods*, and *instance methods*, but Perl only has *class methods* and *object methods*. Actually, Perl only has methods. Whether a method acts as a class or object method is determined solely by actual usage. You could call a class method (one expecting a string argument) on an object or an object method (one expecting a reference) on a class, but you shouldn't expect reasonable results if you do.

A C++ programmer thinks about global (class) constructors and destructors. These correspond to module initialization code and per-module END{} blocks respectively.

From the C++ perspective, all methods in Perl are virtual. This is why their arguments are never checked for function prototypes as regular built-in and user-defined functions can be. Prototypes are checked by the compiler at compile time. You can't determine until run time the function that a method has called.

Philosophical Aside

In its OO programming, Perl gives you a lot of freedom: the ability to do things more than one way (you can bless any data type to make an object), to inspect and modify classes you didn't write (adding functions to their packages), and to use these to write tangled pits of misery — if that's really what you want to do.

Less flexible programming languages are usually more restrictive. Many are fanatically devoted to enforced privacy, compile-time type checking, complex function signatures, and a smorgasbord of other features. Perl doesn't provide these things with objects because it doesn't provide them anywhere else, either. Keep this in mind if you find Perl's object-oriented implementation weird. You only think it's weird because you're used to another language's philosophy. Perl's treatment of OO is perfectly sensible — if you think in Perl. For every problem that you can't solve by writing Perl as though it were Java or C++, there is a native Perl solution that works perfectly. The absolutely paranoid programmer can even have complete privacy: the *perltoot*(1) manpage describes how to bless closures to produce objects that are as private as those in C++ (and more so).

Perl's objects are not wrong; they're differently right.

See Also

The general literature on object-oriented programming rarely refers directly to Perl. The documentation that came with Perl is a good place to begin learning about object-oriented programming, particularly the object tutorial *perltoot*(1). For a reference, read *perlobj*(1) and Chapter 5 of *Programming Perl.* You might need it when you read *perlbot*(1), which is full of object-oriented tricks.

Chapters 7 and 8 of *Advanced Perl Programming* includes a discussion of object-oriented programming in Perl for those who have encountered objects before.

13.1. Constructing an Object

Problem

You want to create a way for your users to generate new objects.

Solution

Make a constructor. In Perl, the constructor method must not only initialize its object, but must also first allocate memory for it, typically using an anonymous hash. C++ constructors, on the other hand, are called with memory already allocated. The rest of the object-oriented world would call C++'s constructors *initializers.*

Here's the canonical object constructor in Perl:

```
sub new {
    my $class = shift;
    my $self  = { };
    bless($self, $class);
    return $self;
}
```

This is the equivalent one-liner:

```
sub new { bless( { }, shift ) }
```

Discussion

Any method that allocates and initializes a new object acts as a constructor. The most important thing to remember is that a reference isn't an object until **bless** has been called on it. The simplest possible constructor, although not particularly useful, is the following:

```
sub new { bless({}) }
```

Let's add some initialization:

```
sub new {
    my $self = { };   # allocate anonymous hash
    bless($self);
    # init two sample attributes/data members/fields
    $self->{START} = time();
    $self->{AGE}   = 0;
    return $self;
}
```

This constructor isn't very useful because it uses the single-argument form of **bless**, which always blesses the object into *the current package*. This means it can't be usefully inherited from; objects it constructs will always be blessed into the class that the **new** function was compiled into. In the case of inheritance, this is not necessarily the class on whose behalf the method was invoked.

To solve this, have the constructor heed its first argument. For a class method, this is the package name. Pass this class name as the second argument to **bless**:

```
sub new {
    my $classname = shift;       # What class are we constructing?
    my $self      = {};          # Allocate new memory
    bless($self, $classname);    # Mark it of the right type
    $self->{START} = time();     # init data fields
    $self->{AGE}   = 0;
    return $self;                # And give it back
}
```

Now the constructor can be correctly inherited by a derived class.

You might also want to separate the memory allocation and blessing step from the instance data initialization step. Simple classes won't need this, but it makes inheritance easier; see Recipe 13.10.

```
sub new {
    my $classname = shift;       # What class are we constructing?
    my $self      = {};          # Allocate new memory
    bless($self, $classname);    # Mark it of the right type
    $self->_init(@_);            # Call _init with remaining args
    return $self;
}

# "private" method to initialize fields.  It always sets START to
# the current time, and AGE to 0.  If called with arguments, _init
# interprets them as key+value pairs to initialize the object with.
sub _init {
    my $self = shift;
    $self->{START} = time();
    $self->{AGE}   = 0;
    if (@_) {
        my %extra = @_;
        @$self{keys %extra} = values %extra;
    }
}
```

See Also

perltoot(1) and *perlobj*(1); Chapter 5 of *Programming Perl*; Recipe 13.6; Recipe 13.9; Recipe 13.10

13.2. Destroying an Object

Problem

You want to run special code whenever an object is no longer used. This is sometimes needed when the object is an interface to the outside world—or contains circular data structures—and must clean up after itself. You might remove temporary files, break circular links, gracefully disconnect from a socket, or kill a spawned subprocess.

Solution

Create a method named DESTROY. This will be called when there are no more references to the object, or else when the program shuts down, whichever comes first. You don't need to do any memory deallocation here, just any finalization code if it makes sense for the class.

```
sub DESTROY {
    my $self = shift;
    printf("$self dying at %s\n", scalar localtime);
}
```

Discussion

Every story has a beginning and an end. The beginning of the object's story is its constructor, explicitly called when the object comes into existence. The end of its story is the *destructor*, a method implicitly called when an object leaves this life. Any per-object clean-up code is placed in the destructor, which must be named DESTROY.

Why can't destructors have arbitrary names? Because, although a constructor is explicitly called by name, a destructor is not. Destruction happens automatically via Perl's garbage collection (GC) system, which is currently implemented as a quick but lazy reference-based GC system. To know what to call, Perl insists that the destructor be named DESTROY. If more than one object goes out of scope at once, Perl doesn't promise to call the destructors in a particular order.

Why is DESTROY in all caps? Perl on occasion uses purely uppercase function names as a convention to indicate that the function will be automatically called by

Perl. Others that are called implicitly include BEGIN, END, AUTOLOAD, plus all methods used by tied objects (see Recipe 13.15), like STORE and FETCH.

The user doesn't care when the destructor is called. It just happens when it's supposed to. In languages without any form of GC, this is undependable, so the programmer must explicitly call the destructor to clean up memory and state, crossing their fingers that it's the right time to do so. This is a terrible state of affairs.

Because of Perl's automatic memory management, an object destructor is rarely needed in Perl. Even when it is, explicit invocation is not only uncalled for, it's downright dangerous. The destructor will be called by the run-time system when the object is no longer in use. Most classes don't need a destructor because Perl takes care of simple matters like memory deallocation.

The only situation where Perl's reference-based garbage collection system won't work for you is when there's a circularity in your data structure, such as:

```
$self->{WHATEVER} = $self;
```

In that case, you must delete the self-reference manually if you expect your program not to leak memory. While admittedly error-prone, this is the best we can do right now. Recipe 13.13 provides an elegant solution to this problem, however. Nonetheless, rest assured that when your program is finished, its objects' destructors are all duly called. At interpreter shutdown time, a second, more sweeping form of garbage collection is performed. Not even unreachable or circular objects can escape this final destruction. So you are guaranteed that an object *eventually* gets properly destroyed, unless a program never exits. If you're running Perl embedded in another application, the second GC pass happens more frequently — whenever an interpreter shuts down.

DESTROY does *not* get called when a program exits via an **exec** call.

See Also

perltoot(1) and *perlobj*(1); the section "A Note on Garbage Collection" in Chapter 5 of *Programming Perl*; Recipe 13.10; Recipe 13.13

13.3. Managing Instance Data

Problem

Each data attribute of an object, sometimes called data members or properties, needs its own method for access. How do you write these functions to manipulate the object's instance data?

Solution

Either write pairs of get and set methods that affect the appropriate key in the object hash, like this:

```
sub get_name {
    my $self = shift;
    return $self->{NAME};
}

sub set_name {
    my $self       = shift;
    $self->{NAME} = shift;
}
```

Or, make single methods that do both jobs depending on whether they're passed an argument:

```
sub name {
    my $self = shift;
    if (@_) { $self->{NAME} = shift }
    return $self->{NAME};
}
```

Sometimes, it's useful to return the previous value when setting a new value:

```
sub age {
    my $self = shift;
    my $prev = $self->{AGE};
    if (@_) { $self->{AGE} = shift }
    return $prev;
}
# sample call of get and set: happy birthday!
$obj->age( 1 + $obj->age );
```

Discussion

Methods are how you implement the public interface to the object. A proper class doesn't encourage anyone to poke around inside its innards. Each data attribute should have a method to update it, retrieve it, or both. If a user writes code like this:

```
$him = Person->new();
$him->{NAME} = "Sylvester";
$him->{AGE}   = 23;
```

then they have violated the interface, so deserve whatever they get.

For nominally private data elements, you may omit methods that access them.

By mandating a strictly functional interface, you are free to alter your internal representation later without fear of breaking code. The functional interface allows you to run arbitrary range checks and take care of any data reformatting or conversion.

Here's a fancy version of the **name** method that demonstrates this:

```
use Carp;
sub name {
    my $self = shift;
    return $self->{NAME} unless @_;
    local $_ = shift;
    croak "too many arguments" if @_;
    if ($^W) {
        /[^\s\w'-]/          && carp "funny characters in name";
        /\d/                 && carp "numbers in name";
        /\S+(\s+\S+)+/       || carp "prefer multiword name";
        /\S/                 || carp "name is blank";
    }
    s/(\w+)/\u\L$1/g;        # enforce capitalization
    $self->{NAME} = $_;
}
```

If users, even other classes through inheritance, had been accessing the "NAME" field directly, you couldn't add this kind of code later. By insisting on only indirect, functional access to all data attributes, you keep your options open.

If you're used to C++ objects, then you're accustomed to being able to get at an object's data members as simple variables from within a method. The Alias module from CPAN provides for this, as well as a good bit more, such as the possibility of private methods that the object can call but folks outside the class cannot.

Here's an example of creating a Person using the Alias module. When you update these magical instance variables, you automatically update value fields in the hash. Convenient, eh?

```
package Person;

# this is the same as before...
sub new {
    my $that  = shift;
    my $class = ref($that) || $that;
    my $self = {
        NAME  => undef,
        AGE   => undef,
        PEERS => [],
    };
    bless($self, $class);
    return $self;
}

use Alias qw(attr);
use vars qw($NAME $AGE @PEERS);

sub name {
    my $self = attr shift;
    if (@_) { $NAME = shift; }
    return     $NAME;
};
```

```perl
sub age {
    my $self = attr shift;
    if (@_) { $AGE = shift; }
    return     $AGE;
}

sub peers {
    my $self = attr shift;
    if (@_) { @PEERS = @_; }
    return     @PEERS;
}

sub exclaim {
    my $self = attr shift;
    return sprintf "Hi, I'm %s, age %d, working with %s",
        $NAME, $AGE, join(", ", @PEERS);
}

sub happy_birthday {
    my $self = attr shift;
    return ++$AGE;
}
```

You need **use vars** because Alias plays with package globals by the same names as the fields. To use globals while **use strict** is in effect, you have to predeclare them. These variables are localized to the block enclosing the `attr()` call, just as though `local` were used on them. That means that they're still considered global package variables with temporary values.

See Also

perltoot(1), *perlobj*(1), and *perlbot*(1); Chapter 5 of *Programming Perl*; the documentation for the Alias module from CPAN; Recipe 13.11; Recipe 13.12

13.4. Managing Class Data

Problem

You need a method to be called on behalf of the whole class, not just on one object. This might be a procedural request, or it might be a global data attribute shared by all instances of the class.

Solution

Instead of expecting a reference as their first argument as object methods do, class methods expect a string containing name of the class. Class methods access package data, not object data, as in the **population** method shown here:

```
package Person;

$Body_Count = 0;

sub population { return $Body_Count }

sub new {                                    # constructor
    $Body_Count++;
    return bless({}, shift);
}

sub DESTROY { --$BodyCount }                  # destructor

# later, the user can say this:
package main;

for (1..10) { push @people, Person->new }
printf "There are %d people alive.\n", Person->population();
```

There are 10 people alive.

Discussion

Normally, each object has its own complete state stored within itself. The value of a data attribute in one object is unrelated to the value that attribute might have in another instance of the same class. For example, setting *her* gender here does nothing to *his* gender, because they are different objects with distinct states:

```
$him = Person->new();
$him->gender("male");

$her = Person->new();
$her->gender("female");
```

Imagine a classwide attribute where changing the attribute for one instance changes it for all of them. Just as some programmers prefer capitalized global variables, some prefer uppercase names when the method affects class data instead of instance data. Here's an example of using a class method called **Max_Bounds**:

```
FixedArray->Max_Bounds(100);                 # set for whole class
$alpha = FixedArray->new();
printf "Bound on alpha is %d\n", $alpha->Max_Bounds();
100
$beta = FixedArray->new();
$beta->Max_Bounds(50);                       # still sets for whole class
printf "Bound on alpha is %d\n", $alpha->Max_Bounds();
50
```

The implementation is simple:

```
package FixedArray;
$Bounds = 7;  # default
sub new { bless( {}, shift ) }
sub Max_Bounds {
    my $proto  = shift;
    $Bounds    = shift if @_;              # allow updates
    return $Bounds;
}
```

To make the value effectively read only, simply remove the update possibility, as in:

```
sub Max_Bounds { $Bounds }
```

If you're deeply paranoid, make $Bounds a lexical variable private to the scope of the file containing the class. Then no one could say $FixedArray::Bounds to discover its values. They'd be forced to go through the method interface instead.

Here's a tip to help build scalable classes: store object data on the object's name-space (in the hash), and store class data in the class namespace (package variables or file-scoped lexicals). Only class methods should directly access classwide attributes. Object methods should only access instance data. If the object method needs access to class data, its constructor should store a reference to that data in the object. Here's an example:

```
sub new {
    my $class = shift;
    my $self = bless({}, $class);
    $self->{Max_Bounds_ref} = \$Bounds;
    return $self;
}
```

See Also

perltoot(1), *perlobj*(1), and *perlbot*(1); the section on "Class Context and the Object" in Chapter 5 of *Programming Perl*; Recipe 13.3; the `places` method in the "Example: Overloaded FixNum Class" example in Recipe 13.14

13.5. Using Classes as Structs

Problem

You're used to structured data types more complex than Perl's arrays and hashes, such as C's structs and Pascal's records. You've heard that Perl's classes are comparable, but you aren't an object-oriented programmer.

Solution

Use the standard Class::Struct module to declare C-like structures:

```
use Class::Struct;         # load struct-building module

struct Person => {         # create a definition for a "Person"
    name    => '$',        #    name field is a scalar
    age     => '$',        #    age field is also a scalar
    peers   => '@',        #    but peers field is an array (reference)
};

my $p = Person->new();     # allocate an empty Person struct

$p->name("Jason Smythe");                      # set its name field
$p->age(13);                                   # set its age field
$p->peers( ["Wilbur", "Ralph", "Fred" ] );    # set its peers field

# or this way:
@{$p->peers} = ("Wilbur", "Ralph", "Fred");

# fetch various values, including the zeroth friend
printf "At age %d, %s's first friend is %s.\n",
    $p->age, $p->name, $p->peers(0);
```

Discussion

The `Class::Struct::struct` function builds struct-like classes on the fly. It creates a class of the name given in the first argument, and gives the class a constructor named **new** and per-field accessor methods.

In the structure layout definition, the keys are the names of the fields and the values are the data type. This type can be one of the three base types, '$' for scalars, '@' for arrays, and '%' for hashes. Each accessor method can be called without arguments to fetch the current value, or with an argument to set the value. In the case of a field whose type is an array or hash, a zero-argument method call returns a reference to the entire array or hash, a one-argument call retrieves the value at that subscript,* and a two-argument call sets the value at that subscript.

The type can even be the name of another named structure—or any class, for that matter—which provides a constructor named **new**.

```
use Class::Struct;

struct Person => {name => '$',      age  => '$'};
struct Family => {head => 'Person', address => '$', members => '@'};

$folks  = Family->new();
```

---

* Unless it's a reference, in which case it uses that as the new aggregate, with type checking.

```
$dad    = $folks->head;
$dad->name("John");
$dad->age(34);

printf("%s's age is %d\n", $folks->head->name, $folks->head->age);
```

If you'd like to impose more parameter checking on the fields' values, supply your own version for the accessor method to override the default version. Let's say you wanted to make sure the age value contains only digits, and that it falls within reasonably human age requirements. Here's how that function might be coded:

```
sub Person::age {
    use Carp;
    my ($self, $age) = @_;
    if    (@_ > 2) {  confess "too many arguments" }
    elsif (@_ == 1) {  return $struct->{'age'}       }
    elsif (@_ == 2) {
        carp "age '$age' isn't numeric"    if $age !~ /^\d+/;
        carp "age '$age' is unreasonable" if $age > 150;
        $self->{'age'} = $age;
    }
}
```

If you want to provide warnings only when the **-w** command-line flag is used, check the $^W variable:

```
if ($^W) {
    carp "age '$age' isn't numeric"    if $age !~ /^\d+/;
    carp "age '$age' is unreasonable" if $age > 150;
}
```

If you want to complain if **-w** is set, but to raise an exception if the user doesn't ask for warnings, do something like the following. Don't be confused by the pointer arrow; it's an indirect function call, not a method call.

```
my $gripe = $^W ? \&carp : \&croak;
$gripe->("age '$age' isn't numeric")    if $age !~ /^\d+/;
$gripe->("age '$age' is unreasonable") if $age > 150;
```

Internally, the class is implemented using a hash, as most classes are. This makes your code easy to debug and manipulate. Consider the effect of printing out a structure in the debugger, for example. But the Class::Struct module also supports an array representation. Just specify the fields within square brackets instead of curly ones:

```
struct Family => [head => 'Person', address => '$', members => '@'];
```

Empirical evidence suggests that selecting the array representation instead of a hash trims between 10% and 50% off the memory consumption of your objects, and up to 33% of the access time. The cost is less informative debugging information and more mental overhead when writing override functions, such as **Person::age** above. Choosing an array representation for the object would make it difficult to use inheritance. That's not an issue here, because C-style structures employ the much more easily understood notion of aggregation instead.

The use fields pragma in the 5.005 release of Perl provides the speed and space of arrays with the expressiveness of hashes, and adds compile-time checking of an object's field names.

If all the fields are the same type, rather than writing it out this way:

```
struct Card => {
    name    => '$',
    color   => '$',
    cost    => '$',
    type    => '$',
    release => '$',
    text    => '$',
};
```

you could use a map to shorten it:

```
struct Card => { map { $_ => '$' } qw(name color cost type release text) };
```

Or, if you're a C programmer who prefers to precede the field name with its type, rather than vice-versa, just reverse the order:

```
struct hostent => { reverse qw{
    $ name
    @ aliases
    $ addrtype
    $ length
    @ addr_list
}};
```

You can even make aliases, in the (dubious) spirit of #define, that allow the same field to be accessed under multiple aliases. In C you can say:

```
#define h_type h_addrtype
#define h_addr h_addr_list[0]
```

In Perl, you might try this:

```
# make (hostent object)->type() same as (hostent object)->addrtype()
*hostent::type = \&hostent::addrtype;

# make (hostenv object)->addr() same as (hostenv object)->addr_list(0)
sub hostent::addr { shift->addr_list(0,@_) }
```

As you see, you can add methods to a class—or functions to a package—simply by declaring a subroutine in the right namespace. You don't have to be in the file defining the class, subclass it, or do anything fancy and complicated. It would be much better to subclass it, however:

```
package Extra::hostent;
use Net::hostent;
@ISA = qw(hostent);
```

```
sub addr { shift->addr_list(0,@_) }
1;
```

That one's already available in the standard Net::hostent class, so you needn't bother. Check out that module's source code as a form of inspirational reading. We can't be held responsible for what it inspires you to do, though.

See Also

perltoot(1), *perlobj*(1), and *perlbot*(1); the documentation for the standard Class::Struct module; the source code for the standard Net::hostent module; the documentation for the Alias module from CPAN; Recipe 13.3

13.6. Cloning Objects

Problem

You want to write a constructor method that might be called on an existing object.

Solution

Start your constructor like this:

```
my $proto  = shift;
my $class  = ref($proto) || $proto;
my $parent = ref($proto) && $proto;
```

The $class variable will contain the class to bless into, and the $parent variable will either be false, or else the object you're cloning.

Discussion

Sometimes you need another object of the same type as the current one. You could do this:

```
$ob1 = SomeClass->new();
# later on
$ob2 = (ref $ob1)->new();
```

but that's not very clear. It's clearer to have a single constructor that can be called on the class or an existing object. As a class method, it should return a new object with the default initialization. As an instance method, it should return a new object initialized from the object it was called on:

```
$ob1 = Widget->new();
$ob2 = $ob1->new();
```

Here's a version of **new** that takes this into consideration:

```
sub new {
    my $proto  = shift;
    my $class  = ref($proto) || $proto;
    my $parent = ref($proto) && $proto;

    my $self;
    # check whether we're shadowing a new from @ISA
    if (@ISA && $proto->SUPER::can('new') ) {
        $self = $proto->SUPER::new(@_);
    } else {
        $self = {};
        bless ($self, $proto);
    }
    bless($self, $class);

    $self->{PARENT}  = $parent;
    $self->{START}   = time();    # init data fields
    $self->{AGE}     = 0;
    return $self;
}
```

Initializing doesn't have to mean simply copying values from the parent. If you're writing a linked list or binary tree class, your constructor can return a new object linked into the list or tree, when called as an instance method.

See Also

perlobj(1) and Chapter 5 of *Programming Perl*; Recipe 13.1; Recipe 13.9; Recipe 13.13

13.7. *Calling Methods Indirectly*

Problem

You want to call a method by a name that isn't known until run time.

Solution

Store the method name as a string in a scalar variable and use it where you would use the real method name to the right of the arrow operator:

```
$methname = "flicker";
$obj->$methname(10);          # calls $ob->flicker(10);

# call three methods on the object, by name
foreach $m ( qw(start run stop) ) {
    $obj->$m();
}
```

Discussion

Sometimes you need to call a method whose name you've stored somewhere. You can't take the address of a method, but you can store its name. If you have a scalar variable $meth containing the method name, call the method on an object $crystal with $crystal->$meth().

```
@methods = qw(name rank serno);
%his_info = map { $_ => $ob->$_() } @methods;

# same as this:

%his_info = (
    'name'  => $ob->name(),
    'rank'  => $ob->rank(),
    'serno' => $ob->serno(),
);
```

If you're desperate to devise a way to get a method's address, you should try to rethink your algorithm. For example, instead of incorrectly taking \$ob-> method(), which simply applies the backslash to that method's return value or values, do this:

```
my $fnref = sub { $ob->method(@_) };
```

Now when it's time to call that indirectly, you would use:

```
$fnref->(10, "fred");
```

and have it correctly really call:

```
$obj->method(10, "fred");
```

This works even if $ob has gone out of scope. This solution is much cleaner.

The code reference returned by the UNIVERSAL can() method should probably not be used as an indirect method call. That's because you have no reason to believe that this will be a valid method when applied to an object of an arbitrary class.

For example, this is highly dubious code:

```
$obj->can('method_name')->($obj_target, @arguments)
    if $obj_target->isa( ref $obj );
```

The problem is that the code ref returned by can might not be a valid method to be called on $obj_target. It's probably safest to only test the can() method in a boolean expression.

See Also

perlobj(1); Recipe 11.8

13.8. Determining Subclass Membership

Problem

You want to know whether an object is an instance of a particular class or that class's subclasses. Perhaps you want to decide whether a particular method can be called on an arbitrary object.

Solution

Use methods from the special UNIVERSAL class:

```
$obj->isa("HTTP::Message");              # as object method
HTTP::Response->isa("HTTP::Message");    # as class method

if ($obj->can("method_name")) { .... }   # check method validity
```

Discussion

Wouldn't it be convenient if all objects were rooted at some ultimate base class? That way you could give every object common methods without having to add to each @ISA. Well, you can. You don't see it, but Perl pretends there's an extra element at the end of @ISA—the package named UNIVERSAL.

In version 5.003, no methods were predefined in UNIVERSAL, but you could put whatever you felt like into it. However, as of version 5.004, UNIVERSAL has a few methods in it already. These are built right into your Perl binary, so they don't take extra time to load. Predefined methods include isa, can, and VERSION. The isa method tells you whether an object or class "is" another one, without having to traverse the hierarchy yourself:

```
$has_io = $fd->isa("IO::Handle");
$itza_handle = IO::Socket->isa("IO::Handle");
```

Arguably, it's usually best to try the method call. Explicit type checks like this are sometimes frowned upon as being too constraining.

The can method, called on behalf of that object or class, reports back whether its string argument is a callable method name in that class. In fact, it gives you back a function reference to that method:

```
$his_print_method = $obj->can('as_string');
```

Finally, the VERSION method checks whether the class (or the object's class) has a package global called $VERSION that's high enough, as in:

```
Some_Module->VERSION(3.0);
$his_vers = $obj->VERSION();
```

However, we don't usually call VERSION ourselves. Remember, in Perl an all-uppercase function name means that the function will be automatically called by Perl in some way. In this case, it happens when you say:

```
use Some_Module 3.0;
```

If you wanted to add version checking to your Person class explained above, add this to Person.pm:

```
use vars qw($VERSION);
$VERSION = '1.01';
```

Then, in the user code say use Person 1.01; to make sure that you have at least that version number or higher available. This is not the same as loading in that exact version number; it just has to be at least that high. Lamentably, no support currently exists for concurrent installation of multiple versions of a module.

See Also

The documentation for the standard UNIVERSAL module; the use keyword in *perlfunc*(1) and in Chapter 3 of *Programming Perl*

13.9. *Writing an Inheritable Class*

Problem

You're not sure whether you've designed your class robustly enough to be inherited.

Solution

Use the "empty subclass test" on your class.

Discussion

Imagine you've implemented a class called Person that supplies a constructor called new, and methods like age and name. Here's the straightforward implementation:

```
package Person;
sub new {
    my $class = shift;
    my $self  = { };
    return bless $self, $class;
}
sub name {
    my $self = shift;
    $self->{NAME} = shift if @_;
```

```
        return $self->{NAME};
    }
    sub age {
        my $self = shift;
        $self->{AGE} = shift if @_;
        return $self->{AGE};
    }
```

You might use the class in this way:

```
    use Person;
    my $dude = Person->new();
    $dude->name("Jason");
    $dude->age(23);
    printf "%s is age %d.\n", $dude->name, $dude->age;
```

Now, consider another class, the one called Employee:

```
    package Employee;
    use Person;
    @ISA = ("Person");
    1;
```

There's not a lot to that one. All it's doing is loading in class Person and stating that Employee will inherit any needed methods from Person. Since Employee has no methods of its own, it will get all of its methods from Person. We rely upon an Employee to behave just like a Person.

Setting up an empty class like this is called the *empty base class test*; that is, it creates a derived class that does nothing but inherit from a base class. If the original base class has been designed properly, then the new derived class can be used as a drop-in replacement for the old one. This means you should be able to change just the class name and everything will still work:

```
    use Employee;
    my $empl = Employee->new();
    $empl->name("Jason");
    $empl->age(23);
    printf "%s is age %d.\n", $empl->name, $empl->age;
```

By proper design, we mean using only the two-argument form of bless, avoiding any direct access of class data, and exporting nothing. In the Person::new() function defined above, we were careful to do these things. We use some package data in the constructor, but the reference to this is stored on the object itself. Other methods access package data via that reference, so we should be okay.

Why did we say the Person::new *function*—is that not actually a method? A method is just a function that expects as its first argument a class name (package) or object (blessed reference). Person::new is the function that the Person->new method and the Employee->new method both end up calling. Although a method call looks a lot like a function call, they aren't the same. If you treat them as the same, very soon you'll be left with nothing but broken programs. First, the actual underlying calling conventions are different: method calls get an extra argument. Second, function calls don't do inheritance, but methods do.

Method Call	Resulting Function Call
Person->new()	Person::new("Person")
Employee->new()	Person::new("Employee")

If you got in the habit of calling:

```
$him = Person::new();                    # WRONG
```

you'd have a subtle problem, because the function wouldn't get an argument of "Person" as it is expecting, and so it couldn't bless into the passed-in class. Still worse, you'd probably want to try to call **Employee::new()** also. But there is no such function! It's just an inherited method call.

So, don't use function calls when you mean to call a method.

See Also

perltoot(1), *perlobj*(1), and *perlbot*(1); Chapter 5 of *Programming Perl*; Recipe 13.1; Recipe 13.10

13.10. Accessing Overridden Methods

Problem

Your constructor method overrides the constructor of a parent class. You want your constructor to call the parent class's constructor.

Solution

Learn about the special class, SUPER.

```
sub meth {
    my $self = shift;
    $self->SUPER::meth();
}
```

Discussion

In languages like C++ where constructors don't actually allocate memory but just initialize the object, all base class constructors are automatically called for you. In languages like Java and Perl, you have to call them yourself.

To call a method in a particular class, the notation `$self->SUPER::meth()` is used. This is an extension of the regular notation to start looking in a particular base class. It is only valid from within an overridden method. Here's a comparison of styles:

```
$self->meth();              # Call wherever first meth is found
$self->Where::meth();       # Start looking in package "Where"
$self->SUPER::meth();       # Call overridden version
```

Simple users of the class should probably limit themselves to the first one. The second is possible, but not suggested. The last must only be called from within the overridden method.

An overriding constructor should call its SUPER's constructor to allocate and bless the object, limiting itself to instantiating any data fields needed. It makes sense here to separate the object allocation code from the object initialization code. We'll name it with a leading underscore, a convention indicating a nominally private method. Think of it as a "Do Not Disturb" sign.

```
sub new {
    my $classname  = shift;         # What class are we constructing?
    my $self        = $classname->SUPER::new(@_);
    $self->_init(@_);
    return $self;                    # And give it back
}

sub _init {
    my $self = shift;
    $self->{START}   = time();    # init data fields
    $self->{AGE}     = 0;
    $self->{EXTRA}   = { @_ };     # anything extra
}
```

Both `SUPER::new` and `_init` have been called with any remaining arguments. That way the user might pass other field initializers in, as in:

```
$obj = Widget->new( haircolor => red, freckles => 121 );
```

Whether you store these user parameters in their own extra hash or not is up to you.

Note that SUPER only works on the first overridden method. If your `@ISA` array has several classes, it only gets the first one. A manual traversal of `@ISA` is possible, but probably not worth the hassle.

```
my $self = bless {}, $class;
for my $class (@ISA) {
    my $meth = $class . "::_init";
    $self->$meth(@_) if $class->can("_init");
}
```

This fragile code assumes that all superclasses initialize their objects with _init instead of initializing in the constructor. It also assumes that a hash reference is used for the underlying object.

See Also

The discussion on the SUPER class in *perltoot*(1) and *perlobj*(1), and in the section on "Method Invocation" in Chapter 5 of *Programming Perl*

13.11. Generating Attribute Methods Using AUTOLOAD

Problem

Your object needs accessor methods to set or get its data fields, and you're tired of writing them all out one at a time.

Solution

Carefully use Perl's AUTOLOAD mechanism as a proxy method generator so you don't have to create them all yourself each time you want to add a new data field.

Discussion

Perl's AUTOLOAD mechanism intercepts all possible undefined method calls. So as not to permit arbitrary data names, we'll store the list of permitted fields in a hash. The AUTOLOAD method will check to verify that the accessed field is in that hash.

```
package Person;
use strict;
use Carp;
use vars qw($AUTOLOAD %ok_field);

# Authorize four attribute fields
for my $attr ( qw(name age peers parent) ) { $ok_field{$attr}++; }

sub AUTOLOAD {
    my $self = shift;
    my $attr = $AUTOLOAD;
    $attr =~ s/.*:://;
    return unless $attr =~ /[^A-Z]/;  # skip DESTROY and all-cap methods
    croak "invalid attribute method: ->$attr()" unless $ok_field{$attr};
    $self->{uc $attr} = shift if @_;
    return $self->{uc $attr};
}
```

```
sub new {
    my $proto  = shift;
    my $class  = ref($proto) || $proto;
    my $parent = ref($proto) && $proto;
    my $self = {};
    bless($self, $class);
    $self->parent($parent);
    return $self;
}
1;
```

This class supports a constructor named new, and four attribute methods: name, age, peers, and parent. Use the module this way:

```
use Person;
my ($dad, $kid);
$dad = Person->new;
$dad->name("Jason");
$dad->age(23);
$kid = $dad->new;
$kid->name("Rachel");
$kid->age(2);
printf "Kid's parent is %s\n", $kid->parent->name;
Kid's parent is Jason
```

This is tricky when producing inheritance trees. Suppose you'd like an Employee class that had every data attribute of the Person class, plus two new ones, like salary and boss. Class Employee can't rely upon an inherited Person::AUTOLOAD to determine what Employee's attribute methods are. So each class would need its own AUTOLOAD function. This would check just that class's known attribute fields, but instead of croaking when incorrectly triggered, it would call its overridden superclass version.

Here's a version that takes this into consideration:

```
sub AUTOLOAD {
    my $self = shift;
    my $attr = $AUTOLOAD;
    $attr =~ s/.*:://;
    return if $attr eq 'DESTROY';

    if ($ok_field{$attr}) {
        $self->{uc $attr} = shift if @_;
        return $self->{uc $attr};
    } else {
        my $superior = "SUPER::$attr";
        $self->$superior(@_);
    }
}
```

If the attribute isn't in our OK list, we'll pass it up to our superior, hoping that it can cope with it. But you can't inherit this AUTOLOAD; each class has to have its own, because it is unwisely accessing class data directly, not through the object.

Even worse, if a class A inherits from two classes B and C, both of which define their own AUTOLOAD, an undefined method call on A will hit the AUTOLOAD in only one of the two parent classes.

We could try to cope with these limitations, but AUTOLOAD eventually begins to feel like a kludge piled on a hack piled on a workaround. There are better approaches for the more complex situations.

See Also

The examples using AUTOLOAD in *perltoot*(1); Chapter 5 of *Programming Perl*; Recipe 10.15; Recipe 13.12

13.12. Solving the Data Inheritance Problem

Problem

You want to inherit from an existing class, augmenting it with a few extra methods, but you don't know which data fields your parent class is using. How can you safely carve out your own namespace in the object hash without trampling on any ancestors?

Solution

Prepend each of your fieldnames with your own class name and a distinctive separator, such as an underscore or two.

Discussion

An irksome problem lurks within the normal Perl OO strategy. The exact class representation must be known, violating the veil of abstraction. The subclass has to get unnaturally chummy with all its parent classes, recursively.

We'll pretend we're a big happy object-oriented family and that everyone always uses hashes for objects, thus dodging the problem of a class choosing an array representation but inheriting from one that instead uses a hash model. (The solution to that problem is aggregation and delegation, as shown in *perlbot*(1).) Even with this assumption, an inherited class can't safely use a key in the hash. Even if we agree to use only method calls to access attributes we don't ourselves set, how do we know that we aren't setting a key that a parent class is using? Imagine wanting to use a count field, but unbeknownst to you, your great-great-grandparent class is using the same thing. Using _count to indicate nominal privacy won't help, since gramps might try the same trick.

One reasonable approach is to prefix your own data members with your package name. Thus if you were class Employee and wanted an **age** field, for safety's sake you could use **Employee_age** instead. Here's a sample access method:

```
sub Employee::age {
    my $self = shift;
    $self->{Employee_age} = shift if @_;
    return $self->{Employee_age};
}
```

In the spirit of the Class::Struct module described in Recipe 13.5, here's a more turnkey solution to the problem. Imagine one file with:

```
package Person;
use Class::Attributes;   # see explanation below
mkattr qw(name age peers parent);
```

and another like this:

```
package Employee;
@ISA = qw(Person);
use Class::Attributes;
mkattr qw(salary age boss);
```

Notice that they both have an **age** attribute? If those are to be logically separate, we can't use **$self->{age}**, even for ourselves inside the module! Here's an implementation of the **Class::Attributes::mkattr** function that solves this:

```
package Class::Attributes;
use strict;
use Carp;
use Exporter ();
use vars qw(@ISA @EXPORT);
@ISA = qw(Exporter);
@EXPORT = qw(mkattr);
sub mkattr {
    my $hispack = caller();
    for my $attr (@_) {
        my($field, $method);
        $method = "${hispack}::$attr";
        ($field = $method) =~ s/:/_/g;
        no strict 'refs'; # here comes the kluglich bit
        *$method = sub {
            my $self = shift;
            confess "too many arguments" if @_ > 1;
            $self->{$field} = shift if @_;
            return $self->{$field};
        };
    }
}
1;
```

This way **$self->{Person_age}** and **$self->{Employee_age}** remain separate. The only funniness is that **$obj->age** would only get the first one. Now, you could write `$obj->Person::age` and `$obj->Employee::age` to distinguish these, but well-written Perl code shouldn't use double colons to specify an exact package except under extreme duress. If you really are forced to, perhaps that library could have been better designed.

If you didn't want to write it that way, then from inside class Person, just use `age($self)` and you'll always get Person's version, whereas from inside class Employee, `age($self)` would get Employee's version. That's because it's a function call, not a method call.

See Also

The documentation on the `use fields` and `use base` pragmas, standard as of Perl 5.005; Recipe 10.14

13.13. Coping with Circular Data Structures

Problem

You have an inherently self-referential data structure so Perl's reference-based garbage collection system won't notice when it's no longer being used. You want to prevent your program from leaking memory.

Solution

Create a non-circular container object that holds a pointer to the self-referential data structure. Define a `DESTROY` method for the containing object's class that manually breaks the self-referential circularities.

Discussion

Many interesting data structures include references back to themselves. This can occur in code as simple as this:

```
$node->{NEXT} = $node;
```

As soon as you do that, you've created a circularity that will hide the data structure from Perl's referenced-based garbage collection system. Destructors will eventually be called when your program exits, but you sometimes don't want to wait that long.

A circular linked list is similarly self-referential. Each node contains a front pointer, a back pointer, and the node's value. If you implement it with references in Perl, you get a circular set of references and the data structure won't naturally be garbage collected when there are no external references to its nodes.

Making each node an instance of class Ring doesn't solve the problem. What you want is for Perl to clean up this structure as it would any other structure—which it will do if you implement your object as a structure that contains a reference to the real circle. That reference will be stored in the "DUMMY" field:

```
package Ring;

# return an empty ring structure
sub new {
    my $class = shift;
    my $node  = { };
    $node->{NEXT} = $node->{PREV} = $node;
    my $self  = { DUMMY => $node, COUNT => 0 };
    bless $self, $class;
    return $self;
}
```

It's the nodes contained in the ring that are circular, not the returned ring object itself. That means code like the following won't cause a memory leak:

```
use Ring;

$COUNT = 1000;
for (1 .. 20) {
    my $r = Ring->new();
    for ($i = 0; $i < $COUNT; $i++) { $r->insert($i) }
}
```

Even though we create twenty rings of a thousand nodes each, each ring is thrown away before a new one is created. The user of the class need do no more to free the ring's memory than they would to free a string's memory. That is, this all happens automatically, just as it's supposed to.

However, the implementer of the class does have to have a destructor for the ring, one that will manually delete the nodes:

```
# when a Ring is destroyed, destroy the ring structure it contains
sub DESTROY {
    my $ring = shift;
    my $node;
    for ( $node  = $ring->{DUMMY}->{NEXT};
          $node != $ring->{DUMMY};
          $node  = $node->{NEXT} )
    {
            $ring->delete_node($node);
    }
    $node->{PREV} = $node->{NEXT} = undef;
}

# delete a node from the ring structure
sub delete_node {
    my ($ring, $node) = @_;
    $node->{PREV}->{NEXT} = $node->{NEXT};
```

```
        $node->{NEXT}->{PREV} = $node->{PREV};
        --$ring->{COUNT};
    }
```

Here are a few other methods you might like in your ring class. Notice how the real work lies within the circularity hidden inside the object:

```
# $node = $ring->search( $value ) : find $value in the ring
# structure in $node
sub search {
    my ($ring, $value) = @_;
    my $node = $ring->{DUMMY}->{NEXT};
    while ($node != $ring->{DUMMY} && $node->{VALUE} != $value) {
        $node = $node->{NEXT};
    }
    return $node;
}


# $ring->insert( $value ) : insert $value into the ring structure
sub insert_value {
    my ($ring, $value) = @_;
    my $node = { VALUE => $value };
    $node->{NEXT} = $ring->{DUMMY}->{NEXT};
    $ring->{DUMMY}->{NEXT}->{PREV} = $node;
    $ring->{DUMMY}->{NEXT} = $node;
    $node->{PREV} = $ring->{DUMMY};
    ++$ring->{COUNT};
}

# $ring->delete_value( $value ) : delete a node from the ring
# structure by value
sub delete_value {
    my ($ring, $value) = @_;
    my $node = $ring->search($value);
    return if $node == $ring->{DUMMY};
    $ring->delete_node($node);
}

1;
```

Here's one for your *fortune* file: Perl's garbage collector abhors a naked circularity.

See Also

The algorithms in this recipe derive in part from pages 206-207 of the wonderful textbook, *Introduction to Algorithms*, by Cormen, Leiserson, and Rivest (MIT Press/McGraw-Hill, 1990); see also the section on "Garbage Collection" in Chapter 5 of *Programming Perl* and in *perlobj*(1)

13.14. *Overloading Operators*

Problem

You want to use familiar operators like `==` or `+` on objects from a class you've written, or you want to define the print interpolation value for objects.

Solution

Use the `use overload` pragma. Here are two of the most common and useful operators to overload:

```
use overload ('<=>' => \&threeway_compare);
sub threeway_compare {
    my ($s1, $s2) = @_;
    uc($s1->{NAME}) cmp uc($s2->{NAME});
}

use overload ( '""' => \&stringify );
sub stringify {
    my $self = shift;
    return sprintf "%s (%05d)",
            ucfirst(lc($self->{NAME})),
            $self->{IDNUM};
}
```

Discussion

When you use built-in types, certain operators apply, like `+` for addition or `.` for string catenation. With the `use overload` pragma, you can customize these operators so they do something special on your own objects.

This pragma takes a list of operator/function call pairs, such as:

```
package TimeNumber;
use overload '+' => \&my_plus,
             '-' => \&my_minus,
             '*' => \&my_star,
             '/' => \&my_slash;
```

Now, those four operators can be used with objects of class TimeNumber, and the listed functions will be called. These functions can do anything you'd like.

Here's a simple example of an overload of `+` for use with an object that holds hours, minutes, and seconds. It assumes that both operands are of a class that has a **new** method that can be called as an object method, and that the structure names are as shown:

```
sub my_plus {
    my($left, $right) = @_;
```

```
my $answer = $left->new();
$answer->{SECONDS} = $left->{SECONDS} + $right->{SECONDS};
$answer->{MINUTES} = $left->{MINUTES} + $right->{MINUTES};
$answer->{HOURS}   = $left->{HOURS}   + $right->{HOURS};

if ($answer->{SECONDS} >= 60) {
    $answer->{SECONDS} %= 60;
    $answer->{MINUTES} ++;
}

if ($answer->{MINUTES} >= 60) {
    $answer->{MINUTES} %= 60;
    $answer->{HOURS}    ++;
}

return $answer;

}
```

It's a good idea to overload numeric operators only when the objects themselves are mirroring some sort of numeric construct, such as complex or infinite precision numbers, vectors, or matrices. Otherwise the code is too hard to understand, leading users to invalid assumptions. Imagine a class that modelled a country. If you can add one country to another, couldn't you subtract one country from another? As you see, using operator overloading for non-mathematical things rapidly becomes ridiculous.

You may compare objects (and, in fact, any reference) using either == or eq, but this only tells you whether the addresses are the same. (Using == is about ten times faster than eq though.) Because an object is a higher-level notion than a raw machine address, you often want to define your own notion of what it takes for two of them to be equal to each other.

Two operators frequently overloaded even for a non-numeric class are the comparison and string interpolation operators. Both the <=> and the cmp operators can be overloaded, although the former is more prevalent. Once the spaceship operator <=>, is defined for an object, you can also use ==, !=, <, <=, >, and >= as well. This lets objects be compared. If ordering is not desired, only overload ==. Similarly, an overloaded cmp is used for lt, gt, and other string comparisons if they aren't explicitly overloaded.

The string interpolation operator goes by the unlikely name of "", that is, two double quotes. This operator is triggered whenever a conversion to a string is called for, such as within double or back quotes or when passed to the print function.

Read the documentation on the overload pragma that comes with Perl. Perl's operator overloading has some elaborate features, such as string and numeric conversion methods, autogenerating missing methods, and reversing operands if needed, as in 5 + $a where $a is an object.

Example: Overloaded StrNum Class

Here's a StrNum class that lets you use strings with numeric operators. Yes, we're about to do something we advised against—that is, use numeric operators on non-numeric entities—but programmers from other backgrounds are always expecting + and == to work on strings. This is a simple way to demonstrate operator overloading. We almost certainly wouldn't use this in a time-critical production program due to performance concerns. It's also an interesting illustration of using a constructor of the same name as the class, something that C++ and Python programmers may take comfort in.

```perl
#!/usr/bin/perl
# show_strnum - demo operator overloading
use StrNum;

$x = StrNum("Red"); $y = StrNum("Black");
$z = $x + $y; $r = $z * 3;
print "values are $x, $y, $z, and $r\n";
print "$x is ", $x < $y ? "LT" : "GE", " $y\n";
```

values are Red, Black, RedBlack, and RedBlackRedBlackRedBlack
Red is GE Black

The class is shown in Example 13-1.

Example 13-1. StrNum

```perl
package StrNum;

use Exporter ();
@ISA = 'Exporter';
@EXPORT = qw(StrNum);   # unusual

use overload          (
        '<=>'    => \&spaceship,
        'cmp'    => \&spaceship,
        '""'     => \&stringify,
        'bool'   => \&boolify,
        '0+'     => \&numify,
        '+'      => \&concat,
        '*'      => \&repeat,
);

# constructor
sub StrNum {
    my ($value) = @_;
    return bless \$value;
}
```

Example 13-1. StrNum

```perl
sub stringify { ${ $_[0] } }
sub numify    { ${ $_[0] } }
sub boolify   { ${ $_[0] } }

# providing <=> gives us <, ==, etc. for free.
sub spaceship {
    my ($s1, $s2, $inverted) = @_;
    return $inverted ? $$s2 cmp $$s1 : $$s1 cmp $$s2;
}

# this uses stringify
sub concat {
    my ($s1, $s2, $inverted) = @_;
    return StrNum($inverted ? ($s2 . $s1) : ($s1 . $s2));

}

# this uses stringify
sub repeat {
    my ($s1, $s2, $inverted) = @_;
    return StrNum($inverted ? ($s2 x $s1) : ($s1 x $s2));
}

1;
```

Example: Overloaded FixNum Class

This class uses operator overloading to control the number of decimal places in
output. It still uses full precision for its operations. A `places()` method can be
used on the class or a particular object to set the number of places of output to
the right of the decimal point.

```perl
#!/usr/bin/perl
# demo_fixnum - show operator overloading
use FixNum;

FixNum->places(5);

$x = FixNum->new(40);
$y = FixNum->new(12);

print "sum of $x and $y is ", $x + $y, "\n";
print "product of $x and $y is ", $x * $y, "\n";

$z = $x / $y;
printf "$z has %d places\n", $z->places;
$z->places(2) unless $z->places;
print "div of $x by $y is $z\n";
print "square of that is ", $z * $z, "\n";
```

sum of STRFixNum: 40 and STRFixNum: 12 is STRFixNum: 52

```
    product of STRFixNum: 40 and STRFixNum: 12 is STRFixNum: 480
    STRFixNum: 3 has 0 places
    div of STRFixNum: 40 by STRFixNum: 12 is STRFixNum: 3.33
    square of that is STRFixNum: 11.11
```

The class itself is shown in Example 13-2. It only overloads the addition, multiplication, and division operations for math operators. Other operators are the spaceship operator, which handles all comparisons, the string-interpolation operator, and the numeric conversion operator. The string interpolation operator is given a distinctive look for debugging purposes.

Example 13-2. FixNum

```perl
package FixNum;

use strict;

my $PLACES = 0;

sub new {
    my $proto   = shift;
    my $class   = ref($proto) || $proto;
    my $parent  = ref($proto) && $proto;

    my $v = shift;
    my $self = {
        VALUE  => $v,
        PLACES => undef,
    };
    if ($parent && defined $parent->{PLACES}) {
        $self->{PLACES} = $parent->{PLACES};
    } elsif ($v =~ /(\.\d*)/) {
        $self->{PLACES} = length($1) - 1;
    } else {
        $self->{PLACES} = 0;
    }
    return bless $self, $class;
}

sub places {
    my $proto = shift;
    my $self  = ref($proto) && $proto;
    my $type  = ref($proto) || $proto;

    if (@_) {
        my $places = shift;
        ($self ? $self->{PLACES} : $PLACES) = $places;
    }
    return $self ? $self->{PLACES} : $PLACES;
}

sub _max { $_[0] > $_[1] ? $_[0] : $_[1] }
```

Example 13-2. FixNum (continued)

```perl
use overload '+'    => \&add,
             '*'    => \&multiply,
             '/'    => \&divide,
             '<=>'  => \&spaceship,
             '""'   => \&as_string,
             '0+'   => \&as_number;

sub add {
    my ($this, $that, $flipped) = @_;
    my $result = $this->new( $this->{VALUE} + $that->{VALUE} );
    $result->places( _max($this->{PLACES}, $that->{PLACES} ));
    return $result;
}

sub multiply {
    my ($this, $that, $flipped) = @_;
    my $result = $this->new( $this->{VALUE} * $that->{VALUE} );
    $result->places( _max($this->{PLACES}, $that->{PLACES} ));
    return $result;
}

sub divide {
    my ($this, $that, $flipped) = @_;
    my $result = $this->new( $this->{VALUE} / $that->{VALUE} );
    $result->places( _max($this->{PLACES}, $that->{PLACES} ));
    return $result;
}

sub as_string {
    my $self = shift;
    return sprintf("STR%s: %.*f", ref($self),
        defined($self->{PLACES}) ? $self->{PLACES} : $PLACES,
            $self->{VALUE});
}

sub as_number {
    my $self = shift;
    return $self->{VALUE};
}

sub spaceship {
    my ($this, $that, $flipped) = @_;
    $this->{VALUE} <=> $that->{VALUE};
}


1;
```

See Also

The documentation for the standard use overload pragma and the Math::BigInt and Math::Complex modules, also in Chapter 7 of *Programming Perl*

13.15. *Creating Magic Variables with tie*

Problem

You want to add special processing to a variable or handle.

Solution

Use the tie function to give your ordinary variables object hooks.

Discussion

Anyone who's ever used a DBM file under Perl has already used tied objects. Perhaps the most excellent way of using objects is such that the user never notices them. With tie, you can bind a variable or handle to a class, after which all access to the tied variable or handle is transparently intercepted by specially named object methods.

The most important tie methods are FETCH to intercept read access, STORE to intercept write access, and the constructor, which is one of TIESCALAR, TIEARRAY, TIEHASH, or TIEHANDLE.

User Code	Executed Code
tie $s, "SomeClass"	SomeClass->TIESCALAR()
$p = $s	$p = $obj->FETCH()
$s = 10	$obj->STORE(10)

Where did that $obj come from? The tie triggers a call to the class's TIESCALAR constructor method. Perl squirrels away the object returned and surreptitiously uses it for later access.

Here's a simple example of a tie class that implements a value ring. Every time the variable is read from, the next value on the ring is displayed. When it's written to, a new value is pushed on the ring. Here's an example:

```
#!/usr/bin/perl
# demo_valuering - show tie class
use ValueRing;
tie $color, 'ValueRing', qw(red blue);
print "$color $color $color $color $color $color\n";
red blue red blue red blue

$color = 'green';
print "$color $color $color $color $color $color\n";
green red blue green red blue
```

The simple implementation is shown in Example 13-3.

Example 13-3. ValueRing

```
package ValueRing;

# this is the constructor for scalar ties
sub TIESCALAR {
    my ($class, @values) = @_;
    bless  \@values, $class;
    return \@values;
}

# this intercepts read accesses
sub FETCH {
    my $self = shift;
    push(@$self, shift(@$self));
    return $self->[-1];
}

# this intercepts write accesses
sub STORE {
    my ($self, $value) = @_;
    unshift @$self, $value;
    return $value;
}

1;
```

This example might not be compelling, but it illustrates how easy it is to write ties of arbitrary complexity. To the user, $color is just a plain old variable, not an object. All the magic is hidden beneath the tie. You don't have to use a scalar reference just because you're tying a scalar. Here we've used an array reference, but you can use anything you'd like. Usually a hash reference will be used irrespective of what's being tied to because it's the most flexible object representation.

For arrays and hashes, more elaborate operations are possible. Tied handles didn't appear until the 5.004 release, and prior to 5.005 use of tied arrays was somewhat limited, but tied hashes have always been richly supported. Because so many object methods are needed to fully support tied hashes, most users choose to inherit from the standard Tie::Hash module, which provides default methods for these.

Following are numerous examples of interesting uses of ties.

Tie Example: Outlaw $_

This curious tie class is used to outlaw unlocalized uses of the implicit variable, $_. Instead of pulling it in with use, which implicitly invokes the class's import()

method, this one should be loaded with no to call the seldom-used unimport ()
method. The user says:

```
no UnderScore;
```

Then, all uses of the unlocalized global $_ will raise an exception.

Here's a little test suite for the module.

```
#!/usr/bin/perl
# nounder_demo - show how to ban $_ from your program
no UnderScore;
@tests = (
    "Assignment"   => sub { $_ = "Bad" },
    "Reading"      => sub { print },
    "Matching"     => sub { $x = /badness/ },
    "Chop"         => sub { chop },
    "Filetest"     => sub { -x },
    "Nesting"      => sub { for (1..3) { print } },
);

while ( ($name, $code) = splice(@tests, 0, 2) ) {
    print "Testing $name: ";
    eval { &$code };
    print $@ ? "detected" : "missed!";
    print "\n";
}
```

The result is the following:

```
Testing Assignment: detected
Testing Reading: detected
Testing Matching: detected
Testing Chop: detected
Testing Filetest: detected
Testing Nesting: 123missed!
```

The reason the last one was missed is that it was properly localized by the for
loop, so it was considered safe.

The UnderScore module itself is shown in Example 13-4. Notice how small it is.
The module itself does the tie in its initialization code.

Example 13-4. UnderScore

```
package UnderScore;
use Carp;
sub TIESCALAR {
    my $class = shift;
    my $dummy;
    return bless \$dummy => $class;
}
sub FETCH { croak "Read access to \$_ forbidden"  }
sub STORE { croak "Write access to \$_ forbidden" }
sub unimport { tie($_, __PACKAGE__) }
```

Example 13-4. UnderScore (continued)

```
sub import { untie $_ }
tie($_, __PACKAGE__) unless tied $_;
1;
```

You can't usefully mix calls to use and no for this class in your program, because they all happen at compile time, not run time. To renege and let yourself use $_ again, localize it.

Tie Example: Make a Hash That Always Appends

The class shown below produces a hash whose keys accumulate in an array.

```
#!/usr/bin/perl
# appendhash_demo - show magic hash that autoappends
use Tie::AppendHash;
tie %tab, 'Tie::AppendHash';

$tab{beer} = "guinness";
$tab{food} = "potatoes";
$tab{food} = "peas";

while (my($k, $v) = each %tab) {
    print "$k => [@$v]\n";
}
```

Here is the result:

```
food => [potatoes peas]
beer => [guinness]
```

To make this class easy, we will use the boilerplate hash tying module from the standard distribution, shown in Example 13-5. To do this, we load the Tie::Hash module and then inherit from the Tie::StdHash class. (Yes, those are different names. The file *Tie/Hash.pm* provides both the Tie::Hash and Tie::StdHash classes, which are slightly different.)

Example 13-5. Tie::AppendHash

```
package Tie::AppendHash;
use strict;
use Tie::Hash;
use Carp;
use vars qw(@ISA);
@ISA = qw(Tie::StdHash);
sub STORE {
    my ($self, $key, $value) = @_;
    push @{$self->{$key}}, $value;
}
1;
```

Tie Example: Case-Insensitive Hash

Here's a fancier hash tie called Tie::Folded. It provides a hash with case-insensitive keys.

```
#!/usr/bin/perl
# folded_demo - demo hash that magically folds case
use Tie::Folded;
tie %tab, 'Tie::Folded';

$tab{VILLAIN}  = "big ";
$tab{herOine}  = "red riding hood";
$tab{villain} .= "bad wolf";

while ( my($k, $v) = each %tab ) {
    print "$k is $v\n";
}
```

The following is the output of this demo program:

heroine is red riding hood
villain is big bad wolf

Because we have to trap more accesses, the class in Example 13-6 is slightly more complicated than the one in Example 13-5.

Example 13-6. Tie::Folded

```
package Tie::Folded;
use strict;
use Tie::Hash;
use vars qw(@ISA);
@ISA = qw(Tie::StdHash);
sub STORE {
    my ($self, $key, $value) = @_;
    return $self->{lc $key} = $value;
    }
sub FETCH {
    my ($self, $key) = @_;
    return $self->{lc $key};
}
sub EXISTS {
    my ($self, $key) = @_;
    return exists $self->{lc $key};
}
sub DEFINED {
    my ($self, $key) = @_;
    return defined $self->{lc $key};
}
1;
```

Tie Example: Hash That Allows Look-Ups by Key or Value

Here is a hash that lets you look up members by key or by value. It does this by having a store method that not only uses the key to store the value, it also uses the value to store the key.

Normally there could be a problem if the value being stored were a reference, since you can't normally use a reference as a key. The standard distribution comes with the Tie::RefHash class that avoids this problem. We'll inherit from it so that we can also avoid this difficulty.

```
#!/usr/bin/perl -w
# revhash_demo - show hash that permits key *or* value lookups
use strict;
use Tie::RevHash;
my %tab;
tie %tab, 'Tie::RevHash';
%tab = qw{
    Red         Rojo
    Blue        Azul
    Green       Verde
};
$tab{EVIL} = [ "No way!", "Way!!" ];

while ( my($k, $v) = each %tab ) {
    print ref($k) ? "[@$k]" : $k, " => ",
        ref($v) ? "[@$v]" : $v, "\n";
}
```

When run, *revhash_demo* produces this:

```
[No way! Way!!] => EVIL
EVIL => [No way! Way!!]
Blue => Azul
Green => Verde
Rojo => Red
Red => Rojo
Azul => Blue
Verde => Green
```

The module is shown in Example 13-7. Notice how small it is!

Example 13-7. Tie::RevHash

```
package Tie::RevHash;
use Tie::RefHash;
use vars qw(@ISA);
@ISA = qw(Tie::RefHash);
sub STORE {
    my ($self, $key, $value) = @_;
    $self->SUPER::STORE($key, $value);
    $self->SUPER::STORE($value, $key);
```

Example 13-7. Tie::RevHash

```
}

sub DELETE {
    my ($self, $key) = @_;
    my $value = $self->SUPER::FETCH($key);
    $self->SUPER::DELETE($key);
    $self->SUPER::DELETE($value);
}

1;
```

Tie Example: Handle That Counts Access

Here's an example of tying a filehandle:

```
use Counter;
tie *CH, 'Counter';
while (<CH>) {
    print "Got $_\n";
}
```

When run, that program keeps printing Got 1, Got 2, and so on until the universe collapses, you hit an interrupt, or your computer reboots, whichever comes first. Its simple implementation is shown in Example 13-8.

Example 13-8. Counter

```
package Counter;
sub TIEHANDLE {
    my $class = shift;
    my $start = shift;
    return bless \$start => $class;
}
sub READLINE {
    my $self = shift;
    return ++$$self;
}
1;
```

Tie Example: Multiple Sink Filehandles

Finally, here's an example of a tied handle that implements a *tee*-like functionality by twinning standard out and standard error:

```
use Tie::Tee;
tie *TEE, 'Tie::Tee', *STDOUT, *STDERR;
print TEE "This line goes both places.\n";
```

Or, more elaborately:

```
#!/usr/bin/perl
# demo_tietee
```

```
    use Tie::Tee;
    use Symbol;

    @handles = (*STDOUT);
    for $i ( 1 .. 10 ) {
        push(@handles, $handle = gensym());
        open($handle, ">/tmp/teetest.$i");
    }

    tie *TEE, 'Tie::Tee', @handles;
    print TEE "This lines goes many places.\n";
```

The *Tie/Tee.pm* file is shown in Example 13-9.

Example 13-9. Tie::Tee

```
package Tie::Tee;

sub TIEHANDLE {
    my $class   = shift;
    my $handles = [@_];

    bless $handles, $class;
    return $handles;
}

sub PRINT {
    my $href = shift;
    my $handle;
    my $success = 0;

    foreach $handle (@$href) {
        $success += print $handle @_;
    }

    return $success == @$href;
}

1;
```

See Also

The `tie` function in *perlfunc*(1); *perltie*(1); the section on "Using Tied Variables" in Chapter 5 of *Programming Perl*

14

Database Access

I only ask for information.
—Charles Dickens
David Copperfield

14.0. Introduction

Everywhere you find data, you find databases. At the simplest level, every file can be considered a database. At the most complex level, expensive and complex relational database systems handle thousands of transactions per second. In between are countless improvised schemes for fast access to loosely structured data. Perl can work with all of them.

Early in the history of computers, people noticed that flat file databases don't scale to large data sets. Flat files were tamed using fixed-length records or auxiliary indices, but updating became expensive, and previously simple applications bogged down with I/O overhead.

After some head-scratching, clever programmers devised a better solution. As hashes in memory provide more flexible access to data than do arrays, hashes on disk offer more convenient kinds of access than array-like text files. These benefits in access time cost you space, but disk space is cheap these days (or so the reasoning goes).

The DBM library gives Perl programmers a simple, easy-to-use database. You use the same standard operations on hashes bound to DBM files as you do on hashes in memory. In fact, that's how you use DBM databases from Perl. You call dbmopen with the name of a hash and the filename holding the database. Then whenever you access the hash, Perl consults or changes the DBM database on disk.

Recipe 14.1 shows how to create a DBM database and gives tips on using it effi-ciently. Although you can do with DBM files the same things you do with regular hashes, their disk-based nature leads to performance concerns that don't exist with in-memory hashes. Recipes 14.2 and 14.4 explain these concerns and show how to work around them. DBM files also make possible operations that aren't available using regular hashes. Recipes 14.6 and 14.7 explain two of these things.

Various DBM implementations offer varying features. The old `dbmopen` function only lets you use the DBM library Perl was built with. If you wanted to use `dbmopen` to access from one type of database and write to another, you were out of luck. Version 5 of Perl remedied this by letting you `tie` a hash to an arbitrary object class, as detailed in Chapter 13, *Classes, Objects, and Ties*.

The table below shows several possible DBM libraries you can choose from:

Feature	NDBM	SDBM	GDBM	DB
Linkage comes with Perl	yes	yes	yes	yes
Source bundled with Perl	no	yes	no	no
Source redistributable	no	yes	gpl[a]	yes
FTPable	no	yes	yes	yes
Easy to build	N/A	yes	yes	ok[b]
Often comes with Unix	yes[c]	no	no[d]	no[d]
Builds ok on Unix	N/A	yes	yes	yes[e]
Builds ok on Windows	N/A	yes	yes	yes[f]
Code size	g	small	big	big[h]
Disk usage	g	small	big	ok
Speed	g	slow	ok	fast
Block size limits	4k	1k[i]	none	none
Byte-order independent	no	no	no	yes
User-defined sort order	no	no	no	yes
Partial key lookups	no	no	no	yes

[a] Using GPLed code in your program places restrictions upon you. See *www.gnu.org* for more details.
[b] See the DB_File library method. Requires symbolic links.
[c] On mixed-universe machines, this may be in the BSD compatibility library, which is often shunned.
[d] Except for free Unix ports like Linux, FreeBSD, OpenBSD, and NetBSD.
[e] Providing you have an ANSI C compiler.
[f] Prior to unification in 5.005, several divergent versions of Perl on Windows systems were widely avail-able, including the standard port built from the normal Perl distribution and several proprietary ports. Like most CPAN modules, DB builds only on the standard port.
[g] Depends on how much your vendor has tweaked it.
[h] Can be reduced if you compile for one access method.
[i] By default, but can be redefined (at the expense of compatibility with older files).

NDBM comes with most BSD-derived machines. GDBM is a GNU DBM implemen-tation. SDBM is part of the X11 distribution and also the standard Perl source distribution. DB refers to the Berkeley DB library. While the others are essentially reimplementations of the original DB library, the Berkeley DB code gives you three different types of database on disk and attempts to solve many of the disk, speed, and size limitations that hinder the other implementations.

Code size refers to the size of the compiled libraries. Disk usage refers to the size of the database files it creates. Block size limits refer to the database's maximum key or value size. Byte-order independence refers to whether the database system relies on hardware byte order or whether it instead creates portable files. A user-defined sort order lets you tell the library what order to return lists of keys in. Partial key lookups let you make approximate searches on the database.

Most Perl programmers prefer the Berkeley DB implementations. Many systems already have this library installed, and Perl can use it. For others, you are advised to fetch and install it from CPAN. It will make your life much easier.

DBM files provide key/value pairs. In relational database terms, you get a database with one table that has only two columns. Recipe 14.8 shows you how to use the MLDBM module from CPAN to store arbitrarily complex data structures in a DBM file.

As good as MLDBM is, it doesn't get around the limitation that you only retrieve rows based on one single column, the hash key. If you need complex queries, the difficulties can be overwhelming. In these cases, consider a separate database management system (DBMS). The DBI project provides modules to work with Oracle, Sybase, mSQL, MySQL, Ingres, and others.

See *http://www.bermetica.com/technologia/perl/DBI/index.html* and *http://www.perl.com/ CPAN/modules/by-category/07_Database_Interfaces/*, which currently contains:

```
AsciiDB    DBI Db     MLDBM     OLE     Pg        Sybase
CDB_File   DBZ_ File  Fame      Msql    ObjStore  Postgres  XBase
DBD        DB_File    Ingperl   MySQL   Oraperl   Sprite
```

14.1. Making and Using a DBM File

Problem

You want to create, populate, inspect, or delete values in a DBM database.

Solution

Use **dbmopen** or `tie` to open the database and make it accessible through a hash. Then use the hash as you normally would. When you're done, call **dbmclose** or `untie`.

dbmopen

```
    use DB_File;                          # optional; overrides default
    dbmopen %HASH, $FILENAME, 0666        # open database, accessed through %HASH
        or die "Can't open $FILENAME:$!\n";

    $V = $HASH{$KEY};                     # retrieve from database
    $HASH{$KEY} = $VALUE;                 # put value into database
    if (exists $HASH{$KEY}) {             # check whether in database
        # ...
    }
    delete $HASH{$KEY};                   # remove from database
    dbmclose %HASH;                       # close the database
```

tie

```
    use DB_File;                          # load database module

    tie %HASH, "DB_File", $FILENAME       # open database, to be accessed
        or die "Can't open $FILENAME:$!\n";      # through %HASH

    $V = $HASH{$KEY};                     # retrieve from database
    $HASH{$KEY} = $VALUE;                 # put value into database
    if (exists $HASH{$KEY}) {             # check whether in database
        # ...
    }
    delete $HASH{$KEY};                   # delete from database
    untie %HASH;                          # close the database
```

Discussion

Accessing a database as a hash is powerful but easy, giving you a persistent hash that sticks around after the program using it has finished running. It's also much faster than loading in a new hash every time; even if the hash has a million entries, your program starts up virtually instantaneously.

The program in Example 14-1 treats the database as though it were a normal hash. You can even call keys or each on it. Likewise, exists and defined are implemented for tied DBM hashes. Unlike a normal hash, a DBM hash does not distinguish between those two functions.

Example 14-1. userstats

```
#!/usr/bin/perl -w
# userstats - generates statistics on who is logged in.
# call with an argument to display totals

use DB_File;

$db = '/tmp/userstats.db';          # where data is kept between runs

tie(%db, 'DB_File', $db)            or die "Can't open DB_File $db : $!\n";
```

Example 14-1. userstats (continued)

```perl
if (@ARGV) {
    if ("@ARGV" eq "ALL") {
        @ARGV = sort keys %db;
    }
    foreach $user (@ARGV) {
            print "$user\t$db{$user}\n";
    }
} else {
    @who = `who`;                           # run who(1)
    if ($?) {
        die "Couldn't run who: $?\n";        # exited abnormally
    }
    # extract username (first thing on the line) and update
    foreach $line (@who) {
        $line =~ /^(\S+)/;
        die "Bad line from who: $line\n" unless $1;
        $db{$1}++;
    }
}

untie %db;
```

We use *who* to get a list of users logged in. This typically produces output like:

```
gnat      ttyp1    May 29 15:39    (coprolith.frii.com)
```

If the *userstats* program is called without any arguments, it checks who's logged on and updates the database appropriately.

If the program is called with arguments, these are treated as usernames whose information will be presented. The special argument "ALL" sets @ARGV to a sorted list of DBM keys. For large hashes with many keys, this is prohibitively expensive—a better solution would be to use the BTREE bindings of DB_File described in Recipe 14.6.

See Also

The documentation for the standard modules GDBM_File, NDBM_File, SDBM_File, DB_File, also in Chapter 7 of *Programming Perl*; *perltie*(1); the section on "Using Tied Variables" in Chapter 5 of *Programming Perl*; the discussion on the effect of your umask on file creation in Recipe 7.1; Recipe 13.15

14.2. Emptying a DBM File

Problem

You want to clear out a DBM file.

Solution

Open the database and assign () to it. Use **dbmopen**:

```
dbmopen(%HASH, $FILENAME, 0666)              or die "Can't open FILENAME: $!\n";
%HASH = ();
dbmclose %HASH;
```

or **tie**:

```
use DB_File;

tie(%HASH, "DB_File", $FILENAME)             or die "Can't open FILENAME: $!\n";
%HASH = ();
untie %HASH;
```

Alternatively, delete the file and reopen with create mode:

```
unlink $FILENAME
    or die "Couldn't unlink $FILENAME to empty the database: $!\n";
dbmopen(%HASH, $FILENAME, 0666)
    or die "Couldn't create $FILENAME database: $!\n";
```

Discussion

It may be quicker to delete the file and create a new one than to reset it, but doing so opens you up to a race condition that trips up a careless program or makes it vulnerable to an attacker. The attacker could make a link pointing to the file */etc/precious* with the same name as your file between the time when you deleted the file and when you recreated it. When the DBM library opens the file, it clobbers */etc/precious*.

If you delete a DB_File database and recreate it, you'll lose any customizable settings like page size, fill-factor, and so on. This is another good reason to assign the empty list to the tied hash.

See Also

The documentation for the standard DB_File module, also in Chapter 7 of *Programming Perl*; the **unlink** function in *perlfunc*(1); Recipe 14.1

14.3. Converting Between DBM Files

Problem

You have a file in one DBM format, but another program expects input in a different DBM format.

Solution

Read the keys and values from the initial DBM file and write them to a new file in the different DBM format as in Example 14-2.

Example 14-2. db2gdbm

```perl
#!/usr/bin/perl -w
# db2gdbm: converts DB to GDBM

use strict;

use DB_File;
use GDBM_File;

unless (@ARGV == 2) {
    die "usage: db2gdbm infile outfile\n";
}

my ($infile, $outfile) = @ARGV;
my (%db_in, %db_out);

# open the files
tie(%db_in, 'DB_File', $infile)
    or die "Can't tie $infile: $!";
tie(%db_out, 'GDBM_File', $outfile, GDBM_WRCREAT, 0666)
    or die "Can't tie $outfile: $!";

# copy (don't use %db_out = %db_in because it's slow on big databases)
while (my($k, $v) = each %db_in) {
    $db_out{$k} = $v;
}

# these unties happen automatically at program exit
untie %db_in;
untie %db_out;
```

Call the program as:

```
% db2gdbm /tmp/users.db /tmp/users.gdbm
```

Discussion

When multiple types of DBM file are used in the same program, you have to use tie, not the dbmopen interface. That's because with dbmopen you can only use one database format, which is why its use is deprecated.

Copying hashes by simple assignment, as in %new = %old, works on DBM files. However, it loads everything into memory first as a list, which doesn't matter with small hashes, but can be prohibitively expensive in the case of DBM files. For database hashes, use each to iterate through them instead.

See Also

The documentation for the standard modules GDBM_File, NDBM_File, SDBM_File, DB_File, also in Chapter 7 of *Programming Perl*; Recipe 14.1

14.4. Merging DBM Files

Problem

You want to combine two DBM files into a single DBM file with original key/value pairs.

Solution

Either merge the databases by treating their hashes as lists:

```
%OUTPUT = (%INPUT1, %INPUT2);
```

or, more wisely, by iterating over each key-value pair.

```
%OUTPUT = ();
foreach $href ( \%INPUT1, \%INPUT2 ) {
    while (my($key, $value) = each(%$href)) {
        if (exists $OUTPUT{$key}) {
            # decide which value to use and set $OUTPUT{$key} if necessary
        } else {
            $OUTPUT{$key} = $value;
        }
    }
}
```

Discussion

This straightforward application of Recipe 5.10 comes with the same caveats. Merging hashes by treating them as lists requires that the hashes be preloaded into memory, creating a potentially humongous temporary list. If you're dealing with large hashes, have little virtual memory, or both, then you want to iterate over the keys with **each** to save memory.

Another difference between these merging techniques is what to do if the same key exists in both input databases. The blind assignment merely overwrites the first value with the second value. The iterative merging technique lets you decide what to do. Possibilities include issuing a warning or error, choosing the first over the second, choosing the second over the first, or concatenating the new value to the old one. If you're using the MLDBM module, you can even store them both, using an array reference to the two values.

See Also

Recipe 5.10; Recipe 14.8

14.5. Locking DBM Files

Problem

You need several concurrently running programs to have simultaneous access to a DBM file.

Solution

Either use the DBM implementation's locking mechanism if it has one, lock the file with `flock`, or use an auxiliary locking scheme as in Recipe 7.21.

Discussion

With SDBM or NDBM, you can't do much to lock the database itself. You must devise an auxiliary locking scheme using an extra lockfile.

GDBM uses the concept of readers and writers: either many readers or one solitary writer may have a GDBM file open at any given time. You specify whether you're a reader or a writer when you open it. This can be annoying.

Version 1 of Berkeley DB gives you access to the file descriptor of the open database, allowing you to `flock` it. The lock applies to the database as a whole, not to individual records. Version 2 implements its own full transaction system with locking.

Example 14-3 shows an example of locking a database using Berkeley DB. Run this repeatedly in the background to see locks granted in proper order.

Example 14-3. dblockdemo

```perl
#!/usr/bin/perl
# dblockdemo - demo locking dbm databases
use DB_File;
use strict;

sub LOCK_SH { 1 }            # In case you don't have
sub LOCK_EX { 2 }            # the standard Fcntl module.  You
sub LOCK_NB { 4 }            # should, but who can tell
sub LOCK_UN { 8 }            # how those chips fall?

my($oldval, $fd, $db, %db, $value, $key);

$key    = shift || 'default';
```

Example 14-3. dblockdemo (continued)

```perl
$value  = shift || 'magic';
$value .= " $$";

$db = tie(%db, 'DB_File', '/tmp/foo.db', O_CREAT|O_RDWR, 0666)
    or die "dbcreat /tmp/foo.db $!";
$fd = $db->fd;                          # need this for locking
print "$$: db fd is $fd\n";
open(DB_FH, "+<&=$fd")
    or die "dup $!";

unless (flock (DB_FH, LOCK_SH | LOCK_NB)) {
    print "$$: CONTENTION; can't read during write update!
            Waiting for read lock ($!) ....";
    unless (flock (DB_FH, LOCK_SH)) { die "flock: $!" }
}
print "$$: Read lock granted\n";

$oldval = $db{$key};
print "$$: Old value was $oldval\n";
flock(DB_FH, LOCK_UN);

unless (flock (DB_FH, LOCK_EX | LOCK_NB)) {
    print "$$: CONTENTION; must have exclusive lock!
            Waiting for write lock ($!) ....";
    unless (flock (DB_FH, LOCK_EX)) { die "flock: $!" }
}

print "$$: Write lock granted\n";
$db{$key} = $value;
$db->sync;  # to flush
sleep 10;

flock(DB_FH, LOCK_UN);
undef $db;
untie %db;
close(DB_FH);
print "$$: Updated db to $key=$value\n";
```

See Also

The documentation for the standard DB_File module, also in Chapter 7 of *Programming Perl*; Recipe 7.11; Recipe 16.12

14.6. Sorting Large DBM Files

Problem

You want to process a large dataset you'd like to commit to a DBM file in a particular order.

Solution

Use the DB_File's B-tree bindings and supply a comparison function of your own devising:

```
use DB_File;

# specify the Perl sub to do key comparison using the
# exported $DB_BTREE hash reference
$DB_BTREE->{'compare'} = sub {
    my ($key1, $key2) = @_ ;
    "\L$key1" cmp "\L$key2" ;
};

tie(%hash, "DB_File", $filename, O_RDWR|O_CREAT, 0666, $DB_BTREE)
    or die "can't tie $filename: $!";
```

Description

An annoyance of hashes, whether in memory or as DBM files, is that they do not maintain proper ordering. The CPAN module Tie::IxHash can make a regular hash in memory maintain its insertion order, but that doesn't help you for DBM databases or arbitrary sorting criteria.

The DB_File module supports a nice solution to this using a B-tree implementation. One advantage of a B-tree over a regular DBM hash is its ordering. When the user defines a comparison function, all calls to keys, values, and each are automatically ordered. For example, Example 14-4 is a program that maintains a hash whose keys will always be sorted case-insensitively.

Example 14-4. sortdemo

```
#!/usr/bin/perl
# sortdemo - show auto dbm sorting
use strict;
use DB_File;

$DB_BTREE->{'compare'} = sub {
    my ($key1, $key2) = @_ ;
    "\L$key1" cmp "\L$key2" ;
};

my %hash;
my $filename = '/tmp/sorthash.db';
tie(%hash, "DB_File", $filename, O_RDWR|O_CREAT, 0666, $DB_BTREE)
    or die "can't tie $filename: $!";

my $i = 0;
for my $word (qw(Can't you go camp down by Gibraltar)) {
    $hash{$word} = ++$i;
}
```

Example 14-4. sortdemo (continued)

```
while (my($word, $number) = each %hash) {
    printf "%-12s %d\n", $word, $number;
}
```

By default, the entries in a B-tree DB_File database are stored alphabetically. Here, though, we provide a case-insensitive comparison function, so using each to fetch all the keys would show:

```
by           6
camp         4
Can't        1
down         5
Gibraltar    7
go           3
you          2
```

This sorting property on hashes is so convenient that it's worth using even without a permanent database. If you pass undef where the filename is expected on the tie, DB_File will create a file in */tmp* and then immediately unlink it, giving an anonymous database:

```
tie(%hash, "DB_File", undef, O_RDWR|O_CREAT, 0666, $DB_BTREE)
        or die "can't tie: $!";
```

Remember these two things if you supply a comparison for your BTREE database. One, the new compare function must be specified when you create the database. Two, you cannot change the ordering once the database has been created; you must use the same compare function every time you access the database.

Using BTREE databases under DB_File also permits duplicate or partial keys. See its documentation for examples.

See Also

Recipe 5.6

14.7. Treating a Text File as a Database Array

Problem

You'd like to treat a text file as an array of lines with read-write privileges. You might want to do that so you could easily update the Nth line.

Solution

The DB_File module lets you `tie` a text file to an array.

```
use DB_File;

tie(@array, "DB_File", "/tmp/textfile", O_RDWR|O_CREAT, 0666, $DB_RECNO)
    or die "Cannot open file 'text': $!\en" ;

$array[4] = "a new line";
untie @array;
```

Description

Updating a textfile in place is surprisingly tricky, as noted in Chapter 7, *File Access.* The RECNO binding provides a nice way to address the file as though it were a simple array of lines—the way everyone always seems to think they can.

Working with files this way can be odd. For one thing, the zeroth element of the tied array is the first line of the file. More importantly, tied arrays aren't as fully featured as tied hashes are. This will be fixed in a future version of Perl—patches are already available, in fact.

As you can see from the example above, the tied array interface is limited. To make the interface more useful, methods supplied with DB_File simulate the standard array operations that are not currently implemented in Perl's tied array interface. Save the return value from `tie` function or retrieve it later from the tied hash using the `tied` function. Use this object to access the following methods:

`$X->push(LIST)`
    Pushes elements of `LIST` to the end of the array.

`$value = $X->pop`
    Removes and returns the last element of the array.

`$X->shift`
    Removes and returns the first element of the array.

`$X->unshift(LIST)`
    Pushes elements of `LIST` to the start of the array.

`$X->length`
    Returns the number of elements in the array.

Example 14-5 is a more complete example using methods described above. It also accesses the direct API interface as described in the DB_File module documentation. (Much of this recipe is derived from the DB_File module documentation,

courtesy of Paul Marquess, author of the Perl port of Berkeley DB. This material is
used with his permission.)

Example 14-5. recno_demo

```perl
#!/usr/bin/perl -w
# recno_demo - show how to use the raw API on recno bindings
use strict;
use vars qw(@lines $dbobj $file $i);
use DB_File;

$file = "/tmp/textfile";
unlink $file;                    # just in case

$dbobj = tie(@lines, "DB_File", $file, O_RDWR|O_CREAT, 0666, $DB_RECNO)
    or die "Cannot open file $file: $!\n";

# first create a text file to play with
$lines[0] = "zero";
$lines[1] = "one";
$lines[2] = "two";
$lines[3] = "three";
$lines[4] = "four";

# Print the records in order.
#
# The length method is needed here because evaluating a tied
# array in a scalar context does not return the number of
# elements in the array.

print "\nORIGINAL\n";
foreach $i (0 .. $dbobj->length - 1) {
    print "$i: $lines[$i]\n";
}

# use the push & pop methods
$a = $dbobj->pop;
$dbobj->push("last");
print "\nThe last record was [$a]\n";

# and the shift & unshift methods
$a = $dbobj->shift;
$dbobj->unshift("first");
print "The first record was [$a]\n";

# Use the API to add a new record after record 2.
$i = 2;
$dbobj->put($i, "Newbie", R_IAFTER);

# and a new record before record 1.
$i = 1;
$dbobj->put($i, "New One", R_IBEFORE);

# delete record 3
```

Example 14-5. recno_demo (continued)

```
$dbobj->del(3);

# now print the records in reverse order
print "\nREVERSE\n";
for ($i = $dbobj->length - 1; $i >= 0; -- $i) {
    print "$i: $lines[$i]\n";
}

# same again, but use the API functions instead
print "\nREVERSE again\n";
my ($s, $k, $v)  = (0, 0, 0);
for ($s = $dbobj->seq($k, $v, R_LAST);
     $s == 0;
     $s = $dbobj->seq($k, $v, R_PREV))
{
    print "$k: $v\n"
}

undef $dbobj;
untie @lines;
```

This is what it outputs:

```
ORIGINAL
0: zero
1: one
2: two
3: three
4: four

The last record was [four]
The first record was [zero]

REVERSE
5: last
4: three
3: Newbie
2: one
1: New One
0: first

REVERSE again
5: last
4: three
3: Newbie
2: one
1: New One
0: first
```

Note that rather than iterating through the array, **@lines**, like this:

```
foreach $item (@lines) { }
```

you must use either this:

```
foreach $i (0 .. $dbobj->length - 1) { }
```

or this:

```
for ($done_yet = $dbobj->get($k, $v, R_FIRST);
     not $done_yet;
     $done_yet = $dbobj->get($k, $v, R_NEXT) )
{
    # process key or value
}
```

Also, when we used the put method, we specified the record index using a variable, $i, rather than passing the literal value itself. This is because put returns the record number of the inserted line in that parameter, altering its contents.

See Also

The documentation for the standard DB_File module, also in Chapter 7 of *Programming Perl*, in its discussion of $DB_RECNO bindings.

14.8. *Storing Complex Data in a DBM File*

Problem

You want values in a DBM file to be something other than scalars. For instance, you use a hash of hashes in your program and want to store them in a DBM file for other programs to access, or you want them to persist across process runs.

Solution

Use the CPAN module MLDBM to store more complex values than strings and numbers.

```
use MLDBM 'DB_File';
tie(%HASH, 'MLDBM', [... other DBM arguments]) or die $!;
```

Discussion

MLDBM uses Data::Dumper (see Recipe 11.14) to convert data structures to and from strings so that they can be stored in a DBM file. It doesn't store references, instead it stores the data that the references refer to:

```
# %hash is a tied hash
$hash{"Tom Christiansen"} = [ "book author", 'tchrist@perl.com' ];
$hash{"Tom Boutell"} = [ "shareware author", 'boutell@boutell.com' ];

# names to compare
```

```
$name1 = "Tom Christiansen";
$name2 = "Tom Boutell";

$tom1 = $hash{$name1};       # snag local pointer
$tom2 = $hash{$name2};       # and another

print "Two Toming: $tom1 $tom2\n";
```

Tom Toming: ARRAY(0x73048) ARRAY(0x73e4c)

Each time MLDBM retrieves a data structure from the DBM file, it generates a new copy of that data. To compare data that you retrieve from a MLDBM database, you need to compare the values within the structure:

```
if ($tom1->[0] eq $tom2->[0] &&
    $tom1->[1] eq $tom2->[1]) {
    print "You're having runtime fun with one Tom made two.\n";
} else {
    print "No two Toms are ever alike.\n";
}
```

This is more efficient than:

```
if ($hash{$name1}->[0] eq $hash{$name2}->[0] &&      # INEFFICIENT
    $hash{$name1}->[1] eq $hash{$name2}->[1]) {
    print "You're having runtime fun with one Tom made two.\n";
} else {
    print "No two Toms are ever alike.\n";
}
```

Each time we say `$hash{...}`, the DBM file is consulted. The inefficient code above accesses the database four times, whereas the code using the temporary variables `$tom1` and `$tom2` only accesses the database twice.

Current limitations of Perl's `tie` mechanism prevent you from storing or modifying parts of a MLDBM value directly:

```
$hash{"Tom Boutell"}->[0] = "Poet Programmer";      # WRONG
```

Always get, change, and set pieces of the stored structure through a temporary variable:

```
$entry = $hash{"Tom Boutell"};                      # RIGHT
$entry->[0] = "Poet Programmer";
$hash{"Tom Boutell"} = $entry;
```

If MLDBM uses a database with size limits on values, like SDBM, you'll quickly hit those limits. To get around this, use GDBM_File or DB_File, which don't limit the size of keys or values. DB_File is the better choice because it is byte-order neutral, which lets the database be shared between both big- and little-endian architectures.

See Also

The documentation for the Data::Dumper, MLDBM, and Storable modules from CPAN; Recipe 11.13; Recipe 14.9

14.9. Persistent Data

Problem

You want your variables to retain their values between calls to your program.

Solution

Use a MLDBM to store the values between calls to your program:

```
use MLDBM 'DB_File';

my ($VARIABLE1,$VARIABLE2);
my $Persistent_Store = '/projects/foo/data';
BEGIN {
    my %data;
    tie(%data, 'MLDBM', $Persistent_Store)
        or die "Can't tie to $Persistent_Store : $!";
    $VARIABLE1 = $data{VARIABLE1};
    $VARIABLE2 = $data{VARIABLE2};
    # ...
    untie %data;
}
END {
    my %data;
    tie (%data, 'MLDBM', $Persistent_Store)
        or die "Can't tie to $Persistent_Store : $!";
    $data{VARIABLE1} = $VARIABLE1;
    $data{VARIABLE2} = $VARIABLE2;
    # ...
    untie %data;
}
```

Discussion

An important limitation of MLDBM is that you can't add to or alter the structure in the reference without assignment to a temporary variable. We do this in the sample program in Example 14-6, assigning to $array_ref before we push. You simply can't do this:

```
push(@{$db{$user}}, $duration);
```

For a start, MLDBM doesn't allow it. Also, $db{$user} might not be in the database (the array reference isn't automatically created as it would be if %db weren't tied to a DBM file). This is why we test `exists $db{$user}` when we give `$array_ref` its initial value. We're creating the empty array for the case where it doesn't already exist.

Example 14-6. mldbm-demo

```
#!/usr/bin/perl -w
# mldbm_demo - show how to use MLDBM with DB_File

use MLDBM "DB_File";

$db = "/tmp/mldbm-array";

tie %db, 'MLDBM', $db
  or die "Can't open $db : $!";

while(<DATA>) {
    chomp;
    ($user, $duration) = split(/\s+/, $_);
    $array_ref = exists $db{$user} ? $db{$user} : [];
    push(@$array_ref, $duration);
    $db{$user} = $array_ref;
}

foreach $user (sort keys %db) {
    print "$user: ";
    $total = 0;
    foreach $duration (@{ $db{$user} }) {
        print "$duration ";
        $total += $duration;
    }
        print "($total)\n";
    }

__END__
gnat        15.3
tchrist     2.5
jules       22.1
tchrist     15.9
gnat        8.7
```

Newer versions of MLDBM allow you to select not just the database module (we recommend DB_File), but also the serialization module (we recommend Storable). Previous versions limited you to Data::Dumper for serializing, which is slower than Storable. Here's how you use DB_File with Storable:

```
    use MLDBM qw(DB_File Storable);
```

See Also

The documentation for the Data::Dumper, MLDBM, and Storable modules from CPAN; Recipe 11.13; Recipe 14.8

14.10. Executing an SQL Command Using
DBI and DBD

Problem

You want to send SQL queries to a database system such as Oracle, Sybase, mSQL, or MySQL, and process their results.

Solution

Use the DBI (DataBase Interface) and DBD (DataBase Driver) modules available from CPAN:

```
use DBI;

$dbh = DBI->connect('DBI:driver:database', 'username', 'auth',
          { RaiseError => 1, AutoCommit => 1});
$dbh->do($SQL);
$sth = $dbh->prepare($SQL);
$sth->execute();
while (@row = $sth->fetchrow_array) {
    # ...
}
$sth->finish();
$dbh->disconnect();
```

Discussion

DBI acts as an intermediary between your program and any number of DBMS-specific drivers. For most actions you need a database handle ($dbh in the example). This is attached to a specific database and driver using the DBI->connect call.

The first argument to DBI->connect is a single string with three colon-separated fields. It represents the *data source*—the DBMS you're connecting to. The first field is always DBI, and the second is the name of the driver you're going to use (Oracle, mysql, etc.). The rest of the string is passed by the DBI module to the requested driver module (DBD::mysql, for example) where it identifies the database.

The second and third arguments authenticate the user.

The fourth argument is an optional hash reference defining attributes of the connection. Setting PrintError to true makes DBI warn whenever a DBI method fails. Setting RaiseError is like PrintError except that die is used instead of warn. Auto-Commit says that you don't want to deal with transactions (smaller DBMSs don't support them, and if you're using a larger DBMS then you can read about transactions in the DBMS documentation).

You can execute simple SQL statements (those that don't return rows of data) with a database handle's do method. This returns Boolean true or false. SQL statements that return rows of data (like SELECT) require that you first use the database handle's prepare method to create a statement handle. Then call the execute method on the statement handle to perform the query, and retrieve rows with a fetch method like fetchrow_array or fetchrow_hashref (which returns a reference to a hash mapping column name to value).

Statement handles and database handles often correspond to underlying connections to the database, so some care must be taken with them. A connection is automatically cleaned up when its handle goes out of scope. If a database handle goes out of scope while there are active statement handles for that database, though, you will get a warning like this:

```
disconnect(DBI::db=HASH(0x9df84)) invalidates 1 active cursor(s)
    at -e line 1.
```

The finish method ensures the statement handle is inactive (some old drivers need this). The disconnect method, er, disconnects from the database.

The DBI module comes with a FAQ (perldoc DBI::FAQ) and regular documentation (perldoc DBI). The driver for your DBMS also has documentation (perldoc DBD::mysql, for instance). The DBI API is larger than the simple subset we've shown here; it provides diverse ways of fetching results, and it hooks into DBMS-specific features like stored procedures. Consult the driver module's documentation to learn about these.

The program in Example 14-7 creates, populates, and searches a MySQL table of users. It uses the RaiseError attribute so it doesn't have to check the return status of every method call.

Example 14-7. dbusers

```perl
#!/usr/bin/perl -w
# dbusers - manage MySQL user table
use DBI;
use User::pwent;

$dbh = DBI->connect('DBI:mysql:dbname:mysqlserver.domain.com:3306',
                    'user', 'password',
                    { RaiseError => 1, AutoCommit => 1 })

$dbh->do("CREATE TABLE users (uid INT, login CHAR(8))");

$sql_fmt = "INSERT INTO users VALUES( %d, %s )";
while ($user = getpwent) {
    $sql = sprintf($sql_fmt, $user->uid, $dbh->quote($user->name));
    $dbh->do($sql);
}
```

Example 14-7. dbusers (continued)

```
$sth = $dbh->prepare("SELECT * FROM users WHERE uid < 50");
$sth->execute;

while ((@row) = $sth->fetchrow_array) {
    print join(", ", map {defined $_ ? $_ : "(null)"} @row), "\n";
}
$sth->finish;

$dbh->do("DROP TABLE users");

$dbh->disconnect;
```

See Also

The documentation for the DBI and relevant DBD modules from CPAN; *http://www.symbolstone.org/technology/perl/DBI/* and *http://www.perl.com/CPAN/modules/by-category/07_Database_Interfaces/*

14.11. Program: ggh—Grep Netscape Global History

This program divulges the contents of Netscape's *history.db* file. It can be called with full URLs or with a (single) pattern. If called without arguments, it displays every entry in the history file. The *~/.netscape/history.db* file is used unless the **-database** option is given.

Each output line shows the URL and its access time. The time is converted into `localtime` representation with **-localtime** (the default), `gmtime` representation with **-gmtime**—or left in raw form with **-epochtime**, which is useful for sorting by date.

To specify a pattern to match against, give one single argument without a `://`.

To look up one or more URLs, supply them as arguments:

```
% ggh http://www.perl.com/index.html
```

To find out a link you don't quite recall, use a regular expression (a single argument without a `://` is a pattern):

```
% ggh perl
```

To find out all the people you've mailed:

```
% ggh mailto:
```

To find out the FAQ sites you've visited, use a snazzy Perl pattern with an embedded /i modifier:

```
% ggh -regexp '(?i)\bfaq\b'
```

If you don't want the internal date converted to localtime, use **-epoch**:

```
% ggh -epoch http://www.perl.com/perl/
```

If you prefer gmtime to localtime, use **-gmtime**:

```
% ggh -gmtime http://www.perl.com/perl/
```

To look at the whole file, give no arguments (but perhaps redirect to a pager):

```
% ggh | less
```

If you want the output sorted by date, use the **-epoch** flag:

```
% ggh -epoch | sort -rn | less
```

If you want it sorted by date into your local time zone format, use a more sophisticated pipeline:

```
% ggh -epoch | sort -rn | perl -pe 's/\d+/localtime $&/e' | less
```

The Netscape release notes claim that they're using NDBM format. This is misleading: they're actually using Berkeley DB format, which is why we require DB_File (not supplied standard with all systems Perl runs on) instead of NDBM_File (which is). The program is shown in Example 14-8.

Example 14-8. ggh

```
#!/usr/bin/perl -w
# ggh - grovel global history in netscape logs
$USAGE = <<EO_COMPLAINT;
usage: $0 [-database dbfilename] [-help]
          [-epochtime | -localtime | -gmtime]
          [ [-regexp] pattern] | href ... ]
EO_COMPLAINT

use Getopt::Long;

($opt_database, $opt_epochtime, $opt_localtime,
 $opt_gmtime,   $opt_regexp,    $opt_help,
 $pattern,                               )      = (0) x 7;

usage() unless GetOptions qw{ database=s
                              regexp=s
                              epochtime localtime gmtime
                              help
                        };

if ($opt_help) { print $USAGE; exit; }

usage("only one of localtime, gmtime, and epochtime allowed")
```

Example 14-8. ggh (continued)

```
    if $opt_localtime + $opt_gmtime + $opt_epochtime > 1;

if ( $opt_regexp ) {
    $pattern = $opt_regexp;
} elsif (@ARGV && $ARGV[0] !~ m(://)) {
    $pattern = shift;
}

usage("can't mix URLs and explicit patterns")
    if $pattern && @ARGV;

if ($pattern && !eval { '' =~ /$pattern/; 1 } ) {
    $@ =~ s/ at \w+ line \d+\.//;
    die "$0: bad pattern $@";
}

require DB_File; DB_File->import();  # delay loading until runtime
$| = 1;                              # feed the hungry PAGERs

$dotdir  = $ENV{HOME}    || $ENV{LOGNAME};
$HISTORY = $opt_database || "$dotdir/.netscape/history.db";

die "no netscape history dbase in $HISTORY: $!" unless -e $HISTORY;
die "can't dbmopen $HISTORY: $!" unless dbmopen %hist_db, $HISTORY, 0666;

# the next line is a hack because the C programmers who did this
# didn't understand strlen vs strlen+1.  jwz told me so. :-)
$add_nulls   = (ord(substr(each %hist_db, -1)) == 0);

# XXX: should now do scalar keys to reset but don't
#      want cost of full traverse, required on tied hashes.
#    better to close and reopen?

$nulled_href = "";
$byte_order  = "V";         # PC people don't grok "N" (network order)

if (@ARGV) {
    foreach $href (@ARGV) {
        $nulled_href = $href . ($add_nulls && "\0");
        unless ($binary_time = $hist_db{$nulled_href}) {
            warn "$0: No history entry for HREF $href\n";
            next;
        }
        $epoch_secs = unpack($byte_order, $binary_time);
        $stardate   = $opt_epochtime ? $epoch_secs
                                 : $opt_gmtime ? gmtime    $epoch_secs
                                        : localtime $epoch_secs;
        print "$stardate $href\n";
    }
} else {
    while ( ($href, $binary_time) = each %hist_db ) {
        chop $href if $add_nulls;
        next unless defined $href && defined $binary_time;
```

Example 14-8. ggh (continued)

```
        # gnat reports some binary times are missing
        $binary_time = pack($byte_order, 0) unless $binary_time;
        $epoch_secs = unpack($byte_order, $binary_time);
        $stardate   = $opt_epochtime ? $epoch_secs
                                     : $opt_gmtime ? gmtime    $epoch_secs
                                                   : localtime $epoch_secs;
        print "$stardate $href\n" unless $pattern && $href !~ /$pattern/o;
    }
}

sub usage {
    print STDERR "@_\n" if @_;
    die $USAGE;
}
```

See Also

Recipe 6.17

15

User Interfaces

> *And then the Windows failed—and then*
> *I could not see to see—*
> —Emily Dickinson
> "I heard a Fly buzz—when I died"

15.0. Introduction

Everything we use has a user interface: VCRs, computers, telephones, even books. Our programs have user interfaces: do we have to supply arguments on the command line? Can we drag and drop files into the program? Do we have to press Enter after every response we make, or can the program read a single keystroke at a time?

This chapter won't discuss *designing* user interfaces: entire bookshelves are filled with books written on the subject. Instead, we'll focus on *implementing* user interfaces—parsing command-line arguments, reading a character at a time, writing anywhere on the screen, and writing a graphical user interface.

The simplest user interface is what we'll call *line mode* interfaces. Line mode programs normally read lines at a time and write characters or entire lines. Filters like *grep* and utilities like *mail* exemplify this type of interface. We don't really talk much about this type of interface in this chapter, because so much of the rest of the book does.

A more complex interface is what we'll call *full-screen mode*. Programs like *vi*, *elm*, and *lynx* have full-screen interfaces. They read single characters at a time and can write to any character position on the screen. We address this type of interface in Recipes 15.4, 15.6, 15.9, 15.10, and 15.11.

The final class of interface is the GUI (graphical user interface). Programs with GUIs can address individual pixels, not just characters. GUIs often follow a windowing metaphor, in which a program creates windows that appear on the user's display device. The windows are filled with widgets, things like scrollbars to drag or buttons to click. Netscape Navigator provides a full graphical user interface, as does your window manager. Perl can use many GUI toolkits, but here we'll cover the Tk toolkit, since it's the most well-known and portable. See Recipes 15.14, 15.15, and 15.19.

A program's user interface is different from the environment you run it in. Your environment determines the type of program you can run. If you're logged in through a terminal capable of full-screen I/O, you can run line mode applications but not GUI programs. Let's look briefly at the environments.

Some environments only handle programs that have a bare line mode interface. This includes executing programs with backticks, over *rsh*, or from *cron*. Their simple interface allows them to be combined creatively and powerfully as reusable components in larger scripts. Line mode programs are wonderful for automation, because they don't rely on a keyboard or screen. They rely on only STDIN and STDOUT—if that. These are often the most portable programs because they use nothing but the basic I/O supported by virtually all systems.

The typical login session, where you use a terminal with a screen and keyboard, permits both line mode and full-screen interfaces. Here the program with the full-screen interface talks to the terminal driver and has intimate knowledge of how to make the terminal write to various positions on the screen. To automate such a program you need to create a pseudo-terminal for the program to talk to, as shown in Recipe 15.13.

Finally, some window systems let you run line mode and full-screen programs as well as programs that use a GUI. For instance, you can run *grep* (line-mode programs) from within *vi* (a full-screen program) from an *xterm* window (a GUI program running in a window system environment). GUI programs are difficult to automate unless they provide an alternative interface through remote procedure calls.

Toolkits exist for programming in full-screen and GUI environments. These toolkits (*curses* for full-screen programs; Tk for GUI programs) increase the portability of your programs by abstracting out system-specific details. A curses program can run on virtually any kind of terminal without the user worrying about which particular escape sequences they need to use. Tk programs will run unmodified on Unix and Windows systems—providing you don't use operating-system specific functions.

There are other ways to interact with a user, most notably through the Web. We cover the Web in Chapters 19 and 20, so we make no further mention of it here.

15.1. Parsing Program Arguments

Problem

You want to let users change your program's behavior by giving options on the command line. For instance, you want to allow the user to control the level of output that your program produces with a -v (verbose) option.

Solution

Use the standard Getopt::Std module to permit single-character options:

```
use Getopt::Std;

# -v ARG, -D ARG, -o ARG, sets $opt_v, $opt_D, $opt_o
getopt("vDo");
# -v ARG, -D ARG, -o ARG, sets $args{v}, $args{D}, $args{o}
getopt("vDo", \%args);

getopts("vDo:");            # -v, -D, -o ARG, sets $opt_v, $opt_D, $opt_o
getopts("vDo:", \%args); # -v, -D, -o ARG, sets $args{v}, $args{D}, $args{o}
```

Or, use the standard Getopt::Long module to permit named arguments:

```
use Getopt::Long;

GetOptions( "verbose"  => \$verbose,      # --verbose
            "Debug"    => \$debug,        # --Debug
            "output=s" => \$output );     # --output=string or --output string
```

Discussion

Most traditional programs like *ls* and *rm* take single-character options (also known as flags or switches), such as -l and -r. In the case of *ls -l* and *rm -r*, the argument is Boolean: either it is present or it isn't. Contrast this with *gcc -o compiledfile source.c*, where *compiledfile* is a value associated with the option -o. We can combine Boolean options into a single option in any order. For example:

```
% rm -r -f /tmp/testdir
```

Another way of saying this is:

```
% rm -rf /tmp/testdir
```

The Getopt::Std module, part of the standard Perl distribution, parses these types of traditional options. Its `getopt` function takes a single string of characters, each corresponding to an option that takes a value, parses the command-line arguments stored in @ARGV, and sets a global variable for each option. For example, the value for the -D option will be stored in $opt_D. All options parsed though getopt are value options, not Boolean options.

Getopt::Std also provides the getopts function, which lets you specify whether each option is Boolean or takes a value. Arguments that take a value, like the -o option to *gcc*, are indicated by a :, as in this code:

```
use Getopt::Std;
getopts("o:");
if ($opt_o) {
    print "Writing output to $opt_o";
}
```

Both getopt and getopts can take a second argument, a reference to a hash. If present, option values are stored in $hash{X} instead of $opt_X:

```
use Getopt::Std;

%option = ();
getopts("Do:", \%option);

if ($option{D}) {
    print "Debugging mode enabled.\n";
}

    # if not set, set output to "-".  opening "-" for writing
    # means STDOUT
    $option{o} = "-" unless defined $option{o};

print "Writing output to file $option{o}\n" unless $option{o} eq "-";
open(STDOUT, "> $option{o}")
        or die "Can't open $option{o} for output: $!\n";
```

You can specify some programs' options using full words instead of single characters. These options are (usually) indicated with two dashes instead of one:

```
% gnutar --extract --file latest.tar
```

The value for the --**file** option could also be given with an equals sign:

```
% gnutar --extract --file=latest.tar
```

The Getopt::Long module's GetOptions function parses this style of options. It takes a hash whose keys are options and values are references to scalar variables:

```
use Getopt::Long;

GetOptions( "extract" => \$extract,
            "file=s"  => \$file );

if ($extract) {
    print "I'm extracting.\n";
```

```
    }
```

```
    die "I wish I had a file" unless defined $file;
    print "Working on the file $file\n";
```

If a key in the hash is just an option name, it's a Boolean option. The corresponding variable will be set to false if the option wasn't given, or to 1 if it was. Getopt::Long provides fancier options than just the Boolean and value of Getopt::Std. Here's what the option specifier can look like:

Specifier	Value?	Comment
option	No	Given as --option or not at all
option!	No	May be given as --option or --nooption
option=s	Yes	Mandatory string parameter: --option=somestring
option:s	Yes	Optional string parameter: --option or --option=somestring
option=i	Yes	Mandatory integer parameter: --option=35
option:i	Yes	Optional integer parameter: --option or --option=35
option=f	Yes	Mandatory floating point parameter: --option=3.141
option:f	Yes	Optional floating point parameter: --option or --option=3.141

See Also

The documentation for the standard Getopt::Long and Getopt::Std modules; examples of argument parsing by hand can be found in Recipe 1.5, Recipe 1.17, Recipe 6.22, Recipe 7.7, Recipe 8.19, and Recipe 15.12

15.2. Testing Whether a Program Is Running Interactively

Problem

You want to know whether your program is being called interactively or not. For instance, a user running your program from a shell is interactive, whereas the program being called from *cron* is not.

Solution

Use -t to test STDIN and STDOUT:

```
    sub I_am_interactive {
        return -t STDIN && -t STDOUT;
    }
```

If you're on a POSIX system, test process groups:

```
use POSIX qw/getpgrp tcgetpgrp/;

sub I_am_interactive {
    local *TTY;   # local file handle
    open(TTY, "/dev/tty") or die "can't open /dev/tty: $!";
    my $tpgrp = tcgetpgrp(fileno(TTY));
    my $pgrp  = getpgrp();
    close TTY;
    return ($tpgrp == $pgrp);
}
```

Discussion

The -t operator tells whether the filehandle or file is a tty device. Such devices are signs of interactive use. This only tells you whether your program has been redirected. Running your program from the shell and redirecting STDIN and STDOUT makes the -t version of I_am_interactive return false. Called from *cron*, I_am_interactive also returns false.

The POSIX test tells you whether your program has exclusive control over its tty. A program whose input and output has been redirected still can control its tty if it wants to, so the POSIX version of I_am_interactive returns true. A program run from *cron* has no tty, so I_am_interactive returns false.

Whichever I_am_interactive you choose to use, here's how you'd call it:

```
while (1) {
    if (I_am_interactive()) {
        print "Prompt: ";
    }
    $line = <STDIN>;
    last unless defined $line;
    # do something with the line
}
```

Or, more clearly:

```
sub prompt { print "Prompt: " if I_am_interactive() }
for (prompt(); $line = <STDIN>; prompt()) {
    # do something with the line
}
```

See Also

The documentation for the standard POSIX module, also in Chapter 7 of *Programming Perl*; the -t file-test operator in Chapter 2 of *Programming Perl* and in *perlop*(1)

15.3. Clearing the Screen

Problem

You want to clear the screen.

Solution

Use the Term::Cap module to send the appropriate character sequence. Use POSIX Termios to get the output speed of the terminal (or guess 9600 bps). Use `eval` to trap errors that may arise using POSIX Termios::

```
use Term::Cap;

$OSPEED = 9600;
eval {
    require POSIX;
    my $termios = POSIX::Termios->new();
    $termios->getattr;
    $OSPEED = $termios->getospeed;
};

$terminal = Term::Cap->Tgetent({OSPEED=>$OSPEED});
$terminal->Tputs('cl', 1, STDOUT);
```

Or, just run the *clear* command:

```
system("clear");
```

Discussion

If you clear the screen a lot, cache the return value from the termcap or *clear* command:

```
$clear = $terminal->Tputs('cl');
$clear = `clear`;
```

Then you can clear the screen a hundred times without running *clear* a hundred times:

```
print $clear;
```

See Also

Your system's *clear*(1) and *termcap*(5) manpages (if you have them); the documentation for the standard module Term::Cap module, also in Chapter 7 of *Programming Perl*; the documentation for the Term::Lib module from CPAN

15.4. Determining Terminal or Window Size

Problem

You need to know the size of the terminal or window. For instance, you want to format text so that it doesn't pass the right-hand boundary of the screen.

Solution

Either use the `ioctl` described in Recipe 12.14, or else use the CPAN module Term::ReadKey:

```
use Term::ReadKey;

($wchar, $hchar, $wpixels, $hpixels) = GetTerminalSize();
```

Discussion

`GetTerminalSize` returns four elements: the width and height in characters and the width and height in pixels. If the operation is unsupported for the output device (for instance, if output has been redirected to a file), it returns an empty list.

Here's how you'd graph the contents of `@values`, assuming no value is less than 0:

```
use Term::ReadKey;

($width) = GetTerminalSize();
die "You must have at least 10 characters" unless $width >= 10;

$max = 0;
foreach (@values) {
    $max = $_ if $max < $_;
}

$ratio = ($width-10)/$max;               # chars per unit
foreach (@values) {
    printf("%8.1f %s\n", $_, "*" x ($ratio*$_));
}
```

See Also

The documentation for the Term::ReadKey module from CPAN; Recipe 12.14

15.5. Changing Text Color

Problem

You want text to appear in different colors on the screen. For instance, you want to emphasize a mode line or highlight an error message.

Solution

Use the CPAN module Term::ANSIColor to send the ANSI color-change sequences to the user's terminal:

```
use Term::ANSIColor;

print color("red"), "Danger, Will Robinson!\n", color("reset");
print "This is just normal text.\n";
print colored("<BLINK>Do you hurt yet?</BLINK>", "blink");
```

Or, you can use convenience functions from Term::ANSIColor:

```
use Term::ANSIColor qw(:constants);

print RED, "Danger, Will Robinson!\n", RESET;
```

Discussion

Term::ANSIColor prepares escape sequences that some (but far from all) terminals will recognize. For example, if you normally launch a *color-xterm*, this recipe will work. If you normally use the normal *xterm* program, or have a vt100 in your kitchen, it won't.

There are two ways of using the module: either by calling the exported functions `color($attribute)` and `colored($text, $attribute)`, or by using convenience functions like BOLD, BLUE, and RESET.

Attributes can be a combination of colors and controls. The colors are black, red, green, yellow, blue, magenta, on_block, on_red, on_green, on_yellow, on_blue, on_magenta, on_cyan, and on_white. (Apparently orange and purple don't matter.) The controls are clear, reset, bold, underline, underscore, blink, reverse, and concealed. Clear and reset are synonyms, as are underline and underscore. Reset restores the colors to the way they were when the program started, and concealed makes foreground and background colors the same.

You can combine attributes:

```
# rhyme for the deadly coral snake
print color("red on_black"),  "venom lack\n";
print color("red on_yellow"), "kill that fellow\n";
```

```
print color("green on_cyan blink"), "garish!\n";
print color("reset");
```

We could have written this as:

```
print colored("venom lack\n", "red", on_black");
print colored("kill that fellow\n", "red", "on_yellow");

print colored("garish!\n", "green", "on_cyan", "blink");
```

or as:

```
use Term::ANSIColor qw(:constants);

print BLACK, ON_WHITE, "black on white\n";
print WHITE, ON_BLACK, "white on black\n";
print GREEN, ON_CYAN, BLINK, "garish!\n";
print RESET;
```

Here, **BLACK** is a function exported from Term::ANSIColor.

It's important to **print RESET** or **color("reset")** at the end of your program if you're not calling **colored** for everything. Failure to reset your terminal will leave it displaying odd colors. You may want to use:

```
END { print color("reset") }
```

to ensure the colors will be reset when your program finishes.

Attributes that span lines of text can confuse some programs or devices. If this becomes a problem, either manually set the attributes at the start of each line, or use **colored** after setting the variable **$Term::ANSIColor::EACHLINE** to the line terminator:

```
$Term::ANSIColor::EACHLINE = $/;
print colored(<<EOF, RED, ON_WHITE, BOLD, BLINK);
This way
each line
has its own
attribute set.
EOF
```

See Also

The documentation for the Term::AnsiColor module from CPAN

15.6. Reading from the Keyboard

Problem

You want to read a single character from the keyboard. For instance, you've displayed a menu of one-character options, and you don't want to require the user to press Enter to make their selection.

Solution

Use the CPAN module Term::ReadKey to put the terminal into **cbreak** mode, read characters from STDIN, and then put the terminal back into its normal mode:

```
use Term::ReadKey;

ReadMode 'cbreak';
$key = ReadKey(0);
ReadMode 'normal';
```

Discussion

Term::ReadKey can put the terminal into many modes—**cbreak** is just one of them. **cbreak** mode makes each character available to your program as it is typed (see Example 15-1). It also echoes the characters to the screen; see Recipe 15.10 for an example of a mode that does not echo.

Example 15-1. sascii

```
#!/usr/bin/perl -w
# sascii - Show ASCII values for keypresses

use Term::ReadKey;
ReadMode('cbreak');
print "Press keys to see their ASCII values.  Use Ctrl-C to quit.\n";

while (1) {
    $char = ReadKey(0);
    last unless defined $char;
    printf(" Decimal: %d\tHex: %x\n", ord($char), ord($char));
}

ReadMode('normal');
```

Using **cbreak** mode doesn't prevent the terminal's device driver from interpreting end-of-file and flow-control characters. If you want to be able to read a real Ctrl-C (which normally sends a **SIGINT** to your process) or a Ctrl-D (which indicates end-of-file under Unix), you want to use **raw** mode.

An argument of 0 to ReadKey indicates that we want a normal read using getc. If no input is available, the program will pause until there is some. We can also pass -1 to indicate a non-blocking read, or a number greater than 0 to indicate the number of seconds to wait for input to become available; fractional seconds are allowed. Non-blocking reads and timed-out reads return either undef when no input is available or a zero-length string on end of file.

Recent versions of Term::ReadKey also include limited support for non-Unix systems.

See Also

The getc and sysread functions in Chapter 3 of *Programming Perl,* and in *perlfunc*(1); the documentation for the Term::ReadKey module from CPAN; Recipe 15.8; Recipe 15.9

15.7. Ringing the Terminal Bell

Problem

You want to sound an alarm on the user's terminal.

Solution

Print the "\a" character to sound a bell:

```
print "\aWake up!\n";
```

Or, use the "vb" terminal capability to show a visual bell:

```
use Term::Cap;

$OSPEED = 9600;
eval {
    require POSIX;
    my $termios = POSIX::Termios->new();
    $termios->getattr;
    $OSPEED = $termios->getospeed;
};

$terminal = Term::Cap->Tgetent({OSPEED=>$OSPEED});
$vb = "";
eval {
    $terminal->Trequire("vb");
    $vb = $terminal->Tputs('vb', 1);
};

print $vb;                                # ring visual bell
```

Discussion

The "\a" escape is the same as "\cG", "\007", and "\x07". They all correspond to the ASCII BEL character and cause an irritating ding. In a crowded terminal room at the end of the semester, this beeping caused by dozens of *vi* novices
all trying to get out of insert mode at once can be maddening. The visual bell is a
workaround to avoid irritation. Based upon the polite principle that terminals
should be seen and not heard (at least, not in crowded rooms), some terminals let
you briefly reverse the foreground and background colors to give a flash of light
instead of an audible ring.

Not every terminal supports the visual bell, which is why we `eval` the code that
finds it. If the terminal doesn't support it, `Trequire` will `die` without having
changed the value of $vb from "". If the terminal does support it, the value of
$vb will be set to the character sequence to flash the bell.

There's a better approach to the bell issue in graphical terminal systems like *xterm*.
Many of these let you enable the visual bell from the enclosing application itself,
allowing all programs that blindly output a `chr(7)` to become less noisy.

See Also

The section on "String Literals" in Chapter 2 of *Programming Perl* or the section on
"Quote and Quote-like Operators" in *perlop*(1); the documentation for the standard Term::Cap module

15.8. Using POSIX termios

Problem

You'd like to manipulate your terminal characteristics directly.

Solution

Use the POSIX `termios` interface.

Description

Think of everything you can do with the *stty* command—you can set everything
from special characters to flow control and carriage-return mapping. The standard
POSIX module provides direct access to the low-level terminal interface to implement *stty*-like capabilities in your program.

Example 15-2 finds what your tty's erase and kill characters are (probably backspace and Ctrl-U). Then it sets them back to their original values out of antiquity, # and @, and has you type something. It restores them when done.

Example 15-2. demo POSIX termios

```perl
#!/usr/bin/perl -w
# demo POSIX termios

use POSIX qw(:termios_h);

$term = POSIX::Termios->new;
$term->getattr(fileno(STDIN));

$erase = $term->getcc(VERASE);
$kill = $term->getcc(VKILL);
printf "Erase is character %d, %s\n", $erase, uncontrol(chr($erase));
printf "Kill is character %d, %s\n", $kill, uncontrol(chr($kill));

$term->setcc(VERASE, ord('#'));
$term->setcc(VKILL, ord('@'));
$term->setattr(1, TCSANOW);

print("erase is #, kill is @; type something: ");
$line = <STDIN>;
print "You typed: $line";

$term->setcc(VERASE, $erase);
$term->setcc(VKILL, $kill);
$term->setattr(1, TCSANOW);

sub uncontrol {
    local $_ = shift;
    s/([\200-\377])/sprintf("M-%c",ord($1) & 0177)/eg;
    s/([\0-\37\177])/sprintf("^%c",ord($1) ^ 0100)/eg;
    return $_;
}
```

Here's a module called HotKey that implements a **readkey** function in pure Perl. It doesn't provide any benefit over Term::ReadKey, but it shows POSIX termios in action:

```perl
# HotKey.pm
package HotKey;

@ISA = qw(Exporter);
@EXPORT = qw(cbreak cooked readkey);

use strict;
use POSIX qw(:termios_h);
my ($term, $oterm, $echo, $noecho, $fd_stdin);

$fd_stdin = fileno(STDIN);
```

```
$term     = POSIX::Termios->new();
$term->getattr($fd_stdin);
$oterm    = $term->getlflag();

$echo     = ECHO | ECHOK | ICANON;
$noecho   = $oterm & ~$echo;

sub cbreak {
    $term->setlflag($noecho);  # ok, so i don't want echo either
    $term->setcc(VTIME, 1);
    $term->setattr($fd_stdin, TCSANOW);
}

sub cooked {
    $term->setlflag($oterm);
    $term->setcc(VTIME, 0);
    $term->setattr($fd_stdin, TCSANOW);
}

sub readkey {
    my $key = '';
    cbreak();
    sysread(STDIN, $key, 1);
    cooked();
    return $key;
}

END { cooked() }

1;
```

See Also

POSIX Programmer's Guide, by Donald Lewine; O'Reilly & Associates (1991); the documentation for the standard POSIX module, also in Chapter 7 of *Programming Perl*; Recipe 15.6; Recipe 15.9

15.9. Checking for Waiting Input

Problem

You want to know whether keyboard input is waiting without actually reading it.

Solution

Use the CPAN module Term::ReadKey, and try to read a key in non-blocking mode by passing it an argument of −1:

```
use Term::ReadKey;
```

```
ReadMode ('cbreak');

if (defined ($char = ReadKey(-1)) ) {
    # input was waiting and it was $char
} else {
    # no input was waiting
}

ReadMode ('normal');                    # restore normal tty settings
```

Discussion

The -1 parameter to ReadKey indicates a non-blocking read of a character. If no character is available, ReadKey returns undef.

See Also

The documentation for the Term::ReadKey module from CPAN; Recipe 15.6

15.10. Reading Passwords

Problem

You want to read input from the keyboard without the keystrokes being echoed on the screen. For instance, you want to read passwords as *passwd* does, i.e. without displaying the user's password.

Solution

Use the CPAN module Term::ReadKey, set the input mode to noecho, and then use ReadLine:

```
use Term::ReadKey;

ReadMode('noecho');
$password = ReadLine(0);
```

Discussion

Example 15-3 shows how to verify a user's password. If your system uses shadow passwords, only the superuser can get the encrypted form of the password with getpwuid. Everyone else just gets * as the password field of the database, which is useless for verifying passwords.

Example 15-3. checkuser

```perl
#!/usr/bin/perl -w
# checkuser - demonstrates reading and checking a user's password

use Term::ReadKey;

print "Enter your password: ";
ReadMode 'noecho';
$password = ReadLine 0;
chomp $password;
ReadMode 'normal';

print "\n";

($username, $encrypted) = ( getpwuid $< )[0,1];

if (crypt($password, $encrypted) ne $encrypted) {
    die "You are not $username\n";
} else {
    print "Welcome, $username\n";
}
```

See Also

The documentation for the Term::ReadKey module from CPAN; the `crypt` and `getpwuid` functions in Chapter 3 of *Programming Perl* and in *perlfunc*(1), which demonstrate using the *stty*(1) command; your system's *crypt*(3) and *passwd*(5) manpages (if you have them)

15.11. Editing Input

Problem

You want a user to be able to edit a line before sending it to you for reading.

Solution

Use the standard Term::ReadLine library along with the Term::ReadLine::Gnu module from CPAN:

```perl
use Term::ReadLine;

$term = Term::ReadLine->new("APP DESCRIPTION");
$OUT = $term->OUT || *STDOUT;

$term->addhistory($fake_line);
$line = $term->readline(PROMPT);

print $OUT "Any program output\n";
```

Discussion

The program in Example 15-4 acts as a crude shell. It reads a line and passes it to the shell to execute. The `readline` method reads a line from the terminal, with editing and history recall. It automatically adds the user's line to the history.

Example 15-4. vbsh

```perl
#!/usr/bin/perl -w
# vbsh -  very bad shell
use strict;

use Term::ReadLine;
use POSIX qw(:sys_wait_h);

my $term = Term::ReadLine->new("Simple Shell");
my $OUT = $term->OUT() || *STDOUT;
my $cmd;

while (defined ($cmd = $term->readline('$ ') )) {
    my @output = `$cmd`;
    my $exit_value  = $? >> 8;
    my $signal_num  = $? & 127;
    my $dumped_core = $? & 128;
    printf $OUT "Program terminated with status %d from signal %d%s\n",
            $exit_value, $signal_num,
            $dumped_core ? " (core dumped)" : "";
    print @output;
    $term->addhistory($cmd);
}
```

If you want to seed the history with your own functions, use the `addhistory` method:

```perl
$term->addhistory($seed_line);
```

You can't seed with more than one line at a time. To remove a line from the history, use the `remove_history` method, which takes an index into the history list. 0 is the first (least recent) entry, 1 the second, and so on up to the most recent history lines.

```perl
$term->remove_history($line_number);
```

To get a list of history lines, use the `GetHistory` method, which returns a list of the lines:

```perl
@history = $term->GetHistory;
```

See Also

The documentation for the standard Term::ReadLine module and the Term::ReadLine::Gnu from CPAN

15.12. Managing the Screen

Problem

You want to control the screen layout or highlighting, detect when special keys are pressed, or present full-screen menus, but you don't want to think about what kind of display device the user has.

Solution

Use the Curses module from CPAN, which makes use of your native *curses*(3) library.

Description

The *curses* library provides easy access to the full screen display in an efficient and device-independent fashion. (By display, we mean any cursor-addressable monitor.) With Curses, you write high-level code to put data on the logical display, building it up character by character or string by string. When you want output to show up, call the `refresh` function. The library generates output consisting only of the changes on the virtual display since the last call to `refresh`. This is particularly appreciated on a slow connection.

The example program in Example 15-5, called *rep*, demonstrates this. Call it with arguments of the program to run, like any of these:

```
% rep ps aux
% rep netstat
% rep -2.5 lpq
```

The *rep* script will repeatedly call the listed command, printing its output to the screen, updating only what has changed since the previous run. This is most effective when the changes between runs are small. It maintains the current date in reverse video at the bottom-right corner of your screen.

By default, *rep* waits 10 seconds before rerunning the command. You can change this delay period by calling it an optional number of seconds (which can be a decimal number) as shown above when calling *lpq*. You may also hit any key during the pause for it to run the command right then.

Example 15-5. rep

```
#!/usr/bin/perl -w
# rep - screen repeat command
use strict;
use Curses;
```

Example 15-5. rep (continued)

```perl
my $timeout = 10;
if (@ARGV && $ARGV[0] =~ /^-(\d+\.?\d*)$/) {
    $timeout = $1;
    shift;
}

die "usage: $0 [ -timeout ] cmd args\n" unless @ARGV;

initscr();             # start screen
noecho();
cbreak();
nodelay(1);            # so getch() is non-blocking

$SIG{INT} = sub { done("Ouch!") };
sub done { endwin(); print "@_\n"; exit; }

while (1) {
    while ((my $key = getch()) ne ERR) {      # maybe multiple keys
        done("See ya") if $key eq 'q'
    }
    my @data = `(@ARGV) 2>&1`;                 # gather output+errors
    for (my $i = 0; $i < $LINES; $i++) {
        addstr($i, 0, $data[$i] || ' ' x $COLS);
    }

    standout();
    addstr($LINES-1, $COLS - 24, scalar localtime);
    standend();

    move(0,0);
    refresh();                                 # flush new output to display

    my ($in, $out) = ('', '');
    vec($in,fileno(STDIN),1) = 1;              # look for key on stdin
    select($out = $in,undef,undef,$timeout);   # wait up to this long
}
```

Curses lets you tell whether the user typed one of the arrow keys or those other funny keys, like HOME or INSERT. This is normally difficult, because those keys send multiple bytes. With Curses, it's easy:

```perl
keypad(1);                    # enable keypad mode
$key = getch();
if ($key eq 'k'     ||        # vi mode
    $key eq "\cP"   ||        # emacs mode
    $key eq KEY_UP)           # arrow mode
{
    # do something
}
```

Other Curses functions let you read the text at particular screen coordinates, control highlighting and standout mode, and even manage multiple windows.

The perlmenu module, also from CPAN, is built on top of the lower-level Curses module. It provides·high-level access to menus and fill-out forms. Here's a sample form from the perlmenu distribution:

```
              Template Entry Demonstration

    Address Data Example                        Record # ____

    Name: [_____]
    Addr: [_____]
    City: [_____]     State: [__]     Zip: [\\\\\]

    Phone: (\\\) \\\-\\\\                 Password: [^^^^^^^^]

    Enter all information available.
    Edit fields with left/right arrow keys or "delete".
    Switch fields with "Tab" or up/down arrow keys.
    Indicate completion by pressing "Return".
    Refresh screen with "Control-L".
    Abort this demo here with "Control-X".
```

The user types in the areas indicated, with regular text indicated by underline fields, numeric data by backslashed fields, and starred-out data with circumflexed fields. This is reminiscent of Perl's formats, except that forms are used for output, not input.

See Also

Your system's *curses*(3) manpage (if you have it); the documentation for the Curses and the perlmenu modules from CPAN; the section on "Formats" in Chapter 2 of *Programming Perl*, or *perlform*(1); Recipe 3.10

15.13. *Controlling Another Program with Expect*

Problem

You want to automate interaction with a full-screen program that expects to have a terminal behind STDIN and STDOUT.

Solution

Use the Expect module from CPAN:

```
    use Expect;

    $command = Expect->spawn("program to run")
        or die "Couldn't start program: $!\n";
```

```
# prevent the program's output from being shown on our STDOUT
$command->log_stdout(0);

# wait 10 seconds for "Password:" to appear
unless ($command->expect(10, "Password")) {
    # timed out
}

# wait 20 seconds for something that matches /[1L]ogin: ?/
unless ($command->expect(20, -re => '[1L]ogin: ?')) {
    # timed out
}

# wait forever for "invalid" to appear
unless ($command->expect(undef, "invalid")) {
    # error occurred; the program probably went away
}

# send "Hello, world" and a carriage return to the program
print $command "Hello, world\r";

# if the program will terminate by itself, finish up with
$command->soft_close();

# if the program must be explicitly killed, finish up with
$command->hard_close();
```

Discussion

This module requires two other modules from CPAN: IO::Pty and IO::Stty. It sets up a pseudo-terminal to interact with programs that insist on using talking to the terminal device driver. People often use this for talking to *passwd* to change passwords. *telnet* (Net::Telnet, described in Recipe 18.6, is probably more suitable and portable) and *ftp* are also programs that expect a real tty.

Start the program you want to run with **Expect->spawn**, passing a program name and arguments either in a single string or as a list. Expect starts the program and returns an object representing that program, or **undef** if the program couldn't be started.

To wait for the program to emit a particular string, use the **expect** method. Its first argument is the number of seconds to wait for the string, or **undef** to wait forever. To wait for a string, give that string as the second argument to **expect**. To wait for a regular expression, give **"-re"** as the second argument and a string containing the pattern as the third argument. You can give further strings or patterns to wait for:

```
$which = $command->expect(30, "invalid", "succes", "error", "boom");
if ($which) {
```

```
        # found one of those strings
    }
```

In scalar context, expect returns the number of arguments it matched. In the example above, expect would return 1 if the program emitted "invalid", 2 if it emitted "succes", and so on. If none of the patterns or strings matches, expect returns false.

In list context, expect returns a five-element list. The first element is the number of the pattern or string that matched, the same as its return value in scalar context. The second argument is a string indicating why expect returned. If there were no error, the second argument will be undef. Possible errors are "1:TIME-OUT", "2:EOF", "3:spawn id(...)died" and "4:...". (See the *Expect*(3) manpage for the precise meaning of these messages.) The third argument of expect's return list is the string matched. The fourth argument is text before the match, and the fifth argument is text after the match.

Sending input to the program you're controlling with Expect is as simple as using print. The only catch is that terminals, devices, and sockets all vary in what they send and expect as the line terminator—we've left the sanctuary of the C standard I/O library, so the behind-the-scenes conversion to "\n" isn't taking place. We recommend trying "\r" at first. If that doesn't work, try "\n" and "\r\n".

When you're finished with the spawned program, you have three options. One, you can continue with your main program, and the spawned program will be forcibly killed when the main program ends. This will accumulate processes, though. Two, if you know the spawned program will terminate normally either when it has finished sending you output or because you told it to stop—for example, *telnet* after you exit the remote shell—call the soft_close method. If the spawned program could continue forever, like *tail -f,* then use the hard_close method; this kills the spawned program.

See Also

The documentation for the Expect, IO::Pty, and IO::Stty modules from CPAN; *Exploring Expect,* by Don Libes, O'Reilly & Associates (1995).

15.14. Creating Menus with Tk

Problem

You want to create a window that has a menu bar at the top.

Solution

Use the Tk Menubutton and Frame widgets:

```
use Tk;

$main = MainWindow->new();

# Create a horizontal space at the top of the window for the
# menu to live in.
$menubar = $main->Frame(-relief              => "raised",
                        -borderwidth         => 2)
                ->pack (-anchor              => "nw",
                        -fill                => "x");

# Create a button labeled "File" that brings up a menu
$file_menu = $menubar->Menubutton(-text       => "File",
                                  -underline => 1)
                ->pack      (-side        => "left" );
# Create entries in the "File" menu
$file_menu->command(-label    => "Print",
                    -command => \&Print);
```

This is considerably easier if you use the **-menuitems** shortcut:

```
$file_menu = $menubar->Menubutton(-text       => "File",
                                  -underline => 1,
                                  -menuitems => [
                [ Button => "Print",-command  => \&Print ],
                [ Button => "Save",-command   => \&Save  ] ])
                    ->pack(-side           => "left");
```

Discussion

Menus in applications can be viewed as four separate components working together: Frames, Menubuttons, Menus, and Menu Entries. The Frame is the horizontal bar at the top of the window that the menu resides in (the *menubar*). Inside the Frame are a set of Menubuttons, corresponding to Menus: File, Edit, Format, Buffers, and so on. When the user clicks on a Menubutton, the Menubutton brings up the corresponding Menu, a vertically arranged list of Menu Entries.

Options on a Menu are *labels* (Open, for example) or *separators* (horizontal lines dividing one set of entries from another in a single menu).

The *command* entry, like Print in the File menu above, has code associated with it. When the entry is selected, the command is run by invoking the callback. These are the most common:

```
$file_menu->command(-label    => "Quit Immediately",
                    -command => sub { exit } );
```

Separators don't have any action associated with them:

```
$file_menu->separator();
```

A *checkbutton* menu entry has an on value, an off value, and a variable associated with it. If the variable has the on value, the checkbutton menu entry has a check beside its label. If the variable has the off value, it does not. Selecting the entry on the menu toggles the state of the variable.

```
$options_menu->checkbutton(-label    => "Create Debugging File",
                           -variable => \$debug,
                           -onvalue  => 1,
                           -offvalue => 0);
```

A group of *radiobuttons* is associated with a single variable. Only one radiobutton associated with that variable can be on at any time. Selecting a radiobutton gives the variable the value associated with it:

```
$debug_menu->radiobutton(-label    => "Level 1",
                         -variable => \$log_level,
                         -value    => 1);

$debug_menu->radiobutton(-label    => "Level 2",
                         -variable => \$log_level,
                         -value    => 2);

$debug_menu->radiobutton(-label    => "Level 3",
                         -variable => \$log_level,
                         -value    => 3);
```

Create nested menus with the *cascade* menu entry. For instance, under *Netscape Navigator*, the File menu button at the left has a cascade menu entry New that brings up a selection of new windows. Creating a cascading menu entry is trickier than creating the other menu entries. You must create a cascade menu entry, fetch the new menu associated with that menu entry, and create entries on that new menu.

```
# step 1: create the cascading menu entry
$format_menu->cascade            (-label    => "Font");

# step 2: get the new Menu we just made
$font_menu = $format_menu->cget("-menu");

# step 3: populate that Menu
$font_menu->radiobutton          (-label    => "Courier",
                                  -variable => \$font_name,
                                  -value    => "courier");
$font_menu->radiobutton          (-label    => "Times Roman",
                                  -variable => \$font_name,
                                  -value    => "times");
```

A *tear-off* menu entry lets the user move the menu that it is on. By default, all Menubuttons and cascade menu entries make Menus that have a tear-off entry at the top of them. To create Menus without that default, use the -tearoff option:

```
$format_menu = $menubar->Menubutton(-text      => "Format",
                                    -underline => 1
                                    -tearoff   => 0)
              ->pack;

$font_menu  = $format_menu->cascade(-label     => "Font",
                                    -tearoff   => 0);
```

The -menuitems option to Menubutton is a shorthand for creating these menubuttons. Pass it an array reference representing the options on the Menubutton. Each option is itself an anonymous array. The first two elements of the option array are the button type ("command", "radiobutton", "checkbutton", "cascade", or "tearoff") and the menu name.

Here's how to use menuitems to make an Edit menu:

```
my $f = $menubar->Menubutton(-text => "Edit", -underline => 0,
                             -menuitems =>
    [
        [Button => 'Copy',      -command => \&edit_copy ],
        [Button => 'Cut',       -command => \&edit_cut ],
        [Button => 'Paste',     -command => \&edit_paste ],
        [Button => 'Delete',    -command => \&edit_delete ],
        [Separator => ''],
        [Cascade => 'Object ...', -tearoff => 0,
                                  -menuitems => [
            [ Button => "Circle",  -command => \&edit_circle ],
            [ Button => "Square",  -command => \&edit_square ],
            [ Button => "Point",   -command => \&edit_point ] ] ],
    ])->grid(-row => 0, -column => 0, -sticky => 'w');
```

See Also

The documentation for the Tk module from CPAN

15.15. Creating Dialog Boxes with Tk

Problem

You want to create a dialog box, i.e., a new top-level window with buttons to make the window go away. The dialog box might also have other items, such as labels and text entry widgets for creating a fill-out form. You could use such a dialog box to collect registration information, and you want it to go away when registration is sent or if the user chooses not to register.

Solution

For simple jobs, use the Tk::DialogBox widget:

```
use Tk::DialogBox;

$dialog = $main->DialogBox( -title   => "Register This Program",
                            -buttons => [ "Register", "Cancel" ] );

# add widgets to the dialog box with $dialog->Add()

# later, when you need to display the dialog box
$button = $dialog->Show();
if ($button eq "Register") {
    # ...
} elsif ($button eq "Cancel") {
    # ...
} else {
    # this shouldn't happen
}
```

Discussion

A DialogBox has two parts: the bottom is a set of buttons, and the top has the widgets of your choosing. Showing a DialogBox pops it up and returns the button the user selected.

Example 15-6 contains a complete program demonstrating the DialogBox.

Example 15-6. tksample3

```
#!/usr/bin/perl -w
# tksample3 - demonstrate dialog boxes

use Tk;
use Tk::DialogBox;

$main = MainWindow->new();

$dialog = $main->DialogBox( -title   => "Register",
                            -buttons => [ "Register", "Cancel" ],
                          );

# the top part of the dialog box will let people enter their names,
# with a Label as a prompt

$dialog->add("Label", -text => "Name")->pack();
$entry = $dialog->add("Entry", -width => 35)->pack();

# we bring up the dialog box with a button
$main->Button( -text    => "Click Here For Registration Form",
               -command => \&register)    ->pack(-side => "left");
$main->Button( -text    => "Quit",
```

Example 15-6. tksample3 (continued)

```
                    -command => sub { exit } ) ->pack(-side => "left");

MainLoop;

#
# register
#
# Called to pop up the registration dialog box
#

sub register {
    my $button;
    my $done = 0;

    do {
        # show the dialog
        $button = $dialog->Show;

        # act based on what button they pushed
        if ($button eq "Register") {
                my $name = $entry->get;

            if (defined($name) && length($name)) {
                print "Welcome to the fold, $name\n";
                $done = 1;
            } else {
                print "You didn't give me your name!\n";
            }
        } else {
            print "Sorry you decided not to register.\n";
            $done = 1;
        }
    } until $done;
}
```

The top part of this DialogBox has two widgets: a label and a text entry. To collect more information from the user, we'd have more labels and text entries.

A common use of dialog boxes is to display error messages or warnings. The program in Example 15-7 demonstrates how to display Perl's **warn** function in a DialogBox.

Example 15-7. tksample4

```
#!/usr/bin/perl -w
# tksample4 - popup dialog boxes for warnings

use Tk;
use Tk::DialogBox;

my $main;
```

Example 15-7. tksample4 (continued)

```
# set up a warning handler that displays the warning in a Tk dialog box

BEGIN {
    $SIG{__WARN__} = sub {
        if (defined $main) {
            my $dialog = $main->DialogBox( -title   => "Warning",
                                           -buttons => [ "Acknowledge" ]);
            $dialog->add("Label", -text => $_[0])->pack;
            $dialog->Show;
        } else {
            print STDOUT join("\n", @_), "n";
        }
    };
}

# your program goes here

$main = MainWindow->new();

$main->Button( -text    => "Make A Warning",
               -command => \&make_warning) ->pack(-side => "left");
$main->Button( -text    => "Quit",
               -command => sub { exit } )  ->pack(-side => "left");

MainLoop;

# dummy subroutine to generate a warning

sub make_warning {
    my $a;
    my $b = 2 * $a;
}
```

See Also

The Tk::DialogBox manpage in the documentation for the Tk module from CPAN; the *menu*(n) manpage (if you have it)

15.16. Responding to Tk Resize Events

Problem

You've written a Tk program, but your widget layout goes awry when the user resizes their window.

Solution

You can prevent the user from resizing the window by intercepting the Configure event:

```
use Tk;

$main = MainWindow->new();

$main->bind('<Configure>' => sub {
    $xe = $main->XEvent;
    $main->maxsize($xe->w, $xe->h);
    $main->minsize($xe->w, $xe->h);
});
```

Or you can use **pack** to control how each widget resizes and expands when the user resizes its container:

```
$widget->pack( -fill => "both", -expand => 1 );
$widget->pack( -fill => "x",    -expand => 1 );
```

Discussion

By default, packed widgets resize if their container changes size—they don't scale themselves or their contents to the new size. This can lead to empty space between widgets, or cropped or cramped widgets if the user resizes the window.

One solution is to prevent resizing. We **bind** to the **<Configure>** event, which is sent when a widget's size or position changes, registering a callback to reset the window's size. This is how you'd ensure a popup error-message box couldn't be resized.

You often want to let the user resize the application's windows. You must then define how each widget will react. Do this through the arguments to the **pack** method: **-fill** controls the dimensions the widget will resize in, and **-expand** controls whether the widget's size will change to match available space. The **-expand** option takes a Boolean value, true or false. The **-fill** option takes a string indicating the dimensions the widget can claim space in: **"x"**, **"y"**, **"both"**, or **"none"**.

The solution requires both options. Without **-fill**, **-expand** won't claim space to grow into. Without **-expand**, **-fill** will claim empty space but won't expand in it.

Different parts of your application will behave differently. The main area of a web browser, for example, should probably change size in both dimensions when the window is resized. You'd pack the widget like this:

```
$mainarea->pack( -fill => "both", -expand => 1);
```

The menubar above the main area, though, should expand horizontally but not vertically. You'd pack the widget thus:

```
$menubar->pack( -fill => "x", -expand => 1 );
```

Associated with resizing is the need to anchor a widget to part of its container. Here's how you'd anchor the menubar to the top left corner of its container when you call pack:

```
$menubar->pack (-fill      => "x",
                -expand    => 1,
                -anchor    => "nw" );
```

Now when you resize it, the menubar stays at the top of the window where it belongs, instead of being centered in wide open space.

See Also

The *pack*(n), *XEvent*(3), and *XConfigureEvent*(3) manpages (if you have them); *Tcl and the Tk Toolkit,* by John Ousterhout, Addison-Wesley (1994)

15.17. Removing the DOS Shell Window with Windows Perl/Tk

Problem

You have written a Perl program for the Windows port of Perl and Tk, but you get a DOS shell window every time you start your program.

Solution

Start your program through another Perl script. The Perl script in Example 15-8 is a loader that starts *realprogram* without the DOS window.

Example 15-8. loader

```
#!/usr/bin/perl -w
# loader - starts Perl scripts without the annoying DOS window
use strict;
use Win32;
use Win32::Process;

# Create the process object.

Win32::Process::Create($Win32::Process::Create::ProcessObj,
    'C:/perl5/bin/perl.exe',         # Whereabouts of Perl
    'perl realprogram',              #
    0,                               # Don't inherit.
    DETACHED_PROCESS,                #
```

Example 15-8. loader (continued)

```
    ".") or                          # current dir.
die print_error();

sub print_error() {
    return Win32::FormatMessage( Win32::GetLastError() );
}
```

Description

This program isn't as cryptic as it looks. You get the DOS box because your Perl binary was compiled as a console application. It needs a DOS window open to read STDIN and write STDOUT. This is fine for command-line applications, but there's no need for it if you're using Tk for all your user interaction.

This loader uses the Win32::Process module to run the real program in a new process. The process is detached from the current one, so when the loader ends, its DOS window will go away. Your real program will continue on in glorious freedom without the shackles of the past.

Should trouble strike and your real program not load, the loader dies with the Windows error message.

See Also

The documentation for the Win32::Process module, which is included with distributions of Perl destined for Microsoft systems

15.18. Program: Small termcap program

Description

This program clears your screen and scribbles all over it until you interrupt it. It shows how to use Term::Cap to clear the screen, move the cursor, and write anywhere on the screen. It also uses Recipe 16.6.

The program text is shown in Example 15-9.

Example 15-9. tcapdemo

```
#!/usr/bin/perl -w
# tcapdemo - show off direct cursor placement

use POSIX;
use Term::Cap;

init();                    # Initialize Term::Cap.
zip();                     # Bounce lines around the screen.
```

Example 15-9. tcapdemo (continued)

```perl
finish();                          # Clean up afterward.
exit();

# Two convenience functions.  clear_screen is obvious, and
# clear_end clears to the end of the screen.
sub clear_screen { $tcap->Tputs('cl', 1, *STDOUT) }
sub clear_end    { $tcap->Tputs('cd', 1, *STDOUT) }

# Move the cursor to a particular location.
sub gotoxy {
    my($x, $y) = @_;
    $tcap->Tgoto('cm', $x, $y, *STDOUT);
}

# Get the terminal speed through the POSIX module and use that
# to initialize Term::Cap.
sub init {
    $| = 1;
    $delay = (shift() || 0) * 0.005;
    my $termios = POSIX::Termios->new();
    $termios->getattr;
    my $ospeed = $termios->getospeed;
    $tcap = Term::Cap->Tgetent ({ TERM => undef, OSPEED => $ospeed });
    $tcap->Trequire(qw(cl cm cd));
}

# Bounce lines around the screen until the user interrupts with
# Ctrl-C.
sub zip {
    clear_screen();
    ($maxrow, $maxcol) = ($tcap->{_li} - 1, $tcap->{_co} - 1);

    @chars = qw(* - / | \ _);
    sub circle { push(@chars, shift @chars); }

    $interrupted = 0;
    $SIG{INT} = sub { ++$interrupted };

    $col = $row = 0;
    ($row_sign, $col_sign) = (1,1);

    do {
        gotoxy($col, $row);
        print $chars[0];
        select(undef, undef, undef, $delay);

        $row += $row_sign;
        $col += $col_sign;

        if    ($row == $maxrow) { $row_sign = -1; circle; }
        elsif ($row == 0 )      { $row_sign = +1; circle; }

        if    ($col == $maxcol) { $col_sign = -1; circle; }
        elsif ($col == 0 )      { $col_sign = +1; circle; }
```

Example 15-9. tcapdemo (continued)

```
    } until $interrupted;

}

# Clean up the screen.
sub finish {
    gotoxy(0, $maxrow);
    clear_end();
}
```

This is what it looks like in mid-run:

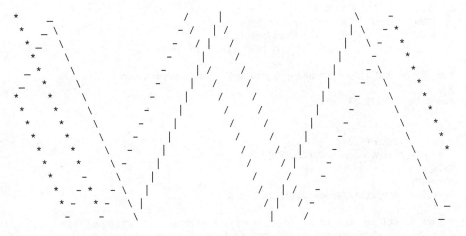

See Also

termcap(5) (if you have it); the documentation for the standard Term::Cap module

15.19. Program: tkshufflepod

This short program uses Tk to list the =head1 sections in the file using the Listbox widget, and it lets you drag the sections around to reorder them. When you're done, press **"s"** or **"q"** to save or quit. You can even double-click on a section to view it with the Pod widget. It writes the section text to a temporary file in */tmp* and removes the file when the Pod widget is destroyed.

Call it with the name of the Pod file to view:

```
% tkshufflepod chap15.pod
```

We used this a lot when we wrote this book.

The program text is shown in Example 15-10.

Example 15-10. tkshufflepod

```perl
#!/usr/bin/perl -w
# tkshufflepod - reorder =head1 sections in a pod file

use Tk;
use strict;

# declare variables

my $podfile;       # name of the file to open
my $m;             # main window
my $l;             # listbox
my ($up, $down);   # positions to move
my @sections;      # list of pod sections
my $all_pod;       # text of pod file (used when reading)

# read the pod file into memory, and split it into sections.

$podfile = shift || "-";

undef $/;
open(F, "< $podfile")
   or die "Can't open $podfile : $!\n";
$all_pod = <F>;
close(F);
@sections = split(/(?==head1)/, $all_pod);

# turn @sections into an array of anonymous arrays.  The first element
# in each of these arrays is the original text of the message, while
# the second element is the text following =head1 (the section title).

foreach (@sections) {
    /(.*)/;
    $_ = [ $_, $1 ];
}

# fire up Tk and display the list of sections.

$m = MainWindow->new();
$l = $m->Listbox('-width' => 60)->pack('-expand' => 1, '-fill' => 'both');

foreach my $section (@sections) {
    $l->insert("end", $section->[1]);
}

# permit dragging by binding to the Listbox widget.
$l->bind( '<Any-Button>'        => \&down );
$l->bind( '<Any-ButtonRelease>' => \&up );

# permit viewing by binding double-click
$l->bind( '<Double-Button>'     => \&view );
```

Example 15-10. tkshufflepod (continued)

```
# 'q' quits and 's' saves
$m->bind( '<q>'      => sub { exit } );
$m->bind( '<s>'      => \&save );

MainLoop;

# down(widget): called when the user clicks on an item in the Listbox.

sub down {
    my $self = shift;
    $down = $self->curselection;;
}

# up(widget): called when the user releases the mouse button in the
# Listbox.

sub up {
    my $self = shift;
    my $elt;

    $up = $self->curselection;;

    return if $down == $up;

    # change selection list
    $elt = $sections[$down];
    splice(@sections, $down, 1);
    splice(@sections, $up, 0, $elt);

    $self->delete($down);
    $self->insert($up, $sections[$up]->[1]);
}

# save(widget): called to save the list of sections.

sub save {
    my $self = shift;

    open(F, "> $podfile")
      or die "Can't open $podfile for writing: $!";
    print F map { $_->[0] } @sections;
    close F;

    exit;
}

# view(widget): called to display the widget.  Uses the Pod widget.

sub view {
    my $self = shift;
    my $temporary = "/tmp/$$-section.pod";
```

Example 15-10. tkshufflepod (continued)

```
    my $popup;

    open(F, "> $temporary")
        or warn ("Can't open $temporary : $!\n"), return;
    print F $sections[$down]->[0];
    close(F);
    $popup = $m->Pod('-file' => $temporary);

    $popup->bind('<Destroy>' => sub { unlink $temporary } );
}
```

16

Process Management and Communication

It is quite a three-pipe problem, and I beg that you won't speak to me for fifty minutes.

—Sherlock Holmes
The Red-Headed League

16.0. Introduction

Perl may be many things to many people, but to most of us it is the glue that connects diverse components. This chapter is about launching commands and connecting separate processes together. It's about managing their creation, communication, and ultimate demise. It's about systems programming.

When it comes to systems programming, Perl, as usual, makes easy things easy and hard things possible. If you want to use it as you would the shell, Perl is happy to assist you. If you want to roll up your sleeves for low-level hacking like a hardcore C programmer, you can do that, too.

Because Perl lets you get so close to the system, portability issues can sneak in. This chapter is the most Unix-centric chapter of the book. It will be tremendously useful to those on Unix systems, but only of limited use to others. We deal with features that aren't as universal as strings and numbers and basic arithmetic. Most basic operations work more or less the same everywhere. But if you're not using some kind of Unix or other POSIX conformant system, most of the interesting features in this chapter may work differently for you—or not at all. Check the documentation that came with your Perl port if you aren't sure.

Process Creation

In this chapter, we cover the proper care and feeding of your own child processes. Sometimes this means launching a stand-alone command and letting it have its own way with the world (using `system`). Other times it means keeping a tight rein on your child, feeding it carefully filtered input or taking hold of its output stream (backticks and piped `open`s). Without even starting a new process, you can use `exec` to replace your current program with a completely different program.

We first show how to use the most portable and commonly used operations for managing processes: backticks, `system`, `open`, and the manipulation of the `%SIG` hash. Those are the easy things, but we don't stop there. We also show what to do when the simple approach isn't good enough.

For example, you might want to interrupt your program while it's running a different program. Maybe you need to process a child program's standard error separately from its standard output. Perhaps you need to control both the input and output of a program simultaneously. When you tire of having just one thread of control and begin to take advantage of multitasking, you'll want to learn how to split your current program into several, simultaneously running processes that all talk to each other.

For tasks like these, you have to drop back to the underlying system calls: `pipe`, `fork`, and `exec`. The `pipe` function creates two connected filehandles, a reader and writer, whereby anything written to the writer can be read from the reader. The `fork` function is the basis of multitasking, but unfortunately it has not been supported on all non-Unix systems. It clones off a duplicate process identical in virtually every aspect to its parent, including variable settings and open files. The most noticable changes are the process ID and parent process ID. New programs are started by forking, then using `exec` to replace the program in the child process with a new one. You don't always both `fork` and `exec` together, so having them as separate primitives is more expressive and powerful than if all you could do is run `system`. In practice, you're more apt to use `fork` by itself than `exec` by itself.

When a child process dies, its memory is returned to the operating system, but its entry in the process table isn't freed. This lets a parent check the exit status of its child processes. Processes that have died but haven't been removed from the process table are called *zombies*, and you should clean them up lest they fill the whole process table. Backticks and the `system` and `open` functions automatically take care of this, and will work on most non-Unix systems. You have more to worry about when you go beyond these simple portable functions and use low-level primitives to launch programs. One thing to worry about is signals.

Signals

Your process is notified of the death of a child it created with a *signal.* Signals are a kind of notification delivered by the operating system. They are used for errors (when the kernel says, "Hey, you can't touch that area of memory!") and for events (death of a child, expiration of a per-process timer, interrupt with Ctrl-C). If you're launching processes manually, you normally arrange for a subroutine of your choosing to be called whenever one of your children exits.

Each process has a default disposition for each possible signal. You may install your own handler or otherwise change the disposition of most signals. Only SIGKILL and SIGSTOP cannot be changed. The rest you can ignore, trap, or block.

Briefly, here's a rundown of the more important signals:

SIGINT
> is normally triggered by Ctrl-C. This requests that a process interrupt what it's doing. Simple programs like filters usually just die, but more important ones like shells, editors, or FTP programs usually use SIGINT to stop long-running operations so you can tell them to do something else.

SIGQUIT
> is also normally generated by a terminal, usually Ctrl-\. Its default behavior is to generate a core dump.

SIGTERM
> is sent by the *kill* shell command when no signal name is explicitly given. Think of it as a polite request for a process to die.

SIGUSR1 and SIGUSR2
> are never caused by system events, so user applications can safely use them for their own purposes.

SIGPIPE
> is sent by the kernel when your process tries to write to a pipe or socket when the process on the other end has closed its connection, usually because it no longer exists.

SIGALRM
> is sent when the timer set by the **alarm** function expires, as described in Recipe 16.21.

SIGHUP
> is sent to a process when its controlling terminal gets a hang-up (e.g., the modem lost its carrier), but it also often indicates that a program should restart or reread its configuration.

SIGCHLD

is probably the most important signal when it comes to low-level systems programming. The system sends your process a SIGCHLD when one of its child processes stops running—or, more likely, when that child exits. See Recipe 16.19 for more on SIGCHLD.

Signal names are a convenience for humans. Each signal has an associated number that the operating system uses instead of names. Although we talk about SIGCHLD, your operating system only knows it as a number, like 20 (these numbers vary across operating systems). Perl translates between signal names and numbers for you, so you can think in terms of signal names.

Recipes 16.15, 16.17, 16.21, 16.18, and 16.20 run the full gamut of signal handling.

16.1. Gathering Output from a Program

Problem

You want to run a program and collect its output into a variable.

Solution

Either use backticks:

```
$output = `program args`;   # collect output into one multiline string
@output = `program args`;   # collect output into array, one line per element
```

Or use Recipe 16.4:

```
open(README, "program args |") or die "Can't run program: $!\n";
while(<README>) {
    $output .= $_;
}
close(README);
```

Discussion

The backticks are a convenient way to run other programs and gather their output. The backticks do not return until the called program exits. Perl goes to some trouble behind the scenes to collect the output, so it is inefficient to use the backticks and ignore their return value:

```
`fsck -y /dev/rsd1a`;       # BAD AND SCARY
```

Both the **open** function and the backtick operator call the shell to run their commands. This makes them unsafe when used in a program with special privileges.

A high-level workaround is given in Recipe 19.6. Here's a low-level workaround, using `pipe`, `fork`, and `exec`:

```
use POSIX qw(:sys_wait_h);

pipe(README, WRITEME);
if ($pid = fork) {
    # parent
    $SIG{CHLD} = sub { 1 while ( waitpid(-1, WNOHANG)) > 0 };
    close(WRITEME);
} else {
    die "cannot fork: $!" unless defined $pid;
    # child
    open(STDOUT, ">&=WRITEME")       or die "Couldn't redirect STDOUT: $!";
    close(README);
    exec($program, $arg1, $arg2)     or die "Couldn't run $program : $!\n";
}

while (<README>) {
    $string .= $_;
    # or  push(@strings, $_);
}
close(README);
```

See Also

The section on "Cooperating with Strangers" in Chapter 6 of *Programming Perl*, or *perlsec*(1); Recipe 16.2; Recipe 16.4; Recipe 16.10; Recipe 16.19; Recipe 19.6

16.2. Running Another Program

Problem

You want to run another program from your own, pause until the other program is done, and then continue. The other program should have same STDIN and STD-OUT as you have.

Solution

Call `system` with a string to have the shell interpret the string as a command line:

```
$status = system("vi $myfile");
```

If you don't want the shell involved, pass `system` a list:

```
$status = system("vi", $myfile);
```

Discussion

The **system** function is the simplest and most generic way to run another program in Perl. It doesn't gather the program's STDOUT like backticks or **open**.
Instead, its return value is (essentially) that program's exit status. While the new
program is running, your main program is suspended, so the new program can
read from your STDIN and write to your STDOUT so users can interact with it.

Like **open**, **exec**, and backticks, **system** uses the shell to start the program whenever it's called with one argument. This is convenient when you want to do redirection or other tricks:

```
system("cmd1 args | cmd2 | cmd3 >outfile");
system("cmd args <infile >outfile 2>errfile");
```

To avoid the shell, call **system** with a list of arguments:

```
$status = system($program, $arg1, $arg);
die "$program exited funny: $?" unless $status == 0;
```

The returned status value is not just the exit value: it includes the signal number (if
any) that the process died from. This is the same value that **wait** sets $? to. See
Recipe 16.19 to learn how to decode this value.

The **system** function ignores SIGINT and SIGQUIT while child processes are running. That way those signals will kill only the child process. If you want your main
program to die as well, check the return value of **system**, or the value of the $?
variable.

```
if (($signo = system(@arglist)) &= 127) {
    die "program killed by signal $signo\n";
}
```

To get the effect of a **system** that ignores SIGINT, install your own signal handler
and then manually **fork** and **exec**:

```
if ($pid = fork) {
    # parent catches INT and berates user
    local $SIG{INT} = sub { print "Tsk tsk, no process interruptus\n" };
    waitpid($pid, 0);
} else {
    die "cannot fork: $!" unless defined $pid;
    # child ignores INT and does its thing
    $SIG{INT} = "IGNORE";
    exec("summarize", "/etc/logfiles")           or die "Can't exec: $!\n";
}
```

A few programs examine their own program name. Shells look to see whether
they were called with a leading minus to indicate interactivity. The *expn* program
at the end of Chapter 18 behaves differently if called as *vrfy*, which can happen if

you've installed the file under two different links as suggested. This is why you shouldn't trust that $0 is really the pathname to the invoked program—you could have been lied to in a number of ways.

If you want to fib to the program you're executing about its own name, specify the real path as the "indirect object" in front of the list passed to system. (This also works with exec.) The indirect object has no comma following it, just like using printf with a filehandle or making object methods without the pointer arrow.

```
$shell = '/bin/tcsh';
system $shell '-csh';          # pretend it's a login shell
```

Or, more directly:

```
system {'/bin/tcsh'} '-csh';     # pretend it's a login shell
```

In the next example, the program's real pathname is supplied in the indirect object slot as {'/home/tchrist/scripts/expn'}. The fictitious name 'vrfy' is given as the first real function argument, which the program will see stored in $0.

```
# call expn as vrfy
system {'/home/tchrist/scripts/expn'} 'vrfy', @ADDRESSES;
```

Using an indirect object with system is also more secure. This usage forces interpretation of the arguments as a multivalued list, even if the list had just one argument. That way you're safe from the shell expanding wildcards or splitting up words with whitespace in them.

```
@args = ( "echo surprise" );

system @args;# subject to shell escapes if @args == 1
system { $args[0] } @args;  # safe even with one-arg list
```

The first version, the one without the indirect object, ran the *echo* program, passing it "surprise" an argument. The second version didn't—it tried to run a program literally called "echo surprise", didn't find it, and set $? to a non-zero value indicating failure.

See Also

The section on "Cooperating with Strangers" in Chapter 6 of *Programming Perl*, or *perlsec*(1); the waitpid, fork, exec, system, and open functions in Chapter 3 of *Programming Perl* or *perlfunc*(1); Recipe 16.1; Recipe 16.4; Recipe 16.19; Recipe 19.6; *Advanced Programming in the UNIX Environment*, by Richard W. Stevens; Addison-Wesley (1992)

16.3. *Replacing the Current Program with a Different One*

Problem

You want to replace the running program with another, as when checking parameters and setting up the initial environment before running another program.

Solution

Use the built-in **exec** function. If **exec** is called with a single argument containing metacharacters, the shell will be used to run the program:

```
exec("archive *.data")
    or die "Couldn't replace myself with archive: $!\n";
```

If you pass **exec** more than one argument, the shell will not be used:

```
exec("archive", "accounting.data")
    or die "Couldn't replace myself with archive: $!\n";
```

If called with a single argument containing no shell metacharacters, the argument will be split on whitespace and then interpreted as though the resulting list had been passed to **exec**:

```
exec("archive accounting.data")
    or die "Couldn't replace myself with archive: $!\n";
```

Discussion

The **exec** function in Perl is a direct interface to the *execlp*(2) system call, which replaces the current program with another, leaving the process intact. The program that calls **exec** gets wiped clean, and its place in the operating system's process table is taken by the program specified in the arguments to **exec**. As a result, the new program has the same process ID ($$) as the original program. If the specified program couldn't be run, **exec** returns a false value and the original program continues. Be sure to check for this.

If you **exec** yourself into a different program, neither your END blocks nor any object destructors will be automatically run as they would if your process actually exited.

See Also

The **exec** function in Chapter 3 of *Programming Perl* and in *perlfunc*(1); your system's *execlp*(2) manpage (if you have it); Recipe 16.2

16.4. Reading or Writing to Another Program

Problem

You want to run another program and either read its output or supply the program with input.

Solution

Use **open** with a pipe symbol at the beginning or end. To read from a program, put the pipe symbol at the end:

```
$pid = open(README, "program arguments |")  or die "Couldn't fork: $!\n";
while (<README>) {
    # ...
}
close(README)                           or die "Couldn't close: $!\n";
```

To write to the program, put the pipe at the beginning:

```
$pid = open(WRITEME, "| program arguments") or die "Couldn't fork: $!\n";
print WRITEME "data\n";
close(WRITEME)                          or die "Couldn't close: $!\n";
```

Discussion

In the case of reading, this is similar to using backticks, except you have a process ID and a filehandle. As with the backticks, **open** uses the shell if it sees shell-special characters in its argument, but it doesn't if there aren't any. This is usually a welcome convenience, because it lets the shell do filename wildcard expansion and I/O redirection, saving you the trouble.

However, sometimes this isn't desirable. Piped **opens** that include unchecked user data would be unsafe while running in taint mode or in untrustworthy situations. Recipe 19.6 shows how to get the effect of a piped **open** without risking using the shell.

Notice how we specifically call **close** on the filehandle. When you use **open** to connect a filehandle to a child process, Perl remembers this and automatically waits for the child when you close the filehandle. If the child hasn't exited by then, Perl waits until it does. This can be a very, very long wait if your child doesn't exit:

```
$pid = open(F, "sleep 100000|");    # child goes to sleep
close(F);                           # and the parent goes to lala land
```

To avoid this, you can save the PID returned by open to kill your child, or use a manual pipe-fork-exec sequence as described in Recipe 16.10.

If you attempt to write to a process that has gone away, your process will receive a SIGPIPE. The default disposition for this signal is to kill your process, so the truly paranoid install a SIGPIPE handler just in case.

If you want to run another program and be able to supply its STDIN yourself, a similar construct is used:

```
$pid = open(WRITEME, "| program args");
print WRITEME "hello\n";              # program will get hello\n on STDIN
close(WRITEME);                       # program will get EOF on STDIN
```

The leading pipe symbol in the filename argument to open tells Perl to start another process instead. It connects the opened filehandle to the process's STDIN. Anything you write to the filehandle can be read by the program through its STDIN. When you close the filehandle, the opened process will get an eof when it next tries to read from STDIN.

You can also use this technique to change your program's normal output path. For example, to automatically run everything through a pager, use something like:

```
$pager = $ENV{PAGER} || '/usr/bin/less';  # XXX: might not exist
open(STDOUT, "| $pager");
```

Now, without changing the rest of your program, anything you print to standard output will go through the pager automatically.

As with opening a process for reading, text passed to the shell here is subject to shell metacharacter interpretation. To avoid the shell, a similar solution is called for. As before, the parent should also be wary of close. If the parent closes the filehandle connecting it to the child, the parent will block while waiting for the child to finish. If the child doesn't finish, neither will the close. The workaround as before is either to kill your child process prematurely, or else use the low-level pipe-fork-exec scenario.

When using piped opens, always check return values of both open and close, not just of open. That's because the return value from open does not indicate whether the command was succesfully launched. With a piped open, you fork a child to execute the command. Assuming the system hadn't run out of processes, the fork immediately returns the PID of the child it just created.

By the time the child process tries to exec the command, it's a separately scheduled process. So if the command can't be found, there's effectively no way to communicate this back to the open function, because that function is in a different process!

Check the return value from close to see whether the command was successful. If the child process exits with non-zero status—which it will do if the command isn't found—the close returns false and $? is set to the wait status of that process. You can interpret its contents as described in Recipe 16.19.

In the case of a pipe opened for writing, you should also install a SIGPIPE handler, since writing to a child that isn't there will trigger a SIGPIPE.

See Also

The open function in Chapter 3 of *Programming Perl* and in *perlfunc*(1); Recipe 16.10; Recipe 16.15; Recipe 16.19; Recipe 19.6

16.5. Filtering Your Own Output

Problem

You want to postprocess your program's output without writing a separate program to do so.

Solution

Use the forking form of open to attach a filter to yourself. For example, this will restrict your program to a hundred lines of output:

```
head(100);
while (<>) {
    print;
}

sub head {
    my $lines = shift || 20;
    return if $pid = open(STDOUT, "|-");
    die "cannot fork: $!" unless defined $pid;
    while (<STDIN>) {
        print;
        last unless --$lines ;
    }
    exit;
}
```

Discussion

It's easy to add an output filter. Just use the forking *open* on your own STDOUT, and let the child filter STDIN to STDOUT, performing whatever alterations you care about. Notice that we install the output filter *before* we generate the output. This makes sense—you can't filter your output if it has already left your program.

Any such filters should be applied in LIFO order—the last one inserted is the first one run.

Here's an example that uses two output filters. One numbers lines; the other quotes the lines like a mail reply. When run on */etc/motd*, you get something like:

```
1: > Welcome to Linux, version 2.0.33 on a i686
2: >
3: >      "The software required 'Windows 95 or better',
4: >       so I installed Linux."
```

If you reversed the order of the two filters, you'd get:

```
> 1: Welcome to Linux, Kernel version 2.0.33 on a i686
> 2:
> 3:      "The software required 'Windows 95 or better',
> 4:       so I installed Linux."
```

The program is in Example 16-1.

Example 16-1. qnumcat

```perl
#!/usr/bin/perl
# qnumcat - demo additive output filters

number();                   # push number filter on STDOUT
quote();                    # push quote filter on STDOUT

while (<>) {                # act like /bin/cat
    print;
}
close STDOUT;               # tell kids we're done--politely
exit;

sub number {
    my $pid;
    return if $pid = open(STDOUT, "|-");
    die "cannot fork: $!" unless defined $pid;
    while (<STDIN>) { printf "%d: %s", $., $_ }
    exit;
}

sub quote {
    my $pid;
    return if $pid = open(STDOUT, "|-");
    die "cannot fork: $!" unless defined $pid;
    while (<STDIN>) { print "> $_" }
    exit;
}
```

As with all process forks, doing this a zillion times has some cost, but it's fine for a couple of processes, or even a couple dozen. If the system was actually designed to be multitasking right from the start, as Unix was, this is far cheaper than you imagine. Virtual memory and copy-on-write makes this efficient. Forking is an elegant and inexpensive solution to many, if not most, multitasking needs.

See Also

The open function in Chapter 3 of *Programming Perl* and in *perlfunc*(1); Recipe 16.4

16.6. Preprocessing Input

Problem

You'd like your programs to work on files with funny formats, such as compressed files or remote web documents specified with a URL, but your program only knows how to access regular text in local files.

Solution

Take advantage of Perl's easy pipe handling by changing your input files' names to pipes before opening them.

To autoprocess gzipped or compressed files by decompressing them with *gzip,* use:

```
@ARGV = map { /\.(gz|Z)$/ ? "gzip -dc $_ |" : $_  } @ARGV;
while (<>) {
    # .......
}
```

To fetch URLs before processing them, use the *GET* program from LWP (see Chapter 20, *Web Automation*):

```
@ARGV = map { m#^\w+://# ? "GET $_ |" : $_ } @ARGV;
while (<>) {
    # .......
}
```

You might prefer to fetch just the text, of course, not the HTML. That just means using a different command, perhaps *lynx -dump.*

Discussion

As shown in Recipe 16.1, Perl's built-in open function is magical: you don't have to do anything special to get Perl to open a pipe instead of a file. (That's why it's sometimes called *magic open* and, when applied to implicit ARGV processing, *magic ARGV.*) If it looks like a pipe, Perl will open it like a pipe. We take advantage of this by rewriting certain filenames to include a decompression or other preprocessing stage. For example, the file `"09tails.gz"` becomes `"gzcat -dc 09tails.gz|"`.

This technique has further applications. Suppose you wanted to read */etc/passwd* if the machine isn't using NIS, and the output of *ypcat passwd* if it is. You'd use the output of the *domainname* program to decide if you're running NIS, and then set the filename to open to be either `"< /etc/passwd"` or `"ypcat passwd|"`:

```
$pwdinfo = `domainname` =~ /^(\(none\))?$/
                ? '< /etc/passwd'
                : 'ypcat  passwd |';

open(PWD, $pwdinfo)                    or die "can't open $pwdinfo: $!";
```

The wonderful thing is that even if you didn't think to build such processing into your program, Perl already did it for you. Imagine a snippet of code like this:

```
print "File, please? ";
chomp($file = <>);
open (FH, $file)                       or die "can't open $file: $!";
```

The user can enter a regular filename—or something like `"webget http:// www.perl.com |"` instead—and your program would suddenly be reading from the output of some *webget* program. They could even enter –, a lone minus sign, which, when opened for reading, interpolates standard input instead.

This also comes in handy with the automatic ARGV processing we saw in Recipe 7.7.

See Also

Recipe 7.7; Recipe 16.4

16.7. Reading STDERR from a Program

Problem

You want to run a program as you would with **system**, backticks, or **open**, but you don't want its STDERR to be sent to your STDERR. You would like to be able to either ignore or read the STDERR.

Solution

Use the shell's numeric redirection and duplication syntax for file descriptors. (We don't check the return value from **open** here, to make the examples easier to read, but you should always check it in your programs!)

To capture a command's STDERR and STDOUT together:

```
$output = `cmd 2>&1`;                        # with backticks
# or
$pid = open(PH, "cmd 2>&1 |");               # with an open pipe
while (<PH>) { }                             # plus a read
```

To capture a command's STDOUT and discard its STDERR:

```
$output = `cmd 2>/dev/null`;                 # with backticks
# or
$pid = open(PH, "cmd 2>/dev/null |");        # with an open pipe
while (<PH>) { }                             # plus a read
```

To capture a command's STDERR and discard its STDOUT:

```
$output = `cmd 2>&1 1>/dev/null`;            # with backticks
# or
$pid = open(PH, "cmd 2>&1 1>/dev/null |");   # with an open pipe
while (<PH>) { }                             # plus a read
```

To exchange a command's STDOUT and STDERR, i.e., capture the STDERR but have its STDOUT come out on our old STDERR:

```
$output = `cmd 3>&1 1>&2 2>&3 3>&-`;         # with backticks
# or
$pid = open(PH, "cmd 3>&1 1>&2 2>&3 3>&-|"); # with an open pipe
while (<PH>) { }                             # plus a read
```

To read both a command's STDOUT and its STDERR separately, it's easiest and safest to redirect them separately to files, and then read from those files when the program is done:

```
system("program args 1>/tmp/program.stdout 2>/tmp/program.stderr");
```

Discussion

When you launch a command with backticks, a piped open, or system on a single string, Perl checks for characters special to the shell. These allow you to redirect the new program's file descriptors. STDIN is file descriptor number 0, STDOUT number 1, and STDERR number 2. You can then use 2>*file* to redirect STDERR to a file. The special notation &N where N is a file descriptor number is used to redirect to a file descriptor. Therefore, 2>&1 points STDERR at STDOUT.

Here is a table of interesting shell file descriptor redirections:

Redirection	Meaning
0</dev/null	Make STDIN give immediate EOF
1>/dev/null	Discard STDOUT
2>/dev/null	Discard STDERR
2>&1	Send STDERR to STDOUT instead

Redirection	Meaning
2>&-	Close STDERR (not recommended)
3<>/dev/tty	Open fd 3 to */dev/tty* in read-write mode

Using this, let's examine the most complicated of the redirection sequences from the solution section:

```
$output = `cmd 3>&1 1>&2 2>&3 3>&-`;
```

There are four steps here:

Step A: 3>&1

Make a new file descriptor, number 3, be a copy of number 1. This saves where STDOUT had been destined in the new file descriptor we've just opened.

Step B: 1>&2

Make STDOUT go wherever STDERR had been going. We still have the saved destination squirreled away in descriptor 3.

Step C: 2>&3

Make file descriptor 2 a copy of number 3. That means that STDERR is now going out where STDOUT had been originally going.

Step D: 3>&-

Since we're done moving streams around, keep everything nice and tidy and close our temporary file descriptor. This avoids file descriptor leaks.

If that's confusing, it might help to think in terms of regular variables and a sequence of assignment statements, with $fd1 representing STDOUT and $fd2 representing STDERR. If you wanted to exchange the two variables, you'd use a temporary to hold one value. That's all we're doing here.

```
$fd3 = $fd1;
$fd1 = $fd2;
$fd2 = $fd3;
$fd3 = undef;
```

When all's said and done, the string returned from the backticks is the command's STDERR, and its STDOUT has been diverted to the original STDERR.

Ordering is important in all these examples. That's because the shell processes file descriptor redirections in strictly left to right order.

```
system("prog args 1>tmpfile 2>&1");
system("prog args 2>&1 1>tmpfile");
```

The first command sends both standard out and standard error to the temporary file. The second command sends only the old standard output there, and the old standard error shows up on the old standard out. If that's confusing, think in terms of assignments to variables representing file descriptors:

```
# system ("prog args 1>tmpfile 2>&1");
$fd1 = "tmpfile";          # change stdout destination first
$fd2 = $fd1;               # now point stderr there, too
```

is very different from:

```
# system("prog args 2>&1 1>tmpfile");
$fd2 = $fd1;               # stderr same destination as stdout
$fd1 = "tmpfile";          # but change stdout destination
```

See Also

Your system's *sh*(1) manpage (if you have one) for details about file descriptor redirection; the `system` function in Chapter 3 of *Programming Perl* and in *perlfunc*(1)

16.8. Controlling Input and Output of Another Program

Problem

You want to both write to and read from another program. The **open** function lets you do one or the other, but not both.

Solution

Use the standard IPC::Open2 module:

```
use IPC::Open2;

open2(*README, *WRITEME, $program);
print WRITEME "here's your input\n";
$output = <README>;
close(WRITEME);
close(README);
```

Discussion

Wanting simultaneous read and write access to another program is very common, but surprisingly perilous. That's why **open** doesn't let you say:

```
open(DOUBLE_HANDLE, "| program args |")      # WRONG
```

The big problem here is buffering. Because you can't force the other program to unbuffer its output, you can't guarantee that your reads won't block. If you block trying to read at the same time the other process blocks waiting for you to send something, you've achieved the unholy state of deadlock. There you'll both stay, wedged, until someone kills your process or the machine reboots.

If you control the other process's buffering because you wrote the other program and know how it works, then IPC::Open2 may be the module for you. The first two arguments to open2 that IPC::Open2 exports into your namespace are filehandles. Either pass references to typeglobs as in the Solution, or create your own IO::Handle objects and pass them in:

```
use IPC::Open2;
use IO::Handle;

($reader, $writer) = (IO::Handle->new, IO::Handle->new);
open2($reader, $writer, $program);
```

If you pass in objects, you must have created them (with `IO::Handle->new`, for instance) first. The open2 function will not create handles for you if you pass in variables that don't contain filehandles.

Alternatively, you can pass in arguments that look like `"<&OTHERFILEHANDLE"` or `">&OTHERFILEHANDLE"`, which specify existing filehandles for the child process to read from or write to. These filehandles don't have to be controlled by your program—they may be connected to other programs, files, or sockets.

You can specify the program either as a list (where the first element is the program name and the remaining elements are arguments to the program) or as a single string (which is passed to the shell as a command to start the program). If you also want control over the process's standard error, use the IPC::Open3 module and see the next recipe.

If an error occurs, open2 and open3 do not return. Instead, they die with an error message that begins with `"open2"` or `"open3"`. To test for failure, use the eval BLOCK construct:

```
eval {
    open2($readme, $writeme, @program_and_arguments);
};
if ($@) {
    if ($@ =~ /^open2/) {
        warn "open2 failed: $!\n$@\n";
        return;
    }
    die;            # reraise unforeseen exception
}
```

See Also

The documentation for the IPC::Open2 and IPC::Open3 modules; Recipe 10.12; the eval function in Chapter 3 of *Programming Perl* and in *perlfunc*(1); the $@ variable in the section on "Global Special Variables" in Chapter 2 of *Programming Perl* and in *perlvar*(1)

16.9. Controlling the Input, Output, and Error of Another Program

Problem

You want full control over a command's input, output, and error streams.

Solution

Carefully use the standard IPC::Open3 module, possibly in conjunction with the IO::Select module. (IO::Select is new as of the 5.004 distribution.)

Discussion

If you're interested in only one of the program's STDIN, STDOUT, or STDERR, the task is simple. When you want to manage two or more of these, however, it abruptly stops being simple. Multiplexing multiple I/O streams is never a pretty picture. Here's an easy workaround:

```
@all = `($cmd | sed -e 's/^/stdout: /' ) 2>&1`;
for (@all) { push @{ s/stdout: // ? \@outlines : \@errlines }, $_ }
print "STDOUT:\n", @outlines, "\n";
print "STDERR:\n", @errlines, "\n";
```

If you don't have *sed* on your system, you'll find that for simple cases like this, *perl -pe* works just as well as *sed -e*.

However, that's not really simultaneous processing. All we're doing is marking STDOUT lines with `"stdout:"` and then stripping them back out once we've read all the STDOUT and STDERR the program produced.

You can use the standard IPC::Open3 module for this. Mysteriously, the argument order is different for IPC::Open3 than for IPC::Open2.

```
open3(*WRITEHANDLE, *READHANDLE, *ERRHANDLE, "program to run");
```

Using this has even *more* potential for chaos than using open2. If you're reading the program's STDERR as it is trying to write more than one buffer's worth to its STDOUT, the program will block on the write because its buffers are full, and you will block on the read because there's nothing available.

You can avoid this deadlock by mimicking open3 with fork, open, and exec; making all the filehandles unbuffered; and using sysread, syswrite, and select to decide which readable filehandle to read a byte from. This makes your program slower and bulkier, though, and it doesn't solve the classic **open2** deadlock where each program is expecting the other to say something.

```
use IPC::Open3;
$pid = open3(*HIS_IN, *HIS_OUT, *HIS_ERR, $cmd);
close(HIS_IN);  # give end of file to kid, or feed him
@outlines = <HIS_OUT>;              # read till EOF
@errlines = <HIS_ERR>;              # XXX: block potential if massive
print "STDOUT:\n", @outlines, "\n";
print "STDERR:\n", @errlines, "\n";
```

As if deadlock weren't bad enough, this approach is subtly error-prone. There are at least three worrisome situations: both the child and the parent trying to read at the same time, causing deadlock; full buffers causing the child to block as it tries to write to STDERR while the parent is blocked trying to read from the child's STDOUT; and full buffers causing the parent to block writing to the child's STDIN while the child is blocked writing to either its STDOUT or STDERR. The first problem is generally unsolvable, although you can work around it by setting timers with **alarm** and preventing blocking operations from restarting if a **SIGALRM** is received.

We use the IO::Select module (you could also do this with the built-in function **select**) to learn which filehandles (if any) can be read from. This solves the second problem, but not the third. To solve the third, you also need **alarm** and non-restarting **SIGALRM**.

If you want to send input to the program, read its output, and either read or ignore its error, you need to work much harder. (See Example 16-2.)

Example 16-2. cmd3sel

```
#!/usr/bin/perl
# cmd3sel - control all three of kids in, out, and error.
use IPC::Open3;
use IO::Select;

$cmd = "grep vt33 /none/such - /etc/termcap";
$pid = open3(*CMD_IN, *CMD_OUT, *CMD_ERR, $cmd);

$SIG{CHLD} = sub {
    print "REAPER: status $? on $pid\n" if waitpid($pid, 0) > 0
};

print CMD_IN "This line has a vt33 lurking in it\n";
close(CMD_IN);

$selector = IO::Select->new();
$selector->add(*CMD_ERR, *CMD_OUT);

while (@ready = $selector->can_read) {
```

Example 16-2. cmd3sel (continued)

```
    foreach $fh (@ready) {
        if (fileno($fh) == fileno(CMD_ERR)) {print "STDERR: ", scalar <CMD_ERR>}
        else                                {print "STDOUT: ", scalar <CMD_OUT>}
        $selector->remove($fh) if eof($fh);
    }
}
close(CMD_OUT);
close(CMD_ERR);
```

We sent only a short line as input, then closed the handle. This avoids the dead-lock situation of two processes each waiting for the other to write something.

See Also

The documentation for the standard IO::Select, IPC::Open2, and IPC::Open3 modules; the **alarm** function in Chapter 3 of *Programming Perl* or *perlfunc*(1); Recipe 16.8; Recipe 16.15; Recipe 16.16

16.10. Communicating Between Related Processes

Problem

You have two related processes that need to communicate, and you need better control than you can get from **open**, **system**, and backticks.

Solution

Use **pipe** and then **fork**:

```
    pipe(READER, WRITER);
    if (fork) {
        # run parent code, either reading or writing, not both
    } else {
        # run child code, either reading or writing, not both
    }
```

Or use a special forking form of **open**:

```
    if ($pid = open(CHILD, "|-")) {
            # run parent code, writing to child
    } else {
        die "cannot fork: $!" unless defined $pid;
        # otherwise run child code here, reading from parent
    }
```

Or, going the other way:

```
if ($pid = open(CHILD, "-|")) {
    # run parent code, reading from child
} else {
    die "cannot fork: $!" unless defined $pid;
    # otherwise run child code here, writing to parent
}
```

Discussion

Pipes are simply two connected filehandles, where data written to one filehandle can be read by the other. The **pipe** function creates two filehandles linked in this way, one writable and one readable. Even though you can't take two already existing filehandles and link them, **pipe** can be used for communication between processes. One process creates a pair of filehandles with the **pipe** functions, then forks off a child, resulting in two distinct processes both running in the same program, each with a copy of the connected filehandles.

It doesn't matter which process is the reader and which is the writer, so long as one of them takes one role and its peer process takes the other. You can only have one-way communication. (But read on.)

We'll pull in the IO::Handle module so we can call its **autoflush()** method. (You could instead play the **select** games described in Chapter 7, if you prefer a lightweight solution.) If we didn't, our single line of output would get lodged in the pipe and not make it through to the other side until we closed that handle.

The version of the parent writing to the child is shown in Example 16-3.

Example 16-3. pipe1

```
#!/usr/bin/perl -w
# pipe1 - use pipe and fork so parent can send to child

use IO::Handle;
pipe(READER, WRITER);
WRITER->autoflush(1);

if ($pid = fork) {
    close READER;
    print WRITER "Parent Pid $$ is sending this\n";
    close WRITER;
    waitpid($pid,0);
} else {
    die "cannot fork: $!" unless defined $pid;
    close WRITER;
    chomp($line = <READER>);
    print "Child Pid $$ just read this: '$line'\n";
    close READER;   # this will happen anyway
    exit;
}
```

In the examples in this recipe, most error checking has been left as an exercise for the reader. This is so you can more clearly see how the functions interact. In real life, test the return values of all system calls.

The version of the child writing to the parent is shown in Example 16-4.

Example 16-4. pipe2

```perl
#!/usr/bin/perl -w
# pipe2 - use pipe and fork so child can send to parent

use IO::Handle;
pipe(READER, WRITER);
WRITER->autoflush(1);

if ($pid = fork) {
    close WRITER;
    chomp($line = <READER>);
    print "Parent Pid $$ just read this: '$line'\n";
    close READER;
    waitpid($pid,0);
} else {
    die "cannot fork: $!" unless defined $pid;
    close READER;
    print WRITER "Child Pid $$ is sending this\n";
    close WRITER;   # this will happen anyway
    exit;
}
```

In most code, both halves would go into loops, with the reader continuing to read until end of file. This happens when the writer closes or exits.

Because piped filehandles are not bidirectional, each process uses just one of the pair and closes the filehandle it doesn't use. The reason is subtle; picture the situation where the reader does not close the writable filehandle. If the writer then exits while the reader is trying to read something, the reader will hang forever. This is because the system won't tell the reader that there's no more data to be read until all copies of the writable filehandle are closed.

The **open** function, when passed as its second argument either `"-|"` or `"|-"` will implicitly pipe and fork. This makes the piping code above slightly easier. The child talks to the parent over STDIN or STDOUT, depending on whether `"-|"` or `"|-"` was used.

Using **open** this way, if the parent wants to write to the child, it does something like what's shown in Example 16-5.

Example 16-5. pipe3

```perl
#!/usr/bin/perl -w
# pipe3 - use forking open so parent can send to child
```

Example 16-5. pipe3 (continued)

```
use IO::Handle;
if ($pid = open(CHILD, "|-")) {
    CHILD->autoflush(1);
    print CHILD "Parent Pid $$ is sending this\n";
    close(CHILD);
} else {
    die "cannot fork: $!" unless defined $pid;
    chomp($line = <STDIN>);
    print "Child Pid $$ just read this: '$line'\n";
    exit;
}
```

Since the child already has STDIN set to the parent, the child could **exec** some other program that expects to read from standard input, such as *lpr*. In fact, this is useful and commonly done.

If the child wants to write to the parent, it does something like what's shown in Example 16-6.

Example 16-6. pipe4

```
#!/usr/bin/perl -w
# pipe4 - use forking open so child can send to parent

use IO::Handle;
if ($pid = open(CHILD, "-|")) {
    chomp($line = <CHILD>);
    print "Parent Pid $$ just read this: '$line'\n";
    close(CHILD);
} else {
    die "cannot fork: $!" unless defined $pid;
    STDOUT->autoflush(1);
    print STDOUT "Child Pid $$ is sending this\n";
    exit;
}
```

Again, since the child already has its STDOUT connected to the parent, this child could **exec** some other program to produce something interesting on its standard output. That output would be available to the parent as input from <CHILD>.

When using **open** this way, we don't have to manually call **waitpid** since we didn't do a manual fork. We do have to call **close**, though. In both cases, the $? variable will have the child's wait status in it (see Recipe 16.19 to see how to interpret this status value).

The preceding examples were unidirectional. What if you want both processes talking to each other? Just make two calls to **pipe** before forking. You must be

careful about who tells whom what and when, though, or you're apt to deadlock.
(See Example 16-7.)

Example 16-7. pipe5

```
#!/usr/bin/perl -w
# pipe5 - bidirectional communication using two pipe pairs
#          designed for the socketpair-challenged
use IO::Handle;
pipe(PARENT_RDR, CHILD_WTR);
pipe(CHILD_RDR,  PARENT_WTR);
CHILD_WTR->autoflush(1);
PARENT_WTR->autoflush(1);

if ($pid = fork) {
    close PARENT_RDR; close PARENT_WTR;
    print CHILD_WTR "Parent Pid $$ is sending this\n";
    chomp($line = <CHILD_RDR>);
    print "Parent Pid $$ just read this: '$line'\n";
    close CHILD_RDR; close CHILD_WTR;
    waitpid($pid,0);
} else {
    die "cannot fork: $!" unless defined $pid;
    close CHILD_RDR; close CHILD_WTR;
    chomp($line = <PARENT_RDR>);
    print "Child Pid $$ just read this: '$line'\n";
    print PARENT_WTR "Child Pid $$ is sending this\n";
    close PARENT_RDR; close PARENT_WTR;
    exit;
}
```

That's getting complicated. It just so happens that there's a special system call,
shown in Example 16-8, that makes the last example simpler. It's called **socketpair**, and it works like **pipe**, except that both handles can be used for reading
and for writing.

Example 16-8. pipe6

```
#!/usr/bin/perl -w
# pipe6 - bidirectional communication using socketpair
#    "the best ones always go both ways"

use Socket;
use IO::Handle;
# We say AF_UNIX because although *_LOCAL is the
# POSIX 1003.1g form of the constant, many machines
# still don't have it.
socketpair(CHILD, PARENT, AF_UNIX, SOCK_STREAM, PF_UNSPEC)
    or  die "socketpair: $!";

CHILD->autoflush(1);
PARENT->autoflush(1);
```

Example 16-8. pipe6 (continued)

```
if ($pid = fork) {
    close PARENT;
    print CHILD "Parent Pid $$ is sending this\n";
    chomp($line = <CHILD>);
    print "Parent Pid $$ just read this: '$line'\n";
    close CHILD;
    waitpid($pid,0);
} else {
    die "cannot fork: $!" unless defined $pid;
    close CHILD;
    chomp($line = <PARENT>);
    print "Child Pid $$ just read this: '$line'\n";
    print PARENT "Child Pid $$ is sending this\n";
    close PARENT;
    exit;
}
```

In fact, some systems have historically implemented pipes as two half-closed ends of a socketpair. They essentially define `pipe(READER, WRITER)` this way:

```
socketpair(READER, WRITER, AF_UNIX, SOCK_STREAM, PF_UNSPEC);
shutdown(READER, 1);        # no more writing for reader
shutdown(WRITER, 0);        # no more reading for writer
```

On Linux kernels before 2.0.34, the *shutdown(2)* system call was broken. Instead of telling the reader not to write and the writer not to read, you had to tell the reader not to read and the writer not to write.

See Also

Chapter 3 of *Programming Perl* or *perlfunc*(1) for all functions used here; the documentation for the standard IPC::Open2 module; *Advanced Programming in the Unix Environment*; Recipe 16.8; Recipe 19.6

16.11. *Making a Process Look Like a File with Named Pipes*

Problem

You want a process to intercept all access to a file. For instance, you want to make your ~/.*plan* file a program that returns a random quote.

Solution

Use named pipes. First create one, probably from your shell:

```
% mkfifo /path/to/named.pipe
```

Here's a reader for it:

```
open(FIFO, "< /path/to/named.pipe")           or die $!;
while (<FIFO>) {
    print "Got: $_";
}
close(FIFO);
```

Here's a writer for it:

```
open(FIFO, "> /path/to/named.pipe")           or die $!;
print FIFO "Smoke this.\n";
close(FIFO);
```

Discussion

A named pipe, or FIFO as they are also known, is a special file that acts as a buffer to connect processes on the same machine. Ordinary pipes also allow processes to communicate, but those processes must have inherited the filehandles from their parents. To use a named pipe, a process need know only the named pipe's filename. In most cases, processes don't even need to be aware that they're reading from a FIFO.

Named pipes can be read from and written to just as though they were ordinary files (unlike Unix-domain sockets as discussed in Chapter 17). Data written into the FIFO is buffered up by the operating system, then read back in the order it was written in. Because a FIFO acts as a buffer to connect processes, opening one for reading will block until another process opens it for writing, and vice versa. If you **open** for read and write using the +< mode to **open**, you won't block (on most systems) because your process could be both reader and writer.

Let's examine how to use a named pipe so people will get a different file each time they *finger* you. To create a named pipe, use *mkfifo* or *mknod* to create a named pipe called *.plan* in your home directory:

```
% mkfifo ~/.plan            # isn't this everywhere yet?
% mknod  ~/.plan p          # in case you don't have mkfifo
```

On some systems, you must use *mknod*(8). The location and names of these programs aren't uniform or necessarily obvious, so consult your system documentation to find out where these programs are.

The next step is to create a program to feed data to the programs that read from your ~/.plan file. We'll just print the date and time, as shown in Example 16-9.

Example 16-9. dateplan

```
#!/usr/bin/perl -w
# dateplan - place current date and time in .plan file
while (1) {
    open(FIFO, "> $ENV{HOME}/.plan")
```

Example 16-9. dateplan (continued)

```
        or die "Couldn't open $ENV{HOME}/.plan for writing: $!\n";
    print FIFO "The current time is ", scalar(localtime), "\n";
    close FIFO;
    sleep 1;
}
```

Unfortunately, this won't always work, because some *finger* programs and their attendant daemons check the size of the *.plan* file before trying to read it. Because named pipes appear as special files of zero size on the filesystem, such clients and servers will not try to open or read from our named pipe, and the trick will fail.

In our *.plan* example, the writer was a daemon. It's not uncommon for readers to be daemons as well. Take, for instance, the use of a named pipe to centralize logging from many processes. The log server reads log messages from the named pipe and can send them to a database or file. Clients write their messages to the named pipe. This removes the distribution logic from the clients, making changes to message distribution easy to implement.

Example 16-10 is a simple program to read two-line messages where the first line is the name of the service and the second line is the message being logged. All messages from `httpd` are ignored, while all messages from `login` are saved to */var/log/login*.

Example 16-10. fifolog

```
#!/usr/bin/perl -w
# fifolog - read and record log msgs from fifo

use IO::File;

$SIG{ALRM} = sub { close(FIFO) };     # move on to the next queued process

while (1) {
    alarm(0);                         # turn off alarm for blocking open
    open(FIFO, "< /tmp/log")          or die "Can't open /tmp/log : $!\n";
    alarm(1);                         # you have 1 second to log

    $service = <FIFO>;
    next unless defined $service;     # interrupted or nothing logged
    chomp $service;

    $message = <FIFO>;
    next unless defined $message;     # interrupted or nothing logged
    chomp $message;

    alarm(0);                         # turn off alarms for message processing

    if ($service eq "http") {
        # ignoring
    } elsif ($service eq "login") {
```

Example 16-10. fifolog (continued)

```
        # log to /var/log/login
        if ( open(LOG, ">> /tmp/login") ) {
            print LOG scalar(localtime), " $service $message\n";
            close(LOG);
        } else {
            warn "Couldn't log $service $message to /var/log/login : $!\n";
        }
    }
}
```

This program is more complicated than the *.plan* program for several reasons. First
and foremost, we don't want our logging server to block would-be writers for
long. It's easy to imagine a situation where an attacker or misbehaving writer
opens the named pipe for writing, but doesn't send a complete message. To prevent this, we use `alarm` and `SIGALRM` to signal us if we get stuck reading.

Only two exceptional conditions can happen when using named pipes: a writer
can have its reader disappear, or vice versa. If a process is reading from a named
pipe and the writer closes its end, the reading process will get an end of file (<>
returns `undef`). If the reader closes the connection, though, the writer will get a
`SIGPIPE` when it next tries to write there. If you disregard broken pipe signals
with `$SIG{PIPE} = 'IGNORE'`, your `print` will return a false value and `$!` will be
set to `EPIPE`:

```
use POSIX qw(:errno_h);

$SIG{PIPE} = 'IGNORE';
# ...
$status = print FIFO "Are you there?\n";
if (!$status && $! == EPIPE) {
    warn "My reader has forsaken me!\n";
    next;
}
```

You may be asking "If I have 100 processes all trying simultaneously to write to
this server, how can I be sure that I'll get 100 separate entries and not a jumbled
mishmash with characters or lines from different processes?" That's a good question. The POSIX standard says that writes of less than `PIPE_BUF` bytes in size will
be delivered atomically, i.e. not jumbled. You can get the `PIPE_BUF` constant from
`POSIX`:

```
use POSIX;
print PIPE_BUF, "\n";
```

Fortunately, the POSIX standard also requires `PIPE_BUF` to be *at least* 512 bytes.
This means that all we have to do is ensure that our clients don't try to log more
than 512 bytes at a time.

What if you want to log more than 512 bytes at a time? Then you split each large message into several smaller (fewer than 512 bytes) messages, preface each with the unique client identifier (process ID, say) and have the server reassemble them. This is similar to the processing involved in TCP/IP message fragmentation and reassembly.

Because a single named pipe doesn't allow bidirectional access between writer and reader, authentication and similar ways of preventing forged messages are hard to do (if not impossible). Rather than struggle to force such things on top of a model that doesn't accommodate them, you are better off using the filesystem's access control to restrict access to the file through the owner and group permissions on the named pipe.

See Also

mkfifo(8) or *mknod(8)* (if you have them); Recipe 17.6

16.12. Sharing Variables in Different Processes

Problem

You want to share variables across forks or between unrelated processes.

Solution

Use SysV IPC, if your operating system supports it.

Discussion

While SysV IPC (shared memory, semaphores, etc.) isn't as widely used as pipes, named pipes, and sockets for interprocess communication, it still has some interesting properties. Normally, however, you can't expect to use shared memory via shmget or the *mmap(2)* system call to share a variable among several processes. That's because Perl would reallocate your string when you weren't wanting it to.

The CPAN module IPC::Shareable takes care of that. Using a clever `tie` module, SysV shared memory, and the Storable module from CPAN allows data structures of arbitrary complexity to be shared among cooperating processes on the same machine. These processes don't even have to be related to each other.

Example 16-11 is a simple demonstration of the module.

Example 16-11. sharetest

```perl
#!/usr/bin/perl
# sharetest - test shared variables across forks
use IPC::Shareable;

$handle = tie $buffer, 'IPC::Shareable', undef, { destroy => 1 };
$SIG{INT} = sub { die "$$ dying\n" };

for (1 .. 10) {
    unless ($child = fork) {           # i'm the child
        die "cannot fork: $!" unless defined $child;
        squabble();
        exit;
    }
    push @kids, $child;  # in case we care about their pids
}

while (1) {
    print "Buffer is $buffer\n";
    sleep 1;
}
die "Not reached";

sub squabble {
    my $i = 0;
    while (1) {
        next if $buffer =~ /^$$\b/o;
        $handle->shlock();
        $i++;
        $buffer = "$$ $i";
        $handle->shunlock();
    }
}
```

The starting process creates the shared variable, forks off 10 children, and then sits back and prints out the value of the buffer every second or so, forever, or until you hit Ctrl-C.

Because the SIGINT handler was set before any forking, it got inherited by the squabbling children as well, so they'll also bite the dust when the process group is interrupted. Keyboard interrupts send signals to the whole process group, not just one process.

What do the kids squabble over? They're bickering over who gets to update that shared variable. Each one looks to see whether someone else was here or not. So long as the buffer starts with their own signature (their PID), they leave it alone. As soon as someone else has changed it, they lock the shared variable using a special method call on the handle returned from the `tie`, update it, and release the lock.

The program runs much faster by commenting out the line that starts with `next` where each process is checking that they were the last one to touch the buffer.

The `/^$$\b/o` may look suspicious, since `/o` tells Perl to compile the pattern once only, but then went and changed the variable's value by forking. Fortunately, the value isn't locked at program compile time, but only the first time the pattern is itself compiled in each process, during whose own lifetime `$$` does not alter.

The IPC::Sharable module also supports sharing variables among unrelated processes on the same machine. See its documentation for details.

See Also

The `semctl`, `semget`, `semop`, `shmctl`, `shmget`, `shmread`, and `shmwrite` functions in Chapter 3 of *Programming Perl* and in *perlfunc*(1); the documentation for the IPC::Shareable module from CPAN

16.13. Listing Available Signals

Problem

You want to know the signals your operating system provides.

Solution

If your shell has a built-in *kill -l* command, use it:

```
% kill -l
HUP INT QUIT ILL TRAP ABRT BUS FPE KILL USR1 SEGV USR2 PIPE
ALRM TERM CHLD CONT STOP TSTP TTIN TTOU URG XCPU XFSZ VTALRM
PROF WINCH POLL PWR
```

Or using just Perl, print the keys in `%SIG` if you have release 5.004 or later:

```
% perl -e 'print join(" ", keys %SIG), "\n"'
XCPU ILL QUIT STOP EMT ABRT BUS USR1 XFSZ TSTP INT IOT USR2 INFO TTOU
ALRM KILL HUP URG PIPE CONT SEGV VTALRM PROF TRAP IO TERM WINCH CHLD
FPE TTIN SYS
```

Before version 5.004, you had to use the Config module:

```
% perl -MConfig -e 'print $Config{sig_name}'
ZERO HUP INT QUIT ILL TRAP ABRT EMT FPE KILL BUS SEGV SYS PIPE ALRM
TERM URG STOP TSTP CONT CHLD TTIN TTOU IO XCPU XFSZ VTALRM PROF WINCH
INFO USR1 USR2 IOT
```

Discussion

If your version of Perl is before 5.004, you have to use **signame** and **signo** in Config to find the list of available signals, since **keys %SIG** wasn't implemented then.

The following code retrieves by name and number the available signals from Perl's standard Config.pm module. Use **@signame** indexed by number to get the signal name, and **%signo** indexed by name to get the signal number.

```
use Config;
defined $Config{sig_name} or die "No sigs?";
$i = 0;                          # Config prepends fake 0 signal called "ZERO".
foreach $name (split(' ', $Config{sig_name})) {
    $signo{$name} = $i;
    $signame[$i] = $name;
    $i++;
}
```

See Also

The documentation for the standard Config module, also in Chapter 7 of *Programming Perl*; the "Signals" sections in Chapter 6 of *Programming Perl* and in *perlipc*(1)

16.14. Sending a Signal

Problem

You want to send a signal to a process. This could be sent to your own process or to another on the same system. For instance, you caught SIGINT and want to pass it on to your children.

Solution

Use **kill** to send a signal by name or number to the process IDs listed in the remaining arguments:

```
kill  9     => $pid;          # send $pid a signal 9
kill  -1    => $pgrp;         # send whole job a signal 1
kill  USR1  => $$;            # send myself a SIGUSR1
kill  HUP   => @pids;         # send a SIGHUP to processes in @pids
```

Discussion

Perl's **kill** function is an interface to the system call of the same name. The first argument is the signal to send, identified by number or by name; subsequent arguments are process IDs to send the signal to. It returns the count of processes successfully signaled. You can only send signals to processes running under the same real or saved UID as your real or effective UID—unless you're the superuser.

If the signal number is negative, Perl interprets remaining arguments as process group IDs and sends that signal to all those groups' processes using the *killpg*(2) system call.

A process group is essentially a job. It's how the operating system ties related processes together. For example, when you use your shell to pipe one command into another, you've started two processes, but only one job. When you use Ctrl-C to interrupt the current job, or Ctrl-Z to suspend it, this sends the appropriate signals to the entire job, which may be more than one process.

kill can also check whether a process is alive. Sending the special pseudo-signal number 0 checks whether it's legal for you to send a signal to the process—without actually sending one. If it returns true, the process is still alive. If it returns false, the process has either changed its effective UID (in which case $! will be set to EPERM) or no longer exists (and $! is ESRCH). Zombie processes (as described in Recipe 16.19) also report back as ESRCH.

```
use POSIX qw(:errno_h);

if (kill 0 => $minion) {
    print "$minion is alive!\n";
} elsif ($! == EPERM) {                # changed uid
    print "$minion has escaped my control!\n";
} elsif ($! == ESRCH) {
    print "$minion is deceased.\n";  # or zombied
} else {
    warn "Odd; I couldn't check on the status of $minion: $!\n";
}
```

See Also

The "Signals" sections in Chapter 6 of *Programming Perl* and in *perlipc*(1); your system's *sigaction*(2), *signal*(3), and *kill*(2) manpages (if you have them); the kill function in Chapter 3 of *Programming Perl* and *perlfunc*(1)

16.15. Installing a Signal Handler

Problem

You want to control how your program responds to signals. You need to do this if you want to catch Ctrl-C, avoid accumulating finished subprocesses, or prevent your process from dying when it writes to a child that has gone away.

Solution

Use the `%SIG` hash to install your own handler by name or by code reference:

```
$SIG{QUIT} = \&got_sig_quit;        # call &got_sig_quit for every SIGQUIT
$SIG{PIPE} = 'got_sig_pipe';        # call main::got_sig_pipe for every SIGPIPE
$SIG{INT}  = sub { $ouch++ };       # increment $ouch for every SIGINT
```

`%SIG` also lets you ignore a signal:

```
$SIG{INT} = 'IGNORE';               # ignore the signal INT
```

It also restores handling for that signal to the default:

```
$SIG{STOP} = 'DEFAULT';             # restore default STOP signal handling
```

Discussion

Perl uses the `%SIG` hash to control what happens when signals are received. Each key in `%SIG` corresponds to a signal. Each value is the action to take when Perl receives the corresponding signal. Perl provides two special behaviors: `"IGNORE"` to take no action when a particular signal is received, and `"DEFAULT"` to perform the default Unix action for that signal.

Although a C programmer might think of a signal as SIGINT, Perl uses just INT. Perl figures you only use signal names in functions that deal with signals, so the SIG prefix is redundant. This means that you'll assign to $SIG{CHLD} to change what your process does when it gets a SIGCHLD.

If you want to run your own code when a given signal is received, you have two choices of what to put in the hash: either a code reference or a subroutine name. (This means you can't name a signal handler IGNORE or DEFAULT if you store the string, but they'd be mighty strange names for signal handlers anyway.) If you use a subroutine name that isn't qualified by a package, Perl will interpret this name to be a function in the `main::` package, not one in the package in which the handler was installed. A code reference refers to a subroutine in a particular package, so it is a better choice.

Perl calls your handler code with a single argument: the name of the signal that triggered it, like `"INT"` or `"USR1"`. Returning from a signal handler takes you back to whatever you were doing when the signal hit.

Perl defines two special signals, `__DIE__` and `__WARN__`, whose handlers are called whenever a Perl program emits warnings through `warn` or dies through `die`. This lets you catch such warnings, and selectively trap or propagate them. The `die` and `warn` handlers are disabled while they run, so you can safely `die` from a `__DIE__` handler or `warn` from a `__WARN__` handler without fear of recursion.

See Also

The "Signals" sections in Chapter 6 of *Programming Perl* and in *perlipc*(1); your system's *sigaction*(2), *signal*(3), and *kill*(2) manpages (if you have them)

16.16. Temporarily Overriding a Signal Handler

Problem

You want to install a signal handler only for a particular subroutine. For instance, your subroutine catches SIGINT, and you don't want to disturb SIGINT handling outside the subroutine.

Solution

Use `local` to temporarily override a signal's behavior:

```
# the signal handler
sub ding {
    $SIG{INT} = \&ding;
    warn "\aEnter your name!\n";
}

# prompt for name, overriding SIGINT
sub get_name {
    local $SIG{INT} = \&ding;
    my $name;

    print "Kindly Stranger, please enter your name: ";
    chomp( $name = <> );
    return $name;
}
```

Discussion

You must use `local` rather than **my** to save away one value out of **%SIG**. The change remains in effect throughout the execution of that block, including in anything called from it. In this case, that's the **get_name** subroutine. If the signal is delivered while another function that your function calls is running, your signal handler is triggered—unless the called subroutine installs its own signal handler. The previous value of the hash is automatically restored when the block exits. This is one of the (few) places where dynamic scoping is more convenient than confusing.

See Also

Recipe 10.13; Recipe 16.15; Recipe 16.18

16.17. Writing a Signal Handler

Problem

You want to write a subroutine that will be called whenever your program receives a signal.

Solution

A signal handler is just a subroutine. With some risk, you can do anything in a signal handler you'd do in any Perl subroutine, but the more you do, the riskier it gets.

Some systems require you to reinstall your signal handler after each signal:

```
$SIG{INT} = \&got_int;
sub got_int {
    $SIG{INT} = \&got_int;          # but not for SIGCHLD!
    # ...
}
```

Some systems restart blocking operations, such as reading data. In such cases, you must call **die** within the handler and trap it with **eval**:

```
my $interrupted = 0;

sub got_int {
    $interrupted = 1;
    $SIG{INT} = 'DEFAULT';          # or 'IGNORE'
    die;
}

eval {
    $SIG{INT} = \&got_int;
    # ... long-running code that you don't want to restart
};

if ($interrupted) {
    # deal with the signal
}
```

Discussion

Installing a custom signal handling subroutine is a lot like playing with fire. It may seem like a lot of fun, but, sooner or later, you're going to get burned unless you're exceedingly careful. By installing Perl code to deal with signals, you're exposing yourself to two dangers. First, few system library functions are re-entrant. If the signal interrupts while Perl is executing one function (like *malloc*(3) or *printf*(3)), and your signal handler then calls the same function again, you could get unpredictable behavior—often, a core dump. Second, Perl isn't itself re-entrant at the lowest levels. (Release 5.005 of Perl supports lightweight processes called *threads*.) If the signal interrupts Perl while Perl is changing its own internal data structures, unpredictable behavior may result—usually random core dumps.

You have two options: be paranoid or be pragmatic. The paranoid approach is to do as little as possible in your signal handler, as exemplified by the `eval` and `die` code in the Solution—set a variable that already has a value, and then bail. Even this is cavalier for the true paranoiac, who avoids `die` in a handler because the system *is* out to get you. The pragmatic approach is to say "I know the risks, but prefer the convenience," and to do anything you want in your signal handler.

Signals have been implemented in many different operating systems, often in slightly different flavors. The two situations where signal implementations vary the most are when a signal occurs when its signal handler is active (*reliability*), and when a signal interrupts a blocking system call like `read` or `accept` (*restarting*).

The initial implementation of signals was unreliable, meaning that while a handler was running, further occurrences of the same signal would cause the default action, likely aborting the program. Later systems addressed this (each in their own subtly different way, of course) by providing a way to block the delivery of further signals of that number until the handler has finished. If Perl detects that your system can use reliable signals, it generates the proper system calls to achieve this saner, safer behavior. You can use POSIX signals to block signal delivery at other times, as described in Recipe 16.20.

For truly portable code, the paranoid programmer will assume the worst case (unreliable signals) and reinstall the signal handler manually, usually as the first statement in a function:

```
$SIG{INT} = \&catcher;
sub catcher {
    $SIG{INT} = \&catcher;
    # ...
}
```

In the special case of catching SIGCHLD, see Recipe 16.19. System V has bizarre behavior that can trip you up.

Use the Config module to find out whether you have reliable signals:

```
use Config;
print "Hurrah!\n" if $Config{d_sigaction};
```

Just because you have reliable signals doesn't mean you automatically get reliable programs. But without them, you certainly won't.

The first implementation of signals interrupted slow system calls, functions that require the cooperation of other processes or device drivers. If a signal comes in while those system calls are still running, they (and their Perl counterparts) return an error value and set the error to EINTR, "Interrupted system call". Checking for this condition made programs so complicated that most didn't check, and therefore misbehaved or died if a signal interrupted a slow system call. Most modern versions of Unix allow you to change this behavior. Perl will always make system calls restartable if it is on a system that support it. If you have a POSIX system, you can control restarting using the POSIX module (see Recipe 16.20).

To determine whether your interrupted system calls will automatically restart, look at your system's C *signal.h* include file:

```
% egrep 'S[AV]_(RESTART|INTERRUPT)' /usr/include/*/signal.h
```

Two signals are untrappable and unignorable: SIGKILL and SIGSTOP. Full details of the signals available on your system and what they mean can be found in the *signal*(3) manpage.

See Also

The "Signals" sections in Chapter 6 of *Programming Perl* and in *perlipc*(1); your system's *sigaction*(2), *signal*(3), and *kill*(2) manpages (if you have them). *Porting UNIX Software*, by Greg Lehey, O'Reilly & Associates, (1995); *Advanced Programming in the Unix Environment*

16.18. Catching Ctrl-C

Problem

You want to intercept Ctrl-C, which would otherwise kill your whole program. You'd like to ignore it or run your own function when the signal is received.

Solution

Set a handler for SIGINT. Set it to "IGNORE" to make Ctrl-C have no effect:

```
$SIG{INT} = 'IGNORE';
```

Or, set it to a subroutine of your own devising to respond to Ctrl-C:

```
$SIG{INT} = \&tsktsk;

sub tsktsk {
```

```
     $SIG{INT} = \&tsktsk;              # See ''Writing A Signal Handler''
     warn "\aThe long habit of living indisposeth us for dying.\n";
 }
```

Discussion

Ctrl-C isn't directly affecting your program. The terminal driver processing your keystrokes recognizes the Ctrl-C combination (or whatever you've set your terminal to recognize as the interrupt character), and sends a SIGINT to every process in the foreground process group (*foreground job*) for that terminal. The foreground job normally comprises all programs started from the shell on a single command line, plus any other programs run by those programs. See the section on "Signals" in the Introduction to this chapter for details.

The interrupt character isn't the only special character interpreted by your terminal driver. Type `stty -a` to find out your current settings:

```
% stty -a
speed 9600 baud; 38 rows; 80 columns;
lflags: icanon isig iexten echo echoe -echok echoke -echonl echoctl
        -echoprt -altwerase -noflsh -tostop -flusho pendin -nokerninfo
        -extproc
iflags: -istrip icrnl -inlcr -igncr ixon -ixoff ixany imaxbel -ignbrk
        brkint -inpck -ignpar -parmrk
oflags: opost onlcr oxtabs
cflags: cread cs8 -parenb -parodd hupcl -clocal -cstopb -crtscts -dsrflow
        -dtrflow -mdmbuf
cchars: discard = ^O; dsusp = ^Y; eof = ^D; eol = <undef;>
        eol2 = <undef; erase = ^H; intr = ^C; kill = ^U; lnext = ^V;>
        min = 1; quit = ^\; reprint = ^R; start = ^Q; status = <undef;>
        stop = ^S; susp = ^Z; time = 0; werase = ^W;
```

The last section, `cchars:`, is the list of special characters. Recipe 15.8 shows you how to change these from your script without calling the *stty* program.

See Also

Your system's *stty*(1) manpage (if you have one); Recipe 15.8; Recipe 16.17

16.19. Avoiding Zombie Processes

Problem

Your program forks children, but the dead children accumulate, fill up your process table, and aggravate your system administrator.

Solution

If you don't need to record the children that have terminated, use:

```
$SIG{CHLD} = 'IGNORE';
```

To keep better track of deceased children, install a SIGCHLD handler to call `waitpid`:

```
use POSIX ":sys_wait_h";

$SIG{CHLD} = \&REAPER;
sub REAPER {
    my $stiff;
    while (($stiff = waitpid(-1, &WNOHANG)) > 0) {
        # do something with $stiff if you want
    }
    $SIG{CHLD} = \&REAPER;                   # install *after* calling waitpid
}
```

Discussion

When a process exits, the system keeps it in the process table so the parent can check its status—whether it terminated normally or abnormally. Fetching a child's status (thereby freeing it to drop from the system altogether) is rather grimly called *reaping* dead children. (This entire recipe is full of ways to harvest your dead children. If this makes you queasy, we understand.) It involves a call to `wait` or `waitpid`. Some Perl functions (piped `opens`, `system`, and backticks) will automatically reap the children they make, but you must explicitly wait when you use `fork` to manually start another process.

To avoid accumulating dead children, simply tell the system that you're not interested in them by setting `$SIG{CHLD}` to `"IGNORE"`. If you want to know which children die and when, you'll need to use `waitpid`.

The `waitpid` function reaps a single process. Its first argument is the process to wait for—use `-1` to mean any process—and its second argument is a set of flags. We use the WNOHANG flag to make `waitpid` immediately return 0 if there are no dead children. A flag value of 0 is supported everywhere, indicating a blocking wait. Call `waitpid` from a SIGCHLD handler, as we do in the Solution, to reap the children as soon as they die.

The `wait` function also reaps children, but it does not have a non-blocking option. If you inadvertently call it when there are running child processes but none have exited, your program will pause until there is a dead child.

Because the kernel keeps track of undelivered signals using a bit vector, one bit per signal, if two children die before your process is scheduled, you will get only a single SIGCHLD. You must always loop when you reap in a SIGCHLD handler, and so you can't use `wait`.

Both `wait` and `waitpid` return the process ID that they just reaped and set $? to the wait status of the defunct process. This status is actually two 8-bit values in one 16-bit number. The high byte is the exit value of the process. The low 7 bits represent the number of the signal that killed the process, with the 8th bit indicating whether a core dump occurred. Here's one way to isolate those values:

```
$exit_value  = $? >> 8;
$signal_num  = $? & 127;
$dumped_core = $? & 128;
```

The standard POSIX module has macros to interrogate status values: WIFEXITED, WEXITSTATUS, WIFSIGNALLED, and WTERMSIG. Oddly enough, POSIX doesn't have a macro to test whether the process core dumped.

Beware of two things when using SIGCHLD. First, the system doesn't just send a SIGCHLD when a child exits; it also sends one when the child stops. A process can stop for many reasons—waiting to be foregrounded so it can do terminal I/O, being sent a SIGSTOP (it will wait for the SIGCONT before continuing), or being suspended from its terminal. You need to check the status with the **WIFEXITED**[*] function from the POSIX module to make sure you're dealing with a process that really died, and isn't just suspended.

```
use POSIX qw(:signal_h :errno_h :sys_wait_h);

$SIG{CHLD} = \&REAPER;
sub REAPER {
    my $pid;

    $pid = waitpid(-1, &WNOHANG);

    if ($pid == -1) {
        # no child waiting.  Ignore it.
    } elsif (WIFEXITED($?)) {
        print "Process $pid exited.\n";
    } else {
        print "False alarm on $pid.\n";
    }
    $SIG{CHLD} = \&REAPER;          # in case of unreliable signals
}
```

The second trap with SIGCHLD is related to Perl, not the operating system. Because **system, open,** and backticks all fork subprocesses and the operating system sends your process a SIGCHLD whenever any of its subprocesses exit, you could get called for something you weren't expecting. The built-in operations all

---

* Not SPOUSEXITED, even on a PC.

wait for the child themselves, so sometimes the SIGCHLD will arrive before the `close` on the filehandle blocks to reap it. If the signal handler gets to it first, the zombie won't be there for the normal close. This makes `close` return false and set `$!` to `"No child processes"`. Then, if the `close` gets to the dead child first, `waitpid` will return 0.

Most systems support a non-blocking `waitpid`. Use Perl's standard Config.pm module to find out:

```
use Config;
$has_nonblocking = $Config{d_waitpid} eq "define" ||
                   $Config{d_wait4}   eq "define";
```

System V defines SIGCLD, which has the same signal number as SIGCHLD but subtly different semantics. Use SIGCHLD to avoid confusion.

See Also

The "Signals" sections in Chapter 6 of *Programming Perl* and in *perlipc*(1); the `wait` and `waitpid` functions in Chapter 3 of *Programming Perl* and in *perlfunc*(1); the documentation for the standard POSIX module, in Chapter 7 of *Programming Perl*; your system's *sigaction*(2), *signal*(3), and *kill*(2) manpages (if you have them); Recipe 16.17

16.20. Blocking Signals

Problem

You'd like to delay the reception of a signal, possibly to prevent unpredictable behavior from signals that can interrupt your program at any point.

Solution

Use the POSIX module's interface to the `sigprocmask` system call. This is only available if your system is POSIX conformant.

To block a signal around an operation:

```
use POSIX qw(:signal_h);

$sigset = POSIX::SigSet->new(SIGINT);     # define the signals to block
$old_sigset = POSIX::SigSet->new;         # where the old sigmask will be kept

unless (defined sigprocmask(SIG_BLOCK, $sigset, $old_sigset)) {
    die "Could not block SIGINT\n";
}
```

To unblock:

```
unless (defined sigprocmask(SIG_UNBLOCK, $old_sigset)) {
    die "Could not unblock SIGINT\n";
}
```

Discussion

The POSIX standard introduced `sigaction` and `sigprocmask` to give you better control over how signals are delivered. The `sigprocmask` function controls delayed delivery of signals and `sigaction` installs handlers. If available, Perl uses `sigaction` when you change `%SIG`.

To use `sigprocmask`, first build a signal set using `POSIX::SigSet->new`. This takes a list of signal numbers. The POSIX module exports functions named after the signals, which return their signal numbers.

```
use POSIX qw(:signal_h);

$sigset = POSIX::SigSet->new( SIGINT, SIGKILL );
```

Pass the POSIX::SigSet object to `sigprocmask` with the SIG_BLOCK flag to delay signal delivery, SIG_UNBLOCK to restore delivery of the signals, or SIG_SETMASK to block only signals in the POSIX::SigSet. The most paranoid of programmers block signals for a `fork` to prevent a signal handler in the child process being called before Perl can update the child's `$$` variable, its process id. If the signal handler were called immediately and reported `$$` in that handler, it could possibly report its parent's `$$`, not its own. This issue does not arise often.

See Also

Your system's *sigprocmask*(2) manpage (if you have one); the documentation for the standard POSIX module in Chapter 7 of *Programming Perl*

16.21. Timing Out an Operation

Problem

You want to make sure an operation doesn't take more than a certain amount of time. For instance, you're running filesystem backups and want to abort if it takes longer than an hour. Or, you want to schedule an event for the next hour.

Solution

To interrupt a long-running operation, set a SIGALRM handler to call `die`. Set an alarm with `alarm`, then `eval` your code:

```
$SIG{ALRM} = sub { die "timeout" };

eval {
    alarm(3600);
    # long-time operations here
    alarm(0);
};

if ($@) {
    if ($@ =~ /timeout/) {
                                # timed out; do what you will here
    } else {
        alarm(0);               # clear the still-pending alarm
        die;                    # propagate unexpected exception
    }
}
```

Discussion

The **alarm** function takes one argument: the integer number of seconds before your process receives a SIGALRM. It may be delivered after that time in busy time-sharing systems. The default action for SIGALRM is to terminate your program, so you should install your own signal handler.

You cannot (usefully) give the **alarm** function a fractional number of seconds; if you try, it will be truncated to an integer. For precise timers, see Recipe 3.9.

See Also

The "Signals" sections in Chapter 6 of *Programming Perl* and in *perlipc*(1); the **alarm** function in Chapter 3 of *Programming Perl* and in *perlfunc*(1); Recipe 3.9

16.22. *Program: sigrand*

Description

The following program gives you random signatures by using named pipes. It expects the signatures file to have records in the format of the *fortune* program—that is, each possible multiline record is terminated with "%%\n". Here's an example:

```
Make is like Pascal: everybody likes it, so they go in and change it.
                            --Dennis Ritchie
%%
I eschew embedded capital letters in names; to my prose-oriented eyes,
they are too awkward to read comfortably. They jangle like bad typography.
                            --Rob Pike
%%
God made the integers; all else is the work of Man.
```

```
                                             --Kronecker
%%
I'd rather have :rofix than const.          --Dennis Ritchie
%%
If you want to program in C, program in C.  It's a nice language.
I use it occasionally...    :-)             --Larry Wall
%%
Twisted cleverness is my only skill as a programmer.
                                        --Elizabeth Zwicky
%%
Basically, avoid comments. If your code needs a comment to be understood,
it would be better to rewrite it so it's easier to understand.
                                --Rob Pike
%%
Comments on data are usually much more helpful than on algorithms.
                                --Rob Pike
%%
Programs that write programs are the happiest programs in the world.
                                --Andrew Hume
%%
```

We check whether we're already running by using a file with our PID in it. If sending a signal number 0 indicates that PID still exists (or, rarely, that something else has reused it), we just exit. We also look at the current Usenet posting to decide whether to look for a per-newsgroup signature file. That way, you can have different signatures for each newsgroup you post to. For variety, a global signature file is still on occasion used even if a per-newsgroup file exists.

You can even use *sigrand* on systems without named pipes if you remove the code to create a named pipe and extend the sleep interval before file updates. Then *.signature* would just be a regular file. Another portability concern is that the program forks itself in the background, which is almost like becoming a daemon. If you have no `fork` call, just comment it out.

The full program is shown in Example 16-12.

Example 16-12. sigrand

```perl
#!/usr/bin/perl -w
# sigrand - supply random fortunes for .signature file

use strict;

# config section variables
use vars qw( $NG_IS_DIR $MKNOD $FULLNAME $FIFO $ART $NEWS $SIGS $SEMA
             $GLOBRAND $NAME );

# globals
use vars qw( $Home $Fortune_Path @Pwd );

###############################################################
# begin configuration section
```

Example 16-12. sigrand (continued)

```
# should really read from ~/.sigrandrc

gethome();

# for rec/humor/funny instead of rec.humor.funny
$NG_IS_DIR       = 1;

$MKNOD           = "/bin/mknod";
$FULLNAME        = "$Home/.fullname";
$FIFO            = "$Home/.signature";
$ART             = "$Home/.article";
$NEWS            = "$Home/News";
$SIGS            = "$NEWS/SIGNATURES";
$SEMA            = "$Home/.sigrandpid";
$GLOBRAND        = 1/4;  # chance to use global sigs anyway

# $NAME should be (1) left undef to have program guess
# read address for signature maybe looking in ~/.fullname,
# (2) set to an exact address, or (3) set to empty string
# to be omitted entirely.

$NAME            = '';              # means no name used
## $NAME         = "me\@home.org\n";

# end configuration section -- HOME and FORTUNE get autoconf'd
##############################################################

setup();                # pull in inits
justme();               # make sure program not already running
fork && exit;           # background ourself and go away

open (SEMA, "> $SEMA")     or die "can't write $SEMA: $!";
print SEMA "$$\n";
close(SEMA)                or die "can't close $SEMA: $!";

# now loop forever, writing a signature into the
# fifo file.  if you don't have real fifos, change
# sleep time at bottom of loop to like 10 to update
# only every 10 seconds.
for (;;) {
    open (FIFO, "> $FIFO")or die "can't write $FIFO: $!";
    my $sig = pick_quote();
    for ($sig) {
        s/^((:?[^\n]*\n){4}).*$/$1/s;    # trunc to 4 lines
        s/^(.{1,80}).*? *$/$1/gm;        # trunc long lines
    }
    # print sig, with name if present, padded to four lines
    if ($NAME) {
        print FIFO $NAME, "\n" x (3 - ($sig =~ tr/\n//)), $sig;
    } else {
        print FIFO $sig;
    }
```

Example 16-12. sigrand (continued)

```perl
    close FIFO;

    # Without a microsleep, the reading process doesn't finish before
    # the writer tries to open it again, which since the reader exists,
    # succeeds.  They end up with multiple signatures.  Sleep a tiny bit
    # between opens to give readers a chance to finish reading and close
    # our pipe so we can block when opening it the next time.

    select(undef, undef, undef, 0.2);   # sleep 1/5 second
}
die "XXX: NOT REACHED";                 # you can't get here from anywhere

###################################################################

# Ignore SIGPIPE in case someone opens us up and then closes the fifo
# without reading it; look in a .fullname file for their login name.
# Try to determine the fully qualified hostname.  Look our for silly
# ampersands in passwd entries.  Make sure we have signatures or fortunes.
# Build a fifo if we need to.

sub setup {
    $SIG{PIPE} = 'IGNORE';

    unless (defined $NAME) {             # if $NAME undef in config
        if (-e $FULLNAME) {
            $NAME = `cat $FULLNAME`;
            die "$FULLNAME should contain only 1 line, aborting"
                if $NAME =~ tr/\n// > 1;
        } else {
            my($user, $host);
            chop($host = `hostname`);
            ($host) = gethostbyname($host) unless $host =~ /\./;
            $user = $ENV{USER} || $ENV{LOGNAME} || $Pwd[0]
                or die "intruder alert";
            ($NAME = $Pwd[6]) =~ s/,.*//;
            $NAME =~ s/&/\u\L$user/g; # can't believe some folks still do this
            $NAME = "\t$NAME\t$user\@$host\n";
        }
    }

    check_fortunes() if !-e $SIGS;

    unless (-p $FIFO) {          # -p checks whether it's a named pipe
        if (!-e _) {
            system("$MKNOD $FIFO p") && die "can't mknod $FIFO";
            warn "created $FIFO as a named pipe\n";
        } else {
            die "$0: won't overwrite file .signature\n";
        }
    } else {
        warn "$0: using existing named pipe $FIFO\n";
    }
```

Example 16-12. sigrand (continued)

```perl
    # get a good random number seed.  not needed if 5.004 or better.
    srand(time() ^ ($$ + ($$ << 15)));
}

# choose a random signature
sub pick_quote {
    my $sigfile = signame();
    if (!-e $sigfile) {
        return fortune();
    }
    open (SIGS, "< $sigfile" )or die "can't open $sigfile";
    local $/  = "%%\n";
    local $_;
    my $quip;
    rand($.) < 1 && ($quip = $_) while <SIGS>;
    close SIGS;
    chomp $quip;
    return $quip || "ENOSIG: This signature file is empty.\n";
}

# See whether ~/.article contains a Newsgroups line.  if so, see the first
# group posted to and find out whether it has a dedicated set of fortunes.
# otherwise return the global one.  also, return the global one randomly
# now and then to spice up the sigs.
sub signame {
    (rand(1.0) > ($GLOBRAND) && open ART) || return $SIGS;
    local $/  = '';
    local $_  = <ART>;
    my($ng)   = /Newsgroups:\s*([^,\s]*)/;
    $ng =~ s!\.!/!g if $NG_IS_DIR;      # if rn -/,  or SAVEDIR=%p/%c
    $ng = "$NEWS/$ng/SIGNATURES";
    return -f $ng ? $ng : $SIGS;
}

# Call the fortune program with -s for short flag until
# we get a small enough fortune or ask too much.
sub fortune {
    local $_;
    my $tries = 0;
    do {
        $_ = `$Fortune_Path -s`;
    } until tr/\n// < 5 || $tries++ > 20;
    s/^/ /mg;
    $_ || " SIGRAND: deliver random signals to all processes.\n";
}

# Make sure there's a fortune program.  Search
# for its full path and set global to that.
sub check_fortunes {
    return if $Fortune_Path;       # already set
    for my $dir (split(/:/, $ENV{PATH}), '/usr/games') {
```

Example 16-12. sigrand (continued)

```
        return if -x ($Fortune_Path = "$dir/fortune");
    }
    die "Need either $SIGS or a fortune program, bailing out";
}


# figure out our directory
sub gethome {
    @Pwd = getpwuid($<);
    $Home = $ENV{HOME} || $ENV{LOGDIR} || $Pwd[7]
        or die "no home directory for user $<";
}


# "There can be only one."  --the Highlander
sub justme {
    if (open SEMA) {
        my $pid;
        chop($pid = <SEMA>);
        kill(0, $pid)and die "$0 already running (pid $pid), bailing out";
        close SEMA;
    }
}
```

17

Sockets

Glendower: I can call spirits from the vasty deep.
Hotspur: Why so can I, or so can any man,
But will they come when you do call for them?

—Shakespeare
King Henry IV Part I, Act III Scene 1

17.0. Introduction

Sockets are endpoints for communication. Some types of sockets provide reliable communications. Others offer few guarantees, but consume low system overhead. Socket communication can be used to let processes talk on just one machine or over the Internet.

In this chapter we consider the two most commonly used types of sockets: *streams* and *datagrams.* Streams provide a bidirectional, sequenced, and reliable channel of communication—similar to pipes. *Datagram* sockets do not guarantee sequenced, reliable delivery, but they do guarantee that message boundaries will be preserved when read. Your system may support other types of sockets as well; consult your *socket*(2) manpage or equivalent documentation for details.

We also consider both the Internet and Unix domains. The Internet domain gives sockets two-part names: a host (an IP address in a particular format) and a port number. In the Unix domain, sockets are named using files (e.g., */tmp/mysock*).

In addition to domains and types, sockets also have a *protocol* associated with them. Protocols are not very important to the casual programmer, as there is rarely more than one protocol for a given domain and type of socket.

Domains and types are normally identified by numeric constants (available through functions exported by the Socket and IO::Socket modules). Stream sockets have the type SOCK_STREAM, and datagram sockets have the type SOCK_DGRAM. The Internet domain is PF_INET, and the Unix domain PF_UNIX. (POSIX uses PF_LOCAL instead of PF_UNIX, but PF_UNIX will almost always be an acceptable constant simply because of the preponderance of existing software that uses it.) You should use these symbolic names instead of numbers because the numbers may change (and historically, have).

Protocols have names like tcp and udp, which correspond to numbers that the operating system uses. The getprotobyname function (built into Perl) returns the number when given a protocol name. Pass protocol number 0 to socket functions to have the system select an appropriate default.

Perl has built-in functions to create and manipulate sockets; these functions largely mimic their C counterparts. While this is good for providing low-level, direct access to every part of the system, most of us prefer something more convenient. That's what the IO::Socket::INET and IO::Socket::UNIX classes are for—they provide a high-level interface to otherwise intricate system calls.

Let's look at the built-in functions first. They all return undef and set $! if an error occurs. The socket function makes a socket, bind gives a socket a local name, connect connects a local socket to a (possibly remote) one, listen readies a socket for connections from other sockets, and accept receives the connections one by one. You can communicate over a stream socket with print and <> as well as with syswrite and sysread, or over a datagram socket with send and recv. (Perl does not currently support *sendmsg(2)*.)

A typical server calls socket, bind, and listen, then loops in a blocking accept call that waits for incoming connections (see Recipe 17.2 and Recipe 17.5). A typical client calls socket and connect (see Recipe 17.1 and Recipe 17.4). Datagram clients are special. They don't have to connect to send data because they can specify the destination as an argument to send.

When you bind, connect, or send to a specific destination, you must supply a socket name. An Internet domain socket name is a host (an IP address packed with inet_aton) and a port (a number), packed into a C-style structure with sockaddr_in:

```
use Socket;

$packed_ip   = inet_aton("208.146.240.1");
$socket_name = sockaddr_in($port, $packed_ip);
```

A Unix domain socket name is a filename packed into a C structure with sockaddr_un:

```
use Socket;

$socket_name = sockaddr_un("/tmp/mysock");
```

To take a packed socket name and turn it back into a filename or host and port, call sockaddr_un or sockaddr_in in list context:

```
($port, $packed_ip) = sockaddr_in($socket_name);    # for PF_INET sockets
($filename)         = sockaddr_un($socket_name);    # for PF_UNIX sockets
```

Use inet_ntoa to turn a packed IP address back into an ASCII string. It stands for "numbers to ASCII" and inet_aton stands for "ASCII to numbers."

```
$ip_address = inet_ntoa($packed_ip);
$packed_ip  = inet_aton("204.148.40.9");
$packed_ip  = inet_aton("www.oreilly.com");
```

Most recipes use Internet domain sockets in their examples, but nearly everything that applies to the Internet domain also applies to the Unix domain. Recipe 17.6 explains the differences and pitfalls.

Sockets are the basis of network services. We provide three ways to write servers: one where a child process is created for each incoming connection (Recipe 17.11), one where the server forks in advance (Recipe 17.12), and one where the server process doesn't fork at all (Recipe 17.13).

Some servers need to listen to many IP addresses at once, which we demonstrate in Recipe 17.14. Well-behaved servers clean up and restart when they get a HUP signal; Recipe 17.16 shows how to implement that behavior in Perl. We also show how to put a name to both ends of a connection; see Recipe 17.7 and Recipe 17.8.

Unix Network Programming and the three-volume *TCP/IP Illustrated* by W. Richard Stevens are indispensable for the serious socket programmer. If you want to learn the basics about sockets, it's hard to beat the original and classic reference, *An Advanced 4.4BSD Interprocess Communication Tutorial*. It's written for C, but almost everything is directly applicable to Perl. It's available in */usr/share/doc* on most BSD-derived Unix systems. We also recommend you look at *The Unix Programming Frequently Asked Questions List* (Gierth and Horgan), and *Programming UNIX Sockets in C—Frequently Asked Questions* (Metcalf and Gierth), both of which are posted periodically to the *comp.unix.answers* newsgroup.

17.1. Writing a TCP Client

Problem

You want to connect to a socket on a remote machine.

Solution

This solution assumes you're using the Internet to communicate. For TCP-like communication within a single machine, see Recipe 17.6.

Either use the standard (as of 5.004) IO::Socket::INET class:

```
use IO::Socket;

$socket = IO::Socket::INET->new(PeerAddr => $remote_host,
                                PeerPort => $remote_port,
                                Proto    => "tcp",
                                Type     => SOCK_STREAM)
    or die "Couldn't connect to $remote_host:$remote_port : $@\n";

# ... do something with the socket
print $socket "Why don't you call me anymore?\n";

$answer = <$socket>;

# and terminate the connection when we're done
close($socket);
```

or create a socket by hand for better control:

```
use Socket;

# create a socket
socket(TO_SERVER, PF_INET, SOCK_STREAM, getprotobyname('tcp'));

# build the address of the remote machine
$internet_addr = inet_aton($remote_host)
    or die "Couldn't convert $remote_host into an Internet address: $!\n";
$paddr = sockaddr_in($remote_port, $internet_addr);

# connect
connect(TO_SERVER, $paddr)
    or die "Couldn't connect to $remote_host:$remote_port : $!\n";

# ... do something with the socket
print TO_SERVER "Why don't you call me anymore?\n";

# and terminate the connection when we're done
close(TO_SERVER);
```

Discussion

While coding this by hand requires a lot of steps, the IO::Socket::INET class wraps them all in a convenient constructor. The important things to know are where you're going (the PeerAddr and PeerPort parameters) and how you're getting there (the Type parameter). IO::Socket::INET tries to determine these things from what you've given it. It deduces Proto from the Type and Port if possible, and assumes tcp otherwise.

PeerAddr is a string containing either a hostname ("www.oreilly.com") or an IP address ("204.148.40.9"). PeerPort is an integer, the port number to connect to. You can embed the port number in the address by giving an address like "www.oreilly.com:80". Type is the kind of socket to create: SOCK_DGRAM for datagrams, or SOCK_STREAM for streams.

If you want a SOCK_STREAM connection to a port on a particular machine with no other options, pass a single string to IO::Socket::INET->new consisting of the hostname and port separated by a colon:

```
$client = IO::Socket::INET->new("www.yahoo.com:80")
    or die $@;
```

If an error occurs, IO::Socket::INET will return **undef** and $@ (*not* $!) will be set to the error message.

```
$s = IO::Socket::INET->new(PeerAddr => "Does not Exist",
                           Peerport => 80,
                           Type     => SOCK_STREAM )
    or die $@;
```

If your packets are disappearing into a network void, it can take a while for your inability to connect to a port to be recognized. You can decrease this time by specifying a **Timeout** parameter to IO::Socket::INET->new():

```
$s = IO::Socket::INET->new(PeerAddr => "bad.host.com",
                           PeerPort => 80,
                           Type     => SOCK_STREAM,
                           Timeout  => 5 )
    or die $@;
```

If you do this, though, there's no way to tell from $! or $@ whether you couldn't connect or whether you timed out. Sometimes it's better to set it up by hand instead of using a module.

If you have several network interfaces, the kernel decides which one to use based on your current routes. If you wish to override this default, add a **LocalAddr** parameter to your call to IO::Socket::INET->new. If coding by hand code, do this:

```
$inet_addr = inet_aton("208.146.240.1");
$paddr     = sockaddr_in($port, $inet_addr);
bind(SOCKET, $paddr)            or die "bind: $!";
```

If you know only the name, do this:

```
$inet_addr = gethostbyname("www.yahoo.com")
                            or die "Can't resolve www.yahoo.com: $!";
$paddr     = sockaddr_in($port, $inet_addr);
bind(SOCKET, $paddr)            or die "bind: $!";
```

See Also

The socket, bind, connect, and gethostbyname functions in Chapter 3 of *Programming Perl* and in *perlfunc*(1); the documentation for the standard Socket, IO::Socket, and Net::hostent modules; the section on "Internet TCP Clients and

Servers" in Chapter 6 of *Programming Perl* and in *perlipc*(1); *Unix Network Programming*, by W. Richard Stevens, published by Prentice Hall (1992); Recipe 17.2; Recipe 17.3

17.2. *Writing a TCP Server*

Problem

You want to write a server that waits for clients to connect over the network to a particular port.

Solution

This recipe assumes you're using the Internet to communicate. For TCP-like communication within a single Unix machine, see Recipe 17.6.

Use the standard (as of 5.004) IO::Socket::INET class:

```
use IO::Socket;

$server = IO::Socket::INET->new(LocalPort => $server_port,
                                Type      => SOCK_STREAM,
                                Reuse     => 1,
                                Listen    => 10 )   # or SOMAXCONN
    or die "Couldn't be a tcp server on port $server_port : $@\n";

while ($client = $server->accept()) {
    # $client is the new connection
}

close($server);
```

Or, craft it by hand for better control:

```
use Socket;

# make the socket
socket(SERVER, PF_INET, SOCK_STREAM, getprotobyname('tcp'));

# so we can restart our server quickly
setsockopt(SERVER, SOL_SOCKET, SO_REUSEADDR, 1);

# build up my socket address
$my_addr = sockaddr_in($server_port, INADDR_ANY);
bind(SERVER, $my_addr)
    or die "Couldn't bind to port $server_port : $!\n";

# establish a queue for incoming connections
listen(SERVER, SOMAXCONN)
    or die "Couldn't listen on port $server_port : $!\n";
```

```
# accept and process connections
while (accept(CLIENT, SERVER)) {
    # do something with CLIENT
}

close(SERVER);
```

Discussion

Setting up a server is more complicated than being a client. The optional `listen` function tells the operating system how many pending, unanswered connections to queue up waiting for your server. The `setsockopt` function used in the Solution allows you to avoid waiting two minutes after killing your server before you restart it again (valuable in testing). The `bind` call registers your server with kernel so others may find you. Finally, `accept` takes the incoming connections one by one.

The numeric argument to `listen` is the number of unaccepted connections that the operating system should queue before clients start getting "connection refused" errors. Historically, the maximum `listen` value was 5, and even today, many operating systems silently limit this queue size to around 20. With busy web servers becoming commonplace, many vendors have increased this value. Your documented system maximum can be found in the SOMAXCONN constant from the Socket module.

The `accept` function takes two arguments: the filehandle to connect to the remote client and the server filehandle. It returns the client's port and IP address, as packed by `inet_ntoa`:

```
use Socket;

while ($client_address = accept(CLIENT, SERVER)) {
    ($port, $packed_ip) = sockaddr_in($client_address);
    $dotted_quad = inet_ntoa($packed_ip);
    # do as thou wilt
}
```

With the IO::Socket classes, `accept` is a method of the server filehandle:

```
while ($client = $server->accept()) {
    # ...
}
```

If you call the `accept` method in list context, it returns the client socket and its address:

```
while (($client,$client_address) = $server->accept()) {
    # ...
}
```

If no connection is waiting, your program blocks in the `accept` until a connection comes in. If you want to ensure that your `accept` won't block, use nonblocking sockets:

```
use Fcntl qw(F_GETFL F_SETFL O_NONBLOCK);

$flags = fcntl(SERVER, F_GETFL, 0)
            or die "Can't get flags for the socket: $!\n";

$flags = fcntl(SERVER, F_SETFL, $flags | O_NONBLOCK)
            or die "Can't set flags for the socket: $!\n";
```

Now, when you `accept` and nothing is waiting for you, `accept` will return `undef` and set `$!` to `EWOULDBLOCK`.

You might fear that when the return flags from F_GETFL are 0, that this would trigger the `die` just as a failure from `undef` would. Not so—as with `ioctl`, a non-error return from `fcntl` is mapped by Perl to the special value `"0 but true"`. This special string is even exempt from the -w flag's pesky non-numeric warnings, so feel free to use it in your functions when you want to return a value that's numerically zero yet still true. It probably should have been `"0 and sneaky"` instead.

See Also

The `socket`, `bind`, `listen`, `accept`, `fcntl`, and `setsockopt` functions in Chapter 3 of *Programming Perl* and in *perlfunc*(1); your system's *fcntl*(2), *socket*(2), *setsockopt*(2) manpages (if you have them); the documentation for the standard Socket, IO::Socket, and Net::hostent modules; the section on "Internet TCP Clients and Servers" in Chapter 6 of *Programming Perl* and in *perlipc*(1); *Unix Network Programming*; *Beej's Guide to Network Programming* at *http://www.ecst.csuchico.edu/ ~beej/guide/net*; Recipe 7.13; Recipe 7.14; Recipe 17.1; Recipe 17.3; Recipe 17.7

17.3. Communicating over TCP

Problem

You want to read or write data over a TCP connection.

Solution

This recipe assumes you're using the Internet to communicate. For TCP-like communication within a single machine, see Recipe 17.6.

Use `print` or `<>` :

```
print SERVER "What is your name?\n";
chomp ($response = <SERVER>);
```

Or, use `send` and `recv`:

```
defined (send(SERVER, $data_to_send, $flags))
    or die "Can't send : $!\n";

recv(SERVER, $data_read, $maxlen, $flags)
    or die "Can't receive: $!\n";
```

Or, use the corresponding methods on an IO::Socket object:

```
use IO::Socket;

$server->send($data_to_send, $flags)
    or die "Can't send: $!\n";

$server->recv($data_read, $flags)
    or die "Can't recv: $!\n";
```

To find out whether data can be read or written, use the **select** function, which is nicely wrapped by the standard IO::Socket class:

```
use IO::Select;

$select = IO::Select->new();
$select->add(*FROM_SERVER);
$select->add($to_client);

@read_from = $select->can_read($timeout);
foreach $socket (@read_from) {
    # read the pending data from $socket
}
```

Discussion

Sockets handle two completely different types of I/O, each with attendant pitfalls and benefits. The normal Perl I/O functions used on files (except for **seek** and **sysseek**) work for stream sockets, but datagram sockets require the system calls **send** and **recv**, which work on complete records.

Awareness of buffering issues is particularly important in socket programming. That's because buffering, while designed to enhance performance, can interfere with the interactive feel that some programs require. Gathering input with `<>` may try to read more data from the socket than is yet available as it looks for a record separator. Both **print** and `<>` use **stdio** buffers, so unless you've changed autoflushing (see the Introduction to Chapter 7, *File Access*) on the socket handle, your data won't be sent to the other end as soon as you **print** it. Instead, it will wait until a buffer fills up.

For line-based clients and servers, this is probably okay, so long as you turn on autoflushing for output. Newer versions of IO::Socket do this automatically on the anonymous filehandles returned by IO::Socket->new.

But stdio isn't the only source of buffering. Output (print, printf, or syswrite—or send on a TCP socket) is further subject to buffering at the operating system level under a strategy called *The Nagle Algorithm*. When a packet of data has been sent but not acknowledged, further to-be-sent data is queued and is sent as soon as another complete packet's worth is collected or the outstanding acknowledgment is received. In some situations (mouse events being sent to a windowing system, keystrokes to a real-time application) this buffering is inconvenient or downright wrong. You can disable the Nagle Algorithm with the TCP_ NODELAY socket option:

```
use Socket;
require "sys/socket.ph";     # for &TCP_NODELAY

setsockopt(SERVER, SOL_SOCKET, &TCP_NODELAY, 1)
    or die "Couldn't disable Nagle's algorithm: $!\n";
```

Re-enable it with:

```
setsockopt(SERVER, SOL_SOCKET, &TCP_NODELAY, 0)
    or die "Couldn't enable Nagle's algorithm: $!\n";
```

In most cases, TCP_NODELAY isn't something you need. TCP buffering is there for a reason, so don't disable it unless your application is one of the few real-time packet-intensive situations that need to.

Load in TCP_NODELAY from *sys/socket.ph*, a file that isn't automatically installed with Perl, but can be easily built. See Recipe 12.14 for details.

Because buffering is such an issue, you have the select function to determine which filehandles have unread input, which can be written to, and which have "exceptional conditions" pending. The select function takes three strings interpreted as binary data, each bit corresponding to a filehandle. A typical call to select looks like this:

```
$rin = '';                          # initialize bitmask
vec($rin, fileno(SOCKET), 1) = 1;   # mark SOCKET in $rin
# repeat calls to vec() for each socket to check

$timeout = 10;                      # wait ten seconds

$nfound = select($rout = $rin, undef, undef, $timeout);
if (vec($rout, fileno(SOCKET),1)){
    # data to be read on SOCKET
}
```

The four arguments to `select` are: a bitmask indicating which filehandles to check for unread data; a bitmask indicating which filehandles to check for safety to write without blocking; a bitmask indicating which filehandles to check for exceptional conditions on; and a time in seconds indicating the maximum time to wait (this can be a floating point number).

The function changes the bitmask arguments passed to it, so that when it returns, the only bits set correspond to filehandles ready for I/O. This leads to the common strategy of assigning an input mask (`$rin` above) to an output one (`$rout` about), so that `select` can only affect `$rout`, leaving `$rin` alone.

You can specify a timeout of 0 to *poll* (check without blocking). Some beginning programmers think that blocking is bad, so they write programs that "busy wait"— they poll and poll and poll and poll. When a program blocks, the operating system recognizes that the process is pending on input and gives CPU time to other programs until input is available. When a program busy-waits, the system can't let it sleep because it's always doing something—checking for input! Occasionally, polling is the right thing to do, but far more often it's not. A timeout of `undef` to `select` means "no timeout," and your program will patiently block until input becomes available.

Because `select` uses bitmasks, which are tiresome to create and difficult to interpret, we use the standard IO::Select module in the Solution section. It bypasses bitmasks and is, generally, the easier route.

A full explanation of the exceptional data tested for with the third bitmask in `select` is beyond the scope of this book. Consult Stevens's *Unix Network Programming* for a discussion of out-of-band and urgent data.

Other `send` and `recv` flags are listed in the manpages for those system calls.

See Also

The `send`, `recv`, `fileno`, `vec`, `setsockopt`, and `select` functions in Chapter 3 of *Programming Perl* and in *perlfunc*(1); the sections on "I/O Operators" and on "Bitwise String Operators" in *perlop*(1); your system's *setsockopt*(2) manpage (if you have one); the documentation for the standard Socket and IO::Socket modules; the section on "Internet TCP clients and servers" in Chapter 6 of *Programming Perl* and in *perlipc*(1); *Unix Network Programming*; Recipe 17.1; Recipe 17.2

17.4. *Setting Up a UDP Client*

Problem

You want to exchange messages with another process using UDP (datagrams).

Solution

To set up a UDP socket handle, use either the low-level Socket module on your own filehandle:

```
use Socket;
socket(SOCKET, PF_INET, SOCK_DGRAM, getprotobyname("udp"))
    or die "socket: $!";
```

or else IO::Socket, which returns an anonymous one:

```
use IO::Socket;
$handle = IO::Socket::INET->new(Proto => 'udp')
    or die "socket: $@";      # yes, it uses $@ here
```

Then to send a message to a machine named $HOSTNAME on port number $PORTNO, use:

```
$ipaddr   = inet_aton($HOSTNAME);
$portaddr = sockaddr_in($PORTNO, $ipaddr);
send(SOCKET, $MSG, 0, $portaddr) == length($MSG)
        or die "cannot send to $HOSTNAME($PORTNO): $!";
```

To receive a message of length no greater than $MAXLEN, use:

```
$portaddr = recv(SOCKET, $MSG, $MAXLEN, 0)      or die "recv: $!";
($portno, $ipaddr) = sockaddr_in($portaddr);
$host = gethostbyaddr($ipaddr, AF_INET);
print "$host($portno) said $MSG\n";
```

Discussion

Datagram sockets are unlike stream sockets. Streams provide sessions, giving the illusion of a stable connection. You might think of them as working like a telephone call—expensive to set up, but once established, reliable and easy to use. Datagrams, though, are more like the postal system—it's cheaper and easier to send a letter to your friend on the other side of the world than to call them on the phone. Datagrams are easier on the system than streams. You send a small amount of information one message at a time. But your messages' delivery isn't guaranteed, and they might arrive in the wrong order. Like a small post box, the receiver's queue might fill up and cause further messages to be dropped.

Why then, if datagrams are unreliable, do we have them? Because some applications are most sensibly implemented in terms of datagrams. For instance, in streaming audio, it's more important that the stream as a whole be preserved than that every packet get through, especially if packets are being dropped because there's not enough bandwidth for them all. Another use for datagrams is broadcasting, which corresponds to mass mailing of advertisements in the postal model, and is equally popular in most circles. One use for broadcast packets is to send out a message to your local subnet saying "Hey, is there anybody around here who wants to be my server?"

Because datagrams don't provide the illusion of a lasting connection, you get a little more freedom in how you use them. You don't have to **connect** your socket to the remote end that you're sending data. Instead, address each datagram individually when you **send**. Assuming $remote_addr is the result of a call to **sockaddr_in**, do this:

```
send(MYSOCKET, $msg_buffer, $flags, $remote_addr)
    or die "Can't send: $!\n";
```

The only flag argument used much is MSG_OOB, which lets you send and receive out-of-band data in advanced applications.

The remote address should be a port and internet address combination returned by the Socket module's **sockaddr_in** function. If you want, call **connect** on that address instead. Then you can omit the last argument to your **sends**, after which they'll all go to that recipient. Unlike streams, you are free to reconnect to another machine with the same datagram socket.

Example 17-1 is a small example of a UDP program. It contacts the UDP time port of the machine whose name is given on the command line, or of the local machine by default. This doesn't work on all machines, but those with a server will send you back a 4-byte integer packed in network byte order that represents the time that machine thinks it is. The time returned, however, is in the number of seconds since 1900. You have to subtract the number of seconds between 1900 and 1970 to feed that time to the localtime or gmtime conversion functions.

Example 17-1. clockdrift

```perl
#!/usr/bin/perl
# clockdrift - compare another system's clock with this one
use strict;
use Socket;

my ($host, $him, $src, $port, $ipaddr, $ptime, $delta);
my $SECS_of_70_YEARS     = 2_208_988_800;

socket(MsgBox, PF_INET, SOCK_DGRAM, getprotobyname("udp"))
    or die "socket: $!";
$him = sockaddr_in(scalar(getservbyname("time", "udp")),
    inet_aton(shift || '127.1'));
defined(send(MsgBox, 0, 0, $him))
```

Example 17-1. clockdrift (continued)

```
    or die "send: $!";
defined($src = recv(MsgBox, $ptime, 4, 0))
    or die "recv: $!";
($port, $ipaddr) = sockaddr_in($src);
$host = gethostbyaddr($ipaddr, AF_INET);
my $delta = (unpack("N", $ptime) - $SECS_of_70_YEARS) - time();
print "Clock on $host is $delta seconds ahead of this one.\n";
```

If the machine you're trying to contact isn't alive or if its response is lost, you'll only know because your program will get stuck in the recv waiting for an answer that will never come.

See Also

The send, recv, gethostbyaddr, and unpack functions in Chapter 3 of *Programming Perl* and in *perlfunc*(1); the documentation for the standard Socket and IO::Socket modules; the section on "UDP: message passing" in Chapter 6 of *Programming Perl* and in *perlipc*(1); *Unix Network Programming*; Recipe 17.5

17.5. Setting Up a UDP Server

Problem

You want to write a UDP server.

Solution

First bind to the port the server is to be contacted on. With IO::Socket, this is easily accomplished:

```
use IO::Socket;
$server = IO::Socket::INET->new(LocalPort => $server_port,
                                Proto     => "udp")
    or die "Couldn't be a udp server on port $server_port : $@\n";
```

Then, go into a loop receiving messages:

```
while ($him = $server->recv($datagram, $MAX_TO_READ, $flags)) {
    # do something
}
```

Discussion

Life with UDP is much simpler than life with TCP. Instead of accepting client connections one at a time and committing yourself to a long-term relationship, take messages from clients as they come in. The recv function returns the address of the sender, which you must then decode.

Example 17-2 is a small UDP-based server that just sits around waiting for messages. Every time a message comes in, we find out who sent it and send them a message based on the previous message, and then save the new message.

Example 17-2. udpqotd

```perl
#!/usr/bin/perl -w
# udpqotd - UDP message server
use strict;
use IO::Socket;
my($sock, $oldmsg, $newmsg, $hisaddr, $hishost, $MAXLEN, $PORTNO);
$MAXLEN = 1024;
$PORTNO = 5151;
$sock = IO::Socket::INET->new(LocalPort => $PORTNO, Proto => 'udp')
    or die "socket: $@";
print "Awaiting UDP messages on port $PORTNO\n";
$oldmsg = "This is the starting message.";
while ($sock->recv($newmsg, $MAXLEN)) {
    my($port, $ipaddr) = sockaddr_in($sock->peername);
    $hishost = gethostbyaddr($ipaddr, AF_INET);
    print "Client $hishost said ''$newmsg''\n";
    $sock->send($oldmsg);
    $oldmsg = "[$hishost] $newmsg";
}
die "recv: $!";
```

This program is easier using IO::Socket than the raw Socket module. We don't have to say where to send the message because the library keeps track of who sent the last message and stores that information away on the $sock object. The peername method retrieves it for decoding.

You can't use the *telnet* program to talk to this server. You have to use a dedicated client. One is shown in Example 17-3.

Example 17-3. udpmsg

```perl
#!/usr/bin/perl -w
# udpmsg - send a message to the udpquotd server

use IO::Socket;
use strict;

my($sock, $server_host, $msg, $port, $ipaddr, $hishost,
    $MAXLEN, $PORTNO, $TIMEOUT);

$MAXLEN  = 1024;
$PORTNO  = 5151;
$TIMEOUT = 5;
```

Example 17-3. udpmsg (continued)

```
$server_host = shift;
$msg         = "@ARGV";
$sock = IO::Socket::INET->new(Proto     => 'udp',
                              PeerPort   => $PORTNO,
                              PeerAddr   => $server_host)
    or die "Creating socket: $!\n";
$sock->send($msg) or die "send: $!";

eval {
    local $SIG{ALRM} = sub { die "alarm time out" };
    alarm $TIMEOUT;
    $sock->recv($msg, $MAXLEN)        or die "recv: $!";
    alarm 0;
    1;  # return value from eval on normalcy
} or die "recv from $server_host timed out after $TIMEOUT seconds.\n";

($port, $ipaddr) = sockaddr_in($sock->peername);
$hishost = gethostbyaddr($ipaddr, AF_INET);
print "Server $hishost responded ''$msg''\n";
```

This time when we create the socket, we supply a peer host and port at the start, allowing us to omit that information in the send.

We've added an **alarm** timeout in case the server isn't responsive, or maybe not even alive. Because **recv** is a blocking system call that may not return, we wrap it in the standard **eval** block construct for timing out a blocking operation.

See Also

The **send**, **recv**, and **alarm** functions in Chapter 3 of *Programming Perl* and in *perlfunc*(1); the documentation for the standard Socket and IO::Socket modules; the section on "UDP: message passing" in Chapter 6 of *Programming Perl* and in *perlipc*(1); *Unix Network Programming*; Recipe 16.21; Recipe 17.4

17.6. Using UNIX Domain Sockets

Problem

You want to communicate with other processes on only the local machine.

Solution

Use domain sockets. You can use the code and techniques from the preceding Internet domain recipes, with the following changes:

- Because the naming system is different, use **sockaddr_un** instead of **sockaddr_in**.

- Use IO::Socket::UNIX instead of IO::Socket::INET.

- Use PF_UNIX instead of PF_INET, and give PF_UNSPEC as the last argument
  to socket.

- SOCK_STREAM clients don't have to bind to a local address before they connect.

Discussion

Unix domain sockets have names like files on the filesystem. In fact, most systems
implement them as special files; that's what Perl's -S filetest operator looks for—
whether the file is a Unix domain socket.

Supply the filename as the Peer argument to IO::Socket::UNIX->new, or
encode it with sockaddr_un and pass it to connect. Here's how to make server
and client Unix domain datagram sockets with IO::Socket::UNIX:

```
use IO::Socket;

unlink "/tmp/mysock";
$server = IO::Socket::UNIX->new(Local    => "/tmp/mysock",
                                Type     => SOCK_DGRAM,
                                Listen   => 5 )
    or die $@;

$client = IO::Socket::UNIX->new(Peer     => "/tmp/mysock",
                                Type     => SOCK_DGRAM,
                                Timeout  => 10 )
    or die $@;
```

Here's how to use the traditional functions to make stream sockets:

```
use Socket;

socket(SERVER, PF_UNIX, SOCK_STREAM, 0);
unlink "/tmp/mysock";
bind(SERVER, sockaddr_un("/tmp/mysock"))
    or die "Can't create server: $!";

socket(CLIENT, PF_UNIX, SOCK_STREAM, 0);
connect(CLIENT, sockaddr_un("/tmp/mysock"))
    or die "Can't connect to /tmp/mysock: $!";
```

Unless you know what you're doing, set the protocol (the Proto argument to
IO::Socket::UNIX->new, and the last argument to socket) to 0 for PF_UNIX
sockets. You can use both SOCK_DGRAM and SOCK_STREAM types of communication in the Unix domain, with the same semantics as we saw for Internet sockets. Changing the domain doesn't change the characteristics of the type of socket.

Because many systems actually create a special file in the filesystem, you should delete the file before you try to bind the socket. Even though there is a race condition (somebody could create a file with the name of your socket between your calls to unlink and bind), this isn't a security problem, because bind won't overwrite an existing file.

See Also

Recipes 17.1 through 17.5

17.7. Identifying the Other End of a Socket

Problem

You have a socket and want to identify the machine at the other end.

Solution

If you're only interested in the IP address of the remote machine, use:

```
use Socket;

$other_end         = getpeername(SOCKET)
    or die "Couldn't identify other end: $!\n";
($port, $iaddr)    = unpack_sockaddr_in($other_end);
$ip_address        = inet_ntoa($iaddr);
```

If you want its actual host name, use:

```
use Socket;

$other_end          = getpeername(SOCKET)
    or die "Couldn't identify other end: $!\n";
($port, $iaddr)    = unpack_sockaddr_in($other_end);
$actual_ip         = inet_ntoa($iaddr);
$claimed_hostname = gethostbyaddr($iaddr, AF_INET);
@name_lookup       = gethostbyname($claimed_hostname)
    or die "Could not look up $claimed_hostname : $!\n";
@resolved_ips      = map { inet_ntoa($_) }
    @name_lookup[ 4 .. $#name_lookup ];
```

Discussion

For a long time, figuring out who connected to you was considered more straightforward than it really is. The getpeername function returns the IP address of the remote machine in a packed binary structure (or undef if an error occurred). To unpack it, use inet_ntoa. If you want the name of the remote end, call gethostbyaddr to look up the name of the machine in the DNS tables, right?

Not really. That's only half the solution. Because a name lookup goes to the name's owner's DNS server and a lookup of an IP addresses goes to the address's owner's DNS server, you have to contend with the possibility that the machine that connected to you is giving incorrect names. For instance, the machine `evil.crackers.org` could belong to malevolent cyberpirates who tell their DNS server that its IP address (`1.2.3.4`) should be identified as `trusted.dod.gov`. If your program trusts `trusted.dod.gov`, a connection from `evil.crackers.org` will cause `getpeername` to return the right IP address (`1.2.3.4`), but `gethostbyaddr` will return the duplicitous name.

To avoid this problem, we take the (possibly deceitful) name returned by `gethostbyaddr` and look it up again with `gethostbyname`. In the case of `evil.crackers.org`, the lookup of `trusted.dod.gov` will be done through `dod.gov`'s DNS servers, and will return the real IP address(es) for `trusted.dod.gov`. Because many machines have more than one IP address (multihomed web servers are the obvious example), we can't use the simplified form of `gethostbyname`:

```
$packed_ip  = gethostbyname($name) or die "Couldn't look up $name : $!\n";
$ip_address = inet_ntoa($packed_ip);
```

So far we've assumed we're dealing with an Internet domain application. You can also call `getpeername` on a Unix domain socket. If the other end called `bind`, you'll get the filename they bound to. If the other end *didn't* call `bind`, however, `getpeername` may return an empty string (unpacked), a packed string with oddball garbage in it, or `undef` to indicate an error, or your computer may reboot. (These possibilities are listed in descending order of probability and desirability.) This is what we in the computer business call "undefined behavior."

Even this level of paranoia and mistrust isn't enough. It's still possible for people to fake out DNS servers they don't directly control, so don't use hostnames for identification or authentication. True paranoiacs and misanthropes use cryptographically-secure methods.

See Also

The `gethostbyaddr`, `gethostbyname`, and `getpeername` in Chapter 3 of *Programming Perl* and in *perlfunc*(1); the `inet_ntoa` in the standard Socket module; the documentation for the standard IO::Socket and Net::hostnet modules

17.8. Finding Your Own Name and Address

Problem

You want to find your (fully qualified) hostname.

Solution

First, get your (possibly qualified) hostname. Either try the standard Sys::Hostname module:

```
use Sys::Hostname;

$hostname = hostname();
```

or POSIX's uname function:

```
use POSIX qw(uname);
($kernel, $hostname, $release, $version, $hardware) = uname();

$hostname = (uname)[1];                     # or just one
```

Then turn it into an IP address and convert to its canonical name:

```
use Socket;                            # for AF_INET
$address  = gethostbyname($hostname)
    or die "Couldn't resolve $hostname : $!";
$hostname = gethostbyaddr($address, AF_INET)
    or die "Couldn't re-resolve $hostname : $!";
```

Discussion

Sys::Hostname tries to be portable by using knowledge about your system to decide how best to find the hostname. It tries many different ways of getting the hostname, but several involve running other programs. This can lead to tainted data (see Recipe 19.1).

POSIX::uname, on the other hand, only works on POSIX systems and isn't guaranteed to provide anything useful in the nodename field that we are examining. That said, the value *is* useful on many machines and doesn't suffer from the tainted data problem that Sys::Hostname does.

Once you have the name, though, you must consider that it might be missing a domain name. For instance, Sys::Hostname may return you guanaco instead of guanaco.camelids.org. To fix this, convert the name back into an IP address with gethostbyname and then back into a name again with gethostbyaddr. By involving the domain name system, you are guaranteed of getting a full name.

See Also

The `gethostbyname` and `gethostbyaddr` functions in Chapter 3 of *Programming Perl* and in *perlfunc*(1); the documentation for the standard Net::hostent and Sys::Hostname modules

17.9. *Closing a Socket After Forking*

Problem

Your program has forked and you want to tell the other end that you're done sending data. You've tried `close` on the socket, but the remote end never gets an EOF or SIGPIPE.

Solution

Use `shutdown`:

```
shutdown(SOCKET, 0);        # I/we have stopped reading data
shutdown(SOCKET, 1);        # I/we have stopped writing data
shutdown(SOCKET, 2);        # I/we have stopped using this socket
```

On an IO::Socket object, you could also write:

```
$socket->shutdown(0);       # I/we have stopped reading data
```

Discussion

When a process forks, the child has copies of all the parent's open filehandles, including sockets. When you `close` a file or socket, you close only the current process' copy. If another process (parent or child) still has the socket open, the operating system doesn't consider their file or socket closed.

Take the case of a socket that data is being sent to. If two processes have this socket open, one can close it but the socket isn't considered closed by the operating system because the other still has it open. Until the *other* process closes the socket, the process reading from the socket won't get an end-of-file. This can lead to confusion and deadlock.

To avoid this, either `close` unused filehandles after a `fork`, or use `shutdown`. The `shutdown` function is a more insistent form of `close`—it tells the operating system that even though other processes have copies of this filehandle, it should be marked as closed and the other end should get an end-of-file if they read from it, or a SIGPIPE if they write to it.

The numeric argument to shutdown lets you specify which sides of the connection are closed. An argument of 0 says that we're done reading data, so the other end of the socket will get a SIGPIPE if they try writing. 1 says that we're done writing data, so the other end of the socket will get an end-of-file if they try reading. 2 says we're done reading and writing.

Imagine a server that wants to read its client's request until end of file, and send an answer. If the client calls close, that socket is now invalid for I/O, so no answer would ever come back. Instead, the client should use shutdown to half-close the connection.

```
print SERVER "my request\n";        # send some data
shutdown(SERVER, 1);                # send eof; no more writing
$answer = <SERVER>;                 # but you can still read
```

See Also

The close and shutdown functions in Chapter 3 of *Programming Perl* and in *perlfunc*(1); your system's *shutdown*(2) manpage (if you have it)

17.10. Writing Bidirectional Clients

Problem

You want set up a fully interactive client so you can type a line, get the answer, type a line, get the answer, etc., somewhat like *telnet*.

Solution

Once you've connected, fork off a duplicate process. One twin only reads your input and passes it on to the server, and the other only reads the server's output and sends it to your own output.

Discussion

In a client-server relationship, it is difficult to know whose turn it is to talk. Single-threaded solutions involving the four-argument version of select are hard to write and maintain. But there's no reason to ignore multitasking solutions. The fork function dramatically simplifies this problem.

Once you've connected to the service you'd like to chat with, call fork to clone a twin. Each of these two (nearly) identical processes has a simple job. The parent copies everything from the socket to standard output, and the child simultaneously copies everything from standard input to the socket.

The code is in Example 17-4.

Example 17-4. biclient

```perl
#!/usr/bin/perl -w
# biclient - bidirectional forking client
    use strict;
use IO::Socket;
my ($host, $port, $kidpid, $handle, $line);

unless (@ARGV == 2) { die "usage: $0 host port" }
($host, $port) = @ARGV;

# create a tcp connection to the specified host and port
$handle = IO::Socket::INET->new(Proto      => "tcp",
                                PeerAddr   => $host,
                                PeerPort   => $port)
        or die "can't connect to port $port on $host: $!";

$handle->autoflush(1);              # so output gets there right away
print STDERR "[Connected to $host:$port]\n";

# split the program into two processes, identical twins
die "can't fork: $!" unless defined($kidpid = fork());

if ($kidpid) {
    # parent copies the socket to standard output
    while (defined ($line = <$handle>)) {
        print STDOUT $line;
    }
    kill("TERM" => $kidpid);        # send SIGTERM to child
}
else {
    # child copies standard input to the socket
    while (defined ($line = <STDIN>)) {
        print $handle $line;
    }
}
exit;
```

To accomplish the same thing using just one process is remarkably more difficult. It's easier to code two processes, each doing a single task, than it is to code one process to do two different tasks. Take advantage of multitasking by splitting your program into multiple threads of control, and some of your bewildering problems will become much easier.

The kill function in the parent's if block is there to send a signal to the child (currently running in the else block) as soon as the remote server has closed its end of the connection. The kill at the end of the parent's block is there to eliminate the child process as soon as the server on the other end goes away.

If the remote server sends data a byte at time and you need that data immediately without waiting for a newline (which may never arrive), you may wish to replace the while loop in the parent with the following:

```
my $byte;
while (sysread($handle, $byte, 1) == 1) {
    print STDOUT $byte;
}
```

Making a system call for each byte you want to read is not very efficient (to put it mildly), but it is the simplest to explain and works reasonably well.

See Also

The sysread and fork functions in Chapter 3 of *Programming Perl* and in *perlfunc*(1); the documentation for the standard IO::Socket module; Recipe 16.5; Recipe 16.10; Recipe 17.11

17.11. Forking Servers

Problem

You want to write a server that forks a subprocess to handle each new client.

Solution

Fork in the accept loop, and use a $SIG{CHLD} handler to reap the children.

```
# set up the socket SERVER, bind and listen ...
use POSIX qw(:sys_wait_h);

sub REAPER {
    1 until (-1 == waitpid(-1, WNOHANG));
    $SIG{CHLD} = \&REAPER;               # unless $] >= 5.002
}

$SIG{CHLD} = \&REAPER;

while ($hisaddr = accept(CLIENT, SERVER)) {
    next if $pid = fork;                  # parent
    die "fork: $!" unless defined $pid;   # failure
    # otherwise child
    close(SERVER);                        # no use to child
    # ... do something
    exit;                                 # child leaves
} continue {
    close(CLIENT);                        # no use to parent
}
```

Discussion

This approach is very common for SOCK_STREAM servers in the Internet and Unix domains. Each incoming connection gets a cloned server of its own. The model is:

1. Accept a stream connection.

2. Fork off a duplicate to communicate over that stream.

3. Return to 1.

This technique isn't used with SOCK_DGRAM sockets because their method of communication is different. The time it takes to fork makes the forking model impractical for UDP-style servers. Instead of working with a series of stateful, long-running connections, SOCK_DGRAM servers work with a bunch of sporadic datagrams, usually statelessly. With them, the model must become:

1. Read a datagram.

2. Handle the datagram.

3. Return to 1.

The child process deals with the new connection. Because it will never use the SERVER socket, we immediately close it. This is partly to keep a tidy house, but mainly so that the server socket is closed when the parent (server) process exits. If the children do not close the SERVER socket, the operating system considers the socket still open even when the parent dies. For more on this, see Recipe 17.9.

`%SIG` ensures that we clean up after our children when they exit. See Chapter 16 for details.

See Also

The `fork` and `accept` functions in Chapter 3 of *Programming Perl* and in *perlfunc*(1); Recipe 16.15; Recipe 16.19; Recipe 17.12; Recipe 17.13

17.12. Pre-Forking Servers

Problem

You want to write a server that concurrently processes several clients (as in "Forking Servers"), but connections are coming in so fast that forking slows the server too much.

Solution

Have a master server maintain a pool of pre-forked children, as shown in Example 17-5.

Example 17-5. preforker

```perl
#!/usr/bin/perl
# preforker - server who forks first
use IO::Socket;
use Symbol;
use POSIX;

# establish SERVER socket, bind and listen.
$server = IO::Socket::INET->new(LocalPort => 6969,
                                Type      => SOCK_STREAM,
                                Proto     => 'tcp',
                                Reuse     => 1,
                                Listen    => 10 )
    or die "making socket: $@\n";

# global variables
$PREFORK                = 5;        # number of children to maintain
$MAX_CLIENTS_PER_CHILD  = 5;        # number of clients each child should process
%children               = ();       # keys are current child process IDs
$children               = 0;        # current number of children

sub REAPER {                        # takes care of dead children
    $SIG{CHLD} = \&REAPER;
    my $pid = wait;
    $children --;
    delete $children{$pid};
}

sub HUNTSMAN {                      # signal handler for SIGINT
    local($SIG{CHLD}) = 'IGNORE';  # we're going to kill our children
    kill 'INT' => keys %children;
    exit;                          # clean up with dignity
}

# Fork off our children.
for (1 .. $PREFORK) {
    make_new_child();
}

# Install signal handlers.
$SIG{CHLD} = \&REAPER;
$SIG{INT}  = \&HUNTSMAN;

# And maintain the population.
while (1) {
    sleep;                              # wait for a signal (i.e., child's death)
    for ($i = $children; $i < $PREFORK; $i++) {
        make_new_child();               # top up the child pool
```

Example 17-5. preforker (continued)

```
    }
}

sub make_new_child {
    my $pid;
    my $sigset;

    # block signal for fork
    $sigset = POSIX::SigSet->new(SIGINT);
    sigprocmask(SIG_BLOCK, $sigset)
        or die "Can't block SIGINT for fork: $!\n";

    die "fork: $!" unless defined ($pid = fork);

    if ($pid) {
        # Parent records the child's birth and returns.
        sigprocmask(SIG_UNBLOCK, $sigset)
            or die "Can't unblock SIGINT for fork: $!\n";
        $children{$pid} = 1;
        $children++;
        return;
    } else {
        # Child can *not* return from this subroutine.
        $SIG{INT} = 'DEFAULT';        # make SIGINT kill us as it did before

        # unblock signals
        sigprocmask(SIG_UNBLOCK, $sigset)
            or die "Can't unblock SIGINT for fork: $!\n";

        # handle connections until we've reached $MAX_CLIENTS_PER_CHILD
        for ($i=0; $i < $MAX_CLIENTS_PER_CHILD; $i++) {
            $client = $server->accept()      or last;
            # do something with the connection
        }

        # tidy up gracefully and finish

        # this exit is VERY important, otherwise the child will become
        # a producer of more and more children, forking yourself into
        # process death.
        exit;
    }
}
```

Discussion

Whew. Although this is a lot of code, the logic is simple: the parent process never deals with clients but instead forks $PREFORK children to do that. The parent keeps track of how many children it has and forks more to replace dead children. Children exit after having handled $MAX_CLIENTS_PER_CHILD clients.

The code is a reasonably direct implementation of the logic above. The only trick comes with signal handlers: we want the parent to catch SIGINT and kill its children, so we install our signal handler &HUNTSMAN to do this. But we then have to be careful that the child doesn't have the same handler after we fork. We use POSIX signals to block the signal for the duration of the fork (see Recipe 16.20).

When you use this code in your programs, be sure that make_new_child never returns. If it does, the child will return, become a parent, and spawn off its own children. Your system will fill up with processes, your system administrator will storm down the hallway to find you, and you may end up tied to four horses wondering why you hadn't paid more attention to this paragraph.

On some operating systems, notably Solaris, you cannot have multiple children doing an accept on the same socket. You have to use file locking to ensure that only one child can call accept at any particular moment.

See Also

The select function in Chapter 3 or *perlfunc*(1); your system's *fcntl*(2) manpage (if you have one); the documentation for the standard Fcntl, Socket, IO::Select, IO::Socket, and Tie::RefHash modules; Recipe 17.11; Recipe 17.12

17.13. Non-Forking Servers

Problem

You want a server to deal with several simultaneous connections, but you don't want to fork a process to deal with each connection.

Solution

Keep an array of open clients, use select to read information when it becomes available, and deal with a client only when you have read a full request from it, as shown in Example 17-6.

Example 17-6. nonforker

```
#!/usr/bin/perl -w
# nonforker - server who multiplexes without forking
use POSIX;
use IO::Socket;
use IO::Select;
use Socket;
use Fcntl;
use Tie::RefHash;
```

Example 17-6. nonforker (continued)

```perl
$port = 1685;                    # change this at will

# Listen to port.
$server = IO::Socket::INET->new(LocalPort => $port,
                                Listen    => 10 )
  or die "Can't make server socket: $@\n";

# begin with empty buffers
%inbuffer  = ();
%outbuffer = ();
%ready     = ();

tie %ready, 'Tie::RefHash';

nonblock($server);
$select = IO::Select->new($server);

# Main loop: check reads/accepts, check writes, check ready to process
while (1) {
    my $client;
    my $rv;
    my $data;

    # check for new information on the connections we have

    # anything to read or accept?
    foreach $client ($select->can_read(1)) {

        if ($client == $server) {
            # accept a new connection

            $client = $server->accept();
            $select->add($client);
            nonblock($client);
        } else {
            # read data
            $data = '';
            $rv   = $client->recv($data, POSIX::BUFSIZ, 0);

            unless (defined($rv) && length $data) {
                # This would be the end of file, so close the client
                delete $inbuffer{$client};
                delete $outbuffer{$client};
                delete $ready{$client};

                $select->remove($client);
                close $client;
                next;
            }

            $inbuffer{$client} .= $data;
```

Example 17-6. nonforker (continued)

```perl
                    # test whether the data in the buffer or the data we
                    # just read means there is a complete request waiting
                    # to be fulfilled.  If there is, set $ready{$client}
                    # to the requests waiting to be fulfilled.
                    while ($inbuffer{$client} =~ s/(.*\n)//) {
                        push( @{$ready{$client}}, $1 );
                    }
                }
            }
        }

        # Any complete requests to process?
        foreach $client (keys %ready) {
            handle($client);
        }

        # Buffers to flush?
        foreach $client ($select->can_write(1)) {
            # Skip this client if we have nothing to say
            next unless exists $outbuffer{$client};

            $rv = $client->send($outbuffer{$client}, 0);
            unless (defined $rv) {
                # Whine, but move on.
                warn "I was told I could write, but I can't.\n";
                next;
            }
            if ($rv == length $outbuffer{$client} ||
                $! == POSIX::EWOULDBLOCK) {
                substr($outbuffer{$client}, 0, $rv) = '';
                delete $outbuffer{$client} unless length $outbuffer{$client};
            } else {
                # Couldn't write all the data, and it wasn't because
                # it would have blocked.  Shutdown and move on.
                delete $inbuffer{$client};
                delete $outbuffer{$client};
                delete $ready{$client};

                $select->remove($client);
                close($client);
                next;
            }
        }

        # Out of band data?
        foreach $client ($select->has_exception(0)) {  # arg is timeout
            # Deal with out-of-band data here, if you want to.
        }
    }

    # handle($socket) deals with all pending requests for $client
    sub handle {
        # requests are in $ready{$client}
```

Example 17-6. nonforker (continued)

```
        # send output to $outbuffer{$client}
        my $client = shift;
        my $request;

        foreach $request (@{$ready{$client}}) {
            # $request is the text of the request
            # put text of reply into $outbuffer{$client}
        }
        delete $ready{$client};
}

# nonblock($socket) puts socket into nonblocking mode
sub nonblock {
        my $socket = shift;
        my $flags;

        $flags = fcntl($socket, F_GETFL, 0)
                or die "Can't get flags for socket: $!\n";
        fcntl($socket, F_SETFL, $flags | O_NONBLOCK)
                or die "Can't make socket nonblocking: $!\n";
}
```

Discussion

As you see, handling multiple simultaneous clients within one process is more complicated than forking dedicated clones. You end up having to do a lot of operating system-like work to split your time between different connections and to ensure you don't block while reading.

The `select` function tells which connections have data waiting to be read, which can have data written to them, and which have unread out-of-band data. We could use the `select` function built into Perl, but it would take more work to find out which filehandles are available. So we use the standard (as of 5.004) IO::Select module.

We use `getsockopt` and `setsockopt` to turn on the non-blocking option for the server socket. Without it, a single client whose socket buffers filled up would cause the server to pause until the buffers emptied. Using nonblocking I/O, however, means that we have to deal with the case of partial reads and writes—we can't simply use <> to block until an entire record can be read, or use `print` to send an entire record with `print`. `%inbuffer` holds the incomplete command read from clients, `%outbuffer` holds data not yet sent, and `%ready` holds arrays of unhandled messages.

To use this code in your program, do three things. First, change the IO::Socket::INET call to specify your service's port. Second, change the code that moves records from the `inbuffer` to the `ready` queue. Currently it treats each line (text ending in \n) as a request. If your requests are not lines, you'll want to change this.

```
while ($inbuffer{$client} =~ s/(.*\n)//) {
    push( @{$ready{$client}}, $1 );
}
```

Finally, change the middle of the loop in **handler** to actually create a response to the request. A simple echoing program would say:

```
$outbuffer{$client} .= $request;
```

Error handling is left as an exercise to the reader. At the moment, we assume any read or write that caused an error is reason to end that client's connection. This is probably too harsh, because "errors" like EINTR and EAGAIN don't warrant termination (although you *should* never get an EAGAIN when using **select** ( )).

See Also

The **select** function in Chapter 3 or *perlfunc*(1); your system's *fcntl*(2) manpage (if you have one); the documentation for the standard Fcntl, Socket, IO::Select, IO::Socket, and Tie::RefHash modules; Recipe 17.11; Recipe 17.12

17.14. Writing a Multi-Homed Server

Problem

You want to write a server that knows that the machine it runs on has multiple IP addresses, and that it should possibly do different things for each address.

Solution

Don't bind your server to a particular address. Instead, bind to **INADDR_ANY**. Then, once you've **accepted** a connection, use **getsockname** on the client socket to find out which address they connected to:

```
use Socket;

socket(SERVER, PF_INET, SOCK_STREAM, getprotobyname('tcp'));
setsockopt(SERVER, SOL_SOCKET, SO_REUSEADDR, 1);
bind(SERVER, sockaddr_in($server_port, INADDR_ANY))
    or die "Binding: $!\n";

# accept loop
while (accept(CLIENT, SERVER)) {
    $my_socket_address = getsockname(CLIENT);
    ($port, $myaddr)   = sockaddr_in($my_socket_address);
}
```

Discussion

Whereas `getpeername` (as discussed in Recipe 17.7) returns the address of the remote end of the socket, `getsockname` returns the address of the local end. When we've bound to `INADDR_ANY`, thus accepting connections on any address the machine has, we need to use `getsockname` to identify which address the client connected to.

If you're using IO::Socket::INET, your code will look like this:

```
$server = IO::Socket::INET->new(LocalPort => $server_port,
                                Type      => SOCK_STREAM,
                                Proto     => 'tcp',
                                Listen    => 10)
    or die "Can't create server socket: $@\n";

while ($client = $server->accept()) {
    $my_socket_address = $client->sockname();
    ($port, $myaddr)   = sockaddr_in($my_socket_address);
    # ...
}
```

If you don't specify a local port to `IO::Socket::INET->new`, your socket will be bound to `INADDR_ANY`.

If you want your server to listen only for a *particular* virtual host, don't use `INADDR_ANY`. Instead, bind to a specific host address:

```
use Socket;

$port = 4269;                   # port to bind to
$host = "specific.host.com";    # virtual host to listen on

socket(Server, PF_INET, SOCK_STREAM, getprotobyname("tcp"))
    or die "socket: $!";
bind(Server, sockaddr_in($port, inet_aton($host)))
    or die "bind: $!";
while ($client_address = accept(Client, Server)) {
    # ...
}
```

See Also

The `getsockname` function in Chapter 3 of *Programming Perl* and in *perlfunc*(1); the documentation for the standard Socket and IO::Socket modules; the section on "Sockets" in Chapter 6 of *Programming Perl* or *perlipc*(1)

17.15. Making a Daemon Server

Problem

You want your program to run as a daemon.

Solution

If you are paranoid and running as root, **chroot** to a safe directory:

```
chroot("/var/daemon")
    or die "Couldn't chroot to /var/daemon: $!";
```

Fork once, and let the parent exit.

```
$pid = fork;
exit if $pid;
die "Couldn't fork: $!" unless defined($pid);
```

Dissociate from the controlling terminal that started us and stop being part of whatever process group we had been a member of.

```
use POSIX;

POSIX::setsid()
    or die "Can't start a new session: $!";
```

Trap fatal signals, setting a flag to indicate we need to gracefully exit.

```
$time_to_die = 0;

sub signal_handler {
    $time_to_die = 1;
}

$SIG{INT} = $SIG{TERM} = $SIG{HUP} = \&signal_handler;
# trap or ignore $SIG{PIPE}
```

Wrap your actual server code in a loop:

```
until ($time_to_die) {
    # ...
}
```

Discussion

Before POSIX, every operating system had its own way for a process to tell the operating system "I'm going it alone, please interfere with me as little as possible." POSIX makes it much cleaner. That said, you can still take advantage of any operating system-specific calls if you want to.

The `chroot` call is one of those non-POSIX calls. It makes a process change where it thinks the directory / is. For instance, after `chroot "/var/daemon"`, if the process tries to read the file */etc/passwd*, it will read */var/daemon/etc/passwd*. A chrooted process needs copies of any files it will run made available inside its new /, of course. For instance, our chrooted process would need */var/daemon/ bin/csh* if it were going to glob files. For security reasons, only the superuser may `chroot`. This is done by FTP servers if you login to them anonymously. It isn't really necessary to become a daemon.

The operating system expects a child's parent to wait when the child dies. Our daemon process has no particular parent to do this, so we need to disinherit it. This we do by `fork`ing once and having our parent exit, so that the child is not associated with the process that started the parent. The child then closes all the filehandles it got from its parent (STDIN, STDERR, and STDOUT) and calls `POSIX::setsid` to ensure that it is completely dissociated from its parent's terminal.

Now we're almost ready to begin. We don't want signals like SIGINT to kill us immediately (its default behavior), so we use `%SIG` to catch them and set a flag saying it's time to exit. Then our main program simply becomes: "While we weren't killed, do something."

The signal SIGPIPE is a special case. It's easy to get (by writing to a filehandle whose other end is closed) and has unforgiving default behavior (it terminates your process). You probably want to either ignore it (`$SIG{PIPE} = 'IGNORE'`) or define your own signal handler to deal with it appropriately.

See Also

Your system's *setsid*(2) and *chroot*(1) manpage (if you have them); the `chroot` function in Chapter 3 of *Programming Perl* and in *perlfunc*(1); the Unix Socket FAQ at *http://www.ibrado.com/sock-faq/*. *Unix Network Programming*

17.16. Restarting a Server on Demand

Problem

You want your server to shutdown and restart when it receives a HUP signal, just like `inetd` or `httpd`.

Solution

Catch the `SIGHUP` signal, and re-execute your program:

```
$SELF = "/usr/local/libexec/myd";    # which program I am
```

```
@ARGS = qw(-l /var/log/myd -d);        # program arguments

$SIG{HUP} = \&phoenix;

sub phoenix {
    # close all your connections, kill your children, and
    # generally prepare to be reincarnated with dignity.
    exec($SELF, @ARGS)                 or die "Couldn't restart: $!\n";
}
```

Discussion

It sure looks simple ("when I get a HUP signal, restart") but it's tricky. You must
know your own program name, and that isn't easy to find out. You could use $0
or the FindBin module. For normal programs, this is fine, but critical system utilities must be more cautious, as there's no guarantee that $0 is valid. You can hard-
code the filename and arguments into your program, as we do here. That's not
necessarily the most convenient solution, however, so you might want to read the
program and arguments from an external file (using the filesystem's protections to
ensure it hasn't been tampered with).

Be sure and install your signal handler *after* you define $SELF and @ARGS, other-
wise there's a race condition when a SIGHUP could run **restart** but you don't
know the program to run. This would cause your program to die.

Some servers don't want restart on receiving a SIGHUP—they just want to reread
their configuration file.

```
$CONFIG_FILE = "/usr/local/etc/myprog/server_conf.pl";
$SIG{HUP} = \&read_config;
sub read_config {
    do $CONFIG_FILE;
}
```

Some clever servers even autoload their configuration files when they notice that
those files have been updated. That way you don't have to go out of your way to
signal them.

See Also

The **exec** function in Chapter 3 of *Programming Perl* and in *perlfunc*(1);
Recipe 8.16; Recipe 8.17; Recipe 16.15

17.17. Program: backsniff

This program logs attempts to connect to ports. It uses the Sys::Syslog module (it
in turn wants the *syslog.ph* library, which may or may not come with your system)
to log the connection attempt as level LOG_NOTICE and facility LOG_DAEMON. It

uses getsockname to find out what port was connected to and getpeername to find out what machine made the connection. It uses getservbyport to convert the local port number (e.g., 7) into a service name (e.g, "echo").

It produces entries in the system log file like this:

> **May 25 15:50:22 coprolith sniffer: Connection from 207.46.131.141 to 207.46.130.164:echo**

Install it in the *inetd.conf* file with a line like this:

> **echo   stream tcp nowait   nobody /usr/scripts/snfsqrd sniffer**

The program is shown in Example 17-7.

Example 17-7. backsniff

```perl
#!/usr/bin/perl -w
# backsniff - log attempts to connect to particular ports

use Sys::Syslog;
use Socket;

# identify my port and address
$sockname           = getsockname(STDIN)
                        or die "Couldn't identify myself: $!\n";
($port, $iaddr)     = sockaddr_in($sockname);
$my_address         = inet_ntoa($iaddr);

# get a name for the service
$service = (getservbyport ($port, "tcp"))[0] || $port;
# now identify remote address
$sockname           = getpeername(STDIN)
                            or die "Couldn't identify other end: $!\n";
($port, $iaddr)     = sockaddr_in($sockname);
$ex_address         = inet_ntoa($iaddr);

# and log the information
openlog("sniffer", "ndelay", "daemon");
syslog("notice", "Connection from %s to %s:%s\n", $ex_address,
        $my_address, $service);
closelog();
exit;
```

17.18. Program: fwdport

Imagine that you're nestled deep inside a protective firewall. Somewhere in the outside world is a server that you'd like access to, but only processes on the firewall can reach it. You don't want to login to the firewall machine each time to access that service.

For example, this might arise if your company's ISP provides a news-reading service that seems to come from your main firewall machine, but rejects any NNTP connections from any other address. As the administrator of the firewall, you don't want dozens of people logging on to it, but you would like to let them read and post news from their own workstations.

The program in Example 17-8, *fwdport*, solves this problem in a generic fashion. You may run as many of these as you like, one per outside service. Sitting on the firewall, it can talk to both worlds. When someone wants to access the outside service, they contact this proxy, which connects on their behalf to the external service. To that outside service, the connection is coming from your firewall, so it lets it in. Then your proxy forks off twin processes, one only reading data from the external server and writing that data back to the internal client, the other only reading data from the internal client and writing that data back to the external server.

For example, you might invoke it this way:

```
% fwdport -s nntp -l fw.oursite.com -r news.bigorg.com
```

That means that the program will act as the server for the NNTP service, listening for local connections on the NNTP port on the host *fw.oursite.com*. When one comes in, it contacts *news.bigorg.com* (on the same port), and then ferries data between the remote server and local client.

Here's another example:

```
% fwdport -l myname:9191 -r news.bigorg.com:nntp
```

This time we listen for local connections on port 9191 of the host *myname*, and patch those connecting clients to the remote server *news.bigorg.com* on its NNTP port.

In a way, *fwdport* acts as both a server and a client. It's a server from the perspective of inside the firewall and a client from the perspective of the remote server outside. The program summarizes this chapter well because it demonstrates just about everything we've covered here. It has server activity, client activity, collecting of zombie children, forking and process management, plus much more thrown in.

Example 17-8. fwdport

```perl
#!/usr/bin/perl -w
# fwdport -- act as proxy forwarder for dedicated services

use strict;                    # require declarations
use Getopt::Long;              # for option processing
use Net::hostent;              # by-name interface for host info
use IO::Socket;                # for creating server and client sockets
```

Example 17-8. fwdport (continued)

```perl
use POSIX ":sys_wait_h";      # for reaping our dead children

my (
    %Children,              # hash of outstanding child processes
    $REMOTE,                # whom we connect to on the outside
    $LOCAL,                 # where we listen to on the inside
    $SERVICE,               # our service name or port number
    $proxy_server,          # the socket we accept() from
    $ME,                    # basename of this program
);

($ME = $0) =~ s,.*/,,;        # retain just basename of script name

check_args();                 # processing switches
start_proxy();                # launch our own server
service_clients();            # wait for incoming
die "NOT REACHED";            # you can't get here from there

# process command line switches using the extended
# version of the getopts library.
sub check_args {
    GetOptions(
        "remote=s"    => \$REMOTE,
        "local=s"     => \$LOCAL,
        "service=s"   => \$SERVICE,
    ) or die <<EOUSAGE;
    usage: $0 [ --remote host ] [ --local interface ] [ --service service ]
EOUSAGE
    die "Need remote"              unless $REMOTE;
    die "Need local or service"    unless $LOCAL || $SERVICE;
}

# begin our server
sub start_proxy {
    my @proxy_server_config = (
        Proto     => 'tcp',
        Reuse     => 1,
        Listen    => SOMAXCONN,
    );
    push @proxy_server_config, LocalPort => $SERVICE if $SERVICE;
    push @proxy_server_config, LocalAddr => $LOCAL    if $LOCAL;
    $proxy_server = IO::Socket::INET->new(@proxy_server_config)
                or die "can't create proxy server: $@";
    print "[Proxy server on ", ($LOCAL || $SERVICE), " initialized.]\n";
}


sub service_clients {
    my (
        $local_client,          # someone internal wanting out
        $lc_info,               # local client's name/port information
        $remote_server,         # the socket for escaping out
```

Example 17-8. fwdport (continued)

```
        @rs_config,                     # temp array for remote socket options
        $rs_info,                       # remote server's name/port information
        $kidpid,                        # spawned child for each connection
);

$SIG{CHLD} = \&REAPER;                  # harvest the moribund

accepting();

# an accepted connection here means someone inside wants out
while ($local_client = $proxy_server->accept()) {
    $lc_info = peerinfo($local_client);
    set_state("servicing local $lc_info");
    printf "[Connect from $lc_info]\n";

    @rs_config = (
        Proto       => 'tcp',
        PeerAddr    => $REMOTE,
    );
    push(@rs_config, PeerPort => $SERVICE) if $SERVICE;

    print "[Connecting to $REMOTE...";
    set_state("connecting to $REMOTE");                     # see below
    $remote_server = IO::Socket::INET->new(@rs_config)
                  or die "remote server: $@";
    print "done]\n";

    $rs_info = peerinfo($remote_server);
    set_state("connected to $rs_info");

    $kidpid = fork();
    die "Cannot fork" unless defined $kidpid;
    if ($kidpid) {
        $Children{$kidpid} = time();            # remember his start time
        close $remote_server;                   # no use to master
        close $local_client;                    # likewise
        next;                                   # go get another client
    }

    # at this point, we are the forked child process dedicated
    # to the incoming client.  but we want a twin to make i/o
    # easier.

    close $proxy_server;                        # no use to slave

    $kidpid = fork();
    die "Cannot fork" unless defined $kidpid;

    # now each twin sits around and ferries lines of data.
    # see how simple the algorithm is when you can have
    # multiple threads of control?
```

Example 17-8. fwdport (continued)

```
            # this is the fork's parent, the master's child
            if ($kidpid) {
                set_state("$rs_info --> $lc_info");
                select($local_client); $| = 1;
                print while <$remote_server>;
                kill('TERM', $kidpid);      # kill my twin cause we're done
                }
            # this is the fork's child, the master's grandchild
            else {
                set_state("$rs_info <-- $lc_info");
                select($remote_server); $| = 1;
                print while <$local_client>;
                kill('TERM', getppid());    # kill my twin cause we're done
            }
            exit;                           # whoever's still alive bites it
    } continue {
        accepting();
    }
}

# helper function to produce a nice string in the form HOST:PORT
sub peerinfo {
    my $sock = shift;
    my $hostinfo = gethostbyaddr($sock->peeraddr);
    return sprintf("%s:%s",
                    $hostinfo->name || $sock->peerhost,
                    $sock->peerport);
}

# reset our $0, which on some systems make "ps" report
# something interesting: the string we set $0 to!
sub set_state { $0 = "$ME [@_]" }

# helper function to call set_state
sub accepting {
    set_state("accepting proxy for " . ($REMOTE || $SERVICE));
}

# somebody just died.  keep harvesting the dead until
# we run out of them.  check how long they ran.
sub REAPER {
    my $child;
    my $start;
    while (($child = waitpid(-1,WNOHANG)) > 0) {
        if ($start = $Children{$child}) {
            my $runtime = time() - $start;
            printf "Child $child ran %dm%ss\n",
                $runtime / 60, $runtime % 60;
            delete $Children{$child};
        } else {
            print "Bizarre kid $child exited $?\n";
        }
}
```

Example 17-8. fwdport (continued)

```
    }
    # If I had to choose between System V and 4.2, I'd resign. --Peter Honeyman
    $SIG{CHLD} = \&REAPER;
};
```

See Also

Getopt::Long(3),   *Net::hostent*(3),   *IO::Socket*(3),   *POSIX*(3),   Recipe 16.19,
Recipe 17.10

18

Internet Services

*This "telephone" has too many shortcomings to
be seriously considered as a means of
communication. The device is inherently
of no value to us.*

——Western Union internal memo, 1876

18.0. Introduction

Correct use of sockets is only part of network communicating programs. Once you have a way for two programs to talk, you still need a *protocol* for communication. This protocol lets each party know when to talk, and it precisely defines who is responsible for which part of the service.

Common Internet protocols are:

Protocol	Meaning	Action
FTP	File Transfer Protocol	Copying files between remote machines
telnet		Remote login
rsh and rcp	Remote shell and Remote copy	Remote login and remote file copying
NNTP	Network News Transfer Protocol	Reading and posting USENET news
HTTP	Hypertext Transfer Protocol	Transferring documents on the Web
SMTP	Simple Mail Transfer Protocol	Sending mail
POP3	Post Office Protocol	Reading mail

Even something as relatively simple as connecting to a remote computer requires intricate negotiations between client and server and has numerous dynamically configurable options. If you had to write the Perl code to implement these protocols each time you wanted to use a network service, you'd probably end up writing a lot of buggy programs, try to get demoted into a management position, or both.

Fortunately, CPAN has modules for these protocols. Most modules implement the client side of the protocol rather than the server side. This means your program can use these modules to send mail, but not to be a mail server that other clients connect to; to read and post news, but not be a news server that other clients connect to; to transfer files to and from an FTP server, but not to be an FTP server that other clients connect to; and so on.

Most of these modules fall under the Net:: hierarchy. We'll be using Net::FTP to send and receive files using FTP, Net::NNTP to read and post Usenet news, Net::Telnet to simulate a connection to another machine, Net::Whois to find out information about a domain name, Net::Ping to check whether a machine is alive, and Net::POP3 and Mail::Mailer to receive and send mail. We deal with the CGI protocol in Chapter 19, *CGI Programming*, and HTTP in Chapter 20, *Web Automation*.

You can thank Graham Barr for most of these modules, whose IO::Socket modules we used for low-level network communication in Chapter 17, *Sockets*. He wrote Net::FTP, Net::NNTP, Net::POP3, and Mail::Mailer. Jay Rogers wrote Net::Telnet, and Chip Salzenberg wrote Net::Whois. Thank these folks that you don't have to reinvent these tricky wheels!

18.1. Simple DNS Lookups

Problem

You want to find the IP address of a host or turn an IP address into a name. Network servers do this to authenticate their clients, and clients do it when the user gives them a hostname but Perl's socket library requires an IP address. Furthermore, many servers produce log files containing IP addresses, but hostnames are more useful to analysis software and humans.

Solution

If you have a name like **www.perl.com**, use `gethostbyname` if you want all the addresses:

```
use Socket;
```

```
@addresses = gethostbyname($name)    or die "Can't resolve $name: $!\n";
@addresses = map { inet_ntoa($_) } @addresses[4 .. $#addresses];
# @addresses is a list of IP addresses ("208.201.239.48", "208.201.239.49")
```

Or, use `inet_aton` if you only need the first:

```
use Socket;

$address = inet_ntoa(inet_aton($name));
# $address is a single IP address "208.201.239.48"
```

If you have an IP address like `"208.201.239.48"`, use:

```
use Socket;

$name = gethostbyaddr(inet_aton($address), AF_INET)
            or die "Can't resolve $address: $!\n";
# $name is the hostname ("www.perl.com")
```

Discussion

This process is complicated because the functions are mere wrappers for the C
system calls, so this means you have to convert IP addresses from ASCII strings
(`"208.146.240.1"`) into their C structures. The standard Socket module gives you
`inet_aton` to convert from ASCII to the packed numeric format and `inet_ntoa`
to convert back:

```
use Socket;
$packed_address = inet_aton("208.146.140.1");
$ascii_address  = inet_ntoa($packed_address);
```

The `gethostbyname` function takes a string containing the hostname (or IP
address). In scalar context, it returns the IP address of the remote host suitable for
passing to `inet_ntoa` (or `undef` on error). In list context, it returns a list of at
least five elements (or an empty list in case of error). The returned list is:

Index	Meaning
0	Official name of host
1	Aliases (space-separated string)
2	Address Type (normally AF_INET)
3	Length of Address Structure (irrelevant)
4,5, ...	Address Structures

A hostname may have more than one address, particularly busy web sites, where
many machines serve identical web pages to share the load. In such situations, the
DNS server that provides you the addresses rotates them to balance the load. If

you need to pick an IP address to connect to, it is sufficient to always select the first (but if it doesn't work, try the rest as well):

```
$packed = gethostbyname($hostname)
            or die "Couldn't resolve address for $hostname: $!\n";
$address = inet_ntoa($packed);
print "I will use $address as the address for $hostname\n";
```

If you're using hostnames to permit or refuse access to a service, be careful. Anyone can set their DNS server to identify their machine as www.whitehouse.gov, www.yahoo.com, or this.is.not.funny. You can't know whether the machine really has the name it claims to have until you use gethostbyname and check that the original address is in the address list for the name.

```
# $address is the IP address I'm checking, like "128.138.243.20"
use Socket;
$name     = gethostbyaddr(inet_aton($address), AF_INET)
            or die "Can't look up $address : $!\n";
@addr     = gethostbyname($name)
            or die "Can't look up $name : $!\n";
$found    = grep { $address eq inet_ntoa($_) } @addr[4..$#addr];
```

It turns out that even with this algorithm, you can't be absolutely sure of the name due to a variety of methods that can be used to circumvent even this technique. Even the IP address from which the packets appear to be coming can be spoofed, so you shouldn't ever rely on the network layer for authentication. Always do authentication yourself (with passwords, or cryptographic challenges) when it really matters, because the IPv4 network was not designed to provide security.

More information is kept about a host than just addresses and aliases. To fully access this information, use the Net::DNS module from CPAN. For instance, Example 18-1 shows how to retrieve the MX (mail exchange) records for an arbitrary host.

Example 18-1. mxhost

```
#!/usr/bin/perl
# mxhost - find mx exchangers for a host
use Net::DNS;

$host = shift;
$res = Net::DNS::Resolver->new();
@mx = mx($res, $host)
    or die "Can't find MX records for $host (".$res->errorstring.")\n";

foreach $record (@mx) {
    print $record->preference, " ", $record->exchange, "\n";
}
```

Here's some output:

```
% mxhost cnn.com
```

```
10 mail.turner.com
30 alfw2.turner.com
```

The inet_aton function takes a string containing a hostname or IP address, as does gethostbyname, but it only returns the first IP address for the host. If you want to find them all, you'll need to add some more code. The Net::hostent provides for by-name access that will let you do that. Example 18-2 shows an example of its use.

Example 18-2. hostaddrs

```
#!/usr/bin/perl
# hostaddrs - canonize name and show addresses
use Socket;
use Net::hostent;
$name = shift;
if ($hent = gethostbyname($name)) {
    $name     = $hent->name;                    # in case different
    $addr_ref = $hent->addr_list;
    @addresses = map { inet_ntoa($_) } @$addr_ref;
}
print "$name => @addresses\n";
```

Here's the output:

```
% hostaddrs www.ora.com
helio.ora.com => 204.148.40.9

% hostaddrs www.whitehouse.gov
www.whitehouse.gov => 198.137.240.91 198.137.240.92
```

See Also

The gethostbyname and gethostbyaddr functions in Chapter 3 of *Programming Perl* and in *perlfunc*(1); the documentation for the Net::DNS module from CPAN; the documentation for the standard Socket and Net::hostent modules

18.2. Being an FTP Client

Problem

You want to connect to an FTP server and get or put files. You might want to automate the one-time transfer of many files or automatically mirror an entire section of an FTP server, for example.

Solution

Use the CPAN module Net::FTP:

```
use Net::FTP;

$ftp = Net::FTP->new("ftp.host.com")      or die "Can't connect: $@\n";
$ftp->login($username, $password)          or die "Couldn't login\n";
$ftp->cwd($directory)                      or die "Couldn't change directory\n";
$ftp->get($filename)                       or die "Couldn't get $filename\n";
$ftp->put($filename)                       or die "Couldn't put $filename\n";
```

Discussion

Using the Net::FTP module is a three-part process: *connect* to a server, identify and *authenticate* yourself, and *transfer* files. All interaction with the FTP server happens through method calls on a Net::FTP object. If an error occurs, methods return undef in scalar context or an empty list in list context.

The connection is established with the **new** constructor. If an error occurs, $@ is set to an error message and **new** returns undef. The first argument is the hostname of the FTP server and is optionally followed by named options:

```
$ftp = Net::FTP->new("ftp.host.com",
                        Timeout => 30,
                        Debug   => 1)
    or die "Can't connect: $@\n";
```

The Timeout option gives the number of seconds all operations wait before giving up. Debug sets the debugging level (non-zero sends copies of all commands to STDERR). Firewall takes a string as an argument, specifying the machine acting as an FTP proxy. Port lets you specify an alternate port number (the default is 21, the standard port for FTP). Finally, if the Passive option is set to true, all transfers are done passively (some firewalls and proxies require this). The Firewall and Passive options override the environment variables FTP_FIREWALL and FTP_PASSIVE.

Having connected, the next step is to authenticate. Normally, you'll want to call login with up to three arguments: username, password, and account.

```
$ftp->login()
    or die "Couldn't authenticate.\n";

$ftp->login($username)
    or die "Still couldn't authenticate.\n";

$ftp->login($username, $password)
    or die "Couldn't authenticate, even with explicit username
            and password.\n";

$ftp->login($username, $password, $account)
    or die "No dice.  It hates me.\n";
```

If you call `login` with no arguments, Net::FTP uses the Net::Netrc module to find settings for the host you've connected to. If none are found there, anonymous login is attempted (username `anonymous`, password `username@hostname`). If no password is given and the username `anonymous` is used, the user's mail address is supplied as the password. The optional account argument is not used on most systems. If the authentication fails, `login` returns `undef`.

Once authenticated, the usual FTP commands are available as methods called on your Net::FTP object. The `get` and `put` methods fetch and send files. To send a file, use:

```
$ftp->put($localfile, $remotefile)
    or die "Can't send $localfile: $!\n";
```

If you omit the second argument, the remote file will have the same name as the local file. You can also send from a filehandle (in which case the remote filename must be given as the second argument):

```
$ftp->put(*STDIN, $remotefile)
    or die "Can't send from STDIN: $!\n";
```

If the transfer is interrupted, the remote file is not automatically deleted. The `put` method returns the remote filename if it succeeded, or `undef` if an error occurred.

To fetch a file, use the `get` method, which returns the local filename, or `undef` if there was an error:

```
$ftp->get($remotefile, $localfile)
    or die "Can't fetch $remotefile : $!\n";
```

You can also `get` into a filehandle, in which case the filehandle is returned (or `undef` if there was an error):

```
$ftp->get($remotefile, *STDOUT)
    or die "Can't fetch $remotefile: $!\n";
```

Pass `get` an optional third argument, an offset into the remote file, to begin the transfer at that offset. Received bytes are appended to the local file.

The `type` method changes the file translation mode. Pass it a string (`"A"`, `"I"`, `"E"`, or `"L"`) and it will return the previous translation mode. The `ascii`, `binary`, `ebcdic`, and `byte` methods call `type` with the appropriate string. If an error occurs (the FTP server does not do EBCDIC, for example), `type` and its helper methods return `undef`.

Use `cwd($remotedir)` and `pwd` to set and fetch the current remote directory. They both return true if successful, false otherwise. If you `cwd("..")`, the `cdup` method is called to change the directory to the parent of the current directory. Call `cwd` without an argument to change to the root directory.

```
$ftp->cwd("/pub/perl/CPAN/images/g-rated");
```

```
print "I'm in the directory ", $ftp->pwd(), "\n";
```

mkdir($remotedir) and rmdir($remotedir) make and delete directories on the remote machine. You have the built-in mkdir and rmdir functions to make and delete directories on the local machine. To create all directories up to the given directory, pass a true second argument to mkdir. For instance, if you want to make */pub*, */pub/gnat*, and */pub/gnat/perl*, say:

```
$ftp->mkdir("/pub/gnat/perl", 1)
    or die "Can't create /pub/gnat/perl recursively: $!\n";
```

If mkdir succeeds, the full path to the newly created directory is returned. If it fails, mkdir returns undef.

The ls and dir methods get a list of files in a remote directory. Traditionally, dir gives you a more verbose listing than ls, but neither has a standard format. Most Unix FTP servers return the output of *ls* and *ls -l* respectively, but you can't guarantee that behavior from every FTP server. These methods, in list context, return the list of lines returned by the server. In scalar context, they return a reference to an array.

```
@lines = $ftp->ls("/pub/gnat/perl")
    or die "Can't get a list of files in /pub/gnat/perl: $!";
$ref_to_lines = $ftp->dir("/pub/perl/CPAN/src/latest.tar.gz")
    or die "Can't check status of latest.tar.gz: $!\n";
```

When you're done and want to close up gracefully, use the quit method:

```
$ftp->quit()     or warn "Couldn't quit.  Oh well.\n";
```

Other methods rename, change ownership and permissions of remote files, check the size of the remote file, and so on. Read the Net::FTP documentation for details.

If you want to mirror files between machines, use the excellent *mirror* program written in Perl by Lee McLoughlin. Look for it on the Web at *http://sunsite.doc.ic.ac.uk/packages/mirror/*.

See Also

Your system's *ftp*(1) and *ftpd*(8) manpages (if you have them); the documentation for the Net::FTP module from CPAN

18.3. Sending Mail

Problem

You want your program to send mail. Some programs monitor system resources like disk space and notify appropriate people by mail when disk space becomes dangerously low. CGI script authors may not want their programs to report errors like "the database is down" to the user, preferring instead to send mail to the database administrator notifying them of the problem.

Solution

Use the CPAN module Mail::Mailer:

```
use Mail::Mailer;

$mailer = Mail::Mailer->new("sendmail");
$mailer->open({ From    => $from_address,
                To      => $to_address,
                Subject => $subject,
              })
    or die "Can't open: $!\n";
print $mailer $body;
$mailer->close();
```

Or, use the **sendmail** program directly:

```
open(SENDMAIL, "|/usr/lib/sendmail -oi -t -odq")
                    or die "Can't fork for sendmail: $!\n";
print SENDMAIL <<"EOF";
From: User Originating Mail <me\@host>
To: Final Destination <you\@otherhost>
Subject: A relevant subject line

Body of the message goes here, in as many lines as you like.
EOF
close(SENDMAIL)       or warn "sendmail didn't close nicely";
```

Discussion

You have three choices for sending mail from your program. You can use another program that users normally use to send mail, like *Mail* or *mailx*; these are called MUAs or *Mail User Agents*. You can use a system-level mail program like *sendmail*; this is an MTA, or *Mail Transport Agent*. Or you can connect to an SMTP (Simple Mail Transfer Protocol) server. Unfortunately, there's no standard user-level mail program, *sendmail* doesn't have a standard location, and SMTP isn't particularly simple. The CPAN module Mail::Mailer hides these complexities from you.

When Mail::Mailer is installed, it looks for *mail*, *Mail*, and other names mail-sending programs tend to hide under. It also looks in common locations for *sendmail*. When you create a Mail::Mailer object, you get convenient access to those programs (and SMTP mail servers) without needing to know their argument structure or how they return errors.

Create a Mail::Mailer object with `Mail::Mailer->new`. If you don't pass any arguments, it uses the default mail sending method (probably a program like *mail*). Arguments to new let you pick an alternative way of sending the message. The first argument is the type of delivery method (`"mail"` for a Unix mail user agent, `"sendmail"` for sendmail, and `"smtp"` to open a connection to an SMTP server). The optional second argument is the path to the program.

For instance, here is how to instruct Mail::Mailer to use *sendmail* instead of its default:

```
$mailer = Mail::Mailer->new("sendmail");
```

Here's how to tell it to use `/u/gnat/bin/funkymailer` instead of *mail*:

```
$mailer = Mail::Mailer->new("mail", "/u/gnat/bin/funkymailer");
```

Here's how to use SMTP with the machine *mail.myisp.com* as the mail server:

```
$mailer = Mail::Mailer->new("smtp", "mail.myisp.com");
```

If an error occurs at any part of Mail::Mailer, `die` is called. This means if you want to check for errors, you need to wrap your mail-sending code in `eval` and check `$@` afterward:

```
eval {
    $mailer = Mail::Mailer->new("bogus", "arguments");
    # ...
};
if ($@) {
    # the eval failed
    print "Couldn't send mail: $@\n";
} else {
    # the eval succeeded
    print "The authorities have been notified.\n";
}
```

The new constructor raises an exception if you provide arguments it doesn't understand or if you specify no arguments and it doesn't have a default method. Mail::Mailer won't run a program or connect to the SMTP server until you call the open method with the headers of the message:

```
$mailer->open( { From    => 'Nathan Torkington <gnat@frii.com>',
                 To      => 'Tom Christiansen <tchrist@perl.com>',
                 Subject => 'The Perl Cookbook' } );
```

The open method raises an exception if the program or server couldn't be opened. If open succeeds, you may treat `$mailer` as a filehandle and print the body of your message to it:

```
print $mailer <<EO_SIG;
Are we ever going to finish this book?
My wife is threatening to leave me.
She says I love EMACS more than I love her.
```

```
Do you have a recipe that can help me?

Nat
EO_SIG
```

When you're done, call the `close` function on the Mail::Mailer object:

```
close($mailer)                          or die "can't close mailer: $!";
```

If you want to go it alone and communicate with *sendmail* directly, use something like this:

```
open(SENDMAIL, "|/usr/sbin/sendmail -oi -t -odq")
            or die "Can't fork for sendmail: $!\n";
print SENDMAIL <<"EOF";
From: Tom Christiansen <tchrist\@perl.com>
To: Nathan Torkington <gnat\@frii.com>
Subject: Re: The Perl Cookbook

(1) We will never finish the book.
(2) No man who uses EMACS is deserving of love.
(3) I recommend coq au vi.

tom
EOF
close(SENDMAIL);
```

This is a straightforward use of `open` to run another program (see Recipe 16.4). You need to specify the full path to `sendmail` because its location varies from machine to machine. It is often found in places like */usr/lib* or */usr/sbin*. The flags we give to *sendmail* say to not exit when a line with only a dot is read (`-oi`), to read the headers of the message to decide whom to send it to (`-t`), and to insert the message into the queue instead of attempting to deliver it immediately (`-odq`). This last option is only important when you're sending a lot of mail—omitting it would quickly swamp the machine with *sendmail* processes. If you want immediate delivery of your message (for instance, you're testing your program or the mail is urgent) remove `-odq` from the command line.

We `print` an entire message, headers and then body, separated by a blank line. There are no special escapes to insert new lines (as some user mail programs have), so all text is literal. *sendmail* adds headers like `Date` and `Message-ID` (which you shouldn't generate yourself anyway).

Some ports of Perl (Windows and Mac particularly) don't have *sendmail* or *mail* to use. In these cases, you should find an SMTP server you can send mail through.

See Also

The open function in Chapter 3 of *Programming Perl* and in *perlfunc*(1); Recipe 16.4; Recipe 16.10; Recipe 16.19; Recipe 19.6; the RFCs dictating the SMTP protocol, RFC 821, *Simple Mail Transfer Protocol,* as amended by later RFCs

18.4. *Reading and Posting Usenet News Messages*

Problem

You want to connect to a Usenet news server to read and post messages. Your program could send a periodic posting to a newsgroup,* summarize a newsgroup, or identify first-time contributors in a newsgroup so you can send them a helpful welcome message.

Solution

Use the CPAN module Net::NNTP:

```
use Net::NNTP;

$server = Net::NNTP->new("news.host.dom")
    or die "Can't connect to news server: $@\n";
($narticles, $first, $last, $name) = $server->group( "misc.test" )
    or die "Can't select misc.test\n";
$headers  = $server->head($first)
    or die "Can't get headers from article $first in $name\n";
$bodytext = $server->body($first)
    or die "Can't get body from article $first in $name\n";
$article  = $server->article($first)
    or die "Can't get article $first from $name\n";

$server->postok()
    or warn "Server didn't tell me I could post.\n";

$server->post( [ @lines ] )
    or die "Can't post: $!\n";
```

Discussion

Usenet is a distributed news system. Servers exchange messages to ensure that each server gets all the messages for the newsgroups it carries. Each server sets its own expiration criteria to decide how long messages stay on the server. Client

---

* If so, be sure to check out Ian Kluft's *auto-faq* program at *http://www.novia.net/~pschleck/auto-faq/.*

newsreaders connect to their designated server (usually belonging to their company, ISP, or university) and can read existing postings and contribute new ones.

Each message (or article, as they're also known) has a set of headers and a body, separated by a blank line. Articles are identified in two ways: the *message ID* header and an *article number* within a newsgroup. An article's message ID is stored in the message itself and is guaranteed to be unique no matter which news server the article was read from. When an article references others, it does so by message ID. A message ID is a string like:

```
<0401@jpl-devvax.JPL.NASA.GOV>
```

An article can also be identified by a newsgroup and an article number within the group. Each news server assigns its own article numbers to the articles it has, so they're only guaranteed to be good for the news server you got them from.

The Net::NNTP constructor connects to the specified news server. If the connection couldn't be made, it returns undef and sets $@ to an error message. If the connection was successfully made, new returns a new Net::NNTP object:

```
$server = Net::NNTP->new("news.mycompany.com")
    or die "Couldn't connect to news.mycompany.com: $@\n";
```

Once connected, you can get a list of newsgroups with the list method. This returns a reference to a hash whose keys are newsgroup names. Each value is a reference to an array consisting of the first valid article number in the group, the last valid article number in the group, and a string of flags. The flags are typically "y", meaning you may post, but could be "m" for moderated or =NAME, meaning that the group is an alias for the newsgroup NAME. There are over 17,000 newsgroups that your server might carry, so fetching a list of all the groups can take a while.

```
$grouplist = $server->list()
    or die "Couldn't fetch group list\n";

foreach $group (keys %$grouplist) {
    if ($grouplist->{$group}->[2] eq 'y') {
        # I can post to $group
    }
}
```

Much as FTP has the concept of a current directory, the Network News Transfer Protocol (NNTP) has the concept of a current group. Make a group the current group with the group method:

```
($narticles, $first, $last, $name) = $server->group("comp.lang.perl.misc")
    or die "Can't select comp.lang.perl.misc\n";
```

The group method returns a four-element list: the number of articles in the group, the first article number, the last article number, and the name of the group. If the group does not exist, it returns an empty list.

There are two ways to retrieve articles: call `article` with a message ID, or select a group with `group` and then call `article` with an article number. In scalar context, it returns a reference to an array of lines. In list context, `article` returns a list of lines. If an error occurs, `article` returns false:

```
@lines = $server->article($message_id)
    or die "Can't fetch article $message_id: $!\n";
```

You can fetch an article's header or body with the **head** and **body** methods. Like `article`, these methods take an article number or message ID, and return a list of lines or an array reference.

```
@group = $server->group("comp.lang.perl.misc")
    or die "Can't select group comp.lang.perl.misc\n";
@lines = $server->head($group[1])
    or die "Can't get headers from first article in comp.lang.perl.misc\n";
```

To post an article, use the **post** method. Give it a list of lines or a reference to an array of lines, and it returns true if the post succeeded, false if the article couldn't be posted.

```
$server->post(@message)
    or die "Can't post\n";
```

Use the **postok** method to find out whether the server said that you may post:

```
unless ($server->postok()) {
    warn "You may not post.\n";
}
```

Read the manpage for Net::NNTP for a complete list of methods.

See Also

The documentation for the Net::NNTP module from CPAN; RFC 977, *Network News Transfer Protocol*; your system's *trn*(1) and *innd*(8) manpages (if you have them)

18.5. Reading Mail with POP3

Problem

You want to fetch mail from a POP3 server. This lets you write a program to summarize your unread mail, move it from a remote server to a local mailbox, or toggle between Internet and local mail systems.

Solution

Use the CPAN module Net::POP3:

```
$pop = Net::POP3->new($mail_server)
    or die "Can't open connection to $mail_server : $!\n";
defined ($pop->login($username, $password))
    or die "Can't authenticate: $!\n";
$messages = $pop->list
    or die "Can't get list of undeleted messages: $!\n";
foreach $msgid (keys %$messages) {
    $message = $pop->get($msgid);
    unless (defined $message) {
        warn "Couldn't fetch $msgid from server: $!\n";
        next;
    }
    # $message is a reference to an array of lines
    $pop->delete($msgid);
}
```

Discussion

Traditionally, mail has been a three-party system: the *MTA* (Mail Transport Agent, a system program like *sendmail*) delivers mail to the *spool*, where it is read by the *MUA* (Mail User Agent, a program like *mail*). This dates from the days of big servers holding mail and users reading it through dumb terminals. As PCs and networks entered the picture, the need arose for MUAs like Pine to run on different machines than the one housing the spool. The Post Office Protocol (POP) implements efficient message listing, reading, and deleting over a TCP/IP session.

The CPAN module Net::POP3 is a POP client. That is, it lets your Perl program act as an MUA. The first step in using Net::POP3 is to create a new Net::POP3 object. Pass **new** the name of the POP3 server:

```
$pop = Net::POP3->new( "pop.myisp.com" )
    or die "Can't connect to pop.myisp.com: $!\n";
```

All Net::POP3 functions return **undef** or the empty list () if an error occurs, depending on the context they were called in. If an error occurs, $! may contain a meaningful error message (but also may not).

You may optionally pass further arguments to **new** in a hash-like fashion, indicating a timeout value (in seconds) for network operations:

```
$pop = Net::POP3->new( "pop.myisp.com",
                       Timeout => 30 )
    or die "Can't connect to pop.myisp.com : $!\n";
```

Authenticate yourself to the POP3 server with the **login** method. It takes two arguments, username and password, but both are optional. If the username is

omitted, the current username is used. If the password is omitted, Net::POP3 tries
to use Net::Netrc to find a password:

```
defined ($pop->login("gnat", "S33kr1T Pa55w0rD"))
    or die "Hey, my username and password didn't work!\n";

defined ($pop->login( "midget" ))              # use Net::Netrc to find password
    or die "Authentication failed.\n";

defined ($pop->login())                        # current username and Net::Netrc
    or die "Authentication failed.  Miserably.\n";
```

The login method sends the password in plain text across the network. This is
undesirable, so if you have the MD5 module from CPAN, you can use the apop
method. It works exactly like login, except that it encrypts the password:

```
$pop->apop( $username, $password )
    or die "Couldn't authenticate: $!\n";
```

Once authenticated, you may then access the spool with list, get, and delete.
The list method gives you a list of undeleted messages in the spool. It returns a
hash, where each key is a message number and each value is the size of the corresponding message in bytes:

```
%undeleted = $pop->list();
foreach $msgnum (keys %undeleted) {
$msgsize = $undeleted->{msgnum};
    print "Message $msgnum is $undeleted{$msgnum} bytes long.\n";
}
```

To retrieve a message, call get with the message number. It returns a reference an
array of lines in the message:

```
print "Retrieving $msgnum : ";
$message = $pop->get($msgnum);
if ($message) {
    # succeeded
    print "\n";
    print @$message;                        # print the message
} else {
        # failed
    print "failed ($!)\n";
}
```

The delete method marks a message as deleted. When you call quit to terminate your POP3 session, the messages marked as deleted are removed from the
mailbox. The reset method undoes any delete calls made during the session. If
the session is terminated by the Net::POP3 object being destroyed because it went
out of scope, the reset will be called automatically.

You have probably noticed there's no way to *send* mail. POP3 only supports reading and deleting existing messages. To send new ones, you still have to use pro-

grams like *mail* or *sendmail,* or do SMTP. In other words, you still need to use Recipe 18.3.

The task attempted by POP3—connecting mail clients and mail servers—is also attempted by the IMAP protocol. IMAP has more features and is more typically seen on very large sites.

See Also

The documentation for the Net::POP3 module from CPAN; RFC 1734, *POP3 AUTHentication command;* RFC 1957, *Some Observations on Implementations of the Post Office Protocol*

18.6. Simulating Telnet from a Program

Problem

You want to simulate a *telnet* connection from your program by logging into a remote machine, issuing commands, and reacting to what is sent. This has many applications, from automating tasks on machines you can telnet to but which don't support scripting or *rsh,* to simply testing whether a machine's telnet daemon is still running.

Solution

Use the CPAN module Net::Telnet:

```
use Net::Telnet;

$t = Net::Telnet->new( Timeout => 10,
                       Prompt  => '/%/',
                       Host    => $hostname );

$t->login($username, $password);
@files = $t->cmd("ls");
$t->print("top");
(undef, $process_string) = $t->waitfor('/\d+ processes/');
$t->close;
```

Discussion

Net::Telnet provides an object-oriented interface to the telnet protocol. Create a connection with Net::Telnet->new, and then interact with the remote machine using method calls on the resulting object.

Give the new method named parameters, passed in hash-like form. We'll only cover only a few of many possible parameters. The most important is Host, the machine you're telnetting to. The default host is localhost. If you want to telnet to a port other than one telnet normally uses, specify this in the Port option. Error handling is done through the function whose reference is specified in the Errmode parameter.

Another important option is Prompt. When you log in or run a command, Net::Telnet uses the Prompt pattern to determine when the login or command has completed. The default Prompt is:

```
/[\$%#>] $/
```

which matches the common shell prompts. If the prompt on the remote machine doesn't match the default pattern, you have to specify your own. Remember to include the slashes.

Timeout lets you control how long (in seconds) network operations wait before they give up. The default is 10 seconds.

If an error or timeout occurs in the Net::Telnet module, the default behavior is to raise an exception, which, if uncaught, prints a message to STDERR and exits. To change this, pass a subroutine reference to new in the Errmode argument. If instead of a code subroutine, you specify the string "return" as the Errmode, methods return undef (in scalar context) or an empty list (in list context) on error, with the error message available via the errmsg method:

```
$telnet = Net::Telnet->new( Errmode => sub { main::log(@_) }, ... );
```

The login method is used to send a username and password to the remote machine. It uses the Prompt to decide when the login is complete and times out if the machine doesn't reply with a prompt:

```
$telnet->login($username, $password)
    or die "Login failed: @{[ $telnet->errmsg() ]}\n";
```

To run a program and gather its output, use the cmd method. Pass it the string to send, and it returns the output of the command. In list context, it returns one line per list element. In scalar context, it returns one long line. It waits for the Prompt before returning.

You can separate the sending of the command from the reception of its output with the print and waitfor methods, as we do in the Solution. The waitfor method takes either a single string containing a Perl regular expression match operator:

```
$telnet->waitfor('/--more--/')
```

or named arguments. Timeout lets you specify a timeout to override the default, Match is a string containing a match operator as above, and String is a literal string to find:

```
$telnet->waitfor(String => 'greasy smoke', Timeout => 30)
```

In scalar context, `waitfor` returns true if the pattern or string was found. If it is not found, the `Errmode` action is performed. In list context, it returns two strings: all the text before the match, and the text that matched.

See Also

The documentation for the Net::Telnet module from CPAN; RFCs 854-856, as amended by later RFCs

18.7. Pinging a Machine

Problem

You want to test whether a machine is alive. Network and system monitoring software often use the `ping` program as an indicator of availability.

Solution

Use the standard Net::Ping module:

```
use Net::Ping;

$p = Net::Ping->new()
    or die "Can't create new ping object: $!\n";
print "$host is alive" if $p->ping($host);
$p->close;
```

Discussion

Testing whether a machine is up isn't as easy as it sounds. It's not only possible but it's also unpleasantly common for machines to respond to the *ping* command and have no working services. It's better to think of a *ping* as testing whether a machine is reachable, rather than whether the machine is doing its job. To check the latter, you must try to use its services (telnet, FTP, web, NFS, etc).

In the form shown in the Solution, Net::Ping attempts to connect to the UDP *echo* port (port number 7) on the remote machine, send a datagram, and receive the echoed response. The machine is considered unreachable if it can't connect, if the reply datagram isn't received, or if the reply differs from the original datagram. The `ping` method returns true if the machine was reachable, false otherwise.

You can also ping using other protocols by passing the protocol name to new. Valid protocols are *tcp*, *udp*, and *icmp* (all lowercase). A TCP ping attempts to connect to the echo port (TCP port 7) on the remote machine, and returns true if the connection could be established, false otherwise (unlike UDP ping, no data is sent to be echoed). An ICMP ping uses the ICMP protocol, as does the *ping*(8) command. On Unix machines, you must be the superuser to use the ICMP protocol:

```
# use TCP if we're not root, ICMP if we are
$pong = Net::Ping->new( $> ? "tcp" : "icmp" );

(defined $pong)
    or die "Couldn't create Net::Ping object: $!\n";

if ($pong->ping("kingkong.com")) {
    print "The giant ape lives!\n";
} else {
    print "All hail mighty Gamera, friend of children!\n";
}
```

All these ping methods are prone to failure. Some sites filter the ICMP protocol at their router, so Net::Ping will say such machines are down even though you can connect using other protocols. Similarly, many machines disable the TCP and UDP *echo* services, causing TCP and UDP pings to fail. There is no way to know whether the ping failed because the service is disabled or filtered, or because the machine is actually down.

See Also

The documentation for the Net::Ping module from CPAN; your system's *ping*(8), *tcp*(4), *udp*(4), and *icmp*(4) manpages (if you have them); RFC 792 and 950

18.8. Using Whois to Retrieve Information from the InterNIC

Problem

You want to find out who owns a domain, as if you'd used the Unix whois command.

Solution

Use the CPAN module Net::Whois:

```
use Net::Whois;

$domain_obj = Net::Whois::Domain->new($domain_name)
    or die "Couldn't get information on $domain_name: $!\n";

# call methods on $domain_obj to get name, tag, address, etc.
```

Discussion

Whois is a service provided by domain name registration authorities to identify owners of domain names. Historically, queries were made with the *whois*(1) program on Unix systems, which returned about fifteen lines of information, including the names, addresses, and phone numbers of the administrative, technical, and billing contacts for the domain.

The `Net::Whois` module is a client for the whois service, just like *whois*(1). It connects to a whois server (the default is `whois.internic.net`, the master server for the `".com"`, `".org"`, `".net"`, and `".edu"` domains) and gives you access to the information through method calls on an object.

To request information on a domain, create a new Net::Whois::Domain object. For instance, to look up information on `perl.org`:

```
$d = Net::Whois::Domain->new( "perl.org" )
    or die "Can't get information on perl.org\n";
```

The only guaranteed fields are the domain name and the tag—the domain's unique identifier in the NIC records:

```
print "The domain is called ", $d->domain, "\n";
print "Its tag is ", $d->tag, "\n";
```

Information that may be present includes: *name* of the domain's company or product (e.g., `"The Perl Institute"`), the *address* of the company (a list of lines, e.g., `("221B Baker Street", "London")`), and the *country* the address is valid for (e.g., `"United Kingdom"` or its two-letter abbreviation "uk").

```
print "Mail for ", $d->name, " should be sent to:\n";
print map { "\t$_\n" } $d->address;
print "\t", $d->country, "\n";
```

In addition to information about the domain, you can also get information on the domain's *contacts*. The `contact` method returns a reference to a hash mapping contact type (e.g., `"Billing"` or `"Administrative"`) onto an array of lines.

```
$contact_hash = $d->contacts;
if ($contact_hash) {
    print "Contacts:\n";
    foreach $type (sort keys %$contact_hash) {
        print "  $type:\n";
        foreach $line (@{$contact_hash->{$type}}) {
            print "    $line\n";
        }
    }
} else {
    print "No contact information.\n";
}
```

See Also

The documentation for the Net::Whois module from CPAN; your system's *whois*(8) manpage (if you have one); RFC 812 and 954

18.9. Program: expn and vrfy

This program talks directly to an SMTP server and uses the EXPN and VRFY commands to figure out whether an address is going to work. It isn't perfect, because it relies on the remote SMTP giving meaningful information with the EXPN and VRFY commands. It uses Net::DNS if available, but can also work without.

This program inspects $0 (the program name) to see how it was called. If run as *expn*, it uses the EXPN command; if called as *vrfy*, it uses the VRFY command. Use links to install it with two names:

```
% cat > expn
#!/usr/bin/perl -w
...
^D
% ln expn vrfy
```

When you run it with an email address, the program reports what the mail server says when you try to EXPN or VRFY the address. If you have Net::DNS installed, it tries all hosts listed as mail exchangers in the DNS entry for the address.

Here's what it looks like without Net::DNS:

```
% expn gnat@frii.com
Expanding gnat at frii.com (gnat@frii.com):
calisto.frii.com Hello coprolith.frii.com [207.46.130.14],
    pleased to meet you
<gnat@mail.frii.com>
```

And here's the same address with Net::DNS installed:

```
% expn gnat@frii.com
Expanding gnat at mail.frii.net (gnat@frii.com):
deimos.frii.com Hello coprolith.frii.com [207.46.130.14],
    pleased to meet you
Nathan Torkington <gnat@deimos.frii.com>

Expanding gnat at mx1.frii.net (gnat@frii.com):
phobos.frii.com Hello coprolith.frii.com [207.46.130.14],
    pleased to meet you
<gnat@mail.frii.com>

Expanding gnat at mx2.frii.net (gnat@frii.com):
europa.frii.com Hello coprolith.frii.com [207.46.130.14],
    pleased to meet you
<gnat@mail.frii.com>
```

```
Expanding gnat at mx3.frii.net (gnat@frii.com):
ns2.winterlan.com Hello coprolith.frii.com [207.46.130.14],
    pleased to meet you
550 gnat... User unknown
```

The program is shown in Example 18-3.

Example 18-3. expn

```perl
#!/usr/bin/perl -w
# expn -- convince smtp to divulge an alias expansion
use strict;
use IO::Socket;
use Sys::Hostname;

my $fetch_mx = 0;
# try loading the module, but don't blow up if missing
eval {
    require Net::DNS;
    Net::DNS->import('mx');
    $fetch_mx = 1;
};

my $selfname = hostname();
die "usage: $0 address\@host ...\n" unless @ARGV;

# Find out whether called as "vrfy" or "expn".
my $VERB = ($0 =~ /ve?ri?fy$/i)  ? 'VRFY' : 'EXPN';
my $multi = @ARGV > 1;
my $remote;

# Iterate over addresses give on command line.
foreach my $combo (@ARGV) {
    my ($name, $host) = split(/\@/, $combo);
    my @hosts;
    $host ||= 'localhost';
    @hosts = map { $_->exchange } mx($host)     if $fetch_mx;
    @hosts = ($host)    unless @hosts;

    foreach my $host (@hosts) {
        print $VERB eq 'VRFY' ? "Verify" : "Expand",
            "ing $name at $host ($combo):";

        $remote = IO::Socket::INET->new(
                Proto    => "tcp",
                PeerAddr => $host,
                PeerPort => "smtp(25)",
            );

        unless ($remote) {
            warn "cannot connect to $host\n";
            next;
        }
        print "\n";
```

Example 18-3. expn (continued)

```
        $remote->autoflush(1);

        # use CRLF network line terminators
        print $remote "HELO $selfname\015\012";
        print $remote "$VERB $name\015\012";
        print $remote "quit\015\012";
        while (<$remote>) {
            /^220\b/ && next;
            /^221\b/ && last;
            s/250\b[\-\s]+//;
            print;
        }
        close($remote)or die "can't close socket: $!";
        print "\n"; #  if @ARGV;
    }
}
```

19

CGI Programming

A successful tool is one that was used to do
something undreamt of by its author.
—Stephen C. Johnson

19.0. Introduction

Changes in the environment or the availability of food can make certain species more successful than others at getting food or avoiding predators. Many scientists believe a comet struck the earth millions of years ago, throwing an enormous cloud of dust into the atmosphere. Subsequent radical changes to the environment proved too much for some organisms, say dinosaurs, and hastened their extinction. Other creatures, such as mammals, found new food supplies and freshly exposed habitats to compete in.

Much as the comet altered the environment for prehistoric species, the Web has altered the environment for modern programming languages. It's opened up new vistas, and although some languages have found themselves eminently unsuited to this new world order, Perl has positively thrived. Because of its strong background in text processing and system glue, Perl has readily adapted itself to the task of providing information using text-based protocols.

Architecture

The Web is driven by plain text. Web servers and web browsers communicate using a text protocol called HTTP, Hypertext Transfer Protocol. Many of the documents exchanged are encoded in a text markup system called HTML, Hypertext Markup Language. This grounding in text is the source of much of the Web's flexibility, power, and success. The only notable exception to the predominance of plain text is the Secure Socket Layer (SSL) protocol that encrypts other protocols like HTTP into binary data that snoopers can't decode.

Web pages are identified using the Uniform Resource Locator (URL) naming scheme. URLs look like this:

```
http://www.perl.com/CPAN/
http://www.perl.com:8001/bad/mojo.html
ftp://gatekeeper.dec.com/pub/misc/netlib.tar.Z
ftp://anonymous@myplace:gatekeeper.dec.com/pub/misc/netlib.tar.Z
file:///etc/motd
```

The first part (`http`, `ftp`, `file`) is called the *scheme,* and identifies how the file is retrieved. The next part (`://`) signifies a hostname will follow, whose interpretation depends on the scheme. After the hostname comes the *path* identifying the document. This path information is also called a *partial URL.*

The Web is a client-server system. Client browsers like Netscape and Lynx request documents (identified by a partial URL) from web servers like Apache. This browser-to-server dialog is governed by the HTTP protocol. Most of the time, the server merely sends back the contents of a file. Sometimes, however, the web server will run another program to send back a document that could be HTML text, an image, or any other document type. The server-to-program dialog is governed by the CGI (Common Gateway Interface) protocol, so the program that the server runs is a *CGI program* or *CGI script.*

The server tells the CGI program what page was requested, what values (if any) came in through HTML forms, where the request came from, who they authenticated as (if they authenticated at all), and much more. The CGI program's reply has two parts: headers to say "I'm sending back an HTML document," "I'm sending back a GIF image," or "I'm not sending you anything, go to this page instead," and a document body, perhaps containing GIF image data, plain text, or HTML.

The CGI protocol is easy to implement wrong and hard to implement right, which is why we recommend using Lincoln Stein's excellent CGI.pm module. It provides convenient functions for accessing the information the server sends you, and for preparing the CGI response the server expects. It is so useful, it is included in the standard Perl distribution as of the 5.004 release, along with helper modules like CGI::Carp and CGI::Fast. We show it off in Recipe 19.1.

Some web servers come with a Perl interpreter embedded in them. This lets you use Perl to generate documents without starting a new process. The system overhead of reading an unchanging page isn't noticable on infrequently accessed pages, even when it's happening several times a second. CGI accesses, however, bog down the machine running the web server. Recipe 19.5 shows how to use `mod_perl`, the Perl interpreter embedded in the Apache web server, to get the benefits of CGI programs without the overhead.

Behind the Scenes

CGI programs are called each time the web server needs a dynamic document generated. It is important to understand that your CGI program doesn't run continuously, with the browser calling different parts of the program. Each request for a partial URL corresponding to your program starts a new copy. Your program generates a page for that request, then quits.

A browser can request a document in a number of ways called *methods*. (Don't confuse HTTP methods with the methods of object-orientation. They have nothing to do with each other). The GET method is the most common, indicating a simple request for a document. The HEAD method is used when the browser wants to know about the document without actually fetching it. The POST method is used to submit form values.

Form values can be encoded in both GET and POST methods. With the GET method, values are encoded in the URL, leading to ugly URLs like this:

```
http://mox.perl.com/cgi-bin/program?name=Johann&born=1685
```

With the POST method, values are in a different part of the HTTP request that the browser sends the server. If the form values in the example URL above were sent with a POST request, the user, server, and CGI script all see the URL:

```
http://mox.perl.com/cgi-bin/program
```

The GET and POST methods differ in another respect: *idempotency*. This simply means that making a GET request for a particular URL once or multiple times should be no different. This is because the HTTP protocol definition says that a GET request may be cached by the browser, or server, or an intervening proxy. POST requests cannot be cached, because each request is independent and matters. Typically, POST requests changes or depends on the state of the server (query or update a database, send mail, or purchase a computer).

Most servers log requests to a file (the *access log*) for later analysis by the webmaster. Error messages produced by CGI programs don't go to the browser by default. Instead they are also logged to a file (the *error log*), and the browser simply gets a "500 Server Error" message saying that the CGI program didn't uphold its end of the CGI bargain.

Error messages are useful in debugging any program, but they are especially so with CGI scripts. Sometimes, though, the authors of CGI programs either don't have access to the error log or don't know where it is. Having error messages sent to a more convenient location is discussed in Recipe 19.2. Tracking down errors is covered in Recipe 19.3.

Recipe 19.9 shows how to learn what your browser and server are really saying to one another. Unfortunately, some browsers do not implement the HTTP specification correctly, and you can use the tools in this recipe to investigate whether your program or your browser is the cause of a problem.

Security

CGI programs let anyone run a program on your system. Sure, you get to pick the program, but the anonymous user from Out There can send it unexpected values and try to trick it into doing the wrong thing. Thus security is a big concern on the Web.

Some sites address this concern by banning CGI programs. Sites that can't do without the power and utility of CGI programs must find ways to secure their CGI programs. Recipe 19.4 gives a checklist of considerations for writing a secure CGI script, and it briefly covers Perl's tainting mechanism for guarding against accidental use of unsafe data. Recipe 19.6 shows how your CGI program can safely run other programs.

HTML and Forms

Some HTML tags let you create forms, where the user can fill in values that will be submitted to the server. The forms are composed of widgets, like text entry fields and check boxes. CGI programs commonly return HTML, so the CGI module has helper functions to create HTML for everything from tables to form widgets.

In addition to Recipe 19.7, this chapter also has Recipe 19.11, which shows how to create forms that retain their values over multiple calls. Recipe 19.12 shows how to make a single CGI script that produces and responds to a set of pages, for example, a product catalog and ordering system.

Web-Related Resources

Unsurprisingly, some of the best references on the Web are found on the Web:

WWW Security FAQ
> *http://www.w3.org/Security/Faq/*

Web FAQ
> *http://www.boutell.com/faq/*

CGI FAQ
> *http://www.webthing.com/tutorials/cgifaq.html*

HTTP Specification
> *http://www.w3.org/pub/WWW/Protocols/HTTP/*

HTML Specification

　　http://www.w3.org/TR/REC-html40/

　　http://www.w3.org/pub/WWW/MarkUp/

CGI Specification

　　http://www.w3.org/CGI/

CGI Security FAQ

　　http://www.go2net.com/people/paulp/cgi-security/safe-cgi.txt

We recommend Lincoln Stein's fine book, *Official Guide to Programming with Cgi.pm* (John Wiley and Associates, 1998), Tom Boutell's aging but worthwhile *CGI Programming in C and Perl* (Addison-Wesley, 1996) and *HTML: The Definitive Guide* (3rd Edition; O'Reilly & Associates, 1998) by Chuck Musciano and Bill Kennedy. The best periodical to date is the monthly *Web Techniques* magazine, targeted at web programmers.

19.1. Writing a CGI Script

Problem

You want to write a CGI script to process the contents of an HTML form. In particular, you want to access the form contents, and produce valid output in return.

Solution

A CGI script is a server-side program launched by a web server to generate a dynamic document. It receives encoded information from the remote client (user's browser) via STDIN and environment variables, and it must produce a valid HTTP header and body on STDOUT. The standard CGI module, shown in Example 19-1, painlessly manages the encoding of input and output.

Example 19-1. hiweb

```perl
#!/usr/bin/perl -w
# hiweb - load CGI module to decode information given by web server
use strict;

use CGI qw(:standard escapeHTML);

# get a parameter from a form
my $value = param('PARAM_NAME');

# output a document
print header(), start_html("Howdy there!"),
      p("You typed: ", tt(escapeHTML($value))),
      end_html();
```

Discussion

CGI is just a protocol, a formal agreement between a web server and a separate program. The server encodes the client's form input data, and the CGI program decodes the form and generates output. The protocol says nothing regarding which language the program must be written in; programs and scripts that obey the CGI protocol have been written in C, shell, Rexx, C++, VMS DCL, Smalltalk, Tcl, Python, and (of course) Perl.

The full CGI specification lays out which environment variables hold which data (such as form input parameters) and how it's all encoded. In theory, it should be easy to follow the protocol to decode the input, but in practice, it is surprisingly tricky to get right. That's why we *strongly* recommend using Lincoln Stein's excellent CGI module. The hard work of handling the CGI requirements correctly and conveniently has already been done, freeing you to write the core of your program without tedious network protocols.

CGI scripts are called in two main ways, referred to as *methods*—but don't confuse HTTP methods with Perl object methods! The HTTP GET method is used in document retrievals where an identical request will produce an identical result, such as a dictionary lookup. A GET stores form data in the URL. This means it can be conveniently bookmarked for canned requests, but has limitations on the total size of the data requested. The HTTP POST method sends form data separate from the request. It has no such size limitations, but cannot be bookmarked. Forms that update information on the server, like mailing in feedback or modifying a database entry, should use POST. Client browsers and intervening proxies are free to cache and refresh the results of GET requests behind your back, but they may not cache POST requests. GET is only safe for short read-only requests, whereas POST is safe for forms of any size, as well as for updates and feedback responses. Therefore, by default, the CGI module uses POST for all forms it generates.

With a few exceptions mainly related to file permissions and highly interactive work, CGI scripts can do nearly anything any other program can do. They can send back results in many formats: plain text, HTML documents, sound files, pictures, or anything else specified in the HTTP header. Besides producing plain text or HTML text, they can also redirect the client browser to another location, set server cookies, request authentication, and give errors.

The CGI module provides two different interfaces, a procedural one for casual use, and an object-oriented one for power users with complicated needs. Virtually all CGI scripts should use the simple procedural interface, but unfortunately, most of CGI.pm's documentation uses examples with the original object-oriented approach. Due to backwards compatibility, if you want the simple procedural interface, you need to specifically ask for it using the :standard import tag. See Chapter 12, *Packages, Libraries, and Modules*, for more on import tags.

To read the user's form input, pass the **param** function a field name to get. If you had a form field name "favorite", then **param("favorite")** would return its value. With some types of form fields like scrolling lists, the user can choose more than one option. For these, **param** returns a list of values, which you could assign to an array.

For example, here's a script that pulls in values of three form fields, the last one having many return values:

```
use CGI qw(:standard);
$who   = param("Name");
$phone = param("Number");
@picks = param("Choices");
```

Called without any arguments, **param** returns a list of valid form parameters in list context, or in scalar context, how many form parameters there were.

That's all there is to accessing the user's input. Do with it whatever you please, and then generate properly formatted output. This is nearly as easy. Remember that unlike regular programs, a CGI script's output must be formatted in a particular way: it must first emit a set of headers followed by a blank line before it can produce normal output.

As shown in the Solution above, the CGI module helps with output as well as input. The module provides functions for generating HTTP headers and HTML code. The **header** function builds the text of a header for you. By default, it produces headers for a text/html document, but you can change the Content-Type and supply other optional header parameters as well:

```
print header( -TYPE    => 'text/plain',
              -EXPIRES => '+3d' );
```

CGI.pm can also be used to generate HTML. It may seem trivial, but this is where the CGI module shines: the creation of dynamic forms, especially stateful ones such as shopping carts. The CGI module even has functions for generating forms and tables.

When printing form widgets, the characters &, <, >, and " in HTML output are automatically replaced with their entity equivalents. This is not the case with arbitary user output. That's why the Solution imports and makes use of the **escapeHTML** function—if the user types any of those special characters, they won't cause formatting errors in the HTML.

For a full list of functions and their calling conventions, see CGI.pm's documentation, included as POD source within the module itself.

See Also

The documentation for the standard CGI module; Chapter 19 of *Learning Perl* on "CGI Programming"; *http://www.w3.org/CGI/*; Recipe 19.7

19.2. Redirecting Error Messages

Problem

You're having trouble tracking down your script's warnings and error messages, or your script's STDERR output is confusing your server.

Solution

Use the CGI::Carp module from the standard Perl distribution to cause all messages going out STDERR to be prefixed with the name of the application and the current date. You can also send warnings and errors to a file or the browser if you wish.

Discussion

Tracking down error messages from CGI scripts is notoriously annoying. Even if you manage to find the server error log, you still can't determine which message came from which script, or at what time. Some unfriendly web servers even abort the script if it has the audacity to emit anything out its STDERR before the `Content-Type` header is generated, which means the -w flag can get you into trouble.

Enter the CGI::Carp module. It replaces **warn** and **die**, plus the normal Carp module's **carp**, **croak**, and **confess** functions with more verbose and safer versions. It still sends them to the normal server error log.

```
use CGI::Carp;
warn "This is a complaint";
die "But this one is serious";
```

The following use of CGI::Carp also redirects errors to a file of your choice, placed in a BEGIN block to catch compile-time warnings as well:

```
BEGIN {
    use CGI::Carp qw(carpout);
    open(LOG, ">>/var/local/cgi-logs/mycgi-log")
        or die "Unable to append to mycgi-log: $!\n";
    carpout(*LOG);
}
```

You can even arrange for fatal errors to return to the client browser, which is nice for your own debugging but might confuse the end user.

```
use CGI::Carp qw(fatalsToBrowser);
die "Bad error here";
```

Even if the error happens before you get the HTTP header out, the module will try to take care of this to avoid the dreaded 500 Server Error. Normal warnings still go out to the server error log (or wherever you've sent them with carpout) with the application name and date stamp prepended.

See Also

The documentation for the standard CGI::Carp module, the discussion on BEGIN in Recipe 12.3

19.3. Fixing a 500 Server Error

Problem

Your CGI script gives you a 500 Server Error.

Solution

Follow the checklist given in the discussion. It's aimed at a Unix audience, but the general principles embodied in the questions apply to all systems.

Discussion

Make sure the web server can run the script.

Check ownership and permissions with *ls -l*. The appropriate read and execute bits must be set on the script before the web server can run it. The script should be readable and executable by everyone (or at least by whomever the server runs scripts as). Use *chmod 0755 scriptname* if it's owned by you, otherwise *chmod 0555 scriptname* if owned by the designated anonymous web user, assuming you are running as that user or the superuser. All directories in the path must also have their execute bit set.

Make sure the script can be identified as a script by the web server. Most web servers have a system-wide *cgi-bin*, and all files in that directory will be run as scripts. Some servers identify a CGI script as any file whose name ends in a particular extension, like *.cgi* or *.plx*. Some servers have options to permit access via the GET method alone, and not through the POST method that your form likely uses. Consult your web server documentation, configuration files, webmaster, and (if all else fails) technical support.

If you're running on Unix, do you have the right path to the Perl executable on the #! line? The #! line must be the first line in the script; you can't even have blank lines before the #! line. Some operating systems have ridiculously short limits on the number of characters that can be in this line, so you may need to make a link (e.g., from */home/richh/perl* to */opt/installed/third-party/software/perl-5.004/ bin/perl*, to pick a hypothetical pathological example).

If you're running on Win32, have you associated your Perl scripts with the correct Perl executable?

Make sure the script has permissions to do what it's trying to do.

Identify the user the script runs as by replacing with the simple code shown in Example 19-2.

Example 19-2. webwhoami

```
#!/usr/bin/perl
# webwhoami - show web users id
print "Content-Type: text/plain\n\n";
print "Running as ", scalar getpwuid($>), "\n";
```

This prints the username the script is running as.

Identify the resources the script is trying to access. List the files, network connections, system calls, and so on, which require special privilege. Then make sure they can be accessed by the user the script is running as. Are there disk or network quotas? Do the protections on the file allow access? Are you trying to get to the encrypted password field using **getpwent** on a shadow password system (since usually only the superuser can get shadow passwords)?

Set permissions on any files the script needs to write to at 0666, or better yet to 0644 if they're owned up the effective user ID the script is running under. If new files are to be created or old ones moved or removed, write and execute permission on enclosing directory of those files is also needed.

Is the script valid Perl?

Try to run it from a shell prompt. CGI.pm lets you run and debug your scripts from the command line or from standard input. Here, ^D represents whatever you type to get an End of File.

```
% perl -wc cgi-script        # just compilation

% perl -w  cgi-script        # parms from stdin
(offline mode: enter name=value pairs on standard input)
name=joe
number=10
^D
```

```
% perl -w  cgi-script name=joe number=10    # run with mock form input
% perl -d  cgi-script name=joe number=10    # ditto, under the debugger

# POST method script in csh
% (setenv HTTP_METHOD POST; perl -w cgi-script name=joe number=10)
# POST method script in sh
% HTTP_METHOD=POST perl -w cgi-script name=joe number=10
```

Check the server's error log. Most web servers redirect CGI process's STDERR into a file. Find that file (try */usr/local/etc/httpd/logs/error_log*, */usr/local/www/logs/ error_log*, or just ask your administrator) and see whether any warnings or error messages are showing up there.

Are you using an old version of Perl? Type *perl -v* to find out. If you're not using 5.004 or better, you or your admins should upgrade, because 5.003 and earlier releases were not protected against buffer overruns. This is a grave security matter.

Are you using an old version of the libraries? You can either *grep -i version* in the library file (probably in */usr/lib/perl5/*, */usr/local/lib/perl5*, */usr/lib/perl5/site_perl*, or some such). For CGI.pm, and in fact, with any module, you can do this to figure out which version you're using:

```
% perl -MCGI -le 'print CGI->VERSION'
2.49
```

Are you running the latest version of your web server? It's not often that it happens, but sometimes a web server has bugs that can interfere with your scripts.

Are you running with the **-w** switch? This makes Perl gripe about things like using uninitialized variables, reading from a write-only filehandle, and so on.

Are you running with the **-T** flag? If Perl complains about insecure actions, you might be assuming things about your script's input and environment that aren't true. Make it taint-clean (read Recipe 19.4, see the *perlsec* manpage to find out about tainting and its consequences for your program, and check the CGI Security FAQ for particular web traps to avoid) and you may sleep easier at night as well as have a working script.

Are you running with **use strict**? It makes you declare variables before you use them and quote your strings to avoid any confusion with subroutines, and in doing so finds a lot of errors.

Are you checking the return values of each and every one of your system calls? Many people blindly believe that every **open** or **system** or **rename** or **unlink** in their programs will work all the time. These functions return a value so you can find out whether they worked or not—check them!

Can Perl find the libraries you're using? Write a small script that just prints @INC (Perl's array of directories it looks for modules and libraries in). Check the permissions on the libraries (they must be readable by the user the script runs as). Don't try to copy modules from one machine to another—a lot of them have compiled and autoloaded components hidden away in the Perl library directory. Install them yourself from scratch.

Is Perl giving you warnings or errors? Try using CGI::Carp (see Recipe 19.2) to send Perl's error messages and warnings to the browser or a file you have access to.

Is the script upholding its end of the CGI protocol?

The HTTP header must come before the text or image you return. Don't forget the blank line between the header and body. Also, because STDOUT is not automatically autoflushed but STDERR is, if your script generates warnings or errors to STDERR the web server might see them before it sees your HTTP header and can generate an error on some servers. Add this at the top of your script (after the #! line) to also flush STDOUT:

```
$| = 1;
```

Don't ever try to decode the incoming form data by parsing the environment and standard input yourself. There are just too many places where it can go wrong. Use the CGI module and spend your time writing cool programs or reading Usenet instead of tracking down bugs in your implementation of an arcane protocol.

Asking for help elsewhere.

Check the FAQs and other documents mentioned at the end of the Introduction to this chapter. There is still a chance that you have made a common mistake on whatever system you're using—read the relevant FAQs to make sure you don't embarrass yourself by asking the CGI equivalent of "why doesn't my car run when it's out of gas and oil?"

Ask a friend. Almost everyone knows somebody they can ask for help. You'll probably get a reply much sooner than if you asked the Net.

Post to `comp.infosystems.www.authoring.misc` if your question is about a CGI script (the CGI module, decoding cookies, finding out where the user is coming from, etc.).

See Also

Recipe 19.2; the discussion on buffering in the introduction of Chapter 8, *File Contents*; the CGI FAQ at *http://www.webthing.com/tutorials/cgifaq.html*

19.4. Writing a Safe CGI Program

Problem

Because CGI programs allow external users to run programs on systems they would not otherwise have access on, all CGI programs represent a potential security risk. You want to minimize your exposure.

Solution

- Use taint mode (the -T switch on the #! line).

- Don't blindly untaint data. (See below.)

- Sanity-check everything, including all form widget return values, even hidden widgets or values generated by JavaScript code. Many people naïvely assume that just because they tell JavaScript to check the form's values before the form is submitted, the form's values will actually be checked. Not at all! The user can trivially circumvent this by disabling JavaScript in their browser, by downloading the form and altering the JavaScript, or quit by talking HTTP without a browser using any of the examples in Chapter 20, *Web Automation*.

- Check return conditions from system calls.

- Be conscious of race conditions (described below).

- Run with -w and use strict to make sure Perl isn't assuming things incorrectly.

- Don't run anything setuid unless you absolutely must. If you must, think about running setgid instead if you can. Certainly avoid setuid root at all costs. If you must run setuid or setgid, use a wrapper unless Perl is convinced your system has secure setuid scripts and you know what this means.

- Always encode login passwords, credit card numbers, social security numbers, and anything else you'd not care to read pasted across the front page of your local newspaper. Use a secure protocol like SSL when dealing with such data.

Discussion

Many of these suggestions are good ideas for any program—using -w and checking the return values of your system calls are obviously applicable even when security isn't the first thing on your mind. The -w switch makes Perl issue warnings about dubious constructs, like using an undefined variable as though it had a legitimate value, or writing to a read-only filehandle.

Apart from unanticipated shell escapes, the most common security threat lies in forged values in a form submission. It's trivial for anyone to save the source to your form, edit the HTML, and submit the altered form. Even if you're certain that a field can return only `"yes"` or `"no"`, they can always edit it up to return `"maybe"` instead. Even fields marked as type HIDDEN in the form can be tampered. If the program at the other end blindly trusts its form values, it can be fooled into deleting files, creating new user accounts, mailing password or credit card databases, or innumerable other malicious abuses. This is why you must never blindly trust data (like prices) stored in hidden fields when writing CGI shopping cart applications.

Even worse is when the CGI script uses a form value as the basis of a filename to open or a command to run. Bogus values submitted to the script could trick it into opening arbitrary files. Situations like this are precisely why Perl has a taint mode. If a program runs setuid, or else has the -T switch active, any data coming in through program arguments, environment variables, directory listings, or a file, are considered tainted, and cannot be used directly or indirectly to affect the outside world.

Running under taint mode, Perl insists that you set your path variable first, even if specifying a complete pathname when you call a program. That's because you have no assurance that the command you run won't turn around and invoke some other program using a relative pathname. You must also untaint any externally derived data for safety.

For instance, when running in taint mode:

```
#!/usr/bin/perl -T
open(FH, "> $ARGV[0]") or die;
```

Perl warns with:

Insecure dependency in open while running with -T switch at ...

This is because $ARGV[0] (having come from outside your program) is not trustworthy. The only way to change tainted data into untainted data is by using regular expression backreferences:

```
$file = $ARGV[0];                                   # $file tainted
unless ($file =~ m#^([\w.-]+)$#) {                  # $1 is untainted
    die "filename '$file' has invalid characters.\n";
}
$file = $1;                                          # $file untainted
```

Tainted data can come from anything outside your program, such as from your program arguments or environment variables, the results of reading from filehandles or directory handles, and stat or locale information. Operations considered insecure with tainted data include system(STRING), exec(STRING), backticks, glob, open with any mode except read-only, unlink, mkdir, rmdir, chown, chmod, umask, link, symlink, the -s command-line switch, kill, require, eval, truncate, ioctl, fcntl, socket, socketpair, bind, connect, chdir, chroot, setpgrp, setpriority, and syscall.

A common attack exploits what's known as a *race condition*. That's a situation where, between two actions of yours, an attacker can race in and change something to make your program misbehave. A notorious race condition occurred in the way older Unix kernels ran setuid scripts: between the kernel reading the file to find which interpreter to run, and the now-setuid interpreter reading the file, a malicious person could substitute their own script.

Race conditions crop up even in apparently innocuous places. Consider what would happen if not one but many copies of the following code ran simultaneously.

```
unless (-e $filename) {                         # WRONG!
    open(FH, "> $filename");
    # ...
}
```

There's a race between testing whether the file exists and opening it for writing. Still worse, if someone replaced the file with a link to something important, like one of your personal configuration files, the above code would erase that file. The correct way to do this is to do a non-destructive create with the sysopen function, described in Recipe 7.1.

A setuid CGI script runs with different permissions than the web server does. This lets the CGI script access resources (files, shadow password databases, etc) that it otherwise could not. This can be convenient, but it can also be dangerous. Weaknesses in setuid scripts may let crackers access not only files that the low-privilege web server user can access, but also any that could be accessed by the user the script runs as. For a poorly written setuid root script, this could let anyone change passwords, delete files, read credit card records, and other malicious acts. This is why you should always make sure your programs run with the lowest possible privilege, normally the user the web server runs as: nobody.

Finally (and this recommendation may be the hardest to follow) be conscious of the physical path your network traffic takes. Are you sending passwords over an unencrypted connection? Do these unencrypted passwords travel through insecure networks? A form's PASSWORD input field only protects you from someone looking over your shoulder. Always use SSL when real passwords are involved. If you're serious about security, fire up your browser and a packet sniffer to see how easily your traffic is decoded.

See Also

The section on "Cooperating with Strangers" in Chapter 6 of *Programming Perl*; *perlsec*(1); the CGI and HTTP specs and the CGI Security FAQ, all mentioned in the Introduction to this chapter; the section on "Avoiding Denial of Service Attacks" in the standard CGI module documentation; Recipe 19.6

19.5. Making CGI Scripts Efficient

Problem

Your CGI script is called often, and the web server is suffering as a result. You'd like to lessen the load your CGI script causes.

Solution

Use `mod_perl` in the Apache web server along with the following section in your *httpd.conf* file:

```
Alias /perl/ /real/path/to/perl/scripts/

<Location /perl>
SetHandler  perl-script
PerlHandler Apache::Registry
Options ExecCGI
</Location>

PerlModule Apache::Registry
PerlModule CGI
PerlSendHeader On
```

Discussion

Using the `mod_perl` Apache web server module, you can write Perl code that will step in at any part of a request's processing. You can write your own logging and authentication routines, define virtual hosts and their configuration, and write your own handlers for certain types of request.

The snippet above says that requests with URLs starting in */perl/* are actually in */real/path/to/perl/scripts/* and that they should be handled by Apache::Registry. This runs them in a CGI environment. `PerlModule CGI` preloads the CGI module, and `PerlSendHeader On` makes most of your CGI scripts work out of the box with `mod_perl`.

/perl/ works analogously to */cgi-bin/*. To make the suffix *.perl* indicate `mod_perl`
CGI scripts just as the suffix *.cgi* indicates regular CGI scripts, use the following in
your Apache configuration file:

```
<Files *.perl>
SetHandler  perl-script
PerlHandler Apache::Registry
Options ExecCGI
</Files>
```

Because the Perl interpreter that runs your CGI script doesn't shut down when
your script is done (as normally happens when the web server runs your script as
a separate program), you cannot rely on your global variables being undefined
when the program starts. -w and use strict check for many bad habits in these
kinds of scripts. There are other gotchas, too—see the *mod_perl_traps* manpage.

Don't worry about how big your web server processes appear to grow from pre-
loading all these scripts. They need to find their way into memory eventually, and
it's better to happen before Apache forks off kids. That way each script has to be
in memory only once, because forked children have shared memory pages (under
all modern operating systems). In other words, it only appears to take up more
memory this way. It actually takes less!

An interface to Netscape's server is also available at *http://www.perl.com/*
CPAN-local/modules/by-module/Netscape/nsapi_perl-0.24.tar.gz that effects a similar performance gain by avoiding forking.

See Also

The documentation for Bundle::Apache, Apache, Apache::Registry, from CPAN;
http://perl.apache.org/, mod_perl FAQ at *http://perl.apache.org/faqa/*, the *mod_*
perl(3) and *cgi_to_mod_perl*(1) manpages (if you have them)

19.6. Executing Commands Without Shell
Escapes

Problem

You need to use a user's input as part of a command, but you don't want to allow
the user to make the shell run other commands or look at other files. If you just
blindly call the **system** function or backticks on a single string containing a command line, the shell might be used to run the command. This would be unsafe.

Solution

Unlike its single-argument version, the list form of the `system` function is safe from shell escapes. When the command's arguments involve user input from a form, never use this:

```
system("command $input @files");              # UNSAFE
```

Write it this way instead:

```
system("command", $input, @files);            # safer
```

Discussion

Because Perl was designed as a glue language, it's easy to use it to call other programs—too easy, in some cases.

If you're merely trying to run a shell command but don't need to capture its output, it's easy enough to call `system` using its multiple argument form. But what happens if you're using the command in backticks or as part of a piped open? Now you have a real problem, because those don't permit the multiple argument form that `system` does. The solution is to manually `fork` and `exec` the child processes on your own. It's more work, but at least stray shell escapes won't be ruining your day.

It's safe to use backticks in a CGI script only if the arguments you give the program are purely internally generated, as in:

```
chomp($now = `date`);
```

But if the command within the backticks contains user-supplied input, perhaps like this:

```
@output = `grep $input @files`;
```

you have to be much more careful.

```
die "cannot fork: $!" unless defined ($pid = open(SAFE_KID, "-|"));
if ($pid == 0) {
    exec('grep', $input, @files) or die "can't exec grep: $!";
} else {
    @output = <SAFE_KID>;
    close SAFE_KID;                    # $? contains status
}
```

This works because `exec`, like `system`, permits a calling convention that's proof against shell escapes. When passed a list, no shell is called, and so no escapes can occur.

Similar circumlocutions are needed when using open to start up a command. Here's a safe backtick or piped open for read. Instead of using this unsafe code:

```
open(KID_TO_READ, "$program @options @args |");    # UNSAFE
```

Use this more complicated but safer code:

```
# add error processing as above
die "cannot fork: $!" unless defined($pid = open(KID_TO_READ, "-|"));

if ($pid) {    # parent
   while (<KID_TO_READ>) {
       # do something interesting
   }
   close(KID_TO_READ)                 or warn "kid exited $?";

} else {       # child
   # reconfigure, then
   exec($program, @options, @args)  or die "can't exec program: $!";
}
```

Here's a safe piped open for writing. Instead of using this unsafe code:

```
open(KID_TO_WRITE, "|$program $options @args");   # UNSAFE
```

Use this more complicated but safer code:

```
die "cannot fork: $!" unless defined($pid = open(KID_TO_WRITE, "-|"));
$SIG{ALRM} = sub { die "whoops, $program pipe broke" };

if ($pid) {  # parent
   for (@data) { print KID_TO_WRITE $_ }
   close(KID_TO_WRITE)                or warn "kid exited $?";

} else {     # child
   # reconfigure, then
   exec($program, @options, @args)  or die "can't exec program: $!";
}
```

At the point where the comment in the code says reconfigure, then you can put in any extra security measures you'd like. You're in the child process now, where changes won't propagate back to the parent. You can change environment variables, reset temporary user or group ID values, change directories or umasks, etc.

All this doesn't help you, of course, if your system call runs a setuid program that can be exploited with the data you give it. The mail program *sendmail* is a setuid program commonly run from CGI scripts. Know the risks before you call *sendmail* or any other setuid program.

See Also

The system, exec, and open functions in Chapter 3 of *Programming Perl* and in *perlfunc*(1); the section on "Cooperating with Strangers" in Chapter 6 of *Programming Perl*; *perlsec*(1); Recipe 16.1; Recipe 16.2; Recipe 16.3

19.7. *Formatting Lists and Tables with HTML Shortcuts*

Problem

You have several lists and tables to generate and would like helper functions to make these easier to output.

Solution

The CGI module provides HTML helper functions which, when passed array references, apply themselves to each element of the referenced array:

```
print ol( li([ qw(red blue green)]) );
<OL><LI>red</LI> <LI>blue</LI> <LI>green</LI></OL>
@names = qw(Larry Moe Curly);
print ul( li({ -TYPE => "disc" }, \@names) );
<UL><LI TYPE="disc">Larry</LI> <LI TYPE="disc">Moe</LI>
    <LI TYPE="disc">Curly</LI></UL>
```

Discussion

The distributive behavior of the HTML generating functions in CGI.pm can significantly simplify generation of lists and tables. Passed a simple string, they just produce HTML for that string. But passed an array reference, they work on all those strings.

```
print li("alpha");
    <LI>alpha</LI>
print li( [ "alpha", "omega"] );
    <LI>alpha</LI> <LI>omega</LI>
```

The shortcut functions for lists will be loaded when you use the :standard import tag, but you need to ask for :html3 explicitly to get helper functions for working with tables. There's also a conflict between the <TR> tag, which would normally make a tr() function, and Perl's built-in tr/// operator. Therefore, to make a table row, use the Tr() function.

This example generates an HTML table starting with a hash of arrays. The keys will be the row headers, and the array of values will be the columns.

```
use CGI qw(:standard :html3);

%hash = (
    "Wisconsin"  => [ "Superior", "Lake Geneva", "Madison" ],
    "Colorado"   => [ "Denver", "Fort Collins", "Boulder" ],
    "Texas"      => [ "Plano", "Austin", "Fort Stockton" ],
    "California" => [ "Sebastopol", "Santa Rosa", "Berkeley" ],
);

$\ = "\n";

print "<TABLE> <CAPTION>Cities I Have Known</CAPTION>";
print Tr(th [qw(State Cities)]);
for $k (sort keys %hash) {
    print Tr(th($k), td( [ sort @{$hash{$k}} ] ));
}
print "</TABLE>";
```

That generates text that looks like this:

```
<TABLE> <CAPTION>Cities I Have Known</CAPTION>
    <TR><TH>State</TH> <TH>Cities</TH></TR>
    <TR><TH>California</TH> <TD>Berkeley</TD> <TD>Santa Rosa</TD>
        <TD>Sebastopol</TD> </TR>
    <TR><TH>Colorado</TH> <TD>Boulder</TD> <TD>Denver</TD>
        <TD>Fort Collins</TD> </TR>
    <TR><TH>Texas</TH> <TD>Austin</TD> <TD>Fort Stockton</TD>
        <TD>Plano</TD></TR>
    <TR><TH>Wisconsin</TH> <TD>Lake Geneva</TD> <TD>Madison</TD>
        <TD>Superior</TD></TR>
</TABLE>
```

You can produce the same output using one print statement, although it is slightly trickier, because you have to use a map to create the implicit loop. This print statement produces output identical to that displayed above:

```
print table
        caption('Cities I have Known'),
        Tr(th [qw(State Cities)]),
        map { Tr(th($_), td( [ sort @{$hash{$_}} ] )) } sort keys %hash;
```

This is particularly useful for formatting the results of a database query, as in Example 19-3 (see Chapter 14, *Database Access*).

Example 19-3. salcheck

```
#!/usr/bin/perl
# salcheck - check for salaries
use DBI;
use CGI qw(:standard :html3);

$limit = param("LIMIT");

print header(), start_html("Salary Query"),
      h1("Search"),
```

Example 19-3. salcheck (continued)

```
        start_form(),
        p("Enter minimum salary", textfield("LIMIT")),
        submit(),
        end_form();

if (defined $limit) {
    $dbh = DBI->connect("dbi:mysql:somedb:server.host.dom:3306",
        "username", "password")
        or die "Connecting: $DBI::errstr";
    $sth = $dbh->prepare("SELECT name,salary FROM employees
        WHERE salary > $limit")
        or die "Preparing: ", $dbh->errstr;
    $sth->execute
        or die "Executing: ", $sth->errstr;

    print h1("Results"), "<TABLE BORDER=1>";

    while (@row = $sth->fetchrow_array()) {
        print Tr( td( \@row ) );
    }

    print "</TABLE>\n";
    $sth->finish;
    $dbh->disconnect;
}

print end_html();
```

See Also

The documentation for the standard CGI module; Recipe 14.10

19.8. Redirecting to a Different Location

Problem

You need to tell the client's browser to look elsewhere for a page.

Solution

Instead of a normal header, just issue a location redirect and exit. Don't forget the extra newline at the end of the header.

```
$url = "http://www.perl.com/CPAN/";
print "Location: $url\n\n";
exit;
```

Discussion

Sometimes your CGI program doesn't need to generate the document on its own. It only needs to tell the client at the other end to fetch a different document instead. In that case, the HTTP header needs to include this directive as a **Location** line followed by the URL you want to send them to. Make sure to use an absolute URL, not a relative one.

The direct and literal solution given above is usually sufficient. But if you already have the CGI module loaded, use the `redirect` function. You might use this code if you are building and setting a cookie, as shown in Example 19-4.

Example 19-4. oreobounce

```perl
#!/usr/bin/perl -w
# oreobounce - set a cookie and redirect the browser
use CGI qw(:cgi);

$oreo = cookie( -NAME    => 'filling',
                -VALUE   => "vanilla crème",
                -EXPIRES => '+3M',      # M for month, m for minute
                -DOMAIN  => '.perl.com');

$whither = "http://somewhere.perl.com/nonesuch.html";

print redirect( -URL    => $whither,
                -COOKIE => $oreo);
```

That would produce:

```
Status: 302 Moved Temporarily
Set-Cookie: filling=vanilla%20cr%E4me; domain=.perl.com;
    expires=Tue, 21-Jul-1998 11:58:55 GMT
Date: Tue, 21 Apr 1998 11:55:55 GMT
Location: http://somewhere.perl.com/nonesuch.html
Content-Type: text/html
B<<blank line here>>
```

Example 19-5 is a complete program that looks at the client browser name and redirects it to a page in Eric Raymond's *Jargon File* that talks about the user's browser. It's also a nice example of a different approach to building a switch statement in Perl.

Example 19-5. os_snipe

```perl
#!/usr/bin/perl
# os_snipe - redirect to a Jargon File entry about current OS
$dir = 'http://www.wins.uva.nl/%7Emes/jargon';
for ($ENV{HTTP_USER_AGENT}) {
    $page  =    /Mac/            && 'm/Macintrash.html'
           ||   /Win(dows )?NT/  && 'e/evilandrude.html'
           ||   /Win|MSIE|WebTV/ && 'm/MicroslothWindows.html'
           ||   /Linux/          && 'l/Linux.html'
```

Example 19-5. os_snipe (continued)

```
        || /HP-UX/          && 'h/HP-SUX.html'
        || /SunOS/          && 's/ScumOS.html'
        ||                     'a/AppendixB.html';
}
print "Location: $dir/$page\n\n";
```

The *os_snipe* program shows a good use of dynamic redirection, because you don't always send every user to the same place. If you did, it would usually make more sense to arrange for a static redirect line in the server's configuration file, since that would be easier on the web server than running a CGI script for each redirection.

Telling the client's browser that you don't plan to produce any output is not the same as redirecting nowhere:

```
    use CGI qw(:standard);
    print header( -STATUS => '204 No response' );
```

That produces this:

```
Status: 204 No response
Content-Type: text/html
<blank line here>
```

Use this, for instance, when the user will submit a form request but you don't want their page to change or even update.

It may seem silly to provide a content type and then no content, but that's what the module does. If you were hand-coding this, it wouldn't be required.

```
    #!/bin/sh

    cat <<EOCAT
    Status: 204 No response

    EOCAT
```

See Also

The documentation for the standard CGI module

19.9. Debugging the Raw HTTP Exchange

Problem

Your CGI script is misbehaving strangely with your browser, and you suspect something in the HTTP header is missing. You want to find out exactly what your browser is sending to the server in the HTTP header.

Solution

Create your own fake web server, and point your browser at it, as shown in Example 19-6.

Example 19-6. dummyhttpd

```perl
#!/usr/bin/perl -w
# dummyhttpd - start an HTTP daemon and print what the client sends

use strict;
use HTTP::Daemon;   # need LWP-5.32 or better

my $server = HTTP::Daemon->new(Timeout => 60, LocalPort => 8989);
print "Please contact me at: <URL:", $server->url, ">\n";

while (my $client = $server->accept) {
  CONNECTION:
    while (my $answer = $client->get_request) {
        print $answer->as_string;
        $client->autoflush;
      RESPONSE:
        while (<STDIN>) {
            last RESPONSE   if $_ eq ".\n";
            last CONNECTION if $_ eq "..\n";
            print $client $_;
        }
        print "\nEOF\n";
    }
    print "CLOSE: ", $client->reason, "\n";
    $client->close;
    undef $client;
}
```

Discussion

It's hard to keep track of which versions of all the different browsers still have which bugs. The fake server program can save you days of head scratching, because sometimes a misbehaving browser doesn't send the server the right thing. Historically, we have seen aberrant browsers lose their cookies, mis-escape a URL, send the wrong status line, and do other even less obvious things.

To use the fake server, it's best to run it on the same machine as the real server. That way your browser will still send it any cookies destined for that domain. Then instead of pointing your browser at:

```
http://somewhere.com/cgi-bin/whatever
```

use the alternate port given in the **new** constructor above. You don't need to be the superuser to run the server if you use the alternate port.

```
http://somewhere.com:8989/cgi-bin/whatever
```

If you convince yourself that the client is behaving properly but wonder about the server, it's easiest to use the *telnet* program to manually talk to the remote server.

```
% telnet www.perl.com 80
GET /bogotic HTTP/1.0
<blank line here>
HTTP/1.1 404 File Not Found
Date: Tue, 21 Apr 1998 11:25:43 GMT
Server: Apache/1.2.4
Connection: close
Content-Type: text/html

<HTML><HEAD>
<TITLE>404 File Not Found</TITLE>
</HEAD><BODY>
<H1>File Not Found</H1>
The requested URL /bogotic was not found on this server.<P>
</BODY></HTML>
```

If you have LWP installed on your system, you can use the *GET* alias for the *lwp-request* program. This will follow any redirection chains, which can shed light on your problem. For example:

```
% GET -esuSU http://mox.perl.com/perl/bogotic
GET http://language.perl.com/bogotic
Host: mox.perl.com
User-Agent: lwp-request/1.32

GET http://mox.perl.com/perl/bogotic --> 302 Moved Temporarily
GET http://www.perl.com/perl/bogotic --> 302 Moved Temporarily
GET http://language.perl.com/bogotic --> 404 File Not Found
Connection: close
Date: Tue, 21 Apr 1998 11:29:03 GMT
Server: Apache/1.2.4
Content-Type: text/html
Client-Date: Tue, 21 Apr 1998 12:29:01 GMT
Client-Peer: 208.201.239.47:80
Title: Broken perl.com Links

<HTML>
<HEAD><TITLE>An Error Occurred</TITLE></HEAD>
<BODY>
<H1>An Error Occurred</h1>
404 File Not Found
</BODY>
</HTML>
```

See Also

The documentation for the standard CGI module; Recipe 19.10

19.10. Managing Cookies

Problem

You want to get or set a cookie to help manage sessions or user preferences.

Solution

Using CGI.pm, retrieve an existing cookie like this:

```
$preference_value = cookie("preference name");
```

To prepare a cookie, do this:

```
$packed_cookie = cookie( -NAME    => "preference name",
                         -VALUE   => "whatever you'd like",
                         -EXPIRES => "+2y");
```

To save a cookie back to the client browser, you must include it in the HTTP header, probably using either the **header** or **redirect** functions:

```
print header(-COOKIE => $packed_cookie);
```

Discussion

Cookies store information on the client's browser. If you're using Netscape under Unix, you can inspect your own *~/.netscape/cookies* file, although this doesn't show your current set of cookies. It only holds those cookies present when you last exited the browser. Think of them as per-application user preferences or a way to help with transactions. Benefits of cookies are that they can be shared between several different programs on your server, and they persist even across browser invocations.

However, cookies can be used for dubious tricks like traffic analysis and click tracing. This makes some folks very nervous about who is collecting their personal data and what use will be made of their page viewing habits. Cookies don't travel well, either. If you use a browser at home or in someone else's office, it won't have the cookies from the browser in your office. For this reason, do not expect every browser to accept the cookies you give it. As if that wasn't bad enough, browsers can randomly toss cookies. Here's an excerpt from the HTTP State Management Mechanism draft at *http://portal.research.bell-labs.com/~dmk/cookie-2.81-3.1.txt*:

> Because user agents have finite space in which to store cookies, they may also discard older cookies to make space for newer ones, using, for example, a least-recently-used algorithm, along with constraints on the maximum number of cookies that each origin server may set.

Due to their unreliability, you should probably not place too much faith in cookies. Use them for simple, stateful transactions, and avoid traffic analysis for reasons of privacy.

Example 19-7 is a complete program that remembers the user's last choice.

Example 19-7. ic_cookies

```perl
#!/usr/bin/perl -w
# ic_cookies - sample CGI script that uses a cookie
use CGI qw(:standard);

use strict;

my $cookname = "favorite ice cream";
my $favorite = param("flavor");
my $tasty    = cookie($cookname) || 'mint';

unless ($favorite) {
    print header(), start_html("Ice Cookies"), h1("Hello Ice Cream"),
            hr(), start_form(),
                p("Please select a flavor: ", textfield("flavor",$tasty)),
                    end_form(), hr();
    exit;
}

my $cookie = cookie(
                -NAME    => $cookname,
                -VALUE   => $favorite,
                -EXPIRES => "+2y",
            );

print header(-COOKIE => $cookie),
        start_html("Ice Cookies, #2"),
        h1("Hello Ice Cream"),
        p("You chose as your favorite flavor '$favorite'.");
```

See Also

The documentation for the standard CGI module

19.11. Creating Sticky Widgets

Problem

You want the default values for the fields in your form to be the last values submitted. For instance, you want to create a search form like AltaVista (*http://altavista.digital.com/*) where the keywords you're searching with appear in the search dialog above the results.

Solution

Use CGI.pm's HTML shortcuts to create your form, which will automatically provide previous values as defaults:

```
print textfield("SEARCH");        # previous SEARCH value is the default
```

Discussion

Example 19-8 is a simple script for querying the list of users currently logged in.

Example 19-8. who.cgi

```
#!/usr/bin/perl -wT
# who.cgi - run who(1) on a user and format the results nicely

$ENV{IFS}='';
$ENV{PATH}='/bin:/usr/bin';

use CGI qw(:standard);

# print search form
print header(), start_html("Query Users"), h1("Search");
print start_form(), p("Which user?", textfield("WHO")); submit(), end_form();

# print results of the query if we have someone to look for
$name = param("WHO");
if ($name) {
    print h1("Results");
    $html = '';

    # call who and build up text of response
    foreach ('who') {
        next unless /^$name\s/o;        # only lines matching $name
        s/&/&amp;/g;                    # escape HTML
        s/</&lt;/g;
        s/>/&gt;/g;
        $html .= $_;
    }
    # nice message if we didn't find anyone by that name
    $html = $html || "$name is not logged in";

    print pre($html);
}

print end_html();
```

The call to `textfield` generates HTML for a text entry field whose parameter name is WHO. After printing the form, we check whether we were called with a value for the WHO parameter. If so, we try to find the lines in the output from *who* for that user.

See Also

The documentation for the standard CGI module; Recipe 19.4; Recipe 19.7

19.12. *Writing a Multiscreen CGI Script*

Problem

You want to write a single CGI script that can return several different pages to the browser. For instance, you want a single CGI script for administering a database of products. The script will be called to display the form to add a product, to process the add-product form, to display a list of products to delete, to process the delete-product form, to display a list of product to edit, to display a form of the product's attributes for the user to change, and to process the edit-product form. You can use these multiscreen CGI scripts to form an elementary shopping-cart-type application.

Solution

Use a hidden field to encode the current screen.

Discussion

It is easy to generate sticky hidden fields with the CGI module. The `hidden` function returns HTML for a hidden widget and will use the widget's current value if you only give `hidden` the widget name:

```
use CGI qw(:standard);
print hidden("bacon");
```

To determine which page ("display product list", "display all items in shopping cart", "confirm order") to display, use another hidden field. We'll call this one `.State` so it won't conflict with any field we might have called `State` (for instance, in credit card billing information). To let the user move from page to page, use submit buttons that set `.State` to the name of the page to go to. For instance, to make a button to take the user to the "Checkout" page, use:

```
print submit(-NAME => ".State", -VALUE => "Checkout");
```

We wrap this in a function to make it easier to type:

```
sub to_page { return submit( -NAME => ".State", -VALUE => shift ) }
```

To decide what code to display, check the `.State` parameter:

```
$page = param(".State") || "Default";
```

Put the code to generate each page in separate subroutines. You could decide which subroutine to call with a long `if` ... `elsif` ... `elsif`:

```
if ($page eq "Default") {
    front_page();
} elsif ($page eq "Checkout") {
    checkout();
} else {
    no_such_page();        # when we get a .State that doesn't exist
}
```

This is tedious and clumsy. Instead use a hash that maps a page name to a subroutine. This is another strategy for implementing a C-style `switch` statement in Perl.

```
%States = (
    'Default'      => \&front_page,
    'Shirt'        => \&shirt,
    'Sweater'      => \&sweater,
    'Checkout'     => \&checkout,
    'Card'         => \&credit_card,
    'Order'        => \&order,
    'Cancel'       => \&front_page,
);

if ($States{$page}) {
    $States{$page}->();    # call the correct subroutine
} else {
    no_such_page();
}
```

Each page will have some persistent widgets. For instance, the page that lets the user order t-shirts will want the number of t-shirts to persist even when the user continues and orders shoes as well. We do this by calling the page-generating subroutines with a parameter that lets them know whether they're the active page. If they're not the active page, they should only send back hidden fields for any persistent data:

```
while (($state, $sub) = each %States) {
    $sub->( $page eq $state );
}
```

The `eq` comparison returns true if the page is the current page, and false if it isn't. The page-generating subroutine then looks like this:

```
sub t_shirt {
    my $active = shift;

    unless ($active) {
        print hidden("size"), hidden("color");
        return;
    }
```

```
print p("You want to buy a t-shirt?");
print p("Size: ", popup_menu('size', [ qw(XL L M S XS) ]));
print p("Color:", popup_menu('color', [ qw(Black White) ]));

print p( to_page("Shoes"), to_page("Checkout") );
}
```

Because the subroutines all generate HTML, we have to print the HTTP header and start the HTML document and form before we call the subroutines. This lets us print a standard header and footer for all the pages, if we want. Here, we assume we have subroutines `standard_header` and `standard_footer` for printing the headers and footers:

```
print header("Program Title"), start_html();
print standard_header(), begin_form();
while (($state, $sub) = each %States) {
    $sub->( $page eq $state );
}
print standard_footer(), end_form(), end_html();
```

Don't make the mistake of encoding prices in the forms. Calculate prices based on the values of the hidden widgets, and sanity-check the information where you can. For example, compare against known products, to make sure they're not trying to order a burgundy XXXXXXL t-shirt.

Using hidden data is more robust than using cookies, because you can't rely on the browser supporting or accepting cookies. A full explanation is in Recipe 19.10.

We show a simple shopping cart application as the program *chemiserie* at the end of this chapter.

See Also

The documentation for the standard CGI module.

19.13. *Saving a Form to a File or Mail Pipe*

Problem

Your CGI script needs to save or mail the entire form contents to a file.

Solution

To store a form, use the CGI module's `save_parameters` function or `save` method, which take a filehandle argument. You can save to a file:

```
# first open and exclusively lock the file
open(FH, ">>/tmp/formlog")              or die "can't append to formlog: $!";
flock(FH, 2)                            or die "can't flock formlog: $!";
```

```
# either using the procedural interface
use CGI qw(:standard);
save_parameters(*FH);                        # with CGI::save

# or using the object interface
use CGI;
$query = CGI->new();
$query->save(*FH);

close(FH)                            or die "can't close formlog: $!";
```

Or, save to a pipe, such as one connected to a mailer process:

```
use CGI qw(:standard);
open(MAIL, "|/usr/lib/sendmail -oi -t") or die "can't fork sendmail: $!";
print MAIL <<EOF;
From: $0 (your cgi script)
To: hisname\@hishost.com
Subject: mailed form submission

EOF
save_parameters(*MAIL);
close(MAIL)                          or die "can't close sendmail: $!";
```

Discussion

Sometimes all you want to do with form data is to save it for later use. The save_
parameters function and save method in CGI.pm write form parameters to an
open filehandle. That filehandle can be attached to an open file (preferably one
opened in append mode and locked, as in the solution), or to a pipe whose other
end is a mail program.

File entries are stored one per line as variable=value pairs, with any funny
characters URL-escaped. Each record is separated by a line with a single equals
sign. These are typically read back by calling the CGI->new method with a filehandle argument that manages all the unescaping automatically, as described
below.

If you want to add extra information to your query before you save it, the param
function (or method, if you're using the object-oriented interface) can be called
with more than one argument, setting the value(s) of a form parameter. For example, here's how you would save a time stamp and the entire environment:

```
param("_timestamp", scalar localtime);
param("_environs", %ENV);
```

Once you've got the forms in a file, process them by using the object interface.

To load a query object from a filehandle, call the new method with a filehandle
argument. Each time you do this, it returns a complete form. When end of file is
hit, the returned form has no parameters. The following code demonstrates this

approach. It keeps a running total of all the `"items request"` parameters, but only if the form was not submitted from a *perl.com* site. Remember, we added the `_environs` and `_timestamp` parameters when we wrote the file.

```
use CGI;
open(FORMS, "< /tmp/formlog")          or die "can't read formlog: $!";
flock(FORMS, 1)                        or die "can't lock formlog: $!";
while ($query = CGI->new(*FORMS)) {
    last unless $query->param();       # means end of file
    %his_env = $query->param('_environs');
    $count  += $query->param('items requested')
            unless $his_env{REMOTE_HOST} =~ /(^|\.)perl\.com$/
}
print "Total orders: $count\n";
```

File ownership and access permissions are an issue here, as they are in any files created by CGI script.

See Also

Recipe 18.3; Recipe 19.3

19.14. Program: chemiserie

The CGI script in Example 19-9 lets people order t-shirts and sweaters over the Web, using techniques described in Recipe 19.12. Its output isn't elegant or beautiful, but illustrating the multiscreen technique in a short program was challenging enough without trying to make it pretty as well.

The **shirt** and **sweater** subroutines check their widget values. If the user somehow submits an invalid color or size, the value is reset to the first in the list of allowable colors or sizes.

Example 19-9. chemiserie

```
#!/usr/bin/perl -w
# chemiserie - simple CGI shopping for shirts and sweaters

use strict;
use CGI qw(:standard);
use CGI::Carp qw(fatalsToBrowser);

my %States;                # state table mapping pages to functions
my $Current_Screen;        # the current screen

# Hash of pages and functions.

%States = (
    'Default'       => \&front_page,
    'Shirt'         => \&shirt,
```

Example 19-9. chemiserie (continued)

```
    'Sweater'        => \&sweater,
    'Checkout'       => \&checkout,
    'Card'           => \&credit_card,
    'Order'          => \&order,
    'Cancel'         => \&front_page,
);

$Current_Screen = param(".State") || "Default";
die "No screen for $Current_Screen" unless $States{$Current_Screen};

# Generate the current page.

standard_header();

while (my($screen_name, $function) = each %States) {
    $function->($screen_name eq $Current_Screen);
}
standard_footer();
exit;


##############################
# header, footer, menu functions
##############################

sub standard_header {
    print header(), start_html(-Title => "Shirts", -BGCOLOR=>"White");
    print start_form(); # start_multipart_form() if file upload
}

sub standard_footer { print end_form(), end_html() }

sub shop_menu {
    print p(defaults("Empty My Shopping Cart"),
        to_page("Shirt"),
        to_page("Sweater"),
        to_page("Checkout"));
}


##############################
# subroutines for each screen
##############################

# The default page.
sub front_page {
    my $active = shift;
    return unless $active;

    print "<H1>Hi!</H1>\n";
    print "Welcome to our Shirt Shop!  Please make your selection from ";
    print "the menu below.\n";

    shop_menu();
```

Example 19-9. chemiserie (continued)

```perl
}

# Page to order a shirt from.
sub shirt {
    my $active = shift;
    my @sizes  = qw(XL L M S);
    my @colors = qw(Black White);

    my ($size, $color, $count) =
      (param("shirt_size"), param("shirt_color"), param("shirt_count"));

    # sanity check
    if ($count) {
        $color = $colors[0] unless grep { $_ eq $color } @colors;
        $size  = $sizes[0]  unless grep { $_ eq $size  } @sizes;
        param("shirt_color", $color);
        param("shirt_size",  $size);
    }

    unless ($active) {
        print hidden("shirt_size")  if $size;
        print hidden("shirt_color") if $color;
        print hidden("shirt_count") if $count;
        return;
    }

    print h1("T-Shirt");
    print p("What a shirt!  This baby is decked out with all the options.",
        "It comes with full luxury interior, cotton trim, and a collar",
        "to make your eyes water!  Unit price: \$33.00");

    print h2("Options");
    print p("How Many?", textfield("shirt_count"));
    print p("Size?",  popup_menu("shirt_size",  \@sizes ),
        "Color?", popup_menu("shirt_color", \@colors));

    shop_menu();
}

# Page to order a sweater from.
sub sweater {
    my $active = shift;
    my @sizes  = qw(XL L M);
    my @colors = qw(Chartreuse Puce Lavender);

    my ($size, $color, $count) =
      (param("sweater_size"), param("sweater_color"), param("sweater_count"));

    # sanity check
    if ($count) {
        $color = $colors[0] unless grep { $_ eq $color } @colors;
        $size  = $sizes[0]  unless grep { $_ eq $size  } @sizes;
```

Example 19-9. chemiserie (continued)

```perl
        param("sweater_color", $color);
        param("sweater_size",  $size);
    }

    unless ($active) {
        print hidden("sweater_size")  if $size;
        print hidden("sweater_color") if $color;
        print hidden("sweater_count") if $count;
        return;
    }

    print h1("Sweater");
    print p("Nothing implies preppy elegance more than this fine",
        "sweater.  Made by peasant workers from black market silk,",
        "it slides onto your lean form and cries out ``Take me,",
        "for I am a god!''.  Unit price: \$49.99.");

    print h2("Options");
    print p("How Many?", textfield("sweater_count"));
    print p("Size?",  popup_menu("sweater_size",  \@sizes));
    print p("Color?", popup_menu("sweater_color", \@colors));

    shop_menu();
}

# Page to display current order for confirmation.
sub checkout {
    my $active = shift;

    return unless $active;

    print h1("Order Confirmation");
    print p("You ordered the following:");
    print order_text();
    print p("Is this right?  Select 'Card' to pay for the items",
        "or 'Shirt' or 'Sweater' to continue shopping.");
    print p(to_page("Card"),
        to_page("Shirt"),
        to_page("Sweater"));
}

# Page to gather credit-card information.
sub credit_card {
    my $active = shift;
    my @widgets = qw(Name Address1 Address2 City Zip State Phone Card Expiry);

    unless ($active) {
        print map { hidden($_) } @widgets;
        return;
    }

    print pre(p("Name:            ", textfield("Name")),
```

Example 19-9. chemiserie (continued)

```
        p("Address:        ", textfield("Address1")),
        p("                 ", textfield("Address2")),
        p("City:           ", textfield("City")),
        p("Zip:            ", textfield("Zip")),
        p("State:          ", textfield("State")),
        p("Phone:          ", textfield("Phone")),
        p("Credit Card #: ", textfield("Card")),
        p("Expiry:         ", textfield("Expiry")));

    print p("Click on 'Order' to order the items.  Click on 'Cancel' to return
shopping.");

    print p(to_page("Order"), to_page("Cancel"));
}

# Page to complete an order.
sub order {
    my $active = shift;

    unless ($active) {
        return;
    }

    # you'd check credit card values here

    print h1("Ordered!");
    print p("You have ordered the following toppings:");
    print order_text();

    print p(defaults("Begin Again"));
}

# Returns HTML for the current order ("You have ordered ...")
sub order_text {
    my $html = '';

    if (param("shirt_count")) {
        $html .= p("You have ordered ", param("shirt_count"),
            " shirts of size ",  param("shirt_size"),
            " and color ", param("shirt_color"), ".");
    }
    if (param("sweater_count")) {
        $html .= p("You have ordered ",  param("sweater_count"),
            " sweaters of size ", param("sweater_size"),
            " and color ", param("sweater_color"), ".");
    }
    $html = p("Nothing!") unless $html;
    $html .= p("For a total cost of ", calculate_price());
    return $html;
}
```

Example 19-9. chemiserie (continued)

```
sub calculate_price {
    my $shirts   = param("shirt_count")    || 0;
    my $sweaters = param("sweater_count")  || 0;
    return sprintf("\$%.2f", $shirts*33 + $sweaters * 49.99);
}

sub to_page { submit(-NAME => ".State", -VALUE => shift) }
```

20

Web Automation

*The web, then, or the pattern, a web
at once sensuous and logical, an elegant and
pregnant texture: that is style, that is the
foundation of the art of literature.*

—Robert Louis Stevenson,
*On some technical Elements of Style in Literature
(1885)*

20.0. Introduction

Chapter 19, *CGI Programming*, concentrated on responding to browser requests and producing documents using CGI. This one approaches the Web from the other side: instead of responding to a browser, you pretend to be one, generating requests and processing returned documents. We make extensive use of modules to simplify this process, because the intricate network protocols and document formats are tricky to get right. By letting existing modules handle the hard parts, you can concentrate on the interesting part—your own program.

The relevant modules can all be found under the following URL:

```
http://www.perl.com/CPAN/modules/by-category/15_World_Wide_Web_HTML_HTTP_CGI/
```

There are modules for computing credit card checksums, interacting with Netscape or Apache server APIs, processing image maps, validating HTML, and manipulating MIME. The largest and most important modules for this chapter, though, are found in the libwww-perl suite of modules, referred to collectively as LWP. Here are just a few of the modules included in LWP:

Module Name	Purpose
LWP::UserAgent	WWW user agent class
LWP::RobotUA	Develop robot applications
LWP::Protocol	Interface to various protocol schemes
LWP::Authen::Basic	Handle 401 and 407 responses
LWP::MediaTypes	MIME types configuration (text/html, etc.)
LWP::Debug	Debug logging module
LWP::Simple	Simple procedural interface for common functions
HTTP::Headers	MIME/RFC822 style headers
HTTP::Message	HTTP style message
HTTP::Request	HTTP request
HTTP::Response	HTTP response
HTTP::Daemon	A HTTP server class
HTTP::Status	HTTP status code (200 OK etc)
HTTP::Date	Date parsing module for HTTP date formats
HTTP::Negotiate	HTTP content negotiation calculation
WWW::RobotRules	Parse *robots.txt* files
File::Listing	Parse directory listings

The HTTP:: and LWP:: modules let you request documents from a server. The LWP::Simple module, in particular, offers a very basic way to fetch a document. LWP::Simple, however, lacks the ability to access individual components of the HTTP response. To access these, use HTTP::Request, HTTP::Response, and LWP::UserAgent. We show both sets of modules in Recipes 20.1, 20.2, and 20.10.

Closely allied with LWP, but not distributed in the LWP bundle, are the HTML:: modules. These let you parse HTML. They provide the basis for Recipes 20.5, 20.4, 20.6, 20.3, 20.7, and the programs *htmlsub* and *hrefsub*.

Recipe 20.12 gives a regular expression to decode the fields in your web server's log files and shows how to interpret the fields. We use this regular expression and the Logfile::Apache module in Recipe 20.13 to show two ways of summarizing the data in web server log files.

20.1. *Fetching a URL from a Perl Script*

Problem

You have a URL that you want to fetch from a script.

Solution

Use the get function from by the CPAN module LWP::Simple, part of LWP.

```
use LWP::Simple;
$content = get($URL);
```

Discussion

The right library makes life easier, and the LWP modules are the right ones for this task.

The get function from LWP::Simple returns undef on error, so check for errors this way:

```
use LWP::Simple;
unless (defined ($content = get $URL)) {
    die "could not get $URL\n";
}
```

When it's run that way, however, you can't determine the cause of the error. For this and other elaborate processing, you'll have to go beyond LWP::Simple.

Example 20-1 is a program that fetches a document remotely. If it fails, it prints out the error status line. Otherwise it prints out the document title and the number of bytes of content. We use three modules from LWP and one other from CPAN.

LWP::UserAgent

This module creates a virtual browser. The object returned from the new constructor is used to make the actual request. We've set the name of our agent to "Schmozilla/v9.14 Platinum" just to give the remote webmaster browser-envy when they see it in their logs.

HTTP::Request

This module creates a request but doesn't send it. We create a GET request and set the referring page to a fictitious URL.

HTTP::Response

This is the object type returned when the user agent actually runs the request. We check it for errors and contents.

URI::Heuristic

This curious little module uses Netscape-style guessing algorithms to expand partial URLs. For example:

Simple	Guess
perl	*http://www.perl.com*
www.oreilly.com	*http://www.oreilly.com*
ftp.funet.fi	*ftp://ftp.funet.fi*
/etc/passwd	*file:/etc/passwd*

Although these aren't legitimate URLs (their format is not in the URI specification), Netscape tries to guess the URL they stand for. Because Netscape does it, most other browsers do too.

The source is in Example 20-1.

Example 20-1. titlebytes

```
#!/usr/bin/perl -w
# titlebytes - find the title and size of documents
use LWP::UserAgent;
use HTTP::Request;
use HTTP::Response;
use URI::Heuristic;
my $raw_url = shift                   or die "usage: $0 url\n";
my $url = URI::Heuristic::uf_urlstr($raw_url);
$| = 1;                               # to flush next line
printf "%s =>\n\t", $url;
my $ua = LWP::UserAgent->new();
$ua->agent("Schmozilla/v9.14 Platinum"); # give it time, it'll get there
my $req = HTTP::Request->new(GET => $url);
$req->referer("http://wizard.yellowbrick.oz");
                                  # perplex the log analysers
my $response = $ua->request($req);
if ($response->is_error()) {
    printf " %s\n", $response->status_line;
  } else {
    my $count;
    my $bytes;
    my $content = $response->content();
    $bytes = length $content;
    $count = ($content =~ tr/\n/\n/);
    printf "%s (%d lines, %d bytes)\n", $response->title(), $count, $bytes; }
```

When run, the program produces output like this:

```
% titlebytes http://www.tpj.com/
http://www.tpj.com/ =>
      The Perl Journal (109 lines, 4530 bytes)
```

Yes, "referer" is not how "referrer" should be spelled. The standards people got it wrong when they misspelled HTTP_REFERER. Please use two r's when referring to things in English.

See Also

The documentation for the CPAN module LWP::Simple, and the *lwpcook*(1) manpage that came with LWP; the documentation for the modules LWP::User-Agent, HTTP::Request, HTTP::Response, and URI::Heuristic; Recipe 20.2

20.2. Automating Form Submission

Problem

You want to submit form values to a CGI script from your program.

Solution

If you're submitting form values using the GET method, create a URL and encode the form using the `query_form` method:

```
use LWP::Simple;
use URI::URL;

my $url = url('http://www.perl.com/cgi-bin/cpan_mod');
$url->query_form(module => 'DB_File', readme => 1);
$content = get($url);
```

If you're using the POST method, create your own user agent and encode the content appropriately:

```
use HTTP::Request::Common qw(POST);
use LWP::UserAgent;

$ua = LWP::UserAgent->new();
my $req = POST 'http://www.perl.com/cgi-bin/cpan_mod',
               [ module => 'DB_File', readme => 1 ];
$content = $ua->request($req)->as_string;
```

Discussion

For simple operations, the procedural interface of the LWP::Simple module is sufficient. For fancier ones, the LWP::UserAgent module provides a virtual browser object, which you manipulate using method calls.

The format of a query string is:

```
field1=value1&field2=value2&field3=value3
```

In GET requests, this is encoded in the URL being requested:

```
http://www.site.com/path/to/
    script.cgi?field1=value1&field2=value2&field3=value3
```

Fields must still be properly escaped, so setting the `arg` form parameter to `"this isn't <EASY>&<FUN>"` would yield:

```
http://www.site.com/path/to/
    script.cgi?arg=%22this+isn%27t+%3CEASY%3E+%26+%3CFUN%3E%22
```

The `query_form` method called on a URL object correctly escapes the form values for you, or you could use the `URI::Escape::uri_escape` or `CGI::escape_html` functions on your own. In POST requests, the query string is the body of the HTTP document sent to the CGI script.

We can use the LWP::Simple module to submit data in a GET request, but there is no corresponding LWP::Simple interface for POST requests. Instead, the HTTP::Request::Common module's POST function conveniently creates a properly formatted request with everything properly escaped.

If you need to go through a proxy, construct your user agent and tell it to use a proxy this way:

```
$ua->proxy(['http', 'ftp'] => 'http://proxy.myorg.com:8081');
```

That says that both HTTP and FTP requests through this user agent should be routed through the proxy on port 8081 at *proxy.myorg.com*.

See Also

The documentation for the CPAN modules LWP::Simple, LWP::UserAgent, HTTP::Request::Common, URI::Escape, and URI::URL; Recipe 20.1

20.3. Extracting URLs

Problem

You want to extract all URLs from an HTML file.

Solution

Use the HTML::LinkExtor module from CPAN:

```
use HTML::LinkExtor;

$parser = HTML::LinkExtor->new(undef, $base_url);
$parser->parse_file($filename);
@links = $parser->links;
```

```
foreach $linkarray (@links) {
    my @element = @$linkarray;
    my $elt_type = shift @element;                          # element type

    # possibly test whether this is an element we're interested in
    while (@element) {
        # extract the next attribute and its value
        my ($attr_name, $attr_value) = splice(@element, 0, 2);
        # ... do something with them ...
    }
}
```

Discussion

You can use HTML::LinkExtor in two different ways: either to call `links` to get a
list of all links in the document once it is completely parsed, or to pass a code reference in the first argument to **new**. The referenced function will be called on each
link as the document is parsed.

The `links` method clears the link list, so you can call it only once per parsed document. It returns a reference to an array of elements. Each element is itself an
array reference with an HTML::Element object at the front followed by a list of
attribute name and attribute value pairs. For instance, the HTML:

```
<A HREF="http://www.perl.com/">Home page</A>
<IMG SRC="images/big.gif" LOWSRC="images/big-lowres.gif">
```

would return a data structure like this:

```
[
    [ a,    href   => "http://www.perl.com/" ],
    [ img,  src    =>"images/big.gif",
            lowsrc => "images/big-lowres.gif" ]
]
```

Here's an example of how you would use the $elt_type and the $attr_name to
print out and anchor an image:

```
if ($elt_type eq 'a' && $attr_name eq 'href') {
    print "ANCHOR: $attr_value\n"
        if $attr_value->scheme =~ /http|ftp/;
}
if ($elt_type eq 'img' && $attr_name eq 'src') {
    print "IMAGE:  $attr_value\n";
}
```

Example 20-2 is a complete program that takes as its arguments a URL, like *file:////tmp/testing.html* or *http://www.ora.com/*, and produces on standard output an alphabetically sorted list of unique URLs.

Example 20-2. xurl

```
#!/usr/bin/perl -w
# xurl - extract unique, sorted list of links from URL
use HTML::LinkExtor;
use LWP::Simple;

$base_url = shift;
$parser = HTML::LinkExtor->new(undef, $base_url);
$parser->parse(get($base_url))->eof;
@links = $parser->links;
foreach $linkarray (@links) {
    my @element  = @$linkarray;
    my $elt_type = shift @element;
    while (@element) {
        my ($attr_name , $attr_value) = splice(@element, 0, 2);
        $seen{$attr_value}++;
    }
}
for (sort keys %seen) { print $_, "\n" }
```

This program does have a limitation: if the get of $base_url involves a redirection, your links will all be resolved with the original URL instead of the URL at the end of the redirection. To fix this, fetch the document with LWP::UserAgent and examine the response code to find out if a redirection occurred. Once you know the post-redirection URL (if any), construct the HTML::LinkExtor object.

Here's an example of the run:

```
% xurl http://www.perl.com/CPAN
ftp://ftp@ftp.perl.com/CPAN/CPAN.html
http://language.perl.com/misc/CPAN.cgi
http://language.perl.com/misc/cpan_module
http://language.perl.com/misc/getcpan
http://www.perl.com/index.html
http://www.perl.com/gifs/lcb.xbm
```

Often in mail or Usenet messages, you'll see URLs written as:

```
<URL:http://www.perl.com>
```

This is supposed to make it easy to pick URLs from messages:

```
@URLs = ($message =~ /<URL:(.*?)>/g);
```

See Also

The documentation for the CPAN modules LWP::Simple, HTML::LinkExtor, and HTML::Entities; Recipe 20.1

20.4. Converting ASCII to HTML

Problem

You want to convert ASCII text to HTML.

Solution

Use the simple little encoding filter in Example 20-3.

Example 20-3. text2html

```perl
#!/usr/bin/perl -w -p00
# text2html - trivial html encoding of normal text
# -p means apply this script to each record.
# -00 mean that a record is now a paragraph

use HTML::Entities;
$_ = encode_entities($_, "\200-\377");

if (/^\s/) {
    # Paragraphs beginning with whitespace are wrapped in <PRE>
    s{(.*)$}          {<PRE>\n$1</PRE>\n}s;            # indented verbatim
} else {
    s{^(>.*)}         {$1<BR>}gm;                      # quoted text
    s{<URL:(.*?)>}    {<A HREF="$1">$1</A>}gs          # embedded URL   (good)
                      ||
    s{(http:\S+)}     {<A HREF="$1">$1</A>}gs;         # guessed URL    (bad)
    s{\*(\S+)\*}      {<STRONG>$1</STRONG>}g;          # this is *bold* here
    s{\b_(\S+)\_\b}   {<EM>$1</EM>}g;                  # this is _italics_ here
    s{^}              {<P>\n};                         # add paragraph tag
}
```

Discussion

Converting arbitrary plain text to HTML has no general solution because there are
too many different, conflicting ways of representing formatting information in a
plain text file. The more you know about the input, the better the job you can do
of formatting it.

For example, if you knew that you would be fed a mail message, you could add
this block to format the mail headers:

```perl
    BEGIN {
        print "<TABLE>";
        $_ = encode_entities(scalar <>);
        s/\n\s+/ /g;  # continuation lines
        while ( /^(\S+?:)\s*(.*)$/gm ) {               # parse heading
            print "<TR><TH ALIGN='LEFT'>$1</TH><TD>$2</TD></TR>\n";
        }
        print "</TABLE><HR>";
    }
```

See Also

The documentation for the CPAN module HTML::Entities

20.5. Converting HTML to ASCII

Problem

You want to convert an HTML file into formatted plain ASCII.

Solution

If you have an external formatter like *lynx*, call an external program:

```
$ascii = 'lynx -dump $filename';
```

If you want to do it within your program and don't care about the things that the HTML::TreeBuilder formatter doesn't yet handle (tables and frames):

```
use HTML::FormatText;
use HTML::Parse;

$html = parse_htmlfile($filename);
$formatter = HTML::FormatText->new(leftmargin => 0, rightmargin => 50);
$ascii = $formatter->format($html);
```

Discussion

These examples both assume you have the HTML text in a file. If your HTML is in a variable, you need to write it to a file for *lynx* to read. If you are using HTML::FormatText, use the HTML::TreeBuilder module:

```
use HTML::TreeBuilder;
use HTML::FormatText;

$html = HTML::TreeBuilder->new();
$html->parse($document);

$formatter = HTML::FormatText->new(leftmargin => 0, rightmargin => 50);

$ascii = $formatter->format($html);
```

If you use Netscape, its "Save as" option with the type set to "Text" does the best job with tables.

See Also

The documentation for the CPAN modules HTML::Parse, HTML::TreeBuilder, and HTML::FormatText; your system's *lynx*(1) manpage; Recipe 20.6

20.6. *Extracting or Removing HTML Tags*

Problem

You want to remove HTML tags from a string, leaving just plain text.

Solution

The following oft-cited solution is simple but wrong on all but the most trivial
HTML:

```
($plain_text = $html_text) =~ s/<[^>]*>//gs;        #WRONG
```

A correct but slower and slightly more complicated way is to use the HTML-Tree
bundle of modules from CPAN:

```
use HTML::Parse;
use HTML::FormatText;
$plain_text = HTML::FormatText->new->format(parse_html($html_text));
```

Discussion

As with almost everything else, there is more than one way to do it. Each solution
attempts to strike a balance between speed and flexibility. Occasionally you may
find HTML that's simple enough that a trivial command line call will work:

```
% perl -pe 's/<[^>]*>//g' file
```

However, this will break on with files whose tags cross line boundaries, like this:

```
<IMG SRC = "foo.gif"
    ALT = "Flurp!">
```

So, you'll see people doing this instead:

```
% perl -0777 -pe 's/<[^>]*>//gs' file
```

or its scripted equivalent:

```
{
    local $/;                # temporary whole-file input mode
    $html = <FILE>;
    $html =~ s/<[^>]*>//gs;
}
```

But even that isn't good enough except for simplistic HTML without any interesting bits in it. This approach fails for the following examples of valid HTML (among
many others):

```
<IMG SRC = "foo.gif" ALT = "A > B">

<!-- <A comment> -->
```

```
<script>if (a<b && a>c)</script>

<# Just data #>

<![INCLUDE CDATA [ >>>>>>>>>>> ]]>
```

If HTML comments include other tags, those solutions would also break on text like this:

```
<!-- This section commented out.
    <B>You can't see me!</B>
-->
```

The only solution that works well here is to use the HTML parsing routines from CPAN. The second code snippet shown above in the Solution demonstrates this better technique.

For more flexible parsing, subclass the HTML::Parser class and only record the text elements you see:

```
package MyParser;
use HTML::Parser;
use HTML::Entities qw(decode_entities);

@ISA = qw(HTML::Parser);

sub text {
    my($self, $text) = @_;
    print decode_entities($text);
}

package main;
MyParser->new->parse_file(*F);
```

If you're only interested in simple tags that don't contain others nested inside, you can often make do with an approach like the following, which extracts the title from a non-tricky HTML document:

```
($title) = ($html =~ m#<TITLE>\s*(.*?)\s*</TITLE>#is);
```

Again, the regex approach has its flaws, so a more complete solution using LWP to process the HTML is shown in Example 20-4.

Example 20-4. htitle

```
#!/usr/bin/perl
# htitle - get html title from URL

die "usage: $0 url ...\n" unless @ARGV;
require LWP;

foreach $url (@ARGV) {
    $ua = LWP::UserAgent->new();
    $res = $ua->request(HTTP::Request->new(GET => $url));
```

Example 20-4. htitle (continued)

```
    print "$url: " if @ARGV > 1;
    if ($res->is_success) {
        print $res->title, "\n";
    } else {
        print $res->status_line, "\n";
    }
}
```

Here's an example of the output:

```
% htitle http://www.ora.com
www.oreilly.com -- Welcome to O'Reilly & Associates!

% htitle http://www.perl.com/ http://www.perl.com/nullvoid
http://www.perl.com/: The www.perl.com Home Page
http://www.perl.com/nullvoid: 404 File Not Found
```

See Also

The documentation for the CPAN modules HTML::TreeBuilder, HTML::Parser, HTML::Entities, and LWP::UserAgent; Recipe 20.5

20.7. Finding Stale Links

Problem

You want to check whether a document contains invalid links.

Solution

Use the technique outlined in Recipe 20.3 to extract each link, and then use the LWP::Simple module's head function to make sure that link exists.

Discussion

Example 20-5 is an applied example of the link-extraction technique. Instead of just printing the name of the link, we call the LWP::Simple module's head function on it. The HEAD method fetches the remote document's metainformation to determine status information without downloading the whole document. If it fails, then the link is bad so we print an appropriate message.

Because this program uses the get function from LWP::Simple, it is expecting a URL, not a filename. If you want to supply either, use the URI::Heuristic module described in Recipe 20.1.

Example 20-5. churl

```perl
#!/usr/bin/perl -w
# churl - check urls

use HTML::LinkExtor;
use LWP::Simple qw(get head);

$base_url = shift
    or die "usage: $0 <start_url>\n";
$parser = HTML::LinkExtor->new(undef, $base_url);
$parser->parse(get($base_url));
@links = $parser->links;
print "$base_url: \n";
foreach $linkarray (@links) {
    my @element  = @$linkarray;
    my $elt_type = shift @element;
    while (@element) {
        my ($attr_name , $attr_value) = splice(@element, 0, 2);
        if ($attr_value->scheme =~ /\b(ftp|https?|file)\b/) {
            print "  $attr_value: ", head($attr_value) ? "OK" : "BAD", "\n";
        }
    }
}
```

Here's an example of a program run:

```
% churl http://www.wizards.com
http://www.wizards.com:
  FrontPage/FP_Color.gif:  OK
  FrontPage/FP_BW.gif:  BAD
  #FP_Map:  OK
  Games_Library/Welcome.html:  OK
```

This program has the same limitation as the HTML::LinkExtor program in
Recipe 20.3.

See Also

The documentation for the CPAN modules HTML::LinkExtor, LWP::Simple,
LWP::UserAgent, and HTTP::Response; Recipe 20.8

20.8. Finding Fresh Links

Problem

Given a list of URLs, you want to determine which have been most recently modified.

Solution

The program in Example 20-6 reads URLs from standard input, rearranges by date, and prints them back to standard output with those dates prepended.

Example 20-6. surl

```perl
#!/usr/bin/perl -w
# surl - sort URLs by their last modification date

use LWP::UserAgent;
use HTTP::Request;
use URI::URL qw(url);

my($url, %Date);
my $ua = LWP::UserAgent->new();

while ( $url = url(scalar <>) ) {
    my $ans;
    next unless $url->scheme =~ /^(file|https?)$/;
    $ans = $ua->request(HTTP::Request->new("HEAD", $url));
    if ($ans->is_success) {
        $Date{$url} = $ans->last_modified || 0;   # unknown
    } else {
        print STDERR "$url: Error [", $ans->code, "] ", $ans->message, "!\n";
    }
}

foreach $url ( sort { $Date{$b} <=> $Date{$a} } keys %Date ) {
    printf "%-25s %s\n", $Date{$url} ? (scalar localtime $Date{$url})
                                     : "<NONE SPECIFIED>", $url;
}
```

Discussion

The *surl* script works more like a traditional filter program. It reads from standard input one URL per line. (Actually, it reads from <ARGV>, which defaults to STDIN if @ARGV is empty.) The last-modified date on each URL is fetched using a HEAD request. That date is stored in a hash using the URL for a key. Then a simple sort by value is run on the hash to reorder the URLs by date. On output, the internal date is converted into `localtime` format.

Here's an example of using the *xurl* program from the earlier recipe to extract the URLs, then running that program's output to feed into *surl*.

```
% xurl http://www.perl.com/   | surl | head
Mon Apr 20 06:16:02 1998  http://electriclichen.com/linux/srom.html
Fri Apr 17 13:38:51 1998  http://www.oreilly.com/
Fri Mar 13 12:16:47 1998  http://www2.binevolve.com/
Sun Mar  8 21:01:27 1998  http://www.perl.org/
Tue Nov 18 13:41:32 1997  http://www.perl.com/universal/header.map
Wed Oct  1 12:55:13 1997  http://www.songline.com/
```

```
Sun Aug 17 21:43:51 1997  http://www.perl.com/graphics/perlhome_header.jpg
Sun Aug 17 21:43:47 1997  http://www.perl.com/graphics/perl_id_313c.gif
Sun Aug 17 21:43:46 1997  http://www.perl.com/graphics/ora_logo.gif
Sun Aug 17 21:43:44 1997  http://www.perl.com/graphics/header-nav.gif
```

Having a variety of small programs that each do one thing and that can be combined into more powerful constructs is the hallmark of good programming. You could even argue that *xurl* should work on files, and that some other program should actually fetch the URL's contents over the Web to feed into *xurl*, *churl*, or *surl*. That program would probably be called *gurl*, except that a program by that name already exists: the LWP module suite has a program called *lwp-request* with aliases *HEAD*, *GET*, and *POST* to run those operations in shell scripts.

See Also

The documentation for the CPAN modules LWP::UserAgent, HTTP::Request, and URI::URL; Recipe 20.7

20.9. Creating HTML Templates

Problem

You want to store a parameterized template in an external file, read it in from your CGI script, and substitute your own variables for escapes embedded in the text. This way you can separate your program from the static parts of the document.

Solution

To expand only variable references, use this **template** function:

```
sub template {
    my ($filename, $fillings) = @_;
    my $text;
    local $/;                      # slurp mode (undef)
    local *F;                      # create local filehandle
    open(F, "< $filename\0")   || return;
    $text = <F>;                   # read whole file
    close(F);                      # ignore retval
    # replace quoted words with value in %$fillings hash
    $text =~ s{ %% ( .*? ) %% }
              { exists( $fillings->{$1} )
                    ? $fillings->{$1}
                    : ""
              }gsex;
    return $text;
}
```

On a data file like this:

```
<!-- simple.template for internal template() function -->
<HTML><HEAD><TITLE>Report for %%username%%</TITLE></HEAD>
<BODY><H1>Report for %%username%%</H1>
%%username%% logged in %%count%% times, for a total of %%total%% minutes.
```

Or use the CPAN module Text::Template to expand full expressions if you can guarantee the data file is secure from tampering. A data file for Text::Template looks like this:

```
<!-- fancy.template for Text::Template -->
<HTML><HEAD><TITLE>Report for {$user}</TITLE></HEAD>
<BODY><H1>Report for {$user}</H1>
{ lcfirst($user) } logged in {$count} times, for a total of
{ int($total / 60) } minutes.
```

Discussion

Parameterized output for your CGI scripts is a good idea for many reasons. Separating your program from its data lets you give other people (art directors, for instance) the ability to change the HTML but not the program. Even better, two programs can share the same template, so style changes in the template will be immediately reflected in both.

For example, suppose you have stored the first template from the Solution in a file. Then your CGI program contains the definition of the **template** subroutine above and makes appropriate settings for variables $username, $count, and $total. You can fill in the template by simply using:

```
%fields = (
                username => $whats_his_name,
                count    => $login_count,
                total    => $minute_used,
);

print template("/home/httpd/templates/simple.template", \%fields);
```

The template file contains keywords surrounded with double percent symbols (%%KEYWORD%%). These keywords are looked up in the %$fillings hash whose reference was passed as the second argument to **template**. Example 20-7 is a more elaborate example using an SQL database.

Example 20-7. userrep1

```
#!/usr/bin/perl -w
# userrep1 - report duration of user logins using SQL database

use DBI;
use CGI qw(:standard);

# template() defined as in the Solution section above
```

Example 20-7. userrep1 (continued)

```
$user = param("username")                      or die "No username";

$dbh = DBI->connect("dbi:mysql:connections:mysql.domain.com",
    "connections", "seekritpassword")          or die "Couldn't connect\n";
$sth = $dbh->prepare(<<"END_OF_SELECT")        or die "Couldn't prepare SQL";
    SELECT COUNT(duration),SUM(duration)
    FROM logins WHERE username='$user'
END_OF_SELECT

# this time the duration is assumed to be in seconds
if (@row = $sth->fetchrow_array()) {
    ($count, $seconds) = @row;
} else {
    ($count, $seconds) = (0,0);
}

$sth->finish();
$dbh->disconnect;

print header();
print template("report.tpl", {
    'username' => $user,
    'count'    => $count,
    'total'    => $total
});
```

If you want a fancier, more flexible solution, look at the second template in the
Solution section, which relies upon the CPAN module Text::Template. Contents of
braces found within the template file are evaluated as Perl code. Ordinarily, these
substitutions will just be simple variables:

```
You owe: {$total}
```

but they can also include full expressions:

```
The average was {$count ?  ($total/$count) : 0}.
```

Example 20-8 is an example of how you could use that template.

Example 20-8. userrep2

```
#!/usr/bin/perl -w
# userrep2 - report duration of user logins using SQL database

use Text::Template;
use DBI;
use CGI qw(:standard);

$tmpl = "/home/httpd/templates/fancy.template";
$template = Text::Template->new(-type => "file", -source => $tmpl);
$user = param("username")                      or die "No username";

$dbh = DBI->connect("dbi:mysql:connections:mysql.domain.com",
    "connections", "secret passwd")            or die "Couldn't db connect\n";
```

Example 20-8. userrep2 (continued)

```
$sth = $dbh->prepare(<<"END_OF_SELECT")       or die "Couldn't prepare SQL";
    SELECT COUNT(duration),SUM(duration)
    FROM logins WHERE username='$user'
END_OF_SELECT

$sth->execute()                               or die "Couldn't execute SQL";

if (@row = $sth->fetchrow_array()) {
    ($count, $total) = @row;
} else {
    $count = $total = 0;
}

$sth->finish();
$dbh->disconnect;

print header();
print $template->fill_in();
```

The more powerful approach raises security concerns. Anyone who can write to the template file can insert code that your program will run. See Recipe 8.17 for ways to lessen this danger.

See Also

The documentation for the CPAN module Text::Template; Recipe 8.16; Recipe 14.10

20.10. Mirroring Web Pages

Problem

You want to keep a local copy of a web page up-to-date.

Solution

Use LWP::Simple's `mirror` function:

```
use LWP::Simple;
mirror($URL, $local_filename);
```

Discussion

Although closely related to the `get` function discussed in Recipe 20.1, the `mirror` function doesn't download the file unconditionally. It adds the `If-Modified-Since` header to the GET request it creates, so the server will not transfer the file unless it has been updated.

The `mirror` function mirrors only a single page, not a full tree. To mirror a set of pages, use this recipe in conjunction Recipe 20.3. A good solution to mirroring an entire remote tree can be found in the *w3mir* program, also found on CPAN.

Be careful! It's possible (and easy) to write programs that run amok and begin downloading all web pages on the net. This is not only poor etiquette, it's also an infinite task, since some pages are dynamically generated. It could also get you into trouble with someone who doesn't want their pages downloaded *en masse*.

See Also

The documentation for the CPAN module LWP::Simple; the HTTP specification at *http://www.w3.org/pub/WWW/Protocols/HTTP/*

20.11. *Creating a Robot*

Problem

You want to create a script that navigates the Web on its own (i.e., a robot), and you'd like to respect the remote sites' wishes.

Solution

Instead of writing your robot to use LWP::UserAgent, have it use LWP::RobotUA instead:

```
use LWP::RobotUA;
$ua = LWP::RobotUA->new('websnuffler/0.1', 'me@wherever.com');
```

Discussion

To avoid having marauding robots and web crawlers hammer their servers, sites are encouraged to create a file with access rules called *robots.txt*. If you're fetching only one document with your script, this is no big deal, but if your script is going to fetch many documents, probably from the same server, you could easily exhaust that site's bandwidth.

When you create your own scripts to run around the Web, it's important to be a good net citizen. That means two things: don't request documents from the same server too often, and heed the advisory access rules in their *robots.txt* file.

The easiest way to handle this is to use the LWP::RobotUA module to create agents instead of LWP::UserAgent. This agent automatically knows to pull things over slowly when repeatedly calling the same server. It also checks each site's *robots.txt* file to see whether you're trying to grab a file that is off limits. If you do, you'll get back a response like this:

```
403 (Forbidden) Forbidden by robots.txt
```

Here's an example *robots.txt* file, fetched using the *GET* program that comes with the LWP module suite:

```
% GET http://www.webtechniques.com/robots.txt
User-agent: *
      Disallow: /stats
      Disallow: /db
      Disallow: /logs
      Disallow: /store
      Disallow: /forms
      Disallow: /gifs
      Disallow: /wais-src
      Disallow: /scripts
      Disallow: /config
```

A more interesting and extensive example is at *http://www.cnn.com/robots.txt*. This file is so big, they even keep it under RCS control!

```
% GET http://www.cnn.com/robots.txt | head
# robots, scram
# $Id : robots.txt,v 1.2 1998/03/10 18:27:01 mreed Exp $
User-agent: *
Disallow: /
User-agent:      Mozilla/3.01 (hotwired-test/0.1)
Disallow:    /cgi-bin
Disallow:    /TRANSCRIPTS
Disallow:    /development
```

See Also

The documentation for the CPAN module LWP::RobotUA(3); *http://info.web-crawler.com/mak/projects/robots/robots.html* for a description of how well-behaved robots act

20.12. Parsing a Web Server Log File

Problem

You want to extract from a web server log file only the information you're interested in.

Solution

Pull apart the log file as follows:

```
while (<LOGFILE>) {
  my ($client, $identuser, $authuser, $date, $time, $tz, $method,
      $url, $protocol, $status, $bytes) =
  /^(\S+) (\S+) (\S+) \[([^:]+):(\d+:\d+:\d+) ([^\]]+)] "(\S+) (.*?) (\S+)"
     (\S+) (\S+)$/;
  # ...
}
```

Discussion

This regular expression pulls apart entries in Common Log Format, an informal standard that most web servers adhere to. The fields are:

client
>   IP address or domain name of browser's machine

identuser
>   If IDENT (RFC 1413) was used, what it returned

authuser
>   If username/password authentication was used, whom they logged in as

date
>   Date of request (e.g., 01/Mar/1997)

time
>   Time of request (e.g., 12:55:36)

tz
>   Time zone (e.g., -0700)

method
>   Method of request (e.g., GET, POST, or PUT)

url
>   URL in request (e.g., */~user/index.html*)

protocol
>   HTTP/1.0 or HTTP/1.1

status
>   Returned status (200 is okay, 500 is server error)

bytes
>   Number of bytes returned (could be "-" for errors, redirects, and other non-document transfers)

Other formats include the referrer and agent information. The pattern needs only minor changes for it to work with other log file formats. Watch out that spaces in the URL field are *not* escaped. This means that we can't use \S* to extract the URL. .* would cause the regex to match the entire string and then backtrack until it could satisfy the rest of the pattern. We use .*? and anchor the pattern to the end of the string with $ to make the regular expression engine match nothing and then add characters until the entire pattern is satisfied.

See Also

The CLF spec at *http://www.w3.org/Daemon/User/Config/Logging.html*

20.13. Processing Server Logs

Problem

You need to summarize your server logs, but you don't have a customizable program to do it.

Solution

Parse the error log yourself with regular expressions, or use the Logfile modules from CPAN.

Discussion

Example 20-9 is a sample report generator for an Apache weblog.

Example 20-9. sumwww

```perl
#!/usr/bin/perl -w
# sumwww - summarize web server log activity

$lastdate = "";
daily_logs();
summary();
exit;

# read CLF files and tally hits from the host and to the URL
sub daily_logs {
    while (<>) {
        ($type, $what) = /"(GET|POST)\s+(\S+?) \S+"/ or next;
        ($host, undef, undef, $datetime) = split;
        ($bytes) = /\s(\d+)\s*$/ or next;
        ($date)  = ($datetime =~ /\[([^:]*)/);
        $posts  += ($type eq POST);
        $home++ if m, / ,;
        if ($date ne $lastdate) {
            if ($lastdate) { write_report()    }
            else           { $lastdate = $date }
        }
        $count++;
        $hosts{$host}++;
        $what{$what}++;
```

Example 20-9. sumwww (continued)

```
        $bytesum += $bytes;
    }
    write_report() if $count;
}

# use *typeglob aliasing of global variables for cheap copy
sub summary  {
    $lastdate = "Grand Total";
    *count    = *sumcount;
    *bytesum = *bytesumsum;
    *hosts    = *allhosts;
    *posts    = *allposts;
    *what     = *allwhat;
    *home     = *allhome;
    write;
}

# display the tallies of hosts and URLs, using formats
sub write_report {
    write;

    # add to summary data
    $lastdate     = $date;
    $sumcount    += $count;
    $bytesumsum += $bytesum;
    $allposts    += $posts;
    $allhome     += $home;

    # reset daily data
    $posts = $count = $bytesum = $home = 0;
    @allwhat{keys %what}   = keys %what;
    @allhosts{keys %hosts} = keys %hosts;
    %hosts = %what = ();
}

format STDOUT_TOP =
@|||||||||| @|||||| @||||||| @||||||| @|||||| @|||||| @||||||||||||||
"Date",      "Hosts", "Accesses", "Unidocs", "POST", "Home", "Bytes"
----------- ------- -------- -------- ------- ------- ---------------
.

format STDOUT =
@>>>>>>>>>> @>>>>>> @>>>>>>> @>>>>>>> @>>>>>> @>>>>>> @>>>>>>>>>>>>>>
$lastdate,   scalar(keys %hosts),
            $count, scalar(keys %what),
                        $posts, $home,  $bytesum
.
```

Here's sample output from that program:

Date	Hosts	Accesses	Unidocs	POST	Home	Bytes
19/May/1998	353	6447	3074	352	51	16058246
20/May/1998	1938	23868	4288	972	350	61879643

```
21/May/1998    1775    27872    6596    1064    376       64613798
22/May/1998    1680    21402    4467     735    285       52437374
23/May/1998    1128    21260    4944     592    186       55623059
Grand Total    6050   100849   10090    3715   1248      250612120
```

Use the Logfile::Apache module from CPAN, shown in Example 20-10, to write a similar, but less specific, program. This module is distributed with other Logfile modules in a single Logfile distribution (*Logfile-0.115.tar.gz* at the time of writing).

Example 20-10. aprept

```perl
#!/usr/bin/perl -w
# aprept - report on Apache logs

use Logfile::Apache;

$l = Logfile::Apache->new(
    File  => "-",                    # STDIN
    Group => [ Domain, File ]);

$l->report(Group => Domain, Sort => Records);
$l->report(Group => File,   List => [Bytes,Records]);
```

The **new** constructor reads a log file and builds indices internally. Supply a file-name with the parameter named **File** and the fields to index in the **Group** parameter. The possible fields are **Date** (date request), **Hour** (time of day the request was received), **File** (file requested), **User** (username parsed from request), **Host** (hostname requesting the document), and **Domain** (**Host** translated into "France", "Germany", etc.).

To produce a report on STDOUT, call the **report** method. Give it the index to use with the **Group** parameter, and optionally say how to sort (**Records** is by number of hits, **Bytes** is by number of bytes transferred) or how to further break it down (by number of bytes or number of records).

Here's some sample output:

```
Domain                      Records
===================================
US Commercial           222 38.47%
US Educational          115 19.93%
Network                  93 16.12%
Unresolved               54  9.36%
Australia                48  8.32%
Canada                   20  3.47%
Mexico                    8  1.39%
United Kingdom            6  1.04%


File                          Bytes        Records
==================================================
/                        13008  0.89%      6  1.04%
/cgi-bin/MxScreen        11870  0.81%      2  0.35%
```

/cgi-bin/pickcards	39431	2.70%	48	8.32%
/deckmaster	143793	9.83%	21	3.64%
/deckmaster/admin	54447	3.72%	3	0.52%

See Also

The documentation for the CPAN module Logfile::Apache; *perlform*(1) and the section on "Formats" in Chapter 2 of *Programming Perl*

20.14. Program: htmlsub

This program makes substitutions in HTML files so that the changes only happen in normal text. If you had the file *scooby.html* that contained:

```
<HTML><HEAD><TITLE>Hi!</TITLE></HEAD><BODY>
<H1>Welcome to Scooby World!</H1>
I have <A HREF="pictures.html">pictures</A> of the crazy dog
himself.  Here's one!<P>
<IMG SRC="scooby.jpg" ALT="Good doggy!"><P>
<BLINK>He's my hero!</BLINK>  I would like to meet him some day,
and get my picture taken with him.<P>
P.S. I am deathly ill.  <A HREF="shergold.html">Please send
cards</A>.
</BODY></HTML>
```

You can use *htmlsub* change every occurrence of the word "picture" in the document text to read "photo". It prints the new document on STDOUT:

```
% htmlsub picture photo scooby.html
<HTML><HEAD><TITLE>Hi!</TITLE></HEAD><BODY>
<H1>Welcome to Scooby World!</H1>
I have <A HREF="pictures.html">photos</A> of the crazy dog
himself.  Here's one!<P>
<IMG SRC="scooby.jpg" ALT="Good doggy!"><P>
<BLINK>He's my hero!</BLINK>  I would like to meet him some day,
and get my photo taken with him.<P>
P.S. I am deathly ill.  <A HREF="shergold.html">Please send
cards</A>.
</BODY></HTML>
```

The program is shown in Example 20-11.

Example 20-11. htmlsub

```perl
#!/usr/bin/perl -w
# htmlsub - make substitutions in normal text of HTML files
# from Gisle Aas <gisle@aas.no>

sub usage { die "Usage: $0 <from> <to> <file>...\n" }

my $from = shift or usage;
my $to   = shift or usage;
usage unless @ARGV;

# Build the HTML::Filter subclass to do the substituting.

package MyFilter;
require HTML::Filter;
@ISA=qw(HTML::Filter);
use HTML::Entities qw(decode_entities encode_entities);

sub text
{
    my $self = shift;
    my $text = decode_entities($_[0]);
    $text =~ s/\Q$from/$to/go;         # most important line
    $self->SUPER::text(encode_entities($text));
}

# Now use the class.

package main;
foreach (@ARGV) {
    MyFilter->new->parse_file($_);
}
```

20.15. Program: hrefsub

hrefsub makes substitutions in HTML files, so that the changes only apply to the text in HREF fields of <A HREF="..."> tags. For instance, if you had the *scooby.html* file from the previous example, and you've moved *shergold.html* to be *cards.html*, you need simply say:

```
% hrefsub shergold.html cards.html scooby.html
<HTML><HEAD><TITLE>Hi!</TITLE></HEAD><BODY>
<H1>Welcome to Scooby World!</H1>
I have <A HREF="pictures.html">pictures</A> of the crazy dog
himself.  Here's one!<P>
<IMG SRC="scooby.jpg" ALT="Good doggy!"><P>
<BLINK>He's my hero!</BLINK>  I would like to meet him some day,
and get my picture taken with him.<P>
P.S. I am deathly ill.  <a href="cards.html">Please send
```

cards</A>.
</BODY></HTML>

The HTML::Filter manual page has a BUGS section that says:

> Comments in declarations are removed from the declarations and then inserted as
> separate comments after the declaration. If you turn on `strict_comment()`, then
> comments with embedded "-\|-" are split into multiple comments.

This version of *hrefsub* will always lowercase the `<a>` and the attribute names
within this tag when substitution occurs. If `$foo` is a multiword string, then the
text given to `MyFilter->text` may be broken such that these words do not come
together; i.e., the substitution does not work. There should probably be a new
option to HTML::Parser to make it not return text until the whole segment has
been seen. Also, some people may not be happy with having their 8-bit Latin-1
characters replaced by ugly entities, so *htmlsub* does that, too.

Example 20-12. hrefsub

```perl
#!/usr/bin/perl -w
# hrefsub - make substitutions in <A HREF="..."> fields of HTML files
# from Gisle Aas <gisle@aas.no>

sub usage { die "Usage: $0 <from> <to> <file>...\n" }

my $from = shift or usage;
my $to   = shift or usage;
usage unless @ARGV;

# The HTML::Filter subclass to do the substitution.

package MyFilter;
require HTML::Filter;
@ISA=qw(HTML::Filter);
use HTML::Entities qw(encode_entities);

sub start {
    my($self, $tag, $attr, $attrseq, $orig) = @_;
    if ($tag eq 'a' && exists $attr->{href}) {
        if ($attr->{href} =~ s/\Q$from/$to/g) {
            # must reconstruct the start tag based on $tag and $attr.
            # wish we instead were told the extent of the 'href' value
            # in $orig.
            my $tmp = "<$tag";
            for (@$attrseq) {
                my $encoded = encode_entities($attr->{$_});
                $tmp .= qq( $_="$encoded ");
            }
            $tmp .= ">";
            $self->output($tmp);
            return;
        }
    }
}
```

Example 20-12. hrefsub (continued)

```
    $self->output($orig);
}

# Now use the class.

package main;
foreach (@ARGV) {
        MyFilter->new->parse_file($_);
}
```

Index

Symbols

&& operator, 7–8
* to store filehandles, 222, 255–258
@_ array, 335–337
\ (backslash)
   escape characters, 28–30
   operator, 342, 377–378
` (backtick)
   expanding, 22
   operator, 554, 683
   qx( ), 92
, (comma)
   printing lists with commas, 93–95
   (see also CSV)
$' variable, 163
$^W variable, 458
$+ variable, 163
$' variable, 163
$; variable, 318
$/ variable, 274
$_ variable,
   accidental clobbering, 99
   outlawing unauthorized use, 482–484
$| variable, 225, 248
. in numbers, 64–65
.. and ... (range) operators, 177
=> (comma arrow) operator, 129
=~ operator, s///, m//, and tr/// with, 5
-> (infix) notation, 365
-> operator, 443
< access mode, 223
< > for globbing, 320–322

< > (diamond) operator, 224, 236–240, 274,
   602
<&= and <& open modes, 261
<=> (comparison) operator, 115–116
% for hashes, 129
> access mode, 223
>> access mode, 223
/ (root directory), 309
~ (tilde) in filenames, expanding, 231
_ (file stat cache), 310
|| operator, 6–8
||= (assignment) operator, 6, 8

Numbers

"0 but true", 348, 608
-0 command-line option, 275
$1, $2, ... (backreferences), 163
   finding duplicate words, 194
"1 while", 16
"500 Server Error", fixing, 675–678

A

a escape for terminal bell, 525–526
abbreviations, matching, 208–210
accept( ), 602, 607
access log (web server), 669
access modes, 223
access to database (see database access)
access_log files, 726–731
addresses (email), matching, 206–208
advisory locking, 245–247
alarm, ringing, 525–526

About the Authors

Tom Christiansen is an author and lecturer who's been intimately involved with Perl development on a daily basis since Larry Wall first released it to the general public in 1987. After working for several years for TSR Hobbies (of Dungeons and Dragons fame), he set off for college where he spent a year in Spain and five in America pursuing a classical education in computer science, mathematics, music, linguistics, and Romance philology. He eventually escaped UW-Madison without a PhD, but with a BA in Spanish and in Computer Science, plus an MS in Computer Science specializing in operating systems design and in computational linguistics.

Co-author of *Programming Perl*, *Learning Perl*, and *Learning Perl on Win32 Systems* from O'Reilly & Associates, Tom is also the major caretaker of Perl's free online documentation, developer of the *www.perl.com* web site, co-author of the Perl Frequently Asked Questions list, president of *The Perl Journal*, and frequent technical reviewer for O'Reilly & Associates. Tom served two terms on the USENIX Association Board of Directors.

Tom lives high in idyllic Boulder, Colorado, where he gives public seminars on all aspects of Perl programming. When he can be coaxed out of the People's Republic of Boulder, Tom travels around the world giving public and private lectures and workshops on Unix, Perl, and the Web on five continents and in three languages. He takes the summers off to pursue his hobbies of reading, back-packing, gardening, birding, gaming, music making, and recreational programming.

Nathan Torkington has never climbed Mount Kilimanjaro. He adamantly maintains that he was nowhere near the grassy knoll. He has never mustered superhuman strength to lift a burning trolleycar to free a trapped child, and is yet to taste human flesh. Nat has never served as a mercenary in the Congo, line-danced, run away to join the circus, spent a year with the pygmies, finished the Death By Chocolate, or been miraculously saved when his cigarillo case stopped the bullet.

Nat is not American, though he is learning the language. He is from Ti Point, New Zealand. People from Ti Point don't do these things. They grow up on fishing boats and say things like "She'll be right, mate." Nat did. He went to high school at Mahurangi College, university at Victoria University of Wellington, and moved to America when he met his wife, Jenine. His hobbies are bluegrass music and Perl. When he's not being a system administrator and family man, Nat teaches Perl and writes and edits for *The Perl Journal*.

Colophon

The animal featured on the cover of *Perl Cookbook* is a bighorn sheep. Bighorn sheep (Ovis canadensis) are wild sheep noted, not surprisingly, for their large, curved horns. Male bighorns grow to approximately 5 feet long and 40 inches tall to the shoulder and weigh up to 350 pounds. Their horns measure up to 18 inches in circumference and 4 feet long and can weigh up to 30 pounds. Despite their bulk, bighorns are adept at negotiating mountainous terrains. With their sharp, cloven hooves they can walk on ledges as thin as two inches. They have excellent eyesight that enables them to locate footholds and to accurately judge distances between ledges. They can jump as far as 20 feet from ledge to ledge.

Competition for ewes is intense and often leads to fierce battles that can continue for a full day. During the battle two rams race at each other at speeds of up to 20 miles an hour, clashing their horns together. The skull of the bighorn sheep is double-layered to provide protection from these blows. Horn size is a significant factor in determining rank, and rams will only fight other rams with an equivalently sized horn. Mature males usually stay apart from the females and young. In these "bachelor flocks" the lower-ranking males often play the part of ewes and behave in a submissive manner toward the dominant males. The dominant male, in turn, behaves like a courting ram and mounts the lower-ranking male. This behavior is believed to enable the rams to live together without rank disputes that might otherwise drive the lower-ranking males out of the flock.

Bighorns can be found in the Rocky Mountains from Canada to Colorado and in the desert from California to west Texas and Mexico. They are threatened with extinction as a result of disease, habitat reduction, and hunting.

Clairemarie Fisher O'Leary was the production editor and project manager for this book. Steven Kleinedler copyedited, Kristin Barendsen and Kristine Simmons proofread, and Jane Ellin and Sheryl Avruch provided quality control reviews. Trisha Manoni, Sebastian Banker, and Kimo Carter provided production assistance. Seth Maislin wrote the index. The illustrations were created in Macromedia Freehand 7.0 by Robert Romano. Edie Freedman designed the cover, using a 19th-century engraving from the Dover Pictorial Archive. The cover layout was produced with Quark XPress 3.32 using the ITC Garamond font. The inside layout was designed by Edie Freedman and modified by Nancy Priest and implemented in FrameMaker by Mike Sierra. The text and heading fonts are ITC Garamond Light and Garamond Book. This colophon was written by Clairemarie Fisher O'Leary.

Whenever possible, our books a durable and flexible lay-flat binding, either RepKover™ or Otabind™. If the page count exceeds the maximum bulk possible for this type of binding, perfect binding is used.

More Titles from O'Reilly

Perl

Learning Perl, 2nd Edition

By Randal L. Schwartz & Tom Christiansen
Foreword by Larry Wall
2nd Edition July 1997
302 pages, ISBN 1-56592-284-0

In this update of a bestseller, two leading
Perl trainers teach you to use the most
universal scripting language in the age of the
World Wide Web. Current for Perl version
5.004, this hands-on tutorial includes a
lengthy chapter on CGI programming, while touching also on the
use of library modules, references, and Perl's object-oriented
constructs.

Learning Perl on Win32 Systems

By Randal L. Schwartz,
Erik Olson & Tom Christiansen
1st Edition August 1997
306 pages, ISBN 1-56592-324-3

In this carefully paced course, leading
Perl trainers and a Windows NT practitioner
teach you to program in the language that
promises to emerge as the scripting language
of choice on NT. Based on the "llama" book,
this book features tips for PC users and new NT-specific examples,
along with a foreword by Larry Wall, the creator of Perl, and Dick
Hardt, the creator of Perl for Win32.

Learning Perl/Tk

By Nancy Walsh
1st Edition January 1999
376 pages, ISBN 1-56592-314-6

This tutorial for Perl/Tk, the extension to
Perl for creating graphical user interfaces,
shows how to use Perl/Tk to build graphical,
event-driven applications for both Windows
and UNIX. Rife with illustrations, it teaches
how to implement and configure each
Perl/Tk graphical element.

Mastering Regular Expressions

By Jeffrey E. F. Friedl
1st Edition January 1997
368 pages, ISBN 1-56592-257-3

Regular expressions, a powerful tool for
manipulating text and data, are found in
scripting languages, editors, programming
environments, and specialized tools. In this
book, author Jeffrey Friedl leads you through
the steps of crafting a regular expression that
gets the job done. He examines a variety of tools and uses them in
an extensive array of examples, with a major focus on Perl.

Perl in a Nutshell

By Ellen Siever, Stephen Spainhour &
Nathan Patwardhan
1st Edition December 1998
674 pages, ISBN 1-56592-286-7

The perfect companion for working
programmers, *Perl in a Nutshell* is a
comprehensive reference guide to the
world of Perl. It contains everything you
need to know for all but the most obscure
Perl questions. This wealth of information
is packed into an efficient, extraordinarily usable format.

Perl Resource Kit – Win32 Edition

By Dick Hardt, Erik Olson, David Futato &
Brian Jepson
1st Edition August 1998
1,832 pages, Includes 4 books & CD-ROM
ISBN 1-56592-409-6

The *Perl Resource Kit–Win32 Edition* is an
essential tool for Perl programmers who are
expanding their platform expertise to include
Win32, and for Win32 Webmasters and system
administrators who have discovered the power and flexibility of Perl.
The Kit contains some of the latest commercial Win32 Perl software
from Dick Hardt's ActiveState Tool Corp., along with a collection of
Perl modules that run on Win32, and a definitive documentation set
from O'Reilly.

Perl

Mastering Algorithms with Perl

By Jon Orwant, Jarkko Hietaniemi &
John Macdonald
1st Edition August 1999
704 pages, ISBN 1-56592-398-7

There have been dozens of books on
programming algorithms, but never before
has there been one that uses Perl. Whether
you are an amateur programmer or know a
wide range of algorithms in other languages,
this book will teach you how to carry out traditional programming
tasks in a high-powered, efficient, easy-to-maintain manner with
Perl. Topics range in complexity from sorting and searching to
statistical algorithms, numerical analysis, and encryption.

Programming Perl, 3rd Edition

Larry Wall, Tom Christiansen & Jon Orwant
3rd Edition July 2000
1104 pages, ISBN 0-596-00027-8

Programming Perl is not just a book about
Perl; it is also a unique introduction to the
language and its culture, as one might expect
only from its authors. This third edition has
been expanded to cover Version 5.6 of Perl.
New topics include threading, the compiler,
Unicode, and other features that have been added or improved
since the previous edition.

Advanced Perl Programming

By Sriram Srinivasan
1st Edition August 1997
434 pages, ISBN 1-56592-220-4

This book covers complex techniques for
managing production-ready Perl programs
and explains methods for manipulating
data and objects that may have looked
like magic before. It gives you necessary
background for dealing with networks,
databases, and GUIs, and includes a discussion of internals to
help you program more efficiently and embed Perl within C or
C within Perl.

The Perl CD Bookshelf

By O'Reilly & Associates, Inc.
1st Edition July 1999
Features CD-ROM
ISBN 1-56592-462-2

Perl programmer alert! Six bestselling
O'Reilly Animal Guides are now available
on CD-ROM, easily accessible with your
favorite Web browser: *Perl in a Nutshell*;
Programming Perl, 2nd Edition; *Perl
Cookbook*; *Advanced Perl Programming*;
Learning Perl; and *Learning Perl on Win32 Sytems*. As a bonus,
the new hard-copy version of *Perl in a Nutshell* is also included.

CGI Programming with Perl, 2nd Edition

By Shishir Gundavaram
2nd Edition July 2000
470 pages, ISBN 1-56592-419-3

Completely rewritten, this comprehensive
explanation of CGI for those who want to
provide their own Web servers features
Perl 5 techniques and shows how to use two
popular Perl modules, CGI.pm and CGI_lite.
It also covers speed-up techniques, such as
FastCGI and mod_perl, and new material on searching and indexing,
security, generating graphics through ImageMagick, database access
through DBI, Apache configuration, and combining CGI with
JavaScript.

Perl 5 Pocket Reference, 3rd Edition

By Johan Vromans
3rd Edition May 2000
96 pages, ISBN 0-596-00032-4

Revised to cover Perl version 5.6, this quick
reference provides a complete overview of the
Perl programming language in a convenient,
carry-around booklet. *The Perl 5 Pocket
Reference* is the perfect companion to
Programming Perl, Learning Perl, and
the *Perl Cookbook.*

Hand-held Computing

Palm Programming: The Developer's Guide

By Neil Rhodes & Julie McKeehan
1st Edition December 1998
482 pages, Includes CD-ROM
ISBN 1-56592-525-4

Emerging as the bestselling hand-held computers of all time, PalmPilots have spawned intense developer activity and a fanatical following. Used by Palm in their developer training, this tutorial-style book shows intermediate to experienced C programmers how to build a Palm application from the ground up. Includes a CD-ROM with source code and third-party developer tools.

PalmPilot: The Ultimate Guide, 2nd Edition

By David Pogue
2nd Edition June 1999
624 pages, Includes CD-ROM
ISBN 1-56592-600-5

This new edition of O'Reilly's runaway bestseller is densely packed with previously undocumented information. The bible for users of Palm VII and all other Palm models, it contains hundreds of timesaving tips and surprising tricks, plus an all-new CD-ROM (for Windows 9x, NT, or Macintosh) containing over 3,100 PalmPilot programs from the collection of palmcentral.com, the Internet's largest Palm software site.

How to stay in touch with O'Reilly

1. Visit Our Award-Winning Web Site

http://www.oreilly.com/

★ "Top 100 Sites on the Web" —*PC Magazine*
★ "Top 5% Web sites" —*Point Communications*
★ "3-Star site" —*The McKinley Group*

Our web site contains a library of comprehensive product information (including book excerpts and tables of contents), downloadable software, background articles, interviews with technology leaders, links to relevant sites, book cover art, and more. File us in your Bookmarks or Hotlist!

2. Join Our Email Mailing Lists

New Product Releases

To receive automatic email with brief descriptions of all new O'Reilly products as they are released, send email to:
ora-news-subscribe@lists.oreilly.com
Put the following information in the first line of your message (*not* in the Subject field):
subscribe ora-news

O'Reilly Events

If you'd also like us to send information about trade show events, special promotions, and other O'Reilly events, send email to:
ora-news-subscribe@lists.oreilly.com
Put the following information in the first line of your message (*not* in the Subject field):
subscribe ora-events

3. Get Examples from Our Books via FTP

There are two ways to access an archive of example files from our books:

Regular FTP

- ftp to:
  ftp.oreilly.com
  (login: anonymous
  password: your email address)
- Point your web browser to:
  ftp://ftp.oreilly.com/

FTPMAIL

- Send an email message to:
  ftpmail@online.oreilly.com
  (Write "help" in the message body)

4. Contact Us via Email

order@oreilly.com
To place a book or software order online. Good for North American and international customers.

subscriptions@oreilly.com
To place an order for any of our newsletters or periodicals.

books@oreilly.com
General questions about any of our books.

software@oreilly.com
For general questions and product information about our software. Check out O'Reilly Software Online at **http://software.oreilly.com/** for software and technical support information. Registered O'Reilly software users send your questions to: **website-support@oreilly.com**

cs@oreilly.com
For answers to problems regarding your order or our products.

booktech@oreilly.com
For book content technical questions or corrections.

proposals@oreilly.com
To submit new book or software proposals to our editors and product managers.

international@oreilly.com
For information about our international distributors or translation queries. For a list of our distributors outside of North America check out:
http://www.oreilly.com/distributors.html

5. Work with Us

Check out our website for current employment opportunites:
http://jobs.oreilly.com/

O'Reilly & Associates, Inc.
101 Morris Street, Sebastopol, CA 95472 USA
TEL   707-829-0515 or 800-998-9938
          (6am to 5pm PST)
FAX   707-829-0104

O'REILLY®

TO ORDER: **800-998-9938** • order@oreilly.com • http://www.oreilly.com/
OUR PRODUCTS ARE AVAILABLE AT A BOOKSTORE OR SOFTWARE STORE NEAR YOU.
FOR INFORMATION: **800-998-9938** • **707-829-0515** • info@oreilly.com

Titles from O'Reilly

PROGRAMMING

C++: The Core Language
Practical C++ Programming
Practical C Programming, 3rd Ed.
High Performance Computing, 2nd Ed.
Programming Embedded Systems in
    C and C++
Mastering Algorithms in C
Advanced C++ Techniques
POSIX 4: Programming for the Real
    World
POSIX Programmer's Guide
Power Programming with RPC
UNIX Systems Programming for
    SVR4
Pthreads Programming
CVS Pocket Reference
Advanced Oracle PL/SQL
Oracle PL/SQL Guide to Oracle8i
    Features
Oracle PL/SQL Programming, 2nd Ed.
Oracle Built-in Packages
Oracle PL/SQL Developer's
    Workbook
Oracle Web Applications
Oracle PL/SQL Language Pocket
    Reference
Oracle PL/SQL Built-ins Pocket
    Reference
Oracle SQL*Plus: The Definitive
    Guide
Oracle SQL*Plus Pocket Reference
Oracle Essentials
Oracle Database Administration
Oracle Internal Services
Oracle SAP
Guide to Writing DCE Applications
Understanding DCE
Visual Basic Shell Programming
VB/VBA in a Nutshell: The Language
Access Database Design &
    Programming, 2nd Ed.
Writing Word Macros
Applying RCS and SCCS
Checking C Programs with Lint
VB Controls in a Nutshell
Developing Asp Components, 2nd Ed.
Learning WML & WMLScript
Writing Excel Macros
Windows 32 API Programming with
    Visual Basic
ADO: The Definitive Guide

USING THE INTERNET

Internet in a Nutshell
Smileys
Managing Mailing Lists

SOFTWARE

WebSite Professional™ 2.0
Polyform™
WebBoard™ 4.0

WEB

Apache: The Definitive Guide,
    2nd Ed.
Apache Pocket Reference
ASP in a Nutshell, 2nd Ed.
Cascading Style Sheets
Designing Web Audio
Designing with JavaScript, 2nd Ed.
DocBook: The Definitive Guide
Dynamic HTML: The Definitive
    Reference
HTML Pocket Reference
Information Architecture for the
    WWW
JavaScript: The Definitive Guide,
    3rd Ed.
Java and XML
JavaScript Application Cookbook
JavaScript Pocket Reference
Practical Internet Groupware
PHP Pocket Reference
Programming Coldfusion
Photoshop for the Web, 2nd Ed.
Web Design in a Nutshell
Webmaster in a Nutshell, 2nd Ed.
Web Navigation: Designing the
    User Experience
Web Performance Tuning
Web Security & Commerce
Writing Apache Modules with
    Perl and C

UNIX

SCO UNIX in a Nutshell
Tcl/Tk in a Nutshell
The Unix CD Bookshelf, 2nd Ed.
UNIX in a Nutshell, System V Edition,
    3rd Ed.
Learning the Unix Operating System,
    4th Ed.
Learning vi, 6th Ed.
Learning the Korn Shell
Learning GNU Emacs, 2nd Ed.
Using csh & tcsh
Learning the bash Shell, 2nd Ed.
GNU Emacs Pocket Reference
Exploring Expect
TCL/TK Tools
TCL/TK in a Nutshell
Python Pocket Reference

USING WINDOWS

Windows Millenium: The Missing
    Manual
PC Hardware in a Nutshell
Optimizing Windows for Games,
    Graphics, and Multimedia
Outlook 2000 in a Nutshell
Word 2000 in a Nutshell
Excel 2000 in a Nutshell
Paint Shop Pro 7 in a Nutshell
Windows 2000 Pro: The Missing
    Manual

JAVA SERIES

Developing Java Beans
Creating Effective JavaHelp
Enterprise Java Beans, 2nd Ed.
Java Cryptography
Java Distributed Computing
Java Enterprise in a Nutshell
Java Examples in a Nutshell,
    2nd Ed.
Java Foundation Classes in a
    Nutshell
Java in a Nutshell, 3rd Ed.
Java Internationalization
Java I/O
Java Native Methods
Java Network Programming,
    2nd Ed.
Java Performance Tuning
Java Security
Java Servlet Programming
Java ServerPages
Java Threads, 2nd Ed.
Jini in a Nutshell
Learning Java

GRAPHICS & MULTIMEDIA

MP3: The Definitive Guide
Photoshop 6 in a Nutshell, 3rd Ed.
Director in a Nutshell
Lingo in a Nutshell
FrontPage 2000 in a Nutshell

X WINDOW

Vol. 1: Xlib Programming Manual
Vol. 2: Xlib Reference Manual
Vol. 4M: X Toolkit Intrinsics
    Programming Manual, Motif Ed.
Vol. 5: X Toolkit Intrinsics Reference
    Manual
Vol. 6A: Motif Programming Manual
Vol. 6B: Motif Reference Manual, 2nd
    Ed.

PERL

Advanced Perl Programming
CGI Programming with Perl,
    2nd Ed.
Learning Perl, 2nd Ed.
Learning Perl for Win32 Systems
Learning Perl/Tk
Mastering Algorithms with Perl
Mastering Regular Expressions
Perl Cookbook
Perl in a Nutshell
Programming Perl, 3rd Ed.
Perl CD Bookshelf
Perl Resource Kit – Win32 Ed.
Perl/TK Pocket Reference
Perl 5 Pocket Reference,
    3rd Ed.

MAC

AppleScript in a Nutshell
AppleWorks 6: The Missing Manual
Crossing Platforms
iMovie: The Missing Manual
Mac OS in a Nutshell
Mac OS 9: The Missing Manual
Photoshop Cookbook
REALbasic: The Definitive Guide

LINUX

Building Linux Clusters
Learning Debian GNU/Linux
Learning Red Hat Linux
Linux Device Drivers
Linux Network Administrator's
    Guide, 2nd Ed.
Running Linux, 3rd Ed.
Linux in a Nutshell, 3rd Ed.
Linux Multimedia Guide

SYSTEM ADMINISTRATION

Practical UNIX & Internet Security,
    2nd Ed.
Building Internet Firewalls, 2nd Ed.
PGP: Pretty Good Privacy
SSH, The Secure Shell: The
    Definitive Guide
DNS and Bind, 3rd Ed.
The Networking CD Bookshelf
Virtual Private Networks, 2nd Ed.
TCP/IP Network Administration,
    2nd Ed.
sendmail Desktop Reference
Managing Usenet
Using & Managing PPP
Managing IP Networks with Cisco
    Routers
Networking Personal Computers
    with TCP/IP
Unix Backup & Recovery
Essential System Administration,
    2nd Ed.
Perl for System Administration
Managing NFS and NIS
Volume 8: X Window System
    Administrator's Guide
Using Samba
Unix Power Tools, 2nd Ed.
DNS on Windows NT
Windows NT TCP/IP Network
    Administration
DHCP for Windows 2000
Essential Windows NT System
    Administration
Managing Windows NT Logons
Managing the Windows 2000
    Registry

OTHER TITLES

PalmPilot: The Ultimate Guide, 2nd Ed.
Palm Programming:
    The Developer's Guide

O'REILLY®

TO ORDER: **800-998-9938** • **order@oreilly.com** • **http://www.oreilly.com/**
OUR PRODUCTS ARE AVAILABLE AT A BOOKSTORE OR SOFTWARE STORE NEAR YOU.
FOR INFORMATION: **800-998-9938** • **707-829-0515** • **info@oreilly.com**

International Distributors

UK, EUROPE, MIDDLE EAST AND AFRICA (EXCEPT FRANCE, GERMANY, AUSTRIA, SWITZERLAND, LUXEMBOURG, AND LIECHTENSTEIN)

INQUIRIES
O'Reilly UK Limited
4 Castle Street
Farnham
Surrey, GU9 7HS
United Kingdom
Telephone: 44-1252-711776
Fax: 44-1252-734211
Email: information@oreilly.co.uk

ORDERS
Wiley Distribution Services Ltd.
1 Oldlands Way
Bognor Regis
West Sussex PO22 9SA
United Kingdom
Telephone: 44-1243-843294
UK Freephone: 0800-243207
Fax: 44-1243-843302 (Europe/EU orders)
or 44-1243-843274 (Middle East/Africa)
Email: cs-books@wiley.co.uk

FRANCE

INQUIRIES & ORDERS
Éditions O'Reilly
18 rue Séguier
75006 Paris, France
Tel: 33-1-40-51-52-30
Fax: 33-1-40-51-52-31
Email: france@oreilly.fr

GERMANY, SWITZERLAND, AUSTRIA, LUXEMBOURG, AND LIECHTENSTEIN

INQUIRIES & ORDERS
O'Reilly Verlag
Balthasarstr. 81
D-50670 Köln, Germany
Telephone: 49-221-973160-91
Fax: 49-221-973160-8
Email: anfragen@oreilly.de (inquiries)
Email: order@oreilly.de (orders)

CANADA (FRENCH LANGUAGE BOOKS)
Les Éditions Flammarion ltée
375, Avenue Laurier Ouest
Montréal (Québec) H2V 2K3
Tel: 00-1-514-277-8807
Fax: 00-1-514-278-2085
Email: info@flammarion.qc.ca

HONG KONG
City Discount Subscription Service, Ltd.
Unit A, 6th Floor, Yan's Tower
27 Wong Chuk Hang Road
Aberdeen, Hong Kong
Tel: 852-2580-3539
Fax: 852-2580-6463
Email: citydis@ppn.com.hk

KOREA
Hanbit Media, Inc.
Chungmu Bldg. 210
Yonnam-dong 568-33
Mapo-gu
Seoul, Korea
Tel: 822-325-0397
Fax: 822-325-9697
Email: hant93@chollian.dacom.co.kr

PHILIPPINES
Global Publishing
G/F Benavides Garden
1186 Benavides Street
Manila, Philippines
Tel: 632-254-8949/632-252-2582
Fax: 632-734-5060/632-252-2733
Email: globalp@pacific.net.ph

TAIWAN
O'Reilly Taiwan
1st Floor, No. 21, Lane 295
Section 1, Fu-Shing South Road
Taipei, 106 Taiwan
Tel: 886-2-27099669
Fax: 886-2-27038802
Email: mori@oreilly.com

INDIA
Shroff Publishers & Distributors Pvt. Ltd.
12, "Roseland", 2nd Floor
180, Waterfield Road, Bandra (West)
Mumbai 400 050
Tel: 91-22-641-1800/643-9910
Fax: 91-22-643-2422
Email: spd@vsnl.com

CHINA
O'Reilly Beijing
SIGMA Building, Suite B809
No. 49 Zhichun Road
Haidian District
Beijing, China PR 100080
Tel: 86-10-8809-7475
Fax: 86-10-8809-7463
Email: beijing@oreilly.com

JAPAN
O'Reilly Japan, Inc.
Yotsuya Y's Building
7 Banch 6, Honshio-cho
Shinjuku-ku
Tokyo 160-0003 Japan
Tel: 81-3-3356-5227
Fax: 81-3-3356-5261
Email: japan@oreilly.com

THAILAND
TransQuest Publishers (Thailand)
535/49 Kasemsuk Yaek 5
Soi Pracharat-Bampen 15
Huay Kwang, Bangkok
Thailand 10310
Tel: 662-6910421 or 6910638
Fax: 662-6902235
Email: puripat@.inet.co.th

ALL OTHER ASIAN COUNTRIES
O'Reilly & Associates, Inc.
101 Morris Street
Sebastopol, CA 95472 USA
Tel: 707-829-0515
Fax: 707-829-0104
Email: order@oreilly.com

AUSTRALIA
Woodslane Pty., Ltd.
7/5 Vuko Place
Warriewood NSW 2102
Australia
Tel: 61-2-9970-5111
Fax: 61-2-9970-5002
Email: info@woodslane.com.au

NEW ZEALAND
Woodslane New Zealand, Ltd.
21 Cooks Street (P.O. Box 575)
Waganui, New Zealand
Tel: 64-6-347-6543
Fax: 64-6-345-4840
Email: info@woodslane.com.au

ARGENTINA
Distribuidora Cuspide
Suipacha 764
1008 Buenos Aires
Argentina
Phone: 5411-4322-8868
Fax: 5411-4322-3456
Email: libros@cuspide.com

O'REILLY®

O'REILLY™

O'Reilly & Associates, Inc.
101 Morris Street
Sebastopol, CA 95472-9902
1-800-998-9938

Visit us online at:
http://www.oreilly.com/
orders@oreilly.com

O'REILLY WOULD LIKE TO HEAR FROM YOU

Nineteenth century wood engraving
of a bear from the O'Reilly &
Associates Nutshell Handbook®
Using & Managing UUCP.

POST CARD

BUSINESS REPLY MAIL

FIRST CLASS MAIL   PERMIT NO. 80   SEBASTOPOL, CA

Postage will be paid by addressee

O'Reilly & Associates, Inc.
101 Morris Street
Sebastopol, CA 95472-9902